EGYPT

SARAH SMIERCIAK

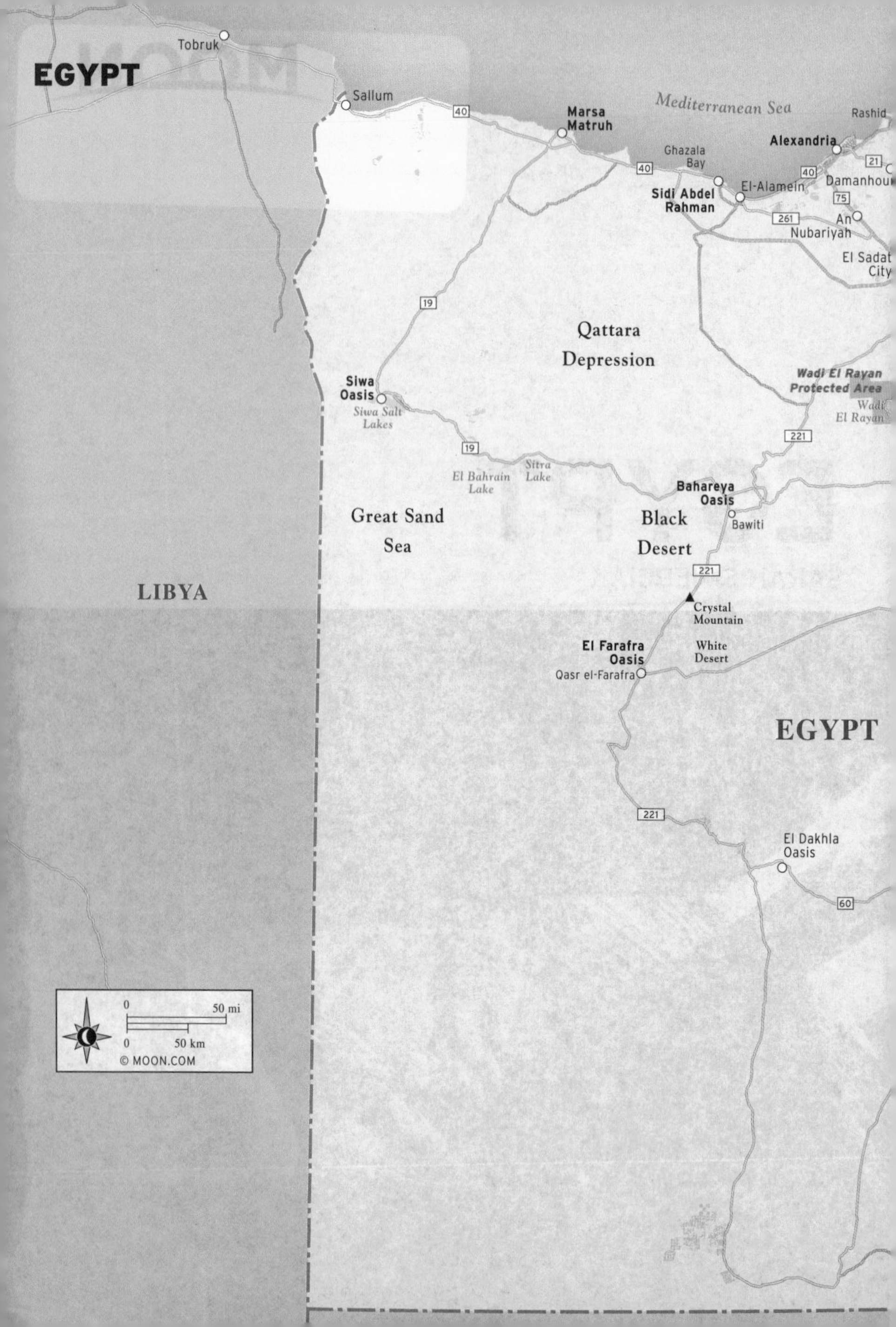
EGYPT
Tobruk
Sallum
40
Marsa
Matruh
Mediterranean Sea
Rashid
Alexandria
Ghazala
Bay
40
40
21
Damanhou
Sidi Abdel
Rahman
El-Alamein
75
261
An
Nubariyah
El Sadat
City
19
Qattara
Depression
Wadi El Rayan
Protected Area
Wadi
El Rayan
Siwa
Oasis
Siwa Salt
Lakes
221
19
El Bahrain
Lake
Sitra
Lake
Bahareya
Oasis
Bawiti
Great Sand
Sea
Black
Desert
221
LIBYA
Crystal
Mountain
El Farafra
Oasis
White
Desert
Qasr el-Farafra
EGYPT
221
El Dakhla
Oasis
60
0
50 mi
0
50 km
© MOON.COM

JERUSALEM
Hebron
Gaza
Mediterranean Sea
Be'er Sheva
ISRAEL
Damietta
Port Said
Arish
Kafr Al-Sheikh
Mansoura
Tanta
Banha
El Obour City
CAIRO
Giza
New Cairo City
6th of October City
Suez
Nekhel
JORDAN
Sinai
Peninsula
Ras Sedr
Eilat
Taba
Aqaba
Fayoum
Gulf of Suez
Zaafaranah
Abu Zenima
Ras Shaitan
Tarabeen Bay
Wadi Gharba
Nuweibaa
Gulf of Aqaba
Beni Suef
Ras Abu Rudeis
Ras Abu Galum Protectorate
St Katherine
Mount Sinai
Dahab
Tabuk
Ras Ghareb
El Tor
Sharma
Minya
Sharm el Sheikh
Ashrafi Island
Ras Mohammed National Park
Mallawi
Shedwan Island
SAUDI ARABIA
Tell el-Amarna
El Gouna
Hurghada
Duba
Asyut Al Gadida City
Asyut
Giftun Islands
Safaga
Red Sea
Nile
Sohag
Al Wajh
Abydos
Qena
El Quseir
Luxor
Port Ghalib
Kharga Oasis
Esna
Umluj
Marsa Alam
Edfu
Wadi el Gemal National Park
Kom Ombo
Yanbu
Aswan
Ras Banas
Toshka Lakes
Lake Nasser
Al Shalaten
Abu Ramad
Halayeb
Abu Simbel
Wadi Halfa
SUDAN

Contents

Although every effort was made to make sure the information in this book was accurate when going to press, research was impacted by the COVID-19 pandemic and things may have changed since the time of writing. Be sure to confirm specific details, like opening hours, closures, and travel guidelines and restrictions, when making your travel plans. For more detailed information, see page 442.

DISCOVER

Egypt

Welcome to Egypt: a land of rich cultural heritage, dramatic landscapes, and friendly people with an infectious sense of humor. The diversity of the country's treasures astounds. You'll find vibrant cities, towering pyramids, stunning beaches, underwater paradises, rolling desert hills, and sub-nationalities you've probably never heard of.

When I'm away from Cairo, what I miss most is its intensity. The constant stimulation of the senses. The sweet smell of mango in the summer emanating from the tired fridges of downtown juice shops. The taste of a warm sweet potato in the winter, expertly roasted on roaming carts with makeshift ovens. The colorful party boats that dance across the Nile, pulsating with neon lights and Egypt's latest pop hits. The spellbinding contralto of 20th-century diva Umm Kulthum cast through the radios of nostalgic taxi drivers. In Egypt's frenetic capital, the sheer density of human beings breaks down barriers, creating an air of familiarity between the city's some 20 million inhabitants.

Clockwise from top left: black tea with fresh mint; diving in the Red Sea; Hanging Church in Cairo; boats moored near the Qaitbay Citadel in Alexandria; bread delivery in Cairo; Mortuary Temple of Hatshepsut.

If the energy of Cairo overwhelms, a quiet escape is just a bus ride away. Standing under the star-speckled sky of the Western Desert, listening to the waves roll in on a Sinai beach, or sailing on a felucca along the golden hills of Aswan, you'll forget the clamor of the city completely.

Around every turn you'll gain a new perspective—and, if you wish, a new friend.

Clockwise from top left: view of Cairo from Gezira/Zamalek; camels near the Great Pyramids of Giza; traditional Egyptian koshary; statue of god Anubis from Tutankhamun's tomb now in the Grand Egyptian Museum.

12 TOP EXPERIENCES

1 **Horseback riding near the Great Pyramids of Giza:** Gallop through the desert in the cool evening air alongside the only surviving wonder of the ancient world (page 114).

^^^

2 Exploring Islamic Cairo's backstreet souqs: Wind through the colorful markets in the alleys behind Islamic Cairo's main attractions. You can buy fresh camel meat, choose your chickens live, or just take a stimulating stroll (page 76).

3 Snorkeling in Ras Mohammed National Park: Explore the dazzling underwater life in this unique corner of the Sinai, where protected fish and fringing reefs create a kaleidoscope of colors (page 351).

>>>

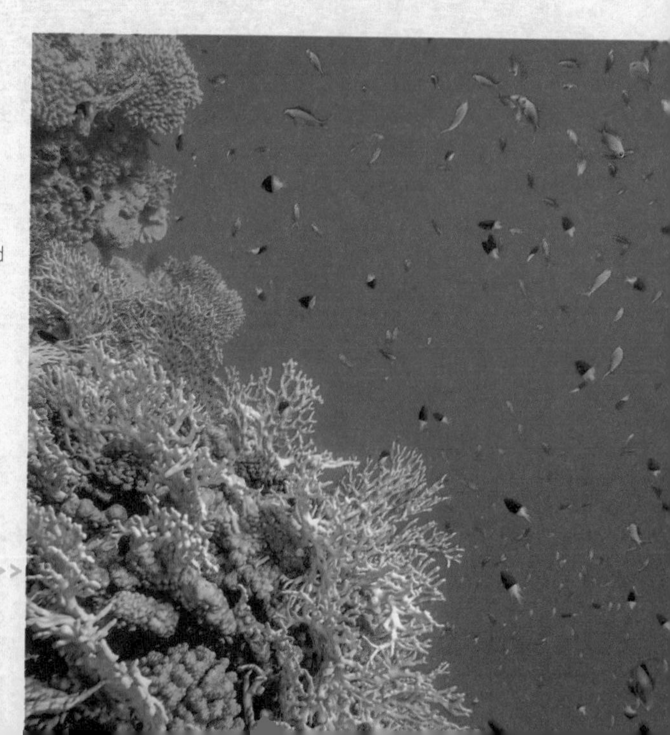

4 **Summiting Mt. Sinai at dawn:** Ascend the historic mountain to watch the sun rise over the rocky landscape from the point where Moses is said to have received the Ten Commandments (page 367).

^
^
^

5 **Camping in the White Desert:** Sleep under the stars in this lunar landscape where mushroom-shaped rocks spring out of snow-white waves of limestone (page 387).

6 Wandering in the shadows of kings at Karnak Temple: This sprawling complex with origins nearly 4,000 years old is separated into pockets of ancient architectural treasures. Stroll down the Avenue of Sphinxes, visit the Sacred Lake, and feel small in the Grand Hypostyle Hall that boasts 134 decorated columns, some close to 25 meters (80 ft) tall (page 171).

7 Riding the dunes in the Great Sand Sea: Hold on tight as your local guide speeds along Siwa's undulating dunes in an off-road vehicle, with nothing but dramatic hills of sand stretching as far as the eye can see (page 403).

>>>

8 Floating in Siwa's Salt Mines: Experience the buoyancy of super-saline water in these striking turquoise pools surrounded by mounds of glittering salt (page 402).

>>>

9 Sailing on the Nile: Escape the chaos of Cairo's streets (page 72) or glide alongside Aswan's lush green islands and golden hills (page 233) on a traditional wooden sailboat steered by expert hands.

>>>

10 Cycling around the City of the Dead: Pedal your way to the breathtaking mortuary temples of Egypt's greatest pharaohs and their colorful tombs in the Valley of the Kings (page 190).

<<<

11 Swimming with the dugong: A cousin of the manatee and distant relative of the elephant, the dugong has a smile that's contagious. Visit their seagrass feeding grounds along the Red Sea Coast for a chance to spot one swimming serenely among playful fish (page 327).

>>>

12 **Exploring Wadi el-Hitan, "Valley of the Whales":** Contemplate the mysteries of our magnificent planet as you wind your way past whale skeletons from some 40 million years ago in their sandy resting place that was once a vast sea (page 124).

Planning Your Trip

Where to Go

Cairo

In Egypt's capital and largest city, layers of history meld with cosmopolitan modernity in a veritable kaleidoscope of human civilizations. Urban sprawl abuts ancient ruins, and young lovers snap selfies as they stroll down 10th-century lanes.

Giza and Around Cairo

Technically part of Greater Cairo, the Giza Plateau is home to the legendary **Sphinx** and **Great Pyramid of Giza.** A couple of hours south of Cairo, get a taste of the country's massive Western Desert in Fayoum, where 40-million-year-old fossils lie in the **Valley of the Whales.**

Northern Nile Valley

Often passed up by tourists in favor of Luxor and Aswan, this strip along the Nile Valley between Cairo and Luxor is for the **die-hard antiquity fans.** Stare at the shockingly blue ceiling of the **Hathor Temple**—one of Egypt's best-preserved ancient houses of worship—and visit the golden-hued interior of the 4th-century **Red Monastery.** After experiencing the crowds at some of the more traveled destinations, you'll appreciate the chance to soak up these treasures in peace.

Luxor

Famed city of ancient temples, Luxor is one grand open-air museum. In the East Bank's "City of the Living," modern life buzzes around plots of **millennia-old monuments.** Cross the Nile to the "City of the Dead" to descend into the tombs

Sphinx and Great Pyramid of Giza

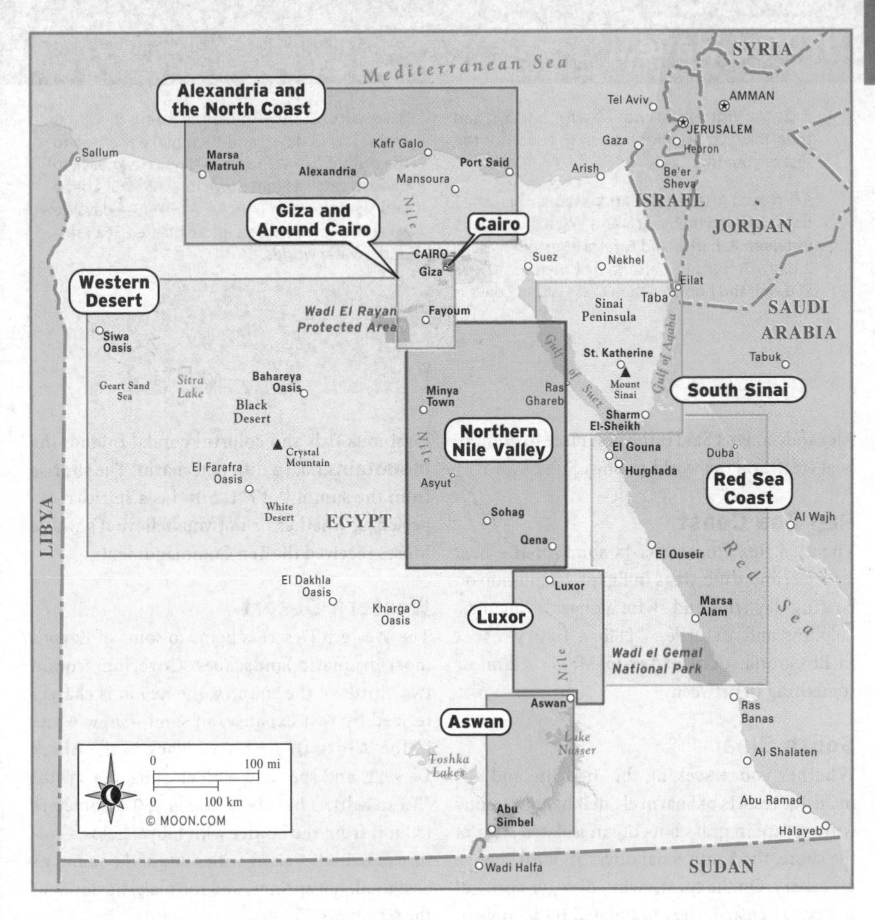

of the **Valley of the Kings** and climb the steps to the elegant **temple of Pharaoh Queen Hatshepsut.**

Aswan

South of Luxor along the Nile, Aswan is the **gateway to Nubia**—home to one of the world's earliest civilizations. Nubians speak their own languages, have their own traditional foods, music, and dance, and are much more relaxed than their compatriots in Egypt's larger cities. The **Abu Simbel Temples** sit at the southern tip of Aswan on Lake Nasser and are two of the country's most impressive.

Alexandria and the North Coast

With its heavy traffic and crowded beaches demanding conservative attire for women, Alexandria is a bit like a miniature Cairo on the Mediterranean (though don't say this to locals). Still, Egypt's second city has its many charms—most notably, artifacts from the days of its namesake, **Alexander the Great,** and Egypt's last female pharaoh, **Queen Cleopatra.** It's also where you'll find some of the country's freshest **seafood.**

If you're looking for a seaside respite with white sand and turquoise waters, continue west to the **resort towns** along the North Coast. East of

If You Have...

- **5 days:** Visit **Cairo** and **Giza** for 2-3 days, and then take a quick flight down to Luxor for the rest of your trip.
- **10 days:** After exploring **Cairo** and **Giza** (3 days), head to the **Black** and **White Deserts** between Bahariya and Farafra (Western Desert; 2 days). Return to Cairo to fly down to **Luxor** (3 days), and hop on a train to **Aswan** (2 days).
- **2 weeks:** Start with the must-sees in **Cairo** and **Giza** (3 days), and then make the trek to the distant **Siwa Oasis** (4 days). Head back to Cairo to catch a flight down to **Luxor** (3-4 days) and swing over to **Marsa Alam** (3-4 days) to relax by the beach or explore the Red Sea's rich underwater worlds.

Alexandria, Port Said is the best place to glimpse boat traffic on the world-famous **Suez Canal.**

Red Sea Coast

The Red Sea Coast boasts some of the best **snorkel** and **dive sites** in Egypt. Island-hop on boating day trips and swim alongside dugongs, dolphins, and sea turtles. Opt for a **luxury resort** in El Gouna, **ecolodges** in Marsa Alam, or something in between.

South Sinai

Whether you're seeking the nightlife and all-inclusive resorts of Sharm el Sheikh, or harmony with nature in grass huts on an isolated strip of the shore, the South Sinai offers an ideal change of scenery. On the coast, swim, **dive,** or **snorkel** in crystal-clear waters populated by schools of luminous fish and colorful corals. Inland, the **mountains** hold a different charm. The sunrise from the summit of **Mt. Sinai** is a spiritual experience, whether or not you believe it's where Moses received the Ten Commandments.

Western Desert

The Western Desert is home to some of Egypt's most dramatic landscapes. Covering around two-thirds of the country, the region is characterized by vast expanses of sand—snow white in the **White Desert,** coal black in the **Black Desert,** and speckled with crystals on **Crystal Mountain.** The **Siwa Oasis,** 50 kilometers (30 mi) from the border with Libya, holds a culture unto itself—along with some of the country's best food, hot springs, and the majestic dunes of the **Great Sand Sea.**

When to Go

Different parts of the country have different high and low seasons, as indicated below. Some general advice: You may want to avoid traveling in summer (June-Aug.) if you can. Cairo, Luxor, and other inland destinations are less crowded, but for good reason—they are sweltering—while the North Coast sees its biggest crowds. In all regions, the **shoulder seasons** listed are generally the best time to visit, when the weather is excellent and the tourists are few.

Dates to avoid: During Egypt's major holidays (**Eid el Fitr,** which immediately follows Ramadan; **Eid el Adha,** whose dates vary according to the lunar calendar; and **Sham el Nassim,** which coincides with Orthodox Easter) local tourism to the seaside is booming. The week of

Christmas and **New Year's** brings tourists to destinations all around the country, with prices of hotels and cruises typically much higher than usual. Finally, outside of Aswan, the **Abu Simbel Sun Festival** (Feb. 22 and Oct. 22), when the sun illuminates the inner sanctum of the Abu Simbel Temples, is impressive, but crowded enough that some might want to make a point to skip it.

Traveling during **Ramadan** is not an issue—see page 447 for more information.

Cairo/Giza, Nile Valley (including Luxor and Aswan), and the Western Desert

- **High season (Dec.-Feb.):** Egypt's coolest months tend to be the busiest in the country's inland destinations, especially Luxor and Aswan.
- **Low season (May-Sept.):** Sweltering summers keep visitors away, especially in the Western Desert and along the Nile Valley.
- **Shoulder seasons (Mar.-Apr. and Oct.-Nov.)**

Alexandria and the North Coast

- **High season (June-Aug.):** Egyptians flock to the North Coast to escape the hot interior.
- **Low season (Oct.-Apr.):** Most signs of life disappear from the vacation villages along the Mediterranean outside summer (a phenomenon I will never understand). Restaurants and grocery stores close, and transportation is hard to come by. The major cities (Alexandria, Port Said, and Marsa Matruh) are still fully functioning and busy with their year-round residents, but much less crowded than in the summers. The weather still pleasant at this time, but December-February is a bit cold for swimming.
- **Shoulder seasons (Sept. and May)**

South Sinai

- **High season (Apr.-May and Oct.-Dec., plus July-Aug. for Sharm el Sheikh):** Dahab, Nuweiba to Taba, and St. Katherine in the interior are at their most crowded, but the crowds here are rarely overwhelming.

Sharm el Sheikh

Europeans head to the resort town of Sharm el Sheikh for summer vacation (July-Aug.) in addition to the other months listed.

- **Low season (Jan.-Feb. and June-Aug.):** Weather is pleasant for hanging in the sea (though summers are hot), and tourists are fewer, making these months fine times to visit.
- **Shoulder seasons (Mar. and Sept.)**

Red Sea Coast

- **High season (Apr.-May and Sept.-Nov.):** The high season along the Red Sea Coast corresponds with the region's best weather.
- **Low season (Dec.-Feb. and July-Aug.):** Many avoid the Red Sea Coast's high temperatures, while winter might be too cool for comfort for some snorkelers and divers.
- **Shoulder seasons (Mar and June)**

Before You Go

Passports and Visas

Visas ($25, or the Egyptian Pound equivalent; valid for 30 days with a 14-day grace period) are available to citizens of the **US, Canada, UK, EU, New Zealand,** and **Australia** upon arrival at any Egyptian airport. You must have at least six months left on your **passport** before expiration to be granted the visa. EVisas are also available for citizens of these countries but are not recommended at this point.

Visitors from **South Africa** will have to apply for a visa well in advance of travel to Egypt.

Transportation

Most travelers to Egypt arrive by air. To get around the country, taking a **bus** or hiring a **private driver** is often the way to go. **Flying** is fast but expensive, and **trains** are an option for travel from Cairo to Alexandria or down the Nile Valley to Aswan.

Language

Egyptians working in the tourism industry (in hotels, on cruises, and in upscale restaurants) will likely have a good command of English. Many average Egyptians also speak some English, but it's often very limited. Some helpful Arabic words and phrases to have on hand before you go include:

- Ahlan: hello
- Shukran: thank you
- Low Samaht: please
- La: no
- Aywa: yes

For a longer list, see page 453.

Best of Egypt: Cairo, the Pyramids, and Luxor

If it's your first trip to Egypt, you won't want to miss Cairo, the Giza pyramids, and the other antiquities that make the country famous, which are largely concentrated around Luxor. This itinerary also gives you a taste of the expansive Western Desert in Fayoum and a dose of Nubian history in Aswan.

If you want to add snorkeling to this trip, head to **Marsa Alam** (4 hours from Luxor by private car) on the Red Sea Coast instead of Aswan on day 6. Explore the house reef at your ecolodge, try to spot a dugong, and swim alongside dolphins.

Day 1: Cairo

Follow the **Highlights of Cairo** itinerary (page 41) to see the city's top attractions, including **Ibn Tulun Mosque,** a bustling **souq,** and rambling **Mu'izz Street.**

Day 2: Giza Pyramids and the Sphinx

Day trip from central Cairo (up to 1 hour by private car)

Hire a guide to take you to the pyramids of **Giza,** the **Sphinx,** and the newly opened **Grand Egyptian Museum,** returning to your Cairo hotel in the evening.

Day 3: Fayoum and Valley of the Whales

Day trip from Cairo (2 hours by private car)

Hire a private driver to pick you up from your hotel in Cairo and bring you to Fayoum's Wadi el-Rayan Protected Area with a short stop in **Tunis Village** for pottery shopping. Get a glimpse of Egypt's expansive **Western Desert** and check out 40-million-year-old whale fossils at the **Valley of the Whales.** Head back to Cairo after sundown.

café in Cairo's Khan el-Khalili bazaar

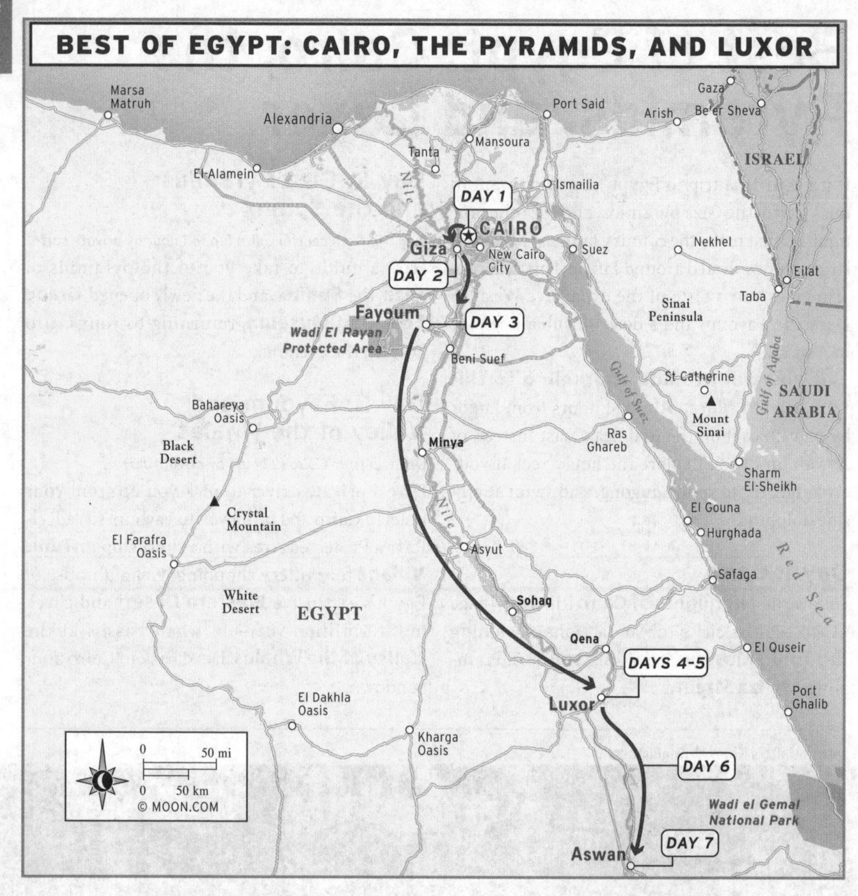

Days 4-5: Luxor

1 hour from Cairo by plane

On your first day in Luxor, explore the East Bank's sprawling **Karnak Temple Complex,** treasure-filled **Luxor Museum,** and **Luxor Temple,** rising out of the modern city center.

On your second day, take a **hot-air balloon** over the West Bank at sunrise, and spend the rest of the day exploring the elaborate **mortuary temples** you've just seen from above. Don't miss the **Mortuary Temple of Hatshepsut** and **Medinet Habu Temple,** plus the colorful tombs in the **Valley of the Kings** and **Deir el-Medina.**

Day 6: Luxor to Aswan

8 hours from Luxor to Aswan by private car (including stops)

Hire a private driver to bring you and your luggage down to Aswan, stopping at the Greco-Roman temples in **Esna, Edfu,** and **Kom Ombo** along the way.

Day 7: Aswan

Check out the beautiful **Nubia Museum** before visiting the reassembled **Philae Temple** on an island in the reservoir between the Low and High Dams. Then, **kayak** in the surrounding waters with **Heissa Camp** and ask them to organize an evening of **Nubian music** and dancing.

Egypt's Best...

felucca sailing on the Nile river

PYRAMIDS, TEMPLES, AND MONUMENTS

- The **Giza Pyramid Complex** with the **Sphinx** and **Great Pyramid of Giza** is probably Egypt's number one draw.
- **Luxor's** temples and burial sites come in a close second.
- Travelers who don't mind the extra commute head to the **Abu Simbel Temples** near Egypt's southern border with Sudan.

DIVING AND SNORKELING

With chances to experience untouched beaches and magnificent dive sites, Egypt's **Red Sea Coast** and **South Sinai** are major highlights. All of these places have options suitable for beginners as well as advanced snorkelers and divers.

- The main outpost for diving and snorkeling on the Red Sea Coast is the resort town of **Hurghada.**
- Those looking for lesser developed seaside escapes might prefer a trip to the Red Sea Coast's **Marsa Alam.**
- On the Sinai Peninsula, head to the resort town of **Sharm el Sheikh.**
- Travelers in search of simplicity will enjoy the strip of the Sinai between **Nuweiba and Taba** with its hut-lined beach camps—difficult to find on mainland Egypt's coast.

NILE SAILING AND CRUISES

- Enjoy a short sunset sail on a traditional wooden sailboat (**felucca**) in Cairo, Luxor, and Aswan, or spend more time on the Nile with a **multiday cruise.** Choose from a luxury ship with pools and restaurants, boutique dahabiya (large two-masted sailboat), or basic felucca. The most popular routes go between Luxor and Aswan over 3-5 nights, stopping at temples along the way.
- Larger cruise ships also offer 3-4-night trips across the placid **Lake Nasser,** departing from Aswan and arriving at the dramatic Abu Simbel Temples.

DESERT SAFARIS

Venturing into Egypt's slice of the Sahara is an unparalleled experience.

- Traverse the dunes of the far-flung **Great Sand Sea.**
- Cross the color-shifting sands of the **Black and White Deserts.**
- Take a day trip to **Fayoum** for an experience near Cairo.

South Sinai: Snorkeling and More

A trip to the South Sinai encapsulates some of Egypt's most impressive landscapes, from colorful reefs to majestic mountains.

From Cairo, the best way to get here is to fly into Sharm el Sheikh's international airport (1 hour).

Day 1: Sharm el Sheikh

1 hour from Cairo by plane

Hop on a boat for a snorkel or dive along the string of reefs in the **Straits of Tiran.**

Day 2: Ras Mohammed National Park

Day trip from Sharm (45 minutes by private car)

Hire a private driver to explore this rugged national park with some of Egypt's most vibrant fringing reefs. Don't miss the **Shark Observatory** snorkel/dive site and the neighboring **Shark Observatory Clifftop** for fabulous views of where the two arms of the Red Sea meet. Take a dip in the glittering **Enchanted Lake** and swing by the **Mangrove Channel** to check out its unique ecosystem. Head back to your Sharm hotel in the evening.

Day 3: Dahab

1 hour from Sharm by private car

Rent bikes to explore this small seaside village, check out the corals off **A'sala Beach,** swim and stay for sunset at the mountain-ringed **El Laguna,** indulge in a feast of fresh **seafood,** and shop along the seaside promenade, **El Mamsha.**

Day 4: Blue Hole and Ras Abu Galum Protectorate

Day trip from Dahab (20 minutes by private car)

Begin at the **Blue Hole** for a snorkel or dive

Dahab

Best Local Experiences

Egypt isn't just about antiquities. Seek out local experiences and you won't be disappointed.

fresh juice shop in Cairo

IN CAIRO

- Challenge a local to a game of backgammon at a Downtown **ahwa** (street-side café).
- Sip fresh mango juice at a drive-in juice shop like Dokki's **Abo Amr City Drink.**
- Sprinkle some vinegar and garlic sauce (da'a) on your plate of koshary (pasta, rice, lentils, chickpeas, and fried onions) at **Koshary Abou Tarek.**
- Navigate the clamorous **Souq el-Ataba.**
- Watch the sun set over the city from the **Mokattam Corniche.**

LOCAL STAYS

- **Farm House** on Aswan's Elephantine Island offers an opportunity to learn about local nature and Nubian culture. Wander the dusty streets of their close-knit island village, with mud-brick houses and green agricultural fields.
- Have your fill of farm-to-fork meals in the shade of palms at **Fahmi's Garden.** Fahmi built a bungalow of palm fronds and extra rooms to host guests in his lovely Siwa home.

HIKING WITH A BEDOUIN GUIDE

- Break bread with the Bedouins of **St. Katherine** on a mountain hike through their homeland.

SIPPING JEBENA (TRADITIONAL COFFEE)

- Members of the local Ababda tribe operate cafés on a pair of pristine beaches in **Wadi el Gemal National Park.** Have an authentic meal or just a delicious hit of caffeine, and keep an eye out for locals selling handicrafts.

around the coral-filled sinkhole. From here, hop on a shared **boat** to the **First Bedouin Village** for more excellent snorkeling, and then grab a pickup truck taxi to the dazzling **Blue Lagoon.** Cool off in crystal-clear waters or just lay on the beach between the mountains and the sea. Make your way back to Dahab around sunset.

Day 5: St. Katherine

1.5 hours from Dahab by private car

Explore the South Sinai's majestic mountains and Bedouin life with a hike up **Mt. Sinai** with a local guide (4-5 hours round-trip). More serious hikers might prefer the longer (less trodden) trek through hidden wadis and gardens up **Mt. Katherine** (8-10 hours round-trip). Spend the night at a central St. Katherine bed and breakfast.

Day 6-7: Nuweiba to Taba

1.5 hours from St. Katherine by private car

On your first day in this quiet strip of the South Sinai coast, just lounge around your **beach camp** of choice, and maybe saunter into the sea for a swim or snorkel.

On your second day, take a day trip to hike through the psychedelic swirls of the **Colored Canyon.** Return to your camp for more relaxing, swimming, and snorkeling.

Urban Adventure to Desert Dream

This yin-and-yang itinerary lets you steep in Cairo's frenetic buzz before departing for the blissful solitude of the Siwa Oasis and Western Desert.

Day 1: Cairo

Explore the monuments of medieval Cairo on **Mu'izz Street,** shop in the winding streets of the **Khan el-Khalili** bazaar, and enjoy sunset with a view from a green perch in **Azhar Park.**

Day 2: Giza

Day trip from central Cairo (up to 1 hour by private car)

Hire a guide to take you to the famed **Giza Pyramid Complex, Sphinx,** and **Grand Egyptian Museum** just down the street.

Day 3: Cairo

Ascend the minaret of one of Egypt's largest and oldest mosques, **Ibn Tulun Mosque,** and then pop in next door to visit the eccentric home and antiquities collection of a 20th-century Brit at the **Gayer-Anderson Museum.** Admire the elegant arches of the **Mosque & Madrasa of Sultan Hasan** and its neighbor, the younger **Al-Rifa'i Mosque.** Sail along the Nile in a **felucca** for sunset.

Day 4: Cairo to Siwa

9-10 hours from Cairo by private car

Much of this day will be spent on the road. Stop at the seaside town of **Marsa Matruh** for lunch and perhaps a quick dip in the Mediterranean.

Day 5: Siwa

On your first full day in Siwa, climb the honeycombed **Mountain of the Dead** to get the lay of the land, swim in the turquoise **Salt Mines,** visit

Mu'izz Street in Cairo

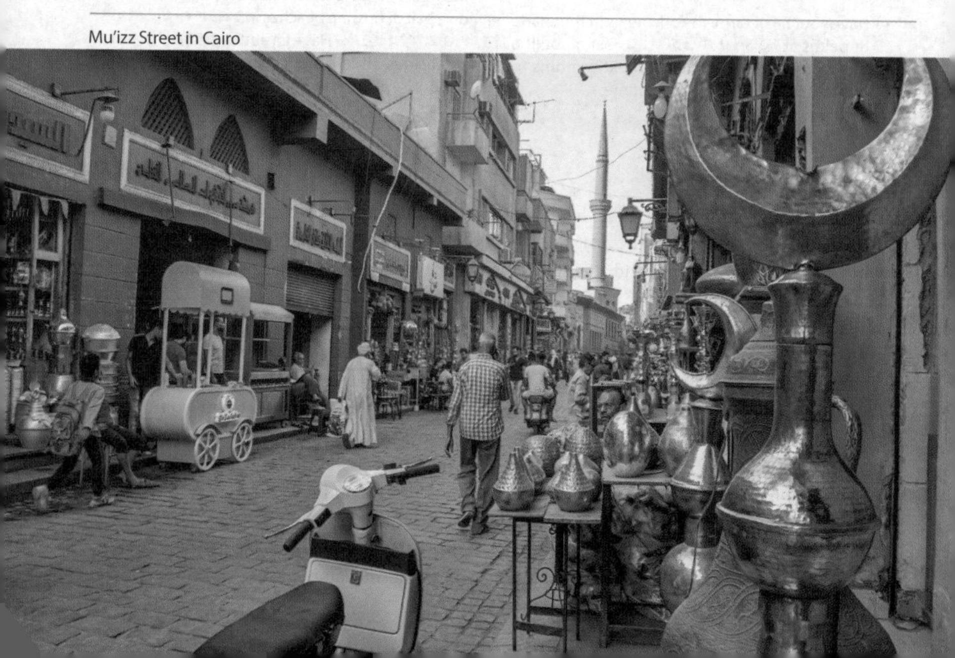

Local Specialties

Each region of Egypt has its own food specialties. Here are a few standouts.

MAGLOUBA

Where to try it: South Sinai

In the Sinai, maglouba (meaning "upside down") is made with rice, vegetables, and a meat (either goat, chicken, or fish). The meat, vegetables, and spices go into the pot first, and are then covered with marinated rice. When it's done cooking, the dish is flipped over onto a large plate with the meat and veg on top. Then everyone grabs a spoon and digs in.

SIWI CUISINE

Where to try it: Siwa Oasis (Western Desert)

The Siwa Oasis has some of the country's best food. Taste the unique flavor of meats marinated and left to cook for hours in a pot buried underground, called **Abu Mardam.** Also sample **leedam,** a tomato-based vegetable dish with onions, coriander, and meat broth served with rice; and **reearin,** a nutritious dish of lentils, hot peppers and **molokhia** (a soupy green). Siwa's classic breakfast spread with a colorful palette of homemade jams (**maraba**)—carrot, fig, date, apricot—is another treat.

SEAFOOD

Where to try it: Alexandria; Port Said; Red Sea Coast; South Sinai

The coasts of the Mediterranean and Red Sea offer delicious seafood—it's so good that people in Cairo travel more than two hours to Alexandria just for lunch! Alexandria or Port Said is the place to go for **fresh shrimp, calamari, crab, oysters,** and Mediterranean fish purchased fresh by the kilo, prepared with Alexandrian or Port Saidian spices and sauces. Along the Red Sea, fish is the main attraction. Try **harid** (parrot fish) for a delicious but inexpensive treat. **Red snapper** and **Red Sea bream** are also tasty options.

molokhia

FATEER MESHALTET

Where to try it: Fayoum (Giza and Around Cairo)

Fateer meshaltet is the specialty of Egypt's rural areas. It's a flaky, layered pastry sometimes made with savory or sweet fillings, but most often left plain and dipped into honey (a'sal) or molasses (a'sal iswid). Homemade ghee, in liberal amounts, is an essential ingredient.

the legendary **Temple of the Oracle,** and watch the sunset from **Fatnas Island.**

Day 6: Great Sand Sea

15 minutes from central Siwa on a guided safari

Ride the undulating dunes in the Great Sand Sea on a 4WD safari. Your local guide/driver will stop at various points to **sandboard** before bringing you to **soak** in **Bir Wahed Hot Spring.** Spend the night **camping** under the stars.

Day 7: Siwa

Explore the 13th-century **Shali Fortress** built of a rock-salt mixture, go **natural spring-hopping,** or relax under the palms in your accommodation's natural spring pool.

Cairo (Al-Qahira)

Twenty-million strong and holding the traces of millennia-old civilizations, Greater Cairo oozes humanity, history, and culture. Material legacies from the pharaohs to the Brits all intermingle to form the foundation of this vibrant city—with stones from the pyramids of Giza integrated into the walls of the 12th-century Citadel, and the 19th-century British-built Ramses Station still the central gateway to Cairo by rail. Belle Époque architecture decorates Downtown and upper-class neighborhoods like Garden City and Zamalek, and unfinished brick buildings stand, sometimes precariously, next to medieval monuments in working-class districts like Sayeda Zeinab and el-Darb el-Ahmar.

Those who come to Egypt for the camels, desert, and pyramids

Highlights

Look for ★ to find recommended sights, activities, dining, and lodging.

★ **Ibn Tulun Mosque:** The pointed arches in this massive 9th-century mosque—Egypt's oldest still standing—inspired European Gothic architecture some 200 years later. Climb the jagged staircase of its minaret for magnificent views of Islamic Cairo (page 46).

★ **Gayer-Anderson Museum:** These medieval-houses-turned-British-Orientalist's-home hide secret passageways and eclectic collections (page 48).

★ **Citadel:** The seat of power in Egypt for nearly 700 years, the Citadel today offers access to fascinating history, peaceful gardens, and the Mohammed Ali Mosque, one of Cairo's most beautiful (page 48).

★ **Bab Zuweila:** Climb to the top of the minarets soaring above this southern gate of the 10th-century Fatimid city to imagine what guards would have seen as they protected their walled city (page 55).

★ **Mu'izz Street:** Some of the best Mamluk monuments are concentrated on this 1-kilometer (0.6-mi) path, once the main thoroughfare of the Fatimid's 10th-century walled city (page 59).

★ **Mokattam Corniche:** See the city sprawled out before you in all its glory from the edge of Mokattam Hills. The corniche is also a fabulous spot to savor the sunset with locals (page 63).

★ **Azhar Park:** This oasis of green space perched on a hill offers the most peaceful stroll you'll have in Cairo, and it's one of the city's most magical spots to watch the sunset (page 70).

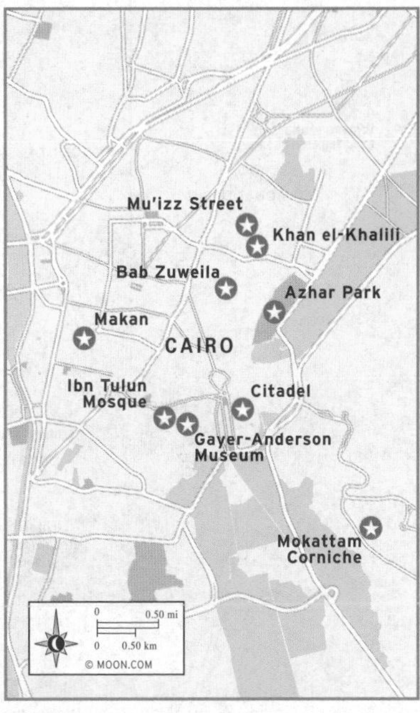

★ **Makan:** Enjoy an evening of spellbinding folk music—all polyrhythmic drumming and full-bodied voices—in this intimate Downtown venue. Wednesday nights offer the best experience (page 73).

★ **Khan el-Khalili:** Visit Cairo's most famous bazaar for high-quality crafts, cheap souvenirs, or just the buzz of commerce (page 76).

Cairo

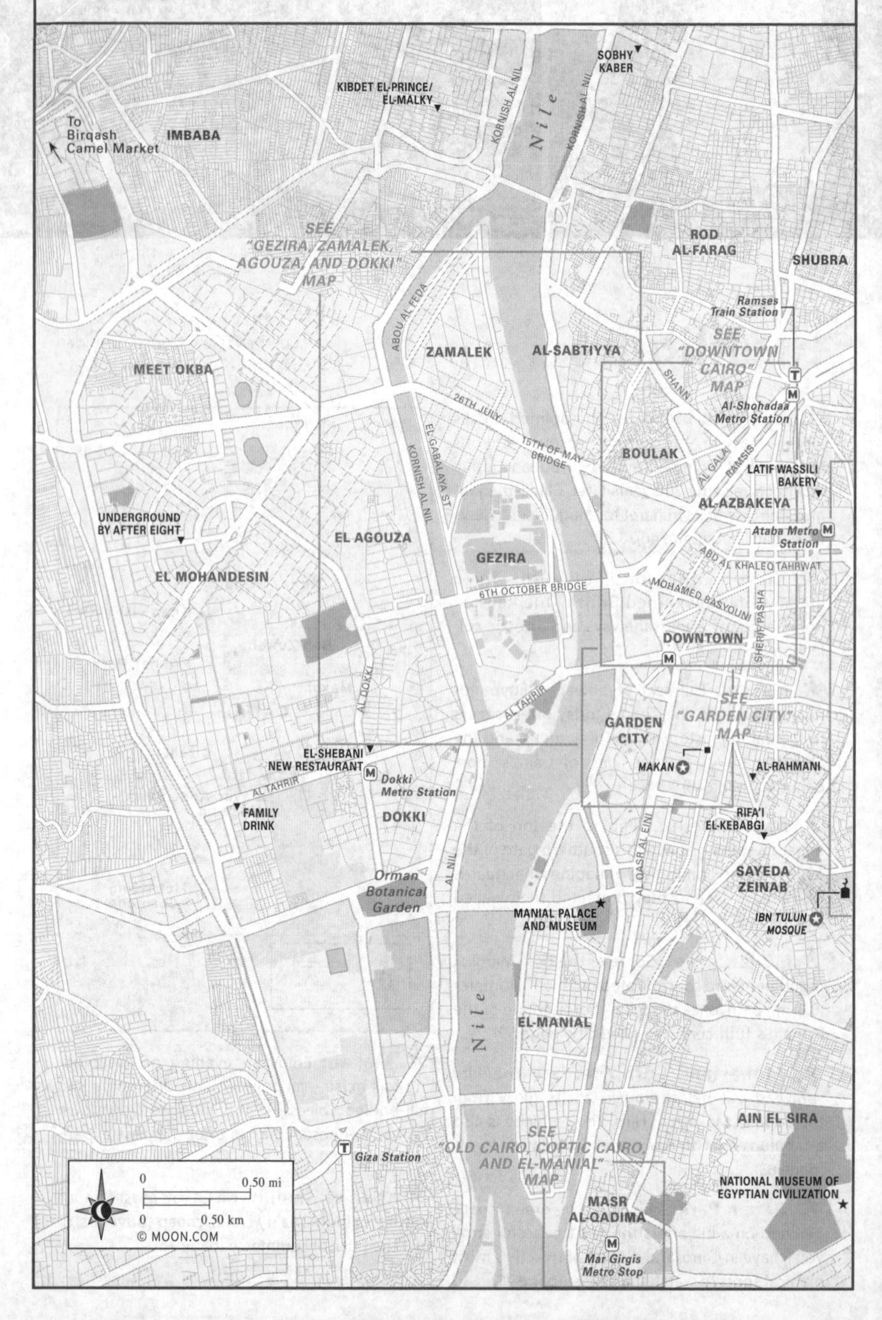
To Birqash Camel Market
IMBABA
KIBDET EL-PRINCE/ EL-MALKY
SOBHY KABER
KORNISH AL NIL
Nile
SEE "GEZIRA, ZAMALEK, AGOUZA, AND DOKKI" MAP
ROD AL-FARAG
SHUBRA
Ramses Train Station
SEE "DOWNTOWN CAIRO" MAP
ABOU AL FEDA
ZAMALEK
AL-SABTIYYA
MEET OKBA
SHANN
Al-Shohadaa Metro Station
26TH JULY
15TH OF MAY BRIDGE
EL-GABALAYA ST
BOULAK
AL GALA
RAMSIS
LATIF WASSILI BAKERY
AL-AZBAKEYA
UNDERGROUND BY AFTER EIGHT
EL AGOUZA
Ataba Metro Station
GEZIRA
ABD AL KHALEQ TAHRWAT
EL MOHANDESIN
6TH OCTOBER BRIDGE
MOHAMED BASYOUNI
DOWNTOWN
SHERIF PASHA
AL DOKKI
AL TAHRIR
SEE "GARDEN CITY" MAP
GARDEN CITY
EL-SHEBANI NEW RESTAURANT
MAKAN
AL-RAHMANI
Dokki Metro Station
FAMILY DRINK
DOKKI
RIFA'I EL-KEBABGI
AL QASR AL EINI
SAYEDA ZEINAB
Orman Botanical Garden
AL NIL
MANIAL PALACE AND MUSEUM
IBN TULUN MOSQUE
EL-MANIAL
AIN EL SIRA
SEE "OLD CAIRO, COPTIC CAIRO, AND EL-MANIAL" MAP
Giza Station
0
0.50 mi
0
0.50 km
© MOON.COM
NATIONAL MUSEUM OF EGYPTIAN CIVILIZATION
MASR AL-QADIMA
Mar Girgis Metro Stop

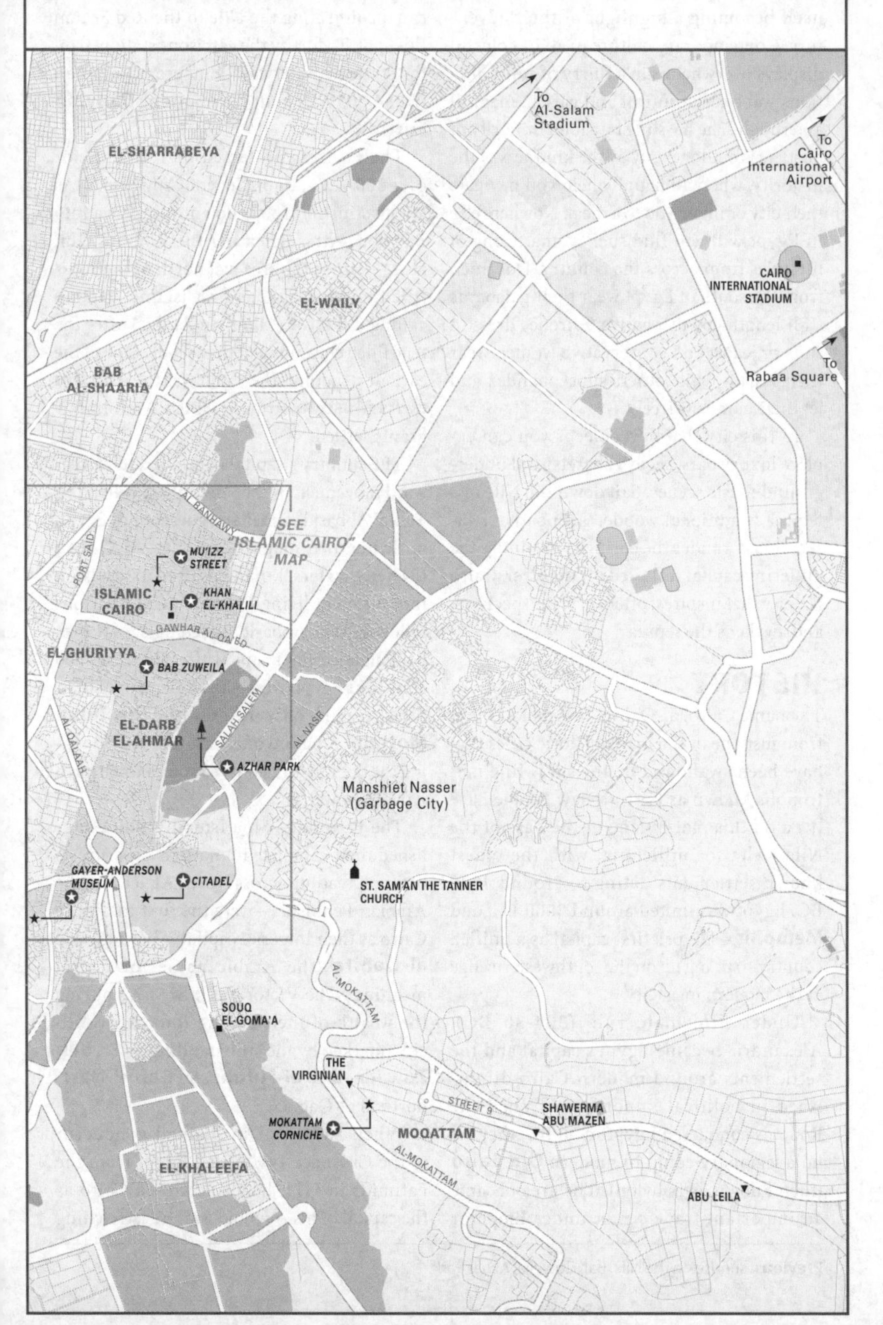
To
Al-Salam
Stadium
To
Cairo
International
Airport
EL-SHARRABEYA
CAIRO
INTERNATIONAL
STADIUM
EL-WAILY
To
Rabaa Square
BAB
AL-SHAARIA
AL BANHAWY
SEE
"ISLAMIC CAIRO"
MAP
PORT SAID
MU'IZZ
STREET
ISLAMIC
CAIRO
KHAN
EL-KHALILI
GAWHAR AL QA'ED
EL-GHURIYYA
BAB ZUWEILA
SALAH SALEM
AL NASR
EL-DARB
EL-AHMAR
AL QALAAH
AZHAR PARK
Manshiet Nasser
(Garbage City)
GAYER-ANDERSON
MUSEUM
CITADEL
ST. SAM'AN THE TANNER
CHURCH
AL-MOKATTAM
SOUQ
EL-GOMA'A
THE
VIRGINIAN
STREET 9
SHAWERMA
ABU MAZEN
MOKATTAM
CORNICHE
MOQATTAM
AL-MOKATTAM
EL-KHALEEFA
ABU LEILA

might be surprised to find the city of Cairo itself becoming a highlight of their adventure. Contemporary culture in all its colorful displays overwhelms in a flurry of contradictions—at once beautiful and garish, magical and rough. The hassling by a loud minority of hustlers is outdone only by the kindness of the majority, who will happily help you navigate their city or invite you to a meal. Nowhere else in Egypt will you find such a smattering of lifestyles from across the country. Doormen from the south of Egypt wear their galabayas (full-length gowns), native Cairenes dress in suits or jeans, and conservative women wear their niqabs while others sport spandex and let their hair flow freely.

In this city that never sleeps you can explore luxury bars, seedy cabarets, and underground music scenes. Sail down the Nile in a felucca (traditional wooden sailboat) at sunset, or just wander the corniche to admire the glittering capital reflected off the river. Cairo is a city that inspires, offers new perspectives, and awakens the senses.

HISTORY

The name Cairo (al-Qahira in Arabic) comes from just one of the many historic cities that have been swallowed by the sprawling metropolis known as Cairo today. People have lived on this plot of land at the base of the Nile Delta for millennia, with the oldest known settlements dating to around 4000 BC. Egypt was united around 3000 BC, and **Memphis**—Egypt's first capital as a unified country—sprang up on the southwestern edge of the modern megacity.

Under Ptolemaic rule (304-30 BC), Alexandria became Egypt's capital and the settlements around modern Cairo diminished in political importance. When the Romans conquered Egypt in 30 BC, they set up a legionary camp in modern **Old Cairo** (then known as Babylon). The area became an important trade center under Emperor Trajan (r. 98-117 AD), who revived an ancient canal connecting the Nile to the Red Sea on this spot. To fortify the garrisons stationed on the strategic waterways, Emperor Diocletian (r. 284-305 AD) built the imposing **Babylon Fortress.**

The Fortress protected its residents for over 300 years, until General Amr Ibn al-As led his Muslim troops down from Syria into Babylon. After defeating the Romans, Ibn al-As claimed the area just north of their fortified town as Egypt's first Islamic capital, calling it **Fustat** ("Tent" in Arabic) after the tent-filled encampment they set up. One of the earliest structures they built was the **Amr ibn al-As Mosque,** around which Arab immigrants settled.

The country's capital continued its northward movement in the 9th century, when Ibn Tulun, Abbasid solider and governor of Egypt, built his own magnificent city, **al-Qata'i** ("The Quarters"), named after its division into different living quarters for his various followers. The Abbasids razed most of the rebellious governor's capital after they regained control of Egypt (which had fallen out of their orbit), leaving only the exquisite **Ibn Tulun Mosque.** A period of unrest followed, opening the door to invasion by a competing North African power.

The Fatimids—Shia Ismailis who established their caliphate in modern-day Tunisia before spreading across North Africa and the Arabian Peninsula—were the first to choose Cairo as their imperial capital. They founded **al-Qahira** (the Arabic name for Cairo, meaning "The Victorious") in 969, pouring the wealth of their empire into the walled city (marked by the still-standing gates, **Bab Zuweila, Bab el-Futuh,** and **Bab el-Nasr**) north of al-Qata'i.

When Salah el-Din—famed conqueror of the Crusaders—wrestled Egypt from the Fatimids in 1171, he also claimed Cairo as the capital of his Ayyubid Empire (stretching

Previous: sunrise on the Nile; Bab Zuweila; Azhar Park.

across half of North Africa, along the Arabian Peninsula, and deep into Greater Syria). He built his own fortified outpost, the **Citadel,** and commissioned a wall (never completed) to surround Fatimid al-Qahira and Fustat.

The Mamluks (meaning "property," or "possessed") were the slave soldiers of the Ayyubid rulers who eventually overthrew their masters in 1250. They took control of the expansive empire they had earlier helped secure and maintained Cairo as their capital. The Mamluks' imperial stronghold became one of the most exquisite cities in the world, with monumental architecture lining **Mu'izz Street** in the Fatimid's walled city all the way down to the Citadel, and beyond.

When the Ottomans conquered Egypt in 1517, they stripped much of Cairo's wealth, sending it instead to their capital, Constantinople. In 1798, Napoleon invaded Egypt, flattening parts of Cairo as his troops quashed riots that erupted periodically during their three-year occupation.

It wasn't until Mohammed Ali—a military commander sent to Egypt to oust the French—became the country's Ottoman viceroy in 1805 that Cairo would begin to regain its status as a regional power center. Mohammed Ali built schools and infrastructure around the city, and embellished the seat of government in the Citadel with multiple palaces and the grand **Mohammed Ali Mosque.**

After Mohammed Ali's death, his descendants ruled Egypt for the next century. His grandson, Khedive Ismail, shifted the heart of the capital toward the Nile to the current Downtown area. Trips to France inspired Ismail to build Egypt's own "Paris on the Nile," and he filled his "modern" Cairo with European-style architecture, building a new seat of government, **Abdeen Palace,** to match.

The British invasion in 1882 brought more transformations to the city. Europeans took up residence in Cairo at a growing pace, bringing with them their Italian restaurants and Parisian cafés. The completion of the Aswan Low Dam in 1902 controlled the annual flooding of the Nile, opening the way for construction even closer to the Nile. Western property developers carved leafy residential neighborhoods like **Garden City** and **Gezira/Zamalek** into the lush Nile-side flora. While affluent foreigners and Egypt-born aristocrats enjoyed increasingly comfortable lives in Cairo, most of the city's natives suffered as the country's wealth went abroad to pay off debts, or toward other projects of the British occupiers' choosing.

When a group of Egyptian military officers ousted the British-backed monarchy in 1952, the city faced another major transformation—something of a reversal of the cosmopolitanization that had begun during the previous century. President Gamal Abdel Nasser's socialist program turned the palaces and gardens of the former ruling elite into public institutions like schools, libraries, and public parks. A campaign of industrialization brought a swell of peasants to the city, which promised opportunities for work and education. This increasing pull of urban centers and the country's population growth as a whole contributed to Greater Cairo's soaring population—reaching an estimated 20 million today, up from under five million in 1960.

ORIENTATION

The Nile separates the Cairo and Giza Governates, with Cairo to the east of the river (for the most part).

Downtown (Wist el-Balad)

Downtown Cairo is the hub of contemporary culture, where the streets are always busy with locals enjoying shisha, tea, and games of backgammon at ahaawi (local coffee shops). This is where you can admire the Belle Époque architecture, take a stroll along the **Nile Corniche,** or sip on Stella (Egypt's most popular local beer) in the cool breeze of the neighborhood's many rooftop bars.

Tahrir Square is the heart of downtown. The **Nile** forms the neighborhood's western border, **Abdeen Palace** and **Ataba Square**

mark the eastern edge, and **Ramses Square,** with its towering neo-Mamluk style train station, sits at the northernmost tip.

Islamic Cairo

East of Downtown just beyond **Port Said Street** begins Islamic Cairo, which can be divided into three major sections from corresponding historical periods. In the north you'll find the original al-Qahira (Cairo)—the 10th-century Fatimid capital—now called the **Gamaleya** district. **Mu'izz Street,** with its multitude of medieval monuments, cuts down the center of this one-time walled city (running north to south). The common entry point to the area is through **Hussein Square** (in front of Hussein Mosque), which leads you first through the **Khan el-Khalili** bazaar before blending into Mu'izz Street.

To the south begins a newer neighborhood, built when the seat of power shifted to the **Citadel** in the 13th century. The Fatimid city is linked to the Citadel through the **el-Darb el-Ahmar** district by a processional road, **Bab el-Wazir Street,** lined with impressive monuments like the **Blue Mosque** and **Khayrbak Funerary Complex.** El-Darb el-Ahmar is bordered to the east by the green gem **Azhar Park,** and beyond that, the **"City of the Dead"** (or **Northern Cemetery**), with an impressive row of medieval mausoleums that stand in a relatively quiet, but thriving (and perfectly safe), working-class neighborhood.

Ibn Tulun Mosque—the last remaining vestige of the 9th-century Tulunid dynasty—roughly marks the southern tip of Islamic Cairo.

Mokattam

The Mokattam neighborhood sits on the hilltop south of Islamic Cairo and offers the best views of the city at the **Mokattam Corniche.**

To the north of Mokattam are middle- to upper-middle class residential areas including **Nasr City.** Visitors aren't likely to spend much time here, but there are spots of political importance on **al-Nasr Road,** such as **Rabaa Square,** where security forces massacred hundreds of protestors staging a sit-in against the military coup in 2013.

Old Cairo and Coptic Cairo

Returning westward to the Nile is the oldest part of Cairo proper—appropriately named Old Cairo—home to the layers of a 2nd-century Roman fortress town, Coptic Cairo and Egypt's first capital built under Muslim rule, Fustat. Here, you'll find the remains of the Romans' **Babylon Fortress,** the beautifully curated **Coptic Museum,** and the **Abu Serga Church,** built on a crypt where the Holy Family is believed to have taken refuge. All are located on a heavily guarded, pedestrian-only street (**Mar Girgis St.**), most easily accessed by the **Mar Girgis** metro stop. Just to the north sits Cairo's former capital, Fustat, with the city's first Muslim house of worship, **Amr ibn al-As Mosque,** and a modern covered market full of handicrafts, **Souq el-Fustat.**

El-Manial

West of Old Cairo on an island in the Nile (Roda Island) is the working- to middle-class district, el-Manial, with a few sights of interest including the lavish **Manial Palace and Museum;** a tribute to Egypt's favorite diva, the **Umm Kulthum Museum & Manasterly Palace;** and the 9th-century **Nilometer,** which measured the annual floods for early Egyptians' agricultural cycles.

Garden City

To the north of Old Cairo and el-Manial along the east bank of the Nile is the upper-class, embassy-rich neighborhood of Garden City, with less activity but plenty of leafy trees, winding streets, and luxury hotels—making it a pleasant base. The green neighborhood is bordered to the east by the busy **Kasr el-Ainy Street,** to the north by Downtown's **Tahrir Square,** and to the west by the **Nile Corniche,** where you can pick up a felucca for a peaceful trip around the Nile.

Gezira and Zamalek

A bit farther north in the middle of the Nile, **Zamalek** is an island in every sense of the word—a self-contained mostly upper-class neighborhood filled with embassies, restaurants, cafés, and bars. The main thoroughfare, **26th of July Street,** is lined with dozens of dining options and sits below the neighborhood's northernmost bridge, **15th of May.** Zamalek occupies the northern half of the island, and the southern half comprises the Gezira district with the sprawling Gezira Youth Club (Markaz Shabab el-Gezira), Cairo Opera House complex, and Nile-side parks (Horreya Garden and Gezira Garden) on either side of the Kasr el-Nil Bridge, which leads to Downtown.

Agouza and Dokki

Crossing the Nile to the west bank (and technically into the Giza Governorate) are the middle-class neighborhoods of Agouza and Dokki, where you can find a handful of good **dining** options. To the north is the working-class neighborhood of **Imbaba.**

PLANNING YOUR TIME

In Egypt all roads lead to Cairo, making it the perfect jumping-off point for visiting the rest of the country. You could spend years exploring the nooks and crannies of this lively city, but give yourself at least three days to make an acquaintance. To avoid wasting time in Cairo's notorious traffic, set up camp in a central location like **Downtown, Zamalek,** or **Garden City** and try to limit your taxi rides by sticking to one walkable area per day.

Most of the city's historic sights are concentrated in **Islamic Cairo,** which you can divide into sections and explore over the course of 2-3 days. The area around the old walled city, Fatimid al-Qahira, (including **Khan el-Khalili, Mu'izz Street, al-Ghouri Complex, al-Azhar Mosque,** and **Azhar Park**) needs at least a day, and another could be spent around the **Citadel** and **el-Darb el-Ahmar.**

A morning in **Old Cairo** can be combined with a visit to **el-Manial** in the afternoon and an evening in **Downtown.** And to enjoy a less touristic day, you can lounge in the parks of **Zamalek** or visit the city outskirts in **Mokattam** and **Manshiet Nasser.**

Unlike some other major cities around the world, in Cairo it's generally not possible to reserve tickets in advance. However, while the city itself is crowded, the tourist attractions typically aren't, so it's unlikely you'll have to wait in long lines.

SIGHTSEEING PASSES

If you plan on visiting a good number of sights in Cairo, Giza, and Luxor, you can combine your purchase of a **Cairo Pass** with a **Luxor Pass** for a 50% discount. See page 167 for more information. The Cairo Pass alone isn't such a great deal (you'd really have to visit all the major sights just to break even), but combined with the Luxor Pass it can save you a bundle.

TOURS AND LOCAL GUIDES

A guide can be a great asset not only for his or her knowledge of Cairo's sights, but also to help you navigate the chaotic city. If you only hire a guide for one day, head to Islamic Cairo where its wealth of medieval monuments will be enriched by an expert escort. Most of the guides and tour providers below also offer trips to the Giza Pyramid Complex.

REAL EGYPT TOURS

tel. 0110 002 2242; www.realegypt.com

Phenomenal guides take you around Cairo (and beyond) on bespoke, private tours. The pampering and professionalism come with more expensive services than many other companies, with prices for 6-8-hour tours based on the size of your group (e.g., $130 for 1 person; $78 per person for 2 people; $40 per person for 5 people), including transportation, guide, and lunch. Entry fees not included.

CAIRO URBAN ADVENTURES

tel. 0109 799 9534; www.urbanadventures.com

Native Cairenes offer a small selection of

Keeping Calm in Cairo

traffic in Cairo

Crowded and mired by traffic, Cairo can be an exhausting city, particularly if you're coming in the hot summer months. You might want to limit your expectations for what can be accomplished in a day and perhaps schedule some time for R&R at your hotel pool if there is one. For a less-crowded experience, keep the following in mind:

- **Friday mornings before noon prayer** is a great time to travel longer distances across the city, or just wander around quiet Downtown streets.
- **Saturdays and Friday afternoons**—when most people are off school and work—also typically have less traffic on the roads, but the Giza pyramids complex and the area around Mu'izz Street can be extra crowded.
- Expect **Thursday and Friday nights** (the weekend) to be busy on the streets. The worst traffic starts around 2pm on Thursday (when many schools get out) and lasts until around 8pm as waves of people leave work.

quality tours around the city, both to main attractions and more intimate experiences like cooking dinner with a local family. Prices are good if you're traveling solo (e.g., $64 per person for a 4-hour tour of Saqqara and Memphis; $53 for a 5-hour tour of the Giza pyramids and local lunch) and groups are small (generally around 5 people with a maximum of 12).

TOUR WITH MYDO

tel. 0114 779 5215

Mydo is an experienced guide with good English who does his best to show his visitors the non-touristic side of Cairo along with the must-see sights. His rates are very reasonable at $100 per 8-10-hour day for a private group of 1-3 people, including door-to-door transportation (but not entrance fees). Contact him to make a trip itinerary for you, or craft your own and he'll execute it expertly.

MOSAIC CLUB

tel. 0100 106 0685; www.mosaicclubegy.com

Mosaic Club offers good free group tours to museums and around Cairo on occasion (check their Facebook page @MosaicClubEgy for event details). You can also get in touch for private tours, but it comes with a heavy price tag of around $150 per 6-hour tour.

BELLIES EN ROUTE

www.belliesenroute.com

Find your favorite Egyptian dish and get acquainted with the city at the same time. This much-loved tour for foodies brings small groups (6-7 people) to eight stops around Downtown for a chance to sample a variety of local cuisine. Enthusiastic local guides make for a fun and informative excursion (4-5 hours; $80 per person). Be sure to book online at their website in advance.

Itinerary Ideas

DAY 1: HIGHLIGHTS OF CAIRO

Jump into modern-day Cairo and navigate the traces of the capital's origins as a walled medieval city.

1 For a proper Egyptian breakfast, head to **Zööba** in Zamalek for a spread of fuul (fava bean stew), ta'maya (Egyptian falafel), eggs, and freshly baked a'ish baladi (local bread).

2 Catch a cab to **Ibn Tulun Mosque** to wander the expansive 9th-century courtyard and ascend the minaret for panoramic views of the frenetic working-class neighborhoods of Sayeda Zeinab, el-Darb el-Ahmar, and beyond.

3 Explore the **Gayer-Anderson Museum** adjacent to the main entrance of the mosque on your way out.

4 Stroll through el-Darb el-Ahmar to **Souq al-Khayamiya (Tentmakers' Souq)** to browse the colorful handmade fabrics. To reach the souq, walk straight from the Gayer-Anderson Museum exit and take the third left onto al-Raeeba Street. Continue straight northward and you'll run into the market after a little over a mile.

5 This covered market will spit you out across the street from the towering **Bab Zuweila.** Climb the steps of the medieval gate and its minarets to orient yourself in Islamic Cairo.

6 Continue your walk toward lunch, which you'll have in a café nestled inside the Khan el-Khalili bazaar. To get there, head through the gate (Bab Zuweila) and continue north for 500 meters (1,600 ft) until you reach Azhar Street. Cross the street using the tunnel in front of al-Azhar Mosque, which will lead you to Hussein Square—the gateway to the bazaar. Resist the urge to browse just yet. Shops are open late and it's lunchtime! Cross the square and take an immediate left onto Sikkat al-Badistan, where you'll find the **Naguib Mahfouz Café** after 120 meters (400 ft). Sample a variety of Egyptian mezzes (appetizers) and try the mixed grill with classic kebab and kofta (both various forms of meatballs).

7 Take a right out of the restaurant and walk 100 meters (330 ft) to **Mu'izz Street.** You have a wealth of choices to explore on this 1-kilometer (0.6-mi) path, but don't miss the Qalawun Complex, Beit al-Suhaymi, and al-Hakim Mosque.

8 Walk through Bab el-Futuh, the gate that marks the northern end of Mu'izz Street, and take a 10-minute taxi trip (15LE) to **Azhar Park.** This sprawling green space perched on a hill is a prime spot to watch the sunset and listen to the cacophony of minarets issue their call to prayer.

9 When hunger strikes, head to the park's **Citadel View Studio Misr** for some hamam (grilled pigeon) or fattah (a traditional rice, bread, and meat dish) and brilliant views of… yes, the citadel, and its colorfully illuminated Mohammed Ali Mosque.

Itinerary Ideas

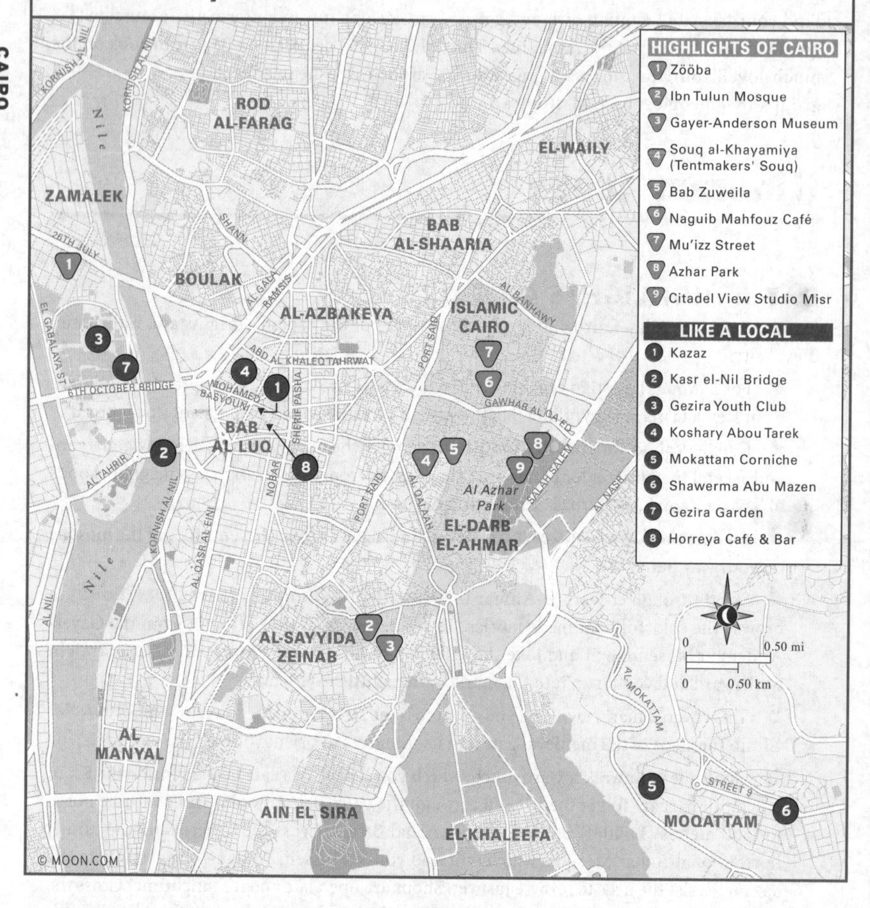

DAY 2: CAIRO LIKE A LOCAL

Have a lie in after your hectic day—Egyptians don't tend to be morning people.

1 Pick up a breakfast of fuul and ta'maya sandwiches from **Kazaz** in Downtown Cairo to eat at an ahwa (outdoor coffee shop) on Hoda Shaarawy Street with a strong Arabic coffee. Ask for a backgammon board to try your hand at a favorite local game.

2 After an unhurried breakfast, walk down Talaat Harb Street through Tahrir Square and cross the **Kasr el-Nil Bridge** into Gezira and Zamalek (less than a mile). Linger and enjoy the breeze off the Nile.

3 Walk due north after the bridge for 650 meters (2,000 ft) to the **Gezira Youth Club** for a leisurely stroll around the 2-kilometer (1-mile) track, or grab a seat in the shade to watch kids play soccer and tennis.

4 For a late lunch, head Downtown for a hearty bowl of koshary at **Koshary Abou Tarek.** It's less than a mile from the club, but you'd have to cross some busy streets, so it's probably easier to take a cab (10LE). To pick one up at a convenient spot, head a few meters south of the club exit and cross the street so the taxi can take the ramp to the 6th of October Bridge.

5 After lunch, take a taxi southeast (11 km/7 mi; 45-50LE) to the **Mokattam Corniche** to enjoy a cup of tea and a glorious sunset over Cairo from this rocky hillside perch.

6 Head to **Shawerma Abu Mazen** on foot or by cab (2 km/1 mi; 10LE) for a dinner of succulent sliced meat or chicken wrapped in Syrian saj bread.

7 Make your way back to central Cairo and hop on a colorful party boat from **Gezira Garden** to cruise the Nile, hear the latest Arabic pop music, and dance with locals.

8 Cap the day with a cold beer at **Horreya Café & Bar** in Falaki Square.

Sights

DOWNTOWN (WIST EL-BALAD)

Tahrir Square

(Midan el-Tahrir)

Midan el-Tahrir, or "Liberation Square," served as center stage for Egypt's 2011 Revolution (though is name predates the momentous event by nearly a century, originating with the 1919 uprising against British occupiers). Tens of thousands of protesters converged here from around the country to demand the ouster of the Mubarak regime. Many set up camp in the square for months on end—even after Mubarak resigned—refusing to surrender their gains to the security forces. Hundreds died on this spot in the process.

Today, Tahrir represents a somewhat sad nostalgia of Egypt's short-lived revolutionary euphoria and the current regime's crackdown on any hint of dissent. Perhaps as a reminder that Egypt is still the land of the pharaohs, the government erected one of Ramses II's obelisks in the center of the square in 2020, surrounded by four ram-headed sphinxes taken from Luxor's Karnak Temple.

You're not likely to linger in this traffic circle, but there are some benches where, depending on the day's security situation, you can sit and soak in the historic space.

Egyptian Museum

(El-Mathaf el-Masri)

Midan el-Tahrir; tel. 02 25796948; https://egymonuments.gov.eg; 9am-5pm daily and 5:30-9pm Sun. and Thurs.; 200LE adults, 100LE students

For over a century, the Egyptian Museum served as the world's main repository of antiquities uncovered around Egypt. The Grand Egyptian Museum near the Giza Pyramid Complex (scheduled to open 2021/22) will—as its name suggests—outshine this original in size and sparkle. But downsizing the Egyptian Museum's collection will likely improve, rather than detract from, the visitor's overall experience, which for decades has been one of the overwhelming disorganization of too many spectacular pieces.

While the royal mummies and King Tut's treasures have left this venue, striking attractions remain. Some of the highlights include the imposing granite statuary in the entrance and the Tanis Treasures—gold funerary masks, dazzling jewelry, and solid silver coffins discovered in the late 1930s in a complex of royal tombs in the Nile Delta.

The neoclassical building is a charming piece of history worth a visit in itself—custom-made to house Egypt's growing pool of ancient riches with soaring ceilings to accommodate colossal kings and queens.

Downtown Cairo

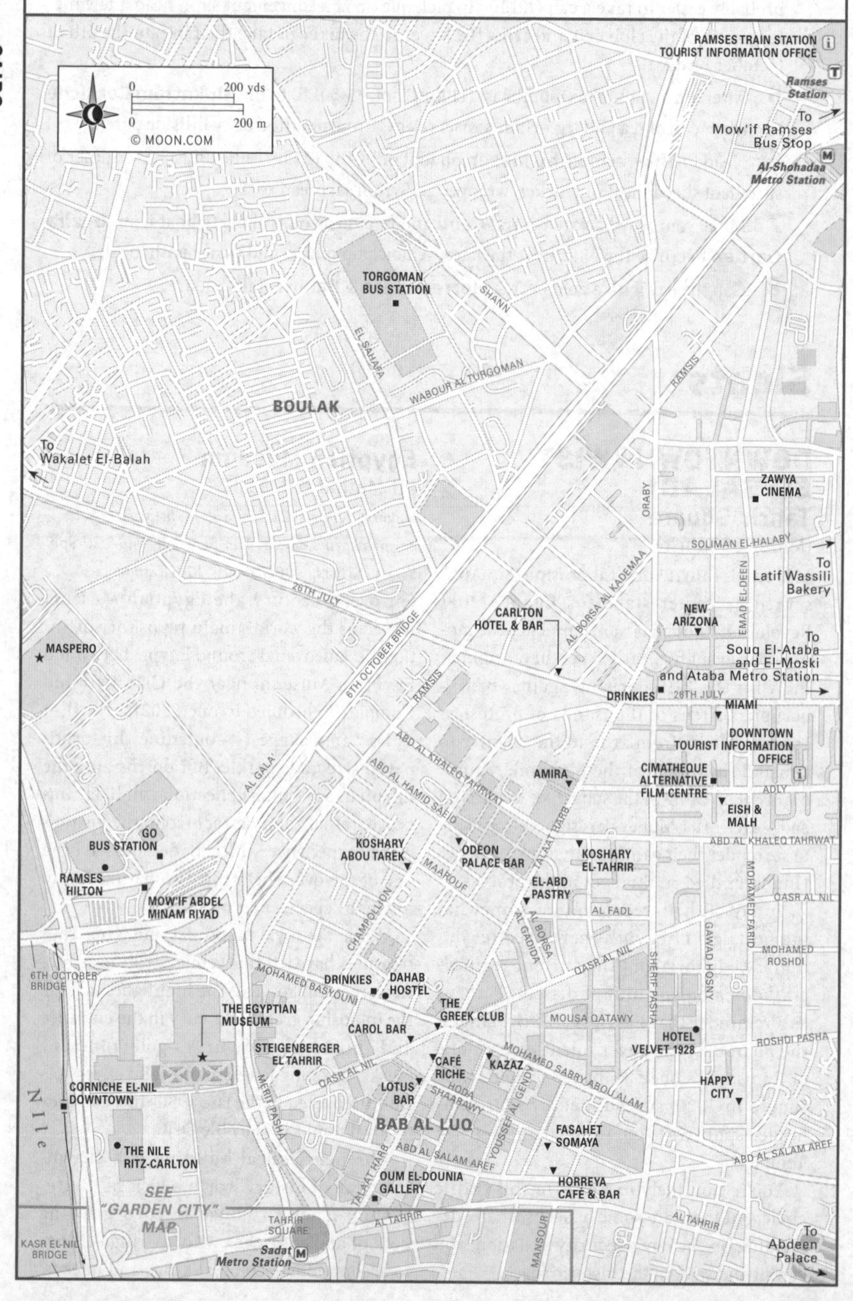

Scenes of the 2011 Revolution

For decades before the 2011 uprising, Egyptians had been suffering under an oppressive system, with arbitrary detentions by the security forces and little recourse to justice in the judiciary. A succession plan for their octogenarian president was widely believed (with good reason) to include a takeover by the president's son, Gamal Mubarak—notorious for his circle of cronies who benefited from the state to earn their billions. With inspiration from their neighbors in Tunisia and a portfolio of grievances, Egypt's young people—who comprise over 65 percent of the population—led the call for a revolution of their own. The protests began on Police Day (January 25, 2011), and after 18 days—during which time some 850 civilians were killed—the 30-year ruler, Hosni Mubarak, stepped down.

After a brief encounter with democracy, the country was plunged yet again into authoritarianism with the 2013 coup that ousted Egypt's first-ever genuinely elected president, Mohamed Morsi. **Tahrir Square (Midan el-Tahrir)** was the epicenter of 2011 Revolution, and as you walk through the city, you can pass through these other seemingly ordinary sights that once witnessed both great and terrible scenes. (Best not to take photos.)

- **Mohammed Mahmoud Street:** Branching off Tahrir Square, this street was a key battle scene during the Revolution, where protesters clashed with security forces for five days and five nights in November 2011. More than 40 people were killed. Once covered in beautiful revolutionary graffiti, the walls that line this street are now painted over—the regime's attempt to erase the memory of resistance.
- **Maspero** (about 1 km/0.6 mi north of Tahrir Square on the Nile Corniche): In October 2011, a group of mostly Coptic Christians protested in front of the Radio and TV Building (better known as Maspero) after a Coptic church was razed in Aswan for allegedly failing to secure the proper license. The peaceful protest—demanding the interim military-led government protect churches—left 27 civilians dead, killed by the army and police.
- **Rabaa Square** (al-Nasr Rd. in Nasr City, 10.6 km/6.6 mi northeast of Tahrir Square): The bloodiest scene of all, on this spot in August 2013, security forces massacred hundreds of civilians who were protesting the military ouster of the democratically elected president, Mohamed Morsi. With this historic "clearing of the squares," the army hammered the final nail in the coffin of Egypt's short-lived democracy, and ushered in military rule that persists to today. The sight is now marked by an abstract pro-military sculpture.

Completed at the turn of the 20th century, the salmon-colored structure has been an unmistakable landmark in the heart of Cairo ever since.

The museum reopens in the evenings on Sundays and Thursdays at 5:30pm, but all visitors must leave at 5pm. Tickets purchased in the morning are not valid for evening re-entry.

Abdeen Palace

Midan el-Gomhoreya; tel. 02 23916909; 9am-3pm Sat.-Thurs.; 100LE adults, 50LE students

Khedive Ismail, 19th-century ruler of Egypt and grandson of Mohammed Ali, began building himself this lavish palace as a "modern" seat of power in 1864. He moved here with his coterie when it was finished a decade later, ending a nearly 700-year tradition of ruling from the Citadel. But Ismail didn't get to enjoy his costly home for long. His profligate projects and mounting debts got him dismissed by the Ottoman sultan in 1879 and prompted the British occupation a few years later. The palace continued to serve as the royal residence until the 1952 coup brought an end to the monarchy.

A small section of the 500-room palace now houses a museum with weapons, medallions, and silverware from the royal family alongside kitsch gifts to the fallen autocrat, Hosni Mubarak. The rest of the palace is used to receive and accommodate important

Medieval Cairo's Public Institutions

Under the Mamluks (r. 1250-1517), Cairo became the cultural center of the Arab Islamic world. Mamluk sultans used wealth from across their empire to embellish the city with exquisite architecture that hosted a range of public institutions. These multifunctional complexes often included a mosque, mausoleum, and one or more of the following. You'll see examples of all of these as you explore Islamic Cairo:

- **Madrasa:** center of learning that focused on theology and law through study of the Quran and Hadith (sayings attributed to the Prophet Mohammed)
- **Sabil:** public drinking fountain
- **Kuttab:** elementary school that focused on literacy and memorization of the Quran
- **Khanqah:** Sufi lodge and place of worship
- **Wikala:** urban commercial center that housed merchants and their goods
- **Maristan:** hospital

foreign delegations, giving them a royal welcome to Egypt.

ISLAMIC CAIRO

★ Ibn Tulun Mosque

Al Saliba St.; 8am-4pm daily; free

In 868, Ibn Tulun—a trusted soldier of the Abbasid caliph—was sent to govern Egypt's then-capital, Fustat; soon after he named himself ruler of the country. He built a new capital north of Fustat, called al-Qata'i (both now part of modern Cairo), with this mosque the crown jewel. After his death, the Abbasids reclaimed the province and razed all the extravagant palaces and monuments, save the mosque, making the structure Ibn Tulun's last remaining material legacy.

Today, the sprawling sand-colored house of worship is still a spectacular sight, with its most majestic feature the minaret's jagged staircase—spiraling around the exterior and echoing that of the Grand Mosque of Samarra in modern day Iraq. A walk to the top offers brilliant views of the surrounding working-class neighborhoods (ask the caretaker to unlock the minaret for you—15-20LE baksheesh, or tip, will be expected).

The mosque is one of Egypt's most unique—the country's largest in terms of land area (designed to accommodate Ibn Tulun's entire congregation for Friday prayer) and the oldest that remains more or less as it was originally built. In the 12th century it served as a caravanserai (a roadside inn) for pilgrims and suffered neglect. The mosque was restored in 1296 by Sultan Lajin, who had earlier hid in its dilapidated nooks and crannies after conspiring in the assassination of the erstwhile Sultan Al Ashraf Khalil. Lajin promised to return the mosque to its former glory if it protected him. Some results of this pact can be seen in the domed building in the courtyard housing the fountain, the wooden minbar (pulpit), the marble surrounding the main mihrab (prayer niche), and the glass mosaic inscription inside it declaring the Islamic creed, "There is no god but God, and Mohammed is his prophet."

Only three of the mosque's 128 windows are original. Can you find them? They're distinguished by their intersecting circles, a common motif of the period. Starting from the left of the qibla wall (the southeastern wall), they are the fifth, sixth, and sixteenth. Also note the stucco decorations covering the red bricks under the arches, and on the wooden panels over the mosque's entrances. This was a quick and economical way to ornament

Islamic Cairo

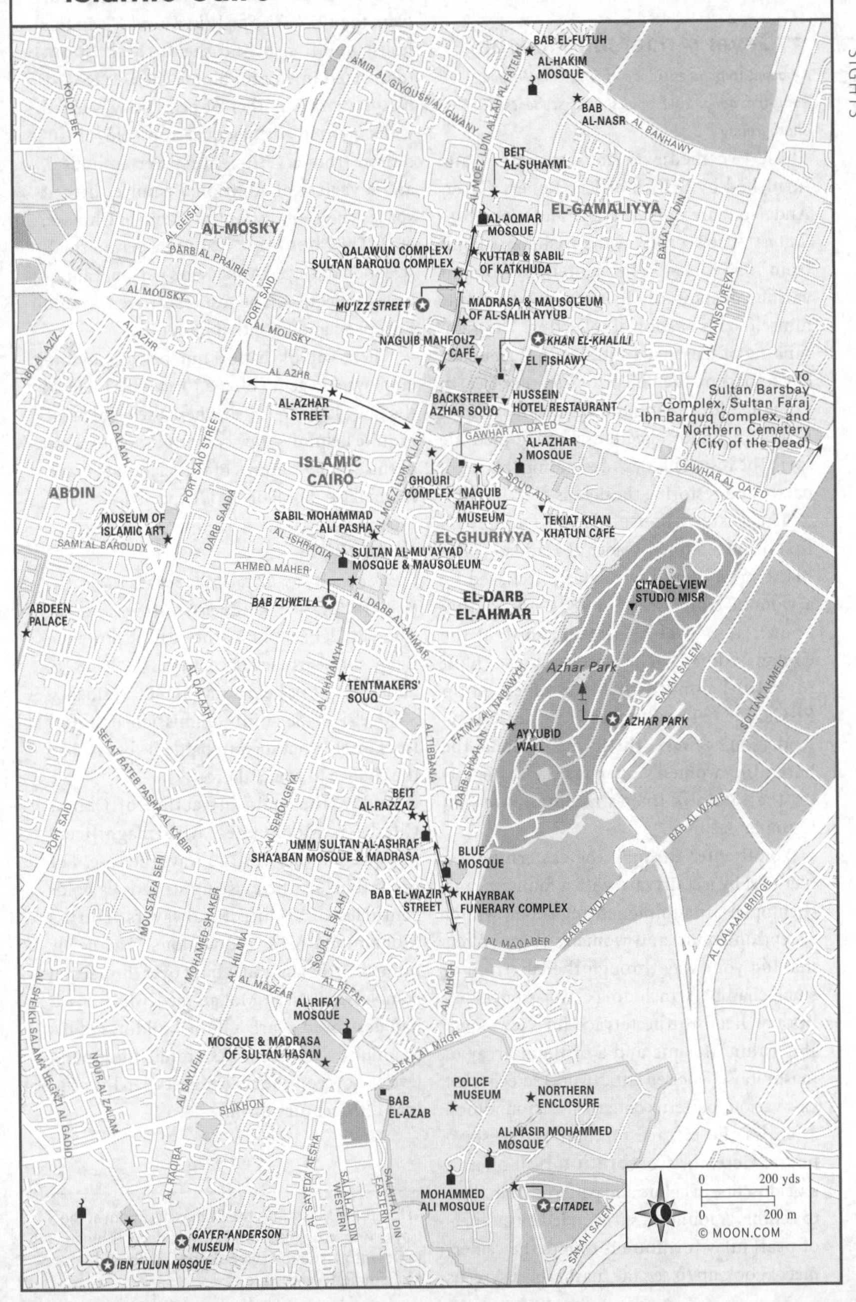

large expanses, achieved with carved wooden molds stamped over wet plaster.

★ Gayer-Anderson Museum

Adjacent to main entrance of Ibn Tulun Mosque; 9am-4pm daily; 60LE adults, 30LE students, 50LE photography

These two medieval houses, merged and furnished by British officer Robert Gayer-Anderson, are quite literally an Orientalist's fantasy. They served as the Irishman's home from 1935 to 1943 after he retired from his various posts in the British army to devote himself to his passion of collecting. The high-ranking officer made a deal with the monarchy to occupy the house for life, rent-free, in exchange for gifting the Egyptian state his furnishings and collections when he died. He spent the rest of his days decorating this small palace and restoring the details of its interior.

The eastern house (dating from 1631) first belonged to Al-Qader al-Haddad ("The Blacksmith"), and was later purchased by a woman from Crete in 1834—becoming known as Beit al-Kretliya, "House of the Cretan Woman." The western house (built in 1540) belonged to Mohammed Salim El-Gazzar ("The Butcher"). Under Gayer-Anderson's tenure, the former became the haremlik (women's quarters), and the latter the salamlik (men's reception area) in Ottoman fashion.

You'll enter through the eastern house, met first by a courtyard with a fountain, and then open-air summer sitting room, winter reception room, and women's room. After making your way through the labyrinth of small chambers, including Gayer-Anderson's library, head to the terrace for views over Ibn Tulun Mosque and a brilliant array of mashrabiya (wooden latticework) screens that cast various patterns onto their surroundings.

Cross the terrace to enter the western house. Here, the **Celebration Hall** offers a kaleidoscope of colors and patterns from floor to ceiling. A fountain surrounded by mother-of-pearl inlay furniture is room's the centerpiece. Look up to see the mashrabiya screens that conceal the women's gallery. This was the setting for a seductive James Bond scene from the 1977 *The Spy Who Loved Me.* In this house you'll also find the **Turkish Room** (decorated in vibrant blues), the **Damascus Room** (with a mother-of-pearl inlay bed and walls painted with lacquer and gold, all acquired from a 17th-century Syrian house), and a variety of additional empire-themed spaces (Persian, Byzantine, British, Chinese, etc.). The **Pharaonic Room** displays a small selection of Gayer-Anderson's personal antiquities collection. The rest is scattered around European and Egyptian museums.

There will likely be a number of museum employees eager to offer a **tour.** This is one of the few places in Cairo where their guidance is quite helpful—they can direct you to some of the unique features of this elaborate maze. A small tip (50LE or so) is expected.

★ Citadel

Salah Salem St.; tel. 02 25121735; 8am-5pm Mon.-Fri., 8am-4pm Sat.-Sun.; 140LE adults, 70LE students

The Citadel served as the seat of power in Egypt for nearly seven centuries (1206-1874), and at its peak held some 10,000 residents. Salah el-Din (Saladin) commissioned the fortress in 1176 but died in battle before he had the chance to reside there.

Today, the main attraction of Cairo's Citadel is Mohammed Ali's magnificent mosque, but this wasn't always the case. The ground below the existing structures holds centuries of architectural layers. During Mohammed Ali's "renovations," the newly minted Ottoman leader built over the palatial complex of al-Nasir Mohammed, who himself had destroyed nearly all the buildings of his Mamluk predecessors. As a result, the ground level is now considerably higher than the original 12th-century form.

1: Ibn Tulun Mosque **2:** the Damascus Room at the Gayer-Anderson Museum **3:** a man delivers bread in Downtown Cairo **4:** view of the Citadel and Mohammed Ali Mosque

1
2
3
4

The Citadel is comprised of two parts: the southern enclosure (which holds the Mohammed Ali Mosque, along with Al-Nasir Mohammed Mosque, the Citadel prison, and Police Museum), and the northern enclosure. The main entrance sends you through the southern enclosure, originally built in the early 13th century as the royal residence. This is a favorite destination for school field trips, so come at opening time if you'd prefer to avoid the crowds of children. A visit should take 1-3 hours.

MOHAMMED ALI MOSQUE

The cherry on top of the Citadel, Mohammed Ali's silver-domed mosque can be seen for miles around Cairo. Its minarets soar 82 meters (269 ft) into the sky, and the interior is elaborately decorated with massive chandeliers (inspired by Istanbul's Blue Mosque) and alabaster walls—chosen to promote the suffering local alabaster industry. Mohammed Ali spent nearly two decades overseeing this monumental endeavor (1830-48) and died before it was completed. His body now lies to the right of the entrance, behind the bronze grille.

The mosque interior and connected courtyard form a massive rectangle about 94 meters long and 52 meters wide (308 ft by 171 ft). Inside, don't miss the opulent gilded ceilings and the exquisite minbars (pulpits). The wooden one with golden accents is Mohammed Ali's original, while the smaller alabaster one was a gift from King Farouk in 1939.

From the courtyard, note the green tower. If Mohammed Ali had written an inscription, it might have read: "I gave the king of France a 3,400-year-old, 75-foot-tall obelisk from the Luxor Temple and all I got was this lousy clock."

Between the mosque and Mohammed Ali's **Gawhara Palace,** built in 1814 in baroque style (and closed for years "for renovations"), a large **terrace** offers beautiful views of the city. Remnants of al-Nasir's Striped Palace (Qasr al-Ablaq) are visible from the north side of the terrace, one floor below.

AL-NASIR MOHAMMED MOSQUE

A short walk northeast from Mohammed Ali Mosque, you'll find the green-domed Al-Nasir Mohammed Mosque—the only Mamluk structure still standing. Completed in 1335, this royal house of worship has seen both better and worse days. It was once intricately decorated and host to as many as 5,000 congregants from al-Nasir Mohammed's court. When the Ottomans conquered the Mamluks in 1517, Sultan Selim stripped the marble panels that lined the interior walls and sent them to Constantinople. The mosque was left to deteriorate under the Ottomans and Mohammed Ali, and when the British occupied Egypt in 1882 (taking the Citadel as their army headquarters), the mosque became a prison and military warehouse with partition walls built between the columns to form the cells and storage rooms. The ancient columns—taken from Pharaonic, Ptolemaic, and Byzantine structures—have witnessed it all.

Today you'll find a well-restored hypostyle mosque with a large courtyard surrounded by traditional Mamluk ablaq (stripes created by alternating stone colors) in black and rust-colored red, and stair-step crenellations along the top. The mosque's most distinctive features—its green-tiled dome and matching minaret—have been beautifully returned.

PRISON AND POLICE MUSEUM

Through the gate across from Al-Nasir Mohammed Mosque (to the west) are the remains of the Citadel **prison**—where former president Anwar Sadat once languished under British rule for espionage. You'll pass by it on your way to the **Police Museum** (in the north corner of the southern enclosure). This museum is small and poorly signed, but it holds a few interesting artifacts like the gun used in an assassination attempt of former president Gamal Abdel Nasser. Inside, a western window offers the best view of the spot where Mohammed Ali massacred the Mamluk ruling elite in 1811 after inviting them to dinner. His guests were on their way out **Bab el-Azab** (once the main entrance) when up to 500 were

Walking Tour of el-Darb el-Ahmar

el-Darb el-Ahmar at dusk

This 2-kilometer (1-mi) walk through the neighborhood of el-Darb el-Ahmar (located within Islamic Cairo) brings you down the path that once served as the lifeline between al-Qahira—the Fatimid's 10th-century walled city—and the new 13th-century seat of power at the Citadel. The sultan's royal procession would pass down this lane (**Bab el-Wazir Street** or "Gate of the Minister," now also called al-Mahgar Street) and empty into the Citadel after beginning at **Bab al-Nasr** on the north side of al-Qahira.

In the 14th century, the Mamluks transformed the area into a center of economic and social activities, which it would remain for nearly 700 years. Along this processional route you'll encounter more than a dozen historical treasures. For a leisurely 3-4-hour walk (or 25 minutes with no stops), try this itinerary:

- Start at the monumental 14th-century **Mosque & Madrasa of Sultan Hasan** and the neighboring 19th-century **Al-Rifa'i Mosque,** where Egypt's last kings are buried.
- Cross the street to the original gate of the Citadel, **Bab el-Azab** (now closed), and turn left for a short walk along the Citadel walls. Take another left onto **Bab el-Wazir Street** (a brown sign should direct you there).
- Another 350 meters (1,100 ft) through this working-class district will bring you to the **Khayrbak Funerary Complex** immediately followed by the **Blue Mosque,** with its stunning blue tiles.
- Continue for 200 meters (650 ft) to **Beit al-Razzaz,** stuck together with the 14th-century **Mosque & Madrasa of Umm Sultan Al-Ashraf Sha'aban** (built by Sultan Sha'aban, a grandson of al-Nasir Mohammed, for his mother). Across the street from Beit al-Razzaz on the second floor is a sadaf (mother-of-pearl inlay) workshop, Warshat Fareed, where the craftsmen are very welcoming. You can buy a beautiful box or just see how it's made.
- Continue north until you encounter **Bab Zuweila,** and ascend its **minarets** to see what you've covered from a new angle.

slaughtered, marking the definitive end to nearly six centuries of Mamluk rule.

NORTHERN ENCLOSURE

The northern enclosure (accessed through **Bab el-Qulla** just north of Al-Nasir Mohammed Mosque) served as military barracks until Mohammed Ali built three interconnected palaces here in 1827. They housed a hospital during WWII and now hold the **National Military Museum,** designed with the help of North Korea (which—with its kitsch propaganda—will become apparent during your visit). While not a must-see attraction, a quick stroll through the museum is worthwhile, whether for the weapons or the palace ceilings of European-meets-Ottoman baroque.

Mosque & Madrasa of Sultan Hasan

Salah al Din Square (el-Darb el-Ahmar); 8am-4:30pm daily; 80LE adults, 40LE students (with Al-Rifa'i Mosque)

Sultan Hasan ascended the throne at age 13 and ruled as a puppet of powerful emirs for a total of 12 years (1347-1351 and 1354-1361). Neither impressive nor popular, he built this massive monument to himself in 1356 with the unclaimed wealth of families killed off by the Black Death. A disgruntled Mamluk prince murdered Hasan, and the young sultan's body never enjoyed the luxurious mausoleum built in the corner of this mosque-madrasa.

With its vaulted interiors and lofty archways, the complex is one of Cairo's most exquisite pieces of architecture. As you approach the structure, note the angled entrance, which allowed the Sultan to admire his masterpiece from his palace in the Citadel. A castle-like passageway brings you to the central courtyard with a large fountain in the center. This was originally intended as decoration (not for ablutions as is the common function), and on special occasions flowed with colorful sherbet.

Surrounding the courtyard are four large iwans (vaulted chambers), each dedicated to one of the four Sunni schools of jurisprudence. The doors in each corner led to the living quarters of the teachers and some 500 students who studied at the madrasa. The largest and most elaborate chamber (the Hanafi madrasa) holds the qibla wall with polychrome marble panels (a traditional Mamluk trait) and Quranic verses spanning the wall in Kufic script. The stone platform in the center of the room served as a stage for Quran readers and helped project their voices across the schools. The mausoleum sits beyond this qibla wall. Hasan's two young sons are buried beneath the wooden centerpiece below the majestic stalactite ceiling.

The views of the Citadel from the top of the minaret are superb. Perseverance and subtle suggestion of baksheesh will likely gain you access, but beware of the precarious steps.

Al-Rifa'i Mosque

Next to Mosque & Madrasa of Sultan Hassan; 8am-4:30pm daily; 80LE adults, 40LE students (with Mosque & Madrasa of Sultan Hassan)

Next to Sultan Hasan's complex in the same gated space sits this much younger sibling, commissioned by Princess Khushyar (mother of Khedive Ismail) in 1869. The mosque-mausoleum was intended to serve as a shrine to the Sufi saint Ahmed al-Rifa'i and as a resting place for the royal family (the descendants of Mohammed Ali). Construction took a 25-year hiatus following the forced abdication of Khedive Ismail by the British, and it wasn't completed until 1912.

Its neo-Malmluk style mimics the grandeur of Sultan Hasan's structure, with matching colors and crenellations. Al-Rifa'i's cenotaph sits in the middle of the room (although he's buried in his birthplace, Iraq). On the far left you'll find a chamber holding the tombs of Egypt's last kings—Farouk and Fouad—and Iran's last shah, Mohammed Pahlavi, who had married into the family and died in Egypt while in exile. More funerary chambers found on the north wall hold Princess Khushyar and Ismail in one room, Ismail's three wives in another, and Ismail's son, Sultan Hussein Kamel, in a third.

Baksheesh and Special Access

"Nothing but baksheesh can purchase a sight" – Mark Twain, *Innocents Abroad* (1869)

Baksheesh (tips) opens many doors. The art of baksheesh can be nuanced or crude—a subtle quid pro quo, or an explicit request for money. Generally speaking, "no" is a flexible word in Egypt, limbered up with a smile and the slip of some folded cash discreetly exchanged in a handshake. If you want to walk up **minarets** or open **locked doors,** baksheesh is usually the ticket. Other services (a quick guided tour, the safeguarding of your shoes at a mosque, "take a picture on my camel") are offered with the expectation of a small reward (a dollar or two). The constant requests may get annoying, but keep in mind people are generally poorly paid, small amounts can go a long way, and aggressive demands can be safely, if tediously, ignored.

Khayrbak Funerary Complex

Bab el-Wazir St., el-Darb el-Ahmar; 9am-3pm daily; free, but baksheesh (tip) expected

Sultan al-Ghouri's trusted emir, Khayrbak, built this mausoleum for himself in 1502. Later, in 1516, Khayrbak defected during a battle against the Ottomans, and the crushing Mamluk defeat paved the way for the Ottoman takeover of Egypt. Khayrbak was rewarded with the position of first Ottoman viceroy of Egypt (1517-22), during which time he added a mosque and sabil-kuttab to his funerary complex (1521). The space beneath the mosque served as a khanqah (Sufi lodge).

This was the last major monument built in Cairo until the Mohammed Ali dynasty some three centuries later (under the Ottomans money flowed, instead, to their capital in Constantinople).

The elegant marble panels and soaring vaulted ceilings—striped ablaq style with octagonal skylights—are some of the architectural highlights. To enter, make your way to the back of the building where you'll find the caretakers. They keep the main door locked, but for 20LE or so they'll take you through the back.

Blue Mosque (Aqsunqur Mosque)

Bab el-Wazir St., el-Darb el-Ahmar; 11am-7:30pm daily; free

The magnificent blue tiles that give this mosque its name were added in 1652—more than 300 years after the original construction. The effect is a somewhat jarring clash of Mamluk-meets-Ottoman styles. Shams el-Din Aqsunqur ("white falcon"), the mosque's original patron, was a powerful Mamluk emir who married both the daughter and widow of Sultan al-Nasir Mohammed. After al-Nasir's death, the Mamluks suffered from decades of instability and child sultans controlled by puppet-master emirs, like Aqsunqur. One of al-Nasir's sons, Sultan al-Ashraf Kuchuk ("the little one"), is buried to the left after the entrance. He was killed at the age of nine by his brother, al-Kamil Sha'ban, who later became sultan. Aqsunqur had Sultan Sha'ban murdered, and was in turn, strangled himself in 1347—the same year his mosque was completed. He is buried in the plain tomb to the far right. The high-ranking Ottoman emir who appropriated the mosque and covered the walls in blue, Ibrahim Agha, is buried in a tomb-chamber to the immediate right.

Don't miss the hieroglyphic inscriptions on the doorsill—yet another layer of history. Ask the caretaker to take you up the minaret to see the processional street (Bab el-Wazir St. leading between the Citadel and the Fatimid walled city of al-Qahira) from a new angle.

Beit al-Razzaz

Bab el-Wazir St., el-Darb el-Ahmar; 9am-3pm Sat.-Thurs.; 40LE

You'd never guess it from the exterior, but this unassuming mansion comprised of two

1
2
3
4

medieval palaces holds over 190 rooms. Sultan Qaitbay built the first small palace you'll encounter in the late 15th century, which was later connected to a newer one also from the Mamluk era. An heir to an Ottoman rice merchant, Ahmed al-Razzaz bought and combined the two palaces with their spacious courtyards in the late 18th century. Don't miss the beautifully restored wooden ceilings and colorful windows of the dazzling reception room—the largest one still intact in all of Cairo.

Museum of Islamic Art

Port Said St., Bab al-Khalq; tel. 02 23901520; https://miaegypt.org; 9am-5pm Sat.-Thurs., 9am-11:30am and 1:30pm-5pm Fri.; 120LE adults, 60LE students

Home to more than 100,000 items, this is one of the world's largest museums dedicated to Islamic art. Only select pieces are on display, but they span 13 centuries—from the 7th-century Umayyad dynasty to the 19th-century Ottoman Empire. With soaring ceilings and well-ordered objects, the museum is a tranquil spot to recollect before returning to the chaotic streets of Islamic Cairo.

The museum is housed in a sizeable neo-Mamluk building completed in 1903 by an Italian architect. The right wing is organized chronologically, while the left is divided thematically (e.g., medicine, weapons, etc.) and incorporates artifacts from outside Egypt. In the left wing, keep an eye out for an Islamic gold dinar from 696—the oldest ever found—and the 12th-century cenotaph of Hussein (the Prophet Mohammed's grandson) taken from his mosque nearby. Other gems include beautifully illustrated 17th-century Iranian manuscripts, a 16th-century herbal medicine book from Andalusia via Turkey, copper compasses from Iran (15th-17th century), and blinged-out swords and daggers of the fashion-conscious rulers from Mughal India to Mamluk Egypt.

A truck bomb targeting the police headquarters across the street tore through the building in 2014, destroying dozens of artifacts. The museum has since been expertly restored. Don't miss the courtyard with lovely marble fountain. Lighting is exceptionally dim in some areas; a flashlight might be useful.

★ Bab Zuweila

Corner of Ahmed Maher St. and Mu'izz li Din Allah St.; 8:30am-5pm daily; 40LE adults, 20LE students

The only remaining southern gate of the medieval Fatimid city, Bab Zuweila was once the stage for public executions and gruesome displays of punishment. Decapitated heads of alleged criminals decorated the spikes above, and the last independent Mamluk, Tumanbay II, met his death here by hanging in 1517.

Bab Zuweila takes its name from a group of Fatimid soldiers from the Berber tribe, al-Zawila, who were quartered near the original gate in 969. After more than a century of wear on the sun-dried brick walls, an Armenian wazir and military commander, Badr al-Jamali, rebuilt this gate and the walls of the city with stone in 1092.

For the entrance, walk through the gate and turn left. The **exhibition hall** at the bottom of the main stairs displays medieval amulets and remnants of a centuries-old coffee shop that used to sit nearby. You can climb to the very top of the lofty **minarets,** which were added in the 1400s as part of the neighboring mosque of Sultan al-Mu'ayyad. The dark (bring a flashlight), awkwardly shaped stairs only allow for passage of one person at a time. But panoramic views at the top—some of the best in Cairo and covering nearly all Islamic Cairo—are worth the harrowing hike.

Sultan al-Mu'ayyad Mosque & Mausoleum

Mu'izz li Din Allah St., next to Bab Zuweila; 9am-5pm daily; free

Constructed between 1415 and 1420, this mosque served primarily as a madrasa and one of the most well-regarded academic

1: Al-Nasir Mohammed Mosque 2: window in Mohammed Ali Mosque 3: Beit al-Razzaz 4: Blue Mosque

Cairo's Imperial Architecture

Sprawling modern-day Cairo has housed the capitals of three empires over the past 1,000-plus years, each of which adorned the city with its own architectural jewels.

FATIMIDS (969-1171 AD)

When the Fatimids invaded Egypt, they chose a corner of modern Cairo as their caliphate's center of power. From this period, we have the three remaining gates of their protected capital, al-Qahira: **Bab el-Futuh** and **Bab el-Nasr** to the north, and **Bab Zuweila** to the south. They built **Mu'izz Street** to connect these walls, with two grand palaces serving as the centerpieces of the royal city. These palaces, along with most of the Fatimid monuments that once lined the thoroughfare, have since been destroyed. But some impressive traces still remain, most notably **al-Aqmar Mosque, al-Hakim Mosque,** and **al-Azhar Mosque.**

AYYUBIDS (1171-1250 AD)

Sultan Salah el-Din, founder of the Ayyubid dynasty and vanquisher of the Fatimids, set about building the heavily fortified **Citadel**—and a stone wall to encircle the Fatimid city and Fustat to the south—to secure his new center of power. Remains of this never-completed **Ayyubid Wall** now run along the border of the el-Darb el-Ahmar neighborhood and Azhar Park.

MAMLUKS (1250-1517 AD)

The Mamluks have left the largest monumental footprint of all, constructing the most impressive of the architectural treasures along **Mu'izz Street** (most notably the **Complexes of Qalawun** and **Sultan Barquq**) and in the **Northern Cemetery,** as well as the **Mosque & Madrasa of Sultan Hasan** at the foot of the Citadel.

institutions of its time. It was built on the site of a prison where the Circassian Mamluk emir, al-Mu'ayyad, kept the company of fleas and lice during the end of Faraj ibn Barquq's reign. The imprisoned emir promised God if he were released, he would convert the place of horrors into a "saintly" one. After successfully conspiring against Sultan Faraj, al-Mu'ayyad gained both his freedom and the sultanate (1412-1421).

To build his complex, al-Mu'ayyad harvested materials from structures built by his predecessors around Cairo—most notably, the mosque's intricate door and much of the marble, including the mismatched columns. He also used the base of Bab Zuweila to support his skyscraping minarets, and borrowed numerous books from the royal library at the Citadel for his impressive collection (they remain quite overdue).

The dome protruding from the top of the mosque is the roof to the mausoleum of Sultan al-Mu'ayyad and his eldest son. To reach the mausoleum, take an immediate left after entering the mosque's main door. Before you go in, look up to admire the exquisite turquoise tiles, enameled glass lamps and muqarnas (miniature pointed niches) hanging from the peak of the entrance. The towering bronze door with embossed geometric patterns—taken from the Mosque & Madrasa of Sultan Hasan—is also a treasure.

More stunning ceiling work awaits in the main entrance and throughout the mosque. Some other features to seek out include the original wood and ivory minbar and its neighboring mihrab with inlaid marble. The Turkish tiles on this wall come from the restoration work by Mohammed Ali's son, Ibrahim Pasha, in the mid-1800s.

Sabil Mohammed Ali Pasha

Mu'izz li Din Allah St. (170 m/560 ft north of Bab Zuweila); 9am-5pm daily; 20LE

In 1820, Mohammed Ali built this functional monument to his favorite son, Tusun, who had been killed by the plague a few years earlier. The façade is typical of the architecture during Mohammed Ali's reign, decorated with bronze grilles, poetic verses, and floral motifs. Upstairs you'll find the kuttab with wooden desks where elementary-age children would memorize the Quran. The main exhibit occupies the ground-floor room where water was once drawn up from the cistern and poured into the pipes of the public drinking fountain, accessed from the outside. The cistern could hold up to 455,000 liters (120,000 gallons) of water, providing up to 4,000 cups a day. Those so inclined can descend the rickety wooden ladder into the 9-meter-deep (30-ft-deep) reservoir and breathe in its mildew-heavy air. Or you can check out the photos on the wall.

Al-Ghouri Complex

Mu'izz li Din Allah St. (known by locals as Al-Ghouriya St.); 9am-5pm daily; 60LE adults, 30LE students

Al-Ghouri, the second to last Mamluk sultan, died in his 70s during a battle against the Ottoman Turks in 1516. His body never returned from the battlefield to rest in this opulent mausoleum, but he did enjoy more than a decade of his multifunction structure. Completed in 1505, the complex includes a mosque-madrasa (to the left if you're coming from Bab Zuweila), and a mausoleum-sabil-kuttab-khanqah to the right. The khanqah and courtyard now hold small theaters. Between the two buildings, the roofed space has hosted market stalls for centuries—the rent from which contributed to the complex's upkeep. Ask nicely if you can take a quick peek from the upper floors for great views the bustling market stalls below and access to the sabil and kuttab on the way up. Baksheesh (20-25LE) will be expected.

Naguib Mahfouz Museum

3 Atfet Al-Afifii Saghira, el-Darb el-Ahmar; tel. 02 27357001; 9am-2pm and 5pm-9pm Wed.-Mon.; 50LE

Literary giant Naguib Mahfouz remains the only Arab winner of the Nobel Prize for Literature. This two-story museum housed in an 18th-century Sufi lodge (called Tekkeyet Mohamed Bey Abu El Dahab) displays Mahfouz's handwritten notes, awards, and personal belongings alongside a public library and full collection of his works.

Mahfouz was born in the Gamaleya neighborhood, just across the street from this memorial, which served as the setting for many of his stories. His life spanned nearly a century (1911-2006) and he wrote over 30 novels, 25 screenplays, and hundreds of short stories and articles.

Al-Azhar Mosque

Al-Azhar St.; 9am-evening prayer (sunset about 6pm in winter, 8pm in summer) daily; free

Students from around the globe still flock to study at al-Azhar—the most prestigious center of theology in Sunni Islam and one of the world's oldest universities. The original mosque was built in 970 by the Shia general, Jawhar, who successfully conquered Egypt for the Fatimid Caliph al-Mu'izz li-Din Allah a year earlier. In 988, the Caliph established a madrasa inside al-Azhar, laying the foundation for the preeminent educational institution it is today. When Salah el-Din conquered the Fatimids, al-Azhar suffered nearly a century of neglect before being converted into a Sunni institution under the Mamluks in 1260.

Layers of history are evident in al-Azhar's construction. The double doors of the main entrance come from the mid-1700s, while renovation of the left side of the façade was commissioned by Khedive Tawfiq in 1888, and the right wing added by his son, Khedive 'Abbas Hilmi, in 1894. Immediately after entering you'll find two Mamluk madrasas on either side of you. These were originally constructed in the ziyada (an enclosed space adjacent to the mosque). The gate to the courtyard dates from 1469 under Mamluk Sultan Qaitbay, who also added the minaret above. The minaret to the left was built with the madrasa below it in 1340, and the one to the right was a gift of Sultan al-Ghouri in the early 16th century.

Once inside the central courtyard, you'll be

1

2

transported back to the Fatimid period. To the right are the residential units that once served as rent-free housing for students of al-Azhar, and at the far end of the mosque sits the mihrab, with original Kufic inscriptions. The interior arches are held up by a hodgepodge of columns originating from Roman, Coptic, and possibly pharaonic monuments—which explains the uneven heights, remedied with platforms. A step up from the mihrab is where Ottoman commander and prolific builder 'Abdel Rahman Katkhuda commissioned an extension in 1751. His tomb lies on the right side of the addition, at the top of a set of stairs.

★ Mu'izz Street

Pop into the **Qalawun Complex** first to buy your multi-sight entrance ticket that covers most of the sights on Mu'izz Street.

QALAWUN COMPLEX

Mu'izz St.; 9am-5pm daily; 100LE adults, 50LE students (multi-sight entrance ticket)

Slave soldier turned sultan al-Mansour Qalawun built his massive mausoleum-madrasa-maristan complex in just one year between 1284 and 1285. Qalawun, a Kipchak (a Turkic nomadic people) Mamluk, ruled from 1279-1290 after rising to influence under Sultan Baybars and stealing power from the latter's young sons. His dynasty lasted for nearly a century—breaking Mamluk tradition that rejected hereditary succession.

Walking through the main entrance, you'll encounter a long corridor. To the right sits the **mausoleum,** the complex's main attraction. Qalawun and his son, al-Nasir Mohammed, are buried beneath the chamber's wooden centerpiece. The mausoleum's mihrab is one of the most exquisite in Egypt—ornamented with marble and mother-of-pearl inlays and topped with kaleidoscopic stained-glass windows. Look up to see the geometric coffered ceilings and more windows with their colors slowly crawling on the walls above. The rose-colored granite columns come from the citadel of Qalawun's former master, Sultan al-Salih Ayyub, on Roda Island (now the el-Manial neighborhood).

Exiting into the corridor, the **madrasa** can be found directly across from the mausoleum. Here, students studied the four Sunni schools of Islamic jurisprudence and medicine. The fountain in the center of the **courtyard** is one of the few remnants of the Fatimid palace that previously occupied this space. The shallow sides of the courtyards once housed students.

At the far end of the corridor opposite the main entrance are the remains of the **hospital.** Now mostly destroyed, it once served as many as 4,000 patients at a time, treated all known diseases (including mental illness), and provided storytellers and musicians to entertain its patients. All classes and races of Muslims were welcomed to receive free treatment. The thorn in this rose is that the hospital, and the rest of the complex, was built by slave labor.

MADRASA & MAUSOLEUM OF AL-SALIH AYYUB

Mu'izz St.; 9am-5pm daily; 100LE adults, 50LE students (multi-sight entrance ticket)

Little remains of al-Salih's once impressive schoolhouse (built in 1243), but its legacy persisted for centuries to come. His was the first madrasa in Egypt to include all four Sunni legal schools (Hanafi, Maliki, Shafi'i, and Hanbali)—a trend that would be imitated through the Mamluk era. After al-Salih's death in 1249, his slave-turned-wife Shagarat al-Durr added the mausoleum, initiating another first (that of a dual madrasa-mausoleum complex) later adopted by most Mamluk monuments. She also set the precedent of burying former rulers within the city walls, rather than in the nearby necropolises. Al-Salih's tomb can be found beneath the dome. To reach the madrasa, head down the alley below the minaret (the only Ayyubid one still standing) and turn left. Only one arch remains (on the east side) of this structure that once covered a long strip of buildings.

1: Sultan al-Mu'ayyad Mosque **2:** vendors at al-Ghouri Complex

Strolling Mu'izz Street

balloon vendor on Mu'izz Street

Tucked away in heart of Islamic Cairo, Mu'izz Street (named after Fatimid ruler al-Mu'izz and located in the Gamaleya district, next to Khan el-Khalili bazaar) is the perfect place for a stroll. This 1-kilometer (0.6-mi) path leads you down the most concentrated selection of Islamic medieval architecture in the world. Today, families and young lovers wander down this 10th-century lane and drink tea beneath the millennium-old walls of their once-fortified city.

BEGIN YOUR WALK

Begin your walk at the neighborhood's main thoroughfare, **al-Azhar Street,** and step into the must-see interiors of the **Qalawun Complex** (housing a 13th-century madrasa and mausoleum), **Beit al-Suhaymi** (a beautifully restored Ottoman-era house), and **al-Hakim Mosque** with vast marble courtyard. **Bab el-Futuh,** one of only three remaining gates to the original Cairo, marks the end of the street to the north. Here you'll find dozens of plastic patio chairs and tables, filled with friends drinking tea and smoking shisha—join them if you like.

WHEN TO GO

In the evenings, especially on **Thursday and Friday nights** (the weekend in Egypt), Mu'izz Street lights up in a carnival atmosphere with splashes of colors in every direction—cotton candy makers spin intricate bouquets of sugar, vendors sell flashing multicolored balloons, and storefronts illuminate the façades of the medieval monuments in pinks, blues, and greens. If you don't mind the crowds, come at this time to experience the street at its most vibrant. For a calmer experience (and to enter the monuments) visit early. It's most peaceful on **Friday mornings** before the noon prayer, but any day between 9am-noon is relatively quiet.

SULTAN BARQUQ COMPLEX

Mu'izz St.; 9am-5pm daily; 100LE adults, 50LE students (multi-sight entrance ticket)

More Mamluk grandeur awaits in Sultan Barquq's mosque-madrasa-khanqah. Built exactly one century after Qalawun's complex (between 1384-1386) and just two doors down, Barquq's monument makes no attempt to conceal its neighbor's influence. Like Qalawun's madrasa, Barquq's school takes a cruciform plan with four vaulted chambers (iwans) surrounding a courtyard. Living quarters in the four corners accommodated the 125 students and 60 Sufis who studied and worshiped here. To the right after entering the courtyard, you'll find the qibla wall. Four red granite columns pilfered from pharaonic structures direct the eyes up toward the dazzling ceiling. In the domed tomb-chamber (entered to the left of the qibla wall) lies Barquq's daughter, Fatima. His own elaborate tomb is in the Northern Cemetery.

Sultan Barquq (in Arabic, "Sultan Plum") was the first ruler to emerge from the Circassian Mamluks, who were originally brought to Egypt from the Caucuses as slaves by Qalawun in the 1200s. Barquq began what became known as the Borgi ("of the tower") Mamluk dynasty, which followed the Bahri ("of the sea") dynasty—their names corresponding to their respective living quarters as slave soldiers in either the Citadel or a castle on the Nile.

KUTTAB & SABIL OF KATKHUDA

Mu'izz St.; 8am-4pm daily; 100LE adults, 50LE students (multi-sight entrance ticket)

Standing proudly where the road forks, Katkhuda's public drinking fountain and elementary school (built in 1744) boasts a beautiful mélange of Mamluk and Ottoman features. The puzzle-like voussoirs (stone wedges of an arch), stalactite niches along the top, and marble mosaics all invoke Mamluk precedents. But the structure was one of the first in Egypt to integrate Ottoman flavors, like the carved floral design beneath the larger arch (which came from the Mongols in China via Constantinople). A cistern sits below the marble panel next to the entrance. On the first floor you'll find stunning blue tiles imported from Syria, with a representation of the Ka'ba in Mecca in the northwest corner. The kuttab upstairs is surrounded with mashrabiya screens and now offers a nice post to people-watch passersby on Mu'izz Street.

AL-AQMAR MOSQUE

Mu'izz St.; 9am-evening prayer (sunset about 6pm in winter, 8pm in summer) daily; free

Despite its relatively small size, al-Aqmar ("The Moonlit") Mosque is one of Egypt's most significant mosques for ushering in a number of firsts. Completed in 1125, it was the first in Cairo to be ornamented with shell-topped niches and muqarnas (stalactite panels), the first to have a decorated stone façade, the first to have embellishments across its entire length, and the first to have its main door face the street rather than the qibla.

Note the pierced medallion in the niche above the entrance. It reads in the center "Mohammed" and "Ali"—the latter the cousin and son-in-law of the Prophet, who Shia followers (like the Fatimids who built it) believe was Mohammed's rightful successor. The script encircling the two revered names reads, in part: "God wishes to remove from you the impurity, oh People of the House, and to purify you" (Quran 33:33).

BEIT AL-SUHAYMI

El-Darb el-Asfar off Mu'izz St.; 9am-5pm daily; 80LE adults, 40LE students

First built in 1648 as the home of an Azhar sheikh, Beit al-Suhaymi offers an excellent example of a traditional upper-class medieval house. Another owner expanded the building in 1699 before a final buyer, Sheikh al-Suhaymi, enlarged the structure further and left it his name in 1796.

If you've visited the medieval houses that make up the Gayer-Anderson Museum, you'll notice a number of shared features. The spaces are divided in traditional Ottoman style with a salamlik ("greeting place") and haramlik ("forbidden place"), which corresponded to the male and female domains. The marble courtyard stays cool in the hot summers, and a seating area on the second floor faces north to enjoy the breeze. From the northwest corner of courtyard, enter the winter hall—also used for more formal hosting. Upstairs you'll find the haramlik, enclosed with beautiful mashrabiya screens to allow the women some fresh air with their mandatory modesty. Note the small rooms for bathing—a feature only found in upper-class houses at a time when most went to the public baths. The upper floors are divided into rooms for the various residents of the estate, with the prime spots saved for men and mothers of sons, and the lesser chambers for concubines and servants.

AL-HAKIM MOSQUE

Mu'izz St.; 9am-night prayer (sunset about 6pm in winter, 8pm in summer) daily; free

At the end of Mu'izz Street, sharing a wall with the once-enclosed medieval city, sits the expansive mosque of al-Hakim. The first Cairo-born Fatimid caliph, al-Hakim took nearly two decades to complete this mosque after his father began construction in 990. The expansive congregational courtyard and stucco-covered brick walls recall Ibn Tulun's Mosque, one century its elder. But the uniquely Fatimid façade of the main entrance integrates themes from the (modern-day) Tunisian birthplace of the dynasty.

Al-Hakim—the "Mad Caliph," as he was sometimes called—dished out cruelty on a whim. He ordered the killing of Cairo's dogs to be spared of their barking, and forbade cobblers from making women's shoes to prevent ladies from leaving the house. He also declared himself divine, and shortly thereafter disappeared in Mokattam Hills, possibly murdered by his sister who succeeded him in the seat of power. Perhaps appropriately, al-Hakim's mosque more often served profane functions throughout its thousand-plus year history—a prison to detain Crusaders, a stable, a warehouse, an art museum, and a boys school—before shedding its patron's original sins and becoming once again a sacred space.

Northern Cemetery ("City of the Dead")

In the mid-14th century, Sufis seeking to escape the earthly distractions of urban life settled in the empty desert on the outskirts of the walled city. Sultan Barquq, the first Circassian Mamluk ruler, requested to be buried among the Sufi sheikhs he revered. His massive mausoleum complex transformed this space into a cemetery of Mamluk caliphs, adding a northern necropolis to its southern counterpart (dominated by Abbasid caliphs).

But Barquq's complex was also intended to serve as a place for the living—an early project to urbanize the desert. In the 15th century, an important caravan route leading to Syria passed through this area, and the complexes of Barquq and his successors provided places of worship and lodging for travelers.

Today, the Northern Cemetery is a proper neighborhood, with residential buildings and shops standing between the monumental tombs. It's also a pleasant place for a historical walk—calmer than much of Cairo, with fewer cars and tuk tuks to compete with on your stroll. If you're coming from the Hussein area on foot, cross the Salah Salem highway via the pedestrian overpass in front of the Fatimid Cairo Hospital.

SULTAN QAITBAY COMPLEX

Northern Cemetery; 9am-4pm daily; free

Qaitbay, the slave soldier of Barsbay (whose tomb lies to the north), became sultan in 1468 and ruled for nearly 30 years. Like his former master, his reign brought relative prosperity. He built this ornate mosque-madrasa-mausoleum complex in 1472 as the centerpiece of his "royal suburb," which housed a palace, hostels, charities, and residential buildings. Inside, don't miss Qaitbay's tomb-chamber, which sits behind an inconspicuous door entered through the qibla wall. If you haven't had enough stairs for the day, ask the caretaker to visit the roof and minaret. Facing the mosque entrance from the exterior, head a few meters to the right to see Qaitbay's reception hall (maq'ad), built over arched storerooms. The unremarkable room was once part of the palace where Qaitbay stayed during his visits to the cemetery suburb. Remains of the lodging that hosted travelers en route to Syria can be seen up the street to the north of Qaitbay's mosque just before Sultan Barsbay's Complex.

SULTAN BARSBAY COMPLEX

Northern Cemetery; 9am-4pm daily; free

Barsbay's complex originally served as a

khanqah when it was built in 1432. The long strip of ruins to your right (when facing the entrance) is where local Sufis lived and worshiped. To the left of the entrance are the mosque, mausoleum, madrasa, and sabil. The dome over the mausoleum marks a turn in decorative designs from the zigzag pattern popular in the first quarter of the 15th century to more intricate, interwoven patterns. Barsbay's reign, which lasted 16 years (1422-1438), marked a period of relative stability in the Mamluk's troubled last century.

SULTAN FARAJ IBN BARQUQ COMPLEX

Northern Cemetery; 9am-4pm daily; free

Sultan Faraj (who took the throne at the tender age of 13) built this complex for his father, the late Sultan Barquq, between 1400-1411. Aside from the mausoleum, the complex served primarily as a khanqah, a Sufi lodge and place of worship, but (in Mamluk fashion) also functioned as a mosque, madrasa, sabil, and kuttab. On either side of the qibla wall you'll find a stunning tomb-chamber. Facing the qibla, Sultan Barquq and his sons are buried to the left, and the female family members lie to the right. The colossal stone domes that top the chambers were the largest of their time. Ask the caretaker to take you up to the roof and minaret for nice views of the necropolis. On your way up, you'll pass by rooms where Sufis once slept and worshiped, and the spacious porch of the kuttab, where young students memorized the Quran.

MOKATTAM

★ Mokattam Corniche

Al-Ahram St.; 24 hours daily; free

The sunset from the Mokattam Corniche is something spectacular. From this perch on the edge of Mokattam Hills you can see straight across the Nile to the Pyramids of Giza towering in the distance. Makeshift ahaawi (cafés) line the sandy cliffside and offer cheap (nonalcoholic) drinks to enjoy with the show. After nightfall, it's a notorious spot for youths "up to no good" to indulge in the forbidden—booze, hashish, and romantic encounters—under the cover of darkness.

OLD CAIRO AND COPTIC CAIRO

Babylon Fortress

Mar Girgis St.; 24 hours daily; free

This rounded tower is the largest remaining wedge of the Roman fortress of Babylon—not to be confused with the ancient Mesopotamian city—built here around AD 300 on what was then the east bank of the Nile. (Its twin to the north was converted into the foundation of St. George's Convent in the early 18th century.) These towers once guarded the mouth of an ancient canal that connected the Nile with the Red Sea. Over the centuries the ground outside the fortress wall has risen some 8 meters (26 ft)—with layers of newer structures built upon the rubble of older ones—and within its gates, 4 meters (13 ft) of encrusted history lie below the churches. The Roman style of alternating red brick and limestone visible here would become a key feature of Mamluk architecture centuries later. Today, the tower welcomes visitors as they enter the heart of Old Cairo.

Coptic Museum

3 Mar Girgis St.; tel. 02 23628766; www.coptic-cairo.com; 8am-4pm daily; 100LE adults, 50LE students, 50LE camera

Located just beyond the Babylon Fortress tower, this museum holds centuries of Coptic art. It was founded in 1908 by Marcus Simaika Pasha, an Egyptian Copt and high-ranking government official, and its collection of some 16,000 pieces continues to grow (although only a fraction is on display). The downstairs contains dozens of friezes, gravestones, and wooden fragments of old Coptic houses, most dating from AD 300-700. On the upper floor you'll find medieval manuscripts, textiles, coins, and icons galore. The museum's brilliant ceilings and stained-glass windows (20th-century constructions) are marvels in themselves. Don't miss the magnificent 6th-7th-century niche carved out of the Apollo Monastery at Bawit

1
2

(350 km/200 mi south of Cairo) with the Virgin Mary and Jesus flanked by the 12 apostles and two interloping local saints. In the breezy courtyard, 7th-century column capitals from the St. Jeremiah Monastery that once stood in Saqqara (30 km/20 mi south of Cairo) now sit perched on concrete posts.

Old Cairo, Coptic Cairo, and El-Manial

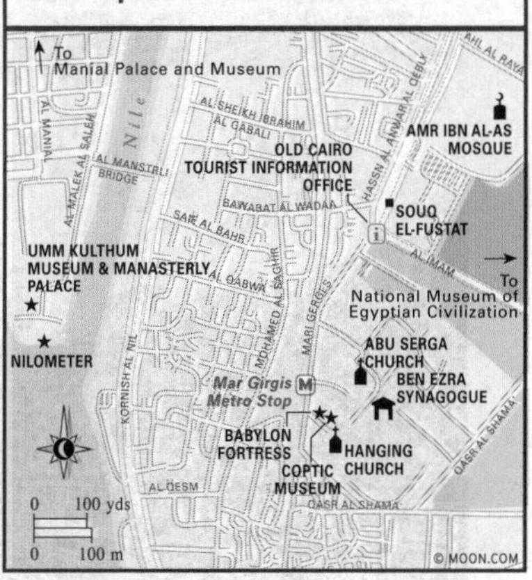

Hanging Church (Church of the Virgin Mary)

Mar Girgis St.; 8am-5pm daily; free

At first glance there seems to be nothing "hanging" about this church. But once inside, a sliver of open floor exposes the hidden ruins of the southern Roman tower over which this structure is, indeed, suspended. The church likely dates from the 9th century, although an earlier version may have existed here as early as the 3rd century. The bone and ivory screens that adorn the interior were added in the 13th century, and the portico is courtesy of a 19th-century restoration. Inside you'll also find over 100 icons depicting a variety of religious figures and events, such as the torture of St. George and the life of John the Baptist. The oldest and most revered icon, the 8th-century "Coptic Mona Lisa," can be found on the far-right wall after the entrance above a strip of votive candles. In the southeastern corner, a door leads to the oldest part of the building, which houses a sanctuary and baptistery. The church became the Coptic pope's residence in the 11th century—a move from his previous home in Alexandria—and remained the holy home for some 200 years. If you're keen to attend a Coptic mass, head over on a Friday or Sunday morning.

Ben Ezra Synagogue

Behind the Church of St. George; tel. 0128 789 6125; 8am-4pm daily; free

The synagogue that once occupied this space was the oldest Jewish house of worship in Egypt, likely dating from the 9th century (though the current structure was built in 1890). Over the centuries, it's been the scene of great achievements. Lore has it Moses spoke to God on this spot, ending a destructive bought of storms and plagues that ravished the pharaoh's land. And the Jewish philosopher Maimonides frequented the synagogue while writing his 12th-century magnum opus, *Mishneh Torah*. Some 700 years later, over 200,000 manuscripts and notes of daily life (some from as early as the 9th century), were found in the geniza (religious storeroom), shedding light on medieval Jewish life. The first floor houses the men's section. To find the women's, head to the second floor via a wooden staircase in the courtyard.

Abu Serga Church

(Saints Sergius and Bacchus Church)

Mar Girgis St.; 8am-4pm daily; free

Founded at the end of the 7th century, Abu Serga is believed to be Cairo's oldest church. The current structure likely dates from the 10th century (followed by many facelifts), but it sits atop an earlier colonnaded church of similar size and style. It's dedicated to Saints Sergius and Bacchus—soldiers in the Roman army who were martyred after refusing the emperor's demand that they denounce Christianity. Look up to see the unique

1: sunset at Mokattam Corniche **2:** Hanging Church (Church of the Virgin Mary)

"Garbage City"

Cave Church

If you're curious where the garbage of 20 million inhabitants goes, take a trip to Manshiet Nasser—Cairo's "Garbage City" at the base of Mokattam Hills. It's the largest of a handful of neighborhoods on the city's outskirts that tend to the urban trash with improvised recycling centers that salvage some 85% of waste.

Pickup trucks piled high with sacks of garbage navigate the narrow streets to drop off the day's collections for sorting. Children climb mountains of trash while they play, and no one seems fazed by the concoction of odors—the smells of fresh deliveries mingling with yesterday's burning refuse.

Start your trip at the **Association for the Protection of Environment (APE)** (5 Hakim Attala St.; 8am-3pm Mon.-Thurs. and Sat.; tel. 02 23412723; www.ape.org.eg), an NGO that collaborates with the zabbaleen (trash collectors). Here you can learn about how the community works and lives, and you can buy recycled products—from rugs to patchwork quilts and paper items.

Then, make your way down the frenetic streets to an oasis of calm at the **"Cave Church,"** or **St. Sam'an the Tanner Church** (1 km/0.6 mi south of APE; www.samaanchurch.com; 8am-6pm daily; free). Add this enormous space carved into the Mokattam cliffside to the list of Egypt's shocking juxtapositions. Aside from the main church, which seats some 20,000 worshipers, three smaller ones cater to this community of zabbaleen, most of whom are Coptic Christians.

To arrange a guided tour of the neighborhood, call APE or **Nader Khattab** (Nader_Khattab1974@hotmail.com; tel. 0100 158 5557), an excellent licensed guide who can pick you up at your hotel for an extra charge. The church also offers tours of the cave complexes, but expect to spend much of the time learning about God's miracles rather than history and architecture.

ceiling, reminiscent of Noah's ark. Don't miss the crypt where legend has it the Holy Family stayed during their flight into Egypt.

Amr ibn al-As Mosque

Sidi Hassan al-Anwar St.; 9am-evening prayer (sunset about 6pm in winter, 8pm in summer) daily; free

Amr ibn al-As led the Muslim conquest of Egypt, taking the Roman fortress of Babylon in 641. From here, he set up camp and set out with his army to conquer Alexandria (the Byzantine seat of power) a few months later. On the spot of this current mosque, ibn al-As built an earlier version to serve as the centerpiece of his new capital, Fustat. After centuries of fires, earthquakes, and the wear of time, nothing remains of the original 7th-century structure. But it continues to be a fascinating monument, with many hands involved in laying its subsequent stones—from Salah el-Din in the 12th century to 15th-century Mamluk sultans and Mohammed Ali in the 19th century. The façade dates from a 1977 government renovation.

National Museum of Egyptian Civilization

Ein El Sira, El Fustat; tel. 02 27412273; www.nmec.gov.eg; 9am-5pm daily; 200LE adults, 100LE students

In 2021, the mummies of Egypt's most illustrious kings and queens passed through Cairo in a lavish parade—relocated from their former resting places in the Egyptian Museum (Tahrir Square) to the basement of the brand-new National Museum of Egyptian Civilization. The haunting collection of 22 corpses—including the Pharaoh Queen Hatshepsut and prolific builder Ramses II—is the highlight of this new house of Egyptian artifacts.

Upstairs, there's one soaring exhibition hall with treasures from across Egyptian history arranged in chronological order. Pharaonic items start to the right (when facing the entrance), before blending into pieces from the Greco-Roman, Coptic, and Islamic periods, and finally paraphernalia of the Mohammed Ali dynasty. There are some striking items, big and small, like the gilded funerary furniture of ancient queens and a 4,000-year-old miniature model of an ancient textile workshop.

When you're done with your visit, head out a side door (to your left before the exit) for beautiful views of the museum garden and Lake Ein el Sira. A visit should take 1-2 hours. On Fridays, the museum reopens in the evening from 6pm-9pm.

EL-MANIAL

Nilometer

2 Abd El-Malek Ln., off El Malek El Saleh St.; 9am-3:45pm daily; 40LE adults, 20LE students

"Egypt is the gift of the Nile" wrote Herodotus in the 5th century BC. Indeed, the Nile's flood cycles—predictable and nourishing—made Egypt an agricultural king and sustained its thriving civilizations. This Nilometer, built in 861, measured the annual flood that once submerged the lands bordering the river, leaving behind a fertile silt. Note the column in the center of the structure marked with engraved lines. It's divided into 16 sections, around 54 centimeters (21 in) each. When the water reached the top, a dam that blocked the medieval canal (the Khalig) would be released, thus controlling any excess flooding.

You can now climb down the steps of this majestic structure without fear of inundation. Since the building of the Aswan High Dam in 1970, the Nile no longer floods, and the three tunnels that led to the river have been sealed up (found beneath the filled arches). The luscious ceiling was Mohammed Ali's touch, and original inscriptions of Quranic verses encircle the interior: "See you not how God sends down water from heaven, so that the earth becomes green?"

Manial Palace and Museum

1 Saray St.; tel. 02 23687495; 9am-4pm daily; 100LE adults, 50LE students

Believe it or not, this opulent palace was the residence of the *lesser* Mohammed Ali—a prince in waiting who never got his turn on the throne. Prince Mohammed Ali, son of Khedive Tawfik, built this home between 1901-1929 in a mélange of art nouveau, rococo, and various Islamic styles. It all makes for a rather busy space, with no inch left uncovered—tiled walls meet coffered ceilings, and elaborate furniture sits on marble floors. The complex is now divided into five separate buildings: a reception room, a mosque (added in 1933), a hunting museum displaying the kills of King Farouk (opened 1963), Prince Mohammed Ali's residence, a throne room of Mohammed Ali senior (the prince's great-great-grandfather), and a museum housing the prince's personal collection of art and antiques (in the southern part of the garden).

Umm Kulthum Museum & Manasterly Palace

1 El Malek El Saleh St.; tel. 02 23631467; 9am-4pm daily; 10LE adults, 5LE students

If you spend more than a few hours in Cairo, you're almost certain to hear Umm Kulthum's entrancing sound. Her voice spills out of taxi windows and booms from the speakers of street-side cafés. Born at the turn of the 20th century, she began her singing career at a young age, dressed as a boy to avoid judgement from her conservative community in the Nile Delta. Her father was a village imam and first trained her voice through Quranic recitation.

This museum holds the traces of her life and brilliant career, which took off in the 20s and flourished through the 60s under Nasser's project of Arab nationalism. You'll find her gowns, iconic scarf, and bedazzled sunglasses that hid her ailing eyes. Other rooms hold awards, photographs, letters exchanged with politicians, and a 25-minute biographical documentary that plays on loop.

The museum is housed in the eastern wing of the Manesterly Palace, built 1851 by one-time Cairo governor Hasan Pasha al-Manasterly. While you're in the neighborhood, the remains of his rococo residence are worth a quick visit. The shady terrace overlooking the Nile is a lovely place for a rest.

GEZIRA AND ZAMALEK

Museum of Modern Egyptian Art

In Opera House Complex; tel. 02 27366665; 10am-4pm Tues.-Thurs. and Sat.-Sun.; 20LE adults, 10LE students

A must-see for modern art lovers, this museum holds some of Egypt's best paintings and sculptures of the 20th and 21st centuries. Works by Egyptian pioneers like painter Mahmoud Said and sculptor Mahmoud Mukhtar decorate the ground floor, while upstairs hosts rotating exhibits. The space itself is also beautiful, with tall ceilings, nice lighting, and gleaming marble floors. Schedule around an hour for a visit and a bit more to roam the well-manicured oasis that is the Opera House Complex grounds.

Cairo Tower (Borg el Qahira)

El Borg St.; tel. 02 27365112; 9am-1am daily; 200LE

This elegant tower inspired by the pharaonic lotus motif belies its original purpose as a middle finger to the US. When the Eisenhower administration reneged on a promise of a large aid package to Egypt, Nasser used the $3 million conciliatory gift secretly sent to him by the CIA to build this 187-meter (614-ft) structure. The tower, completed in 1961, was rumored to be nicknamed "Roosevelt's erection"—after the CIA operative Kermit Roosevelt, who orchestrated the offer. For brilliant views of Cairo head to the open-air **observation deck** or rotating restaurant, **Restaurant el Dawar** (noon-midnight daily; 250LE) on top. If you're hoping to catch the sunset, come early and expect lines.

Mahmoud Mukhtar Museum

5 El Tahrir St.; tel. 02 27351123; 9am-2pm Sat.-Thurs.; 20LE

Born to a peasant family in the Nile Delta and educated in Paris, Mahmoud Mukhtar became Egypt's most renowned sculptor in the 1920s and has retained the title ever since. This museum was built to house his some 85 sculptures of various materials and subjects, most blending pharaonic themes with European styles. The work that made him famous, "Egypt Awakening," is not located in this museum but outside Cairo University. In this first public sculpture unveiled by an Egyptian artist in millennia, a muscular Sphinx with a nose job sits beside a peasant woman—a tribute to the 1919 Revolution and an independent Egypt.

Aisha Fahmy Palace

1 Aziz Abaza St.; tel. 02 27358211; 9am-9pm daily; free

In the whitewashed history of this palace, a respectable aristocrat named Ali Fahmy builds the Nile-side villa for his daughter, Aisha, in

Gezira, Zamalek, Agouza, and Dokki

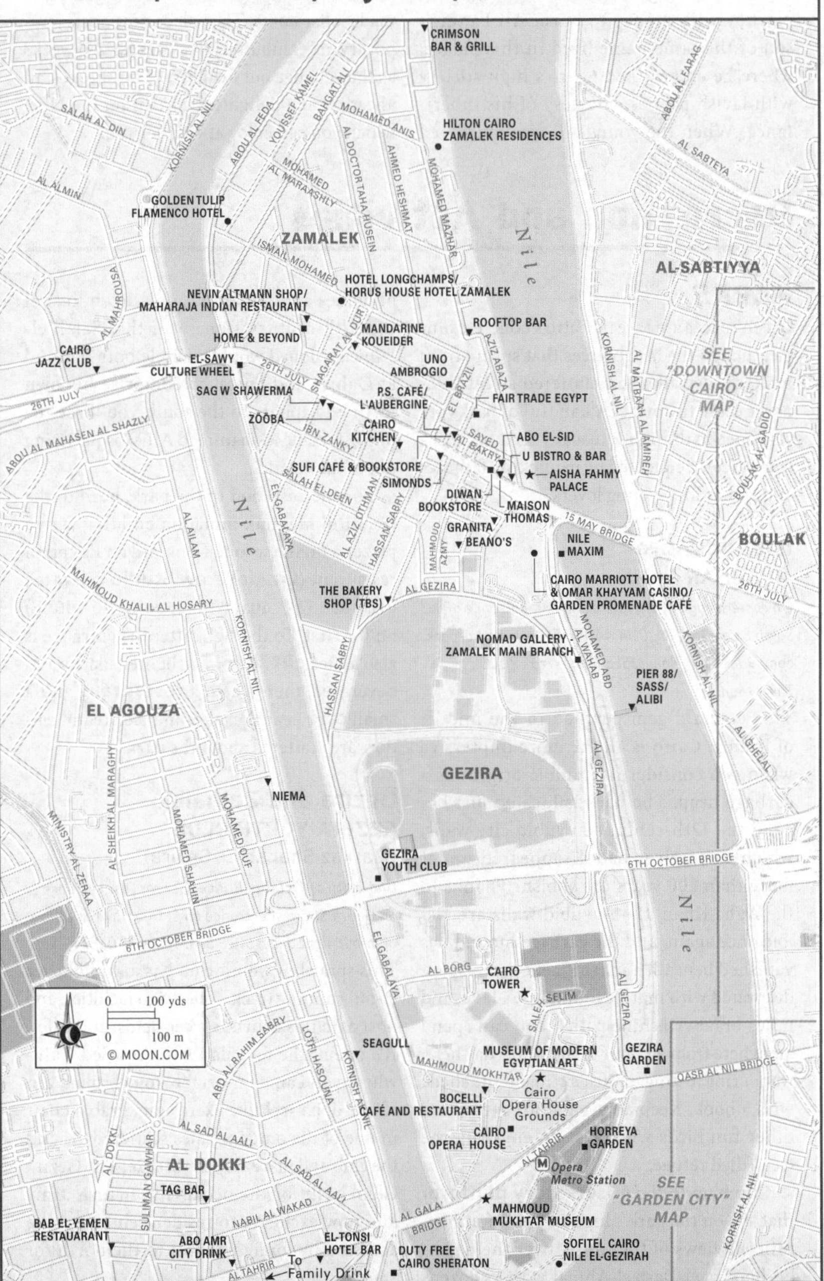

1907. The real version is much racier, involving a French high-end escort and a young playboy with money to burn. Ali Fahmy's son of the same name lived in this palace, where he entertained Cairo's high society with lavish parties, courtesy of his inheritance. When the young Ali was murdered by his prostitute-turned-princess wife, Aisha bought her siblings' shares in the villa and made it her home. The palace now hosts temporary art exhibitions (it closes for 2-6 weeks as they change out exhibits, so be sure to call ahead) and a delightful garden on the Nile, which you can enjoy at your leisure.

Recreation and Activities

PARKS

Green spaces are rare in Cairo's concrete jungle, though the hearty trees that spring from broken sidewalks and cluttered street sides never cease to amaze. A handful of parks are also open to the public (usually for a small entrance fee), frequented by picnicking families and canoodling young lovers.

Islamic Cairo

★ AZHAR PARK

On eastern edge of el-Darb el-Ahmar, entrance off Salah Salem Rd.; tel. 0114 440 0555; www.azharpark.com; 9am-10pm daily; 15LE Mon.-Wed., 20LE Thurs.-Sun.

This emerald gem perched in the middle of Islamic Cairo is all the more impressive when you consider its humble origins as a garbage heap. The park is located just beyond the 12th-century Ayyubid city walls, which themselves had disappeared under more than 500 years of rubbish. Thanks to the Agha Khan, the Ayyubid walls are visible once again, and the garbage mound has vanished beneath a magnificent green space decorated with marble fountains, a lake, and miles of labyrinthine paths. You can spend anywhere from an hour to the whole day here, wandering, eating, or just sitting in the shade with a book. Keep an eye out for egrets and other fun birds who are also enjoying the tree-filled refuge.

Climb up to the **observatory platform** that sits on the park's highest point for magnificent views of the sunset over the neighborhood of el-Darb el-Ahmar with its dozens of domes and minarets. Look down to spot the 12th-century stone wall that Salah el-Din envisioned would encircle both Fatimid al-Qahira and Fustat to comprise his own fortified capital. To the south you'll see the unmistakable Mohammed Ali Mosque rising out of the Citadel.

For the best food in the park, head to the beautiful Mamluk-imitation building with a pizzeria on the second floor and an Egyptian restaurant (**Citadel View Studio Misr;** tel. 0120 727 3747; 10am-10pm daily; 70-100LE) on the first. To the right after the entrance is also a nice **gift shop.** For lighter snacks and beverages, there's also a **restaurant** and a small **café** near the lake, and ice cream vendors are scattered about the park.

Gezira and Zamalek

GEZIRA YOUTH CLUB (Markaz Shabab El-Gezira)

Under 6th of October Bridge, Gezira; east entrance on Gezira St., west entrance on El Gabalaya St.; 6am-midnight daily; 50LE Sun.-Thurs, 100LE Fri.-Sat.

This sprawling youth club has a 2-kilometer (1-mi) running track, equestrian facilities, and host of tennis courts, soccer fields, and cafés. It's one of the few places in crowded Cairo where you can comfortably jog en plein air. If you don't feel like exercising, grab a chair in one of the outdoor cafés scattered around the club and just enjoy the breeze. The Gezira Club, built for the occupying British army and now exclusive to resident elites, can be accessed by foreigners just to the north for 150LE.

Nile-Side Strolls

Garden City Corniche el-Nil

"Corniche el-Nil" is the name given to most roads that run along the Nile. In Cairo, portions along this riverside road are great places for a stroll:

- **People of Egypt's Promenade (Mamsha Ahl Masr):** This section of the Corniche (extending for around 2 km/1.25 mi along the east bank of the Nile between Imbaba Bridge in the north and the 15th of May Bridge in the south) received a serious facelift in 2020, with platforms jutting into the river and pleasant patches of green. It's a great place to walk or sit and watch the boats float by.
- **Downtown Corniche El-Nil:** At the time of writing, this part of the Corniche that borders Downtown (between 15th of May Bridge and Kasr el-Nil Bridge) remained under construction. Plans for the path are not entirely clear, but it will likely be an extension of Mamsha Ahl Masr. The adjacent **Kasr el-Nil Bridge** is one of the best spots to enjoy a cool breeze and admire the river from up close alongside families and young lovers.
- **Garden City Corniche el-Nil:** Lined with benches and beautiful banyan trees, this strip of Nile-side promenade forms the western border of the upper-class Garden City neighborhood. It's a nice place for a stroll (though the busy Corniche el-Nil St. does put a bit of a damper on an otherwise pleasant space). You can pick up a **felucca** here directly in front of the Four Seasons Hotel.

GEZIRA GARDEN

Gezira, just north of Kasr el-Nil Bridge; 9am-11pm daily; 10LE

This space is more of an enclosed Nile-side promenade than a garden, but it does have a few strips of well-manicured trees and views of palms towering in the distance. Scant on shade, it's best enjoyed in the evening when a cool breeze comes off the river and multicolored **party boats** light up from the docks that line the park. For 15LE you can join the fun with a 15-minute spin around the Nile, or gather some friends and rent the boat for yourselves (400LE/hour). Located just north of the Kasr el-Nil Bridge.

HORREYA GARDEN

Gezira, just south of Kasr el-Nil Bridge; 9am-10pm daily; 10LE

This spacious park spotted with statues of

TOP EXPERIENCE

Boating on the Nile

felucca sailing on the Nile

A short cruise along the Nile is a fabulous way to experience the city from a different angle. Chartering a private felucca (traditional wooden sailboat) for sunset is my favorite way to enjoy the river's glittering majesty, but visitors have a range of options to choose from.

- **Feluccas:** Charter a felucca from the **Garden City Nile Corniche** in front of the **Four Seasons** (1089 Corniche el-Nil, Garden City) for the most relaxing trip on the Nile. A 1-hour private sail around the river should only cost around 250-400LE (depending on your haggling skills), plus a tip for your captain (10-20% is the norm).
- **Party Boats:** If you're looking for a livelier ride, hop on a party boat at **Gezira Garden** (15LE for 15 minutes with party included, or 400LE/hour for a private trip) with its neon colors, loud motor, and even louder Arabic pop music. You can pick up a smaller boat (just as colorful) from a couple of small docks on Abu el-Feda Street in Zamalek, across from the KFC. Prices start at 300LE/hour, but you can likely get out for 200LE with some friendly haggling.
- **Private Dining Boats:** For a peaceful meal with good food and drink on the Nile, call **Seagull** restaurant (Agouza Corniche) in advance to reserve their private dining boat (400LE/hour, plus the cost of dinner).
- **Dinner Cruises:** Unfortunately, the large Nile dinner cruises are notorious for their bad food and mediocre belly dancers. But if you go with limited expectations, don't mind crowds, and aren't a picky eater, the **Nile Maxim** (El-Gezira St., in Front of Cairo Marriott Hotel, Zamalek; tel. 02 27388888; www.maximrestaurants.com) dinner cruises can be entertaining.

bygone poets and military heroes is a perfect place for a picnic. Here you can wander among palms or enjoy the shade of beautiful banyan trees. Makeshift cafés also offer coffee and tea.

SPECTATOR SPORTS

Football (soccer) is the king of sports in Egypt. For both of Cairo's main stadiums, you can buy tickets and apply for a required fan ID at **www.tazkarti.com.** Be sure to start the process well in advance—they'll ask you to upload a photo and a copy of your passport and get back to you a few weeks later (ticket prices start around 200LE). But if you want to join in the event as most Egyptians do, skip the stadiums and head to your favorite ahwa (streetside café) in any neighborhood around Cairo.

AL-SALAM STADIUM

Nahdet Masr St., Second al-Salam

The two biggest rivals in Cairo, **Ahly** and **Zamalek,** typically play at the Al-Salam Stadium on the city's outskirts. Confusingly, the home colors of both teams are red and white (although Ahly's uniforms are predominately red with white accents, and Zamalek's the reverse). Each team has its own group of superfans, or "Ultras"—Ahly with their Ultras Ahlawy and Zamalek with their Ultras White Knights—both of which are politically charged and played a significant role in the 2011 Revolution. Matches were closed to fans for years after a 2012 stadium riot in Port Said involving conspiracy by security forces, but the doors have since reopened with tighter security measures (hence the "Fan ID"). Games can still get a bit rowdy, and you might feel more comfortable going with a local. The stadium is quite a trek, located around 29 kilometers (18 mi) northeast of Downtown Cairo—or 16 kilometers (10 mi) past the Cairo International Airport—and is best reached by taxi (about 180-220LE from Downtown).

CAIRO INTERNATIONAL STADIUM

Mamdouh Salem St., Nasr City; www.cairo-stadium.org.eg

The Egyptian national team, also known as the **Pharaohs,** plays at the Cairo International Stadium. Their colors are also red and white, with a splash of black—imitating the Egyptian flag with red on the top, white bottoms, and black socks. Matches between the Pharaohs and their international opponents usually don't get as rambunctious as those between local rivals, but the environment is still charged and exciting. This venue is much easier to get to than al-Salam Stadium, just 10.5 kilometers (6.5 mi) from Downtown Cairo. It's best reached by taxi (70-80LE from Downtown).

Entertainment and Events

PERFORMING ARTS

Islamic Cairo

AL-GHOURI COMPLEX WHIRLING DERVISH PERFORMANCE

Al-Ghouri Complex, 3 Mohamed Abdo St., off al-Azhar St.; tel. 0102 664 4787; info@wekaletelghouri.com; Mon., Wed., and Sat. 7:30pm, doors open 6:30pm; 85LE

For an entrancing whirling dervish performance (tanoura), head to the al-Ghouri Complex any Monday, Wednesday, or Saturday evening. Shows start at 7:30pm and finish around 9pm. Doors open at 6:30pm, so be sure to come early to secure your spot.

Garden City

★ MAKAN

1 Saad Zaghloul St.; tel. 02 2792 0878; www.egyptmusic.org; 11am-midnight Sat.-Thurs.

Some of Cairo's most mesmerizing folk music can be found at the understated venue Makan ("Place" in Arabic), located east of Garden City. If you only make it to one show here, the **Mazaher Ensamble** every Wednesday

Sha'bi Music

Sha'bi music, or "music of the people," began in the 1970s with the invention of the cassette tape and personal recorder, which allowed aspiring (unconnected) musicians to bypass the studio. Using traditional Egyptian instruments, singers, most from low-income communities, spoke to the plight of the masses through witty double entendres and danceable beats—not unlike the fathers of hip-hop in the working-class districts of New York. Before Sha'bi music, classical Egyptian music, particularly of the nationalistic variety, dominated, à la Umm Kulthum and Abdel Halim Hafez.

HEARING SHA'BI IN CAIRO

The modern version of sha'bi music, mahraganat (or "festivals") is a creation of this decade, with autotune its most distinctive "instrument," along with syncopated drums and a healthy dose of sampling. This is the so-called electro-sha'bi music you'll hear pouring out of tuk tuks, ahaawi (local coffee shops), and party boats rocking up and down the Nile.

MAKE A PLAYLIST

If you want to make your own playlist, type "mahraganat" on YouTube or Spotify next to the name of some of Egypt's most popular electro-sha'bi artists: **Wegz, Sadat, Alaa 50, DJ Figo, Okka,** and **Ortega.** You can also keep an eye out for occasional concerts at www.ticketsmarche.com (an entertainment ticket vendor), although they're rare.

night at 8pm (80LE) is not to be missed. Their female-led band boasts some of Egypt's last performers of zar—a community healing ritual, sometimes called an exorcism, with polyrhythmic drumming and sonorous voices. Check out their website for a full schedule, or visit the center during the day to explore their extensive audio archive of traditional music from around Egypt.

Gezira and Zamalek

CAIRO OPERA HOUSE

El Borg Gezira St.; tel. 02 7390132 or 02 7390188; www.cairoopera.org

The Cairo Opera House complex is the heart of the city's performing arts, showcasing both local and international orchestras, operas, ballets, and jazz bands. In addition to its two on-site theaters, the Opera House organizes performances at two affiliated theaters Downtown: **El-Gamhouria Theater** (12 El-Gomhoreya St.; tel. 02 23907707) and the **Arab Music Institute** (22 Ramses St.; tel. 02 25763015). You can buy tickets and access the events schedule for all venues on the Opera House website.

EL-SAWY CULTURE WHEEL (Sa'iyat el-Sawy)

26th of July St., under 15th of May Bridge, Zamalek; tel. 0100 099 9995; www.culturewheel.com; 9am-10pm daily

The el-Sawy Culture Wheel hosts a wide range of performances—from puppet shows to poetry readings, classical Arabic bands, and Arabic pop singers. During the day it functions as a café and favorite hangout spot for Cairo's teens and twentysomethings. With a unique location on the Nile, it's an enjoyable place to come with a book and enjoy the river up close.

CINEMA

Downtown (Wist el-Balad)

CIMATHEQUE ALTERNATIVE FILM CENTRE

19a Adly St.; tel. 02 23924164; 10am-5pm daily; 25LE

The Cimatheque Alternative Film Centre is much more than a cinema. In addition to a 45-seat theater for their screenings of international alternative films, this underground center for cinephiles hosts a co-working space, a film library, occasional workshops, and an archive with old cinematic paraphernalia. Visit during the day to meet fellow filmlovers and explore their collection, or come for an evening screening (4:30pm and 7pm). Check out their Facebook page (@cimathe) for event details. To find this hidden gem, head down the alley to the immediate left of the Hashamayim Synagogue in the same building as the "Select Hotel," and make your way up to the fifth floor.

ZAWYA CINEMA

15 Emad el-Deen St.; tel. 0101 433 1779; www.zawyacinema.com

A champion of independent films, Zawya Cinema showcases local talent alongside some of the best international cinema. They also host the annual **Panorama of the European Film Festival** (www.panoramaeurofilm.com) in November at their Downtown location and affiliated **Zamalek Cinema** (13 Shagaret el-Dorr St., on corner of 26th of July St.; tel. 02 27350320; www.zamalekcinema.com). For showtimes and other programming, head to their website or more active Facebook page (@zawyacinema).

FESTIVALS AND EVENTS

Spring

DOWNTOWN CONTEMPORARY ARTS FESTIVAL (D-CAF)

tel. 02 25923749; https://d-caf.org; over three weeks in Mar.-Apr.

With an eclectic program of local and international theater, music, dance, and film, D-CAF offers something for all art-lovers. The festival takes place across the city in both traditional venues and more creative spaces, like rooftops and secluded street-sides. Visit their website for a full schedule of performances and exhibitions.

INTERNATIONAL FESTIVAL OF DRUMS

www.cdf.gov.eg/tobool; over one week in Apr.

Drummers from around world come to infect their audiences with dance and celebrate the beauty of this powerful instrument. The main performance takes place as a procession down medieval **Mu'izz Street** (beginning at **Bab al-Futuh** to the north and typically starting around 4pm) with additional shows in the **Citadel, al-Ghouri Complex, Opera House Complex,** and **Horreya Garden.**

Fall

CAIRO JAZZ FESTIVAL

28 Falaki St., GrEEK Campus, Downtown; www.cairojazzfest.com; over three days in Oct.

This jazz festival is short but sweet, typically lasting for only three days in October. But if you happen to be in town, it's definitely worth a visit. The main venue for the local and international musicians is the American University in Cairo's old GrEEK Campus just off Tahrir Square, but their (equally talented) overflow typically makes its way to other cultural centers around the city. Check their website for full program lineup.

Winter

CAIRO INTERNATIONAL FILM FESTIVAL

Locations throughout Cairo; www.ciff.org.eg; Nov. or Dec.

The Cairo International Film Festival has been celebrating cinema for over 40 years. The event takes place annually over nine days in November or December with films showing at the **Cairo Opera House, Zawya Cinema,** and **Zamalek Cinema.** In their brimming program you can see debut works of up-and-coming Arab artists alongside independent films from around the world.

Shopping

From medieval commercial centers filled with quality handicrafts to shiny Western-style malls and umbrella-filled street-side souqs, Cairo has a diverse set of shopping venues for its visitors (and 20 million residents) to explore. Each space brings with it an opportunity for a kind of cultural immersion while you shop. Souqs are a sensory experience, while Nomad Gallery and Fair Trade Egypt in Zamalek are highly recommended for gifts.

TOP EXPERIENCE

MARKETS

While the paths to these markets are well-trodden by locals, with the exception of Khan el-Khalili and Souq al-Khayamiya you won't find many tourists at them. These souqs are likely to be more experiential destinations than shopping ones, but you never know what gems you might find.

Downtown (Wist el-Balad)

SOUQ EL-ATABA AND EL-MOSKI

Ataba Square to Hussein Square; 8am-midnight daily

If you've missed the days of demonstrations in Cairo and want to know what it feels like to walk among the throngs, head to Souq el-Ataba. You're not likely to buy much here—unless you're on the lookout for plumbing supplies, polyester pajamas, or plastic toys from China—but the experience of navigating between the street vendors is a unique one. El-Moski is essentially an extension of el-Ataba and offers more of the same. You can find el-Moski along Azhar Bridge (Kobri el-Azhar) after walking east from el-Ataba toward Hussein Square.

WAKALET EL-BALAH

26th of July St., Boulaq Abo el-'Ela; 8am-6pm daily

The name Wakalet el-Balah, meaning "date market," comes from a time when the area served as a central trading spot for the sweet fruit. Today, you can browse through thousands of secondhand clothes on racks lining the streets. To get to this central souq, just grab a cab or walk along the Nile Corniche to the 15th of May Bridge. You'll find the market running below it. Alternatively, take the metro to the Nasser Station and head west to 26th of July Street under the bridge.

Islamic Cairo

★ KHAN EL-KHALILI

Off al-Azhar St., next to Hussein Square; 9am-11pm daily, most shops closed Sun.

Famed market Khan el-Khalili—which sits among the ruins of a commercial center constructed by Sultan al-Ghouri in 1511—continues to be a bustling space of commerce and craft, with storefronts lining labyrinthine lanes and concealing busy workshops. Here, you'll find anything from cheap pyramid statues to handmade treasures, like mother-of-pearl boxes, colorful scarves, and lighting fixtures with arabesque patterns. Other treats to look for are antique trinkets (old records, posters, magazines, etc.) from a bygone Egypt, belly dancing outfits, blown-glass dishware, waterpipes, and custom-made jewelry in silver or gold (you can get your name in elegant Arabic script, or in hieroglyphs on a cartouche). To engage the senses, look for an array of spices to the left before Hussein Square (if you're coming from Azhar St.) and the perfume shops along Azhar Street. A word of caution: Perfume sellers are known for being particularly pushy, so brace yourself and remember "la" means no.

As you shop, keep an eye out for some of Khan el-Khalili's original gates: On **Sikkat al-Badistan** you'll find **Bab al-Badistan** (next to the Naguib Mahfouz Café) and nearby, **Bab al-Ghouri,** full of illuminated lanterns. A few steps down from Bab al-Ghouri is the entrance to **Wikalat al-Silahdar**—a small enclosed market built

Navigating Khan el-Khalili

With narrow, crowded lanes and persistent vendors, Khan el-Khalili can be overwhelming, but the medieval gateways and quality souvenirs make for a worthwhile—and unique—excursion. Keep the following tips in mind to make the most of your visit.

mother-of-pearl boxes

MARKET TIPS

- **Browse as much as you like.** Vendors will often unfurl their scarves, unfold their galabayas, and take things down from high shelves to try to guilt you into buying them. Don't feel bad politely saying nothing strikes your fancy.
- **Ask permission before taking photos.** Most vendors won't mind (and expect it from tourists), but asking is considerate.
- **Hop to another shop** if you're struggling to ditch an aggressive salesperson (just not too nearby, lest they be cousins!) and tell the vendors you're being bothered. For every hustler, you'll find several others ready to help.

HOW TO BARGAIN

Vendors here expect to bargain—it's part of the game. Assume the first price they give is at least double what they'd sell it for, and likely triple. If you're not happy with the price, **walk away politely.** If the price is right, they'll come after you to accept. If not, and you can't find what you want anywhere else (though you likely will—many of the stores have the same or similar items), you can always come back and renegotiate.

And don't forget to **smile.** A sense of humor is appreciated in Egypt, and vendors are much more likely to give you a good price if they like you. Finally, do keep in mind that Egypt has been suffering an economic crisis for over a decade. If you can afford it, paying more than "market rate"—especially for some of the fine handmade goods on offer—is actually a good thing.

KHAN EL-KHALILI'S BEST SOUVENIRS

Now you're ready to shop! Keep an eye out for these handmade treasures as you browse.

- **Mother-of-pearl boxes:** Wooden boxes of various sizes decorated with intricate geometric patterns of iridescent mollusk shell interiors. Most are made of a mix of plastic and genuine mother of pearl. Hold the product up to the light to see if it shines to determine how much of it is authentic.
- **Colorful scarves:** Beautiful scarves of soft Egyptian cotton, with options for both men and women. To be sure you're getting a 100% cotton scarf, ask the seller to put a flame to it for a second (he'll likely do this unprompted). A slow burn and lack of black smoke show there's no polyester or other synthetic fabrics.
- **Lighting fixtures:** Lovely lamps with arabesque patterns that decorate the walls when illuminated. Copper lighting fixtures cost more than the aluminum alternatives but last longer. You can usually tell the difference by color, but some white copper lamps look similar to aluminum. In this case, compare the weights (copper should be heavier).

in 1837 on the spot of a former Mamluk-era khan. (The khan—inn for travelers—was first built here in 1385 by an emir of Sultan Barquq named Jaharkas al-Khalili; hence the market's name. Prior to that, the spot had served as the burial grounds for Fatimid caliphs, whom al-Khalili had disinterred and tossed in the trash.)

Go in the morning for a quieter excursion, but there's also a charm to the evenings, which bring illuminated shopfronts and locals out for a cool stroll. There's not much organization, save for the designated streets of silver and gold, which you can find on Khan el-Khalili's westernmost border—the southern section of Mui'zz Street, before you reach the main stretch of medieval monuments.

Enter the bazaar through Hussein Square across the street from al-Azhar Mosque. A tunnel in front of al-Azhar will bring you safely across the street if you're coming from the south.

BACKSTREET AZHAR SOUQ

Near al-Azhar Mosque; 9am-9pm daily

Facing al-Azhar Mosque, a right will take you down a colorful pocket of Islamic Cairo's sprawling markets. Past mounds of spices, caged chickens, and butcher shops chopping camel meat, you'll find a large vegetable market on your left-hand side to pick your fresh fare or just browse.

SOUQ AL-KHAYAMIYA (TENTMAKERS' SOUQ)

Al-Khayamiya St., el-Darb el-Ahmar; 10am-9pm daily

Dating from the mid-17th century, Souq al-Khayamiya is Cairo's oldest still-standing covered market. The main attractions are the roofed structure itself and the handmade appliqué (for sale) depicting a variety of scenes—from pharaonic ceremonies to exotic birds, dancing dervishes, medieval markets, and Mickey Mouse. The upper floors of the market now sit empty but once housed the shoemakers who originally cobbled in the shops below.

Greater Cairo

SOUQ EL-GOMA'A

Souq el-Goma'a St., just south of el-Khalifa along the Autostrad, Tonsy Bridge; noon-6pm Sat.-Thurs., 6am-noon Fri.

Possibly Cairo's largest flea market, Souq el-Goma'a hosts hundreds of vendors selling everything from furniture and antiques to broken toys bought for scrap. Contrary to the name, Souq el-Goma'a ("Friday Market") is open every day, but Friday mornings bring the widest range of merchants hawking goods and even animals. If you've had anything stolen during your visit to Cairo, chances are it'll end up here, so be sure to keep your bags close. To get here, grab a cab or Uber and tell the driver "Souq el-Goma'a fil Khalifa" (7 km/4 mi southwest of Tahrir Square; 45-50LE).

BIRQASH CAMEL MARKET

Off el-Khatab-Berkash Rd., Birqash; 7am-noon Fri. and Sun.

Take a peek inside Egypt's thriving camel trade. Hundreds of these beasts of burden are gathered here for Friday and Sunday auctions, nearly all to be turned into camel steaks or work animals (read: it's no petting zoo). Well outside the city proper, expect the trip to take around an hour from downtown without traffic. To get there, grab a taxi or Uber and ask to go to "Souq el-Gamal fi Birqash" (expect to pay 400-500LE round-trip including wait time). You can ask the driver to wait for you (an hour or so should be sufficient), or take a microbus back to Imbaba and get a cab from there. Friday mornings are best to avoid traffic. Beware rogue camels.

GIFTS

Downtown (Wist el-Balad)

OUM EL-DOUNIA GALLERY

3 Talaat Harb St., 2nd floor, just off Tahrir Square; tel. 02 23938273; www.oumeldounia.com; 10am-10pm daily

---

1: Sikkat al-Badistan in Khan el-Khalili bazaar
2: Souq al-Khayamiya (Tentmakers' Souq)
3: vegetables for sale in Islamic Cairo 4: backstreet souq in Islamic Cairo

1
2
3
قصر الخضروات
4

If you don't like haggling, Oum el-Dounia is a good place to buy souvenirs. They sell high-quality, handmade goods from across the country with a price tag—albeit one much higher than what you'd pay if you bought it from the source. You can find beaded bags and clothes from the Sinai, pottery from Fayoum, appliqué from Cairo, and other home goods.

Old Cairo and Coptic Cairo

SOUQ EL-FUSTAT

Corner of el-Emam Malik St. and Sidi Hassan al-Anwar St.; 10am-6pm daily

This modern covered market (really a strip of stores rather than a proper souq, as the name suggests) hosts dozens of shops selling Egyptian handicrafts. Built in 2003 on the spot of a 14th-century souq, it now offers works of contemporary artisans, from leather bags to home goods, Bedouin-inspired dresses, and more. Come early if you can—some of the stores close before the official hours.

Gezira and Zamalek

NOMAD GALLERY

14 Saray Elgezira St.; tel. 02 27361917; www.nomadgallery.net; 9am-7:30pm daily

Tucked away on the second floor of a side street behind the Tunisian Embassy, this treasure trove of handmade Egyptian goods offers an array of vibrant rugs, unique jewelry, high-quality scarves (silk or Egyptian cotton), and Bedouin-inspired fashion.

FAIR TRADE EGYPT

27 Yehia Ibrahim St.; tel. 02 27365123; 9am-8pm daily

Fair Trade Egypt works with communities across Egypt to sell their handmade goods in return for fair compensation. They offer quality rugs, scarves, pottery, napkins, jewelry, and funky fusion clothes from around the country.

HOME & BEYOND

17 El-Mansour Mohamed St.; tel. 0122 329 7830; 10am-11pm daily

This colorful shop sells traditional handmade goods alongside trendier interpretations. Choose from an array of high-quality cotton scarves, Egyptian film posters from the 1950s-1990s, or serving trays and teacups decorated with pop art-esque portraits of old movie stars and musicians.

NEVIN ALTMANN SHOP

3 Hassan Assem St.; tel. 0121 119 7337; www.nevinaltmann.com; 9am-9pm daily

The prices here are not for bargain hunters, but Nevin Altmann's Siwa-inspired embroidered bags, shawls, and wallets are elegant and colorful. Browse the catalog on their website before you go to get an idea.

BOOKS

Garden City

AMERICAN UNIVERSITY IN CAIRO (AUC) BOOKSTORE

113 Qasr el-Ainy St., just off Tahrir Square.; tel. 02 27975370; 10am-6pm Sat.-Thurs.

Located in what's left of the historic AUC downtown campus east of Garden City, this shop offers a great selection of books about Egypt—from Egyptology to contemporary politics—Arabic literature in translation, and some international best sellers. If you're in need of reading material for your travels, this is an essential stop. Enter from the Mohammed Mahmoud Street gate.

Gezira and Zamalek

DIWAN BOOKSTORE

159 26th of July St.; tel. 0122 600 0168; www.diwanegypt.com; 9am-11:30pm daily

An official partner of the American University in Cairo, Diwan offers a large English-language selection and many books from AUC Press. There's a good selection of Arabic literature in translation, books about history and politics of Egypt and the Middle East, Arabic language learning materials, and international best sellers. You can enjoy your purchases (or other reading material) with a tea in their small café.

Food

In Cairo you can find bites for all budgets and palates. Downtown has a plethora of casual restaurants—including authentic Egyptian eats and international fast-food chains. For fine dining (or if you enjoy a drink with your meal), head to Zamalek or Garden City. Both neighborhoods offer casual options as well, but the prices will still be inflated compared to restaurants elsewhere in the city (in exchange for hipster flair). Head to the working-class districts of Imbaba, Shubra, or Sayeda Zeinab for the most popular local dining experiences. Or check out Dokki's famed drive-up juice bars and Yemeni restaurants. Alcohol not served at the restaurants below unless otherwise noted.

DOWNTOWN (WIST EL-BALAD)

Egyptian

KOSHARY EL-TAHRIR

92 El-Tahrir St., on corner of Abd El Khalik Tharwat St.; tel. 19719; http://koshary-eltahrir.com; 8am-1am Mon.-Sat., 8am-midnight Sun.; 10-25LE

Koshary el-Tahrir rivals Abou Tarek for the title of Cairo's king of koshary. The dining space isn't as unique as that of its competitor, but dishes here are just as delicious and performatively prepared. You can find additional branches in **Dokki** (132 Tahrir St.) and **Mokattam** (on the corner of Street 9 and Mokattam St.).

★ KOSHARY ABOU TAREK

Champollion Rd.; tel. 16011; 9am-11pm Sat.-Thurs., 10am-11pm Fri.; 15-25LE

Arguably *the* place to try the quintessential Egyptian dish, koshary. Enjoy the layers of pasta, lentils, chickpeas, fried onions, and various sauces in Abou Tarek's eccentric dining space—with aluminum tabletops, funky lighting, fish tanks, and ceilings adorned with chandeliers encircled by faux plants. The three-storied smoke-free space is a rare treat.

KAZAZ

38 Sabry Abou Alam St. off Talaat Harb Sq.; tel. 0101 633 3568; 7am-2am daily; 15-50LE

Grab your favorite Egyptian fast food from this clean and tasty eatery. Kazaz's menu is long and varied, so try something new or stick with the classics, fuul and ta'maya. There's a cramped dining area upstairs, but to enjoy a unique Cairo experience head down the street and eat at an ahwa (street-side café). (These casual cafés don't serve food and don't mind if you bring your own as long as you buy a drink).

FASAHET SOMAYA

10 Hoda Shaarawy St.; tel. 0100 847 0614; 5pm-7pm Mon.-Thurs. and Sat., 7pm-9pm Fri.; 100LE

If you haven't been in Cairo long enough to be invited to a home-cooked meal, Fasahet Somaya is the next best thing. Every night chef Somaya serves up a different dish depending on what's fresh in the markets. The set menu means it's not the best place for picky palates, but adventurous eaters will enjoy this game of culinary roulette where any given night might bring oxtail in chocolate sauce or molokhia with rice. The restaurant only hosts 12 people per night, so be sure to call a day in advance to secure your seat.

International

EISH & MALH

20 Adly St.; tel. 0109 874 4014; 7am-12:30am daily; 75-150LE

Popular with the young and hip, Eish & Malh ("Bread and Salt") uses fresh local ingredients to prepare authentic Italian cuisine. The space is casual with a café feel, and hosts live music events most days during brunch or dinner (call or check their Facebook page @eishmalh for details). Large windows and an interior balcony overlooking the ground floor make for a spacious, well-lit dining area, but the lack of a nonsmoking section dampens the promise of "fresh and healthy" eating. Don't miss their organic market the first Friday of every month.

Cafés and Snacks

LATIF WASSILI BAKERY

8 El-Mahdi St.; tel. 02 25916023; 24 hours daily; 10-20LE

For decades this hole-in-the-wall (quite literally) bakery has been a local favorite for its fresh bread and takeaway treats. If you're curious how the round pretzel-like simit sold in traffic by traveling vendors tastes, this is a good place to try it hot out of the oven. You can also sample the Egyptian favorite, fino bread—similar to a long bread roll.

EL-ABD PASTRY

25 Talaat Harb St.; tel. 02 23938307; 8:30am-11pm Sat.-Wed., 8:30am-12:30am Thurs., 11:45am-12:30am Fri.; 15-50LE

You can't miss this sweet shop with its nearly permanent crowd waiting for an ice cream or pastries by the kilo. El-Abd is a Downtown institution with a mix of European and Middle Eastern treats. Sample the fresh croissants, syrupy basbousa, or crisp baklava (all much better than the ice cream). Come early to avoid the lines.

CAFÉ RICHE

17 Talaat Harb St.; tel. 0100 604 2990; 9am-midnight daily; 70-150LE

This former watering hole for Egypt's intellectuals and revolutionaries has become more of a museum than a restaurant. The food should be avoided, but you can enjoy a strong Arabic coffee, a beer, or some local wine in the space that once served as a hotbed for the Egyptian nationalist struggle. In the 1920s, revolutionaries outfitted the café with a printing press to produce anti-British pamphlets, and decades later, a young Gamal Abdel Nasser met with fellow officers here to plan their coup against the puppet monarchy.

ISLAMIC CAIRO

Egyptian

HUSSEIN HOTEL RESTAURANT

36 Al-Mashhad Al Husseini St.; tel. 02 25918089; 8am-3am daily; 60-100LE

When the crowds of the Khan el-Khalili bazaar overwhelm, make your way to this spacious rooftop restaurant and café above Hussein Hotel. Watch people file by in the narrow streets below from your bird's-eye view in the open-air seating area, or head indoors to watch the hubbub in Hussein Square. Best to just enjoy a tea and fresh air, but the food is fine if hunger strikes (try the shish tawook, grilled chicken shish kebab). To find the entrance, take a left before Hussein Square and an immediate right into the bazaar. The hotel door will be on your right.

CITADEL VIEW STUDIO MISR

In al-Azhar Park; tel. 0120 727 3747; 10am-10pm daily; 70-100LE

From this spacious outdoor patio in al-Azhar Park you can admire the illuminated Mohammed Ali Mosque rising out of the Citadel in the distance, framed by an elegant strip of fountains. The food won't be the best you've had, but the tagines and stuffed pigeon with rice are good enough and worth the enchanting ambiance.

NAGUIB MAHFOUZ CAFÉ

5 Şikkat al-Badistan, Khan el-Khalili; tel. 02 25932262; 10am-1am daily, noon-2am daily summer; 160-200LE

Escape the chaos of the Khan el-Khalili bazaar by ducking into this café for some of Egypt's most delicious dishes and traditional live music (after 7pm daily). Sample the stuffed pigeon or hawawshii (spiced meat in pita) under arched ceilings adorned with classical Islamic patterns and matching mashribiya. As you dine, a classical Egyptian band just might send you into tarab (a trance) with covers of the country's most celebrated musical treasures, from Umm Kulthum to Sayed Darwish.

Cafés and Snacks

★ TEKIAT KHAN KHATUN CAFÉ

3 Mohamed Abdu St., behind al-Azhar Mosque; 5pm-3am daily

Nestled behind al-Azhar Mosque, this café in the courtyard of an Ottoman-era house offers a unique space to enjoy a juice or shisha after a long day of exploring Islamic Cairo. Recent hikes in electricity prices means the soft lighting has been replaced by more environment-friendly (and less romantic) energy-saving bulbs, but there's still a charm to the pillow seating in the tree-lined square. If you're lucky you might catch a whirling dervish show that swings by on occasion.

EL-FISHAWY

5 Sikkat Khan El-Khalili; tel. 0111 388 9611; 24 hours daily; juices and hot drinks 25LE

Foreigners flock to this 200-some-year-old café where Egypt's top literary figures and intellectuals once gathered. It's a great place to recharge with an Arabic coffee and rest your legs, but not your senses—you'll be in the middle of the bazaar bustle, with hawkers hawking and traveling musicians passing through to serenade you with their ouds (a classic instrument in Middle Eastern music similar to a lute). Don't miss the backroom where Nobel laureate Naguib Mahfouz is said to have written much of his famous Cairo Trilogy.

MOKATTAM

Middle Eastern

SHAWERMA ABU MAZEN

Street 9; tel. 0110 121 9675; 9am-5am daily; 40-70LE

If you're in need of snacks for your sunset viewing on Mokattam Corniche, this Syrian restaurant will deliver a filling meal. Shawarma in a rolled saj (Syrian bread) is their signature dish, but they also offer a variety of grilled options. Try the falafel to see if you can tell the difference between the Egyptian version (ta'maya) made with fava beans and the Syrian chickpea-based staple.

Sweets

ABU LEILA

Street 9, across from Zidan Market; tel. 0115 600 4315; 24 hours daily; 15-20LE juice

Blinding lights and mounds of fresh fruit tell you you've arrived at this dessert shop that has something for every type of sweet tooth. Whether you're looking for a healthy fresh mango juice or prefer your fruits covered in ice cream and konafa (syrup-soaked shredded phyllo pastry with clotted cream), you won't be disappointed.

GEZIRA AND ZAMALEK

Egyptian

★ ZÖÖBA

16 26th of July St.; tel. 16082; www.zoobaeats.com; 8am-1am daily; 30-60LE

This hipster rendition of classic Egyptian street food adds a colorful twist to local dining. The fresh local bread ('aish baladi), and traditional fava bean paste (fuul) are worth the trip alone, but if you want to get crazy, try the falafel (ta'maya) with pickled beets or lightly fried cauliflower, and rice pudding with orange zest. There's not much space to dine inside, but just pull up a chair and make a new friend.

CAIRO KITCHEN

118 26th of July St.; tel. 02 27354000; 11am-midnight daily; 40-90LE

Find traditional Egyptian dishes like macarona bechamel (baked pasta with cheese and meat) and chicken yogurt fattah in this casual dining space. Here you can try unique twists on classic dips—tahini with carrot or coriander hummus—and colorful salad plates with various mezzes of eggplants, beans, and potatoes.

★ ABO EL-SID

157 26th of July St.; tel. 02 27359640; www.abouelsid.com; 1pm-1am daily; 100-200LE

Abo el-Sid's rich-colored venue gives a trendy touch to classical Arabic styles. Paintings of

TAREK
1

2
EL FISHAWY

old Egyptian movie stars decorate the walls and dimly lit chandeliers with beaded metal lamps hang from the ceilings. It's an excellent place to sample traditional Egyptian dishes (the stuffed pigeon is delicious) or more colorful fares (like Circassian chicken in walnut sauce) with a glass of wine and nice music.

Middle Eastern

SAG W SHAWERMA

132 26th of July St.; tel. 0115 453 6886; 8am-1am Sat.-Thurs., 11am-1am Fri.; 20-45LE

If you're in need of a quick meal to go, this Syrian shawarma shop won't disappoint. Delicious rolled sandwiches on saj (tortilla-like bread) are served rapid-fire to the crowds that gather around for lunch or a late-night snack. If you're not a fan of fries or pickled veg on your shawarma, make it known. Falafel and kobeba (oblong fried meat in bulgur) are also tasty options.

International

★ GRANITA

5 Michel Lutfallah St., All Saints Cathedral; tel. 0101 279 7522; 7am-10pm daily; 50-120LE

Nestled inside the grounds of the All Saints Cathedral, this hidden gem serves delicious brunches (both Egyptian and international fare), pizzas, pastries, paninis, and crepes. The breezy garden seating and plant-filled interior (a rare nonsmoking venue) are tastefully decorated with colorful accents and fresh-cut flowers. Excellent juices and coffee also available.

MAISON THOMAS

157 26th of July St.; tel. 0122 369 2004; www.maisonthomas.net; 24 hours daily; 55-120LE

At this classic Cairo establishment, you can enjoy your Western meal sans guilt of not eating local. Maison Thomas has been a favorite of Egyptians and foreigners alike since it started serving pizzas nearly a century ago. The checkerboard floors, mirror-lined walls, and bright yellow ceilings make for a nice pizza parlor ambiance.

1: food from Koshary Abou Tarek **2:** El-Fishawy

MAHARAJA INDIAN RESTAURANT

3 Hassan Assem St.; tel. 0128 083 8099; 1pm-midnight daily; 90-150LE

Maharaja dishes out some of the best Indian food you'll find in Cairo. The tender chicken tikka masala and garlic naan are favorites, and for dessert, don't miss the artfully presented coconut ice cream. Check out the second floor with its comfortable couches, warm colors, and walls decorated with images from the East.

CRIMSON BAR & GRILL

16 Kamal Al Tawil St.; tel. 0127 505 5555; 8am-1am daily; 600LE min.

One of Cairo's chicest evening venues, Crimson is the brainchild of Egyptian billionaire Naguib Sawiris. The well-orchestrated lighting, indoor plants, and wall garden make for a charming interior, only to be outdone by the terrace overlooking the Nile. Although most popular at night, it's also a nice place for brunch or sunset drinks. Dress code is smart casual. Call in advance for a table with view.

PIER 88

19 El-Gezira St., on Imperial Boat; https://pier88group.com; tel. 0120 811 1130; 1pm-1am Sat.-Wed., 1pm-2am Thurs.-Fri.; 750LE min.

Another child of Egyptian billionaire Naguib Sawiris, Pier 88 caters to the tastes of Egypt's elites with Italian fine dining prepared by a team of international chefs in an open kitchen. You can enjoy Sawiris's locally produced wine or imported varieties along with a steak tartare on the candle-lit balcony overlooking the Nile. Weekend brunches (Fri.-Sat.) are also popular. Reservations necessary Wednesday-Friday nights. Dress code is (appropriately) "fashionable."

Cafés and Snacks

P.S. CAFÉ

5 Sayed Bakry St.; 24 hours daily; 15-30LE hot drinks

When night falls, this 24-hour outdoor café takes over the street with its plastic patio furniture and glass shisha bottles. The clientele run the gamut, but most are young men and women enjoying a cheap outing in this upper-class district.

THE BAKERY SHOP (TBS)

4D El-Gezirah St.; tel. 16679; www.tbsfresh.com; 7am-midnight daily; 15-30LE pastries

A nice European-style bakery with flaky croissants and sandwiches made to order on your choice of freshly baked bread. Coffee and cakes are also supremely tasty, but limited seating makes it better for a takeaway trip.

SIMONDS

112 26th of July; tel. 02 27359436; 24 hours daily; 15-45LE pastries

Enjoy a slice of history with your morning coffee at this 120-something-year-old pastry shop on Zamalek's main thoroughfare. The fresh croissants and flaky Danishes are delicious, nicely paired with a cappuccino. If you're Downtown, check out its branch on 29 Sherif Basha Street (across from McDonald's).

BOCELLI CAFÉ AND RESTAURANT

Cairo Opera House complex; tel. 0111 116 6605; 25-30LE hot drinks

Tucked inside the Cairo Opera House complex, this café boasts a large patch of outdoor seating with comfortable cushions in the shade of palm trees and umbrellas. It's a great place to grab a tea before or after a show, or just a good excuse to walk through the beautiful grounds of the Opera House. The food can be skipped, but it's good enough for a snack. To find this spot, head through the north entrance off Mohammed Mokhtar Street and it will be on your right. If you're coming from the main entrance in Opera Square, walk straight for about 400 meters (1,300 ft) past the main opera hall and through a second set of gates. The café will be on your right.

BEANO'S

8 Al-Sheikh Al Marsafi St.; tel. 02 33001887; 8am-midnight daily; 25-40LE hot drinks

Something of a local Starbucks, this café serves up delicious espresso drinks in a smoke-free space. Expect to see a number of MacBook companions as Western-educated elites work in their second office. Skip the sandwiches, but nut milks and yogurt pots with chia seeds are available for those missing home.

★ GARDEN PROMENADE CAFÉ

16 Saray El-Gezira St.; tel. 02 27283000; 6am-midnight daily; 30-50LE hot drinks

Relax in the lush garden of the **Mariott Hotel** behind the palace built by Khedive Ismail for the 1869 opening of the Suez Canal. Today, wealthy Egyptians brunch alongside hotel guests in this quiet corner of Cairo. Hide out under a large umbrella during the day, and enjoy a cool breeze beneath rustling trees in the evening. A lovely oasis for a coffee or cold afternoon beer. Food is acceptable, but order early as service can be slow.

SUFI CAFÉ & BOOKSTORE

12 Sayed El-Bakry St.; tel. 02 27381643; 11am-1am daily; 70-100LE mains

Enjoy your coffee surrounded by second-hand books in this hip Sufi-themed space. With its large windows, natural lighting, and chill music, it's a lovely place to start your day or recollect. The food won't be the best you'll have in Cairo, but it's suitable for a snack. Check their Facebook page @Sufibookstoreandmore for evening Sufi chants and other musical events.

Sweets

★ MANDARINE KOUEIDER

17 Shagaret el-Dorr St.; tel. 02 27355010; www.mandarine-koueider.com; 9am-11pm daily; 20LE ice cream

Mandarine Koueider is the crème de la crème of Egyptian sweets. You might have to fight your way to the counter, but it's worth the effort to sample the array of baklava, basbousa (syrup-soaked semolina cake), and cream-filled konafa. The yogurt and berry ice cream is a delightful cap to a hot day of sightseeing. Takeaway only, so scurry back to your hotel or do like the locals and find a perch outside the Victorian-style music school next door.

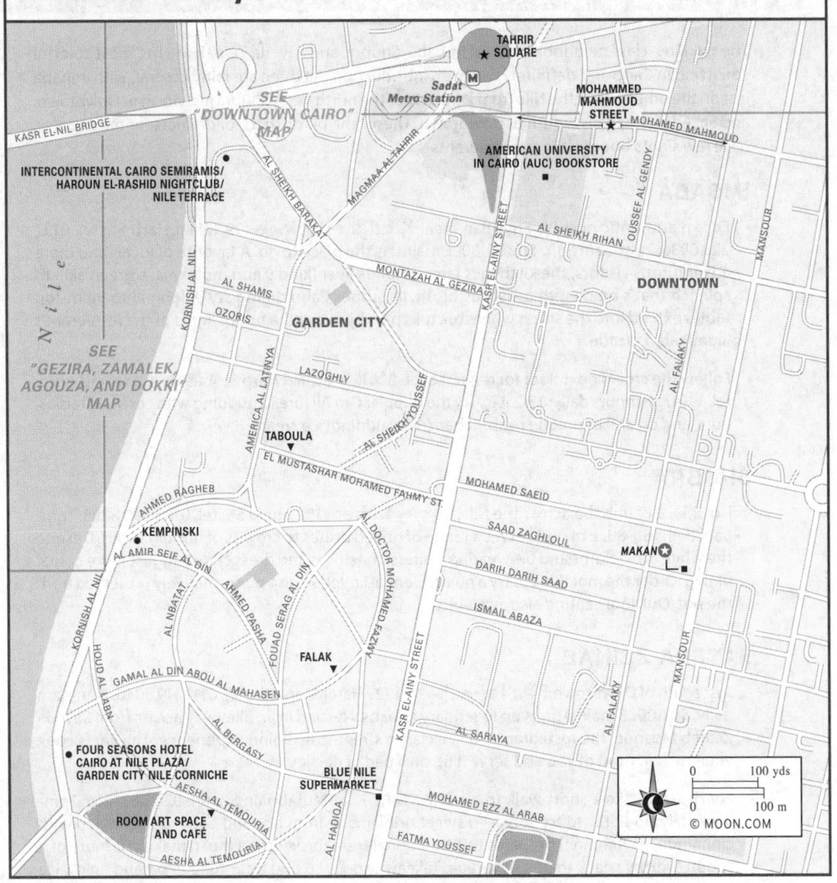

GARDEN CITY

Egyptian

NILE TERRACE

Semiramis Hotel, Corniche el-Nil; tel. 02 27988000; 11am-1am daily; 200-300LE

A wonderful choice for dinner or drinks with a view. The menu is short but sufficient, with grilled meat and chicken dishes, nice mezzes, and a variety of fruity shisha options. Beer, wine, and cocktails also served. Come early to watch the sun set over the Nile and its flocks of feluccas.

Middle Eastern

★ TABOULA

1 Latin America St.; tel. 02 27925261; www.taboula-eg.com; noon-1am daily; 90-150LE

Scrumptious Lebanese dishes are served here with your choice of local wine, beer, or Lebanese liquor. The warm lighting, arabesque patterns, and tangerine-meets-peach color scheme make for a cozy dining experience. Their hummus steals the show, but the array of mezzes, seafood, and grilled meat or chicken plates are also pleasers. Note: It gets smoky in the evenings.

Authentic Cairene Eats

The working-class neighborhoods of Imbaba, Shubra, and Sayeda Zeinab are the most colorful you'll find in Cairo and definitely worth an introduction. All three are fairly central, with Imbaba just on the other side of the Nile from Zamalek (to the northwest), Shubra just north of Downtown, and Sayeda Zeinab just south of Downtown. These "sha'bi" districts, or districts "of the people," have few sights but great local restaurants.

IMBABA

- For an authentic no-frills Egyptian meal, **Kibdet el-Prince** (79 Talaat Harb St.; tel. 0122 220 0836; 2pm-5am Sun.-Fri.; 60-80LE mains) is the place to go. A favorite of locals and more adventurous visitors, the kitchen is famous for its liver (kibda) and molokhia, a green akin to spinach that's made into a viscous broth. In proper Cairo dining style, long aluminum-top tables extend into the street where tuk tuks pass by under the bright lights of the restaurant's illuminated façade.

- Follow the crowd next door for dessert at **el-Malky** (Talaat Harb St., beside Kibdet el-Prince; tel. 19017; 24 hours daily; 15-25LE). Try the popular Om Ali (bread pudding with coconut, raisins, nuts, and cream) or unique roz bi-laban (rice pudding) ice cream.

SHUBRA

- Northeast of Imbaba across the Nile, **Sobhy Kaber** (151 Abeid St.; tel. 0101 598 8898; 1pm-6am daily; 60-80LE mains) serves a range of grilled dishes to crowds of hungry locals. Despite the white tablecloths and tie-wearing waiters, the prices and dress code suggest more casual dining. Order the molokhia to try a quintessential Egyptian dish performatively presented from the pot. Outdoor seating also available.

SAYEDA ZEINAB

- Just south of Downtown, **Rifa'i el-Kebabgi** (29 Haret Mongi St.; tel. 0111 119 8040; 4pm-4am daily; 80-100LE mains) grills up legendary kebabs. Nestled in an alleyway across from Sayeda Zeinab Mosque, the restaurant offers a classic street-side dining experience. The chefs cook your meat in front of you and serve it up on a bed of parsley.

- For dessert, take a short walk to **al-Rahmani** (2 al-Mutabdain St.; tel. 02 23625216; 2pm-3am daily; 15-25LE) to try sobia—a sweet drink made from rice and coconut, sprinkled with cinnamon. Al-Rahmani prepares this traditional treat thicker than most, making it more of a spoon-worthy snack than a beverage. Takeaway only, so find a car to lean on and enjoy. Ice cream also available.

Cafés and Snacks

FALAK

7 Gamal Al-Din Abou Al-Mahasen St.; tel. 0106 477 7808; 9am-11pm daily; 50-75LE

Tall ceilings, art-hung walls, and large balcony doors flung open wide to let in fresh air and natural light make for a particularly pleasant place to breakfast with a book. Located on the ground floor of a Belle Époque residential building, the café has a homey feel. Try an omelet and some orange juice, and peek into their small shop with jewelry, books, framed photographs, and other knickknacks. Outdoor seating also available.

ROOM ART SPACE AND CAFÉ

10 Etehaad Al-Mohamin St.; tel. 0100 068 1539; www.roomart.space; 10am-12:30am daily; 80-200LE mains, 25-40LE coffee

In the basement of Britain's Cairo military headquarters during World War II, this casual café turns into a cultural center in the evening with live music, karaoke, and board game nights (check their website for full events calendar). During the day the space is particularly popular with twentysomethings who come to sip on espressos as they chat with friends or work on their laptops. The ventilation could use improvement and nonsmokers might struggle during crowded evening hours.

AGOUZA AND DOKKI

Egyptian

NIEMA

172 Nile St., Agouza; tel. 02 33365555; 24 hours daily; 15-30LE

The place to enjoy Egyptian fast food at any hour of the day. You'll likely find crowds of people surrounding this takeaway-only restaurant, famous for its shawarma and fries. Families park outside for a drive-in meal, and the those without cars sit on curbsides to enjoy their assortment of sandwiches (other favorites include burger with egg or the classic fuul).

Middle Eastern

EL-SHEBANI NEW RESTAURANT

14 Al-Salwli St., Dokki; tel. 0100 059 0029; 24 hours daily; 60-100LE

Popular with the Yemeni expat community, this restaurant serves up authentic Yemeni food with succulent chicken and lamb dishes. Tasty bean tagines make for a nice vegetarian option. The interior is a bit of an eyesore with clashing patterns of faux stone walls and striped floors, but your taste buds will be pleased.

BAB EL-YEMEN RESTAUARANT

61-63 al-Dokki St., Dokki; tel. 02 33690090; 8am-1am, daily; 80-130LE

Bab el-Yemen ("the Gateway to Yemen") cooks up food that's just as tasty as the other Yemeni restaurants in the neighborhood and puts a bit more effort into the décor. With two floors and plentiful seating, it's a great option for large groups. The flaky Yemeni bread served here is worth the trip alone, but the fasoulia bayda (white bean stew) and chicken mandi (steamed chicken) with rice are also delicious.

Seafood

★ SEAGULL

106 Nile St., Dokki; tel. 02 37606738; www.seagullegypt.net; noon-1:30am daily; 250-350LE

Enjoy some of Cairo's best seafood with a glass of wine at this moored boat on the Nile. You can pick your fresh fish off a bed of ice and have it prepared to order. Snag a seat outside for the best views of the vibrant river life, or if that's not close enough, ask to dine on a private boat (400LE/hour, can hold up to 10 people). Call ahead to reserve.

Sweets

★ ABO AMR CITY DRINK

116 Tahrir St., in front of Dokki metro station; tel. 02 37616178; 24 hours daily; 15-30LE juices

Nets of fresh fruit decorate the exterior of this famed drive-in juice bar where you can get anything from an unadulterated avocado juice to a Twinkie shake. If you don't have a car, find a wall to lean against and indulge.

FAMILY DRINK

17 Tahrir St., on corner of Mohi el-Din Abou el-Ezz St.; tel. 0114 040 3740; 24 hours daily; 15-30LE juices

Family Drink is almost as good as its competitor down the street, with the added bonus of a place to sit. The menu here is much the same with your choice of fresh fruit juices, fruit salads, or candy bar shakes.

Bars and Nightlife

Cairo nightlife comes in many forms. Whether you want to sit en plein air with a shisha and tea, or dance with a cocktail in a New York-style nightclub, you'll have no shortage of ways to spend your time after the sun goes down. Downtown is full of casual rooftop bars, street-side ahaawi (local outdoor cafés) and smoky cabarets. Zamalek and Garden City offer chic bars and restaurants, many of which turn up the dance music on weekend evenings. In Agouza and Dokki you'll find more rooftop bars for chilling, and some fun live music dance clubs with local musicians and DJs.

Nightlife usually picks up on the later side in Cairo (after 10pm) and can last as late as 4am. The most traditional drink of choice is Stella beer, but many places also offer local wine and cocktails. Be sure to check the price before you order any imported liquors—they can be incredibly expensive (like $30 a shot). Without exception, all bars allow smoking indoors. So wear clothes you don't plan on wearing again on your trip, or head to the open-air venues for some extra oxygen.

DOWNTOWN (WIST EL-BALAD)

Bars

CAROL BAR

12 Kasr Al Nil St.; tel. 0102 911 1105; 5pm-4am daily; drinks 55-80LE

A favorite spot of the Downtown intelligentsia, this long, narrow strip of an establishment is a cozy place to grab a drink and enjoy a classy playlist. The space is dimly lit, and the bar illuminated in movie star mirror lights. Decent snacks are available, but avoid the cocktails, which are more water than booze. Call ahead to reserve (especially Thurs.-Fri.) to avoid disappointment.

★ ODEON PALACE BAR

6 Abdel Hamid Said St. off Talaat Harb St.; tel. 02 25776637; 8am-5am daily; drinks 60-100LE

There's nothing palatial about this bar or the hotel it sits above, but the rooftop terrace lined with plants and matching synthetic grass is a nice space to enjoy a cold beer en plein air. The retro elevator prepares you for a return to the '60s that awaits above. While you can skip the food and cocktails, shisha-lovers won't be disappointed.

LOTUS BAR

12 Talaat Harb St.; tel. 02 25750966; www.lotushotel.com; 6pm-2am daily; drinks 50-80LE

Artists and activists gather at this small and somewhat shabby bar, making it a great place for solo travelers looking to meet interesting locals. Grab a beer (the only alcoholic beverage the menu), and sample a popular Egyptian snack, termis (lupini beans). A small balcony offers views of the Downtown bustle and some scarce oxygen with your drinks.

HAPPY CITY

92c Mohamed Farid St.; tel. 02 23959222; 6pm-2am daily; drinks 40-60LE

A classic Downtown bar on the roof of a second-rate hotel—casual and cool, but lacking the view of some of its competitors in the neighborhood. It's an unpretentious space to enjoy a cheap local beer and complimentary mezzes (lupini beans and carrot sticks).

CARLTON HOTEL & BAR

21 26th of July St; tel. 02 25755022; 5pm-2am daily; drinks 60-100LE, 100LE min.

This large and breezy bar atop the 1930s Carlton Hotel is a great place to watch the hectic city below with a cold beer or local wine. Lined with flowers and lush plants, it looks out onto Cairo's colonnaded High Court

Alcohol in Cairo

Barring the odd dry neighborhood, alcohol is not hard to come by in Cairo. The city is brimming with bars and has plenty of liquor stores selling local drinks. Consuming alcohol in public (the street, parks, etc.) is not permitted, but if you do so discreetly, no one will hunt you down for it. That said, with zipping cars, motorcycles, and tuk tuks coming every which way, it's good to keep your wits about you. To pick up drinks for a felucca ride, your hotel, or onward travel outside of Cairo, here are some of your best options:

- **Drinkies** (157 26th of July St., Zamalek; 2 Huissen El Memary Basha St., from Mahmoud Basiony St., Downtown; 41 Talaat Harb Sq., Downtown; 162 26th of July St., Agouza; tel. 19330; www.drinkies.net; noon-midnight Sun.-Wed., noon-2am Thurs.-Sat.): Drinkies has a near monopoly on takeaway alcohol in Cairo. Here you can find local beers, wines, and spirits for cheap. Visit one of their dozens of shops scattered across the city (for full map of locations check their website), or call the Drinkies hotline for a quick delivery.
- **Duty Free Cairo Sheraton** (inside the Sheraton Hotel, Galaa Square, Dokki; tel. 0122 348 0239; 11am-11pm daily): If you're regretting you didn't grab some liquor from the duty free shop at the airport, bring your passport here within three days of arrival to pick some imported booze.
- **Blue Nile Supermarket** (64 Kasr el-Ainy St., Garden City; tel. 02 27920521; 9am-11pm Mon.-Sat.): Shh… You didn't hear it from me, but this miniature supermarket keeps a fridge in the back stocked with beer. They occasionally offer local wine and spirits as well. Just ask at the checkout.
- **Uno Ambrogio** (12 Brazil St., Zamalek; tel. 0100 157 2655; 11am-3am daily): This little liquor store offers the full range of local alcohol options as well as a rare stock of pork—something you're not likely to find much of on your trip to Muslim-majority Egypt. Pork, like alcohol, is Haraam (forbidden) in Islam, and (unlike alcohol) *very* rarely consumed by Egyptian Muslims. Speedy delivery also available.

of Justice and the concrete jungle beyond. Burgers and other bar food available if you're feeling peckish.

THE GREEK CLUB

21 Mahmoud Basiony St., Talaat Harb Sq.; tel. 0225750822; 5pm-midnight, daily; drinks 40-60LE

An inconspicuous entrance off Talaat Harb Square sends you upstairs to a little slice of Greece. The historic club is divided into a main dining room with large balcony overlooking the square, and a delightful blue and white terrace decorated with large posters of Greek scenes on the Mediterranean. Ignore the "members only" sign on the door—a remnant of a time when Cairo's Greek community was large enough to be exclusive. The food can be skipped, but fries or calamari are good options if you'd like snacks with your beer or ouzo. Keep an eye out for the "Misr Life Insurance" sign downstairs if you're having trouble finding the place. Entrance fee: 12LE.

MOKATTAM

Bars

THE VIRGINIAN

3 Al-Ahram street; tel. 02 25083923; 10:30am-2am Sun.-Fri.; beer 50LE

Perched on the edge of Mokattam Hills, this spacious rooftop bar and café offers brilliant views of the city. It's a nice place to read with a late afternoon tea, or to enjoy a beer as you watch the sunset over Cairo. The décor suggests not much has been changed since its heyday in the '70s, but the vintage feel adds to its charm. Food options are minimal. At the time of writing, it was perfectly acceptable to bring your own.

Cabaret Hopping in Downtown Cairo

If you're interested in seeing a different side of Cairo, Downtown's no-frills cabarets featuring amateur belly dancers and sha'bi singers will deliver. These three venues are within 500 meters (1,600 ft) of each other, making for easy late-night bar-hopping. While each has its own character, they share a general flavor that tastes something like fried grasshoppers—not for every palate, but lacking nothing by way of novelty. Stages have seen more graceful dancers and heard more pleasing voices, and yet there's a rawness to the performance that, particularly with a few bottles of local beer and a group of friends, makes for authentic entertainment. Be sure to confirm prices before you order to avoid any unpleasant surprises (a beer should be in the range of 50LE and no cover charge). Women might feel uncomfortable without a big group or a local escort. Acts typically start around midnight.

- **Miami** (26th of July St., down Scarabee Alley near Scarabee Hotel; 6pm-6am daily)
- **New Arizona** (Alfy St., near Talaat Harb Sq.; 6pm-6am daily)
- **Amira** (30 26th of July St., next to Miami Cinema; 4pm-7am daily)

GARDEN CITY

Bars

★ HORREYA CAFÉ & BAR

Falaki Square; tel. 02 23920397; 2pm-5am daily; drinks 40-50LE

With its hanging strips of florescent lights and off-white color scheme, this bar east of Garden City might not be the most flattering of evening venues. But the tall ceilings and mirror-lined walls give the place a certain charm. Horreya, "freedom" in Arabic, offers a slice of just that—an unpretentious space where all are welcome to enjoy a cold Stella (local beer) and sit at their leisure. Feel free to bring snacks.

Clubs

HAROUN EL-RASHID NIGHTCLUB

Semiramis Hotel, Garden City; tel. 02 27988000; midnight-4am Thurs.

Red velvet dominates the décor at this "nightclub" that's really more of a theater with belly dancing and booze. At the time of writing, the legendary Dina "the Dancer" continues to be the main attraction. It's unclear how much longer she'll grace the stage, but the establishment will likely replace her with someone with equal lure to charm an audience alongside the talented classical Arabic band. Tickets start at 1,280LE and includes a set menu sans drinks.

GEZIRA AND ZAMALEK

Bars

★ ROOFTOP BAR

21 Mahmoud Sedky St.; tel. 02 27353471; noon-1am daily; 60-80LE local beer and wine, 100LE min.

What this bar lacks in food quality, it makes up for with spectacular views of the Nile. Sample some local beer or indulge in a shisha while watching the city's lights dance on the river below. The setting is casual with low lighting and attractive beer bottle chandeliers. It can get crowded on the weekends, so come early to snag a choice seat.

L'AUBERGINE

5 Sayed El-Bakry St.; tel. 02 27380080; noon-3am daily; 90-150LE cocktails, 65-100LE mains, 350LE min.

Much-loved by Cairo's media-making crowd, L'Aubergine's interior is less pretentious than its name might imply. The ground floor is a restaurant with a more relaxed vibe and the bar upstairs generally hosts a younger, rowdier crowd—particularly during big football (soccer) games when its sports bar flavor comes alive. Vegetarians will appreciate a large selection (try the pumpkin kobeba), and imported liquor is available if you've tired of Stella. As with most Cairo bars, nonsmokers will suffer. Reservation a must.

★ U BISTRO & BAR

157 26th of July St.; tel. 02 27350543; 1pm-1am Sat.-Tues., 1pm-2am Wed.-Fri.; 250-400LE mains

Head to the second floor of what looks like a residential building—marked only by an unrevealing "Baehler's Mansions"—to find this chic restaurant and bar. Warm lighting, fireplace, and wood-paneled walls make for a romantic evening venue. The Swiss hotelier who built this apartment block in the 1920s, Charles Baehler, once owned Egypt's classiest hotels—from the Winter Palace in Luxor to Cairo's Semiramis. With U Bistro's imported wines and fine dining, Baehler would likely approve. Dress code is smart causal and reservations necessary for Wednesday-Friday evenings (ask for a table with a Nile view).

SASS

19 El-Gezira St., on Imperial Boat; tel. 0120 001 9979; 3pm-1am Sat.-Tues., 7pm-3am Wed.-Fri.; 150-450LE mains, 600LE min.

Tastefully draped in plants with twig and fairy light chandeliers, SASS is a stylish bar and restaurant offering a range of international cuisine—like sushi, orange duck, and tenderloin lollipops. The soft lighting and floor-to-ceiling windows overlooking the Nile make for a romantic setting. On weekend nights, the DJ comes out and the venue turns into a dance club (albeit with more standing than dancing). Smart casual dress code. Reservation recommended.

ALIBI

19 El-Gezira St., on Imperial Boat; 9:30pm-2:30am daily; 150-300LE mains, drinks from 80LE

Alibi offers the same views as its "cooler" neighbors upstairs, without the hefty minimum charge. Plants hang from the ceilings and folding windows let in a cool breeze off the river. The small balcony above the Nile is ideal for a romantic dinner and drinks for two on the quiet weeknights. DJs come Wednesday-Saturday, and the chairs are pushed aside to approximate something of a dance floor.

AGOUZA AND DOKKI

Bars

TAG BAR

20 Abd El-Raheem Sabry, Dokki; tel. 02 33359455; 6pm-2am daily; drinks 55-80LE

If you find yourself on the west side of the city, this casual bar on the roof of **King Hotel** is a nice place to enjoy drinks with a cool evening breeze. The plentiful seating makes it a good option for larger gatherings or just for finding a place to sit on crowded weekends. Nice views of Dokki and the Cairo Tower in the distance.

EL-TONSI HOTEL BAR

143 El-Tahrir St., Dokki; tel. 02 33376908; noon-1am daily; drinks 50-80LE

There's little indication this modest hotel offers such a pleasant rooftop bar open to the public. After the nondescript entrance, a somewhat harrowing elevator ride will bring you up 18 floors to the top of this high-altitude venue. It's a no-nonsense place to enjoy a beer with beautiful views of the Nile and the glittering city below.

Clubs

★ CAIRO JAZZ CLUB

197a, 26th of July St., Agouza; tel. 0106 880 4764; www.cairojazzclub.com; drinks from 100LE

For decades Cairo Jazz Club (CJC) has been the venue of choice for underground music lovers. From jazz to fusion, classical Arabic, house, and more, CJC offers nightly live entertainment. Sets typically run from around 10pm-3am, but check their website for full event details. Reservations highly recommended, and men might be denied entry without a female companion.

GREATER CAIRO

Clubs

UNDERGROUND BY AFTER EIGHT

23B Syria St., Mohandiseen; tel. 0100 339 8000; 9pm-4am daily; drinks from 60LE

Underground by After Eight hosts live music and belly dancing on the weekends, and DJs on the weeknights. It's a great place to see hip new musicians and dance the night away with decent cocktails or a local beer. The venue is located just across the northern border of Dokki into its sister neighborhood (Mohandiseen). Check out their Facebook page @undergroundafter8 for upcoming events, or just show up to be surprised. Reservations (via phone or Facebook) a must on the weekend.

Accommodations

Where you choose as your base in Cairo is more important than in most cities. The intensity of the traffic means that navigating to and from your accommodation can be a major hassle (and waste your precious travel time) if you don't opt for a central location. Downtown is a great place to stay if you want to be in the middle of the bustle, but not the best for those hoping to escape it. If you prefer to retire to calmer quarters, Zamalek or Garden City are the way to go. Both are very close to Downtown, but full of trees and walkable roads. For easy strolls to good restaurants, cafés, and bars, Zamalek certainly beats Garden City (though there are a few nice options in the latter as well).

Airbnb is usually the best choice for accommodation. Rent in Cairo is cheap (and the city doesn't have the same problems with overtourism that some other places have), which means you can find beautifully decorated flats with helpful local hosts for a bargain by US and European standards. Unless you're looking to stay in a hotel with a pool and other five-star amenities, a quick search for flats on Airbnb in the Downtown, Zamalek, or Garden City areas is highly recommended.

DOWNTOWN (WIST EL-BALAD)

Under 800LE

DAHAB HOSTEL

26 Mahmoud Bassiouny St., Rooftop, 7th Floor, Talaat Harb Sq.; tel. 02 25799104; www.dahabhostel.com; 400LE d

Travelers in search of a backpackers' hostel, look no further. Aside from the central Downtown location, the main perk is the beautiful rooftop garden with nice views and shaded spaces to enjoy in the hot summers. The rooms are simple, but clean and inexpensive (cheaper options available with shared bathrooms), and the staff will make you feel at home.

HOTEL VELVET 1928

8 Gawad Hosny St.; tel. 02 23954975; 600LE d

Hidden in a historic Downtown building, this 12-room hotel is perfect for those looking for value, location, and a welcoming staff. Its large windows and high ceilings adorned with chandeliers make for an attractive space, and for a bit extra you can book a room with a balcony where you can enjoy your simple but tasty complimentary breakfast. Downtown is noisy, so request a room on the fifth floor for a quieter stay. Book early for the best prices and your pick of rooms. The location (down a side street) is a bit difficult to find, but people in the area will be happy to help.

1,650-3,300LE

RAMSES HILTON

1115 Corniche el Nil; tel. 02 25777444; www.hilton.com; 1,800LE d

Located in the center of converging streets along the Nile, the Ramses Hilton is conveniently located for excursions by taxi, although not the best jumping-off point for relaxing walks. The décor is nothing special, but you can choose a room with a balcony and stunning views of the Nile. As with all Downtown hotels, ask to stay on an upper floor or bring some earplugs. The large pool overlooking the Nile is a highlight.

STEIGENBERGER EL TAHRIR

2 Kasr el Nil St.; tel. 02 25750777; www.eltahrir.steigenberger.com; 1,900LE d

A stone's throw from Tahrir Square, this brand-new hotel is in the center of the action. The rooms are simple but comfortable, and there's a pleasant (albeit small) pool. For best views with less Downtown noise, ask for a room on the top floors and, if preferred, a nonsmoking one.

Over 3,300LE

THE NILE RITZ-CARLTON

1113 Corniche El Nil; tel. 02 25778899; www.ritzcarlton.com; 3,800LE d

They don't call it "puttin' on the Ritz" for nothing. From the colorful bouquets of freshly cut flowers in the lobby to the chic rooms and plush robes, this hotel screams luxury. The long palm tree-lined pool is a great place to relax after an early morning of sightseeing, or you can hide from the sun in their cave-like spa.

GARDEN CITY

1,650-3,300LE

INTERCONTINENTAL CAIRO SEMIRAMIS

Corniche el-Nil; tel. 02 27988000; www.ihg.com; 2,300LE d

Pretty in pink, this tasteful hotel boasts an elevated pool with a Nile view and a wealth of delicious dining options (in addition to the amenities expected from any five-star hotel). All 700-plus rooms offer balconies looking out onto the river or bustling Tahrir Square. Located just south of the Kasr el-Nil Bridge, across from green Gezira Island, and on the border between vibrant Downtown and tranquil Garden City, it's a great base to explore Cairo with all its faces.

KEMPINSKI

12 Ahmed Ragheb, Kasr el-Nil; tel. 02 27980000; www.kempinski.com; 3,000LE d

A stylish five-star hotel on the Nile with a small outdoor pool overlooking the river from the ninth floor. The breakfast buffet is varied and fresh—a great place to fuel up before starting your day's excursions. Request a room on an upper level to ensure best views of the Nile, and nonsmokers, be sure to reserve a smoke-free room to avoid sleeping in an ashtray.

Over 3,300LE

FOUR SEASONS HOTEL CAIRO AT NILE PLAZA

1089 Corniche el-Nil; tel. 02 27917000; www.fourseasons.com; 3,700LE d

As classy as you'd expect from a Four Seasons, this branch on the Nile has rooms with windows that open to let in the breeze off the river. The hotel lobby doubles as a museum for the Egyptian abstract artist Farouk Hosny, and you can enjoy a range of other five-star amenities, including eight restaurants, a spa, fitness center, heated indoor pool, and large palm-lined outdoor pools.

GEZIRA AND ZAMALEK

800-1,650LE

HORUS HOUSE HOTEL ZAMALEK

21 Ismail Mohamed St.; tel. 02 27353034; 1,000LE d

Located below Hotel Longchamps, Horus House offers similar accommodation for a bit cheaper. The hotel reception has a vintage feel and could use a bit of a facelift, but rooms are clean, beds are comfortable, and there's a pleasant terrace lined with green plants. Room quality varies, so you might want to upgrade to the superior double (much nicer than the standard for around $10 more per night). Breakfast can be skipped.

★ HOTEL LONGCHAMPS

21 Ismail Mohamed St.; tel. 02 27352311; www.hotellongchamps.com; 1,400LE d

This boutique hotel located on the fifth and sixth floors of a residential building is a good option for travelers in search of a more personalized experience. It's not as sleek as the five-star alternatives, but it has much more personality, with each room individually decorated and an extremely helpful owner (Heba) and staff. They can arrange airport pickup/drop-off and trips to the more distant sights around the city (Birqash Camel Market, Saqqara, etc.). The highlight is the terrace where you can enjoy a fresh orange juice in the morning or a glass of wine in the evening. There's not much by way of views, but there are plenty of leafy green trees.

GOLDEN TULIP FLAMENCO HOTEL

2 El-Gezira El-Wosta St.; tel. 02 27350815; www.flamencohotels.com; 1,600LE d

The Flamenco isn't as well-polished as the other international hotels (and no pool), but the rooms are spacious and clean. The views range from stunning Nile to concrete building, so be sure to make your preference known. If you're not happy with your room, chances are an alternative will be available. Staff is friendly and accommodating.

1,650-3,300LE

HILTON CAIRO ZAMALEK RESIDENCES

21 Mohamed Mazhar St.; tel. 02 27370055; www.hilton.com; 1,600LE d

Located on the Nile alongside a row of embassies, this is one of the more economical high-quality hotels on the island. With its 2-3-bedroom suites and a pretty Nile-side pool, this Hilton is a good option for families. There's also a fitness room and spa for adults.

★ CAIRO MARRIOTT HOTEL & OMAR KHAYYAM CASINO

16 Saray el-Gezira Street; tel. 02 27283000; www.marriott.com; 1,900LE d

Built by Khedive Ismail to host foreign dignitaries for the 1869 opening of the Suez Canal, this palace-turned-hotel offers a unique stay. The original palace—which now serves as the main reception area—is flanked by two towers built in the 1970s that can house over 1,000 guests. Many of the rooms have balconies overlooking the Nile or interior garden (be sure to indicate your preference when reserving). The hotel is located on the nicest part of the island, with wide embassy-lined streets shaded by canopies of trees. The pool is open later than most in Cairo's hotels (10pm), so you can take a dip in the warm summer evenings after a long day of exploring. There's also a good 24-hour gym if you still have the energy.

★ SOFITEL CAIRO NILE EL-GEZIRAH

3 El-Thawra Council St; tel. 02 27373737; www.sofitel-cairo-nile-elgezirah.com; 2,500LE d

Perched on the southern edge of Gezira Island, this cylindrical tower offers some of the best views of the Nile and its green island home. Inside is pure luxury with tree-lined courtyards, numerous waterfront dining options, a spa, and an outdoor swimming pool that basically pours into the Nile.

Information and Services

VISITOR INFORMATION

All tourist offices offer complimentary maps and brochures on travel around the country. Be careful not to confuse these official offices sponsored by the Ministry of Tourism for the Downtown travel shops notorious for their scams. The Downtown office location off Ataba Square is the most helpful.

- **Downtown Tourist Information Office:** 5 Adly St., Downtown; tel. 02 3913454; 8am-6pm daily
- **Ramses Train Station Tourist Information Office**
- **Old Cairo Tourist Information Office:** at the north end of the gated section of Mar Girgis St.

EMBASSIES AND CONSULATES

In case of emergency, call your embassy's number listed below. For other routine services, you'll need to make an appointment via email or through the website portals.

- **US Embassy:** 5 Tawfik Diab St., Garden City; tel. 02 27973300; https://eg.usembassy.gov; 8am-4:30pm Sun.-Thurs.
- **British Embassy:** 7 Ahmed Ragheb St., Garden City; tel. 02 27916000; www.gov.uk/world/organisations/british-embassy-cairo; 8am-3:30pm Sun.-Wed., 8am-2pm Thurs.
- **Canadian Embassy:** Nile City Towers, 2005A Corniche El-Nil, South Tower, 18th floor; tel. 02 24612200; cairo@international.gc.ca; 8am-4:30pm Sun.-Wed., 8am-1:30pm Thurs.
- **Australian Embassy:** World Trade Centre 11th Floor, 1191 Corniche El-Nil; tel. 02 27706600; https://egypt.embassy.gov.au; 8am-4:15pm Sun.-Wed., 8am-1:45pm Thurs.

HEALTH AND SAFETY

Emergency Numbers

- **Tourist Police:** 126
- **Ambulance:** 123
- **Fire:** 180

Medical

Generally speaking, the quality of medical facilities in Cairo is not up to Western standards. That said, there are many competent doctors, and in the case of emergency, don't be deterred from seeking help. Avoid public hospitals as they are hopelessly understaffed and poorly maintained.

AS-SALAM INTERNATIONAL HOSPITAL

Corniche el-Nil, El Maadi; tel. 19885; www.assih.com

As-Salam International Hospital is a large private hospital with professional doctors and fairly good equipment.

ANGLO AMERICAN HOSPITAL

El-Borg St., Zamalek; tel. 02 27356162

Anglo American Hospital is a small private hospital and a good option for immediate care if you're in the Zamalek area. While the doctors are good, the equipment is dated and not the best choice for surgical interventions.

Dental Services

BARSOUM DENTAL CLINIC

7 26th of July St, 3rd floor; tel. 0122 101 0257; www.barsoum.com; 10am-7pm Mon.-Thurs. and Sat.; 240LE for preliminary exam

If you have a dental emergency, Barsoum Dental Clinic has a professional team who practice in a hygienic office.

Pharmacies

You'll find a pharmacy on just about every street in Cairo. Pharmacists function more as doctors than they do in the US, and you can ask them for treatment recommendations (prescriptions are typically not necessary). Best to stick to the larger chains for more reliable advice, such as:

- **El-Ezaby:** tel. 19600; www.elezabypharmacy.com; 24 hours daily
- **Misr Pharmacies:** tel. 19110; www.misr-online.com; 24 hours daily
- **Seif Pharmacies:** tel. 19199; www.seif-online.com; 24 hours daily

Transportation

GETTING THERE

Nearly all international visitors will arrive to Cairo by air. Flying is also your quickest/most comfortable option if you're coming from Aswan, Marsa Alam, Hurghada, or Sharm el Sheikh. To get to Cairo from most other locations in Egypt, the bus is usually the best option.

Air

CAIRO INTERNATIONAL AIRPORT

Oruba Road, Heliopolis; tel. 02 26966300; www.cairo-airport.com

Only around 21 kilometers (13 mi) from Downtown, the airport can be reached in anywhere from 25 minutes to 2 hours depending on the traffic. Late-night or early morning arrivals and departures (midnight-6am) make for swift travel to/from airport. There's no need to feel uncomfortable arriving in the middle of the night—Cairo is a safe city, and while there will be few enough people on the roads not to cause traffic, you'll still find people out and about.

There are three terminals, with flights to/from Europe and the US served at Terminals 2 and 3. Terminal 3 is the newest and nicest and serves the Star Alliance airlines. The less glossy Terminal 2 serves the airlines of the Oneworld and SkyTeam Alliances. Both are easy to navigate and generally not too crowded.

The easiest option for travel to and from the airport is via **taxi** or **Uber.** If you opt for a taxi, be sure to request they use the meter. From Downtown, the trip shouldn't cost more than 130LE plus a 20LE card for the car to enter the airport vicinity. From the airport, prices tend to be a bit higher, but you can likely haggle your way down to around the same rate (of course, keep in mind tips are welcome). Before you even exit the airport building, you'll be bombarded with taxi offers. These prices tend to be double or even triple the market rate. Better to find a driver outside.

Train

Travel to Cairo by rail from Aswan or other southern cities along the Nile Valley will bring you to **Giza Station** on the southwest side of the city, or all the way to **Ramses Station** Downtown. If you're coming from Alexandria or elsewhere in the Nile Delta, Ramses Station will be your only Cairo option.

The first-class train that runs between Aswan or Luxor and Cairo is spacious and comfortable, but the train operators have a tendency to leave blinding florescent lights on the entire time, spoiling your chances for sleep on overnight trips. This might be a clever ploy to make you purchase a ticket in an expensive sleeper car (1,900LE for a single cabin instead of around 200LE for a first-class ticket).

In theory, you should be able to book your ticket online at the **Egyptian National Railway** website (www.enr.gov.eg). In reality, this rarely works and you'll likely have to go to the station—preferably a couple of days before you plan to travel, though you can often find a ticket the same day. Again, the best option to reach your final destination in Cairo from either station is via **taxi** or **Uber.**

RAMSES STATION

Ramses Square

Ramses is the city's bustling central railway station. It was remodeled in 2014 and has a shiny new interior with large signs in the main hall indicating arriving/departing train schedules. From the entrance, the **ticket windows** will be located straight ahead and the trains to the right. If you go during the day, you can head to the **Tourist Office** inside the station (8am-6pm daily) for assistance, or just approach any ticket counter and tell them where you want to go and they'll direct you to the appropriate window. The multiple platforms reached by underground passages can sometimes be confusing. Be sure to give yourself plenty of time to figure out where you need to be.

GIZA STATION

El-Sikka el-Hadid St., just south of the Giza Metro Station

The Giza Station is much smaller than Ramses and feels more like a metro stop (though not to be confused with the Giza Metro Station). The ticket windows are located along the outside of the building just before the entrance, which leads directly to the platform.

Bus

If you're coming to Cairo from elsewhere in Egypt by **Go Bus** (tel. 19567; https://go-bus.com), you'll arrive at **Abdel Minam Riyad Square** just next to the Ramses Hilton in Downtown, or the **Nasr City** stop (on the corner of Abu al-Fawares St. and al-Mokhayem el-Daem St.) on the east side of the city.

The Go Bus stations are easy to navigate. In the Downtown location, it's more of a stop than a station and you'll get on/off right on the street or in the parking lot opposite the ticket office. To board, wait at the plastic patio furniture set up on the curb until your bus is called. There will be plenty of Go Bus employees and fellow passengers to help.

To make your way to your final destination in Cairo from any of the stations, **taxis** or **Uber** will be the best option.

TORGOMAN BUS STATION

Boulaq 2, off al-Sahafa St.

Government buses, such as **East Delta, West Delta,** and **Upper Egypt** will bring you to the Torgoman Bus Station (officially the Cairo Gateway Bus Station) in Downtown. Torgoman, which hosts the state-run services, is appropriately confusing. You'll find the buses in the basement of an apparently abandoned mall. From the main entrance, the **ticket office** will be to your right. Head downstairs to find a large waiting room surrounded by the buses on either side, where employees will be around to help you find yours.

GETTING AROUND

Zahma (traffic) in Cairo is a way of life. The city's residents play bumper cars between the hours of 8am and 10pm, with the morning rush hours lasting from around 8am to 10am, and the afternoon rush hours (around 2:30pm-7pm during the school year, and 4pm-7pm in the summer) generally the worst. This also makes walking in Cairo overwhelming at times. Be sure to keep an eye out for rogue motorcycles on sidewalks or going the wrong way down a street or somehow creeping through a tiny sliver between standing cars as you cross. The metro is a mixed blessing during these busier hours—you'll likely reach your destination quicker, but certainly not with your personal space intact. The best way get around the city is generally by cab or Uber, but try to limit your commute by sticking to 1-2 walkable neighborhoods per day.

Taxi and Ride-Hailing Services

By far the easiest way navigate the city, taxis and ride-hailing services (**Uber** and **Careem**) are ubiquitous and inexpensive. Uber bought Careem in 2019 and the two are now essentially interchangeable. Taxis are typically a bit cheaper, and most drivers are kind and respectful, but some (particularly the ones waiting outside tourist destinations) can be aggressive or otherwise unscrupulous. Be sure to ask the taxi driver if the **meter** ('adaad) works before you get in, and if it doesn't, either agree on a price beforehand or flag down another one. Meters start at 7LE.

Many taxi drivers don't speak English, but they will know the main tourist destinations, hotels, etc. Uber/Careem drivers also might not speak English, but the technological intervention of the apps/GPS make that less important. Both are very easy to find throughout almost all of Cairo. Taxis will likely stop for you with no indication that you want one, but just throw up a hand to be sure.

Metro

Although it can get hot and crowded, the metro is a great option for making your way across the city during peak traffic times. The trains run 5:15am-midnight, and ticket prices range from 3-10LE depending on how far you're going. Buy tickets with cash at the station. Every train has a **ladies-only car.** Women aren't required to ride in these, but note that unwanted touching (whether intentional or not) is not an uncommon experience in the shared cars during the super crowded times. During quieter hours, women should have no problem in either section.

The metro is reliable, with trains typically coming every 5-10 minutes. Tickets can be purchased at the manned windows within the station before heading through the turnstiles to the individual tracks. Be sure to check the map before you walk through to make sure you end up on the right platform. Hold on to your ticket—you'll have to insert it into another turnstile on your way out.

The **three lines** (creatively named Lines 1, 2, and 3) converge in downtown at the **Sadat, Al-Shohadaa,** or **Ataba** stations. **Line 1** (with termini **el-Marg el-Gadida** and **Helwan**) is likely to be the most useful for visitors and can bring you from Tahrir Square (Sadat Station) north to Ramses Square (Al-Shohadaa Station) or south to Sayeda Zeinab (**Sayeda Zeinab Station**) and Coptic Cairo (**Mar Girgis Station**).

Line 2 (with termini **el-Monib** and **Shubra**) connects Tahrir Square (Sadat Station) to Ataba Square (Ataba Station) on the east side of Downtown, Ramses Square (Al-Shohadaa Station) in the north, and Gezira (**Opera Station**) and Dokki (**Dokki Station**) in the west.

Line 3, still under construction (with termini Airport and Imbaba or Mohandiseen), will also be useful for visitors if it's ever finished (scheduled completion date is mid-2023), and will eventually go as far as the Cairo International Airport in the east, and pass through Downtown (Ataba and Nasser Stations) and Zamalek (Zamalek Station).

For more information check their website: https://cairometro.gov.eg.

SADAT METRO STATION

Tahrir Square; 5:15am-12:30am daily

A number of entrances are scattered about Tahrir Square, but not all of them are open. Safe bets for functioning staircases into the station include the entrance on the corner of Mohammed Mahmoud Street and Kasr el-Ainy Street (in front of the old American University in Cairo campus) and the one in front of the massive Mogamaa administrative building on the south side of the Square. The station is a labyrinth that sprawls out beneath Tahrir, but it's fairly well marked. Lines 1 and 2 pass through here.

AL-SHOHADAA METRO STATION

Ramses Square; 5:15am-12:30am daily

Enter this busy metro stop in front of the Ramses Railway Station. Lines 1 and 2 pass through here.

ATABA METRO STATION

Ataba Square; 5:15am-12:30am daily

The entrances to this station lie beneath a busy quarter of commerce. You'll likely have to navigate your way past rows of vendors to find the stairways down to the metro. When arriving at this station, follow the exit signs to **Ataba Square** to emerge into the square itself instead of (even more) confusing side streets. From here you can catch a taxi (12LE), microbus (4LE), or walk 1.5 kilometers (1 mi) to **Hussein Square** and its surroundings (Mui'zz Street, al-Azhar Mosque, etc.). Lines 2 and 3 pass through here.

Microbus

The microbus is the king of all public transportation in Cairo. To get around the city like a local, wave one down and shout out your destination (or better yet, learn the hand signals from a local). Another option is to board at the various **microbus stops** (mow'if) around the city, but you'll likely have to wait for the car to fill up (usually around 10-12 people) before heading out. The main three stops are **Mow'if Abdel Minam Riyad** (1 km/0.6 mi north of Tahrir Square under the 6th of October Bridge), **Mow'if Ramses** (in Ramses Square), and **Mow'if Giza** (in Giza Square). Microbuses have defined routes, but they go just about anywhere in the city proper (and beyond). They're relatively clean, with some nicer than others (occasionally missing a side door). Fares should be around 2-6LE depending on your destination.

Public Bus

Much like microbuses, you can either board at a designated stop or just hop on a passing bus. The most useful bus routes for tourists include **Bus M7,** heading to the Mena House, which will drop you off in front of the entrance to the Giza Pyramid Complex (departure point **Mow'if Abdel Minam Riyad**); and **Bus 111,** which will take you to/from the Cairo International Airport (departure point **Mow'if Ramses**). Tickets should cost 2-6LE. For a map of more public bus routes, check https://mobile.mwasalatmisr.com.

Tuk Tuk

In some of the narrow winding roads of working-class neighborhoods, your only option is to walk or hop on a motorized rickshaw, or tuk tuk. These three-wheeled vehicles are typically decked out by their owners in colorful displays of personality, with sticker decals, LED lights, charms, and subwoofers. Just tell them where you want to go and hold on tight. Costs typically 3-10LE, depending on the distance.

Giza and Around Cairo

Near Cairo, travelers will find a handful of worthwhile destinations that can easily be visited as day trips from the city center.

Horseback riding near pyramids at dawn, viewing the iconic Sphinx, and exploring the Grand Egyptian Museum with some of the world's most unique and ancient treasures are just a few of the unforgettable experiences that await near the Giza Plateau. A bit farther south are the Saqqara and Dahshur pyramids—predecessors to those at Giza, and themselves among the most impressive in Egypt. Saqqara claims Egypt's earliest idea of a pyramid, Zoser's Step Pyramid, with a bonus of the well-curated Imhotep Museum displaying treasures found on site, and a sacred bull burial ground, the haunting Serapeum.

Highlights

Look for ★ to find recommended sights, activities, dining, and lodging.

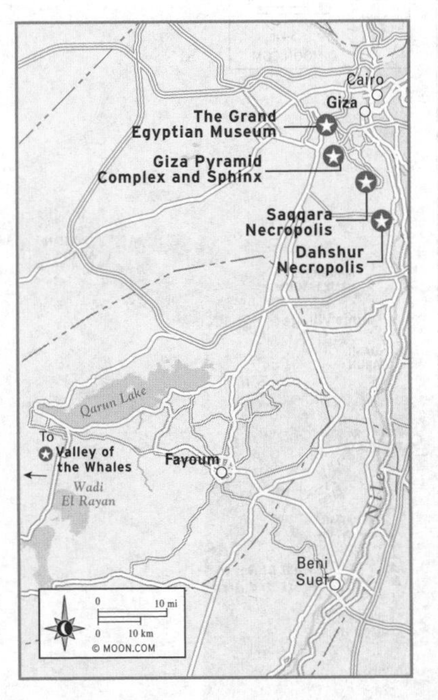

★ **Giza Pyramid Complex and Sphinx:** Admire the world's most iconic tombs from every angle, and then say hello to the Sphinx (page 108).

★ **Grand Egyptian Museum:** After more than a decade of start-and-stop construction, this 5.2-million-square-foot (480,000-square-meter) museum now holds worlds of ancient Egyptian treasures—many of them never before on display (page 113).

★ **Saqqara Necropolis:** Take a lesson in pyramid building at this nearly 5,000-year-old necropolis, Egypt's (and arguably the world's) first attempt at building sky-high royal resting places (page 119).

★ **Dahshur Necropolis:** Blissfully free of crowds, the two massive pyramids at the Dahshur Necropolis have interiors that are open for adventure seekers to explore (page 121).

★ **Valley of the Whales:** Marvel at 37-million-year-old whale fossils unmoved from their sandy grave, which was once a prehistoric sea (page 124).

Giza and Around Cairo

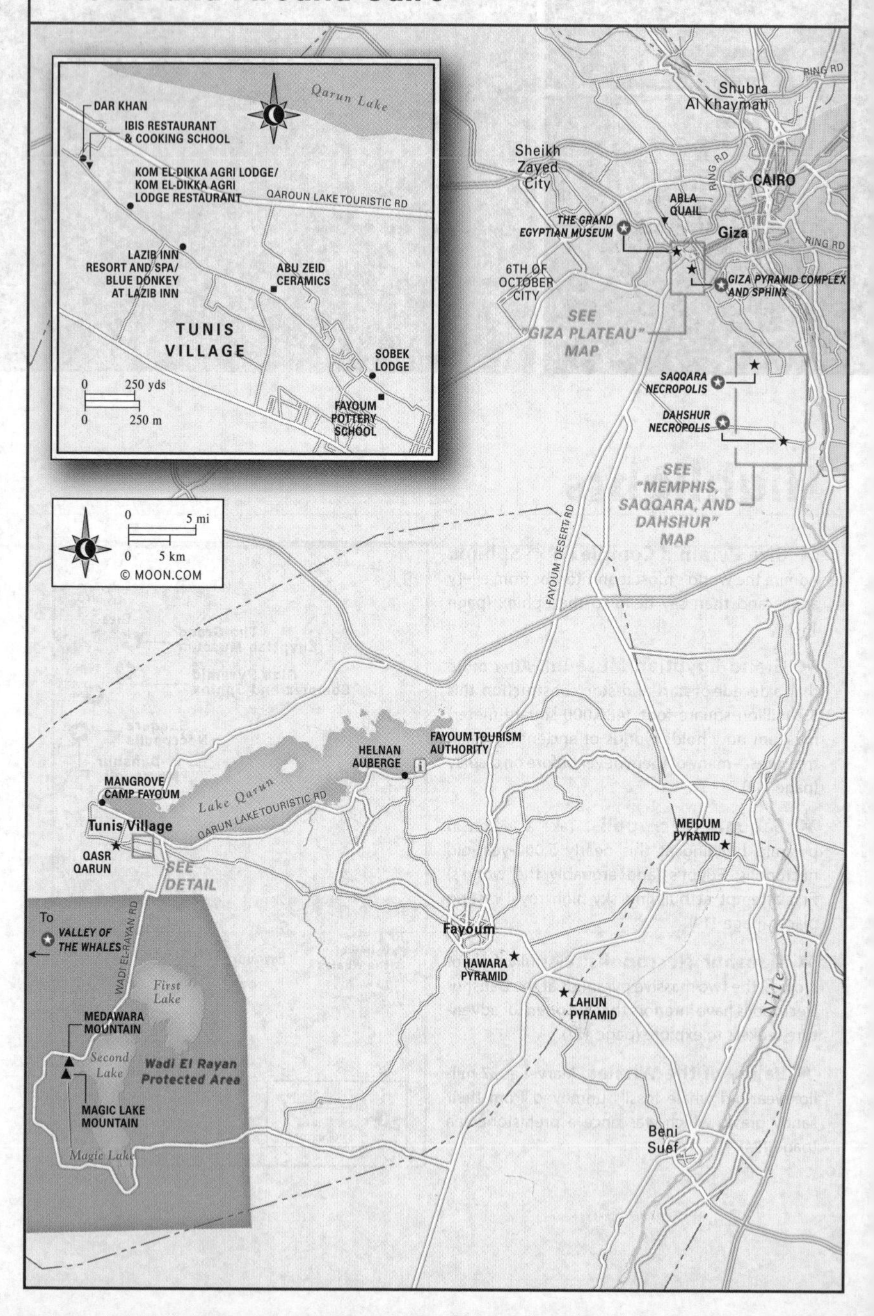

Dahshur holds Egypt's first true pyramid—with proper slanting sides—Snefru's Red Pyramid.

Technically part of the Western Desert, the pseudo-oasis of Fayoum sits close enough to the Nile to secure water from the life source. Fayoum's prehistoric sea-turned-sand holds Egypt's most fantastic traces of marine life, nestled beside dramatic rock formations still striped by the disappeared waters.

ORIENTATION

The Giza Plateau, home to the legendary **Sphinx** and **pyramids of Giza,** is a mere 16 kilometers (10 miles) southwest of Downtown Cairo, best accessed via taxi. Farther south (34 km/21 mi southwest of Downtown Cairo) are the sandy burial grounds of **Saqqara and Dahshur,** along with the ancient capital of **Memphis,** now an open-air museum, a few miles to the east.

Fayoum is a fertile patch that juts off the Nile into the Western Desert 100 kilometers (60 mi) southwest of Cairo.

PLANNING YOUR TIME

You'll want a full day with an early start to visit the **pyramids of Giza, Grand Egyptian Museum,** and necropolis in **Saqqara.** If you haven't exhausted yourself, you can continue your trip down to **Dahshur** (10 km/6 mi south of Saqqara, and 37 km/23 mi southwest of Downtown Cairo), or save that for another day.

Fayoum is a more ambitious jaunt—1.5-2 hours from Cairo, depending on traffic—but still doable as a day trip straight to the highlight of the Wadi el-Rayan Protected Area and its Valley of the Whales (Wadi el-Hitan). Preferably, spend 1-3 nights here to have a full day for a desert safari, and another for exploring the traces of ancient times, wandering the desert on horseback, or just lounging around the verdant gardens of Tunis Village lodges.

TOURS AND LOCAL GUIDES

Most of the guides and tours recommended in Cairo (page 39) also provide excellent tours of Giza, Memphis, Saqqara, and Dahshur. For a list of guides who can take you on a day trip desert safari to Fayoum from Cairo, see page 127.

Itinerary Ideas

ONE DAY IN GIZA

From Cairo, take a day trip back in time (nearly 5,000 years) with a visit to Giza's most impressive remaining monuments.

1 Beat the heat and crowds to the legendary **Giza Pyramid Complex and Sphinx** to explore for a few hours. To get there, grab a cab or Uber (about 16 km/10 mi; 80-100LE) or set out with a guide if you prefer.

2 When you've had enough sun, catch a 10-minute cab (15-20LE) to the brand-new **Grand Egyptian Museum** to hide out in the AC and wander this colossal wonderland of antiquities.

3 Hop into the Mena House Hotel (3 km/2 mi; 10-15LE) directly in front of the Giza Plateau for a late, leisurely lunch at **Alfredo Restaurant** in their massive green yard with a delicious pyramid view.

Previous: camel rests at the Pyramids of Giza; inside the Bent Pyramid; Wadi el-Rayan desert.

4 Head 3 kilometers (2 mi) south to **FB Stables** on the outskirts of the desert, and set out on horseback to watch the sun set over the ancient wonders.

5 See a different side of Cairo at **Abla Quail**—a local favorite in a working-class neighborhood (8 km/5 mi north of the stables; 40-45LE taxi) for a dinner of quail or other classic grilled dishes before returning to your hotel in Cairo.

ONE DAY IN MEMPHIS, SAQQARA, AND DAHSHUR

With plenty of snacks and water, you could easily see Memphis, Saqqara, and Dahshur in a day trip from Cairo. If you plan on entering the tombs in Dahshur, it's best to visit this site first in the early morning before the heat picks up. Hire a driver to take you on this itinerary. Alternatively, if you'd like to explore more of the Saqqara Necropolis with its dozens of tombs and quasi-pyramids (today mostly closed piles of rubble), it's best to go with a guide.

1 Swing by the **Memphis Complex** open-air museum. It's small, so you can see it in about 30 minutes.

2 Head to the Saqqara Necropolis and pop into the **Imhotep Museum,** around 500 meters (1,600 ft) east after Saqqara's main entrance. Watch the short video about Zoser's Step Pyramid (and use the restroom if you have to—this is your only chance to do so!).

3 Walk or (preferably) drive another 1 kilometer (0.6 mi) to a small parking lot and begin your exploration of the **Step Pyramid of Zoser,** whose entrance is at the southern corner of the complex (to your left when coming from the lot).

4 Head next to the **Pyramid of Unas,** with its spooky spells for the afterlife engraved on the walls. It lies 200 meters (650 ft) southwest of the entrance to Zoser's funerary complex.

5 To reach your next sight, the **Pyramid of Teti** with its own set of spells, walk or drive northeast from Zoser's parking lot for 800 meters (0.5 mi).

6 From the Pyramid of Teti, you can get to the **Serapeum** by heading south down the sandy road for 300 meters (1,000 ft) and taking a right for another 1.2 kilometers (0.7 mi).

7 Leave the Saqqara Necropolis and head next for the **Dahshur Necropolis,** the southernmost Memphis burial grounds. The two behemoths that dominate the site, the Red Pyramid and the Bent Pyramid, are located 1.8 kilometers (1.1 mi) apart. Luckily, the sandy roads here are suitable for cars, so your driver can take you close to the entrances where there are small parking lots.

ONE DAY IN FAYOUM

Contact one of the guides listed in the Fayoum section of this chapter to arrange a desert excursion in Fayoum that includes a barbecue meal. Note: This itinerary assumes you're overnighting in Tunis Village in Fayoum. If you're using Cairo as your base, get an early start and make your way back after sunset (#5).

1 Meet up with your driver to take you to Wadi el-Rayan Protected Area with 4WD. Inside the park, explore the fossils of prehistoric whales and their mangrove homes at the **Valley of the Whales** (Wadi el-Hitan).

2 Continue to the dunes of **Qusur el-Arab** to experience the thrill of surfing the sand by car and by board.

3 Head to **Magic Lake** for a barbecue lunch of grilled chicken, rice, and vegetables. If time permits, drive to the top of the neighboring Magic Lake Mountain for brilliant views of the surrounding landscape.

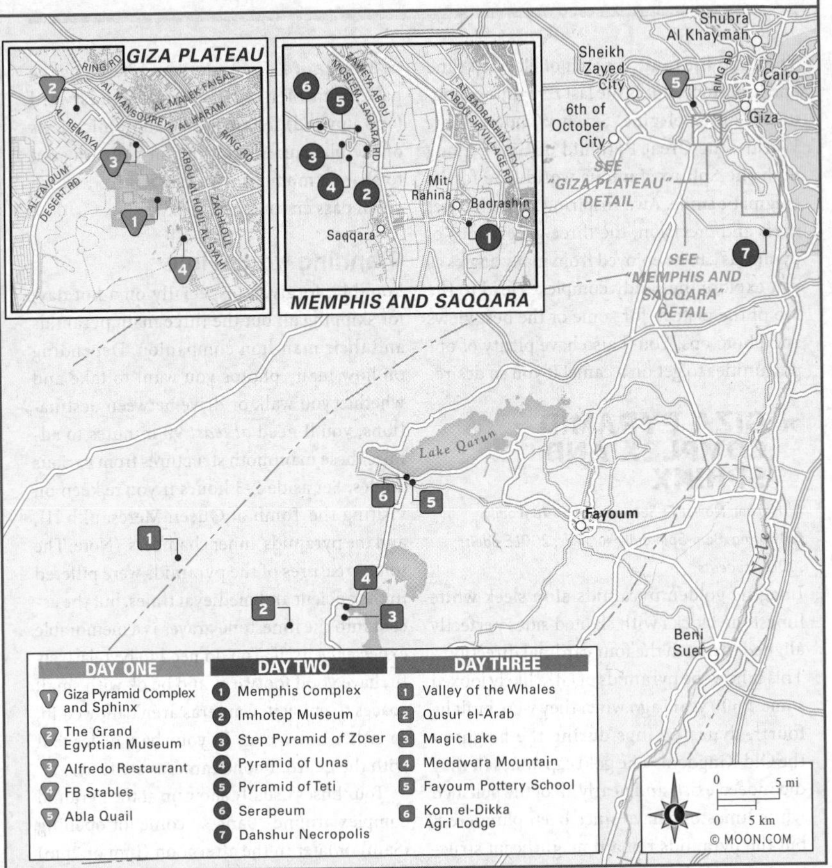

4 Take a short hike up **Medawara Mountain** for the best sunset-watching perch.

5 Return to Tunis Village to visit the rows of pottery workshops and pick up some unique souvenirs. Don't miss **Fayoum Pottery School,** which helped turn the town into a pottery mecca.

6 Enjoy a farm-to-fork dinner at **Kom el-Dikka Agri Lodge.**

Giza Pyramids and the Sphinx

The **Giza Plateau,** a patch of elevated sand and limestone, holds the last remaining monument of the original Seven Wonders of the World—the Great Pyramid of Giza—along with the Sphinx, famous worldwide for its enigmatic smile. Awe-inspiring for their sheer mass and precision, the three generations of pyramids can be enjoyed from many angles as you explore the sandy complex. Head to the top of the plateau for some of the best views and photo ops. You'll also have plenty of opportunities to get on a camel if you so desire.

★ GIZA PYRAMID COMPLEX AND SPHINX

Al-Haram, Nazlet El-Semman; 8am-4pm daily fall-spring, 8am-5pm daily summer; 200LE adults, 100LE students

Imagine golden pyramids atop sleek white limestone blocks with slanted sides perfectly aligned to match the four cardinal directions. This is how the pyramids of Giza likely looked some 4,600 years ago when they were built by fourth-dynasty kings during the height of the Old Kingdom. The gold capstones (if they did indeed exist) and nearly all of the polished white limestone have since been plundered, but the pyramids remain magnificent structures nonetheless.

Orientation

If you walk through the main entrance to the complex, the **Great Pyramid of Giza (Khufu's Pyramid)** will be the first to greet you, with mini **Queens' Pyramids** (built for Khufu's wife and sisters; interior not open) to the east. Immediately east of the Queens' Pyramids, you'll find the **Tomb of Queen Meresankh III** (granddaughter of Khufu and wife of Khafre). Take the path that runs south of the Queen's tomb to the west to reach the **Pyramid of Khafre,** and head south to the significantly smaller **Pyramid of Menkaure.** Continue your hike along the path from Menkaure's Pyramid westward (and upward) for the best panoramic views of the plateau. Make time on your way out to share a moment with the **Sphinx,** which you'll pass en route to the exit.

Planning Your Time

You'll be forgiven (especially on a hot day) for skipping all but the three main pyramids and their man-lion companion. Depending on how many photos you want to take and whether you walk or drive between destinations, you'll need *at least* 90 minutes to admire these mammoth structures from various angles. Set aside 2-3 hours if you're keen on visiting the Tomb of Queen Meresankh III, and the pyramids' inner chambers. (Note: The tomb treasures of the pyramids were pilfered in the ancient and medieval times, but the ascent into the limestone graves is a memorable experience itself. You do need to be relatively fit, have good footwear, and be ok with small spaces to enjoy it. Cameras aren't allowed in, so either hide yours in your bag, or leave it with the guard. Phone cameras are fine.)

Tour buses usually show up at the pyramid complex around 10am, so come for opening (8am) or later in the afternoon (1pm or 2pm) for the best experience. Don't forget to bring water, sunscreen, and your own shade (hats or umbrellas). WCs are located in the main ticket office and near the Sphinx entrance. For a deeper historical understanding of the Giza Plateau, a knowledgeable **guide** can be a great asset.

Tickets

A **combined ticket** to enter the site and the interiors of all open pyramids is 600LE for adults (or 200LE for site entrance; 400LE to enter the Great Pyramid; 100LE to enter either the Pyramid of Khafre or Menkaure). A ticket for the Tomb of Queen Meresankh

Giza Plateau

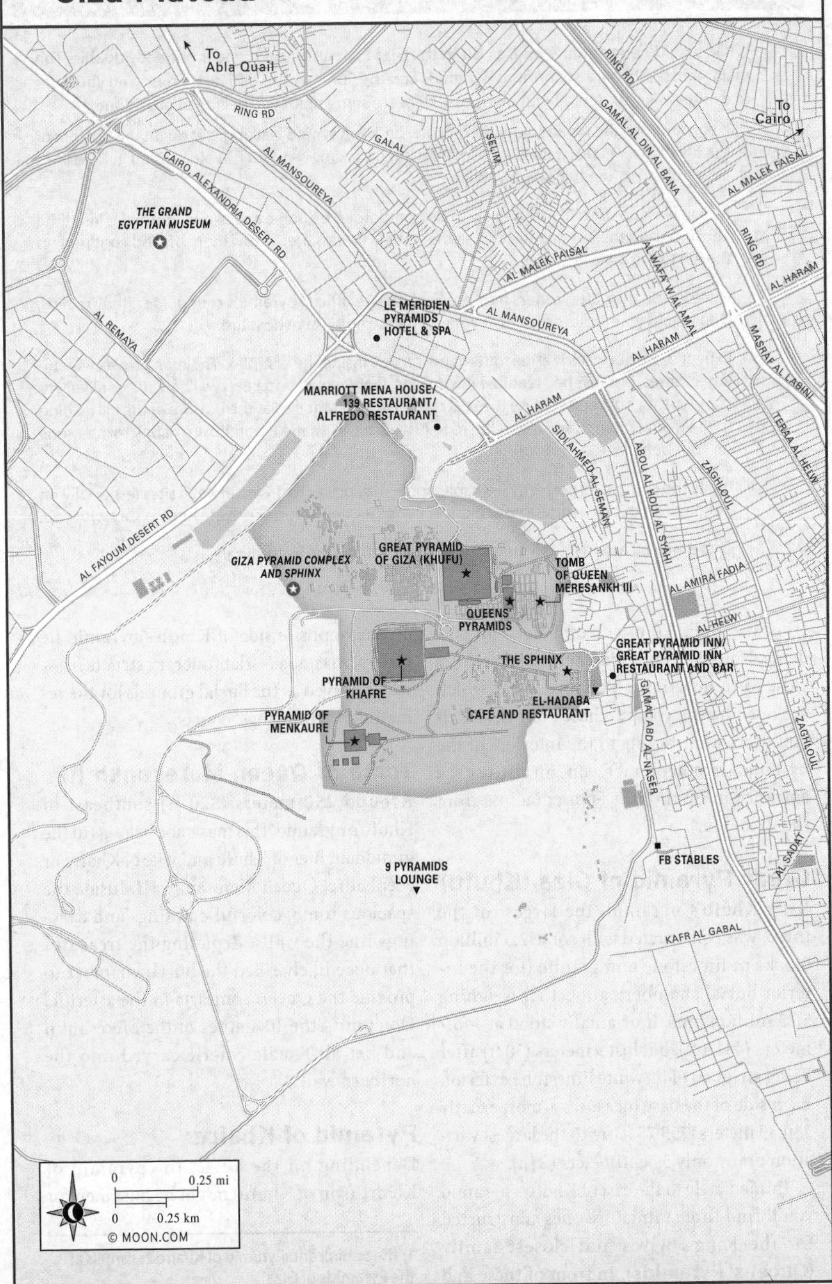

Self-Guided Trips to the Pyramids

While a guide is recommended, a visit to the Giza Plateau without one is perfectly doable. The main sights—the three enormous pyramids and the Sphinx—are difficult to miss, and you'll get to explore the wonders at your own pace. Here are some tips if you decide to go it alone.

- If you arrive to the pyramids by taxi or Uber and don't mind walking, get out at the bottom of the hill (300 m/1,000 ft) that leads to the main gate. This way you'll avoid waiting in long lines as security guards check each vehicle.
- As you walk up the hill, you're likely to be bombarded by horse and camel touts who insist the entrance is to the left (in fact, that's where their stables are). Brush them off and continue up the hill to the main entrance.
- Once inside the gates, others may pretend they're official pyramids tour guides (they're not). Don't hand your tickets over to anyone, lest they hold them hostage.
- Expect more horse and camel touts to pester you inside the complex. They can be overwhelming at times, but just be steadfast in your "no thank yous" and keep walking. It's not likely to come to this, but keep in mind the **tourist police** (stationed at the bottom of the hill leading to the main entrance and along the road just after the Khafre Pyramid) are happy to intervene on your behalf.
- While the complex is perfectly walkable, some may prefer to drive between sites (especially on hot days). In this case, arrange for a driver (whether taxi, Uber, or private hire) to stay with you.
- There may be a long line to purchase your tickets, so plan accordingly.

III costs 50LE. All prices are halved for students. Note: The pyramid interiors sometimes close for renovation, so be sure to ask which are open before you purchase your tickets. If you don't want tickets to the interiors of the pyramids or other tombs, you can also use the entrance in front of the Sphinx (across from the Pizza Hut).

Great Pyramid of Giza (Khufu)

King Khufu's pyramid, the largest of the three, was constructed with some 2.3 million blocks of limestone and granite (for the interior burial chamber), altogether weighing 5.75 million tons. It originally stood at 146.7 meters (481.4 ft), but lost 9 meters (30 ft) after being stripped of its white limestone exterior. Each side of the base measures almost exactly 230.35 meters (755.75 ft), with the largest variation off by only 5 centimeters (2 in).

Immediately to the east of Khufu's pyramid you'll find three miniature ones constructed for the King's wives and closest family (**Queens' Pyramids**). In front of these and on the opposite side of Khufu's pyramid lie rows of mastabas—flat funerary structures—which served as the burial grounds for the remainder of the kings' courts.

Tomb of Queen Meresankh III

Around 250 meters (820 ft) southeast of Khufu's pyramid, this masataba belongs to the granddaughter of Khufu and wife of Khafre or Menkaure, Queen Meresankh III. Inside the spacious tomb, colorful paintings and carvings line the walls, depicting the treasures that once likely filled the burial chamber to provide the Queen comforts in the afterlife. Don't miss the 10 statues of the Meresankh and her all-female coterie carved into the northern wall.

Pyramid of Khafre

Depending on the angle, the pyramid of Khafre (son of Khufu) might be mistaken for

1: the Sphinx and Pyramid of Khafre **2:** camels at the Pyramids of Giza

How the Pyramids Were Built

King Khufu, who commissioned the largest of Giza's pyramids (the Great Pyramid), initiated the monumental building project at Giza around 2560 BC, turning the rocky plateau into a royal burial ground for the ancient Egyptian capital, Memphis, and outdoing his father's (Snefru's) smaller pyramids in Dahshur. Khufu's son, Khafre, would follow in his father's footsteps, building the second largest pyramid tomb, followed by Khafre's son, Menkaure, who built the smallest of the three (with each pyramid named after its respective patron).

Larger complexes once surrounded each pyramid, including mortuary temples where followers could worship the deceased kings (a good remaining example is the temple of Queen Hatshepsut in Luxor). Burial pits with large boats—possibly to sail the departed pharaohs into the afterlife—also lie next to the two largest pyramids.

WHO BUILT THE PYRAMIDS?

Archeological consensus says the pyramids were not, contrary to one-time popular belief, built by aliens, nor—as ancient Greek historian Herodotus claimed—by enslaved people. Excavations in the 1990s discovered the remains of the workers' village and cemetery, which revealed the builders lived in a well-organized community, ate plenty of protein (a rarity at the time), and received relatively advanced medical attention (e.g., broken bones were properly set).

MATERIALS AND CONSTRUCTION

Most of the stones came from a quarry located less than a mile south of the pyramids, while the white limestone was sourced from the other bank of the Nile, around 16 kilometers (10 mi) away, and the granite for the inner chambers was carted some 800 kilometers (500 mi) up the Nile from Aswan. The Nile's annual flooding brought the water to the base of the Giza Plateau, and—according to tomb paintings—men and oxen finished the job by dragging the blocks, some as heavy as three tons, up ramps to reach the higher parts of the pyramid. However, it remains unclear how the upper portions of the pyramids were completed—even with their ingenious ramps, it would be a tremendous feat.

the Great Pyramid. Khafre's monument, built around 2520 BC, is slightly smaller than that of his father—with original dimensions 143.5 meters (471 ft) tall and 215.72 meters (707.75 ft) on each side—but sits on higher ground, conveniently increasing its grandeur. The pyramid of Khafre is also distinguished by its cap of white limestone—the only one to have preserved a bit of its lustrous exterior.

Pyramid of Menkaure

What Menkaure's pyramid lacked in size compared to those of his father and grandfather, it made up for in the complexity of its mortuary temple, now in ruins. Built around 2490 BC, the pyramid originally stood at 65.5 meters (215 ft) tall, and has since lost around 3 meters (11 ft). Aside from its size, the monument is also distinguished by a gash down its northern side, made by a jealous 12th-century king. El-Aziz Othman, son of famed Salah el-Din, tried to dismantle the pyramids to build his father's city wall (the Ayyubid Wall). Fortunately, the task proved too difficult and was soon abandoned.

The Sphinx

This 73-meter-long, 20-meter-tall (240-ft-long, 66-ft-tall) man-lion carved out of a single wall of limestone was built around the same time as the Pyramid of Khafre. It's believed the Sphinx's face was fashioned in Khafre's likeness, and possibly disfigured thousands of years later by a Sufi who wanted to show idolatrous peasants that their object of worship was mere stone. The Sphinx of Giza was the first known appearance of the mythological creature, which would become a popular image in ancient cultures from Greece to Asia. Egyptians know him as Abu el-Hool, Father of Terror, likely because of his large size and the mystery surrounding him.

★ GRAND EGYPTIAN MUSEUM

Alexandria Desert Rd.; tel. 02 33776893 or 02 33777263; www.gem.gov.eg

At the time of writing, the Grand Egyptian Museum (GEM) had yet to celebrate its long-awaited inauguration (scheduled for late 2021/ early 2022). But sneak peeks of the venue reveal it's almost certain to live up to its promise of grandeur.

A **colossus of Pharaoh Ramses II,** standing around 9 meters (30 feet) tall, greets visitors at the museum entrance. And inside, treasures big and small lie tucked in various corners of the sprawling 500,000-square-meter (5,000,000-sq-ft) space. Some of the uncontested highlights include the entire contents of **King Tut's treasures**—comprised of over 5,000 items, many of them covered in gold, and all reunited for the first time since they were unearthed in 1922. The boy-king's solid gold death mask (weighing 24 pounds) will dazzle visitors, as will the array of curios like his golden toe covers and ancient board games.

King Khufu's giant 4,600-year-old **solar boat** is also now on display in the GEM, after it was moved from its home at the base of Khufu's pyramid in 2021. The relic had previously been housed in pod-like museum built over the limestone pit in which it was discovered in the 1950s. Specialists reconstructed the 42-meter-long (140-ft-long) cedar ship—which was found in more than 1,200 pieces—as it was originally built: without nails, and instead sewn together in excellent craftsmanship with rope made of a thick grass. Khufu and other fourth-dynasty kings took the title "Son of Re," after the sun god who had become popular at the time. It's believed this ancient vessel was intended as a vehicle for Khufu's journey into the afterlife and across the sky with the sun god, giving the "solar boat" its name. Some experts also believe the boat may have been the funerary barge used to carry the king's body from Memphis to the necropolis.

Along with the some 100,000 antiquities scheduled to decorate the museum's halls, the space will also hold a variety of souvenir shops, restaurants, and (according to the blueprints) a cinema.

ENTERTAINMENT AND EVENTS

Giza Pyramids Sound and Light Show

Giza Pyramids, Sphinx entrance; 7pm and 8pm daily Oct.-Apr., 7:30pm and 8:30pm daily May-Sept.; 180LE

Narrated by a British Sphinx à la old-time radio stars, the show is mildly entertaining (but mostly cheesy), with the pharaohs coming to life to tell their stories. Holograms and lasers do their best to hold the audience's attention, but at a run time of approximately 50 minutes, the show does drag a bit. If you're curious about the spectacle but don't want to commit an evening to it, the rooftop terrace of the **Great Pyramid Inn Restaurant and Bar** (located just across the street from the Sphinx) is a great place to watch. You can enjoy the multicolored demonstration with a glass of wine or a shisha and some snacks.

FOOD

There aren't a ton of good restaurants in the Giza pyramids area, but visitors won't go hungry. All of the restaurants below are walking distance from the Giza Pyramid Complex, with the exception of Abla Quail.

★ ABLA QUAIL (SIMAN ABLA)

Al-Mansouria Rd., Kerdasah; tel. 0100 797 0670; 4:30pm-3am, daily; 60-80LE

Quail is the specialty of this working-class district's favorite restaurant, housed in a spacious courtyard of a converted villa. Meals are typically enjoyed family style, with an array of dishes (kofta, grilled chicken, salads, etc.) passed around on large platters. The neighborhood is also also known for its camel liver,

TOP EXPERIENCE

Horseback Rides Near the Pyramids

There's perhaps no better way to admire the pharaohs' majestic tombs than while galloping across the golden desert toward the setting sun. Just to the east of the Giza Plateau, you'll find rows of stables full of horses and camels to choose from for your ride. The area around the Saqqara Necropolis also hosts a handful of quality stables. Most are open 24 hours a day and can tailor rides to your liking.

A few things to note:

- Cairo gets extremely hot in the summer, so longer daytime rides might be better enjoyed by visitors coming in the **cooler months** (Nov.-Apr.).
- Fridays tend to have **busier desert traffic** as most people are off school or work.
- The horse and camel touts inside the pyramid complex and at the stables near the pyramid entrance specialize in hassling tourists. It's best to **arrange with a trusted stable** instead, and enjoy the wide-open desert outside the boundaries of the pyramid complex.

Pyramid of Khafre from horseback

You can find cheaper rates, but the treatment of the animals (and visitors) at the stables listed in this book is much better than most of the alternatives. **Camel rides** and **quad bikes** are also available.

FB STABLES

Gamal Abdul Nasser St., Nazlet el-Samman; tel. 0106 507 0288; www.fbstablesgiza.co.uk; 24 hours daily; 300LE/hour

This 24-hour stable located just southeast of the Giza Pyramid Complex offers ultimate flexibility in terms of what type of adventure you're looking for. Want to head out at 5am to watch the sun rise over the Giza pyramids? Easy. Want a midnight ride under the moonlight? No problem. Trips are 300LE/hour for horse or camel ride. You can travel as far as the Dahshur Pyramids 26 kilometers (16 mi) south of the Giza Plateau on a 7-8-hour day trip. Be sure to finalize all price details of your trip before you head out to make sure there are no unexpected costs. Quad bikes also available (350LE/hour).

CAIRO HORSE RIDING SCHOOL

6 km/4 mi north of Saqqara Necropolis, Mansouria Rd., Abu Sir; tel. 0120 736 2425; sunrise-10pm daily; 300LE/hour

The stables here are an idyllic escape—full of purebred Arabian horses and date palms on the edge of the desert. The excellent guide, trainer, and stable master, Tamer Owayan, caters to riders of all levels. You can request a quick tutorial before heading out to the desert, or just take a few laps around the pen to get used to your horse. Choose from a range of excursions starting at 300LE/hour, 500LE/2 hours, or 1,500LE/6-hour trip between Giza and Saqqara. A typical 1-hour route takes riders past Zoser's Step Pyramid (at a distance) and through a lesser-known pyramid field just north of Saqqara called Abu Sir. Contact Tamer if you prefer to take your trip outside opening hours and he'll do his best to accommodate you. Helmets included.

so if you'd like to add some to your order ask a waiter to procure some from a stand next door. There are a number of Abla imitations—keep an eye out for a small "Barbeque Abla" sign on the exterior.

EL-HADABA CAFÉ AND RESTAURANT

2 Abu Aziza St. off of Abu Al Hool el-Siahe St.; tel. 02 33822575; noon-1am daily; 100-130LE

You might have to send out a search party to track down a waiter, but this quirky restaurant has a spacious rooftop terrace with good views of the pyramids. It's a nice place to have a peaceful tea and watch the sunset over the Giza Plateau. The food is decent, with a selection of grilled dishes (kofta, kebab, grilled liver) and tagines, but be sure to order early as it can take close to an hour to arrive. Roof opens at 6pm on occasion, so be sure to call ahead if you're going for sunset in the winter (when sunset is earlier).

★ 9 PYRAMIDS LOUNGE

In Giza Pyramids Complex; tel. 0121 229 999; 9am-5pm daily; 150-250LE mains

On an elevated patch of the Giza Plateau, this stylish restaurant boasts brilliant views of the pyramids and their sandy surroundings. The food is tasty, with a good breakfast menu and large selection of Egyptian treats like mezzes and grilled meats. Fresh juice and cold beer served. Check out their Facebook page for more information (@9PyramidsLounge). Restaurant visitors must first enter through the main entrance of the Giza Pyramids Complex and pay the 200LE per person entry fee (meaning a trip here is best combined with a trip to the Giza pyramids). Doors close at 3:30pm. Reservations required.

GREAT PYRAMID INN RESTAURANT AND BAR

14 Abou Al-Hool Al-Siahe St.; tel. 02 33836386; https://greatpyramidinn.com; 9am-11pm daily; 150-250LE

The rooftop terrace of the Great Pyramid Inn is an excellent place to relax with a cold beer after a trip to the pyramids. Their grilled dishes are also pretty good, but the venue performs better as a bar/café than a restaurant.

ALFREDO RESTAURANT

In Marriott Mena House; 6 Pyramids Rd.; tel. 02 33773222; 9am-11pm daily; 200-300LE

Sample a wide variety of Italian dishes, from simple but tasty pizzas and pastas to succulent grilled rack of lamb or shrimp primavera. You can enjoy the cool breeze on their terrace near the pool and palm trees, or opt for their royal restaurant interior. A range of beers, wines, and cocktails served.

139 RESTAURANT

In Marriott Mena House; 6 Pyramids Road; tel. 02 33773222; 9am-11pm; 200-300LE

This international restaurant has good fish, salads, and a few nice Indian dishes. As delicious as the food is, more memorable will likely be the ambiance—with tables looking out onto expansive green grounds and pools that reflect the colossal pyramids dominating the skyline. It's a popular destination for weddings, so call ahead to check if any large tents are obstructing the view to avoid disappointment. Alcohol available.

ACCOMMODATIONS

Unless you're coming to Cairo *only* to see the pyramids, choosing a more central location is highly advised. The Giza Plateau is around 24 kilometers (15 mi) south of Downtown Cairo, but in traffic it can mean over an hour's drive at an agonizing crawl. On the other hand, these accommodations are great options if you want to wake up to the enchanting monuments, or swim and dine in their company. If you're bookending a trip to Egypt with stays in Cairo, this area would be a perfect base for a night or two to visit Giza and the southern pyramids.

Under 800LE

GREAT PYRAMID INN

14 Abou Al-Hool Al-Siahe Street; tel. 02 33836386; https://greatpyramidinn.com; 800LE d

This boutique hotel offers a much more

personalized experience than the larger chains, and possibly the best views of the pyramids. It's a great choice for those who don't need a pool or fitness center, but still want to bask in the majesty of Giza's monuments. The entrance to the pyramid complex is literally a stone's throw away, and the rooftop terrace is a prime spot to enjoy your complimentary breakfast in the company of the Sphinx. Free airport shuttle service also available upon request.

1,650-3,300LE

LE MÉRIDIEN PYRAMIDS HOTEL & SPA

El-Remaya Square, Pyramids; tel. 02 33777070; www.marriott.com/hotels/travel/caimd-le-meridien-pyramids-hotel-and-spa; 1,700LE d

Not as fancy as the Mena House down the street, Le Méridien is a more economical choice for a similar view. You can lounge by the large pool while sipping a beverage from their swim-up bar and admiring the pyramids in the distance. The rooms are nothing special, but they are comfortable and clean. Be sure to request one with a pyramid view, or suffer street sounds on the busy roads surrounding the hotel grounds.

★ MARRIOTT MENA HOUSE

6 Pyramids Road; tel. 02 33773222; www.marriott.com; 2,700LE d

More of a campus than a hotel, the Mena House encircles a lush green yard with rows of palm trees that decorate the foreground to the imposing pyramids beyond. There's a long, pleasant pool to cool off in, and a series of pond fountains flowing across the grounds. The hotel started as Khedive Ismail's hunting lodge (now the main dining room), before British aristocrats built up rooms around it for wealthy travelers in the late 19th century. Another 300 rooms were added in the 1970s. The illustrious guest list has included the likes of Charlie Chaplin, Winston Churchill, and Frank Sinatra. One major downside is the hotel often hosts weddings and conventions, which can feel like an invasion. If you like to sleep early, you might want to request a room far from the action.

INFORMATION AND SERVICES

GIZA PYRAMIDS TOURIST INFORMATION OFFICE

No tel.; 9am-4pm daily

This tourist info office is located beside the tourist police at the bottom of the hill that leads to the main entrance of the Giza Pyramid Complex. They're not super helpful, but you may be able to snag some brochures and maps for destinations around Egypt.

GETTING THERE

The Giza pyramids in all their grandeur have been nearly enveloped by urban sprawl, making them easily accessible by taxi, Uber, or microbus.

Taxi

If you take a **taxi** or **Uber** from Downtown, the price should be in the 100LE range, although Ubers can be significantly more expensive during peak hours. It's only a 16-kilometer (10-mi) trip, but can easily take over an hour in traffic. You can get there quicker via the Ring Road freeway, or crawl your way down Haram Road (the latter is preferable for those uncomfortable with witnessing crazy Cairo driving). As always, make sure the taxi driver uses the meter. It shouldn't be difficult to find a ride on the way back, but if you prefer to explore the pyramid grounds by car, you can ask your driver to accompany you and keep the meter running, or agree on a set price for the day (350-450LE).

Private Car Hire

You can also hire a private car for the trip for 400-600LE. **Mydo** (tel. 0114 779 5215) is a great driver who doubles as an experienced guide. **Ibrahim el-Sheemy** (tel. 0122 487 8427) and **Moamen Khedr** (tel. 0122 362 3032; moamen_lancer@yahoo.com) are both excellent drivers with comfortable cars. All are best reached by WhatsApp.

Microbus

Microbuses going to **Haram** (near the Giza Plateau) can be found in **Abdel Minam Riyad Square.** These will take you as far as **Arish Street** (11 km/7 mi), where you can grab another microbus heading to **Remaya Square** (another 5 km/3 mi).

Alternatively, microbuses leaving from in front of **Masrah el-Baloon** (Baloon Theater) in **Agouza** go to **Giza Square** (8 km/5 mi), where you can catch a microbus to **Remaya Square** (another 10.5 km/6.5 mi). In either case, you'll pass in front of the Giza pyramids complex. Just make sure to tell the driver you want to go to al-ahramat (the pyramids). Each length of the journey should cost between 3-6LE, and you pay when people start passing their fare to the front. Taxis are so inexpensive that the only reason to choose this route is if you want to try a local experience.

Memphis, Saqqara, and Dahshur

Founded (c. 3000 BC) by Menes, the first king of unified Egypt, Memphis served as the capital for the newly united kingdoms of Upper and Lower Egypt. The city thrived as a power center for nearly 3,000 years—even after the capital was moved elsewhere, and despite suffering a number of sieges in the 7th and 6th centuries BC. The rise of Christianity proved a death knell for the once formidable city, before the Muslim invasion in AD 640 destroyed it completely.

The ruins from these attacks and the cruelty of time can be seen at the Memphis Complex open-air museum, but more interesting sights can be found at the fallen city's burial grounds: Saqqara to the west and Dahshur to the southwest. Saqqara, the original necropolis for the powerful Memphis rulers, holds the origins of Egypt's iconic pyramids (Zoser's Step Pyramid, c. 2665 BC) alongside older tombs. Dahshur, the southernmost Memphis necropolis, boasts Egypt's first true pyramid, the Red Pyramid, and its less-than-perfect predecessor, the Bent Pyramid.

ORIENTATION AND PLANNING

Saqqara and **Dahshur** are 4 kilometers (2.5 mi) west and 12 kilometers (7.5 mi) southwest of Memphis, respectively. The small **Memphis Complex** can be seen in about 30-60 minutes. Depending on how many of the lesser monuments you'd like to see, plan for a 2-3-hour visit at Saqqara, and for up to 2 hours for your visit to Dahshur Necropolis.

While the main attractions of these sights are easily visited without a **guide,** bringing one along will surely enrich the trip. More importantly, you'll want to secure a two-way ride before being dropped off (taxi traffic this far south is light).

SIGHTS

Memphis Complex

Mit Rahina; 8am-4pm daily; 80LE adults, 40LE students

About 5 kilometers (3 mi) toward the Nile from the desert burial grounds of Saqqara, you'll find the remnants of Egypt's ancient capital, Men-Nefer ("enduring and beautiful"), known to the Greeks as Memphis. The desert necropolises of Giza, Saqqara, and Dahshur all served as the royal burial grounds for the ancient capital. While only fragments of this 5,000-year-old city have lived up to the promise of perpetuity, one can imagine how grand the metropolis must have been in its prime.

The modern-day village of Mit Rahina now sits on the former capital and hosts an open-air museum with a scattering of stones, including the smiling **Sphinx of Memphis** (c. 1,500 BC)—much smaller than its older sibling in Giza, but with nose and false beard intact—and a 10-meter-long (32-ft-long)

Memphis, Saqqara, and Dahshur

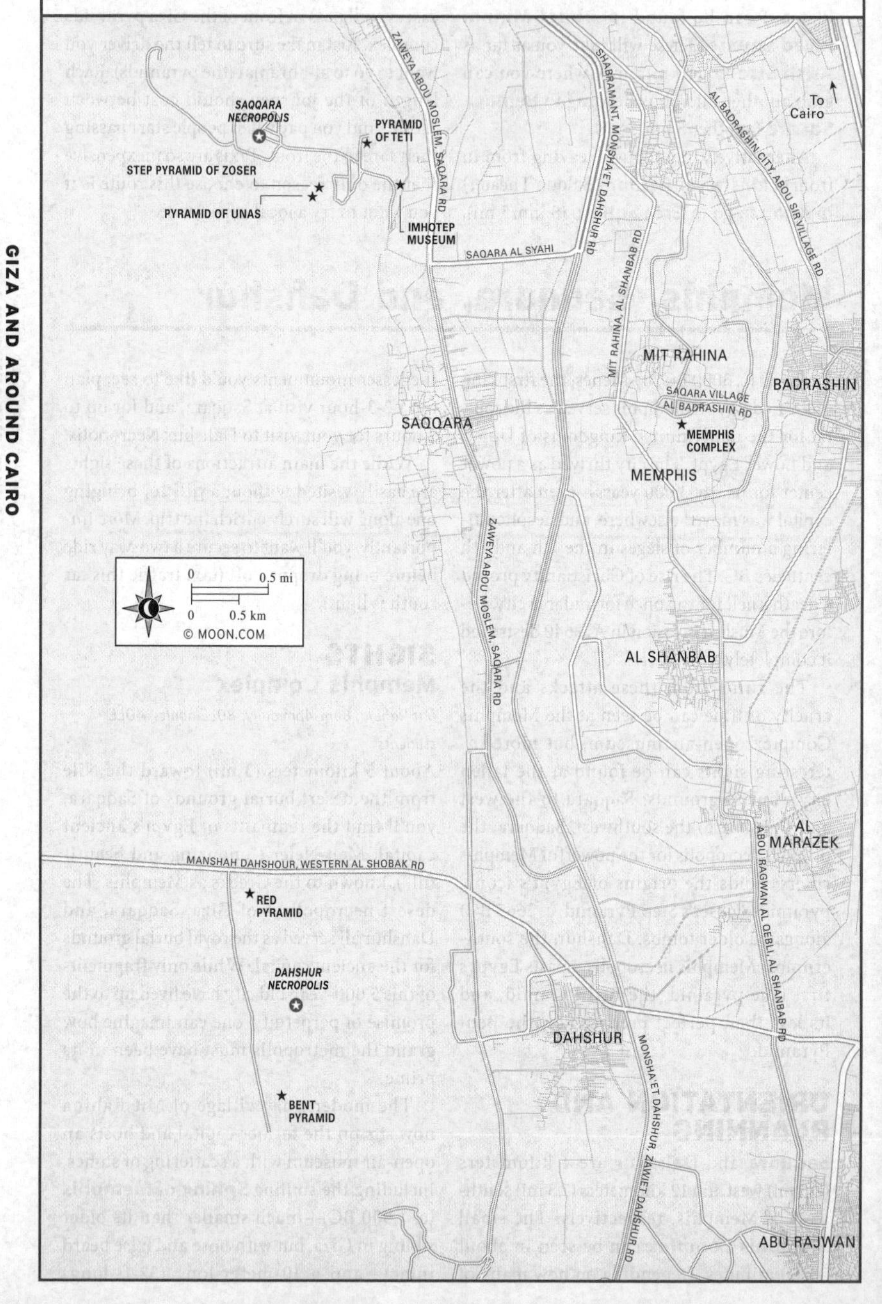

Ramses II Statue, resting on his back in a purpose-built museum for his legless limestone body. You can visit Ramses's clone in full height, also uncovered in Memphis, at the entrance of the Grand Egyptian Museum.

The museum is small (you should only need around 30-60 minutes to visit) but worth a quick detour if you're in the area.

★ Saqqara Necropolis

Saqqara; 8am-4pm daily; 440LE adults, 220LE students for entire site

Dozens of tombs lie scattered across this expansive necropolis, with the **Step Pyramid of Zoser** the undisputed star of the show. True archeology lovers will also enjoy a visit to the surrounding ruins, especially the **Pyramid of Teti,** the **Pyramid of Unas,** and the **Serapeum.** To explore all the nooks and crannies around the necropolis, it's best to bring along an expert **guide.** The sites are spaced a few hundred meters apart from each other, so walking is an option, but driving may be more comfortable. If you only plan to visit select sites, you can also buy individual tickets for a bit cheaper (180LE adults/90LE students for Step Pyramid and Imhotep Museum; 150LE adults/75LE students for Serapeum).

IMHOTEP MUSEUM

Named after Zoser's adviser and the architect behind his pyramid, this little museum is the canapé to the feast of archeological wonders that lay beyond it. Here, you can watch a short video about the Step Pyramid on loop and admire many of the artifacts uncovered in the Saqqara excavation site, including a 4,000 year-old mummy. You might want to pop in before you visit the sandy sites to put them in context, but the AC also makes for a nice post-pyramid cooldown. A visit should only take 20-45minutes.

STEP PYRAMID OF ZOSER

We can thank Zoser, the second king of the third dynasty, for giving Egypt the pyramids. His was the first to be constructed in the whole country, around 2665 BC (a century before Khufu's Great Pyramid of Giza). Zoser's pyramid also represents the first monumental stone structure, as opposed to earlier brick-based monuments. Before Zoser, most kings were buried in mastabas, or flat-topped tombs. His 73-meter (204-ft) step pyramid marks a progression—taking the form of stacked mastabas—before Snefru achieved the ultimate slanted pyramid in Dahshur.

The funerary complex that surrounds the pyramid once stood protected by a wall 9 meters (30 ft) tall and contained a city-like space—with courtyards, shrines, and living quarters for priests covering some 16 hectares (40 ac). The entrance (in the southeast corner of the complex) will lead you down the hypostyle hall into the Great South Court, where King Zoser once ran around a royal track in religious rituals. In the courtyard you'll find a remaining chunk of wall decorated with a frieze of cobras that offered divine protection to the pharaoh.

PYRAMID OF TETI

Teti's Pyramid (built c. 2300 BC) looks much like an unremarkable hill of sand from the outside, but it hosts one of the earliest known instances of the **Pyramid Texts**—incantations intended to liberate the departed pharaoh's soul and shepherd it into the heavens—inscribed on the granite walls and basalt sarcophagus that lie within. This quasi-pyramid can be found to the northeast of Zoser's.

PYRAMID OF UNAS

Another apparent pile of sand and stones, they Pyramid of Unas (built c. 2350 BC) holds the *earliest* known example of the Pyramid Texts—a rough draft for the future **Book of the Dead.** The spells line the antechamber in vertical columns, and the ceiling inside the burial chamber is decorated with stars against a dark blue night sky (now mostly faded). The caretaker may tell you it's closed, but a slip of baksheesh (a tip) will likely gain you entrance. It can be found just south of Zoser's pyramid.

1
2
3
4

SERAPEUM

This temple-cum-burial ground was built c. 1250 BC for sacred bulls called Apis, believed to be the incarnation of Memphis's patron god, Ptah. Inside, you'll find long tunnels with side chambers where the mummified bulls were laid to rest in massive sarcophagi, now empty. The haunting space is a must-see stop on your visit to Saqqara.

★ Dahshur Necropolis

Monshaat Dahshur; 8am-4pm daily; 60LE adults, 30LE students

Few visitors make their way down to this corner of the desert just 10 kilometers (6 mi) south of Saqqara, and you might even have the magnificent site to yourself. Snefru, first king of the fourth dynasty, commissioned the Bent and Red Pyramids here c. 2600 BC. The father of Khufu (of the Great Pyramid), Snefru hadn't yet figured out how to build a perfect pyramid slant when he commissioned the (originally) 105-meter-tall (344-ft-tall) **Bent Pyramid**—resulting in the double slant, or bend. Snefru's engineers tried again with the 104-meter-tall (341-ft-tall) **Red Pyramid** to much greater success, achieving the first "true pyramid" with uniform sides slanted at 43 degrees. This angle approximates that at the top of the Bent Pyramid, contrasting with the 52-degree slant of its base, which proved too steep to support the structure.

Best to wear comfortable shoes, bring a flashlight, and limber up your back to prepare for some crouched exploring. Cameras aren't permitted inside the pyramids, but the caretakers might be persuaded to close their eyes in exchange for a small tip. **WCs** available near the Red Pyramid.

BENT PYRAMID

As of 2019 you can now enter the Bent Pyramid down an 80-meter-long (260-ft-long) tunnel, before crawling (quite literally) up another tunnel into the side chambers (not for the claustrophobic). It wouldn't be a true adventure if there weren't creatures involved—in this case some harmless bats. A tip for making the descent: Try climbing backward as if you were going down a ladder to avoid a long walk at a 90-degree angle. On the way out, watch your head—the tunnel gets progressively smaller as you climb towards the exit.

RED PYRAMID

The entrance to the Red Pyramid's interior can be found on its north side. Inside, the tunnel isn't as cramped as that of the Bent Pyramid, but there's a bit of a musty smell, so you might want to bring a scarf.

GETTING THERE

The best way to visit Memphis and the pyramids of Saqqara and Dahshur on your own is by grabbing a cab or Uber, or hiring a driver with private car. For the most informative trip, going with a guide is recommended. In this case, the guide will likely provide transportation as well.

Taxi

If you take a taxi, ask the driver to use the meter. One way to Dahshur from Downtown Cairo (37 km/23 mi) should be in the neighborhood of 200-250LE for either taxi or Uber, making the round trip around 500-600LE, including wait time.

Private Car Hire

Mydo (tel. 0114 779 5215) is a great driver who doubles as an experienced guide. **Ibrahim el-Sheemy** (tel. 0122 487 8427) and **Moamen Khedr** (tel. 0122 362 3032; moamen_lancer@yahoo.com) are both excellent drivers with comfortable cars. All are best reached by WhatsApp.

Horse, Camel, or Quad Bike

For the real adventure seekers, it's also possible to arrive to the Saqqara and Dahshur necropolises by horse, camel, or quad bike. A reputable list of tour providers can be found on page 114. If you take this option, you likely won't be able to enter the grounds, but can see the pyramids from a distance.

1: Saqqara **2:** Step Pyramid of Zoser **3:** sarcophagus for a sacred bull at the Serapeum **4:** Red and Bent Pyramids in the Dahshur Necropolis

Fayoum

The governorate of Fayoum is a lonely leaf hanging off the stem of the Nile into the Western Desert. In the small villages outside Fayoum City, white egrets spot swaths of growing fava beans, men ride donkeys on cushions of alfalfa, and women walk tall with cauliflower crowns. Lake Qarun glitters in the sunshine, protecting Fayoum's verdant fields from the harshness of the desert that lies beyond it, and sandstone mountains dominate the distant skyline.

Remnants of ancient worlds lie tucked within this pseudo-oasis, including pyramids and ruins of 3rd- and 4th-century BC Ptolemaic settlements that lie along Lake Qarun. The landscape and lifestyle here are a world away from bustling Cairo but can be easily enjoyed as a day trip from the capital or as a relaxing weekend getaway.

Known for its pottery, tiny **Tunis Village** (Qarayat Tunis), with its charming accommodation options and proximity to Lake Qarun and Wadi el-Rayan Protected Area, is the best base for exploring these parts. Its 2-kilometer-long (1-mi-long) main road is lined by boutique lodges with mini swimming pools, simple accommodations, and the workshops of highly skilled local potters.

HISTORY

Like the true oases of the Western Desert, Fayoum sits in depression—its lowest point 45 meters (150 ft) below sea level. In prehistoric times, a natural branch of the Nile poured into the basin to create a massive lake that covered most of the modern-day governorate, Lake Moeris (today called Lake Qarun).

The first attempt to regulate the floods feeding into this fertile land dates to nearly 4,000 years ago, when Pharaoh Senusret II (r. 1844-1837 BC) carved a canal out of the natural waterway and created a network of smaller branches to irrigate new agricultural lands. His grandson, Amenemhet III (r. 1818-1770 BC), expanded the system and reclaimed over 150,000 acres of marsh land for agricultural production, leading to a period of great prosperity. Some 15 centuries later, the Ptolemies initiated yet another major development, draining much of the lake and expanding agriculture in its place.

Senusret II's ancient waterway—the region's umbilical cord branching off the Nile—now takes the form of the Bahr Youssef canal, which snakes from the Nile through Fayoum and empties into Lake Qarun in the north. The pyramids of Fayoum's pharaonic founders (the Pyramids of Lahun and Hawara) sit to the southeast, along the stalk of the heart-shaped leaf that is the governorate. And ruins of 3rd- and 4th-century BC Ptolemaic settlements lie along the water.

ORIENTATION

Fayoum City (which, frankly, can be skipped) is located in the center of the governorate. Bordering the governorate to the north is the sprawling **Lake Qarun** with **Qarun Lake Touristic Road** running along the water's southern edge. The pottery village of **Tunis** sits off this road on the southwest side of the lake, a full hour from Fayoum City.

One kilometer (0.6 mi) beyond Tunis Village, **Wadi el-Rayan Road** branches south off Qarun Lake Touristic Road and brings you to **Wadi el-Rayan Protected Area** (after 26 km/16 mi). After another 13 kilometers (8 mi) south along Wadi el-Rayan Road, **Medawara Mountain** (Gebel el-Medawara) offers beautiful views of the surrounding lakes. To reach the **Valley of the Whales** (Wadi el-Hittan) you need a 4WD with expert driver to head another 38 kilometers (24 mi) northwest into the desert from Medawara Mountain on a sand-covered road. (Knowledgeable local guides can also traverse the unmarked desert to get here.)

Ancient sites lie scattered around the

outskirts of the governorate. **Qasr Qarun** stands 8 kilometers (5 mi) west of Tunis Village, while the ruins of the Greco-Roman town, **Karanis,** can be found just off the **Fayoum Desert Road** that brings you in from Cairo (47 km/29 mi northeast of Tunis Village).

The hill-like **Hawara Pyramid** sits 12 kilometers (7 mi) southeast of Fayoum City, the **Lahun Pyramid** another 15 kilometers (9 mi) southeast of that, and **Meidum Pyramid** 37 kilometers (23 mi) northeast of that.

SIGHTS

Lake Qarun (Buherat Qarun)

North side of Fayoum Governorate

Tens of thousands of years ago, nearly all of the Fayoum depression was submerged in a freshwater lake. This ancient body of water has since been reduced to a much smaller, and saltier, version of itself through a combination of natural and artificial processes. Today Lake Qarun is full of saltwater fish and remains a popular stop-over for migratory birds. The small **Qarn el-Zahabi** island in the middle of the lake is a nesting spot for thousands of feathered friends each year. Locals do cool off in Lake Qarun (hard not to be tempted in the hot summer months), but it's not recommended due to pollution levels.

Karanis and the Kom Aushim Museum

Kom Aushim Village, off Fayoum el-Sahrawy Rd., 77 km/48 mi southwest of Cairo; 9am-4pm daily; 60LE adults, 30LE students

Karanis is Fayoum's most notable Greco-Roman site, with remains of two temples, a bath house, and over a dozen granaries. Ptolemy II sent Greek mercenaries to live and farm here in the 3rd century BC as part of a project to settle his compatriots among native Egyptians. For the next 700-some years an agricultural village inhabited the area—its success waxing and waning depending on how well the government preserved the canals used to irrigate the land. The south temple (the better preserved of the two) dates from the 1st century BC and is dedicated to crocodile gods, the favored deity in Fayoum. Beside the ruins, the **Kom Aushim Museum** (same hours and price) holds interesting archeological artifacts like canopic jars, wooden combs, pottery, and ancient flip-flops (they don't make 'em like they used to).

Karnis is located along the main road coming in from Cairo, so travelers might want to visit the site on their way in to (or out of) Fayoum. The museum is fairly small and a visit to the whole site shouldn't take more than an hour.

Qasr Qarun

8 km/5 mi west of Tunis Village off Wadi el-Rayan Rd.; 8am-4pm daily; 60LE adults, 30LE students

Fayoum's ancient capital, Crocodilopolis, was the center of Egypt's cult of the crocodile god Sobek. This small temple built for the scaly deity in the 3rd century BC is the best of what remains from the large Ptolemaic city, Dionysias. The now sleepy location was once well-trodden—a crossroads of caravans leading north to Alexandria and west to the oases of the Western Desert. You can venture inside to see some of its dozens of empty chambers.

Medinet Maadi

22 km/14 mi east of Wadi el-Rayan, 36 km/22 mi west of Fayoum City; 9am-4pm daily; 50LE adults, 25LE students

The prolific Amenemhet III founded this city (then named Gia, c. late 18th century BC), with its centerpiece a temple dedicated to the cobra goddess of harvest Renenutet and the crocodile god Sobek. To reach the temple and admire its rare Middle Kingdom inscriptions, walk down the avenue lined with crumbling sphinxes and cartoon-like lions. Additional Ptolemaic temples and Roman buildings also layer the site.

A trip here can be combined with a visit to the Wadi el-Rayan Protected Area. A rocky path off the main road within the park (Wadi el-Rayan Rd.) leads to the site after 30 kilometers (19 mi), but it can only be traveled with 4WD. Alternative routes are available for normal cars outside the protected area (39 km/24 mi south of Tunis Village).

Wadi el-Rayan Protected Area

Entrance 9 km/5.5 mi south of Qarun Lake Touristic Rd. in northwest corner of Fayoum Governorate; 9am-5pm daily; 50LE

Covering 1,760 square kilometers (680 sq mi), this protected area offers a wonderful escape into nature. Most of the park is desert with the highlights Qusur el-Arab to the far west, full of massive sand dunes; the Valley of the Whales (Wadi el-Hitan), scattered with whale fossils from a prehistoric sea; and sandstone mountains that rise out of the earth at random intervals.

In the 1970s the two largest lakes—creatively name el-Buhera el-Oola (First Lake) and el-Buhera el-Tania (Second Lake)—were created in Wadi el-Rayan's depression (13 m/42 ft below sea level) to store agricultural runoff. Between the two main lakes is "**Egypt's only waterfall,**" now somewhat anemic due to mismanagement, but still a favorite spot for school field trips. A cafeteria with WCs and a long-forgotten visitor center sit beside the falls, which you can reach with a normal car. If you wish to see the more interesting sites off the paved road, including all the below except Medawara Mountain, you'll need a 4WD with local driver/guide. You can also camp within the park—your guide can make you a package and secure the necessary permits.

MEDAWARA MOUNTAIN (GEBEL EL-MEDAWARA)

17 km/11 mi south of the park entrance; 24 hours daily; free

Climb to the top of this rocky mountain (really more of a hill) for marvelous views of surrounding lakes and shrubs. It's also a great perch for watching the sunset. Ascent time: 3-5 minutes.

MAGIC LAKE

3 km/2 mi south of Medawara Mountain; 24 hours daily; free

If you come to the desert on a hot day, you'll quickly find out where this swimmable lake gets its name. The refreshing water here (as opposed to the polluted Lake Qarun and the irrigation runoff of nearby waters) is a fantastic place to take a quick dip after sandboarding on the neighboring dune. The flat area around the lake is also a nice spot for a late afternoon picnic. Walk or drive up the mountain immediately to the north (**Magic Lake Mountain**) for the best view in all of Fayoum, including the park's "Third Lake," which emerged in a beautiful zigzag pattern after the park's first two lakes were created.

TOP EXPERIENCE

★ VALLEY OF THE WHALES (WADI EL-HITAN)

38 km/24 mi west of Medawara Mountain; 9am-5pm daily; 40LE

If you find it difficult to wrap your head around what desert life looked like 37 million years ago, a visit to this valley might help spark the imagination. Fossils of giant whales lay unmoved from their sandy graves on what was once the floor of the prehistoric Tethys Sea—the remains of which can be found 300 kilometers (200 mi) to the north (for those geographically challenged, that's the Mediterranean).

Now a UNESCO World Heritage Site, this open-air museum is tastefully marked with minimalistic paths of sand lined by local stones that lead visitors to the numbered whales and their mangrove homes. The most striking features to emerge from the hundreds of fossils uncovered here were mini legs and knees, suggesting whales were once land animals that evolved into sea creatures. There's a small indoor **museum** (9am-2pm Sat.-Thurs.; entry with same ticket) beside the main attraction with some interesting information and a short film about the site that plays on loop (about 15 minutes). WCs available.

Qarun Protected Area

North of Lake Qarun; 24 hours daily; 45LE

Few visitors head to these parts, known locally

1: view from Medawara Mountain 2: Wadi el-Rayan waterfalls 3: Third Lake 4: Valley of the Whales

1
2
3
4

as Shimal el-Buhera (North of the Lake), with Wadi el-Rayan to the south a much more popular excursion. But if you have an extra day, this side of the desert is a great place to explore. In the 1,350 square kilometers (523 sq mi) of protected area, you can visit the basalt-covered **Qatrani Mountain** that holds ancient quarries (**Widan el-Faras**), used since at least 3000 BC, and a paved road—said to be the world's first—connecting the quarries to Lake Qarun. Beside the mountain (9 km/6 mi south of Widan el-Faras), you can wander the **Petrified Forest,** or el-Ghaba el-Mutahagara, with scattered stony logs from a woodland that stood here some 55 million years ago. And for a more modern site, you can swing by **Qasr el-Sagha** (at the foot of Qatrani Mountain, 10 km/6 mi north of Lake Qarun)—the unfinished temple built during the Middle Kingdom (2030-1650 BC) of large limestone blocks. A local driver with 4WD is needed to visit these sites (he'll know how to get you there).

Fayoum's Pyramid Circuit

Die-hard pyramid fans will enjoy an outing to Fayoum's skyward tombs on the east side of the governorate (though others may find them less than inspiring). You'd be forgiven for mistaking two out of the three for natural formations—their slanted sides are now reduced to mounds of rubble. But like the Great Pyramid of Giza, these were once the grand resting places of kings.

The best way to visit is with a private car and driver from your Fayoum hotel, or message the reliable **Talaat Fikry** on WhatsApp (tel. 0100 246 5020) who makes the trip (4-6 hours) for around 500LE. For a knowledgeable guide, call or email **Mahmoud Kamel** (tel. 0106 145 4263; fayoumegypt@gmail.com).

HAWARA PYRAMID

11.5 km/7 mi southeast of Fayoum City; 8am-4pm daily; 60LE adults, 30LE students

This pyramid—tomb of Amenemhet III (r. 1818-1770 BC), the pharaoh who helped turn Fayoum into a thriving agricultural area—was originally encased in bright white limestone and surrounded by an intricate mortuary temple. The cult complex was later described by Herodotus as a fabulous labyrinth—"a work beyond words"—with as many as 12 courts and 3,000 chambers. According to the ancient historian, half the chambers were underground and contained the tombs of kings and sacred crocodiles. Romans used the complex as a quarry, and sadly little remains of this former wonder of the ancient world (although some hopefuls contend the maze can still be found underground). As for the pyramid, all that's left is its mud brick core and submerged inner chambers, flooded by a nearby canal. But active imaginations might still be able to conjure the site's lost grandeur.

LAHUN PYRAMID

32 km/20 mi southeast of Fayoum City; 8am-4pm daily; 60LE adults, 30LE students

Amenemhet III's grandfather, Senusret II, built his impressive pyramid (now but a mud-brick mound) here in the late 19th century BC. The ambitious king began Fayoum's massive land reclamation project, converting thousands of acres of marshland into fertile farms. Some 600 years after Senusret II's death, Ramses II plundered the late pharaoh's tomb for his own royal projects, leaving little for visitors to enjoy. But as of 2019, you can now enter the pyramid's surprisingly vast interior and descend into the burial chamber encased in pink granite with matching sarcophagus (long empty, of course). To the north you'll find mastaba tombs where members of the king's court were buried.

Around 4 kilometers (2.5 mi) south of the pyramid you can check out the site of one of the world's oldest dams (**Lahun Dam,** or Sad el-Lahun), originally built by Amenemhet III.

MEIDUM PYRAMID

45 km/28 mi northeast of Fayoum City; 8am-4pm daily; 40LE adults, 20LE students

Remember Snefru—the 26th century BC pharaoh who built the pyramids at Dahshur and fathered Khufu, builder of the Great

Pyramid of Giza? The Meidum Pyramid was yet another of his monumental projects (likely started by his predecessor, King Huni). Some believe Snefru abandoned the undertaking before it was finished to start over in Dahshur with the imperfect Bent Pyramid, before finally achieving Egypt's first true pyramid (the Red Pyramid). Others believe he successfully completed the step pyramid here and filled it in with white limestone to give the appearance of a true pyramid, before it eventually collapsed. Regardless, much more remains of this tomb than those of Hawara and Lahun—even though it's more than 700 years older—and visitors can still see the slanted sides and three of the stacked blocks that once towered eight steps high.

The pyramid is technically not in Fayoum (just over the governorate border in Beni Suef), but it's commonly visited with the pyramids in Fayoum proper, and you can get there in around 45 minutes from either Hawara or Lahun.

RECREATION AND ACTIVITIES

Horseback Riding

STABLE TUNIS

Tunis Village; tel. 0100 209 4774; 6am-11pm daily

Whether you want to ride for 15 minutes or 5 days, Mohammed Salah at Stable Tunis can accommodate. His team takes excellent care of their horses, offers helmets and other safety gear, and is great with everyone—from children to adults, beginners to experts. You can take a short visit from the stables in Tunis Village to the neighboring Lake Qarun (150LE/hour), or have Mohammed organize a multiday camping trip on horseback to the Valley of the Whales (6-8 hours from Tunis Village) and other desert locations (200LE/hour on horse and a bit extra for camping gear and food).

Desert Safaris and Camping

You haven't seen Fayoum if you haven't seen its desert. To get there, you'll need a 4WD with expert driver to bring you safely across the dunes and (for the adventurous) up and down the mushroom rock formations. If you're keen on testing your sandboarding skills, make sure your guide brings his boards.

A trip to **Wadi el-Rayan Protected Area** (including the **Valley of the Whales, Medawara Mountain, Magic Lake,** and/or **Qusur el-Arab**) or to north of Lake Qarun can easily be done as a day trip from Cairo (around 1,400LE for 1-6 people). Guides can also arrange camping and barbecue meals for an extra cost. Organize a trip through your Fayoum hotel, or try out one of these fabulous local guides.

TALAAT FIKRY

tel. 0100 246 5020

Talaat is a fantastic driver who can tailor trips to your liking. A native of Tunis Village, he's been taking visitors on desert excursions for more than a decade. Talaat does an excellent day trip to Fayoum from Cairo (1,200LE round-trip for 1-3 people, plus 1,300LE desert safari for 1-6 people), or longer outings for those who have more time. Don't miss out on his delicious barbecue lunch (120LE per person).

WALEED FEKRY

tel. 0100 469 9359

Waleed has lovely campgrounds (Mangrove Camp Fayoum) for those who enjoy sleeping in a tent but want to take a shower in the morning. He's also been taking visitors out for more than a decade and can organize traditional safaris to Wadi el-Rayan and its surroundings.

ETMAN ABOUD

tel. 0100 133 3781

Etman grew up around Lake Qarun and has been driving visitors around his home and its sandy surroundings for over 15 years. He has a passion for sharing his Bedouin culture with guests.

Tunis Village's Pottery Workshops

The famed Fayoum Pottery School was set up by a Swiss couple in the 1980s to share their love of the art form with the clay-rich region. Today, dozens of the school's graduates continue to work in the field, and many have opened their own workshops in the village. You can't go wrong at even the smallest of Tunis's showrooms—stacked with pieces glazed in striking colors characteristic of the village's pottery—so set aside an hour or two (or three) to stroll the main lane and peruse the shelves. Prices range from around 60-600LE.

FAYOUM POTTERY SCHOOL

At the end of the Main St.; tel. 0100 138 8018; https://nagada.net; 9am-5:30pm daily

This showroom helped turn Tunis into a pottery mecca. It has the widest variety of items in town, with beautiful goblets, plates, teapots, mugs, and decorative dishes. Take a peek into their world with a short taster class (1-1.5 hours; 80LE) or a longer lesson (3 hours; 300LE), where you can make your own plate, cup, or figurine (can be delivered to Cairo for 100LE after two weeks of drying). Best to call a day or two ahead to reserve your spot.

ABU ZEID CERAMICS

Across from Palm Shadows Hotel; tel. 0100 772 6960; 10am-5pm daily

Another exceptional shop to seek out is Abu Zeid Ceramics, whose owner, Ahmed Abu Zeid, helped Fayoum Pottery School founder Evelyn Porret instill the love of pottery-making in Tunis. Ahmed's pieces are unique in the village—merging traditional Egyptian designs with the avant-garde. Check out his Facebook page (@AbouZiedCeramics) for a sample of his work.

MAHMOUD KAMEL

tel. 0106 145 4263; fayoumegypt@gmail.com, https://fayoumegypt.com

If you prefer a guide who can explain the history of places and/or good English is important to you, Mahmoud (a researcher at the Fayoum Tourism Authority) is the best choice. He can arrange for a professional driver and accompany you on a traditional desert safari, a tour of Fayoum's ancient heritage, or other tailored trips. You do pay a premium for his services (e.g., 2,900LE for 2 people to Wadi el-Rayan and the Valley of the Whales versus around 1,400LE for up to 6 people with a skilled driver with basic English).

Sandboarding

QUSUR EL-ARAB

Most of the desert around Fayoum is relatively flat, with the exception of Qusur el-Arab ("Palaces of the Arab" in Arabic)—an area in the southwest corner of Wadi el-Rayan filled with towering dunes of soft sand that snake across the land. Its name comes from the massive rock formations nearby that resemble stately, beige-colored homes. Needless to say, this is the best spot to break out the sandboards.

Swimming

Although it's tempting to swim in Lake Qarun, it's not recommended as pollution levels are high. **Magic Lake** in Wadi el-Rayan Protected Area is good for a dip.

FOOD

All listings below are located in Tunis Village.

SOBEK LODGE

Tunis Village; tel. 0106 888 5423; 8am-10pm daily; 80-150LE mains

Sobek's seating is possibly the nicest in town with palm wood furniture positioned throughout the garden under palm trees and pink bougainvillea. Floor pillows with a low table are also an option. The food here is fresh and flavorful with favorites including stuffed pigeon and duck. Try the fateer (large round flaky pastry) with honey for breakfast.

★ KOM EL-DIKKA AGRI LODGE RESTAURANT

Tunis Village; tel. 0122 244 0012; 8am-10pm daily; 100-200LE mains

At Kom el-Dikka you can pick your own herbs, fruits, and vegetables from their organic gardens, or fish for your meal from their fish farm (call ahead). For breakfast don't miss their fateer dipped in honey or molasses. Their freshly baked bread is worth the visit alone, but the menu has a range of tasty options like grilled chicken, stuffed pigeon, kofta, and salads. Enjoy your meal as you look out over leafy gardens to the distant Lake Qarun.

IBIS RESTAURANT & COOKING SCHOOL

Tunis Village; tel. 0106 090 6048; 9am-9pm daily; 100-200LE mains

Head here for a delicious breakfast of waffles, crepes, or traditional Egyptian fare (including fateer, fuul, and eggs). The fresh fish dishes, pizzas, pastas, and salads are also great for lunch or dinner. And don't miss their irresistible carrot cake or apple crumble with vanilla ice cream for dessert. Reservations a day in advance recommended. Check their Facebook page (@ibisrestaurantandcookingschool) for cooking courses and full menu.

BLUE DONKEY AT LAZIB INN

Tunis Village; tel. 084 282 0000; 8am-midnight daily; 300-450LE mains

The fanciest restaurant in town. Here you can enjoy pretty plating and delectable dishes blending Egyptian and international tastes, like Fayoumi pigeon with stuffed grape leaves or Australian veal chop with caramelized onions. Like the rest of the hotel, the restaurant is full of colorful knickknacks and fresh cut flowers. Dress code: smart casual.

ACCOMMODATIONS

Tunis Village

SOBEK LODGE

Tunis Village; tel. 0106 888 5423; hibourreau@yahoo.fr; 850LE d

Sobek Lodge boasts beautiful gardens with shocking pink bougainvillea, a small swimming pool, and a fabulous gazebo made out of palm trees that looks out to Lake Qarun. The stonewalled rooms are simple with stylish palm wood furniture. They're not as nice as the more expensive options in Tunis Village, but the lodge is a good pick for budget travelers. Price includes breakfast.

★ KOM EL-DIKKA AGRI LODGE

Tunis Village; tel. 0122 244 0012; reservations@komeldikka.com; 1,300LE d

This little patch of paradise doubles as an orchard with orange and olive trees alongside gardens full of herbs and vegetables that you can pick for dinner. A small pool surrounded by palm trees and visiting birds looks out onto Lake Qarun, and a fire pit lights up the cool evenings. Rooms are pristine and match their bucolic setting—some with stone walls and vaulted ceilings, others decorated in a tasteful sand color with cyan accents, and most with fireplaces. You can opt to stay on the ground floor with garden or the upper floor with balcony and lake view. Kom el-Dikka offers the widest range of activities of all accommodations in Fayoum, from fishing in their fish farms to horseback riding, bird-watching, and learning how to compost (all of which you can enjoy for a small fee whether or not you're a guest). They also organize rowboat rides and kayaking on Lake Qarun at a small cost for visitors who stay at their lodge or eat at their restaurant. Delicious breakfast included.

★ DAR KHAN

Tunis Village; tel. 0101 321 0070; 1,600LE d

This little garden retreat with bougainvillea-draped archways is perfect for those in search of privacy. Much smaller than the other lodges here, Dar Khan only has two suites, separated into an East Wing and a West Wing. The East Wing (with two bedrooms and three beds) is the best option for groups of three to four, or those who favor rustic stone walls, decorative windows, and a private balcony. The West Wing (with one bedroom, one bed, and a living room with two couches) is more suitable for two, but can accommodate up to four. Both are tastefully designed with domed ceilings, mashrabiya furniture, and their own full kitchens. Both wings share an inviting pool, fire pit, and rooftop seating area with great views of Lake Qarun. The host prefers booking through Airbnb.

LAZIB INN RESORT AND SPA

Tunis Village; tel. 084 282 0000; https://lazibinn.com; 3,650LE d

Lovers of luxury will find themselves at home here. This exclusive lodge offers 14 spacious suites for double occupancy, all with colorful interiors—peaches, teals, tangerines, deep blues—and eccentric accents alongside wood-burning fireplaces and large Jacuzzis. Upgrade for a terrace, or enjoy the views from the immaculately kept gardens with two small infinity pools (heated in the cooler months) that look out onto Lake Qarun. A (very) small gym, pool table room, and spa with masseuse are also available. Price includes breakfast.

Lake Qarun

MANGROVE CAMP FAYOUM

Immediately west of Lake Qarun, off Qarun Lake Touristic Rd.; tel. 0101 062 0220; 650LE d

This idyllic spot on the edge of the desert (11 km/7 mi northwest of Tunis Village) is a great option for camping lovers who prefer some protection from the elements. Visitors sleep in basic tents but have access to restrooms, showers, fresh food, and a pleasantly shaded reception building with Arabic-style seating. If you prefer an all-inclusive package (breakfast, lunch, dinner), the price is 550LE per person per night. The camp's owner, Waleed, started as a driver/guide and can also take you out on excellent desert safaris to Wadi el-Rayan or North of Lake Qarun (1,400LE for the day, 1-6 people).

HELNAN AUBERGE

Southeast side of Lake Qarun; tel. 084 698 1200; http://helnan.com; 1,650LE d

An opulent reception with marble floors and chandeliers welcomes visitors to King Farouk's former hunting lodge, built in the 1930s. Its expansive grassy grounds with well-manicured hedges and a large swimming pool are perched directly on the edge of Lake Qarun. Additional rooms have been built around the original lodge, with the more expensive ones considerably better than the standards. The nicer rooms are decorated in baroque style with draping curtains and ornate mirrors. This is a good choice for visitors who prefer a traditional hotel feel in contrast to the boutique lodges of Tunis Village. Nonsmokers might take issue with the liberal smoking rules in closed areas. Price includes breakfast buffet and dinner.

INFORMATION AND SERVICES

Visitor Information

FAYOUM TOURISM AUTHORITY

Beside Helnan Auberge on the southeast shore of Lake Qarun; tel. 084 634 2313; http://visitfayoum.net; 8:30am-3pm daily (but inconsistent)

The local tourism authority is not worth a special trip, but you'll pass it en route to Tunis Village and can pop in to pick up some maps and brochures.

ATMs

There's only one lone ATM in Tunis Village. Bring some cash with you just in case it fails. In an emergency, there are plenty of ATMs in Fayoum City and a handful in the neighboring village of Ibshawy, but these are a good distance from Tunis Village (1.5 hours and 40 minutes, respectively). If you're in a bind, ask your hotel to arrange private transportation to the nearest ATM.

GETTING THERE AND AROUND

By far the quickest and easiest way to get to Fayoum is to hire a private car. A regular car can get you to Tunis Village and inside parts of Wadi el-Rayan Protected Area, but it can't take you to the most interesting spots in the park. To journey into the desert, you'll need a 4WD and expert driver.

Private Car Hire

Rates for a private car from Cairo are around 1,200-1,800LE round trip in four-seater car. For a safe and reliable driver, call or WhatsApp **Talaat Fikry** (tel. 0100 246 5020) from Tunis Village who can also take you out on a great desert safari trip. **Moamen Khedr** (tel. 0122 362 3032; moamen_lancer@yahoo.com) is another excellent choice. Without traffic the ride from Cairo to Tunis Village takes around 2 hours.

Your hotel can arrange a private car to take you around Fayoum's ancient sites, or get in touch with **Talaat Fikry** (tel. 0100 246 5020) for what will likely be a much more reasonable price.

Microbus

Microbuses leave all day from **Midan el-Ramaya** near the Giza Pyramids and **Midan Ramses** near Ramses Station (2 hours; 20LE). Unfortunately, there are no direct microbuses to Tunis Village, but if you get off in the village of Ibshaway you can hop in an arabaya sandouk (box car) heading to Mafarek Qarun that will pass in front of Tunis Village (5-10LE). This is only recommended for the adventurous for whom comfort is not important (it's literally a large box on the back of a pickup truck). You can also arrange for your hotel to pick you up in Ibshawy for an extra cost. This route will add around 40 minutes to the trip, and needless to say is much more work that just getting a private car from Cairo. If you're staying at the Helnan Auberge Hotel on Lake Qarun, the microbus should pass directly in front of it and can drop you off along the way. Be sure to tell the driver in advance.

4WD Vehicle

For a trip into the desert, contact: **Talaat Fikry** (tel. 0100 246 5020), **Etman Aboud** (tel. 0100 133 3781), or **Waleed Fekry** (tel. 0100 469 9359). Their English is a bit shaky, meaning the best way to reach them is via WhatsApp message. Your hotel will also be able to arrange a trip.

Microbus and Box Cars (Arabaya Sandouk)

The most common form of transportation between Fayoum's villages are microbuses or pickup trucks with enclosed benches in the back known as box cars (arabaya sandouk). The latter do have windows, but are not recommended for the claustrophobic. Either option should only cost around 5LE.

Bike

The most convenient way to get around the little town of Tunis Village is on foot or by bike. **Kom el-Dikka Agri Lodge** in Tunis Village can organize mountain bike rentals for a nearby 2-kilometer (1-mi) trail (30LE/hour). If you just want a bike to cycle around Tunis, call **Tunis Bike** (tel. 0102 797 7789) and they'll deliver you one (50LE/hour).

Northern Nile Valley

The Northern Nile Valley has some of the most fertile land in the country, appearing from space as a thick ribbon of green before tapering off in the south, where it's hemmed in by encroaching mountains. Since antiquity the region has been an important agricultural hub, with wheat and barley grown here for millennia, later joined by more modern crops like sugarcane and the famous Egyptian cotton.

Before King Menes unified the country for the first time (c. 3000 BC), Upper and Lower Egypt were governed as distinct kingdoms. At various points throughout history the two lands split again, but for most of the next 5,000 years unification prevailed. While Greater Cairo technically serves as the boundary between Upper and Lower

Highlights

Look for ★ to find recommended sights, activities, dining, and lodging.

★ **Beni Hasan:** Admire beautiful wall paintings in these 4,000-year-old rock-cut tombs (page 141).

★ **Tell el-Amarna:** Explore the ruins and rock-cut tombs that remain from heretic king Akhenaten's radical capital city (page 143).

★ **Sohag National Museum:** At this well-curated museum, view superb statues, busts, and everyday items from antiquity that were excavated in the area (page 151).

★ **Red Monastery:** View Egypt's most impressive paintings from the Early Byzantine era inside this beautifully restored monastery church dating to around AD 500 (page 152).

★ **Abydos Temple Complex:** The raised reliefs in the Temple of Seti I in Abydos are some of the finest in all of Egypt. His son, Ramses II, built another "mansion of millions of years" next door (page 156).

★ **Dendera Temple Complex:** Hathor's Temple at Dendera is one of the most splendid in all of Egypt, with polychrome ceilings and magnificent columns topped with the sky goddess's head (page 158).

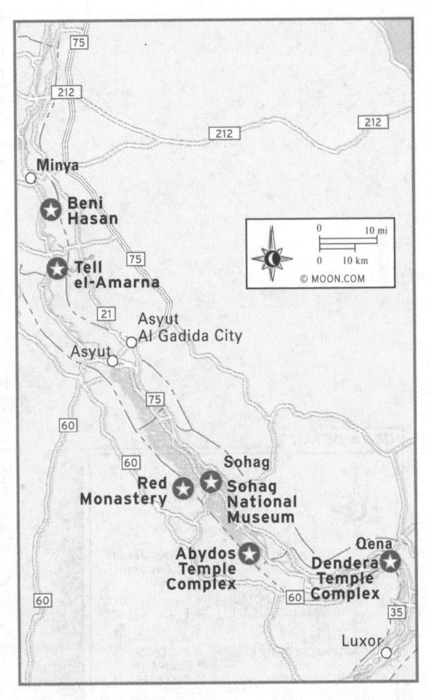

Northern Nile Valley

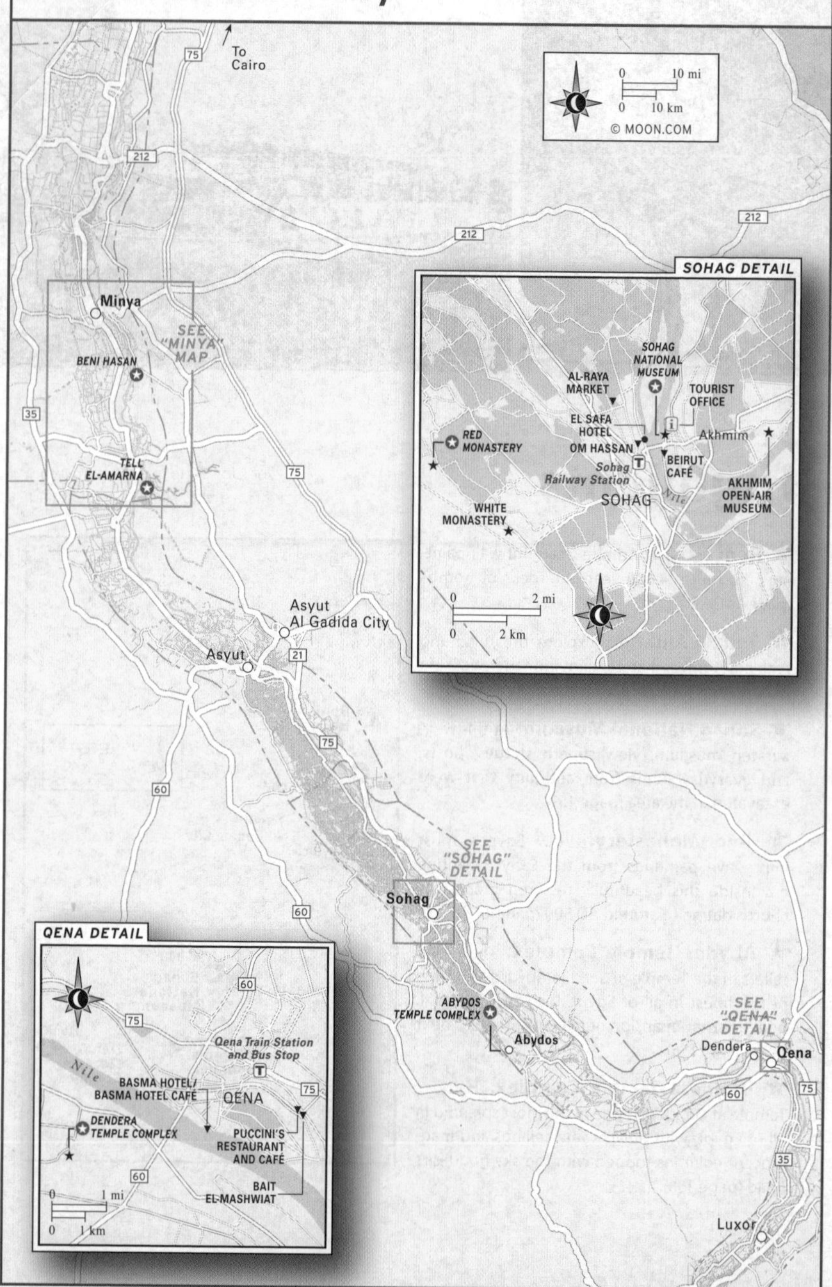

Egypt, beautiful Minya marks the start of the cultural divide—linking the two regions and earning the governorate the name "Bride of Upper Egypt." Scattered throughout modern-day Minya are fascinating relics from its ancient province, with additional off-the-beaten-track treats along the rest of the Valley.

Visitors to Egypt who come for just a week or two might skip this section of the Nile to spend more time in Cairo, Giza, and Luxor—each of which is far more densely packed with sights. But true Egyptology lovers or those looking to see a different side of country will delight in these hidden treasures.

PLANNING YOUR TIME

The city of **Minya,** 280 kilometers (175 mi) south of Cairo, is a great base for exploring the surrounding governorate. **Beni Hasan** is an easy day trip from central Minya (40-minute drive) and often combined with a visit to **Tell el-Amarna** (another 50 minutes south of Beni Hasan). A second common excursion from central Minya is to the area around the towns of el-Ashmunein and Mallawi (including the **El-Ashmunein Open-Air Museum, Tuna el-Gebel,** and **Mallawi Museum** in that order). The drive to el-Ashmunein should take a little over an hour, with Tuna el-Gebel 20 minutes to the southwest, and the Mallawi Museum another 20-30 minutes east of there. If you're short on time, you can even journey to one of these two groups of attractions as a day trip from Cairo, though it would be a *loong* day. Visitors to these lesser-known archeological sites will benefit from bringing an expert guide along to explain their many cryptic symbols.

The sights in **Sohag** can easily be seen in a day, with the best accommodation option a bit to the south in Abydos. **Abydos** and **Qena** can be combined in a day trip from Luxor, or spread out with a night or two in either city.

TOURS AND LOCAL GUIDES

REAL EGYPT TOURS

tel. 0110 002 2242; www.realegypt.com

Real Egypt Tours can arrange for excellent guides and transportation to the many archeological sites around the Northern Nile Valley. A private two-day package from Cairo to Minya's main sites (Beni Hasan, Tell el-Amarna, Tuna el-Gebel) and back costs $430 per person including transportation, tour guide, food, accommodation, and entry fees. For a four-day trip covering the whole Northern Nile Valley between Cairo and Luxor (Minya's main sites, plus Abydos and Dendera), the price for a private party of two will be around $980 per person all-inclusive.

They also offer a great a package to visit **Abydos** and **Qena** from Luxor on a long day trip (11-12 hours). This excursion (including transportation, expert guide, lunch, and entrance fees) comes to around $330 total for two people.

SECURITY

Armed police officers will likely accompany you around Minya's archeological sites and possibly in the city itself. They'll be in clearly marked police uniforms and will typically greet you at your hotel (though don't expect them to speak much English). While they can look intimidating, they escort tourists out of an abundance of caution. There have been no cases of violence against tourists in Minya, but the governorate has seen a number of attacks against Coptic Christians over the years. Security has since been upped around the region, and there's little reason to worry during your travels. But as always, check your government's travel advice before visiting.

Previous: Hathor Temple at Dendera Temple Complex; depiction of Horus at Dendera Temple Complex; dahabiya operated by Real Egypt Tours.

Itinerary Ideas

AROUND MINYA IN ONE DAY

Base yourself in Minya Town—pretty much your only option!—for this itinerary, and hire a driver in advance for a trip around the governorate. A guide would be a helpful addition.

1 Enjoy your hotel's complimentary breakfast before journeying to **Beni Hasan's** cliff-side tombs and temple with a private car hire (40 minutes; 28 km/17 mi).

2 Continue with your driver to **Tell el-Amarna** (55 minutes; 57 km/35 mi) to explore the tombs and city ruins of Akhenaten's revolutionary capital.

3 On your way back to Minya, stop off in the town of Mallawi for a hearty Egyptian lunch at **Tarbush Restaurant and Café** (30 minutes; 17 km/10.5 mi).

4 Walk two blocks west to check out artifacts uncovered from around Minya at the **Mallawi Museum.**

5 Hop back in the car and make a short detour through **el-Ashmunein** to visit the **Open-Air Museum** (25 minutes; 10 km/6 mi).

6 Return to central Minya (50 minutes; 38 km/24 mi) for a dinner of grilled meats or vegetable stews, fresh bread, and rice at **Orkeed Restaurant and Café.**

ABYDOS AND DENDERA IN ONE DAY

From your base in **Luxor,** organize a day trip with a driver or tour operator a few days in advance.

1 Meet your driver at your Luxor hotel around 7am before heading to the **Dendera Temple Complex** to visit the striking Temple of Hathor and its neighbors (2 hours; 80 km/50 mi).

2 Head over the bridge into central Qena for a traditional Egyptian lunch at **Bait el-Mashwiat** (15 minutes; 8 km/5 mi).

3 Continue your journey along a desert road to the **Abydos Temple Complex** (1.5 hours; 100 km/62 mi) to explore the mortuary temples of Seti I and his son, Ramses II.

4 Walk down the street to the House of Life Abydos Hotel for a fresh dinner of local fare at their **Panorama Restaurant.**

5 Return to your **Luxor** hotel (3 hours; 180 km/110 mi) to unwind after a long day.

Minya Town

Central Minya extends just a few miles along the West Bank of the Nile, hugged by emerald green fields and small clusters of palms. To the east, sand-colored mountains form a natural wall—hung with big block letters of "El-Minya" à la the Hollywood Sign—separating the harsh desert from the river's life-giving reach.

The city gets its name from the ancient town of Menat Khufu, ancient Egyptian for "Nursing City of Khufu"—the 25th-century BC builder of the Great Pyramid of Giza whose family originated here. Today it's the capital of the eponymous governorate with a population of around 6 million and rich agricultural land, producing cotton, wheat, and sugarcane. Around half the population here is Coptic Christian (compared to the national tally of about 10 percent), reflected in the dozens of churches that spot the city map. Though there aren't many sights to see in central Minya, its wide boulevards, green islands, and mountainous boundaries make it a beautiful city and great base for exploring the ancient treasures around the governorate.

ORIENTATION

Minya's main thoroughfares are easy to spot. **Corniche Street** follows the Nile on the West Bank and **Taha Hussein Street** runs parallel one street over. Both have a wealth of restaurants, cafés, and shops. The **Nile Bridge** (Kobri el-Nil) brings you to the less-populated East Bank, where the pyramid-shaped **Akhenaten Museum** dominates the skyscape.

SIGHTS

The Corniche

Corniche St., West Bank; no tel.; 24 hours daily; free

A stroll down this wide tree-lined promenade offers brilliant views of the lush river islands and the East Bank's imposing bluffs. It's a favorite picnic spot for locals, who set up camp on benches or blankets beneath the flame-red leaves of royal poincianas. The best section to walk starts near the intersection of

the Akhenaten Museum in Minya

Minya

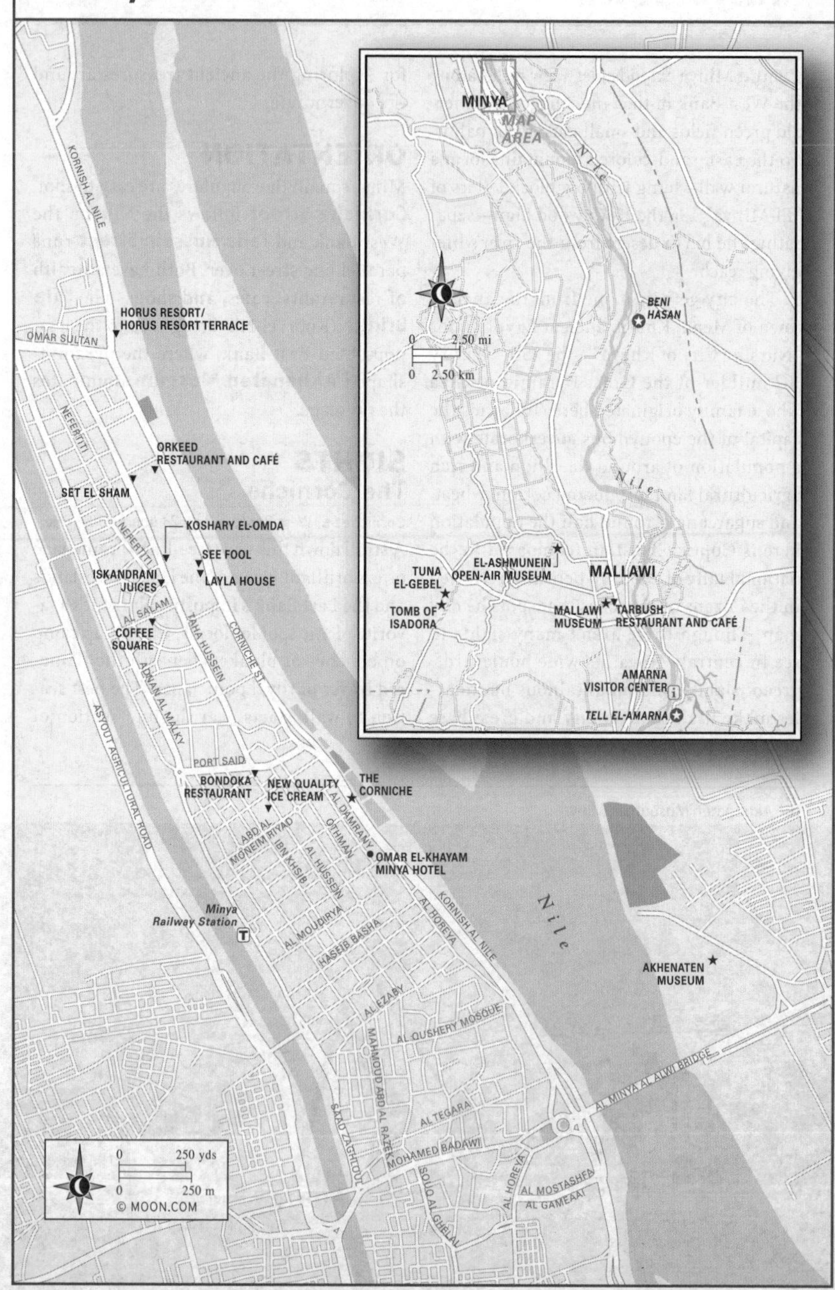
MINYA
MAP AREA
Nile
BENI HASAN
0 2.50 mi
0 2.50 km
EL-ASHMUNEIN OPEN-AIR MUSEUM
TUNA EL-GEBEL
TOMB OF ISADORA
MALLAWI
MALLAWI MUSEUM
TARBUSH RESTAURANT AND CAFÉ
AMARNA VISITOR CENTER
TELL EL-AMARNA
KORNISH AL NILE
HORUS RESORT/ HORUS RESORT TERRACE
OMAR SULTAN
NEFERTITI
ORKEED RESTAURANT AND CAFÉ
SET EL SHAM
KOSHARY EL-OMDA
SEE FOOL
LAYLA HOUSE
ISKANDRANI JUICES
AL SALAM
COFFEE SQUARE
TAHA HUSSEIN
CORNICHE ST.
ADNAN AL MALKY
ASYOUT AGRICULTURAL ROAD
PORT SAID
BONDOKA RESTAURANT
NEW QUALITY ICE CREAM
THE CORNICHE
ABD AL MONEIM RIYAD
IBN KHSIB
AL HUSSEIN
OTHMAN
AL DAMRANY
OMAR EL-KHAYAM MINYA HOTEL
Minya Railway Station
AL MOUDIRYA
HASEIB BASHA
AL HOREYA
AKHENATEN MUSEUM
AL EZARY
AL QUSHERY MOSQUE
MAHMOUD ABD AL RAZEK
AL MINYA AL ALWI BRIDGE
SAAD ZAGHLOUL
AL TEGARA
MOHAMED BADAWI
SOUQ AL GHELAL
AL MOSTASHFA
AL GAMEAAI
0 250 yds
0 250 m
© MOON.COM

Corniche Street and el-Gamhoria Street and continues north for about a mile.

Akhenaten Museum

Sawadah, East Bank, just north of Minya-Assiut Rd.; no tel.

This modern pyramid has been a defining landmark in Minya since the early 2000s, but after years of start-and-stop progress, the work will likely take longer to complete than the Great Pyramid of Giza itself. The massive museum is expected to be a must-see attraction when it finally opens (scheduled for the end of 2022). The main collection includes artifacts from the radical period of Akhenaten's 17-year reign—with items depicting the revolutionary art of his time, known as Amarna style after his new capital in Tell el-Amarna (60 km/40 mi south of the museum).

RECREATION AND ACTIVITIES

Boating

Pick up a colorful motorboat on Corniche Street for a ride up and down Minya's pretty strip of the Nile. Should cost around 60LE per hour.

FOOD

For a filling takeaway lunch to bring with you on a day trip to the "Vicinity of Minya" destinations, pick up some fuul and ta'maya sandwiches from See Fool.

Egyptian

SEE FOOL

Corniche St., next to Minya Sports Club; tel. 086 2324999; 24 hours daily; 15-30LE mains

Grab some fuul and ta'maya from this clean and trusted food stand near the Nile. Do the like locals and take it across the street for a picnic on the Corniche. Other specialties include baba ghanoush and fried cheese (gibna ma'laya).

KOSHARY EL-OMDA

Taha Hussein St., next to Minya Sports Club; tel. 0102 193 6665; 24 hours daily; 15-40LE mains

If you're craving that classic Egyptian dish of pasta, lentils, chickpeas, fried onions, and special sauces, this modest diner has the best koshary in town. As with most legit koshary joints, there's little else on the menu, but you can get similar plates with added meat or a different type of noodle. Be prepared for crowds, especially in the evenings.

★ LAYLA HOUSE

Corniche St.; tel. 0109 477 1188; 10am-midnight daily; 45-100LE mains

The rooftop terrace at Layla House (Beit Layla) offers fabulous views of the Nile and a refreshing breeze. Both Egyptian and international dishes—burgers, pizzas, sandwiches, etc.—are served (go for the Egyptian). A wide selection of shakes and fresh juices also on offer.

BONDOKA RESTAURANT

Port Saeed St. near the south end of Taha Hussein St.; tel. 086 2334141; 9am-midnight daily; 50-100LE mains

Specializing in grilled chicken and meats, Bondoka has a couple of branches around town to cater to its crowds. Most come for the succulent meat dishes, but they also offer a wide array of Egyptian and Syrian treats. Some seats offer a special view of the mountains in the distance and wide boulevard below. The other branch is located on Taha Hussein Street, next to Minya Sports Club (same hours and prices).

★ ORKEED RESTAURANT AND CAFÉ

Corniche St., next to the Engineers' Syndicate; tel. 0100 023 9239; 2pm-midnight daily; 50-150LE mains

For good food with a view of the palm-lined Nile and distant mountains, Orkeed is the place to go. They offer all your favorite Egyptian dishes, like grilled meats, molokhia (a soupy green), and mahshi (stuffed vegetables).

Middle Eastern

SET EL SHAM

Taha Hussein St., near intersection with Street 18; tel. 0106 060 1600; 11am-2am Sat.-Thurs., 1pm-3am Fri.; 30-60LE mains

This Syrian fast-food spot does a great shawarma in saj bread (akin to a big tortilla), usually accompanied by crispy fries, deliciously seasoned rice, and makhalal (pickled vegetables). Enjoy your feast in the bright interior or take it down the street for a picnic on the Corniche.

Cafés and Snacks

ISKANDRANI JUICES

Taha Hussein St. and Nasser Square; tel. 0100 253 6588; 10am-11:30pm daily; 10-30LE juices

Seasonal fruits double as decoration at this no-frills juice bar. Sample the region's famous sugarcane juice (asab el-sukkar)—with its subtly sweet, flora taste and frothy top layer—or other classics like mango, fresh-squeezed orange, or banana and milk. No seating available, so just sip while standing or take it across the street to the benches on the Corniche.

★ COFFEE SQUARE

Al-Salami St., behind the Minya Cultural Palace; tel. 0102 929 2199; 8am-3am daily; 15-35LE drinks

For the best coffee in Minya, head to this industrial chic café. You can sip on the espresso-based drink of your choice under naked bulbs, gilded ventilation ducts, and hanging gardens. Juice and pastries also served.

NEW QUALITY ICE CREAM

El-Houseny St., near intersection with El-Mahakma St.; tel. 0122 533 4418; 11am-2am Mon.-Sat.; 10-40LE ice cream and desserts

Indulge in an ice cream brownie sandwich, chocolate-covered waffle, or just your favorite ice cream flavor at this blindingly bright dessert shop. It's a popular outing destination for families and teens.

BARS AND NIGHTLIFE

Minya is a near-dry city, so if a nightcap is important to you, be sure to bring your own supply.

★ HORUS RESORT TERRACE

At Horus Resort, Corniche St., near intersection with Omar Sultan St.; tel. 0128 221 1141; 8am-11pm daily; 30-60LE hot drinks and beer

If you're in search of a cold beer on the riverside, the terrace café/bar at the Horus Resort is a rare supplier. The view and breeze are unbeatable.

ACCOMMODATIONS

HORUS RESORT

Corniche St., near intersection with Omar Sultan St.; tel. 0128 221 1141; 1,000LE d

Aside from the garish patterns in some of the rooms, the Horus Resort offers a comfortable stay. It's recently received a much-needed facelift, and excellent staff keep the place clean. The large pool beside the Nile is a nice place to sit, though ladies might not feel comfortable in even modest swimwear, and the space is a popular venue for local weddings—a pro or a con depending on how much you value cultural exposure over quiet. Their riverside terrace is one of the few places in town you can find a cold beer. Call to reserve (management hasn't quite figured out email yet).

★ OMAR EL-KHAYAM MINYA HOTEL

3 Damarani St., Downtown; tel. 086 2365666; reservation@okhhotel.com; 1,100LE d

This hotel may not have the Nile-side location of its competitors, but you won't find cleaner, more comfortable rooms in Minya. Added features include a flatscreen TV with Netflix, thoughtful welcome platter, and complimentary breakfast. Management is responsive, and the super helpful staff can help arrange trips to sights around Minya at fair prices.

INFORMATION AND SERVICES

Tourist Office

Corniche St., near intersection with Abdel Minam St.; tel. 086 2372026; 9am-3:30pm Sat.-Thurs.

Located one block south of the Minya Public Library, this unassuming building houses a friendly staff that can help you find a private car or taxi to the sights around the governorate.

ATMs

There are plenty of ATMs around Minya, particularly near the intersection of Corniche Street and el-Gomhoria Street and north along Corniche Street.

Pharmacies

Abdeen Pharmacy (El-Gomhoraya St., near Bahary Club; tel. 19036; 24 hours daily) is a reputable nationwide chain that offers 24/7 delivery.

GETTING THERE

Both train and bus are comfortable options for travel between Cairo and Minya, with about the same prices and trip times. If you take the train, choose the first class "Special Service OD" for the nicest and fastest ride. If you opt for the bus, take the Go Bus "Elite Plus."

Train

Over a dozen trains leave each day for Minya from **Cairo's Ramses Station** (5 hours; 140LE). The **Minya Railway Station** (no tel.; 24 hours daily) is located on Mahatta Square in central Minya.

From Minya, multiple trains leave daily to Cairo, Sohag, and Luxor. Check the Egyptian National Railways website for schedule (www.enr.gov.eg). You can reserve online (when the website's feature is working) or in the station.

Bus

Go Bus (tel. 19567; www.go-bus.com; 5 hours; 120LE) offers several daily trips to Minya, leaving Downtown Cairo from their station at **Abdel Minam Riyad Square,** next to the Ramses Hilton.

The **Upper East Bus Company** also runs a number of daily trips (5-6 hours; 80LE) from Cairo's **Torgoman Station** (Boulaq 2, off al-Sahafa St., near Downtown; no tel.; 24 hours daily).

GETTING AROUND

Central Minya is a very walkable city with plenty of taxis. As always, be sure to agree on a price before you hop in. To get most anywhere in downtown should only be around 10-20LE.

Vicinity of Minya

Stretching some 130 kilometers (80 mi) along the Nile, the Minya governorate is home to a handful of important archeological sites that now lie between the desert and small agricultural villages. All are best visited as day trips with packed lunches from central Minya (the governorate's capital) as there are scant choices for places to eat or sleep.

The wealth of sights means at least two days are needed to see them all, with trips to **Beni Hasan** and **Tell el-Amarna** often combined, and another day reserved for the **El-Ashmunein Open-Air Museum, Tuna el-Gebel,** and **Mallawi Museum.** Ambitious travelers may be able to see them all in one long day with an early start.

★ BENI HASAN

25 km/16 mi south of central Minya, East Bank; 8am-4pm daily; 60LE adults, 30LE students

The ancient cemetery of Beni Hasan, carved into a limestone cliffside, boasts over three dozen rock-cut tombs of note. Most served as resting places for governors of the Oryx province, which extended alongside this necropolis, dating to the 11th and 12th Dynasties

Day Trips from Central Minya

Hiring a private car either through a tour agency or your Minya hotel is the easiest option for exploring the Minya governorate's archaeological sites.

- Visitors who stay at the **Omar el-Khayam Minya Hotel** can take advantage of their private transportation to Beni Hasan and Tell el-Amarna, or to El-Ashmunein, Tuna el-Gebel, and Mallawi Museum (each trip 8 hours; 800LE for car that holds up to 3 people or 1,100LE for minibus up to 8).
- If you prefer to hire a **taxi** yourself, you should find plenty in central Minya. Round-trip excursions to Beni Hasan and Tell el-Amarna, or to El-Ashmunein, Tuna el-Gebel, and Mallawi Museum should be in the range of 650-800LE including wait time. Be sure to agree on a price and exact destinations to be visited ahead of time.

(c. 2125-1795 BC). Only the four listed below are typically open to the public, but the striking wall paintings inside them are worth the trip. Here you'll also encounter some of the best depictions of the popular ancient Egyptian sport of wrestling. Like the other scenes of daily life painted on the walls—among them hunting, music, and dance—the images ensured the tomb owner would be entertained in the afterlife.

The splendor of these tombs for high officials was the product of a unique moment in history, when regional leaders commanded considerable wealth and power. This status gradually diminished during the centralization of the 19th century BC, which depleted the powers of local governors—a development reflected in the less remarkable tombs of later high officials.

Many of the structures here follow a similar plan with an outer court, a pillared chamber, and a niche for the deceased's statue. Hundreds of earlier, less impressive tombs (some more than 4,300 years old) sit on the lower levels and are not accessible.

The ascent up the 100-plus steps on the desert hillside to reach the four open tombs (located just a few meters apart from each other) may be difficult for some, but views of the emerald-green Nile Valley below are almost enough reason for the visit alone. Refreshments and WCs are available at the **Rest House** near the entrance, but be sure to bring water in case it's closed.

TOMB OF AMENEMHAT (NO. 2)

This spacious tomb of a provincial governor holds beautiful wrestling scenes toward the back near the shrine. Other colorful characters can be found in the main four-pillared hall to the left, where an industrious crew of carpenters, potters, farmers, and goldsmiths perform their crafts.

TOMB OF KHNUMHOTEP II (NO. 3)

Overseer of the priests and of the Eastern Desert, Khnumhotep II covered the base of his tomb walls with autobiographical texts applauding his own successes. His tomb also holds a scene so unique it's known by archeologists as "the Beni Hasan painting"—depicting a caravan of Asiatic traders in vibrant garments (to the left in the main hall). The image likely reflects the waves of foreigners who came from the northeast around this time, thought to have been fleeing famine. Keep an eye out for other colorful scenes (particularly on the far-back wall surrounding the shrine), like the tomb's patron catching ducks in a net (above the shrine), and on a papyrus boat hunting birds (left) and spear fishing (right). The hieroglyphics on the frame around the shrine instruct visitors how to make offerings to the departed.

TOMB OF BAQET III (NO. 15)

Another provincial governor, Baqet III served his tenure during a time of domestic strife and wars abroad—some images of which are depicted around his tomb. The highlight of his décor is a wall full of over 100 wrestling positions. Other scenes show activities of daily life, like female acrobats entertaining the governor and his wife (to the left) and farmers, potters, and metalworkers (to the right).

TOMB OF KHETI (NO. 17)

Kheti inherited the post of governor from his father Baqet III along with, it seems, his passion for wrestling. An entire wall in the main hall is covered with a similar manual of the sport's techniques. Other scenes depict daily work (hunting, winemaking) and entertainment (music, dance).

Speos Artemidos

Around 1.5 kilometers (1 mi) south of the tombs in an ancient quarry, Pharaoh Queen Hatshepsut (r. 1479-1457 BC) built a rock-cut temple for the lion-headed goddess Pakhet ("She Who Scratches"). On the façade of the temple a long, faintly visible text decries the damage done by the invading foreign rulers—the Hyksos, who were expelled by her great-grandfather (c. 1550 BC), and praises her work in restoring order: "I never slumbered as one forgetful, but have made strong what was decayed." Inside, a wide chamber—originally with eight columns topped by capitals in the shape of Hathor's head (goddess of the sky)—leads to a smaller inner sanctuary, where a statue of Pakhet once sat. Paintings of Hatshepsut and her favorite deities cover parts of the walls, but Seti I (c.1290-1279 BC) later usurped the space, adding his own cartouche over her work. In the Late Period (747-332 BC) several sacred cats were buried around the temple. The shrine is locally known as Istabl 'Antar (in Arabic, Stable of 'Antar—a 6th-century Arab poet-warrior later dramatized in epic poems).

★ TELL EL-AMARNA

65 km/40 mi south of central Minya, East Bank; 8am-4pm daily; 60LE adults, 30LE students

Son of the long-reigning and prosperous king Amenhotep III, Akhenaten (originally named Amenhotep IV, r. 1353-1335 BC) moved Egypt's capital from Thebes (Luxor) to this spot just a few years into his kingship. The radical pharaoh staged a religious revolution, paring down the pantheon of gods to just one: the Aten, depicted as a sun disc with rays ending in hands.

Akhenaten ("One Who is Effective for the Aten") began his experiment in quasi-monotheism by defacing the names of other gods in the monuments of Thebes, before deciding to build a new cult center altogether. He chose this empty patch of land between the Nile and the cliff-lined desert—where he could see the sun come up over the horizon—and named his new city Akhetaten ("The Horizon of the Sun Disk"). The city grew to a population of 20,000-50,000 people but was inhabited for less than two decades before Akhenaten's son, the famous King Tut, abandoned the monumental project. The child king (encouraged by advisors) changed his name from Tutankhaten to Tutankhamun, restoring Amun as the national god among many.

Akhenaten's successors did their best to erase his memory, leaving little for modern visitors to see compared to the impressive tombs and temples of Luxor. Many of the buildings were taken apart to be used as raw material in other monuments, particularly in nearby Hermopolis, modern el-Ashmunein (Ramses II was a notorious re-appropriator of Akhenaten's city blocks). But Tell el-Amarna remains the best existing example of an Egyptian settlement from the New Kingdom (c. 1539-1075 BC), ancient Egypt's golden age. Many notable relics have also been found here, like the iconic bust of Queen Nefertiti (now in Berlin), excavated by a German archeologist in 1912 from the studio of an ancient sculptor.

Orientation

The **Amarna Visitor Center** (8am-4pm daily) is an excellent place to start your excursion to Akhenaten's capital. From here, head to the **Ticket Office** on the road to the North Tombs to purchase tickets to the monuments. You'll find another restroom, drinks, snacks, and trinkets at the **Rest House** (in front of Ticket Office, though not always open). Following the road east from the Ticket Office, you'll come upon the **North Tombs.** From here you can take a short detour (to the north) to check out the **North Palace.** Head back the way you came 2.5 kilometers (1.5 mi) past the tombs before turning left (about 6 km/4 mi) down a valley to Akhenaten's **Royal Tomb.** To reach the ruins of the **Central City,** return in the direction of the Visitor Center and head south for around 1 kilometer (0.6 mi). Another few kilometers south and 2.5 kilometers (1.5 mi) southeast will bring you to the **South Tombs.**

Planning Your Visit

A car is needed to visit this sprawling site, but even with transportation be prepared for a bit of trekking to reach the tombs. It's best to bring a packed lunch, plenty of water, sun protection, and a flashlight for the dim tomb interiors.

Depending on how many attractions you're keen to see, expect to spend 4-6 hours here. More interesting than the Central City ruins themselves is the surrounding necropolis, which includes two clusters of rock-cut tombs built for high officials (the North Tombs and the South Tombs), and the Royal Tomb for Akhenaten and his family.

For the authoritative source on all things Tell el-Amarna, check out the **Amarna Project** (www.amarnaproject.com)—the joint European-Egyptian effort to preserve the ancient capital and its art—before you visit.

1: Boundary Stela at Tuna el-Gebel **2:** Tomb of Isadora at Tuna el-Gebel **3:** view to the Nile river from Beni Hasan

Visitor Center

Located in a shiny new building on the Nile just north of Akhenaten's Central City ruins, the quasi-museum holds models of reimagined buildings, burial chambers, and landscaping that show how archeologists think the radical king's capital once looked. A full-sized reconstruction of a high official's house is another neat feature. The center also offers useful maps and brochures, both of which are particularly helpful for navigating the Central City, and WCs.

North Tombs

Carved into a cliffside up a sandy hill, these "houses of eternity" for Amarna high officials offer an interesting look into the stages of tomb construction and decoration. Most follow the same design (with a façade, two chambers, and a shrine), and remain unfinished due to the untimely end of the city after Akhenaten's death. Over a thousand years later, Christian monks recycled these ancient resting places as their living quarters. The tombs are close together and not very big, so all can easily be visited in under an hour.

TOMB OF HUYA (NO. 1)

Huya held a position of immense trust in the royal court as steward of Queen Tiye (Akhenaten's mother) as well as the overseer of the royal harem and treasuries. His tomb shows a handful of interesting images, beginning with (as you walk into the first chamber) Huya depicted in prayer with texts praising the sun god, Aten.

Inside the first chamber, the images to the right and left (perpendicular to the entrance) depict royal banquets where Huya serves Queen Tiye, Akhenaten, Nefertiti, and their daughters. On the wall to the far right is a scene of Queen Tiye with Akhenaten at an Amarna temple, worshiping Aten. Huya appears again, bowing in front of the royal pair. The opposite wall illustrates a sumptuous reception of tribute from Syria and Kush. In the rest of the scenes, Huya receives rewards from the royal family for his services or carries out his duties. The second chamber was left undecorated, but holds the shaft leading down to Huya's burial chamber, and gives way to the shrine, with images of Huya's mummified body, his things for the afterlife, and mourning relatives.

TOMB OF MERYRA II (NO. 2)

Just beside the Tomb of Huya lies that of his counterpart in Nefertiti's household. Like Huya, Meryra II also served as steward of the queen and overseer of the harem and treasuries, with the added job of royal scribe.

In the first chamber to the right, Akhenaten, Nefertiti, and their daughters reward Meryra with a gold collar for his loyalty. On the perpendicular wall, the same event of foreign tribute depicted in Huya's tomb appears again in greater detail. Can you spot the pet gazelle held by one of the princesses? The wrestling Egyptian soldiers?

Both the second chamber and shrine were left undecorated, but in some places the walls have been smoothed in preparation for painting.

TOMB OF AHMES (NO. 3)

An indispensable member of Akhenaten's court, Ahmes served as scribe, steward of the King's estate, and fan-bearer "on the King's right hand." His tomb isn't as colorful as others, but visitors will find interesting examples of ink outlines that were never filled in. In the entrance, keep an eye out for Ahmes adoring the king with a fan over his shoulder. On the left wall near the top in the first chamber you can see representations of how the Great Temple once looked. Akhenaten and Nefertiti stand in the courtyard and musicians play in front of the temple. Dozens of Greek graffiti, likely made by mercenaries during the Ptolemaic Period (305-30 BC), can be found carved into the walls around the tomb. To the right of the entrance just outside, one Greek visitor commemorated his climb to the tomb, writing: "Having ascended here, Catullinus has engraved this in the doorway, marveling at the art of the holy quarriers."

TOMB OF MERYRA (NO. 4)

High priest of Aten (and another fan-bearer on the King's right side), Meryra built himself one of the largest tombs in the necropolis. In the entrance and antechamber, Meryra prays to Aten and Akhenaten in a handful of scenes. In the first chamber—with two of four papyrus stem columns remaining—you can see an image of the King's House on the right wall, and a royal visit to the Central City on the left wall. The second chamber and shrine were both unfinished but offer an interesting glimpse into the work process of the stonemasons.

TOMB OF PENTHU (NO. 5)

Penthu was the chief of physicians, a royal scribe, and head servant of Aten. Plaster once covered his tomb to provide a better surface for decorating than the uneven rock below, but much of it (and its adornments) have crumbled. The most interesting images can be found in the first chamber on the left side where the royal family visits a temple to Aten, and in another scene, rewards Penthu with gold collars for his services. The second chamber is undecorated but holds the 12-meter (40-ft) shaft to the burial chamber.

TOMB OF PANEHSY (NO. 6)

During Coptic times, the first chamber in the Tomb of Panehsy (head servant of Aten in the Temple of Aten) was converted into a church. To the left, Panehsy receives rewards from the royal family, and in a second scene below his own household greets him with pride. On the right side, steps still lead to a burial chamber.

Near the entrance to the second chamber on the left, plaster from the Coptic occupants covers part of the scenes showing Akhenaten and Nefertiti offering gifts to Aten in the presence of Panehsy. The second chamber is mostly bare, but has another set of steps down to a burial chamber and leads to the shrine, where a statue of Panehsy once sat. In the image to the right, he sits with his daughter, sister, and nieces before a table of offerings.

North Palace

Though little remains, this is still one of ancient Egypt's best-preserved palaces. It stands north of the Central City past an ancient suburb, and likely served as a residence of the royal family. Some of the walls have been partially rebuilt to help ignite the imagination. You'll need a guide to really bring the palace to life.

The Royal Tombs

To the east of Akhenaten's new city, the pharaoh started a second Royal Valley to replace the original (Valley of the Kings) in Luxor. Akhenaten's Royal Tomb for him and his family was one of the very few to be built before the city and its necropolis were abandoned. The interior is now almost entirely denuded—its decoration done on a thin layer of plaster, which has since crumbled. But despite the lack of images and colors seen in Luxor's tombs, this cavernous resting place is an interesting visit for its unique sprawling nature with sidecars for various family members.

The tombs were looted in ancient times, though a few objects of interest were saved and sent to museums (including the Egyptian Museum in Cairo), like fragments of Akhenaten's sarcophagus and over 200 figurines of the king (called ushabti figures), that were meant to perform the unkingly tasks demanded by the gods in the afterlife.

FIRST TOMB

Visitors enter the tomb down steep steps (with rails). From there, a sloping corridor brings you to the first snaking tomb—jutting off to the right—likely intended for Queen Nefertiti. This space was never finished nor decorated. With Akhenaten's death the main entrance was likely sealed, leaving Nefertiti with no final resting place until a new tomb could be carved out for her down the road (though she disappeared before death and her ultimate burial place remains a mystery).

MEKETATEN'S TOMB

Returning to the sloping corridor, another tomb sticks out to the right after a few meters at the top of a set of stairs. The decayed images here are the best you'll find in the complex. Originally intended for Akhenaten's eldest daughter, Meritaten, the chambers were usurped by her younger sister, Meketaten, who beat her to the afterlife. In the first, on the walls to the far right and left, the royal family worships Aten as the sun rises and sets, respectively. Immediately after the entrance to the right (perpendicular to the door), Akhenaten and Nefertiti mourn the premature loss of their daughter in a rare scene of intimacy. A similar pockmarked mourning scene with the princess's sisters can be seen in the third chamber on the far-left wall.

AKHENATEN'S BURIAL CHAMBER

Exiting the second chamber back to the steps, you'll descend onto a bridge above a shaft and then into Akhenaten's burial chamber. His sarcophagus once sat in the middle of the floor, protected by images of his beloved Nefertiti instead of the four goddesses as was convention for his polytheistic predecessors. Archeologists believe the pharaoh was likely buried here beside his mother, Queen Tiye—a very uncommon arrangement in ancient Egypt. Today little remains save the plinth where the king's sarcophagus once sat and a crumbling column.

Central City

To some, the remains of Akhetaten's Central City may just look like stones in the sand, but the excavated outlines of some of the city's main features make for a unique urban stroll. A series of 16 short, white, cylindrical markers are scattered around the site to point out features of the ruins. Before you explore, be sure to pick up a map and brochures from the Visitor Center for explanations of each marked area. For advanced planning, you can print them out yourself at www.amarnaproject.com.

Start at the **Small Aten Temple,** identified by its lonely column (reconstructed using modern materials), which once stood among many at the back of the temple inside the sanctuary. Crossing a flat, sandy expanse to the southeast, you'll find a small set of stairs leading to a viewing platform that looks over the remains of a private house, likely owned by a high official. The grounds covered the entire area enclosed by the fence, complete with a well, small chapel, kitchen, cattle shed, and grain silos (the circular marks beside the house). Returning to the Small Aten Temple, the **King's House**—likely a small private palace for Akhenaten—is visible at the bottom of a small hill to the north.

South Tombs

Nineteen tombs pepper the cliffside in this southern cluster of resting places. These funerary projects for Amarna high officials are even less finished than those in the north, but the walk to reach them is easier—making them a fine alternative for those not up to the climb to the North Tombs. You'll be forgiven for not hiking to all (there is a sameness about many), but do try to pop into Tombs No. 8, 9, and 25.

TOMB OF TUTU (NO. 8)

One of Akhenaten's highest officials, Tutu (the king's chief servant and overseer of silver and gold), built a relatively spacious tomb for himself. The first chamber is divided by rows of columns into three strips. The wall to the right (perpendicular to the entrance) depicts Akhenaten at his home appointing Tutu as his chief servant from the "Window of Appearance"—where the royal family appeared to the public. To the left, Tutu is appointed head of tax collection. Nearby steps were cut to lead down to a burial chamber, never completed. The second chamber was also abandoned before it was finished.

TOMB OF MAHU (NO. 9)

The Tomb of Mahu, Akhenaten's chief of police, is far from the grandest of the lot, but it is the most complete of all the southern resting places. Visitors can see the stages of decoration from ink outlines to full reliefs. In the short entrance corridor to the left, Akhenaten, Nefertiti, and their eldest daughter, Meritaten, present offerings to Aten. Below this scene, Akhenaten recites a hymn while Mahu looks on dotingly. In the first chamber to the right, Mahu performs his duties, while to the left, an ink sketch depicts the royal family at the "Window of Appearance" ready to grant Mahu his rewards. The second room lacks decoration but has a snaking staircase down to a burial chamber.

TOMB OF AY (NO. 25)

A decade or so after Akhenaten's death Ay would become king, but before that he served as a fan-bearer of the pharaoh, overseer of his horses, and the enigmatic "God's father." Inside holds one large chamber, originally planned to be much larger with 24 carved columns, only four of which were completed in detail. The wall to the left (perpendicular to the entrance) shows one of the best-preserved reward scenes—the traditional tomb illustration of high officials receiving gifts from the royal family—in all of Amarna. The reliefs also show the interior of the King's House and a neighboring house for female musicians, who are shown playing instruments, eating, and doing hair. In the far-left corner of the chamber, stairs lead down to an incomplete burial chamber.

EL-ASHMUNEIN OPEN-AIR MUSEUM

El-Ashmunein, 44 km/27 mi south of central Minya, West Bank; 8am-4pm daily; 40LE adults, 20LE students

Nearly all that's left of the provincial capital of Hermopolis (Greek for "City of Hermes") can be seen in this open-air site, located just north of the modern town of el-Ashmunein.

1: baboon sculpture representing Thoth
2: columns that once formed a Roman marketplace at El-Ashmunein Open-Air Museum

1

2

Originally called Khmun ("Town of Eight" in ancient Egyptian), the area was named after the Ogdoad—a group of eight gods with names like "Infinity" and "Darkness" who represented the world of chaos before creation. The city became a popular cult center for Thoth, god of the moon, wisdom, and learning, who was later worshiped by the Greeks as Hermes.

Today, very little remains of the numerous temples and city structures, save some fallen rocks and the main draws: two fabulous baboon colossi representing Thoth commissioned by Amenhotep III (r. 1390-1353 BC) and a patch of over two dozen columns that once formed a Roman marketplace, and later a Christian basilica. It's not an essential stop, but it's worth a quick look when combined with a trip to Tuna el-Gebel and the Mallawi Museum, which are nearby.

TUNA EL-GEBEL

50 km/30 mi south of central Minya, West Bank; 8am-4pm daily; 60LE adults, 30LE students

This 3-kilometer (2-mi) strip of desert contains Egypt's best Greco-Roman (332 BC-AD 396) necropolis, with around 60 funerary houses built of mud-brick, and nine limestone tombs. It served as the graveyard for the city of Hermopolis—located some 16 kilometers (10 mi) to the northeast—and for others who came in pilgrimage to the revered cult center of Thoth (god of the moon, learning, and writing). It's fun to wander freely around the cemetery, but don't miss the tomb-chapels of Petosiris and Isadora near the entrance (just a few meters apart from each other).

Before the human cemetery spread across the sand, sacred animals affiliated with Thoth were buried in a complex of **catacombs** (in use from c. 1295-100 BC), located just north of the necropolis. One section held mummified ibises and other holy birds, while another housed mummified baboons (one of which remains on display in the catacombs), sometimes interred beside the priests who cared for them.

WCs and refreshments available near the **Ticket Office** on the road that leads to the necropolis.

TOMB OF PETOSIRIS

Petosiris (c. 300 BC) and his family served as high priests at the Temple of Thoth, the chief deity in nearby Hermopolis. His tomb takes the unorthodox shape of a temple—probably modeled on his place of work. In the entrance, a blend of Egyptian and Greek images depict scenes of daily life, with people making offerings to the gods and farmers working the fields. On the walls inside, excerpts from the Book of the Dead guide the deceased into the afterlife, while autobiographical texts proclaim the patron's successes. After a traverse hall, a chamber with four pillars holds the shaft leading down to the burial chamber of Petosiris and his relatives.

TOMB OF ISADORA

Just to the southeast of Petosiris's tomb is that of a Greek woman named Isadora (c. AD 150). The walls are mostly bare, but the deceased's mummy remains in haunting repose. Poems on either side of the entrance suggest poor Isadora likely drowned in the Nile. To the right of the door, the text in Greek reads: "No longer shall I come to make sacrifice with lamentation, daughter, now I have learned that you have become a goddess. With libations and vows praise Isadora, who as a marriageable maiden was snatched away by the Nymphs." The text to the left makes reference to the Greek myth of Hylas, companion of Hercules, who was abducted by the Nymphs to the bottom of a pond.

BOUNDARY STELA

On your way out, swing by the area's oldest monument of note—tucked off the main road, some 750 meters (2,500 ft) north of the ticket office (to your left as you exit). This Boundary Stela carved into the face of a cliff marks the northern edge of Akhetaten (c. 1348-1330 BC), the new capital built by the radical king Akhenaten. The center of his city sat on the East Bank of the Nile some 29 kilometers (18 mi) away in Tell el-Amarna, but this border-marker shows it incorporated a good deal of farmland to the west. The beautiful (relatively well-preserved) relief depicts Aten, the sun-disc god, extending his rays to the royal family. Accessible via a set of stairs.

MALLAWI MUSEUM

Central Mallawi, West Bank, 50 km/30 mi south of central Minya; tel. 0100 662 7575; 9am-5pm daily; 40LE adults, 20LE students

Tucked away in a small village, the Mallawi Museum gained international attention in 2013 when nearly all of the 1,089 items on display were stolen during a period of political unrest. Most of the artifacts have since been recovered, and their home beautifully restored with sleeker curation.

The museum originally opened in 1963 to host the wealth of objects found around the modern-day Minya governorate, particularly at the sites of Tuna el-Gebel, Tell el-Amarna, and El-Ashmunein Open-Air Museum. Spanning from the Old Kingdom (c. 2600 BC) through the Greco-Roman, Coptic, and Islamic periods, the items offer windows into daily life and rituals of death. The striking wooden coffins covered in hieroglyphics and colorful designs are a highlight.

Few visitors make it to these parts, so you'll likely have the place to yourself (unless you happen to run into a school field trip). A visit should take no more than an hour and is best combined with a trip to Tuna el-Gebel Necropolis 18 kilometers (11 mi) to the west and/or Tell el-Amarna 16 kilometers (10 mi) to the southeast.

Food

★ TARBUSH RESTAURANT AND CAFÉ

Al-Galaa St., Mallawi; tel. 0101 090 3934; noon-10:30pm daily; 50-150LE mains

Just a couple of blocks east of the Mallawi Museum, this grill makes some of the best food around. Stuffed pigeon and molokhia are their specialties, along with the traditional grilled chicken and meat dishes. The interior is spacious, bright, and clean. The sign outside is in Arabic, but keep an eye out for the mustache wearing a red hat.

Sohag and Vicinity

The city of Sohag is relatively new on the map of Egypt, only becoming the governorate's capital in 1960 when it took over from a town called Girga to the south. Before that, it was Sohag's sister city across the Nile, Akhmim (known to the Greeks as Panapolis after the Greek god of fertility, Pan), that served as the thriving provincial capital from at least the 27th century BC.

Palm-lined canals snake through Sohag, leaving swaths of green just outside the city center. In the residential areas, redbrick apartment buildings dominate the visual scape, many unfinished with their rebars still reaching for the sky. Few tourists (whether Egyptian or foreign) make it to these parts, but it's a beautiful section of the country with a few worthwhile sights for travelers not on a tight schedule. Central Sohag and Akhmim are an easy day trip from Abydos in the south of the Sohag governorate, just 50 kilometers (30 mi) away (1.5 hours by car).

SIGHTS

★ Sohag National Museum

Akhmim-Al Sawamaa St., El-Khouly, East Bank; no tel.; 9am-5pm daily; 60LE adults, 30LE students

It took some 25 years of start-and-stop construction before the Sohag National Museum finally opened its doors in 2018. The temple-imitation building sits on the bank of the Nile and holds treasures found around the Sohag governorate, many returning home after years in Cairo museums. The most interesting objects come from the expansive archeological site in Abydos and the famous historical textile village of Akhmim. Signage is unfortunately weak—a good guide would be a useful asset.

★ Red Monastery

11 km/7 mi west of central Sohag; no tel.; 7am-sunset daily; 20LE

Since around AD 500 the Church of St. Bishoi—better known as the Red Monastery (Deir el-Ahmar), owing to its redbrick exterior—has served as a center of Coptic worship in Egypt. Centuries of residue from incense and candles left the walls of the church blackened, concealing the colors below. But almost two decades of restoration by an international team have revealed layers of vibrant paintings, nearly all from the Early Byzantine period (6th-8th centuries).

The church's most striking feature is its **sanctuary,** comprised of two levels of niches, each topped by a semi-dome and almost entirely covered in colors. Many of the paints used were wax-based, giving parts an attractive sheen. In the niches, cartoonish monks, popes, saints, and evangelists stare out with bulging eyes. On the upper level, a bright pink and green color scheme with floral patterns looks a bit like 1960s wallpaper, while elsewhere the Virgin Mary suckles baby Jesus and peacocks strut alongside gazelles—all quite ornate for a band of ascetics.

During the medieval period, monks built a mud brick wall to cover the paintings—one reason they're so well-preserved today. Though the sprawling monastery complex was destroyed centuries ago, the church remains active, and the monks are happy to show off their newly refurbished home.

Ask your hotel or the Sohag Tourist Office to help you arrange for a driver to the monastery (30 minutes by car from central Sohag; 200-300LE round-trip including wait time).

White Monastery

3.5 km/2.2 mi south of the Red Monastery; no tel.; 7am-sunset daily; 20LE

Built nearly a century before the Red Monastery, the limestone church at the White Monastery (Deir el-Abyad) retains more of its original structure than that of its neighbor, but far fewer paintings.

Officially called the Monastery of St. Shenute, it's named after the nephew of the founder (Bigol) who took over the post as abbot in 385 after his uncle's death. St. Shenute initiated an extensive expansion of the monastery, stretching it across some 10 square kilometers (4 sq mi) and incorporating thousands of monks and nuns (though the latter group was not always thrilled about his attempts to control their community).

Nearly all of the monastery had been destroyed by the 15th century, with the exception of the **Church of St. Shenute**—founded by the abbot in the mid-5th century as the centerpiece of his monastic community. Shenute was known for his intolerance of Egypt's pagan religions and led a campaign to destroy their nearby temples. The church incorporates granite slabs and column capitals from these houses of worship, and even borrows some of their architectural elements, like the boxy exterior capped with concave molding.

After the entrance, visitors pass through the first room into a large nave, where the congregation attended mass. The roof has since disappeared, and only a few of the columns still stand. These columns and the surrounding walls would have been covered in vibrant paintings, similar to those in the Red Monastery. The sanctuary also takes a similar shape as that of the Red Monastery, with three apses topped by semi-domes. In the central semi-dome, Jesus is surrounded by the four Evangelists writing their Gospels. The small room just north of the sanctuary served as the library, where many invaluable manuscripts were found written in the Coptic language.

Akhmim Open-Air Museum

Central Akhmim, 5 km/3 mi east of central Sohag; no tel.; 9am-5pm daily; 50LE adults, 25LE students

The sleepy textile town of Akhmim, located across the Nile from central Sohag, once overflowed with grand temples—most importantly one dedicated to the Egyptian fertility god, Min. Very little remains of its past glory, save a colossus of the beautiful Meritamun,

1: Red Monastery **2:** White Monastery

1

2

daughter-turned-wife of Ramses II, standing over 9 meters (30 ft) tall—an extremely rare size for known representations of ancient women. A restored colossus of Ramses II himself was erected beside her in 2019, gathered from broken pieces found buried around the site, and a smaller Ramses II sits nearby among mostly Roman ruins.

FOOD

Sohag isn't exactly a dining destination, but you won't go hungry. For snacks check out the supermarket called **Zadk** (Nahda St.; 9am-3am daily), just down the street from the El Safa Hotel, or **Al-Raya Market** (350 m/1,100 ft east of the Sohag National Museum; 8am-3am daily) on the East Bank.

BEIRUT CAFÉ

Corniche St., East Bank; tel. 0 112 740 3222; 10am-2am daily; 20-40LE hot drinks and juice

Just south the Akhmim Bridge (Kobri Akhmim) on the East Bank, this moored boat café boasts a fabulous breeze off the Nile. Locals come to sip tea and shisha en plein air. The upper decks, donned with blue fairy lights, offer the best views. Food is also served, though it can be skipped. Located beside a larger boat hotel called Nile Story.

OM HASSAN

El-Gomhoriya St., in front of El Safa Hotel; tel. 19500; www.omhassan.com; 11am-2am daily; 55-120LE mains

Om Hassan serves up some safe Egyptian food in a bright and roomy dining hall. Popular dishes are grilled chicken and meat (kebab and kofta), molokhia, and tagines (stews cooked and served in a clay pot). Fresh bread also served.

ACCOMMODATIONS

Accommodation options in Sohag are pretty dire. If you're in a bind, the El Safa Hotel is acceptable. Otherwise, stay in Abydos 50 kilometers (30 mi) to the south. Some even visit on a day trip from Luxor, 260 kilometers (160 mi; 4 hours) away.

EL SAFA HOTEL

15 al-Gamhoria St.; tel. 093 2100043; 600 LE d

The view of the Nile from the upper floors is the best thing this hotel has going for it. Rooms are spacious and relatively clean (compared to your other options in town), decorated with fake plants and retro fabrics. Breakfast included.

INFORMATION AND SERVICES

Tourist Office

Next to Sohag Museum, Akhmim-Al Sawamaa St., East Bank; no tel.; 8:30am-3pm Sun.-Thurs.

The friendly staff at this tourist office can help you arrange trips to the few sights around Sohag, but they don't offer too much by way of maps and brochures.

ATMs

You'll find plenty of ATMs in central Sohag (around Nasser Square in particular), with fewer in neighboring Akhmim.

Pharmacies

A reputable nationwide chain, **El-Ezaby** (on corner of al-Gamhoria St. and al-Nahda St.; tel. 19600; 24 hours daily) is located just across from El Safa Hotel.

GETTING THERE

As with most destinations along the Nile Valley, the train is the most scenic (and spacious) way to reach Sohag. Trains leaving from Cairo are typically punctual, but the same can't be said for those departing from the south.

Train

Multiple trains travel every day and night between the **Sohag Railway Station** (al-Mahatta St.; no tel.; 24 hours daily) and **Minya** (3-3.5 hours; 54-99LE), **Luxor** (3-3.5 hours; 52-94LE), or **Cairo's Ramses Station** (6-7 hours; 90-160LE). For the nicest, fastest trains, select the "Special Service OD." Book online at www.enr.gov.eg or at the centrally located station.

Bus

Blue Bus (tel. 16128; www.bluebus.com.eg)

offers multiple trips daily between Cairo near Ramses Station and central Sohag (24 Awlad Nasser St., 1.5 km/0.9 mi northwest of Sohag Railway Station). Less comfortable but more frequent are the trips with **Upper Egypt Bus Co.** (no tel.), which leave from Torgoman Station in Cairo (near Downtown). The trip between Cairo and Sohag for either bus costs around 200-220LE and takes around 7 hours.

Both bus companies typically offer daily trips between Sohag and Hurghada (5 hours), Minya (4.5 hours), Qena (3.5 hours), or Luxor (4.5 hours). Check the schedules at the station as departure times are always changing.

Private Car Hire

Your hotel in Abydos or Luxor will likely be able to arrange for a private car to Sohag and its surrounding sites for a day trip. Sohag is around 1.5 hours by car from Abydos (800-1,200LE round-trip) and 4 hours from Luxor (around 3,000-4,500LE round-trip).

GETTING AROUND

Taxis around the center of town should cost no more than 10-20LE. For trips to the Red and White Monasteries, expect to pay around 200-300LE round-trip depending on how much time you spend there. To Akhmim should be around 100LE round-trip including wait time. As always, be sure to agree on a price with your driver ahead of time. The Tourist Office (beside the Sohag Museum) can help you negotiate with a driver if necessary.

Abydos

Abydos, once a sacred city and the most important burial ground in all of Egypt, today sits on the desert edge of a small modern village by the same name. For casual visitors, the main attractions are the **Temple of Seti I** (c.1290-1279 BC) and yet another monument built by Seti I's prolific son, the **Temple of Ramses II** (c. 1279-1213 BC). But these are just the most outwardly impressive structures in this sprawling necropolis with some 5,000 years' worth of buried treasures, namely mummies and their items for the afterlife. These tombs are still under excavation and not open to the public, but they're extremely important for archeologists as they seek to understand the earliest days of civilization in Egypt.

The most popular way to visit Abydos is from Luxor 175 kilometers (110 mi) away (3-hour drive). The trip is usually combined with a stop at the Dendera Temple Complex in Qena.

HISTORY

Archeologists have been unearthing treasures in this plot of desert for nearly 200 years. Covering 13 square kilometers (5 sq mi), the necropolis contains Egypt's very first royal tombs—over 5,000 years old and predating the pyramids of Saqqara and Giza by centuries. In a pre-dynastic tomb from earlier still, the first known Egyptian writing was discovered dating to around 3300 BC. (To the untrained eye, these archeological wonders look little more than rubble.)

The area morphed from a royal cemetery into the main cult center for Osiris, god of the afterlife, beginning around 2000 BC. With powers to grant immortality—to guide his followers to life after death—Osiris was one of ancient Egypt's most popular deities. His temple (1 km/0.6 mi north of the Temple of Seti I and now all but vanished) served as the hub for his devotees for thousands of years, transforming Abydos into a choice burial spot for his followers, both royal and common. It once stood as the centerpiece to a thriving walled town, and an annual festival drew pilgrims from around the country to enact the god's dramatic death at the hands of his jealous brother, Seth, and resurrection.

★ ABYDOS TEMPLE COMPLEX

Abydos Rd., West Bank; 8am-4pm daily; 80LE adults, 40LE students

One ticket covers entry to Abydos's two main attractions: the Temple of Seti I, where you'll see some of Egypt's best raised reliefs in the second hypostyle hall, and the neighboring Temple of Ramses II.

Temple of Seti I

Seti I (r. 1290-1279 BC), founder and arguably greatest king of the Ramesside dynasty, built this temple to honor himself and Osiris, god of the afterlife—or more specifically the fusion of the two: Seti-as-Osiris. Called "Seti Happy in Abydos," the edifice served as a yet another "mansion of millions of years," built concurrently with the pharaoh's temple in Luxor devoted to Amun (or Seti-as-Amun), king of the gods.

Constructed of a sturdy limestone quarried nearby, much of the imposing structure still stands. A canal once connected the temple to the Nile, which helped workers lug the heavy stones to the building site and brought devotees here with a grand entrance during festival processions.

Outside, two towering pylons (today mostly destroyed) with courts in between them led to two pillared porticoes, which now greet visitors. These outer sections and the **first hypostyle hall** that follows were completed by Seti I's son, Ramses II. Note on the wall that separates the two courts, some of Ramses II's more that 100 children are depicted in procession to honor their grandfather.

It's not until the **second hypostyle hall** that visitors can admire Seti's exquisite attention to detail in his raised reliefs (as opposed to the easier sunken reliefs)—some of the best in all of Egypt. Most depict Seti I making offerings to various gods. In the center of the hall, 36 lotus-bud columns form aisles leading to **seven chapels** dedicated to the divine king and six main deities at the time. From left to right: Seti I takes the first chapel, followed by the gods Ptah (the creator god), Re-Horakhty (a combination of the solar god Re and Horus, god of the sky), Amon-Re (king of gods), Osiris (god of the dead), Isis (goddess of magic and motherhood), and Horus (son of Isis and Osiris). Each chapel is decorated with rituals for worshiping the deities during various festivals. Osiris gets a luxury suite with multiple chambers, decorated in scenes that connect the divine Seti I to Osiris, suggesting he'll follow a similar path of resurrection.

In a hallway off to the left of the chambers is a rare list of 76 Egyptian kings, their names written in cartouches (known as the **Abydos King List**). Seti's selective recordkeeping leaves out the names of pharaohs he considered illegitimate, including the Pharaoh Queen Hatshepsut and the radical Akhenaten.

Behind the temple is the **Osireion,** a symbolic tomb complex for the god of the dead. The false tomb was once entered through a sloping corridor to the north, with walls covered in funerary texts from the Book of the Gates to guide the deceased into the afterlife. Today you can peek into the largely stripped complex and see the bright green pond inside, originally intended to represent the primordial waters of creation.

Temple of Ramses II

A short walk north of Seti I's temple, Ramses II built a smaller one also of limestone (secondary to his main mortuary temple in Luxor). While the roof of the temple has disappeared, the reliefs on the remaining lower parts have maintained some of their vibrant colors. A granite doorway brings you to a court surrounded with pillars in the shape of Osiris. The court ends in a portico with two chapels at each end—the left dedicated to the deified Seti I, and the right to Ramses II and nine gods.

Two hypostyle halls follow, both surrounded by more chapels dedicated to favorite deities of Thebes (Luxor) and Abydos.

1: carving in temple in Abydos **2:** the first hypostyle hall in the Temple of Seti I **3:** Temple of Seti I in Abydos

Many of the images depict traditional scenes of Ramses II making offerings to the gods. On the outside of his temple, Ramses II added yet another set of illustrations of from the Battle of Kadesh (which he nearly lost, though the images don't let on), as he did on the Luxor Temple, Ramesseum, and Abu Simbel.

FOOD AND ACCOMMODATIONS

★ HOUSE OF LIFE ABYDOS

4 Abydos Rd., 600 m/2,000 ft east of the Temple of Seti I; tel. 093 4944045; www.houseoflife.info; 1,600LE d

Brainchild of an Egyptian and Dutch duo who've assumed the names Horus and Isis (after the Egyptian god and goddess), this well-manicured hotel and healing center is a rare find in rural Abydos. With a temple façade, faux lotus columns in the lobby, and a scarab-shaped pool, it's a colorful place to crash for a night or two. The rooms are basic (most accented with the hieroglyphic key of life) but comfortable, each with a balcony. Rooftop terraces look out to the surrounding farmland. Breakfast's included, and for an extra 200LE or so you can choose full board—probably a good idea as there aren't many other dining options around.

The hotel's **Panorama Restaurant** (7am-11pm daily; 50-100LE mains) is open to non-guests and is the best place in town to grab refreshments and a bite to eat.

GETTING THERE

The best way to get to Abydos is by private car hire, most easily arranged through your hotel in Luxor or Abydos. Good hagglers will likely be able to find a better deal with a taxi driver, but it might not be worth the extra effort.

Private Car Hire

If you stay in **House of Life Abydos Hotel,** they can arrange for private car transportation to Abydos from your accommodation in Luxor. They're located walking distance from the Abydos Temple Complex.

Taxi

You shouldn't have trouble finding a taxi in Luxor to make a day trip to Abydos, including a stop in Qena for a visit to the Dendera Temple Complex. Rates for the 10-12-hour trip should be in the range of 1,500-2,000LE round-trip.

Qena and Dendera

Once a provincial capital in antiquity, Dendera (Tantere in ancient Egyptian) has since been reduced to a small farming town on the edge of the desert. The city of Qena on the opposite bank of the river has taken over as the provincial hub, outshining its neighbor in all but the latter's glorious temple complex. The two sit across from each other on the most dramatic kink in Egypt's Nile, where the river nearly flows east to west instead of south to north.

Qena and Dendera are best visited on a day trip from Luxor, which has many accommodation options and is located just around 70 kilometers (40 mi) to the south. The ride is a nice (if sometimes bumpy) trip through farmland, or a longer desert drive.

★ DENDERA TEMPLE COMPLEX

Off Aswan Western Agricultural Rd., West Bank; no tel.; 7am-6pm daily; 120LE adults, 60LE students

Like many of Egypt's best remaining temple complexes, this one was almost entirely built under the Greeks and Romans. Egyptians had erected temples on this site millennia prior—even before the Old Kingdom (c. 2649-2130 BC). No traces of these structures are left to explore, but stunning remnants of more recent times, starting from the 2nd century

BC, do remain, with the Hathor Temple—the most important temple dedicated to the popular deity in all of Egypt—the main attraction.

After passing through a monumental **gateway**—built during the rule of Emperors Domitian (r. AD 81-96) and Trajan (r. AD 98-117)—visitors enter an **open-air museum** with coffins, statues, and other stone artifacts lined up in front of the centerpiece, the **Hathor Temple.** The first structure to the right after the gateway is a **Roman Birth House,** followed by a **basilica, sanitorium, sacred lake,** and the **Temple of the Birth of Isis.** Schedule around 1-2 hours for a visit to explore the ins and outs of the complex.

Hathor Temple

Hathor—goddess of love, fertility, motherhood, and the sky—was often considered the pharaoh's divine mother and protectress. Her affiliation with the sacred cow explains her typical depiction as either a woman with floppy cow ears or the milk-giving creature itself—both forms of which can be seen throughout her temple.

OUTER HYPOSTYLE HALL

In the outer hypostyle hall stand 24 columns with cow-eared Hathor-head capitals, each systematically vandalized by Christians in antiquity. More precisely, the capitals take the shape of sistra (singular, sistrum)—a musical instrument linked to Hathor and used to ward off evil. The instrument was often made with the head of Hathor topped by a box (as seen in these columns), or just as a lightbulb-shaped rattle (depicted on the inner temple walls).

Mesmerizing reliefs cover nearly every inch of these columns and the surrounding walls and ceiling—the latter painted in a brilliant sky blue (appropriate for this house of the sky goddess). The images on the ceiling depict an Egyptian chart of the heavens, with added zodiac signs courtesy of the Romans. In one corner another sky goddess, Nut, swallows the sun, which she births in the morning (in the opposite corner). The hall itself was constructed and decorated over many decades by Roman emperors from Augustus (r. 30 BC-AD 14) to Nero (r. AD 54-68). Colors are original, recently restored after centuries of hiding beneath soot and grime.

INNER HYPOSTYLE HALL

Six columns stand in the inner hypostyle hall (also called the "hall of appearances"), where a statue of Hathor would emerge from her sanctuary during religious ceremonies. On the walls, the king celebrates the construction of the temple. Flanking the hall are six small **chambers** used to prepare for daily rituals. To the right (while facing the back of the temple), a passage leads outside to a well, where priests would collect the water used in the ceremonies.

HATHOR'S SANCTUARY

From the inner hypostyle hall, an offering hall leads to a small vestibule and finally into Hathor's sanctuary—the most sacred section that held the goddess's statue and barque (sacred boat). As with most temples, these inner parts were built first (under the Ptolemies beginning in 125 BC).

Encircling the sanctuary are 11 **small chambers** dedicated to gods and sacred things, with one for Hathor's sistrum and another for a necklace (the Menat collar) worn for divine protection. Below the rear chambers, stairs lead down to **crypts** (accessible, though a tight squeeze!), covered in more reliefs and once home to the temple's treasures.

The stairs heading up bring you to a roof (with brilliant views of the surrounding agriculture), where priests performed the ritual of Hathor's union with the sun disc. The ceiling of a chapel in this hidden corner also holds a copy of the famed **Dendera Zodiac** from 47 BC. (The original is in the Louvre.)

EXTERIOR

When you've had your fill of the interior, check out the southwest external wall with a rare **relief of Cleopatra VII Philopater** (i.e., the famous one) and her son by Caesar, Caesarion, who face Hathor at the head

1
2
3

of a procession of deities. It was under the Pharaoh Queen Cleopatra (r. 51-30 BC), who affiliated herself with the powerful goddesses Hathor and Isis, that most of the temple was completed.

Birth Houses and Basilica

Returning to the main entrance of the complex, the first structure to the right is a **Roman Birth House,** dedicated to Hathor and her son by Horus, Ihy (worshiped by the Ptolemies as god of music). It was commissioned by Augustus soon after his conquest over Cleopatra's Egypt, and later decorated with scenes of Roman emperors making offerings to the goddess. Images of Bes, a short and hairy protective god often affiliated with childbirth and fertility, sit above the columns.

Immediately after the Roman Birth House are ruins from a 5th-century **Christian Basilica,** and then those of an earlier **Birth House** (built by one of the last Egyptian kings, Nectanebo I, r. 380-362 BC)—the oldest remaining structure on the site.

Sanitorium and Sacred Lake

Just past the second Birth House sits a mudbrick **Sanitorium**—something of a sacred spa, where Hathor devotees could camp out, bathe in sacred waters, and wait for the goddess to visit them in their dreams. A few meters to the south, priests performed their ritual cleansings in the **Sacred Lake,** one of the best remaining examples of this traditional temple feature.

Temple of the Birth of Isis

This small temple, located just beyond the lake to the left, was decorated during the reign of Augustus. It's dedicated to Isis—the goddess who appeared after Hathor and adopted many of her characteristics. She too is affiliated with the sacred cow, protection, and motherhood (specifically mother of the sky god, Horus). Hathor had earlier been seen as mother of Horus, but later myths made him instead her consort.

1: hypostyle hall in the Hathor Temple 2: open-air museum and Hathor Temple façade 3: mudbrick walls surrounding the Dendera Temple Complex

FOOD

All of the below are located in Qena.

Egyptian

★ BAIT EL-MASHWIAT

Intersection of el-Rayyah Rd. and Luxor-Qena Rd.; tel. 0111 520 6206; 24 hours daily; 40-120LE mains

Decorated with modern mashrabiya (patterned wood screens), this spotless restaurant serves up some of Qena's best grilled chicken and meats. Their specialty is the kebab and kofta platter, but they also offer a range of pastas and traditional Egyptian dishes like mahshi (eggplant or zucchini stuffed with spiced rice) and fattah (boiled lamb or beef on a bed of rice and fried pita bread with tomato sauce). Try to snag a seat on the upper floor by the window for beautiful views of green fields and a palm-lined canal. Another branch located in central Qena (23 July St.; tel. 0111 114 9879; same hours and prices).

International

PUCCINI'S RESTAURANT AND CAFÉ

Off el-Rayyah Rd., on corner of Luxor St. and Luxor-Qena Rd.; tel. 0103 311 1391; www.pucciniweb.com; 1pm-1am daily; 50-100LE mains

Located just up the street from Bait el-Mashwiat, Puccini's offers more views of sprawling green fields and palm trees. This is a good option if you've had your fill of Egyptian food and are looking for some international fare like burgers and fries, pizza, gyros, or even stromboli. A wide array of desserts and fresh juices also served.

Cafés and Snacks

BASMA HOTEL CAFÉ

El-Mina el-Nahri St., in Basma Hotel; tel. 0101 284 7596; 8am-11pm daily; 20-90LE drinks

This spacious strip of chairs and umbrellas is so close to the Nile you could hop right in (though not recommended). It's a nice place to watch the sunset with a tea or a cold nonalcoholic drink. Food can be skipped.

ACCOMMODATIONS

Qena really only has one sight to see and is just a 1.5-2-hour drive from Luxor, which is full of great hotels, B&Bs, and guesthouses. If you're set on staying the night, the Basma Hotel is your best option.

BASMA HOTEL

El-Mina el-Nahri St.; tel. 0101 284 7596; 1,700 LE

The rooms here are clean and comfortable, but foreigners pay a premium for very mediocre lodging. The highlights are a wide-open Nile-side patio café and balconies with fabulous views of the river. There's also a pool, though ladies are expected to cover up.

GETTING THERE AND AROUND

From Luxor, private car hire is an excellent way to reach Qena and Dendera. The fastest way from Cairo (without spending a ton for a private car hire) is by bus.

Train

Trains leave for **Qena** throughout the day and night from **Cairo's Ramses Station** (9-10 hours; 107-193LE), **Minya** (5.5-6.5 hours; 78-141LE), **Sohag** (2-2.5 hours; 42-73LE), and **Luxor** (1 hour; 27-52LE). Train departures from Qena to these cities are equally as common (same prices and trip time). For the nicest, fastest trains, select the "Special Service OD." Book online at www.enr.gov.eg or at the station.

In Qena the train station is located in Midan Mahatta (Station Square)—10 kilometers (6 mi) northeast of the city's main attraction, the Dendera Temple Complex.

Bus

Go Bus (tel. 19567; www.go-bus.com) offers multiple trips a day from **Cairo** (Abdel Minam Riyad Square, next to the Ramses Hilton) to Qena (8-9 hours; 245LE). Two trips per day usually run between **Hurghada** and Qena (3.5 hours; 125LE). If Go Bus isn't operating for whatever reason, the government's **Upper East Bus Company** (Mahatta Square, across from the train station; no tel.) is fine and offers regular trips to/from Cairo (**Torgoman Station,** Downtown), elsewhere along the Nile Valley, and the Red Sea Coast, like Hurghada, Safaga, and Quseir.

In Qena, the bus stop is just northwest of the train station off Qena-Manfalout Road.

Private Car Hire or Taxi

Many hotels in Luxor can arrange for a private car to take a day trip to Qena (1.5-2 hours each way). Prices should be in the range of 800-1,200LE round-trip. Most taxi drivers in Luxor would also be happy to take you to Qena for around the same price.

Luxor (Al-Aqsur)

If Cairo is the city of a thousand minarets and Giza home of the pyramids, Luxor is the land of grand temples. Nowhere else in Egypt do you find such a concentration of these splendid structures so well preserved, nor of the vivid scenes of the gods once worshiped within their walls.

All of Luxor feels like one grand open-air museum, dripping with millennia-old treasures at every turn. The East Bank—the "City of the Living," where the sun is reborn—houses two dramatic temple complexes, once the domain of the region's favorite deities and their priests. The West Bank—the "City of the Dead," where the sun dies each day—holds the tombs of some of Egypt's most famed pharaohs and their mortuary temples, or "mansions of millions of years." More than 4,000

Highlights

Look for ★ to find recommended sights, activities, dining, and lodging.

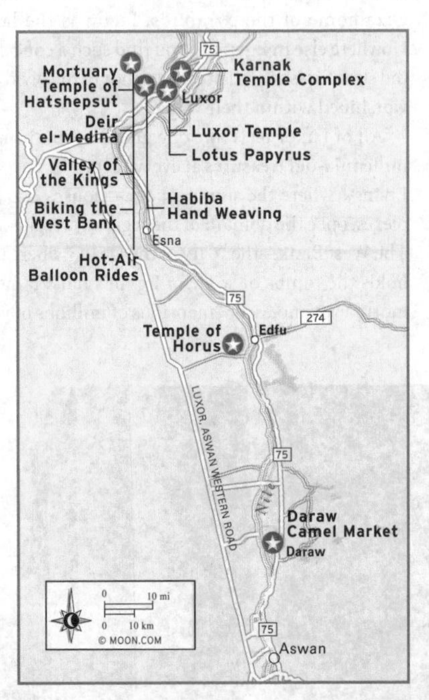

★ **Karnak Temple Complex:** This labyrinthine complex was laid by some of Egypt's greatest kings and queens in tribute to their favorite deities (page 171).

★ **Luxor Temple:** This smaller version of the Karnak Temple Complex served as the "Southern Sanctuary" for Amun, king of the gods, when he visited during the annual Opet festival, celebrating the divine pharaoh's rebirth (page 175).

★ **Deir el-Medina:** Wander the remains of this workmen's village—home to the artisans who built the royal tombs in the Valleys of the Kings and Queens—and visit their vibrant sanctuaries for the afterlife dug into the rocks above (page 182).

★ **Mortuary Temple of Hatshepsut:** Carved into the side of a sandstone mountain, Hatshepsut's temple is a striking legacy of the pharaoh queen's divine rule (page 185).

★ **Valley of the Kings:** Nearly all the New Kingdom (c. 1539-1075 BC) pharaohs were buried in this undulating valley—many in exquisite tombs lined with texts and images to guide them safely into the afterlife (page 188).

★ **Hot-Air Balloon Rides:** Enjoy a dramatic bird's-eye view of the West Bank temples, fields, and mountains, illuminated by the rising sun (page 189).

★ **Biking the West Bank:** Cycle through idyllic farmland to visit the ancient sights of the West Bank at your own pace (page 190).

★ **Lotus Papyrus and Habiba Hand Weaving:** These are two of Luxor's best shops. Take home a souvenir of your favorite tomb paintings on papyrus at Lotus Papyrus, or watch weavers at work and buy a beautiful scarf or carpet at Habiba Hand Weaving (pages 192 and 193).

★ **Temple of Horus:** Located along the route from Luxor to Aswan, Edfu's Greco-Roman house of worship dedicated to the falcon-headed god of the sky is among the best preserved temples in Egypt (page 209).

★ **Daraw Camel Market:** See thousands of animals gathered at an authentic market on the road to Aswan (page 213).

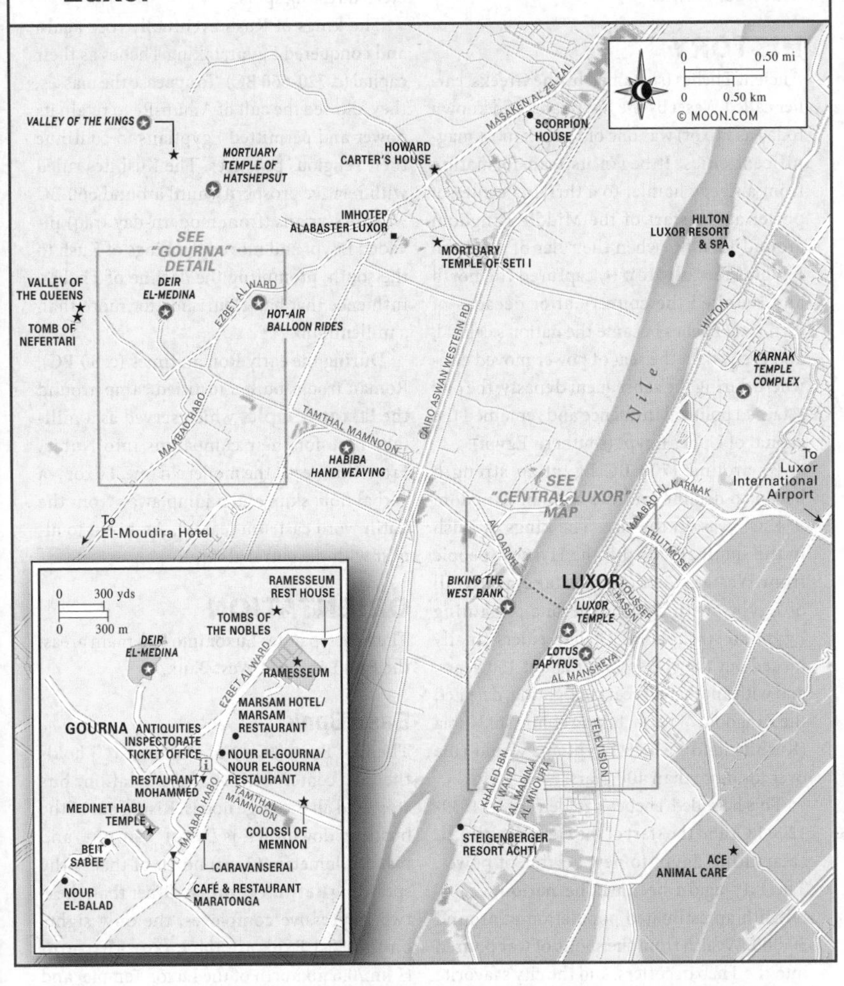

years of history are layered throughout these monuments to immortality, many still standing (or rebuilt) alongside the dramatic landscape from which they were carved.

Alongside this wealth of history is a unique blend of modern urban and rural Egyptian life. Just a few minutes on a ferry from the East to West Bank will transport you from a city of concrete and cars to wide-open fields and wandering donkeys.

South of Luxor en route to Aswan, golden desert and jagged mountains hem in sprawling green fields of sugarcane. Villages spot the stretches of palm-lined fields with more magnificent temples rising out of unexpected places, alongside mosques, concrete

Previous: Karnak Temple Complex; view from cruising the Nile river; Temple of Khnum.

storefronts, and redbrick apartments adorned with rebar crowns.

HISTORY

Ancient Thebes (so named by the Greeks, earlier called Waset by the Egyptians, and known today as Luxor) was one of Egypt's most magnificent cities. It began its transformation from a sleepy hamlet to a thriving center of power at the start of the Middle Kingdom around 1970 BC when the ruler of southern Egypt, **Mentuhotep II,** captured the north and reunited the country after decades of civil war. Thebes became the nation's capital, and even when the seat of power moved elsewhere during the subsequent dynasty, the city retained political influence and remained the capital of Upper Egypt (southern Egypt).

By around 1700 BC Egyptian strength began to decline and the Nubian Kingdom of Kush was on the rise. The kings of Kush in the south allied with the Hyksos (people from Western Asia) to overtake nearly all of Egypt—with Thebes the one remaining Egyptian stronghold. Theban rulers finally kicked out the Hyksos after about 150 years, and with another 50 years of fighting, defeated the Kingdom of Kush, taking control of Nubia (Kushite land), which Egyptians would rule over for more than 400 years.

This heralded Thebes's golden age (c. 1539-1200 BC) and the start of the **New Kingdom,** catapulting Egypt to new heights of power. The city again became the nation's capital with an estimated population of around 50,000. Wealth from the spoils of war poured into the Theban coffers, and the city's favorite god, **Amun-Re,** took on unprecedented importance. Nearly all the magnificent temples and tombs visited in modern-day Luxor date to this period.

During the Ramesside period (c. 1292-1075 BC) initiated by **Ramses I,** the capital shifted to the pharaoh's homeland in the Nile Delta, but for most of this time Thebes remained an important religious and political center. Egypt's rulers continued to build their great "mansions of millions of years" in Thebes and still chose the **Valley of the Kings** as their eternal resting spots.

The kings of Kush eventually rose again and conquered Egypt, taking Thebes as their capital (c. 720-660 BC). To appease the masses, they allowed the cult of Amun-Re to retain its power and permitted Egyptians to continue their religious practices. The Kushites ruled with relative prosperity until around 660 BC when Assyrians (from modern-day Iraq) invaded Egypt and moved the kings of Kush to the south, prompting the decline of Theban influence that had flourished for more than a millennium.

During the early Roman times (c. 30 BC), Roman troops built a fortified camp around the **Luxor Temple,** which served as a military base for their campaigns into Nubia. From this we get the modern name, Luxor—a verbal hop, skip, and a jump away from the Latin word castrum (camp), Arabized to al-qasr with the plural al-aqsur.

ORIENTATION

The Nile separates Luxor into two main areas: the East Bank and West Bank.

East Bank

The East Bank **("City of the Living")** holds the city center with the train station, bus stop, and all the large hotels. Rising out of the bustling downtown is **Luxor Temple,** and just 3 kilometers (2 mi) north of that is the sprawling **Karnak Temple.** Other than these two impressive complexes, the only sights on the East Bank are the **Luxor Museum** (1 km/0.6 mi north of the Luxor Temple) and the **Mummification Museum** (just west of the Luxor Temple). Both are located on a main road that runs along the Nile called **Corniche el-Nil Street.** The Public Ferry Landing to reach the West Bank is also just off this street, 150 meters (500 ft) south of the Mummification Museum.

West Bank

The West Bank **("City of the Dead")** is far less built up than the East—covered in emerald-green fields with the desert necropolis on its western-most border. Nearly all the sights lie along the desert edge in a hamlet called **Gourna** (sometimes spelled Qarna), named after the mountain peak near Valley of the Kings. There are also a handful of excellent guesthouses in the area. Beside the Nile (near the **Public Ferry Landing**) is the hamlet of **Gezirat El Bairat,** where you'll find a number of nice budget hotels and restaurants.

Al Qarna Road is the main thoroughfare that leads from the Nile-side near the ferry to Gourna, turning into **Memnon Street** (also called el-Timsalyn St.) along the way. This continues past the Colossi of Memnon and ends at a traffic circle with the **Antiquities Inspectorate Ticket Office** to the left and the sites of Gourna along the main asphalt road running northeast to southwest.

PLANNING YOUR TIME

Luxor's East Bank can easily be visited in a day. The West Bank needs a minimum of two (and preferably three or four).

Perhaps more than anywhere else in the country it pays to **get an early start** here to avoid both the crowds and the heat, which can become unbearable at midday during the warmer months. If you can muster the strength, try to make it to the big sights for opening (usually 6am but be sure to double check with your hotel as opening times can sometimes be delayed). The cool and quiet really does transform the visit. Best to avoid the main attractions (Valley of the Kings, Mortuary Temple of Hatshepsut, and Karnak Temple Complex) between 10am and noon when large tour groups are most likely to show up. On the East Bank, the must-see Luxor Temple is open late and is beautiful in the evening, so one good strategy is to start at Karnak Temple (another highlight) and visit Luxor Temple later in the day.

Note that for a number of sights on the West Bank you have to pick up tickets at the **Antiquities Inspectorate Ticket Office** (650 m/2,000 ft northwest of Colossi of Memnon on west side of traffic circle; no tel.; 6am-4pm daily) before visiting. Tickets are only valid for one day.

South of Luxor along the Nile, three more cities spot the agricultural land before Aswan. These are **Esna, Edfu,** and **Kom Ombo**—each with an impressive Greco-Roman temple. The best way to visit these parts is as a day trip with a private car and driver as you travel between Luxor and Aswan. It doesn't really matter which city you start from (Luxor or Aswan) unless you want to stop at the Daraw Camel Market (8am-1pm Sat.-Sun.), in which case you'll want to depart from Aswan to make it before closing. This strip can also be enjoyed by boat—either cruise ship, dahabiya (a large two-masted sailboat), or felucca (smaller sailboat)—over 3-5 nights.

Finally, with Luxor's wealth of attractions, many locals—and others coming from around Upper Egypt in search of employment brought by tourism—have learned the trade of hassling visitors for a dollar (or preferably a euro), not unlike the camel touts at Giza's pyramids. While their insistence can be tiresome, they mean no harm and, anyways, are balanced out by the quiet majority. Be prepared with some polite but firm "no thank you"s (beware in particular of pushy horse-drawn carriage drivers). To save yourself the trouble of haggling, organize a trip with a private local guide (who will double as your shield).

SIGHTSEEING PASSES

Premium Luxor Pass

$200 adults, $100 students

The Premium Luxor Pass grants full access to all Luxor's museums and temples for five days—a great resource for ambitious travelers hoping to visit as many sites as possible. You can purchase the pass 9am-3pm daily at the **Karnak Temple,** the **Luxor Inspectorate** (behind the Luxor Museum on the East Bank), the **Antiquities Inspectorate Ticket Office** (after the Colossi of Memnon on the West Bank), or the **Valley of the Kings**

(West Bank). Cash only (**USD** or **euro,** not LE), and you must bring a passport photo and a copy of your passport photo page. They'll issue the pass immediately. You can only enter each site once per day with your pass.

Standard Luxor Pass

$100 adults, $50 student

Cheaper than the premium pass, the Standard Luxor Pass is a good choice if you want to skip the tombs of Seti I and Nefertari. (Tickets for each are 1,000LE and 1,400LE, respectively, if bought individually, so if you do want to visit these sights, you're much better off with the premium pass.) You can only enter each site once per day with your pass.

Luxor Pass/Cairo Pass Combo

If you plan on visiting a good number of sights in Cairo and Giza, for a 50% discount you can combine your Luxor Pass purchase with a **Cairo Pass** ($100 adults, $50 students) and buy both together from the **Ministry of Antiquities in Cairo** (2 el-Malak el-Afdal St., Zamalek; 9am-3pm Sun.-Thurs.). The Cairo Pass alone isn't such a great deal (you'd really have to visit all the major sights just to break even), but combined with the Luxor Pass it can save you a bundle. You can get both the Cairo and Premium Luxor Passes for $200 adults/$100 students (the same price as the Premium Luxor Pass alone) or Cairo Pass and Standard Luxor Pass for $150 adults/$75 students. You choose the date for your Luxor Pass to be activated.

TOURS AND LOCAL GUIDES

Of all the destinations in Egypt, Luxor is where you're likely to benefit most from a guide. **Real Egypt Tours** is particularly good at showing visitors around town.

REAL EGYPT TOURS

tel. 0110 002 2242; www.realegypt.com

Samir Abbass and his team at Real Egypt Tours consistently offer high-quality tours around Luxor (and beyond). Book one of their set programs for 1-5 days around the city, or design your own. Along with private guided trips to Luxor's sites, additional treats like short cooking classes or donkey rides can be arranged. They also organize excellent multiday boat trips by felucca or dahabiya between Esna (just south of Luxor) and Aswan.

DJED EGYPT TRAVEL

70 Mohamed Farid St., East Bank, Luxor; tel. 02 23959124; www.djedegypt.com

Djed (pronounced "Jed") Egypt Travel has an excellent team of guides in Luxor and elsewhere in Egypt. They can be a bit unresponsive during planning time (try calling if emails go unanswered), but the team on the ground is punctual, flexible, and fun. Note: Some do take you to touristy stores for a commission, so if this sounds unappealing make it known early. The company has a fleet of comfortable dahabiyas, making it a good choice if you want to integrate a few nights on the Nile. Choose one of their set itineraries or make your own.

Itinerary Ideas

Plan to be at your first stop on both of your days in Luxor no later than 8am—and, ideally, by 6am—for the best experience. Grab a quick breakfast at your hotel before heading out.

For the first day, you can get around easily on foot or with short cab rides. But for the second day, it's best to hire a driver and/or guide in advance or negotiate a day rate with a taxi (look for cabs near the Public Ferry Landing on the West Bank). For either day, if you're staying on the opposite bank of your destination it's possible to get to the other side by car via a 40-minute detour across the bridge, but it's much quicker to hop on the 3-minute ferry and pick up a cab or meet your driver at the opposite ferry landing.

DAY 1: LUXOR'S EAST BANK

1 Ask your driver to head for the **Karnak Temple Complex.** To avoid the heat and crowds, try to get there as early as possible. Give yourself a good 3-4 hours to wander.

2 Hop into the **Luxor Museum** to cool off and check out some striking statues and other fabulous finds from around the city.

3 Rest your feet in the garden of **Sofra Restaurant & Café** for a tasty lunch of traditional Egyptian dishes and fresh juice.

4 When you've recharged, explore the **Luxor Temple.** A visit should take around 1.5-2.5 hours.

5 Take a spin around the **Luxor Souq** to practice your haggling skills and pick up some nice souvenirs.

6 Watch the sunset with a drink and some snacks on the **Nile Terrace Café and Bar** at the historic Winter Palace Hotel.

7 Enjoy your dinner on a rooftop overlooking downtown and Luxor Temple at **Al-Sahaby Lane.**

DAY 2: LUXOR'S WEST BANK

1 Head straight to the **Mortuary Temple of Hatshepsut** for opening to enjoy the majestic structure at its best.

2 Swing over to the **Valley of the Kings** to explore the colorful tombs of the pharaohs before the crowds come.

3 Pick up tickets for the Medinet Habu Temple and Deir el-Medina at the **Antiquities Inspectorate Ticket Office.**

4 Cross the street to cool off in the shade and enjoy a hearty brunch with some fresh juice at **Nour el-Gourna Restaurant.**

5 Walk off your lunch or drive to **Medinet Habu Temple** to visit Ramses III's mortuary-temple-turned-fortified-city.

6 Head to **Deir el-Medina** to see where the tomb-makers lived, and check out their own colorful homes for the afterlife.

7 On your way back from the sandy outskirts of town, hop out of the car for a few minutes to admire the cracked giants of Amenhotep III, the **Colossi of Memnon.**

Itinerary Ideas

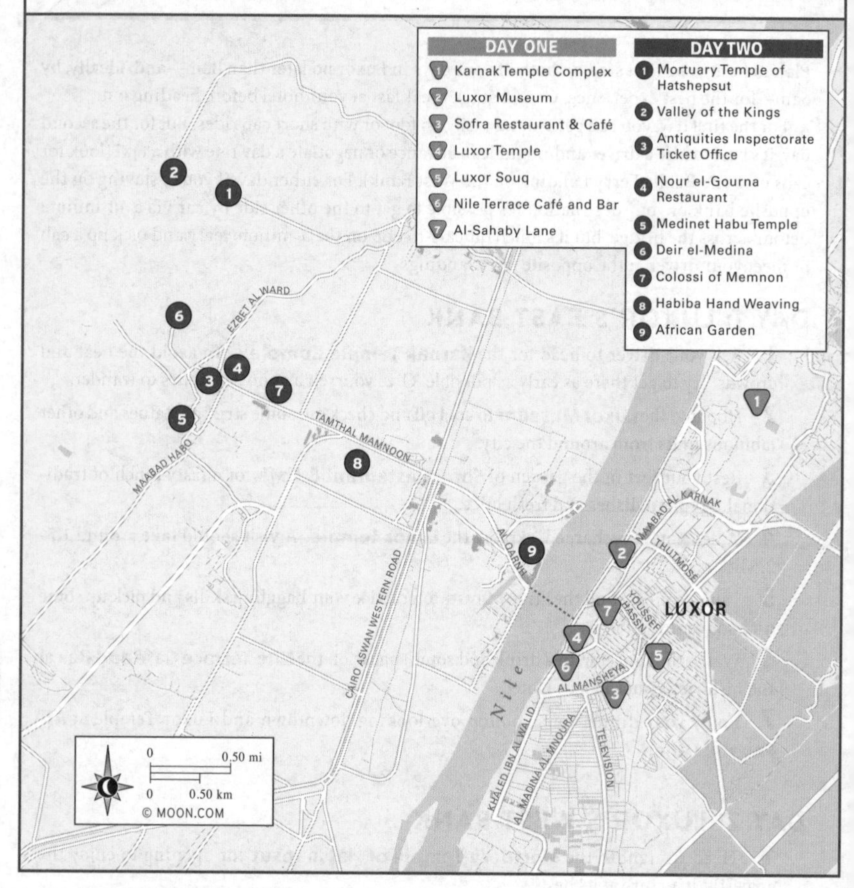

8 Pass by **Habiba Hand Weaving** for some high-quality mementos. Browse their shelves or design your own made-to-order scarf.

9 When hunger strikes, head to **African Garden** for dinner and drinks.

DAY 3: LUXOR TO ASWAN

Take breakfast to go from your hotel and meet up with your private driver early on your journey from Luxor to Aswan.

1 Enjoy the scenic drive (1.5 hours) through farm fields en route to the **Temple of Khnum** in Esna.

2 For the next leg, you'll likely take the desert highway—the fastest route (1.5 hours)—to Edfu's **Temple of Horus.**

3 Grab a lunch of rice, salads, and grilled chicken or meats on the rooftop at **Massa Restaurant** a short walk (350 m/1,000 ft) from the temple.

4 Reunite with your driver for a ride (1.5 hours) down the road separating green fields and desert to explore **Gebel el-Silsila.**

5 After another hour or so you'll arrive at your final temple of the tour, **Temple of Kom Ombo.**

6 Head to **Aswan** (1 hour) to check in to your hotel.

Sights

CENTRAL LUXOR: EAST BANK

TOP EXPERIENCE

★ Karnak Temple Complex

Mabad al-Karnak St.; no tel.; 6am-5:30pm daily; 150LE adults, 75LE students, 40LE adults/20LE students extra for Mut Temple Enclosure

The Karnak Temple Complex is Egypt's most elaborate house of worship—a proper labyrinth nearly a mile long and half a mile wide (1.6 km by 0.8 km), hiding statues, obelisks, columns, and carvings within its numerous nooks and crannies. To decipher the thousands of symbols within is to learn two millennia of ancient Egyptian history. Handfuls of kings and queens have left their marks on this onion of a compound, with awkward layers jutting out in all directions.

The earliest remaining monument here, Senusret I's "White Chapel," dates to some 4,000 years ago. For the next two millennia after the chapel and a matching temple (now destroyed) were built, various parts of the complex were added, subtracted, demolished, and restored.

Today, the site consists of three main enclosures: the **Amun-Re Temple Enclosure,** the largest and best preserved, in the center, flanked by the **Montu Temple Enclosure** to the north, and the **Mut Temple Enclosure** to the south. There's also an open-air museum adjoining the Amun-Re Temple Enclosure. You can easily spend 3-4 hours wandering the site's ins and outs, but if your time is limited, stick to the Amun-Re Temple and just keep walking straight through the structure. This main sanctuary for Thebes's favorite deity holds the most impressive bits of the complex like the stunning Great Hypostyle Hall, towering obelisks, and colossi of god-kings.

Tickets must be purchased at a small **visitor center** beside the parking lot (with WCs and a model of the site), before crossing the modern plaza that leads to the sphinx-lined entrance.

AMUN-RE TEMPLE ENCLOSURE

A large cult formed around Amun—the king of the gods and patron of the pharaohs—in Thebes as early as the 21st century BC, and this monumental complex built in his honor is testament to just how serious Thebans were about pleasing him. Lesser deities are also worshiped throughout the complex, particularly Mut (divine mother and Amun's companion) and Khons (mood god and son of Mut and Amun), who completed the Theban Triad.

The main entrance brings you first down an **alley of ram-headed sphinxes,** a symbol of Amun. The **Amun-Re Temple** covers the entire middle section of the complex, extending along two axes (east-west and north-south), and is surrounded by smaller temples and a sacred lake that was once fed by an underground channel connected to the Nile and used for priests' purification rituals. At the lake's northwest corner, keep an eye out for Amenhotep III's red granite **sacred scarab.**

In the Amun-Re Temple, six pylons with courts between them lead to the main sanctuary, and four more pylons branch off to the south. The entrance through the First Pylon leads to a **Great Court** with a towering 13th-century BC **Ramses II** statue (his miniature

Theban Gods and Goddesses

Each region of ancient Egypt had its favorite gods and goddesses, often in sets of three—father, mother, and child. The preferred deities in Thebes, known as the **Theban Triad,** were Amun-Re, Mut, and Khons. This trio (especially the patriarch, Amun-Re) and their priests received the most attention and resources from the pharaohs to embellish temples in their honor.

As power centers rose and fell across the country, the local gods of the erstwhile ruling province sometimes absorbed admirable qualities of other deities, creating an overlap in representations of different gods or hyphenated forms. For example, when Thebes was at the height of its power, Amun became known as Amun-Re—a combined version of Amun and the sun god, Re, whose cult center was located in Heliopolis (modern Cairo) in the north. Amun's companion, Mut, took on characteristics of the lion-headed goddess of war, Sekhmet, and the cow-headed sky goddess, Hathor.

AMUN/AMUN-RE

- **Who he is:** Amun (or Amun-Re) is the king of the gods and patron of the pharaohs.
- **Name means:** "The Hidden One." His images were often painted blue to suggest invisibility.
- **Symbols:** Ram-headed sphinx, ram horns. Often represented in human form with a beard and double plumed crown or with man's body and ram's head. He's commonly depicted with an erect penis as a symbol of his fertility and his role as a creator god.
- **Best appearances in Luxor:** Karnak Temple Complex; Luxor Temple; Medinet Habu Temple; Ramesseum.
- **Alternative spellings:** Amon-Re, Amon-Ra, Amen-Re, Amen-Ra.

MUT

- **Who she is:** Queen of the gods, divine mother to the pharaoh, and Amun's companion.

daughter standing on his feet) and a lonely column—the remains of **Taharqa's Kiosk** (c. 680 BC), a Nubian king's pavilion for resting during royal processions. To the left immediately after the entrance are three shrines to the Theban Triad. To the right is **Ramses III's Temple,** a side car to Amun-Re's main complex, with the pharaoh's statues lining the inner court.

The **Second Pylon** leads to the temple's most spectacular feature, Seti I's **Great Hypostyle Hall** with 134 papyrus columns that once held up a roof. Second only to the grandeur of the columns are the elaborate reliefs on the walls commissioned by Seti I and his son Ramses II (r. 1279-1213 BC).

The **Third Pylon** opens to a small court with a red granite **obelisk** (its twin no longer standing). After the **Fourth Pylon** Queen Hatshepsut added two more obelisks—one vertical, and the other now fallen—in the 14 columned Hypostyle Hall built by her father. This is the oldest part of the temple still standing.

Don't miss the **Temple of Khons** (located in the southwest corner of the Amun-Re Temple Enclosure). Khons's temple is miniature compared to his father's, Amun-Re, but still impressive. The beautiful colors inside this moon god's temple give an idea of what the rest of the Karnak complex looked like before its polychrome walls faded.

MONTU TEMPLE ENCLOSURE

Amenhotep III built this temple to Montu (located north of Amun-Re's), the falcon-headed god of war who reigned supreme in Thebes before Amun-Re took the stage. There's little

- **Name means:** "Mother."
- **Symbols:** Vulture, lioness. Usually depicted as a woman with a vulture headdress topped with the double crown of Lower and Upper Egypt, a female body with the head of a lioness, or as a woman suckling a child.
- **Best appearances in Luxor:** Mut Temple at the Karnak Temple Complex.

KHONS

- **Who he is:** Mood god, son of Mut and Amun.
- **Name means:** "Wanderer," in a nod to the traveling moon.
- **Symbols:** Hawk, baboon. Usually depicted as a young man with side braid or lock of hair wearing a crown with a lunar disk atop a horizontal crescent moon and a cobra on his forehead.
- **Best appearances in Luxor:** Temple of Khons at the Karnak Temple Complex.
- **Alternative spellings:** Khonsu, Chons.

MONTU

- **Who he is:** God of war, the original favored god of Thebes before Amun's ascendence.
- **Symbols:** Falcon, bull. Often represented with a human body and falcon or bull head with two cobras on his forehead and two plumes sticking out of a sun disk crown.
- **Best appearances in Luxor:** Montu Temple at the Karnak Temple Complex.
- **Alternative spellings:** Mont, Monthu, Mentu, Montu-Ra.

left in Montu's Enclosure and its gate is often locked, but you can ask a guard to open it if you're keen on a comprehensive tour. Ruins of additional places of worship surround Montu's, including the Temple of Ma'at—the only remaining temple (itself in shambles) for this goddess of truth, justice, and order.

MUT TEMPLE ENCLOSURE

40LE adults, 20LE students

A good 600 meters (2,000 ft) south of the Temple of Khons along the excavated alley of sphinxes, the Mut Temple Enclosure is full of mostly broken statues of Sekhmet, the lioness goddess of war affiliated with Mut, with one still beautifully intact. Amenhotep III commissioned hundreds of her statues as well as the temple itself. Mut's temple now lies in ruins, surrounded on three sides by a kidney-shaped sacred lake. Few people make it this far south, and you'll likely have the site to yourself.

OPEN-AIR MUSEUM

The whole Karnak complex is really an open-air museum, but this section—the site of ancient structures reassembled by modern archeologists after they'd been taken apart by kings—is unique. The main attractions are **Senusret I's White Chapel,** a small pavilion made of white limestone that's the oldest remaining monument in Karnak, and **Hatshepsut's Red Chapel,** crafted of deep-red quartzite. Both served as way stations, or resting places, for the barque that held the statue of Amun during ritual processions. In Hatshepsut's chapel, the queen (depicted as a man) offers an

Central Luxor

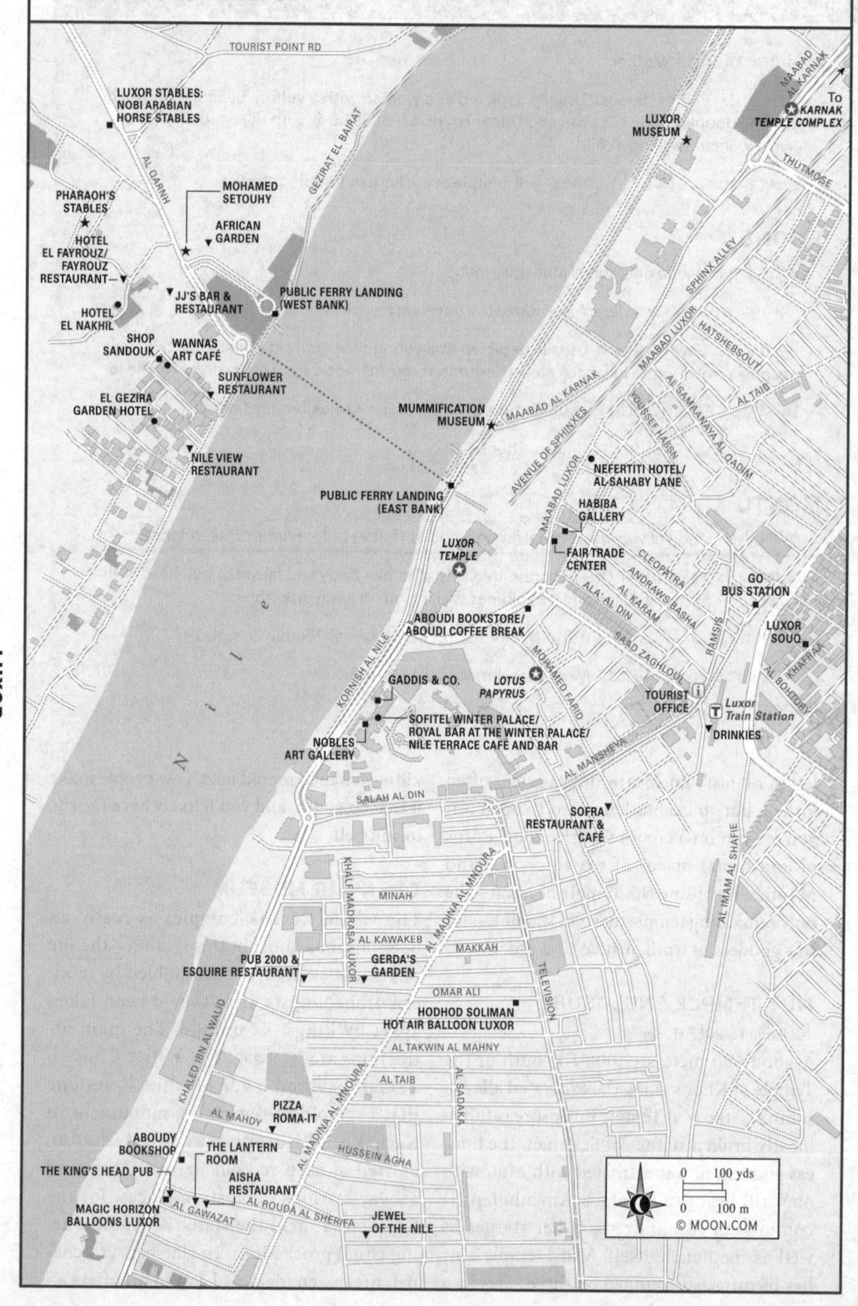

LUXOR SIGHTS

The Opet Festival

The Beautiful Feast of Opet, or Opet Festival, became a major religious celebration in Thebes during the early years of the New Kingdom (c. 1539-1070 BC). The annual jamboree, which coincided with the flood season, centered around a procession that followed a statue of Amun-Re, king of the gods, as he was carried in a sacred barque from his temple in the north (Karnak) to his sanctuary in the south (Luxor Temple). Residents of Thebes marched between the temples along an **Avenue of Sphinxes**—a nearly 3-kilometer-long (2-mi-long) path flanked by hundreds of mostly ram-headed lions (their excavated remains once again visible).

The festivities lasted up to 27 days, culminating in the reunion between the god and ruling king in the **Barque Sanctuary** of Luxor Temple, where the king would make his offerings of incense and flowers, in exchange for the crown and godly powers. If the ritual was not properly performed (so the story went), the world would fall into chaos.

The concept of ka—the divine spirit passed on from ruler to ruler—was central to this ritual. Nowhere else is ka (depicted in hieroglyphs as two raised hands) as prominent as at Luxor Temple. Keep an eye out for the relief scenes here, especially on the wall of **Amenhotep III's Colonnade,** that depict the event. The earliest known images of the Opet Festival are located in **Hatshepsut's Red Chapel** at the Karnak Temple Complex.

erect Amun-Re gifts, and Amun-Re returns the respect. Other reliefs depict her walking behind the sacred barque of Amun-Re, carried on the shoulders of priests during the Opet Festival—the earliest known images of the event. Additional statues and ruins collected throughout the complex have also been moved to these parts.

The open-air museum is located in the northwest section of the Amun-Re Temple Enclosure. To get here, take two lefts at the red obelisk in the middle of Amun's Temple.

Luxor Museum

Corniche el-Nil, 1 km/0.6 mi north of Luxor Temple; tel. 095 237 0569; 9am-2pm and 5pm-9pm daily; 140LE adults, 70LE students

This small-ish but well-curated museum features stunning statues and reliefs, many of which were found beneath courtyards in the Luxor and Karnak Temples, buried by Ptolemaic kings who had no use for earlier rulers' clutter. Objects are well-lit, nicely spaced, and kept cool with strong AC—a godsend after spending the morning in the sun exploring the nearby temple complexes. Plan around 1-3 hours for a visit, depending on how interested you are in reading about the objects (there's great English signage). The attached bookstore offers the museum's catalog and some high-quality books about the region. Clean WCs available. Double check the opening hours as they do change on occasion.

Mummification Museum

Corniche el-Nil, 250 m/800 ft north of Luxor Temple; tel. 095 237 0569; 9am-2pm and 5pm-9pm daily; 100LE adults, 50LE students

This small underground museum dedicated to mummies has some wonderful specimens on display, from humans and monkeys to cats and crocodiles. If you've ever wondered about the ins and outs of mummification, this is the place to come. The items here—like the opened skull filled with linen and resin where the brain once was—show you in gruesome detail what it meant to be preserved for the ages. A visit should only take around 30-45 minutes, and the AC is a nice treat on a hot day. Evening hours are sometimes truncated on a whim, so it's best to pop in earlier.

★ Luxor Temple

Central Luxor, Corniche el-Nil and Mabad al-Karnak St.; no tel.; 6am-9pm daily; 140LE adults, 70LE students

Luxor Temple, originally called the "Southern

1
2
3

Sanctuary," is the town's younger complex, built in its current form mostly by Amenhotep III (r. 1390-1353 BC) and Ramses II (r. 1279-1213)—more than six centuries after the first stones were laid in what's now known as the Karnak Temple.

The 250-meter-long (850-ft-long) structure is divided into two main courts connected by a processional colonnade and followed by a maze of smaller chambers designed for specific rituals. Highlights include the towering statuary and dozens of imposing columns. The man with the erection depicted throughout the temple is the god of honor here, Amun-Re. His depictions in an ithyphallic state remind us he is a creator god, born after impregnating his own mother (which, naturally, begs the question of where his mother came from).

You can spend weeks here examining the details, but 1.5-2 hours should be enough time for a casual visit. The entrance and ticket office are located on the east side of the temple off Mabad el-Karnak Street, smack-dab in the center of downtown Luxor. The site is open late and beautifully illuminated in the evening, so you might want to start at Karnak Temple and visit this one after a leisurely lunch break.

COURTYARD OF RAMSES II

We have Ramses II to thank for the outer parts of the temple: He built the colossal statues of himself and two 25-meter-tall (82-ft-tall) obelisks flanking the towering pylon entrance (one of which now stands in the Place de la Concorde in Paris, gifted by Mohammed Ali to the French in the 1830s). After the entrance, you'll encounter the 74-columned Courtyard of Ramses II decorated with kings and gods (and in case you forgot who built it, more shirtless statues of the serenely smiling pharaoh). To the right sits a **shrine,** built by Queen Hatshepsut and her stepson Thutmose III some 200 years earlier, for the Theban Triad to whom the temple is dedicated: Amun, Mut, and Khons. To the left, the **Mosque of Sheikh Abu el-Haggag** (its minaret dating to the 11th century) rises out of the courtyard, representing a third layer of religion—built on the site of a Coptic church, which was built over part of the ancient god's temple. The mosque is dedicated to the local saint said to have introduced Islam to the town.

1: Ramses II at Karnak Temple Complex **2:** Avenue of Sphinxes outside of Luxor Temple **3:** Ramses II at Luxor Temple

AMENHOTEP III'S COLONNADE

Beyond the courtyard begins Amenhotep III's Colonnade, the original entrance to the temple, with 14 dramatic columns standing 16 meters (52 ft) tall that once held up a roof. Keep an eye out for the relief scenes on the wall of the colonnade that depict the Opet Festival, when a statue of Amun was carried in a sacred barque from his temple in the north (Karnak) to his southern sanctuary (Luxor Temple).

SUN COURT AND BEYOND

The colonnade leads to the spacious **Sun Court of Amenhotep III,** ringed by more columns. After reuniting with Amun in the inner sanctuary during the Opet Festival, the king would emerge here to present himself with renewed divinity to the masses.

The Sun Court connects to a Hypostyle Hall with reliefs of Amenhotep III presenting gifts to Amun and Mut, followed by the Chamber of the Divine King—which was originally dedicated to Amun, but in Roman times became the place to worship the divine emperor. Following a small antechamber with four pillars, you reach the most sacred bit, the Barque Sanctuary, where Amun's image was placed when he visited from Karnak. Alexander the Great (4th century BC) reconstructed the shrine here, adorning it with reliefs of himself as Egyptian pharaoh, on top of Amenhotep III's original.

In the northeast corner of the Barque Sanctuary (to your left as you enter), pass into two connected chambers comprising the Birth Room, depicting the divine birth of Amenhotep III. As the story goes, the pharaoh's mother (Queen Mutemwiya) was impregnated by Amun, an act depicted on the walls here as Amun feeding her the ankh (key of life).

WEST BANK: GOURNA AND AROUND

Be sure to swing by the **Antiquities Inspectorate Ticket Office** (650 m/2,000 ft northwest of Colossi of Memnon on west side of traffic circle; no tel.; 6am-4pm daily) to get your tickets for the **Medinet Habu Temple, Ramesseum, Mortuary Temple of Seti I, Tombs of the Nobles, Deir el-Medina,** and **Howard Carter's House** before you head to those sites (tickets not available at the door). Note that the tickets are only valid for one day, so it might be wise to purchase just a couple at a time or be prepared to stick to a strict time schedule. Admission to the **Mortuary Temple of Hatshepsut,** the **Valley of the Kings,** and the **Valley of the Queens** can be purchased at the entrance to each.

Colossi of Memnon

Memnon St.; no tel.; 24 hours daily; free

These two towering figures of Amenhotep III (r. 1391-1353 BC) stand along the main road that leads to the tombs and temples of the West Bank, welcoming visitors and giving a taste of what's to come.

The colossi are the most impressive remains of Amenhotep III's sprawling mortuary complex, which once rivaled that of Karnak Temple in terms of grandeur but was reduced by floods, earthquakes, and the sticky fingers of later kings. Not even Amenhotep III's name survived in popular parlance—the two colossi were instead named for Memnon, Ethiopian king and son of Eos (goddess of the dawn) from Greek mythology. After they broke in an earthquake during the Roman period, the statue to the right produced a cry as the morning wind blew through its cracks, interpreted by the Greeks as Memnon greeting his mother at dawn. Repairs made in the 3rd century AD quieted the colossus, but his mother still illuminates him each morning in golden hues.

Excavations are ongoing in the plot of land behind the statues, and new discoveries are being re-erected along the way.

Medinet Habu Temple

400 m/1,300 ft southwest of the Antiquities Inspectorate Ticket Office; no tel.; 6am-5pm daily; 100LE adults, 50LE students

This labyrinthine temple rich with reliefs dates back more than 3,500 years. Aside from the sheer size of the structure, the highlights here are the colorful images on the ceiling and columns after the second courtyard, and a handful of beautiful granite statues tucked in the temple's nooks and crannies. A visit should take around 1 hour.

HISTORY

Queen Hatshepsut (r. 1479-1457 BC) and her stepson Thutmose III built a temple to Amun here on the hill where the creator god is said to have appeared for the first time. Their structure was expanded over the centuries, most significantly during the reign of Ramses III (r. 1187-1156 BC) who chose the spot for his mortuary temple, or "mansion of millions of years."

As Egypt was suffering from a string of wars, Ramses III built his mortuary temple as a fortified city complete with workshops, administrative offices, and quarters for priests and officials. The protected outpost became both a place of worship and the administrative center in Thebes—remaining so for centuries. Artisans who lived in the nearby workers' village, Deir el-Medina, moved here around 60 years after Ramses III's death when their town collapsed at the hands of raiding Libyans. In Greco-Roman times, the area was used as a cemetery, and in the 1st millennium AD, a Coptic town grew up around the fortified complex until (it's believed) a plague finally destroyed the town in the 800s AD.

VISITING THE TEMPLE

The temple complex was once connected to the Nile via canal, and the landing quay is still visible beside part of the original fortified gate. Beyond that, an unusual temple

Combatting "Temple Fatigue"

The sheer number of sights—primarily temples and tombs—scattered around Luxor means those short on time (or attention) will be wise to strategize. As magnificent as the monuments are, there can be a sameness to many of them, and casual visitors' eyes may start to glaze over after too many back-to-back visits. To make the most of your trip, keep the following in mind:

- The absolute must-sees are the **Karnak** and **Luxor Temples** on the East Bank, which were sanctuaries for the favored god of Thebes, Amun-Re.
- On the West Bank, the main temples are the pharaohs' **mortuary temples,** or **"mansions of millions of years."** These were built primarily for the deified kings—to keep the cults of the pharaohs active for eternity. Of these, don't miss the **Mortuary Temple of Hatshepsut** and the Mortuary Temple of Ramses III at **Medinet Habu.**
- As with temples, tombs can blend together for visitors who are not particular Egyptology enthusiasts. If you're only interested in checking out a few, head straight to the **Valley of the Kings** on the West Bank.
- Expect a **temple** visit to take around 1-2 hours (with the exception of the Karnak Temple Complex, which easily takes 2-4 hours). Each **tomb** should take around 10 minutes for a visit.

entrance that imitates a Syrian fortress leads to large forecourt with the tomb-chapel of Amun's head priestess to the left. To the right of the tomb-chapel stands the relatively small **Temple of Amun,** with the original structure built by Queen Hatshepsut now found in the inner core. The temple's pylons, court, and columned hall were added over the course of 1,500 years, beginning with Ramses III.

The main attraction, the **Mortuary Temple of Ramses III,** is of classic rectangular style with three main sections and a number of side cars. It starts with the 22-meter-tall (72-ft-tall) pylon adorned with scenes of the pharaoh smiting foreign enemies in front of Amun and Re-Horakhty. Don't miss the reliefs on the outer walls that show the mighty pharaoh's battles against invading "Sea Peoples," alongside images of war preparations and victory celebrations. The naval battle scenes are the oldest recorded depictions of naval warfare in history.

Beyond the first pylon a **courtyard** lined with pillars and statues of Ramses III in Osiris form gives way to the second **pylon** with images of the pharaoh showing off his captives to Amun-Re and his consort, Mut.

The temple was modelled on Ramses II's Ramesseum—Ramses III's predecessor (though not immediate relative), whose achievements the later pharaoh so admired. Demonstrating his veneration, Ramses III offers incense to the sacred barque of Ramses II in carvings within the temple. An inscription above the boat reassures the king he will enjoy his palace for all of eternity: "Beautiful is the monument you have made... your Mansion shall be firmly established like the sky, forever."

To the left of the temple, a mudbrick **palace** (now in ruins) hosted the king during religious festivals. From this angle you also get nice views of the outer temple walls and the sandy mountains in the distance.

Valley of the Queens

1.5 km/0.9 mi northwest of the Antiquities Inspectorate Ticket Office; no tel.; 6am-5pm daily; 100LE adults, 50LE students, 1,400LE extra for Tomb of Nefertari

The wives of pharaohs were buried in these hills on the south side of the protective al-Qurn (the pyramid-shaped mountain affiliated with the sky goddess Hathor), opposite their husbands in the Valley of the Kings.

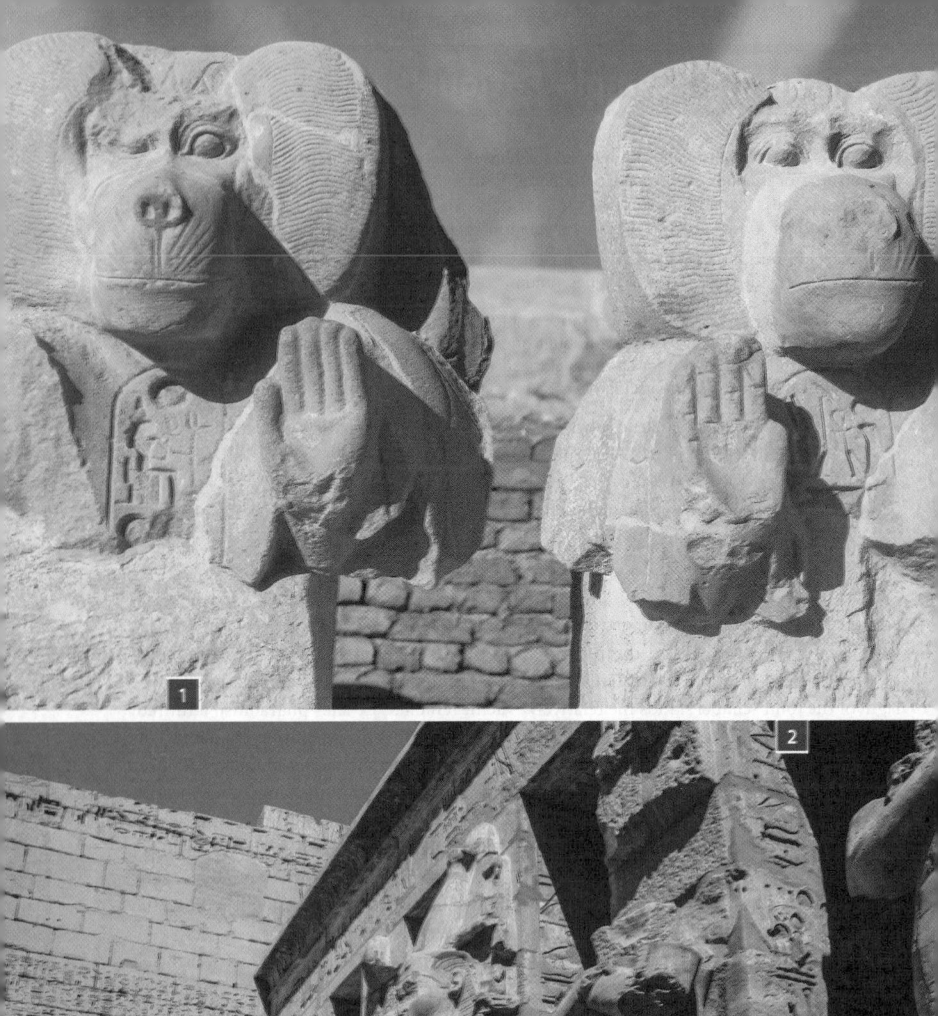
1

2

Royal daughters, sons, and trusted officials also got plots in this necropolis, and by the time the Romans came around, even commoners could rest their bones here.

Today, of the some 100 tombs believed to exist, four are open to the public, three of which are included in your general entrance ticket. The open tombs rotate (usually every few years), and at the time of writing they included the tombs of Queen Titi and two of Ramses III's sons: Amen-khopshef and Khaemwaset. An extra 1,400LE will get you into the fabulous Tomb of Nefertari. Its vibrant colors and rich illustrations are quite magnificent, but the price means it might not be worth it for the casual visitor. (Tip: Do a quick search online for images of the tomb before you go to see if want to drop the cash.)

You can technically only stay in each tomb for 10 minutes, but baksheesh (tips) has the power to slow time. Guides are not allowed to enter. Camera passes cost 300LE, but photography with phones is free.

TOMB OF TITI

Queen Titi's family tree is debated, but she was likely the daughter or wife (or both) of Ramses III. Many of the images on the walls of her tomb are flaked and faded (just think of them as subtle pastels), but it's worth a quick stop while you're in the neighborhood.

TOMBS OF AMEN-KHOPSHEF AND KHAEMWASET

In the tombs of Amen-khopshef and Khaemwaset, their father, Ramses III, leads each son to meet the gods on the young princes' journey into the afterlife. This duty was usually performed by a god, but perhaps the boys' early deaths (both predeceasing dad) made their pharaoh father a more appropriate escort. In the colorful images on their tomb walls, the boys wear the traditional symbol of youth—braided hair fastened to the side by a decorative band—and are depicted behind Ramses III as he embraces the gods.

TOMB OF NEFERTARI

Ramses II built this "house of eternity" for his beloved queen, Nefertari, who died nearly four decades before him (c. 1255 BC). Modeled on the tombs of the Valley of the Kings, it's the most splendid and complex tomb on this lesser hillside—even better than many of the pharaohs' tombs next door—with walls dripping in rich images of the queen's journey to the underworld and her divine rebirth.

The tomb is split into two levels. In the upper rooms, Nefertari meets with the gods who will grant her entrance into the afterlife. When she descends into the burial chamber, she is granted immortality and takes her place beside Osiris, judge of the dead and lord of the underworld.

Above the doorway at the bottom of the steps leading to the burial chamber, Ma'at (goddess of truth, justice, and divine order) sits with extended wings. According to ancient Egyptian mythology, on the day of judgment the heart of the dead would be weighed against her ostrich feather. A heavy heart signified a life lived unjustly, and it would fall into the jaws of Ammit, the goddess of divine retribution—part lion, part crocodile, part hippopotamus.

Throughout the tomb, Nefertari is depicted in her favored headdress—a vulture with hanging wings—and excerpts from the Book of the Dead line the walls, guiding the queen on her journey into the afterworld. The deep blue ceiling covered in stars symbolizes the eternal souls of those who have passed into the afterlife. If the splendor of the tomb isn't testament enough to Ramses II's love for Nefertari, the pharaoh's ode to his late queen engraved on the walls leaves little doubt: "My love is unique; no one can rival her... Gold is nothing compared to her arms, and her fingers are like the lotus flowers... Just by passing, she has stolen away my heart."

In earlier tombs, reliefs were carved directly into the limestone walls, but Nefertari's

1: statues at Ramesseum **2:** statues at Medinet Habu

The Book of the Dead

Ancient Egyptians used a series of texts to help guide and protect them in the afterlife. They called these manuals the "Spells for Going Forth by Day," but 19th-century Egyptologists coined a catchier title: the "Book of the Dead." While the spells were typically recorded on papyrus in hieroglyphs and buried with royals and wealthy officials, during the New Kingdom (c. 1539-1070 BC) rulers began carving the formulas for passage to the afterword on their tomb walls—often substituting the text with colorful images. These spells and their illustrations can be found in the **Valley of the Kings, Valley of the Queens, Tombs of the Nobles,** and the artisans' tombs in **Deir el-Medina.**

is a good example of the later technique, in which the delicate rock was covered in plaster before carving and painting. Her tomb was rediscovered in 1904 by an Italian mission and restored in the early 1990s, but it remained closed to the general public until 2016 (which is why it's still in such good shape).

★ Deir el-Medina

950 m/3,000 ft north of the Antiquities Inspectorate Ticket Office; no tel.; 6am-5pm daily; 100LE adults, 50LE students

The town of Deir el-Medina was likely founded by Thutmose I (r. 1493-1482 BC), the first pharaoh to choose the Valley of the Kings as his resting place. It was home to the artists, artisans, and laborers who dug out the impressive mausoleums we see in the Valleys of the Kings and the Queens and covered them in their exquisite décor. These stonemasons, painters, and carpenters were paid for their services mostly in beer, grain, and oil. At its peak, an estimated 120 families lived here. Around 1165 BC, under Ramses III, the state (in economic crisis) stopped paying workers, prompting one of the first ever recorded strikes. Not coincidentally, for much of the next century tomb robberies devastated the royal resting places. Residents finally abandoned the town in the 11th century BC after repeated raids by Libyans and resettled in the fortified complex of Ramses III's mortuary temple, Medinet Habu.

While not as glamorous as the royal tombs, this workmen's village is every bit as fascinating. Not much remains of the village itself, save the maze-like stubs of their walls. But nestled into the rocks above, the workers built a necropolis of their own, imitating the grand tombs of royalty. It's a striking find in such an unassuming section of the hillside.

On the northeast side of the village stands a small sandstone **temple** from the Greco-Roman period dedicated to the goddesses Hathor and Ma'at. It was later converted into a Coptic church and monastery, giving the site its current name, Deir el-Medina, or Monastery of the City.

You'll find the workmen's tombs up the stairs from the parking lot. The only ones open to the public are those of Sennedjem, Pashedu, Ipuy, and Inherkha. All are included with your entrance ticket. Be sure to purchase your tickets at the **Antiquities Inspectorate Ticket Office** before you come.

TOMB OF SENNEDJEM

Although Sennedjem (spelled "Sennutem" at the site) was but a necropolis functionary, his tomb is fit for a king. He lived in the 13th century BC during the reigns of Seti I and Ramses II. Vibrant images decorate every inch of his walls. On the northeast side, Sennedjem and his wife harvest grain and sow seeds in the afterlife's bountiful fields—an image representing one of the spells from the Book of the Dead. The colors and details are exquisite.

TOMB OF PASHEDU

Pashedu (c. 1290 BC) was the head painter for Seti I's tomb, and his own tomb is as beautifully decorated as you might expect. Through the corridor flanked by images of Anubis (god of embalming), you enter the vaulted burial chamber. On the wall to the immediate right are verses from the Book of the Dead's chapter on "Drinking Water in God's Domain" with a corresponding image of Pashedu beneath a palm tree, drinking from the ground. Note the floating Eyes of Horus symbolizing protection, in this case for the afterlife.

TOMB OF IPUY

Head sculptor of his day, Ipuy (c. 1279-1213 BC) adorned his resting place with scenes from everyday life. His tomb is a tribute to the working man and provides a fascinating window into their world. Paintings depict men weaving fishing nets, washing linens, building structures, and picking grapes while others dance on them to make wine.

TOMB OF INHERKHA

This tomb belongs to a foreman of the necropolis from the days of Ramses III and IV. Bright scenes from the Book of the Dead cover its two vaulted chambers. Keep an eye out for the sun god taking the form of a cat as he slays the serpent of chaos, Apophis, beneath the sacred ished tree (tree of life).

Ramesseum

850 m/2,800 ft northeast of the Antiquities Inspectorate Ticket Office; no tel.; 6am-5pm daily; 80LE adults, 40LE students

The remains of Ramses II's mortuary temple (today known as the Ramesseum) were the inspiration for English poet Percy Bysshe Shelley when he wrote his famous "Ozymandias" (the Greek name for Ramses II)—a sonnet that waxes about the inevitability of man's transience, despite all efforts to achieve an eternal legacy. The great pharaoh's "mansion of millions of years" has suffered the wear of time and the granite heads of his colossal statues lay severed, but major parts of the structure do remain standing (or at least reconstructed) and we still remember his name, which is not bad after more than 3,000 years.

The floor plan for the Ramesseum takes a fairly classic form with two pylons, each followed by a court, then a towering hypostyle hall (a highlight), a series of antechambers with branching rooms, a barque hall, and an inner sanctuary. The pylons depict the pharaoh's famed Battle of Qadesh in Syria, which he nearly lost before it ended in a stalemate (though you'd never know it from the images of him trouncing his Hittite enemies). A more appropriate image might be their signing of a peace treaty—the first recorded in history.

Don't miss the delicate stone toes of Ramses II—all that remains standing from one of the pharaoh's largest colossi—and his truly massive (and now cracked) head, which has fallen behind them. These features alone, along with the beautifully carved sun-worshiping baboons near the entrance to the complex, make the site worth a visit.

Schedule around 30 minutes for this stop, and be sure to pick up your tickets at the Antiquities Inspectorate Ticket Office before you go.

Tombs of the Nobles

550 m/1,800 ft north of the Ramesseum; no tel.; 6am-5pm daily; prices vary

Honeycombed into the hills less than a mile from Deir el-Medina are hundreds of chapels built for high-ranking officials and notables, mostly from the 18th dynasty (c. 1539-1292 BC). The "Tombs of the Nobles," which comprises around 400 such chapels, is a bit of a misnomer as the "tomb" patrons tended to be buried elsewhere (often in pits in the Valley of the Kings). These chambers instead served to commemorate their lives and help their souls reach the afterlife.

With walls covered in images depicting daily scenes of work and play, these gems are worth the visit for those interested in the everyday life of ancient Egyptians. This stop is seldom included in tours and often skipped by casual visitors, so it's likely you'll have the place to yourself. You also have a fairly wide selection to choose from, and tickets combine 2-3 chapels a piece (based on proximity to each other). The tombs of Rekhmire and Sennofer are the best. True art (or history) lovers will enjoy a trip to the other two sets of chapels as well to see a wider variety of motifs from this period.

Buy tickets from the Antiquities Inspectorate Ticket Office before you arrive to the site. The parking lot is just across the street from the Ramesseum. From here, head left to reach the first set of tombs. It's just a few minutes' walk between the tomb groupings, and expect to spend 5-10 minutes in each. Be sure to bring plenty of water, sunscreen, and good walking shoes.

TOMBS OF REKHMIRE AND SENNOFER

40LE adults, 20LE students

If you only visit one set of chapels, these two are far and away the best.

Rekhmire was governor of Thebes under Thutmose III (r. 1479-1425 BC) and Amenhotep II. His oddly shaped chapel takes the form of a small chamber followed by a long narrow corridor (leading nowhere) below a sloping ceiling. Along with some traditional funerary images, there's a wealth of everyday life scenes. At the end of the corridor to the right, the boat and pond surrounded by trees symbolize a "happy land"—the destination of Rekhmire's soul.

Continue around 50 meters (160 ft) uphill and take a left to find the sumptuous chapel of **Sennofer.** Sennofer succeeded Rekhmire as governor of Thebes under king Amenhotep II (r. 1425-1400). After entering down a set of stairs, to the immediate right are images of Sennofer entering the afterlife (after a long, happy life, as the inscriptions tell us). Look up to spot the grapevines on the ceiling, a nod to governor's love of wine. Through the door topped with two symbols of Anubis (the god of embalming) you'll enter a room with four pillars. On the wall to the far right, a priest purifies Sennofer and his sister. On one of Sennofer's necklaces "Alexander" is written in hieroglyphics—a cheeky bit of graffiti from the Greek period.

TOMBS OF RAMOSE, USERHET, AND KHAEMHET

60LE adults, 30LE students

The chapel of **Ramose,** governor of Thebes (c. 1375-1355 BC), is a unique specimen from a period of transition. Work on the tomb began using traditional themes under Amenhotep III, but the style shifted when the king's radical son, Akhenaten, ascended the throne. You enter through a hypostyle hall with columns resembling bundles of papyrus stalks. On either side of the entrance are reliefs that were supposed to be painted, but like the inner part of the chapel, remained unfinished. Akhenaten's revolutionary "Amarna style" is seen on the wall opposite the entrance. A sun with rays terminating in hands shines down—the symbol for the sun disc god, Aten—and the pharaoh and his queen, Nefertiti, honor Ramose from their palace window.

A few meters from the tomb of Ramose you'll find that of **Khaemhet,** a royal scribe and inspector of the granaries under Amenhotep III. His walls have some of the best reliefs in the area. As with many of the chapels in these parts, Khaemhet's is decorated with a blend of themes from his life and traditional funerary images. Immediately after the entrance to the left, the snake goddess Rennut ("Lady of the Granaries") nurses an infant. Beside that, ships full of goods for the royal granaries await unloading in Theban docks.

Just south of Ramose's chapel lies that of **Userhet,** a tutor and scribe under Amenhotep II. Christian hermits destroyed many of the images here (especially those of seductive women), but a good deal still remains if in imperfect condition. On the walls flanking the entrance paintings depict scenes from daily life.

TOMBS OF MENNA AND NAKHT

60LE adults, 30LE students

Menna, scribe of the king's land register under Thutmose IV, has a colorful chapel with a funky zigzag ceiling. Many images have been destroyed, perhaps systematically, with a number of faces scratched out. (It's unclear who's responsible for the destruction or when it took place.) But what's been spared remains in vibrant colors. To the left of the entrance are scenes of planting and harvesting, overseen by a blinded Menna. Through the antechamber into the corridor are scenes of Menna's hobbies in life alongside those to prepare him for the afterlife (a procession of his funerary furniture and cattle). Look for the traditional weighing of the heart ceremony in front of the green-faced god of the afterlife, Osiris, on the right wall—Menna's heart weighed against Ma'at, the goddess of truth and justice, to determine if he's lived a just life.

The small chapel of **Nakht,** scribe of the granaries and astronomer under Thutmose IV, also boasts brilliant zigzag ceilings that seem anachronistic to this 3,400-year-old site. Keep an eye out (to the right of the entrance) for the beautiful scene of Nakht fishing and hunting birds with his family in a patch of reeds. His daughter points out a fish for him to catch, but Nakht died before the artists gave him his spear.

★ Mortuary Temple of Hatshepsut

2.5 km/1.5 mi northeast of the Antiquities Inspectorate Ticket Office; no tel.; 6am-5pm daily; 100LE adults, 50LE students

Queen Hatshepsut's sleek temple rests against the backdrop of a craggy mountain, making its right angles and sharp lines all the more striking. Earthquakes in antiquity destroyed the structure completely, burying it under rocks from the mountain that towers above it. But thanks to a Polish-Egyptian mission and earlier explorers, we have an idea of how grand the monument was some three and a half millennia ago.

Hatshepsut's temple is a refreshing change from the traditional flat, rectangular complexes. Its multi-levels and cliffside home make for a dramatic viewing experience. Ramps lead to progressively higher ground in this three-level structure, from a freestanding base built of local limestone to the rock-cut sanctuary, carved into the face of the mountain.

As the crow flies, the pharaoh queen's

Mortuary Temple of Hatshepsut

Hatshepsut the Pharaoh Queen

Queen Hatshepsut ruled over a peaceful and prosperous Egypt for over two decades (c. 1479-1457 BC) only to be erased from history for thousands of years.

LIFE AND LEGACY

Daughter of warrior king Thutmose I, Hatshepsut married her half-brother (Thutmose II) who became a king for just three years before an untimely death delivered the throne to Thutmose III—child of Thutmose II and a low-status wife in his harem. As aunt and stepmother, Hatshepsut briefly played regent to the boy-king before taking the full title of pharaoh. She commissioned grand statues of herself as a male in traditional pharaonic form (albeit with a slightly more flattering waistline), but kept feminine epithets like "her Majesty."

Her monumental building projects and wildly successful trade missions to the Land of Punt (not to mention her ability to navigate questions of legitimacy as a female pharaoh for so many years) made her one of Egypt's most impressive rulers. But after Hatshepsut's death, Thutmose III led a campaign to destroy the pharaoh queen's legacy. Her stepson wrote his own history—one in which he succeeds his father and assumes the credit for her work. After millennia condemned to oblivion, Hatshepsut's glorious reign was finally returned to the pages of history thanks to the work of modern archeologists.

The late pharaoh queen would no doubt be pleased that some 3,500 years later visitors again stand in awe of her majestic monuments. As she inscribed on one of her obelisks in Karnak: "Now my heart turns this way and that, as I think what the people will say. Those who see my monuments in years to come, and who shall speak of what I have done."

SIGHTS THAT CELEBRATE HATSHEPSUT

- **Mortuary Temple of Hatshepsut** (page 185)
- in the halls of the **Karnak Temple Complex** (page 171)
- in the halls of **Luxor Temple** (page 175)
- **Medinet Habu Temple** (page 178)
- the rock-cut temple **Speos Artemidos** at Beni Hasan (page 143)
- You can visit the queen herself, preserved for the ages, in the Royal Mummies Hall at Cairo's **National Museum of Egyptian Civilization** (page 67).

temple (completed around 1460 BC) is located just a few dozen meters from the Valley of the Kings, where Hatshepsut was laid to rest among her male counterparts some 3,500 years ago. Schedule 1-2 hours for a visit.

LOWER PORTICOS

Reliefs in the **Lower South Portico** (to the left when facing the entrance) depict the celebration of Hatshepsut's 16th year of rule, when obelisks were transported from Aswan to the Temple of Amun in Karnak as part of the Sed festival, or royal jubilee. On the opposite side (the **Lower North Portico**), look for the queen depicted as a mighty sphinx, destroying her enemies.

MIDDLE TERRACE

Ascend the ramp to the Middle Terrace with a colonnade hall for images of Hatshepsut's divine birth. As legend has it, Hatshepsut was born of Queen Ahmose and king of the gods Amun-Re—the act suggested by their position on the edge of a bed (in the north colonnade). A pregnant queen is led to the birth room before Amun-Re declares Hatshepsut queen of all Egypt. Reliefs in the south colonnade show a trade expedition to Punt in Africa.

To the far left of the terrace (when facing the temple) is the **Shrine of Hathor.** From at least the 22nd century BC, locals worshiped this goddess of the sky, love, and fertility on this site. Hathor's prestige continued under Hatshepsut, who built her these two hypostyle halls (with the goddess's head as column capitals), a vestibule, a chamber for the sacred barque, and an inner sanctuary. On the opposite side of the terrace (to the far right) is the Chapel of Anubis, the jackal-headed god of embalming, similarly comprised of a colonnaded hall, a chamber, and an inner sanctuary. The carvings on the hall are some of the temple's best, with vibrant stacks of offerings before Anubis and Amun.

UPPER TERRACE

On the Upper Terrace, 24 statues of the pharaoh queen in the form of Osiris with a false beard and crook and flail once lined the façade. Today, only seven remain. The walls are decorated with images of Hatshepsut's coronation ceremony, in which she was crowned by Horus and Seth with the double crown of Upper and Lower Egypt. The south wall (to the left) is dedicated to her royal *ka,* the queen's divine spirit. **Vaulted rooms** sit on either side of the upper colonnade court, dedicated to herself and her father, Thutmose I, alongside the gods Re-Horakhty and Amun. The niches at the back once held statues of the queen, and an entrance led to the inner sanctuary.

OTHER TEMPLES

Hatshepsut's temple is the main attraction of a larger complex here, Deir al-Bahari, comprised of three temples whose construction spans over 500 years. The earlier **Temple of Mentuhotep** (c. 2040 BC), now in ruins just south of the queen's, served as a resting place for the sacred barque of Amun during the sun god's visit to the West Bank in the annual "Beautiful Feast of the Valley"—a festival to celebrate both Amun and the dead. Hatshepsut's grander mortuary temple became Amun's preferred destination during his hallowed visits to this side of town. After her death, the queen's stepson erected a temple of his own (the **Temple of Thutmose III,** now in ruins on a small terrace between the earlier two). He also redecorated her temple, replacing many of Hatshepsut's images with those of his father (Hatshepsut's late husband), Thutmose II. Many people do choose to skip these temples, dwarfed as they are by Hatshepsut's.

Mortuary Temple of Seti I

Off Wadi el Melook Rd.; no tel.; 6am-5pm daily; 60LE adults, 30LE students

Seti I (r. 1290-1279 BC) built this "mansion of millions of years" for himself and his father, Ramses I, who died after ruling for just two years. Seti I also journeyed into the afterlife before he could finish their home for the rest of eternity, so his son Ramses II saw to the task. Alongside the deified kings, the gods Amun and Re-Horakhty are the center of attention here.

Though the pylons and courtyards have all but disappeared, reducing the temple to only half its original size, the most important part—the covered temple—remains. Inside, more than two dozen massive columns still stand, and sections of walls have managed to hold on to some beautiful reliefs. Few people make it to this "lesser" temple (a very much relative term), making it a great place to visit during the peak hours at the main attractions (around 10am-noon). With the mountains towering in the background and a strip of palm trees for shade, it's also a nice place for a picnic.

Howard Carter's House

Off Wadi el Melook Rd.; no tel.; 6am-5pm daily; 80LE adults, 40LE students

Howard Carter discovered King Tut's tomb in 1922 and left his Luxor home just as it was when he lived there (or at least that's how it's sold). This house-turned-museum offers an intimate peek into the famous British archeologist's life, with letters and photographs strewn on the table, and some neat antique appliances in the kitchen. It's unlikely that all the items actually belonged to Carter, but a good number of them did. Not a must-see attraction, but if you have the extra time it makes for an interesting stop. Purchase tickets at the Antiquities Inspectorate Ticket Office. Behind the house you can also visit an exact replica of Tutankhamun's tomb (same ticket).

★ Valley of the Kings

At north end of Wadi el Melook Rd.; no tel.; 6am-5pm daily; 240LE adults, 120LE students

When it became apparent that the "curse of the pharaoh" didn't prevent tomb robbers from plundering their very visible pyramids, kings turned to more discreet interment. Nearly all the pharaohs of the New Kingdom (1539-1075 BC) were buried in this undulating mountainside known today as Wadi el-Melook, or Valley of the Kings. More than 60 tombs lie carved into the rocks, holding the richly decorated resting places of royalty (including some queens) and high-ranking officials. In each, magical texts decorate the wall alongside images of the tomb owner with the gods. A corridor leads to various halls and a burial chamber where the mummy was laid in a stone sarcophagus, surrounded by possessions for the afterlife.

Unfortunately, despite these later pharaohs' discretion, tomb robbers and successors hoping to boost to their royal coffers stripped most of the chambers of their treasures in antiquity. That of Tutankhamun (r. 1333-1323 BC) was saved from such a fate by fallen rocks until modern explorers stumbled across it in 1922, catapulting the relatively unimportant boy-king to fame. His wealth for the afterlife now sits in the Grand Egyptian Museum in Giza (when not traveling the globe).

VISITING THE TOMBS

Only eight of the 60-some tombs are accessible at any given time with your general entrance ticket, and you have to choose just three. The open tombs rotate throughout the years to minimize damage from visitors' breath and sweat, but they typically stay open for a few years at a time. Each tomb is identified by KV (Kings' Valley) followed by a number. At the time of writing the eight tombs available were those of **Ramses VII** (KV 1), **Ramses IV** (KV2), **Ramses IX** (KV 6), **Merenptah** (KV 8), **Ramses III** (KV 11), **Tausert-Setnakht** (KV 14), **Seti II** (KV 15), and **Siptah** (KV 47).

The tombs do vary quite a bit in quality and levels of preservation, so choose your three wisely. If it's open, don't miss that of **Ramses IV** (KV2) with its long hallway, intricate paintings, bright yellow burial chamber, and granite sarcophagus covered in carvings. The tomb of **Ramses III** (KV 11) is one of the largest, and while its colors aren't the most vibrant of the bunch, the elaborate images and texts lining the walls make up for it. The tomb of **Tausert-Setnakht** (KV 14) is also a unique pick. King Setnakht appropriated Queen Tausert's resting place, expanding her chambers and drawing over her texts and images. The result is one of the most sprawling tombs in the valley.

You can also purchase extra tickets to the tombs of **Ramses V & VI** (KV 9) for 100LE, **Seti I** (KV 17) for 1,000LE, and **Tutankhamun** (KV 62) for 300LE. That of **Ramses V & VI** is well worth the extra cash. It's one of largest, with a stunning astronomical ceiling, long hall, and a number of small staircases leading down to a spacious burial chamber. The tomb of **Seti I** is striking with vibrant colors and ornate imagery, but might not be worth the 1,000LE ticket. In the tomb of **Tutankhamun,** the 19-year-old pharaoh's 3,300-year-old mummy still lies in haunting repose. King Tut's early death meant he didn't have enough time to finish a more elaborate resting place, and instead lies in a smaller tomb not originally intended for royalty. These tombs are always open (not on rotating schedule).

Enter the **Visitor Center** beside the parking lot through the obligatory bazaar aggressively selling cheap souvenirs and overpriced water (yes, this is the only way in… just keep your head down and power through). Inside you can watch a short movie about historic excavations at the site and check out a model of the valley. This is also the best place to use the WC.

The **ticket office** is just through the Visitor Center to the right. Buy the 4LE tram pass here along with your tickets if you want to hitch a ride to the start of the tombs; otherwise, it's a 10-minute walk. If you're keen to check out the maximum number of tombs, you might consider buying a **Luxor Pass** (available for purchase here; $100 adults, $50 students). This will grant you entrance into all eight tombs that are open, plus two of the three (KV 9 and KV 62) that normally require an extra ticket. The **Premium Luxor Pass** ($200 adults, $100 students) is needed to visit the tomb of Seti I.

A bit of baksheesh (tips) to the tomb guards can go a long way and will likely open locked doors and get you into some additional tombs. A camera ticket is an extra 300LE (tripods not permitted), but you can take photos with your phone for free. Guides are not allowed to enter with you. Ticket office closes at 4pm. Around 10-20 minutes for each tomb should be sufficient.

Recreation and Activities

FELUCCA TRIPS

Enjoy the calm of the river as you float between lush farmland and Nile-side temples. The best time of day for the trip is just before sunset or sunrise when the weather is cool and the Nile illuminated in iridescent pinks and blues. Head north for the best views of the green West Bank and its golden mountains.

You can pick up a felucca parked along the East Bank's Nile Corniche (Corniche el-Nil). Trips should cost around 100-150LE/hour for a private boat, plus an extra 20% or so tip for your boat driver if you enjoy the ride.

BIKING

Luxor's West Bank is a fairly flat and easy ride with the exception of the ascent to the Valley of the Kings, which is perfectly doable unless you get a bike with a wonky chain (many of them). Be sure to give it a test ride uphill before you set out.

Rent a bike through your hotel or head to **Mohamed Setouhy** (Al Qarna Rd., 300 m/1,000 ft northwest of Ferry Landing across from Yarra Market, West Bank; tel. 0100 223 9710; 7am-7pm daily; 75-100LE/day). There's a small incline on the street in front of Mohamed's shop where you can test the chain.

★ HOT-AIR BALLOON RIDES

Ballooning over the West Bank's mountains and temples at sunrise is an enchanting way to start the day. Flights usually leave at dawn and last 45-70 minutes (be sure to specify you want the earliest departure to catch sunrise if that's the case). All trips take off from the "Ballooning Airport" on the West Bank (near the Ramesseum), but operators typically include hotel pickup in the package. Book directly with one of these reputable companies to avoid paying extra for commission. Listed prices are for shared balloons (6-32 people) during high season (Nov.-Mar.), or for a premium you can reserve your own. During the low season (summer) or for last-minute bookings, tickets can be around half as much. And as with most things in Luxor, prices are negotiable. Don't forget to tip your guide if you enjoyed the flight. Note: Trips can be canceled at last minute due to weather restrictions (usually related to wind), so if this is a must-do on your list, try not to leave it for the last day.

TOP EXPERIENCE

☆ The West Bank by Bike

In the cooler months (late Oct.-Mar.), getting yourself to the tombs and temples on the West Bank by bike is a marvelous way to explore the "City of the Dead" at your own pace. Be sure to lock your bike up near the security booth at the entrance of each site, and bring more water than you think you need.

Try this 19-kilometer (12-mi) route, or modify it to suit your preferences. For a 12-kilometer (7.5-mi) trip, strike step 2.

sightseeing by bike on the West Bank

1. From the Ferry Landing, take the main road (**Al Qarna Rd.**) northwest until you cross a bridge and it turns into Memnon Street. After 3 kilometers (2 mi), you'll be welcomed by the two massive statues of Amenhotep III, the **Colossi of Memnon.**

2. Continue 650 meters (2,000 ft) to the traffic circle and take a right, and then keep going for 2.6 kilometers (1.6 mi) until you reach another traffic circle. A left and 1 kilometer (0.6 mi) will bring you to the magnificent **Mortuary Temple of Hatshepsut.** (If you feel confident in your bike, you can take a shortcut on the sandy road that passes in front of the Tombs of the Nobles. But chains are known to fall off in these parts, and it would only save you 1 km/0.6 mi of extra cycling.)

3. Head back the way you came to the first traffic circle. Continue straight a few meters and the **Antiquities Inspectorate Ticket Office** will be on your left. Pick up tickets for Medinet Habu Temple, Deir el-Medina, and the Ramesseum.

4. Keep pedaling for 600 meters (2,000 ft) more to reach **Medinet Habu Temple.** If you're in need of a boost, grab lunch, a fresh juice, or some coffee at **Café & Restaurant Maratonga** across the street.

5. Head 1.3 kilometers (0.8 mi) north to **Deir el-Medina** to visit the artisans' village, their colorful tombs, and the small Greco-Roman temple dedicated to goddesses Ma'at and Hathor.

6. Another 1.3 kilometers (0.8 mi) along the same road will loop you down and around to the **Ramesseum.** For another pick-me-up, pop into the **Ramesseum Rest House.**

7. Return to the traffic circle next to the ticket office (1 km/0.6 mi), take a left back down Memnon Street until it turns into Al Qarna Rd., and you'll be back to the Ferry Landing after another flat 4 kilometers (2.5 mi). Replenish your calories in the nearby gardens of **Fayrouz Restaurant.**

ACE Animal Care

El Habil Rd., East Bank; tel. 0100 045 2929; www.ace-egypt.org.uk; 9am-5pm Sat.-Thurs.; free

Tucked away in the green fields on the outskirts of the East Bank, this animal rehabilitation center provides free medical care to Luxor's animals and promotes awareness about animal welfare in the community. The sad state of many of the work animals (mostly donkeys and horses) around Luxor makes this a special place, and worth a visit for those looking to see a different side of the city. They're happy to welcome visitors for a tour of their hospital and stables. True animal lovers can volunteer for a week or more. Donations are appreciated.

The rehabilitation center is about a 10-minute drive from the center (near Luxor Temple). Grab a taxi and ask to go to "mustashfa el-hayawanat" ("the animal hospital").

HODHOD SOLIMAN HOT AIR BALLOON LUXOR

Corner of Television St. and Omar Ali St., East Bank; tel. 0122 2222 811; www.hodhodsolimanballoons.com; 8am-9pm daily; 1,750LE per adult

Hodhod Soliman has been in business since 1993 and has maintained an excellent reputation for safe and fun trips.

MAGIC HORIZON BALLOONS LUXOR

Khaled Ibn El Walid St., opposite Steigenberger Nile Palace, East Bank; tel. 095 227 4060; www.visitluxorinhotairballoon.com; 9am-9pm daily; 2,000LE per adult

Another well-respected company that's been flying over Luxor for decades.

HORSE, CAMEL, AND DONKEY RIDES

Exploring the West Bank on a four-legged friend is a fabulous way to see a different side of Luxor. Sunrise or sunset are the best times to ride through the desert, banana trees, and sugarcane fields. There are two excellent stables to choose from (best to stick to one of these to avoid riding maltreated animals). Wear comfortable shoes and bring plenty of water and sunscreen. The guides rely on tips for much of their income, so if you're happy with your trip, you know what to do.

LUXOR STABLES: NOBI ARABIAN HORSE STABLES

Off al-Qarna Rd. after the Mobil Gas Station, Gezirat El Bairat, West Bank; tel. 0100 504 8558; www.luxorstables.com; 6am-6pm daily; horses and camels 100LE/hour, donkeys 50LE/hour

This is the most professional stable in town. Nobi and his team know how to treat both visitors and animals. They prioritize safety, sending you out with a skilled guide and (if you wish) a helmet. Call ahead or pop in to plan your trip. You can opt for a set route, riding through quaint villages and to some of the West Bank's most beautiful temples, or create your own. Rides typically last 1-4 hours. Hotel pickup available for a small additional cost.

PHARAOH'S STABLES

Gezirat El Bairat, West Bank; tel. 0100 6324961; 5am-5pm daily; horses and camels 100LE/hour, donkeys 70LE/hour

Mustafa and his team also have a beautiful stable full of well-tended animals. They're happy to organize around your schedule—you can ride for an hour or a full day, and stay out later than official opening hours. Expert guides will accompany you and helmets are available. Prices reduced for larger groups. Their stable is a bit more difficult to find, but it's located just beside Amon Hotel—around 650 meters (2,000 ft) west of the Ferry Landing.

Shopping

On the East Bank, most of the good shopping is an easy walk from Luxor Temple. A number of these stores make a point to advertise they're "hassle free," and after a few minutes in Luxor you'll find out why this is such a coveted feature. The labyrinthine Luxor Souq, just 10 minutes on foot to the east of Luxor Temple, cannot make such a claim. But for those who don't mind a bit of pushy salesmanship, it's a fun place to explore. The stores on the West Bank are much more scattered, and you might want to integrate any shopping into your sightseeing schedule when you're already in the neighborhood with a car or bike.

The best items to look for while you're in town are handmade scarves, alabaster statues, and papyrus paintings. You can find the finest samples of each at Habiba Hand Weaving, Imhotep Alabaster Luxor (both on the West Bank), and Lotus Papyrus on the East Bank.

CENTRAL LUXOR: EAST BANK

Markets

LUXOR SOUQ

Corner of el-Souk St. and al-Seka al-Hadid St.; no tel.; 7am-midnight daily

This central market—part covered, part open-air—has a bit of everything. In some sections, locals buy their fruits, spices, meat, and (live) pigeons, and in others, visitors come to snag cheap souvenirs or high-quality handicrafts. A good deal of the items on sale here actually come from Cairo's main bazaar (Khan el-Khalili), but you should be able to find some nice locally made scarves and alabaster statues. Haggling, of course, is key. While the souq is technically open until midnight, it's best to go before 8pm as shopkeepers start to close up early on slower nights.

Gifts

HABIBA GALLERY

Andrawes Pasha St., across from Luxor Temple exit; tel. 0100 124 2026; www.habibagallery.com; 10am-10pm daily

If you don't mind paying a bit extra for a calmer shopping experience, check out this little store brimming with high-quality handicrafts—both from Luxor and elsewhere around Egypt. You can find locally woven scarves, painted wooden dolls from Aswan, embroidered bags from the Sinai, pottery from Fayoum, and silver jewelry from Cairo. The prices are fixed and they pride themselves on "hassle free" shopping (a refreshing change of pace from some other spots in the city).

FAIR TRADE CENTER

Mabad al-Karnak St., near Luxor Temple; tel. 0100 034 7900; ftc@egyptfairtrade.org; 9am-9pm daily

This fair-trade outlet sells well-made handicrafts from around the country: alabaster, scarves, pottery, and needlework from Luxor; wool carpets from Marsa Matruh; and rosewood kitchenware from the nearby village of Hagaza, among other treasures. Prices are fixed (and reasonable), and much of the profits goes to the women-led community projects that produce the goods.

★ LOTUS PAPYRUS

Mohammed Farid St., across from Arabesque Hotel; tel. 0122 564 4604; 4pm-10pm daily

Artist and owner Mohsen Riad is an absolute gem. Visit his small shop after you've explored a few tombs, and he can paint you a custom-made papyrus of your favorite scenes. Otherwise, just pop in and browse his vast collection of papyrus paintings, rich with ancient symbols and stories that he can explain. Portraits also available and prices very reasonable.

NOBLES ART GALLERY

Corniche el-Nil. St., in the Winter Palace Hotel; tel. 0109 124 7625; www.thenoblesluxor.com; 9am-10pm daily

This upscale art gallery doubles as an antique shop, with beautifully carved granite statues and busts of some of the characters you'll see scattered throughout Luxor's tombs, temples, and museums. You can even take home a 19th-century flywhisk made of horsehair or an antique silver dagger. The shop blends seamlessly into the colonial era Winter Palace Hotel within which it's located (to the right after the entrance), and it screams high culture. Prices match the setting, but even window shopping here is a delight (just try not to break anything).

Books

ABOUDI BOOKSTORE

28 Mabad al-Karnak St., next to Luxor Temple; tel. 0101 098 7293; www.aboudi-bookstore.com; 10am-10:30pm daily

Book lovers rejoice! The shelves here are brimming with a fantastic array of English-language books about Luxor and elsewhere in Egypt. Established in 1909, it's a Luxor institution and an official partner of the American University in Cairo Press. You can find everything from the general to the super-niche, with good overarching histories or entire books on single tombs. Fiction, Arabic-language learning books, and small souvenirs also available. Enjoy your purchases upstairs in the café overlooking Luxor Temple.

GADDIS & CO.

Corniche el-Nil. St., at the Winter Palace Hotel; tel. 095 237 2142; 10am-10pm daily

Established in 1907, this shop is part bookstore, part museum. The vintage photos from the lens of its photographer founder, Attiya Gaddis, are a treasure. And the selection of books spans the gamut from historical to contemporary prints. Silver jewelry, papyrus paintings, and other small souvenirs are also available for good (and fixed) prices.

ABOUDY BOOKSHOP

Corner of Khaled Ibn al-Walid St. and Gawazat St., across from Steigenberger Nile Palace Hotel; tel. 0109 701 9410; 8am-10:30pm daily

Distant relatives of the owners of the Aboudi Bookstore, this side of the family didn't get the original shop, but their book selection is nearly as good. In addition to English-language books on Luxor and Egyptology, there's a nice selection of souvenirs with appliqué decorated in pharaonic themes and pretty paintings, posters, and postcards.

CENTRAL LUXOR: WEST BANK

Gifts

SHOP SANDOUK

Gezirat El Bairat; tel. 0100 093 4980; www.shopsandouk.business.site; 10am-10pm Sat.-Thurs.

This jam-packed shop has a wide range of handicrafts from around Egypt. Browse their brass canopic jars, arabesque lamps, alabaster vases, framed proverbs in Arabic calligraphy, and colorful array of unique clothing items handmade in Luxor and surrounding villages.

To get here from the Ferry Landing, walk 500 meters (1,600 ft) along the riverside path south toward Mesala Hotel and turn right. The shop is at end of street to the left.

WEST BANK: GOURNA AND AROUND

Gifts

★ HABIBA HAND WEAVING

Memnon St., 1 km/0.6 mi south of Colossi of Memnon; tel. 0101 644 3494; www.habibahandweaving.com; 8am-6pm daily

Beautiful handmade scarves of 100% Egyptian cotton are the main attraction here, but there's a range of treats to choose from (carpets, bags, jewelry, tablecloths). Peruse the various patterns or put your own personal touch with a made-to-order piece. Come between 8am-3pm Sat.-Thurs. to watch the skilled weavers at work. If the shop is closed, just call and the owners will likely open within minutes (they're probably next door).

CARAVANSERAI

Medinet Habu Rd.; tel. 0122 327 8771; 8am-9pm daily

Cross a little wooden bridge into this spacious den of handicrafts from around Egypt. Jewelry and textiles hang off mudbrick walls, and handblown glass baubles dangle from the thatched ceiling. There's also a nice selection of scarves, pottery, and handwoven palm baskets. Located just 250 meters (800 ft) east of the Medinet Habu Temple complex.

IMHOTEP ALABASTER LUXOR

Off Sawalim Village Rd., 400 m/1,300 ft west of the Mortuary Temple of Seti I; tel. 0100 091 0045; www.the-imhotep-factory-for-alabaster.business.site; 8am-5pm daily

The West Bank is brimming with alabaster shops, but this expansive warehouse is the best by far. Their shelves are stacked with beautiful vases, statues, reliefs, canopic jars, and replicas of busts found around Luxor. Alabaster is the main medium, but additional treasures are available in granite, limestone, and basalt.

Food

Food in Luxor isn't much different from what you find elsewhere in Egypt, with grilled chicken, kebab and kofta (ground meat), and mezze (small salads and dips) on nearly every menu. The good number of British expats and travelers in these parts also means there's a surprisingly large selection of pub food.

CENTRAL LUXOR: EAST BANK

Egyptian

★ SOFRA RESTAURANT & CAFÉ

90 Mohamed Farid St.; tel. 095 235 9752; https://sofra.com.eg; 11am-midnight daily; 80-100LE mains

Tucked away off the busy streets near the train station, Sofra ("dining table" in Arabic) occupies a former house from the 1930s. Arabesque tiles, brass tabletops, and tall ceilings make for a charming setting. You can choose from a tasty array of hot and cold mezze and traditional Egyptian dishes like a lamb shank and okra tagine or rabbit with rice and mokokhiya (soupy greens). Try to snag a seat in the garden covered in creeping vines or on the rooftop terrace for fresh air and the best ambiance. You might want to call ahead to reserve, but it's not entirely necessary. Their seasonal fresh juices are divine.

AL-SAHABY LANE

Al-Sahaby St., off Luxor Temple St.; tel. 095 225 6086; 11am-11pm daily; 80-160LE mains

Hidden in an alleyway near Luxor Temple, Al-Sahaby Lane is a solid spot to satisfy your hunger with some Egyptian fare. The grilled dishes come out on little beds of coals to keep them warm, and the lentil soup is a treat. Sit beneath fairy lights at street level, or on the beautiful rooftop terrace looking out over Luxor Temple.

AISHA RESTAURANT

El Rawda El Sharifa St.; tel. 0100 796 7391; 11am-11pm daily; 80-160LE mains

The chefs at this casual Egyptian restaurant have fun with the plating. Fruit salads come out looking like peacocks and french fries like log cabins. The food is also tasty (try the lamb tagine or vegetable curry), and you can enjoy it with a beer or wine.

International

PIZZA ROMA-IT

St. Joseph St., beside el-Madina Club; tel. 0111 879 9559; noon-midnight Sat.-Thurs.; 1pm-midnight Fri.; 30-100LE mains

Enjoy some of the best pizza in town in this colorful space with soft lighting and photos of Italy tastefully arranged on the walls. Pizza is clearly the main attraction (and you have a wide variety of toppings to choose from), but pasta dishes are also available. Don't miss the garlic bread with pesto.

JEWEL OF THE NILE

El Rawda El Sharifa St.; tel. 0106 432 6698; 5pm-11pm Sat.-Thurs.; 50-100LE mains

The British-Egyptian couple who run this restaurant split the menu between their homelands, offering dishes for a variety of tastes. Each Sunday they serve a proper Sunday roast, and on any day of the week you can enjoy plates like juicy kebab and kofta (grilled meat), succulent steak with mashed potatoes, or seabass with lemon sauce. The décor is a bit tacky with mass-produced papyrus paintings on the walls, but the tablecloths are a nice touch.

GERDA'S GARDEN

Ali Ibn Abi Taleb St., off Khaled Ibn el-Walid St.; tel. 0100 968 7337; 1pm-10pm Tues.-Sun.; 50-125LE mains

German precision meets Egyptian flavor at this cross-cultural creation. The co-owner doubles as chef, and you can tell he's passionate about making the dishes just right. Choose from Egyptian food, like tasty kebab and kofta, or German specialties like hackbraten (meatloaf) or goulash. Food is fresh, fantastic, and made to order. Don't miss the soup.

THE LANTERN ROOM

El Rawda El Sharifa St.; tel. 095 236 1451; 5pm-10:30pm Tues.-Sun.; 100-150LE mains

English pub food tops the menu here with your choice of minced meat pies, mashed potatoes and gravy, or fish-and-chips. Egyptian and other international dishes also available, like naan, coconut curry, and buttered chicken. Beer and wine are, of course, served.

Cafés and Snacks

ABOUDI COFFEE BREAK

Mabad al-Karnak St., near McDonald's; tel. 0101 060 7702; 9am-1am Sat.-Thurs., 12:30pm-1am Fri.; 10-20LE juice and hot drinks

With fabulous views of the Luxor Temple and bustling downtown, this café is a great place to recharge and watch the world go by. The mango juice is delicious, and you can't go wrong with their other fresh juice options. Be sure to tell them you'd like it "taza" (fresh) and "sada" (plain) if you don't want any added sugar or syrups. They also serve a surprisingly long menu of mediocre café food (sandwiches, pasta, pizza, burgers, etc.). It's not exactly a dining destination, but you'll find something edible. You can pick up some good reading material from their sister bookstore below.

★ NILE TERRACE CAFÉ AND BAR

Winter Palace Hotel, 17 Corniche el-Nil St.; tel. 095 238 0422; www.sofitel.accor.com; 4pm-10pm daily; 90-200LE local beer, wine, and cocktails

Watch the sun set behind the Theban mountains while you sip on a fresh juice or harder cocktail from the Winter Palace Hotel's terrace overlooking the Nile. Light snacks and sandwiches also available. While you're here, you can also check out the other parts of the historical Winter Palace.

CENTRAL LUXOR: WEST BANK

Egyptian

FAYROUZ RESTAURANT

At Hotel El Fayrouz, Gezirat El Bairat; tel. 095 231 2709; 6am-11pm daily; 60-80LE mains

Enjoy Egyptian and international treats in spacious garden seating surrounded by lush green flora. Their pasta dishes are a bit pedestrian, but they do a great shish tawook (chicken shish kebab) and wonderful starters. The menu is long and varied, with plenty of vegetarian options, so best to ask what's fresh. Beer, wine, local spirits, and shisha available.

SUNFLOWER RESTAURANT

Gezirat El Bairat, 400 m/1,300 ft south of the Ferry Landing along the riverside; tel. 0100 900 2234; 9am-11pm daily; 70-90LE mains

Sample a dazzling array of tagines (beef, fish, vegetarian), juicy grilled chicken, stuffed pigeon, and salads. The shaded rooftop terrace

1
2
Sprite

decorated with colorful murals is a pleasant place to enjoy a breezy afternoon meal or a cool evening snack with beer or wine. Pizza, pasta, and burgers are also available. It is a bit touristy, but not lacking in quality. Located across from el Mesala Hotel.

NILE VIEW RESTAURANT

Gezirat El Bairat, 450 m/1,500 ft south of the Ferry Landing along the riverside; tel. 0100 656 9957; 8am-midnight daily; 70-100LE mains

Enjoy tasty Egyptian dishes on the riverside or rooftop of this relaxed restaurant—both offering (as the name suggests) lovely views of the Nile. Try the fresh fish, spread of traditional mezze (tahini, baba ghanoush, salads, etc.), and fabulous just-made juice cocktails (non-alcoholic). The service is just as pleasant as the food, and many of the ingredients come straight from the owner's family farm.

★ AFRICAN GARDEN

Off al-Qarna Rd., across from the West Bank Bus Station; tel. 0111 313 1380; 9am-11pm daily; 70-100LE mains

Dine in the garden of this classy oasis surrounded by sweeping vines, pretty tiles, and redbrick arches. The food is fresh and colorfully presented with hearty tagines or lighter fare, like grilled chicken and salad, to choose from. Rice, vegetables, and tasty local bread included. In the evenings, all is warmly illuminated and pleasant music pours from the speakers. Beer and wine available. Not to be confused with Africa Restaurant closer to the Nile.

★ WANNAS ART CAFÉ

Gezirat El Bairat, 150 m/500 ft west of the Nile beside el Mesala Hotel; tel. 106 736 7161; 9am-10pm daily; 100LE mains

Enjoy fresh Egyptian food with a creative twist while admiring the art-covered walls at this vegetarian-restaurant-meets-art-space. The colorful dishes are bursting with flavor and served in pretty pottery from Fayoum. Don't miss the tomato soup, fresh salads, and eggplant tagine. Shaded outdoor seating also available (with warming fire pit on cool nights). The coffee here is also some of the best around.

1: Sofra Restaurant & Café **2:** Egyptian meal served at a restaurant on the Nile

WEST BANK: GOURNA AND AROUND

Egyptian

RESTAURANT MOHAMMED

Gourna, 110 m/360 ft southwest of the Antiquities Inspectorate Ticket Office; tel. 0122 385 0227 or 0101 089 4585; 8am-11pm daily; 75-100LE mains

Tucked in a shady garden lined with trees and thick wood vines, Restaurant Mohammed offers a solid selection of traditional Egyptian dishes. Choose a main (duck, chicken, fish, or beef), and crisp salads, fresh flatbread, rice, and fries will come along with it. Seating is cushioned and comfortable and the family (Mohammed et al.) that owns the place gives a warm welcome. Cold beer available.

★ NOUR EL-GOURNA RESTAURANT

At Nour el-Gourna Hotel, across from the Antiquities Inspectorate Ticket Office; tel. 0114 428 1119; 8am-10pm daily; 80-120LE mains

Cool off in this patch of palm trees as you enjoy delectable dishes from the family farm. The fresh bread from their mudbrick oven is enough to make it worth the visit. Add to that tender orange chicken with complimentary mezze (cucumber and tomato salad, tahini, baba ghanoush, etc.), rice, and vegetables, and it's an essential West Bank stop. There are plenty of vegetarian options and other meats available. Service is friendly and portions generous. Cold beer served.

MARSAM RESTAURANT

At Marsam Hotel, 260 m/850 ft northeast of the Antiquities Inspectorate Ticket Office; tel. 0100 342 6471; www.marsamhotelluxor.com; 6:30am-10pm daily; 140-200LE mains

Though it's a bit pricier than other spots in town, Marsam is a pleasant place to break for lunch while visiting the West Bank sites.

Dine beneath the shade of trees in their well-manicured garden patio, and enjoy the generous portions of Egyptian dishes with a cold beer. Be sure to come hungry (or ready to share). Salads, bread, rice, and vegetables are included with your main dish (grilled chicken, beef, or fish tagines and the like). Many of the ingredients come from the sprawling green fields you see as you enjoy your meal. Kitchen closes 5-7pm.

International

CAFÉ & RESTAURANT MARATONGA

Gourna, in front of Medinet Habu Temple; tel. 0103 224 8447; www.caferestaurantmaratonga.wordpress.com; 5am-9pm daily spring-fall, 6am-7pm daily winter; 90-120LE mains

This Egyptian-German café and restaurant uses only the freshest ingredients for their delicious dishes and juices. There's something for everyone—pizzas, burgers, fish, salads, classic Egyptian fare, cold beer, and even decent coffee. Conveniently located across from Medinet Habu Temple. Seating is open-air, but with plenty of shade and ceiling fans.

Cafés and Snacks

RAMESSEUM REST HOUSE

Gourna, on east side of the Ramesseum; tel. 0106 184 8160; 6am-midnight daily; 70-100LE mains

If you find yourself in need of a boost after visiting the Ramesseum, this is the most convenient spot to recharge. You can enjoy a cold beer, fresh juice, or some simple Egyptian fare on their shaded terrace, surrounded by green and looking out the temple complex.

Bars and Nightlife

There's not much "nightlife" per se in Luxor, but you can easily get a drink or pick up alcohol to go from the Egypt-wide liquor store chain **Drinkies** (Ramsis St., just south of the train station, East Bank; tel. 19330; www.drinkies.net; 10am-10pm daily). If you don't want to drink alone, head to one of Luxor's pubs or bars (smoking, of course, is permitted at all).

Another option for after-dark entertainment is the **Sound and Light Show at Karnak Temple** (Mabad al-Karnak St., Karnak Temple; no tel.; www.soundandlight.show; 7pm Mon.-Tues. and Thurs.-Sat., 8pm Sun. and Wed.; 300LE adults, 150LE children). It isn't the best one in Egypt (and includes a bit of hazardous walking in the dark), but some may enjoy the sight of the majestic temple illuminated at night. Additional times in German, French, and Arabic.

CENTRAL LUXOR: EAST BANK

THE KING'S HEAD PUB

Khaled Ibn El-Waleed St., opposite The Lotus Hotel; tel. 0106 510 2133; noon-midnight daily; 45-70LE beer and wine, cocktails from 100LE

This pub (Luxor's first, though it only dates to 1994) has a bit of a frat house vibe, with a pool table, photos of Che Guevara, a wall covered in visitors' graffiti, and a painting of Mona Lisa smoking shisha. Along with local beer and wine, strong cocktails, simple pub food, and Egyptian mezze are served. The clientele is mostly Western tourists and expats.

PUB 2000 & ESQUIRE RESTAURANT

Ali Ebn Taleb St. off Khaled Ben El-Waleed St.; tel. 0128 659 3103; 1pm-midnight daily; 40-60LE local beer and wine

Another pub covered in British flags with good prices for local beer, wine, and cocktails.

The food here is also surprisingly good (try the chicken shawarma and fries) with a variety of Egyptian and British dishes on offer. Owner and staff extremely friendly and accommodating. The pub may stay open as late as 2am if there are customers. Imported alcohol also available.

ROYAL BAR AT THE WINTER PALACE

At the Winter Palace Hotel, 17 Corniche el-Nil St.; tel. 095 238 0422; www.sofitel.accor.com; 9am-12:30am daily; 90-200LE local beer, wine, and cocktails

For something classy, head to the Royal Bar at the Winter Palace Hotel for a proper cocktail and live piano music (musicians play from 7:30pm Mon.-Sat.). Champagne and French wines are also available, along with tasty mezze and other snacks. Smart casual dress code. If you're not dressed appropriately or prefer to enjoy your drinks en plein air, head to the hotel's **Central Park Bar** (10am-9pm daily) by the pool, where your shorts and flip-flops will be perfectly acceptable.

CENTRAL LUXOR: WEST BANK

JJ'S BAR & RESTAURANT

At El-Gezira Garden Hotel; tel. 0106 426 3878; www.jjsbargezira.weebly.com; 10:30am-11:30pm Thurs.-Mon.; 50-60LE local beer and wine

A casual bar and restaurant owned by an English couple, one of whom (Axel) plays the blues on occasion. Try their classic fish-and-chips or famous double-decker burger, or just come to enjoy a cold beer. The outdoor seating is spacious, shaded, and cool with no shortage of fans. The pair opened the restaurant in 2009 and have since cultivated a community of inviting regulars who attend their range of events, like pub quizzes, karaoke, dance parties, artisan markets, and bingo. Clientele is mostly older and Western. Check their Facebook page for upcoming events.

Accommodations

Luxor has a sweeping array of hotels, from budget to boutique to full-out luxury with options on both sides of the Nile. Stick to the East Bank if you like to be in the center of the bustle, or head to the West Bank for calmer quarters and proximity to most of the sights. The West Bank is also generally cheaper (and just a few minutes on a ferry from the city center). Check out Airbnb for some great economical options. All hotels below have air-conditioning unless otherwise stated.

CENTRAL LUXOR: EAST BANK

Under 800LE

NEFERTITI HOTEL

El Sahabi St.; tel. 0100 0329 991; https://nefertitihotel.com; 470LE d

This nice budget hotel is about as central as it gets. The 30 rooms are spotless, if a bit spartan—but they do have some splashes of color and the occasional towel animal. Enjoy your complimentary breakfast or a delicious evening meal on the rooftop terrace looking out to Luxor Temple. The staff are supremely friendly, always available, and can help arrange outings around town at reasonable prices.

GREATER EAST BANK

1,650-3,300LE

STEIGENBERGER RESORT ACHTI

Khaled Ibn El Waleed Awameya St.; tel. 095 227 4544; www.steigenberger.com; 1,800LE d

After recent renovations and new management, this resort has made leaps forward in quality. Located Nile-side, the sprawling hotel offers fabulous views of the river and West Bank mountains, which you can enjoy while taking a dip in one of the two large pools surrounded by swaying palm trees. Rooms are simple but comfortable with your choice of garden or Nile view. Fabulous suites are also available if you want to splurge. There's scrumptious food on site with four stylish restaurants serving Egyptian and international fare, and a good complimentary breakfast buffet with an array of options. Staff are exceedingly welcoming and helpful.

★ HILTON LUXOR RESORT & SPA

New Karnak; tel. 0100 600 1270; www.hilton.com; 2,200LE d

If you're looking for crisp, clean, modern luxury, the Hilton Luxor is the place to stay. The hotel has its own private promenade lined with chaise longues and an infinity pool that (at the right angle) practically pours into the Nile. Sway in the breeze on canopied hammocks while watching the sun set over the Theban mountains. Sunbathe half-submerged on chairs in the larger pool, or enjoy a drink at their swim-up bar. You can even enjoy the sights while being massaged at the spa or running at the gym—both with floor-to-ceiling windows that look out to the river and mountains.

There's a range of rooms to choose from—from simple with a ground floor garden view to grand suites with balconies overlooking the Nile—all 230-plus of them with supremely comfortable beds. If a large balcony is important to you, be sure to specify as there are some rather dinky ones. The extremely friendly staff can help you arrange trips and tours around the city (including via private felucca directly from the hotel). A great breakfast buffet is included, and you can choose from seven other restaurants or cafés for any other meals or snacks.

★ SOFITEL WINTER PALACE

17 Corniche el-Nil St.; tel. 095 238 0422; www.all.accor.com; 3,000LE d

Built at the turn of the 20th century, the Winter Palace became a favorite spot for wealthy European travelers and the Egyptian royal family. All is colonial décor with heavy drapes, large chandeliers, and the occasional portrait of King Farouq in full regalia.

Grab a room in the new annex (the "Pavilion Winter Luxor") to combine historical charm with modern facilities. The main building (the "Palace") is a bit more vintage—better for true history lovers, but not as shiny (and nearly double the price of the newer wing). You can opt for a garden or Nile view in one of their 100-some rooms, each with its own charms, and balconies available on request. Cool off in the large pool or stroll through the sprawling green gardens dense with palm trees and pink bougainvillea. A nice selection of treats is available at the complimentary breakfast buffet. Elegant restaurants and bars on site.

CENTRAL LUXOR: WEST BANK

Under 800LE

HOTEL EL FAYROUZ

Gezirat El Bairat; tel. 095 231 2709; www.elfayrouz.com; 370LE d

This peach-colored hotel boasts fabulous gardens with all sorts of lush greenery. It's an excellent budget option with 22 rooms—most of them simple (but clean and comfortable) as well as a few more stylish options with niches, balconies, and dome ceilings for a bit extra (430LE). Not all have AC, so be sure to specify if that's your preference. Enjoy your simple complimentary breakfast on the roof while watching the sunrise, or in the cool garden beneath banana trees. Two more rooftop terraces offer comfortable corners—one with pillow floor seating and the other with chaise longues to nap in the sun. Added treats are their small library, fast Wi-Fi, and restaurant serving fresh Egyptian and international fare (plus beer, wine, and shisha).

HOTEL EL NAKHIL

Gezirat El Bairat; tel. 0122 382 1007; www.elnakhil.com; 550LE d

The rooms at this smallish hotel are nothing fancy, but they're pristine with comfortable beds and a few splashes of color here and there. The spacious rooftop terrace with views of the Nile, green fields, and palm trees makes this hotel special. As does the superbly friendly staff and tasty complimentary breakfast. Other fantastically fresh Egyptian dishes are available for lunch and dinner at good prices. Beer and wine served. Conveniently located just a 5-minute walk from the Ferry Landing.

EL GEZIRA GARDEN HOTEL

Gezirat El Bairat; tel. 020 102 85 24 109; www.el-gezira.com; 780LE d

Relax in El Gezira Garden's oasis of green after a long morning of exploring. The hotel is conveniently located—a short drive to the West Bank sights, and a 5-minute walk to the Ferry Landing. Rooms are clean and colorful, if a bit busy, with spacious balconies overlooking the hotel gardens. For more communal lounging, head up to the rooftop terrace with comfortable chaise longues and blissful views of the distant mountains. There are a number of amenities for such a small hotel (just 16 double rooms and 8 suites), including a swimming pool, billiard room, yoga studio, and hotel restaurant that serves tasty Egyptian meals (beer and wine also available) and complimentary breakfast. The friendly staff can help organize excursions at fair prices. Not to be confused with Gezira Hotel, which isn't as nice. To get here, walk 500 meters (1,600 ft) south of the Public Ferry Landing, and then inland 100 meters (300 ft).

WEST BANK: GOURNA AND AROUND

Under 800LE

NOUR EL-GOURNA

Gourna, 700 m/2,300 ft northwest of Colossi of Memnon; tel. 0114 428 1119; www.nourelbaladhotel.com; 500LE d

Tucked away in a mini jungle of trees, this family-run hotel made of mudbrick with thatched ceilings is a quaint escape. Their seven rooms are equipped with the basics and some added comforts—mosquito nets and small balconies to take in the fresh air. Located just across the street from the Antiquities Inspectorate Ticket Office and walking distance from many of the sites themselves, it's a great base for exploring the West Bank's "City of the Dead." The farm-to-fork restaurant here is an added perk, and the price includes a nice breakfast. One possible downside: The bathroom door is just a curtain, so be prepared to get intimate with your roommate.

★ NOUR EL-BALAD

Gourna, 1 km/0.6 mi from Medinet Habu Temple; tel. 0100 129 5812; www.nourelbaladhotel.com; 500LE d

Located between the desert and bright green farm fields, Nour el-Balad is the slightly larger counterpart of Nour el-Gourna. Run by the same family, the hotel offers many similar features with a welcoming atmosphere, fantastic food (breakfast included), shady gardens, and mudbrick rooms that stay cool even on the hottest of days (plus ACs just in case). It's a bit more isolated than their other hotel, but just a 10-minute walk from the temple of Medinet Habu and a 15-minute drive from the Public Ferry Landing. Some added advantages here are the shaded rooftop terrace with brilliant views over their farm, and rooms that are a bit more spacious (though still have curtains for bathroom doors). Brothers Mohammed and Abdu are a fabulous team and can arrange for tours, transportation, bike rentals, and other fun excursions.

SCORPION HOUSE

Gourna; tel. 0100 512 8732; 680LE d

In this beautiful mudbrick guesthouse with azure accents and kaleidoscopic floor tiles, each room is unique. The owner, Tayeb, is an archeologist and a fantastic host—as is his wife, Doaa, who makes delectable homecooked meals tailored to your preferences. The small hotel is full of character, plus there's a garden, rooftop, and other colorful common spaces. Each room has a soaring redbrick dome ceiling and tasteful accents. Delicious breakfast included. Their location isn't the most central, but it's only a 15-minute drive from the Ferry Landing and just a 7-minute drive from the Antiquities Inspectorate Ticket Office. Tayeb can arrange for a trusted private driver at a good price for anywhere you want to go.

★ BEIT SABEE

Gourna, next to Medinet Habu Temple; tel. 0115 400 8100; www.nourelnil.com/guesthouse; 685LE d

Choose between peach, lime, turquoise, or tangerine for your room color scheme at this vibrant guesthouse. Décor is fun and quirky, like the handwoven palm leaf pieces with hypnotic spirals, crisscrossed palm wood furniture, and baroque mirrors in cyan-colored frames. Each of the 15 rooms in this three-story mudbrick house has a unique style, and they range in price according to size (from 685LE for the smallest to double that for the largest). You can enjoy your complimentary breakfast on the rooftop with stunning views of the mountains and the temple complex at Medinet Habu. Delicious local lunch and dinner also available from the kitchen for an extra charge.

800-1,650LE

★ MARSAM HOTEL

Gourna, 260 m/850 ft northeast of the Antiquities Inspectorate Ticket Office; tel. 0100 342 6471; www.marsamhotelluxor.com; 900LE d

With mudbrick walls, tall ceilings, and rustic palm wood furniture, this guesthouse is a minimalist's dream. It started as an archeologists' lodge in the 1920s and has since been expanded to offer a range of rooms (37 in all, 20 with AC), from simple ones for singles to suites with a kitchen and private rooftop terrace. Beds could be more comfortable, but they aren't unbearable. The backyard garden looks out to fabulous fields of green, a few patches of palms, and the occasional grazing camel. Early risers can take their breakfast while watching a flock of hot-air balloons float in front of the rising sun. On the opposite side, the Theban mountains tower in the distance. Food is farm-fresh and delicious with breakfast included. While the hotel's not exactly central, it's an easy cycle (or drive) to all the major West Bank sites and just a 10-minute drive to the Ferry Landing for the East Bank. The staff are extremely helpful and can assist with transportation, camel rides, and sailing trips.

GREATER WEST BANK

1,650-3,300 LE

EL-MOUDIRA HOTEL

9 km/6 mi northwest of Luxor Bridge; tel. 095 255 1440; www.moudira.com; 3,300LE d

El-Moudira really leans into the Oriental motifs, with pillared archways, rich colors, sweeping canopies, and mashrabiya screens. It's one of the most colorful places to stay in Luxor with each of its 50 rooms and suites uniquely decorated. The courtyard dining area and pool surrounded by palms and bougainvillea are the highlights. While not conveniently located, it's still only 25-35 minutes by car to either the East Bank downtown or the West Bank sites, and the hotel staff can arrange for quick and affordable transportation. A mediocre breakfast is included. In the evenings you can dine at their on-site restaurant or enjoy drinks at the bar with self-described "Arabian Nights" flair.

Information and Services

TOURIST OFFICE

Across from Luxor Train Station; tel. 095 237 2215; 9am-8pm daily

Depending who's on duty, the staff here can be very informative and help you plan your trip around Luxor. There's not much on offer by way of maps and brochures, but they say there will be "someday soon."

EMERGENCY NUMBERS

- **Tourist Police:** 126
- **Police:** 122
- **Ambulance:** 123

Transportation

GETTING TO LUXOR FROM CAIRO

If you're not in a hurry, the train (10-11 hours) is a great way to get down to Luxor from Cairo. The bus is generally quicker by an hour or two, but not as spacious. Flying (1 hour) is naturally the fastest, but can be pretty expensive for such a short trip and you miss the scenery along the way.

Air

Round-trip flights from **Cairo International Airport** typically cost 2,000-3,500LE and take 1 hour each way. **EgyptAir** (www.egyptair.com) and **Nile Air** (www.nileair.com) both operate regular trips.

From **Luxor international Airport** (8 km/5 mi east of central Luxor; tel. 095 232 4455) you can get downtown via taxi (15 minutes; 60-100LE), and it will properly induct you into Luxor's world of haggling. Rides to lodging on the West Bank will take considerably longer (45 minutes; 200-250LE), or you can ask to be dropped off at the Public Ferry Landing downtown (East Bank) and take a shortcut. Many hotels also offer pickups for an additional charge, which would likely be a less stressful option.

Train

As many as 10 trains travel from Cairo to Luxor daily. For the most comfortable trip, get a first-class ticket on the **"Special Service"** (10-11 hours; 200LE one-way), which is spacious and fairly clean. The **"Spanish"** (10-11 hours; 114 LE) trains are also nice, but not as roomy. Buy your ticket at the train station in Cairo, either from the central **Ramses Station** (Ramses Square, Downtown) or **Giza Station** (el-Sikka el-Hadid St., just south of the Giza Metro Station) on the southwest side of the city. You should also be able to buy online at the **Egyptian National Railways** website (www.enr.gov.eg), though this often doesn't work. Grab your return ticket online or from the Luxor Train Station when you arrive. It's usually possible to purchase tickets on the same day as travel, but it's better to book in advance.

For a sleeper car, book on the **Watania Sleeping Trains** website (www.wataniasleepingtrains.com)—which does usually work!—or at their office in Cairo's Ramses Station. Trains typically leave from Cairo around 6:30pm and 9:10pm, arriving at Luxor around 10-11 hours later and Aswan 14-15 hours later, and leave from Aswan at 5:10pm and Luxor at 8:05pm. During the high season (Nov.-Mar.), trains leave daily, and in the low season they leave from Cairo on Sunday, Tuesday, and Thursday, and return from Aswan and Luxor on Monday, Wednesday, and Friday. Price is $120 for single cabin (only fits one) or $80 per bed in a double cabin, one-way. Tip: It costs the same whether you travel from Cairo to Luxor or all the way to Aswan, so if you only plan to indulge in a private sleeping cabin for one way, best to make it to Aswan.

Luxor Train Station (Midan al-Mahatta; no tel.) is located on the East Bank. A taxi from the train station to the Public Ferry Landing (5 minutes) should be around 15-20LE. Plenty of taxis will be available at the station.

Bus

GO BUS

tel. 19567; www.go-bus.com

Several buses travel between Luxor and Cairo every day for around 255LE a ticket (9-10 hours). In Cairo, buses leave from the Go Bus Station at Abdel Minam Riyad Square beside the Ramses Hilton in Downtown. Book online at the Go Bus website or in the station. In Luxor, the **Go Bus station** (Ramses St.) is located on the East Bank, 170 meters (560 ft) north of the train station.

UPPER EGYPT BUS COMPANY

This state-run bus isn't as nice as the Go Bus but is fine if you have no other option. Multiple services run between Luxor and Cairo with intermediary stops daily and prices slightly cheaper than Go Bus. They're a bit low-tech and your only option for booking is directly at the station.

In Cairo, buses leave from **Torgoman Bus Station** (Boulaq 2, off al-Sahafa St., no tel.) close to Downtown. In Luxor, the station is located on the East Bank (Ramses St., immediately south of the train station; no tel.; 7am-10pm daily).

Private Car Hire

If you're interested in stopping at the sights along the way between Cairo and Luxor (Minya, Abydos, and Dendera), **Real Egypt Tours** (tel. 0110 002 2242; www.realegypt.com) does a nice three-day tour with private car. Otherwise, flying is a better option (much faster, more comfortable, and likely cheaper).

GETTING TO LUXOR FROM ASWAN

Hiring a driver with a private car is the ideal way to get to Luxor from Aswan if you're keen to see the lesser-visited temples located between the two cities. Train is the best option for cheap and comfortable travel. The government-run bus is fine, but it should be reserved as a last resort. Those with more time might consider a 3-4-day cruise to make the trip.

Train

Multiple trains travel daily to Luxor (3-4 hours; 75-120LE) from the Aswan Railway Station located on the north side of central Aswan in Midan al-Mahatta (Station Square), just 300 meters (1,000 ft) east of the Nile. Tickets can be purchased at the station or online from the **Egyptian National Railways** website (www.enr.gov.eg). It's safer to book a day or two in advance, but same-day tickets are usually available.

Bus

UPPER EGYPT BUS COMPANY

Tickets cost around 50-70LE for the four-hour bus ride. Buses leave from the Aswan Bus Station, located 5 kilometers (3 mi) north of the city center on the East Bank next to the Nile (Al-Khataar-Aswan Rd.). Expect to pay 20-30LE for a taxi from central Aswan.

Private Car Hire

Aswan Individual (tel. 0100 250 9588; www.aswan-individual.com) is a fantastic local travel company that can arrange for professional drivers to get you to Luxor for $90 without stops (3.5 hours) or $120 including stops at the temples in Kom Ombo, Edfu, and Esna along the way (7 hours). If you like your driver, tips (10-20% is good) are very welcome. Cars can hold up to three passengers, and private microbuses (for up to eight passengers) are available for a small surcharge.

Boat

Cruise ships sail between Luxor and Aswan in either direction. You can also travel on a dahabiya (large two-masted sailboat), or felucca (smaller sailboat) between Aswan and Esna (plus a 1.5-hour car ride to Luxor). See page 214 for some of the best companies to sail with.

GETTING TO LUXOR FROM HURGHADA

The most comfortable option for travel to Luxor from Hurghada on the Red Sea Coast is by private car, but the bus is much more economical and an easy ride.

Bus

GO BUS

tel. 19567; www.go-bus.com

A handful of buses travel between Hurghada and Luxor each day for around 135LE a ticket (5-5.5 hours). In Hurghada, buses leave from the Go Bus Station (El-Nasr St., Al-Dahar). Book online at the Go Bus website.

UPPER EGYPT BUS COMPANY

If you can't find a Go Bus that works with your schedule, try this less-than-ideal public bus. Several trips are made to Luxor from Hurghada daily, leaving from El-Nasr Street, Al-Dahar, 1.4 kilometers (0.9 mi) north of the Go Bus Station.

Private Car Hire

Aswan Individual (tel. 0100 250 9588; www.aswan-individual.com) offers a private car service with expert drivers between Hurghada and Luxor for $185 (5 hours) one way.

GETTING AROUND

Taxis are the easiest way to get around Luxor on either side of the Nile. To get between the East and West Banks, ferries are your best bet—much faster (and cheaper) than the circuitous route taken by taxis, which have to cross Luxor Bridge to the south.

Taxi

Unlike in Cairo, meters are rare in Luxor so it's best to agree on a price before you get in. On the East Bank, prices between the train station and the Public Ferry Landing or between Luxor Temple and Karnak Temple should be around 15-20LE. If you want to explore the West Bank by taxi, pick one up just south of the Public Ferry Landing in Gezirat El Bairat. For a full day (8am-5pm) around the West Bank sights, it should be in the neighborhood of 500LE.

Ferry

On the East Bank, the **Public Ferry Landing** is next to Luxor Temple (150 m/500 ft south of Mummification Museum). On the West Bank it's located just north of the al-Qarna Rd. traffic circle in Gezirat El Bairat. The price per person should be around 3LE for the 3-minute ride, and they run every 15-20 minutes 6am-10pm.

If you're in a rush, grab a **private ferry** (30-40LE for the whole boat). These smaller motorboats will take you across without having to wait. On the East Bank, docks line the Corniche from south of the Public Ferry Landing until the Winter Palace Hotel. On the West Bank, you can find them south of the Public Ferry Landing.

Microbus

Microbuses are a good and cheap way to get between well-traveled points (from one side of town to the other along the same road, for example). Less so if you want to travel somewhere off the main roads, unless you ask for help from a local. Flag one down and let them know where you want to go. Or head to the **main microbus station** behind the Luxor Train Station on the East Bank (from here you can get to Karnak Temple for 2-3LE) or near the Public Ferry Landing on the West Bank.

Bicycle

Bikes are a fantastic way to get around the West Bank sights in the cooler months. Most hotels offer rentals, or you can pick one up from **Mohamed Setouhy** (Al Qarna Rd., 300 m/1,000 ft northwest of the Ferry Landing across from Yarra Market, West Bank; tel. 0100 223 9710; 7am-7pm daily; 75-100LE/day). Traffic on the East Bank makes this side much more difficult to navigate by bike, but it's a fine mode of transportation between Karnak and Luxor Temples if you stick to the Corniche along the Nile.

Luxor to Aswan

Along this southern strip of Egypt's Nile, modern life bustles around the traces of ancient civilizations, with Greco-Roman temples encircled by rooftops lined with flocks of satellite dishes. Few tourists outside of cruisers come to these parts, but the quiet agricultural towns offer a new perspective on life in Egypt, and their fabulous temples and are well worth the trip.

Planning and Guides

Most visitors who come to Esna, Edfu, and Kom Ombo typically visit on **day trips** from Luxor or Aswan. This means there aren't many decent options for places to eat or sleep. (Bring snacks.)

The most efficient way to see all three destinations is to hire a private car from Luxor to Aswan (or vice versa) and make the stops en route. Egyptologist **Mena Zaki** (tel. 0127 400 8892; www.aswanluxortravel.com) is a great guide if you choose to tour the area between Luxor and Aswan (starting from either and ending in the other) as a long day trip including Kom Ombo, Gebel el-Silsila, Daraw, Esna, and Edfu (8-10 hours; $220 for 1-2 people including tours and transportation, or less if you opt to stop at fewer sites).

If you don't need a guide, Waleed and his team at **Aswan Individual** (tel. 0100 250 9588; www.aswan-individual.com) can provide comfortable private transportation between Luxor and Aswan (again, starting at either) with stops at your leisure at Esna, as well as Kom Ombo and Edfu for $100 (car for 1-3 people) or $130 (private microbus for up to 8 people). You can also tailor this trip to include more or fewer stops for a slight price change. Or add a guide ($32 for all three stops).

You can also travel by boat on the Nile from Luxor to Aswan (or vice versa), stopping at sights along the way. For more information, see page 214.

ESNA

Esna was a thriving town as early as the 20th century BC—a history revealed by monumental blocks from this time found reused in Coptic churches. To the south of the city, archeologists also uncovered an ancient cemetery of mummified Nile perch—a symbol of Esna's patroness, Neith, the creator goddess who rose from the primordial waters to fashion the world. Under the Greeks, the town was named Latopolis in honor of the goddess (and the fish, called latos in ancient Greek). Later (AD 400-650) a large Coptic community settled here.

Around the town, traces of Fatimid (10th century) and Ottoman (18th century) times are also visible, reminding visitors of the millennia of history Esna has seen. One of Egypt's oldest minarets, the Fatimid Emari Minaret, peeks up from across the Temple of Khnum. To the north of the temple sits the Ottoman caravanserai (Wikalet el-Gedawi)—with a large arched entrance over three niches and a wooden doorway (not open to the public). In the Esna Souq, look up to see the wooden latticework, or mashrabiya, of the town's 19th-century houses.

If you have a morning free in Luxor, Esna is a nice day trip—just over an hour (58 km/36 mi) south of the city. The town center and the main sight of interest, the Temple of Khnum, are on the West Bank, while green fields of sugarcane cover the other side.

Sights

Before making your way down Esna Souq, be sure to purchase your tickets for the Temple of Khnum at the **Temple Ticket Office** just across from the souq entrance.

TEMPLE OF KHNUM

150 m/500 ft west of the Nile, after the Tourist Souq; no tel.; 8am-4:30pm daily; 60LE adults, 30LE students

Luxor to Aswan

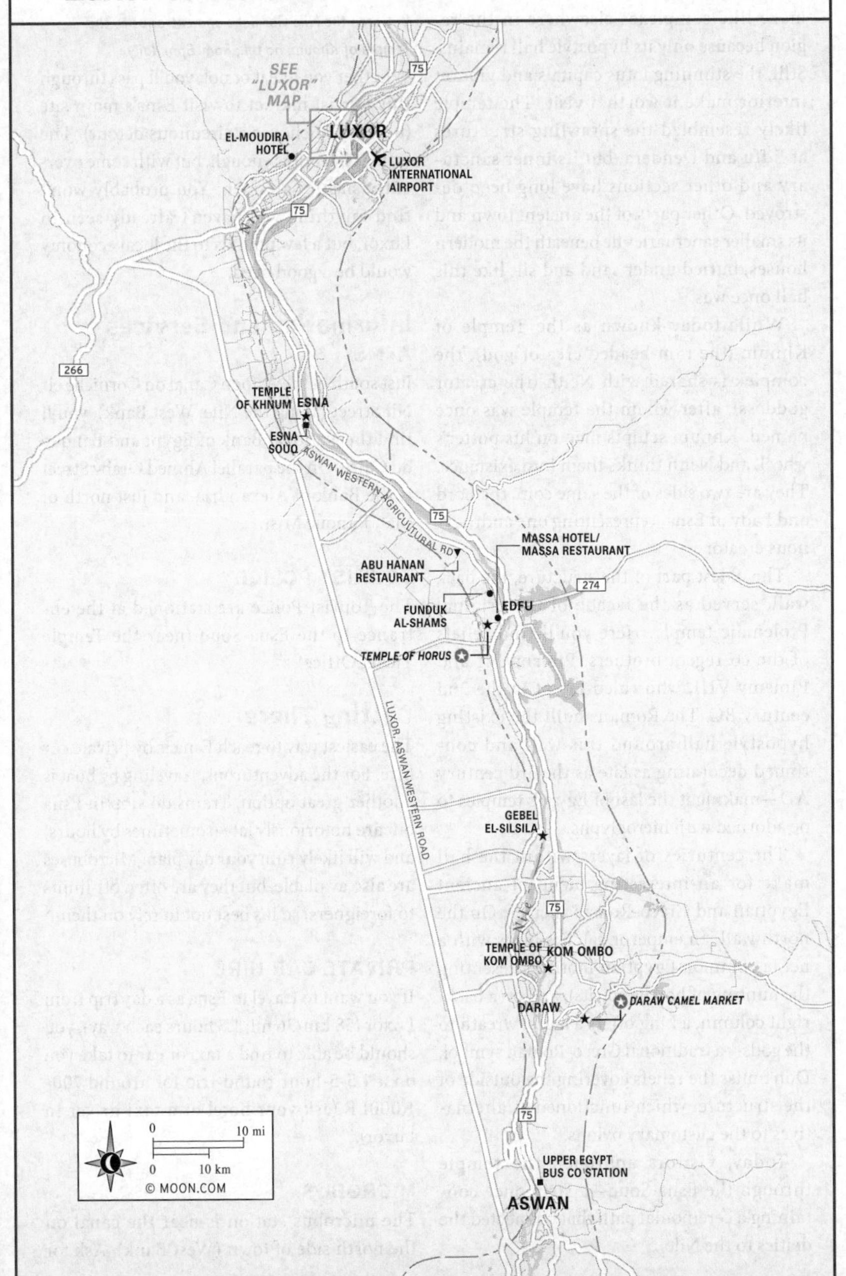

Now some 10 meters (30 ft) below street level, Esna's temple is much smaller than the maze-like complexes elsewhere in the region because only its hypostyle hall remains. Still, the stunning lotus capitals and vibrant interior make it worth a visit. The temple likely resembled the sprawling structures at Edfu and Dendera, but its inner sanctuary and other sections have long been destroyed. Other parts of the ancient town and its smaller sanctuaries lie beneath the modern houses, buried under sand and silt like this hall once was.

While today known as the Temple of Khnum (the ram-headed creator god), the complex is shared with Neith (the creator goddess), after whom the temple was once named. Khnum sculpts men on his potter's wheel, and Neith thinks them into existence. They are two sides of the same coin, the Lord and Lady of Esna, representing one androgynous creator.

The oldest part of the structure, the back wall, served as the façade of the original Ptolemaic temple. Here you'll find reliefs of the co-regent brothers, Ptolemy VI and Ptolemy VIII, who ruled Egypt in the 2nd century BC. The Romans built the existing hypostyle hall around this wall and continued decorating as late as the 3rd century AD—making it the last of Egypt's temples to be adorned with hieroglyphs.

The centuries of layers within the hall make for an interesting blend of ancient Egyptian and Greco-Roman themes. On the north wall, an emperor catches birds with a net (a common Egyptian motif representing the hunting of hostile spirits), and on a back-right column, a king offers a laurel wreath to the gods—a traditional Greco-Roman symbol. Don't miss the reliefs covering the outside of the structure, which functioned as alternatives to the customary pylons.

Today, visitors approach the temple through the Esna Souq—a strip once containing a ceremonial path that connected the deities to the Nile.

Shopping

ESNA SOUQ

Between the Nile Corniche and entrance to the Temple of Khnum; no tel.; 8am-8pm daily

Whether you like it or not, you'll pass through this tourist market to visit Esna's main site (unless you choose a circuitous detour). The walk is harmless enough, but with some over-enthusiastic salesmen. You probably won't find anything you haven't already seen in Luxor, but a few pounds to the local economy would be a good deed.

Information and Services

ATMS

Just south of the Asfoon Canal on Corniche el-Nil Street (along the Nile, West Bank), you'll find the National Bank of Egypt and Banque du Caire. On the parallel Ahmed Oraby Street is the Bank of Alexandria, and just north of that, Banque Misr.

TOURIST POLICE

The Tourist Police are stationed at the entrance to the Esna Souq (near the Temple Ticket Office).

Getting There

The easiest way to reach Esna is by private car hire. For the adventurous, traveling by boat is another great option. Trains do stop in Esna but are notoriously late (sometimes by hours) and will likely ruin your day plan. Microbuses are also available, but they are often off-limits to foreigners, so it's best not to rely on them.

PRIVATE CAR HIRE

If you want to travel to Esna as a day trip from Luxor (58 km/36 mi; 1.5 hours each way), you should be able to find a taxi or car to take you on a 4.5-5-hour round-trip for around 700-1,000LE (ask your hotel or a taxi driver in Luxor).

MICROBUS

The microbus station is near the canal on the north side of town (West Bank). Ask for "mow'if el-microbasaat." You can get to Luxor (12LE), Edfu (12LE), Aswan (30LE), and Kom Ombo (20LE). Foreigners are prohibited from taking this route at times, so be sure to have a plan B.

BOAT

Chartering a felucca or dahabiya between Aswan and Esna is the most romantic way to see this section of the Nile. Smaller boats can't go past Esna because of the lock there (meaning you can't sail on one of these smaller boats from Luxor), but another option is to take a full Nile cruise between Luxor and Aswan.

Getting Around

From the Corniche, it's an easy walk to the Temple of Khnum. Horse carriages (singular, hantour) can also give you an enthusiastic lift around town (about 30LE for a 10-minute ride), but be sure to agree on a price before you get in.

EDFU

Located 50 kilometers (30 mi) south of Esna and 65 kilometers (40 mi) north of Kom Ombo, the sleepy village of Edfu served as the battleground for the legendary confrontation between Horus (god of the sky) and his murderous uncle, Seth (god of chaos and violence). The falcon-headed solar god triumphed and was awarded a temple here some 3,000 years ago. Its stone remains were incorporated into this younger manifestation, a mere 2,260 years old. Traces of the ancient town (still under excavation and closed to visitors) lie just west of the Temple of Horus and under modern buildings around the temple.

Sights

★ TEMPLE OF HORUS

Central Edfu, 1 km/0.6 mi west of Corniche, West Bank; no tel.; 8am-5pm daily; 100LE adults, 50LE students

The vivid symbols that cover the walls of this Ptolemaic temple recount ancient legends, epic battles, and the world's creation. Dedicated to Horus—the falcon-headed sky god and symbol of divine kingship—the imposing sandstone structure is one of Egypt's best-preserved temples thanks to its naturally elevated platform (which protected it from Nile floods), and centuries of hibernation below sand swept in from the neighboring desert.

Ptolemy III commissioned the project in 237 BC on the site of a New Kingdom temple (nearly 1,000 years older). In 122 BC the two hypostyle halls were added, each with 12 splendid columns. Due to Upper Egypt's periodic rebellions and the desire of successive generations to honor Horus in their own style, the complex didn't reach completion until 57 BC under Ptolemy XII (father of the famous Cleopatra). To him we owe the towering entrance pylons and 32-columned courtyard. Romans later made decorative additions.

Two black granite Horus statues in full falcon form meet visitors at the entrance. Beyond that, a sprawling colonnade **courtyard** leads to a **passageway** that rings the inner sections of the temple (one door in each far corner). Through the door to the left (on the western wall of the passageway) you'll find an image of the temple's foundational legend: Horus kills his uncle, Seth (in the form of a hippo) who had earlier killed Horus's father, Osiris. This event was reenacted as a ritual drama here each year by Horus's cult followers.

Pass through the courtyard to the **first hypostyle hall** to find two small chambers to your left and right, one for robing and the other an ancient library. Aromatherapy lovers will enjoy the small chamber in the far-left corner of the **second hypostyle hall,** where perfumes were concocted with scientific precision, their instructions engraved on the walls. Beyond the second hypostyle hall is an **offering hall** and finally the **inner sanctuary** with a shrine of Nectanebo II (the last native Egyptian king, r. 360-343 BC before the Persians invaded). The shrine, 4 meters (13 ft) high and made of a single block of granite, dates from an earlier temple on this site. Encircling the sanctuary are chapels to other gods worshiped here (secondary to Horus), including Min, Osiris, Hathor, and Re.

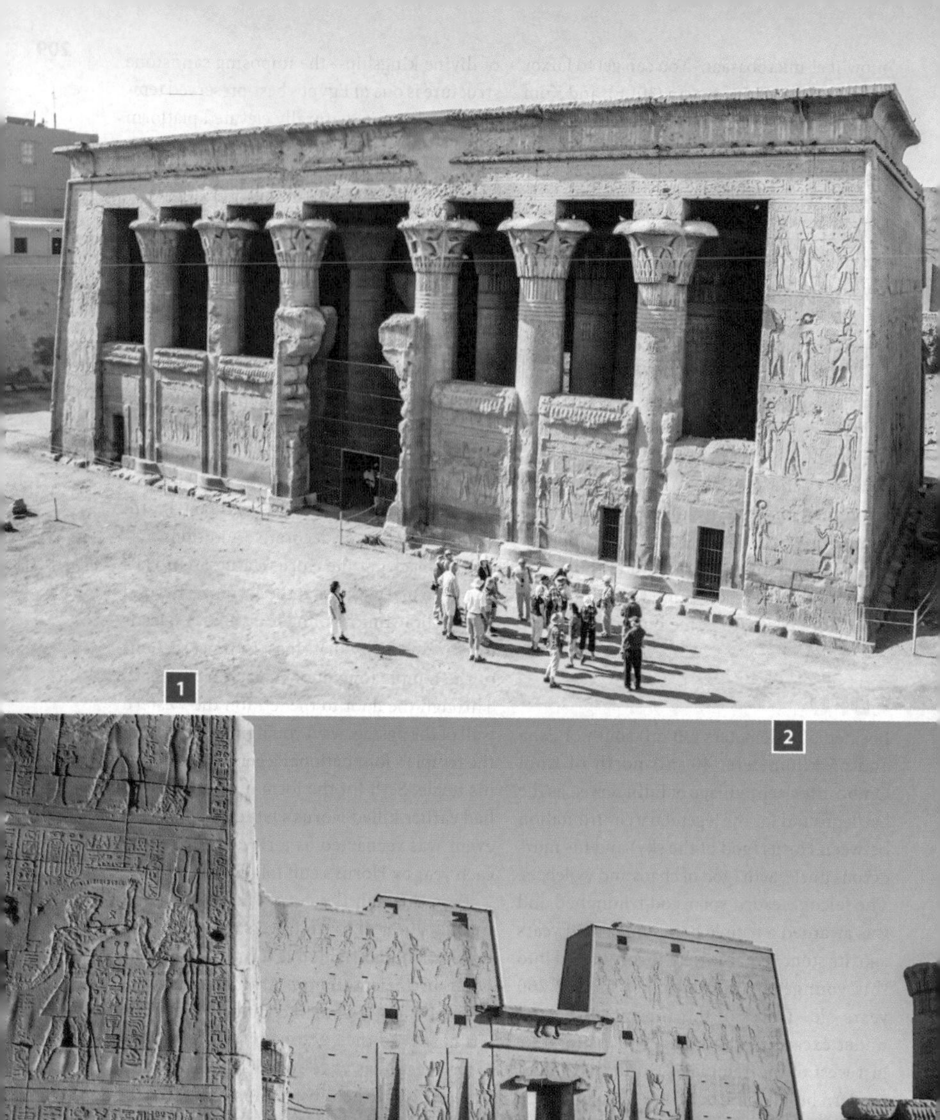
1

2

Remains of a **Birth House** just outside of Horus's Temple (to the left if you're facing the entrance) hold colorful scenes including those of Harsomptus (son of Horus and Hathor) being nursed by goddesses, and Ptolemy VIII (d. 116 BC) making offerings to various deities.

Near the ticket office (just before the temple) you'll find WCs, a cafeteria offering some light refreshments, and a visitor center with a 15-minute movie about the temple's history.

Food

There aren't too many good dining spots in Edfu, but you do have enough to stave off hunger.

ABU HANAN RESTAURANT

Corner of Corniche el-Nil and el-Gomhoria St.; tel. 0114 146 1144; 9am-9pm daily; 60-80LE mains

This modest restaurant with framed Quranic verses decorating the walls is one of the only decent options in town. They provide generous portions of Egyptian food—grilled chicken and meats (kebab and kofta), rice, soups, salads, makhalal (pickled vegetables), tahini, and fresh bread. Simple pasta dishes also available.

MASSA RESTAURANT

At Massa Hotel, El-Souq Mall Abdel Aziz St., central Edfu; tel. 0111 136 0230; 7am-10pm daily; 80-90LE mains

The rooftop restaurant at the Massa Hotel serves a fine traditional Egyptian breakfast of fuul, ta'maya, eggs, and fresh bread. Lunch and dinner bring more Egyptian fare of grilled chicken and meat, rice, bread, and salads.

Accommodations

Visitors don't tend to stay in these parts, instead preferring to set up camp in Luxor or Aswan and visit Edfu on a day trip. If you really want to spend the night, you do have a couple of options.

1: Temple of Khnum **2:** pylon at the Temple of Horus

MASSA HOTEL

El-Souq Mall Abdel Aziz St., central Edfu; tel. 0111 136 0230; 1,000LE d

Just a stone's throw away from the towering Temple of Horus, this modest hotel offers clean rooms with ACs. The decoration is nothing to write home about, but it's the best option by far in central Edfu. Their pleasant rooftop restaurant is also one of the few spots in town where you can get a decent meal.

FUNDUK AL-SHAMS

Off Aswan-Giza Rd., 16 km/10 mi north of central Edfu, West Bank; tel. 0106 182 6314; https://egypt-for-you.com; Oct.-mid-Apr.; 1,700LE d

This colorful guesthouse surrounded by sugarcane fields in a Nile-side village is a gem. Set up to host archeologists working on nearby sites, Funduk al-Shams ("Sun Hotel") offers spotless rooms with palm tree motifs and simple décor. During cooler times you can enjoy the beautiful gardens, or hide from the sun in the large dining hall. The price includes a fabulous breakfast, lunch, and dinner of Austrian-Egyptian fusion with homemade bread and yogurt, and fresh vegetables from their garden. The catch? It's only open between October and mid-April, houses a maximum of 15 people, has no AC (but there are ceiling fans), and is a good 16 kilometers (10 mi) from central Edfu, making it a bit tricky to get to (though the hotel can arrange for pickups). They can also arrange for transportation to the Temple of Horus in central Edfu, the camel market in Daraw, Gebel el-Silsila, or trips to Luxor or Aswan. Be sure to reserve early to get a room.

Getting There

The best way to get to Edfu is by boat or private car hire. Trains do stop in Edfu but aren't reliable. Microbus is another option, but foreigners are often prohibited.

BOAT

Charter a private felucca (about 1,100LE/night) or book a room in a dahabiya (about 20,000LE d for 3 nights) from Aswan (2-3 nights). Almost all Nile cruises between Luxor and Aswan also stop in Edfu.

PRIVATE CAR HIRE

From Luxor, you can hire a car to Edfu for around 1,200-1,400LE round-trip (2.5 hours each way). From Aswan, it takes between 2 hours (via desert road) or 3 hours (via Kom Ombo) to get to Edfu (1,600LE round-trip including stop in Kom Ombo).

MICROBUS

The microbus station is next to Edfu Bridge on the West Bank. You can get to/from Luxor (2.5 hours; 35LE), Aswan (2.5 hours; 35LE), and Kom Ombo (1.5 hours; 25LE). Foreigners are prohibited from taking microbuses in these parts at times, so be sure to have a backup plan.

Getting Around

If you come to Edfu with a driver, he'll take you directly to the town's main site, the Temple of Horus. If you arrive by boat, you can either walk (15 minutes) from the Corniche, or grab a **horse carriage** (hantour) for 40-60LE to the temple. From the microbus station (beside Edfu Bridge on the West Bank Corniche), it's just a 20-minute walk to the temple.

KOM OMBO AND VICINITY

Fifty kilometers (30 mi) north of central Aswan, Kom Ombo served as the cult center of the crocodile god, Sobek. Little remains of the ancient settlement, Pa-Sobek ("the Domain of Sobek"), save a fabulous temple on the East Bank. The Ptolemaic army, who trained their African elephants for warfare in Kom Ombo, helped build and finance the complex in its current form on top of older versions. Today the town is populated by many Nubians, displaced here after their homeland was submerged under Lake Nasser by the building of the Aswan High Dam. There's little to see aside from the famed temple, its tiny crocodile museum, and sprawling fields of sugarcane.

Sights

TEMPLE OF KOM OMBO

Corniche el-Nil, East Bank; no tel.; 8am-8pm daily; 100LE adults, 50LE students

Rising out of a plateau at a bend in the river, this pretty sandstone structure from the Greco-Roman period is a rare "double temple," with perfectly symmetrical halves dedicated to the ancient town's favorite deities. Sobek, the crocodile god of fertility, commands the east side (to the right) and Haroeris ("Horus the Elder")—a mature form the falcon-headed sky god, Horus—the west (left).

Each deity has his own inner sanctuary, but they share the impressive pylon, forecourt (part of which has been eroded by the river), two hypostyle halls with lotus-capital columns, and antechambers—all physically connected but divided by themes according to each respective god. In the forecourt you'll find a double altar to the two gods and broken columns with sharp reliefs and some remaining colors.

Two separate processional paths lead through the temple to the inner sanctuaries, which hid chambers (now visible) where priests would relay oracles from the gods and listen to the supplications of their followers. At the left end of the back wall, notice reliefs of what look to be surgical instruments, likely signifying the curative importance of the temple. Pilgrims came here to petition Haroeris, affiliated with healing, for treatment. In the middle of the sanctuary's back wall is a false door, where the spirit of the dead kings could enter to receive their tributes. Above it, Ma'at (goddess of truth, justice, and order) holds up the sky, flanked by Sobek and Haroeris.

A Greek inscription by Ptolemy VI's (c. 180 BC) troops stationed here dedicates their construction of the temple to their leader, making him the earliest king named on the temple walls. Most of the reliefs and decorations were likely completed around a century later by Ptolemy XII (c. 80 BC), and Romans added the outdoor courtyard and outer corridor.

Other remains on site include ruins of the Birth House (to the left of the entrance) and the Gate of Ptolemy XII (to the right) with a small Shrine to Hathor behind that. Hathor—the mother goddess depicted with cow horns and in some traditions, Sobek's consort, in others, Horus's—is also honored within the temple alongside Sobek. Behind the Birth House, you'll find a deep well and a small pond, at one time full of sacred crocodiles, raised by Sobek's followers. To the north of the temple, you can find what's left of their pets at the Crocodile Museum (same hours and ticket), well worth a visit for the dozens of haunting mummified crocs, croc statues, eggs, and fetuses (and the cool AC). A visit to the whole site should take around 1.5 hours. The ticket office closes at 7pm. WCs available.

GEBEL EL-SILSILA

23 km/14 mi north of central Kom Ombo, West Bank; no tel.; 8am-4pm daily; 50LE adults, 25LE students

Few visitors stop at the rocky hills that slope down into Egypt's narrowest strip of Nile, but they contain the interesting site of Gebel el-Silsila ("Mountain of the Chain")—holding a series of ancient sandstone quarries filled with rock-cut temples that conceal cryptic carvings. For centuries, the quarries served as the main suppliers for pharaohs' monumental building projects, including the sprawling temple at Karnak.

Aside from the dramatic sandstone landscape itself, the main attraction is King Horemheb's (r. 1319-1292 BC) small rock-cut **Temple of Great Speos.** It's dedicated to seven deities, one of whom was the divine pharaoh himself, alongside Amun-Re (king of the gods), Sobek (the crocodile-god affiliated with fertility), Mut (sky goddess and divine mother), Khonsu (god of the moon), Taweret (the hippo-goddess who protected women in childbirth), and Thoth (god of knowledge). You can find the deities on the entrance pillars and seated in a niche carved into the back wall. South of Horemheb's temple, smaller rock-cut shrines were built as cenotaphs by King Seti I, his son (Ramses II), and grandson (Merenptah) in the 13th century BC. The hills are covered in small chambers, stelae, and graffiti, with excavations ongoing.

A guide is highly recommended here to help you find the hidden symbols carved into the walls of these ancient quarries. Otherwise, a guard will likely direct you to the sites in hopes of a tip.

The most common way to reach this site is by private car with short boat trip (1.5 hours one-way; $90 round-trip) or private felucca (2 days, 2 nights; $110 one-way) from Aswan. (Larger cruise ships can't stop here.) Visitors arriving by boat can dock right in front of the Temple of Great Speos. If you come by car, you'll arrive on the East Bank and can catch a motorboat over to the sites on the West Bank (your driver should arrange this). It's a bit tricky to find, so make sure your driver knows exactly where he's going ahead of time (**Aswan Individual** organizes smooth trips by felucca or car).

★ DARAW CAMEL MARKET

9 km/6 mi south of central Kom Ombo, Village of Daraw; no tel.; 8am-1pm Sat.-Sun.; free

On a dusty patch of land surrounded by green sugarcane fields, thousands of Sudanese camels (of the one-humped species, *Camelus dromedarius*) are gathered for this weekend morning market. The sheer quantity of furry humps is a splendid sight to behold, and worth the short trip from Aswan (40 km/25 mi; 1 hour) or Kom Ombo (10 km/6 mi; 20 minutes). Unlike touristic sites where camels don tassels and colorful saddles, Daraw offers a much rawer experience. Here, the beautiful creatures are a commodity, herded up from Sudan via Abu Simbel, where they're loaded onto pickup trucks. Many will continue their journey to the market outside Cairo (Birqash) to be sold for meat or to camel touts who'll bring them to the Giza Pyramids and harass you until you take a ride. The sellers here, by contrast, are friendly as can be and used to the occasional wandering visitor. Don't forget to wear comfortable shoes, conservative clothes (pants preferred, no plunge tops, etc.), and sun protection.

Food and Accommodations

Kom Ombo is a beautiful place to pass through, but for eating and sleeping it's better to stick to Luxor or Aswan. Immediately across the street from the Temple of Kom Ombo entrance (to the south) is a **cafeteria** with a constantly changing name, nice shady seating, and refreshments (8am-8pm daily).

Getting There

PRIVATE CAR HIRE

Hiring a private car is the quickest, easiest way to get to central Kom Ombo and the surrounding sights of Gebel el-Silsila and Daraw. You can visit as a nice day trip from Aswan, or better yet, en route to Luxor from Aswan, or vice versa. Ask your hotel to arrange a car or check out the options at **Aswan Individual** (tel. 0100 250 9588; www.aswan-individual.com). If you want to travel as day trip from Aswan, they can arrange for a private car to Daraw, Kom Ombo, Gebel el-Silsila, and back to Aswan for around $115 (1-3 people). For the same price they can take you all the way to Luxor. If you prefer to start in Luxor, you'll likely miss the Daraw Camel Market (200 km/120 mi away) since it closes around 1pm. A side trip to the Daraw Camel Market from Aswan would only take around 4 hours total ($55 round-trip, 1-3 people). Each way should take a bit under an hour, and you'll want an hour or so to wander around the market there.

FELUCCA

Hire a felucca in Aswan and wake up to the Daraw Camel Market the following morning—a special experience. For more information, see page 222.

CRUISING THE NILE BETWEEN LUXOR AND ASWAN

Nile cruises are a great way to enjoy the river and its rich surroundings. Cruise ships travel between Luxor and Aswan in either direction, and a few also include a quick side trip to Qena—home to the spectacular Dendera Temple. Only on rare occasion do boats travel all the way between Cairo and Aswan due to water-level issues (and previously, security concerns).

Choose between a traditional river cruise ship, dahabiya (a large two-masted sailboat), or felucca (a smaller sailboat). Dahabiyas and feluccas almost exclusively run between Esna and Aswan due to difficulties crossing the Esna Lock and acquiring permits. Both move without a motor but may require the assistance of a tugboat if the winds aren't cooperating.

By Cruise Ship

A traditional river cruise boat is a good option for those looking for the amenities of a hotel on water. Most leave from Luxor on Mondays and from Aswan on Fridays. For all high-quality cruises, meals, guided tours, and entrance tickets to the sights are included. There are dozens to choose from with all budget levels, but here are a few of the finest ships on the Nile. Trips generally last 3-7 nights.

- **Oberoi** (tel. 0100 600 5101; www.oberoi-hotels.com; 21,120LE d per night) has two cruise ships, the *Zahara* and the *Philae*, that are among the most luxurious on the Nile. Each is equipped with a spa, gym, and small pool on the sundeck. Rooms are stylish and comfortable with large windows that open to let in the breeze off the river. Food on both is phenomenal. The *Zahara* has 27 cabins and suites, and the *Philae* is a bit smaller with 22. Choose a four-night cruise between Luxor and Aswan or a six-night cruise that includes a side trip up to Qena (65 km/40 mi north of Luxor). During low season (Apr.-Oct.) prices are considerably less (around 14,000LE d per night).
- **Steam Ship Sudan** (www.steam-ship-sudan.com; 17,700LE d per night) is the most historic cruise ship on the river. Built in 1885 for King Fouad, the *SS Sudan* later became the inspiration for Agatha Christie's 1937 *Death on the Nile*. The boat has since been beautifully refurbished, but still retains original flairs like wood-panels,

brass railings, wicker furniture, and crew in vintage costume. Choose from a four-night cruise (Luxor to Aswan, or the reverse) or five-night trip (including a trip up to Qena). There are only 23 cabins and suites, each with unique décor. The cons: no pool and the old-school engine can be a bit loud.

- **Sanctuary Retreats** (2 Talaat Harb St., Downtown, Cairo; tel. 02 23947820; www.sanctuaryretreats.com; 16,850LE d per night) has a few luxury options, the best of which are the *MS Sun Boat III* (only 18 cabins and suites) and *the MS Sun Boat IV* (40 cabins and suites). They both offer a small pool and attractive lounges. The *MS Sun Boat IV* has nicer rooms with floor-to-ceiling windows that open, a mini gym, and a spa. Choose between four nights (Luxor to Aswan, or the reverse) or eight nights (Luxor to Aswan and back, or vice versa). The *MS Sun Boat III* also sometimes offers a Cairo-Aswan route.
- **Mayfair Cruises** (23 Nabil El Wakkad St., Heliopolis, Cairo; tel. 02 24180021; www.mayfaircruises.com; 7,900LE d per night) offers a choice between three large luxury ships: the *MS Mayflower* (56 cabins and suites), *MS Esplanade* (73) and *MS Mayfair* (74). Each has a spa, a small pool on the sundeck, and pretty rooms with supremely comfortable beds and large windows. Trips last three nights (from Aswan), four nights (from Luxor), or seven nights (Luxor to Aswan and back, or the reverse).
- **Mövenpick** (74 Beirut St., Heliopolis, Cairo; tel. 02 26901756; www.movenpick.com; 7,600LE per night) has a fleet of seven ships to choose from, the best of which are the *MS Darakum* (52 cabins and suites), *MS Hamees* (72), and *MS Royal Lily* (60). Travel in comfort for three nights (from Aswan), four nights (from Luxor), or seven nights (Luxor to Aswan and back). Trips between Cairo and Aswan are available on occasion on the *MS Darakum*. Nightly entertainment on board.

By Dahabiya

If you're looking for more comfort than a felucca but fewer passengers than a cruise ship, a dahabiya is a great option. This medium-sized boat has proper bedrooms, private bathrooms, and sometimes even ACs. The upper deck is typically spacious and half-canopied—perfect for lounging in the shade by day or under the stars at night as you glide along the Nile. Meals are prepared fresh daily on board. Trips generally last 3-5 nights, although longer options are available.

- **Dahabiya Nile Sailing** (Television St., Luxor; tel. 0110 002 2242; www.dahabiya-nilesailing.com; 22,400LE d for 4-night trip) works with a fleet of five beautiful dahabiyas with 4-10 cabins. They offer the widest variety of trips with options of 3-14 nights, typically starting at various points along the Nile and ending in Aswan. With the 14-night package you have the rare opportunity to sail up the river all the way between Cairo and Aswan. Price includes all guided tours, transfers, entry fees, food, and drinks. Owned by the excellent tour operator **Real Egypt Tours** (www.realegypt.com).
- **Nile Dahabiya Boats** (33 Abdel Khalek Tharwat St., Downtown, Cairo; tel. 02 23959124; www.nile-dahabiya.com; 19,650LE d for 3-night trip) has four beautiful dahabiyas: *The Orient, Zekrayaat, Nora,* and *Loulia*. Choose between a three-night downriver trip from Aswan to Esna or four nights upriver from Esna to Aswan. Their boats are on the smaller side—with only 4 double rooms and 1-2 suites—and they sail regardless of the numbers, so you might even get the dahabiya to yourself. Price includes all food and (nonalcoholic) drinks, guided tours, entrance fees to sites, and transfers to/from hotels in Luxor and Aswan. Company owned by the reputable tour operator **Djed Egypt Travel** (www.djedegypt.com).
- **Nour el Nil** (tel. +44 20 3239 0923; www.nourelnil.com; from 41,000LE d for 5-night

trip) has a fleet of six charming boutique dahabiyas. Each boat holds a maximum of 16-24 people. Rooms are pristine with large windows. Price includes full board, car transfer from Luxor to the starting point in Esna, tickets to the visited sites, and expert guide. Alcohol available on board for extra, or you can bring your own from duty free. All trips start on Monday (pickup from your Luxor hotel at 9am) and guests disembark at 9:30am in Aswan on Saturday. Payments are nonrefundable.

By Felucca

For a no-frills adventure, a felucca is the best way to cruise the Nile. Charter a private boat for a solo trip or a group excursion and eat, sleep, and lounge on the boat's shaded deck. If you're on a budget, head to the Nile Corniche in central Aswan (East Bank) and negotiate a rate with a boatman there at least a day in advance. Or for assured quality at a slightly higher cost, try one of these reliable companies:

- **Nubian Sailing** (Corniche el Nil St., Old Cataract Hotel Marina, Aswan; tel. 0100 647 3189; www.nubiansailing.com; 9am-9pm daily): Captain Safy is a lesser-known gem on the Nile. He offers safe and enjoyable trips around Aswan and beyond on his felucca, the *Lion Heart*. Design your own trip (200LE/hour) or choose from one of his set packages, like a three-hour cruise with a superb Nubian lunch or dinner (500LE, plus 100LE per person), a six-hour sightseeing trip around Aswan (1000LE, not including admission), or 2-3 nights to Kom Ombo (1000LE/day, plus 200LE per person for food).
- **Aswan Individual** (Corniche el Nil St., Aswan; tel. 0100 250 9588; www.aswan-individual.com; 8am-10pm daily; 1,050LE/night for up to 5 people) offers a special felucca experience with opportunities to stop along the Nile and visit the village homes of the captain and crew. Fabulous local food is cooked fresh on board daily. Trips last 1-3 nights and travel to the Daraw Camel Market, Kom Ombo, Gebel el-Silsila, and/or Edfu. A bigger boat is available for parties of more than five (1,400LE/night). Those wishing to travel all the way to Luxor can add a private car transfer from the felucca drop-off point (1,600LE). No toilets on board.
- **Egypt Nile Cruise** (44 Haram St., Giza; tel. 0100 564 9180; www.egypt-nile-cruise.com; 9am-6pm daily) arranges excellent tour packages that include 1-3 nights on a felucca with the option of adding hotel stays and tours. An example of their shortest package (2,400LE per person) includes morning pickup in Aswan, overnight sailing (including all meals), a transfer by car to the temples of Kom Ombo and Edfu with expert guided tours, and drop-off in Luxor. They have a fabulous crew that take good care of their guests and cook up delicious dishes on board. Their feluccas include a basic toilet chamber on board to save you from having to go over the side or on land.

Aswan

The belt of green that lines the Nile from the

lotus-like Delta down to the south dissolves in Aswan into speckles of vegetation. Here, the land looks like tahini and molasses (a local breakfast staple), with dark swirls of river encroaching on sesame-colored sand. On the eastern shore, hardy shrubs and palm trees creep out from the folds of pink granite pillows. To the west, dramatic desert hills pour into the Nile. And between the banks, feluccas drift serenely, their white sails propelled by soft breezes.

Aswan once served as the gateway to Nubia—the ancient civilization that stretched south along the Nile from Aswan to Khartoum in modern-day Sudan, and rivaled the mighty kings and queens of Egypt. The Greeks referred to Nubia as Aithiopia (Ethiopia), "Land of Burnt

Highlights

Look for ★ to find recommended sights, activities, dining, and lodging.

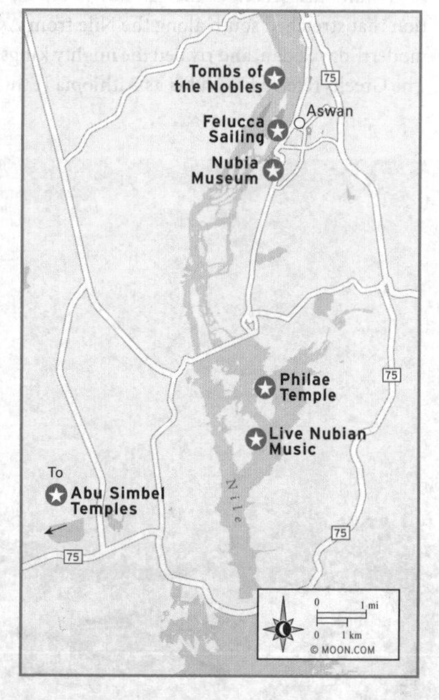

★ **Nubia Museum:** Follow millennia of Nubian history as you examine objects excavated during the construction of Aswan's High Dam (page 225).

★ **Tombs of the Nobles:** Explore tombs that date to the Old and Middle Kingdoms, and then take in stunning hilltop views of Aswan and the Nile (page 228).

★ **Philae Temple:** This sprawling temple complex built for Isis, the goddess of protection and magic, was taken apart block by block and reassembled on a neighboring island to save it from flooding after construction of the Aswan High Dam (page 228).

★ **Felucca Sailing:** For a dose of serenity, hop on a felucca (traditional wooden sailboat) for an hour or two at sunset (page 233).

★ **Live Nubian Music:** Sway to the entrancing beat of the tar drum and unique vocals of Nubians' eclectic music. There are a few places in town to hear it, but **Heissa Camp** is a standout (page 242).

★ **Abu Simbel Temples:** Buried under the sand for centuries, these two towering temples carved into the side of a mountain by Ramses II (c. 1255 BC) are one of Egypt's most fabulous sights (page 245).

Aswan

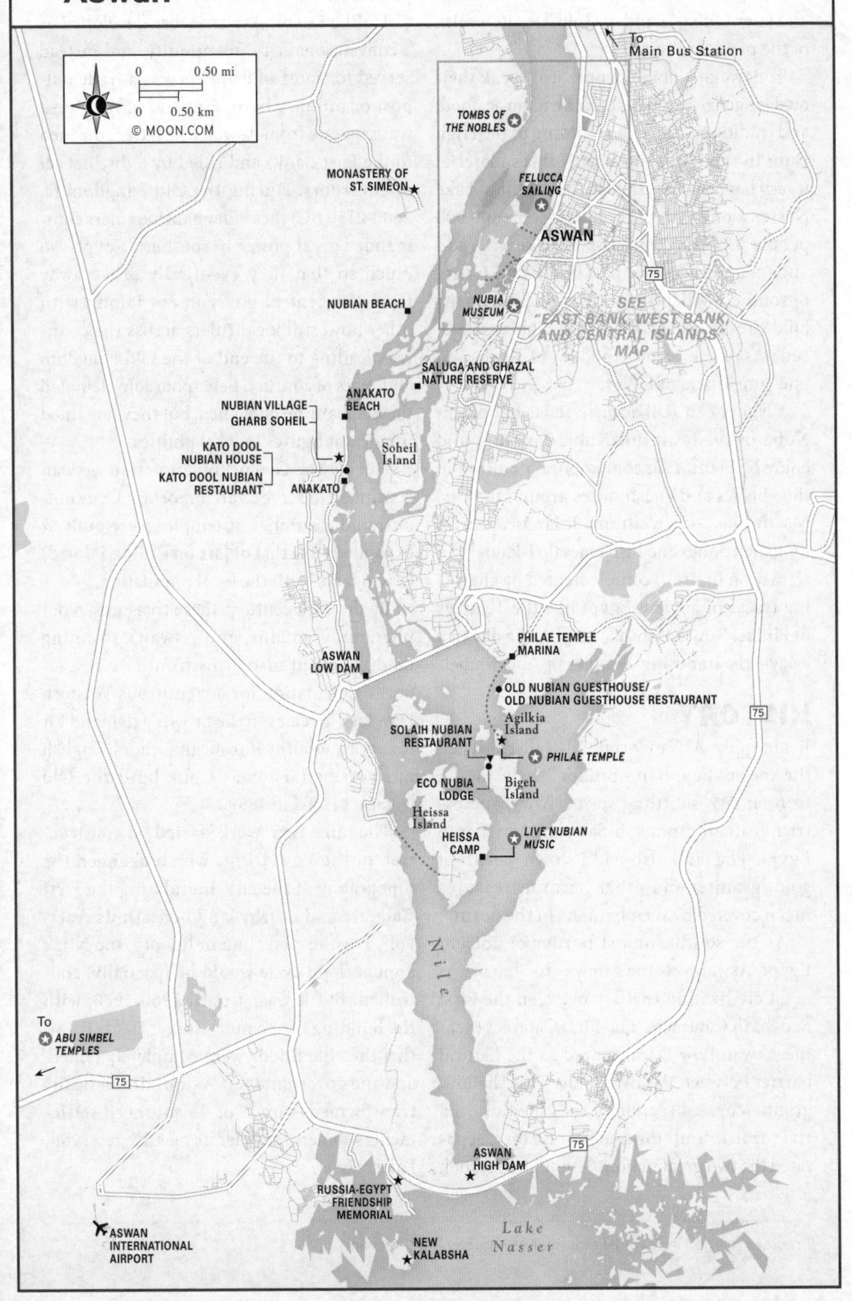

0
0.50 mi
0
0.50 km
© MOON.COM
To
Main Bus Station
TOMBS OF THE NOBLES
MONASTERY OF ST. SIMEON
FELUCCA SAILING
ASWAN
75
NUBIAN BEACH
NUBIA MUSEUM
SEE "EAST BANK, WEST BANK, AND CENTRAL ISLANDS" MAP
SALUGA AND GHAZAL NATURE RESERVE
ANAKATO BEACH
NUBIAN VILLAGE GHARB SOHEIL
KATO DOOL NUBIAN HOUSE
KATO DOOL NUBIAN RESTAURANT
ANAKATO
Soheil Island
PHILAE TEMPLE MARINA
ASWAN LOW DAM
OLD NUBIAN GUESTHOUSE/ OLD NUBIAN GUESTHOUSE RESTAURANT
75
SOLAIH NUBIAN RESTAURANT
Agilkia Island
PHILAE TEMPLE
ECO NUBIA LODGE
Bigeh Island
Heissa Island
HEISSA CAMP
LIVE NUBIAN MUSIC
Nile
To
ABU SIMBEL TEMPLES
75
75
ASWAN HIGH DAM
RUSSIA-EGYPT FRIENDSHIP MEMORIAL
Lake Nasser
ASWAN INTERNATIONAL AIRPORT
NEW KALABSHA

Faces." Egyptians called it Ta Sety, "Land of the Bow," after Nubians' famed archery skills, and later, Nuba, "Land of Gold," for its wealth of the precious metal.

Today, the Nubian people still speak their own language and have their own music, food, and traditions. Since the building of the High Dam in the 1960s, most of Nubia's material legacy has been banished to the depths of Lake Nasser, along with the homes of some 100,000 people. Half of those displaced resettled in Sudan, and the other half in Aswan, Cairo, or southern villages along the Nile. But many hold strong to their identity as Nubians—decedents of the great Kingdom of Kush, and one-time rulers of Egypt.

Visitors can still admire relics of ancient Nuba in the beautiful Nubia Museum and enjoy Nubians' rich contemporary culture in the villages and guesthouses around the city. Meanwhile, Aswan's dramatic landscape with its golden dunes and lush emerald islands is an attraction in itself, complemented by charming traces of ancient Egypt like the Temples of Philae, New Kalabsha, and—just a day trip away—the imposing Temples of Abu Simbel.

HISTORY

In antiquity, Aswan (originally called Swenet, the ancient Egyptian word for "trade") was a frontier city, shuttling spices, ivory, and ostrich feathers from sub-Saharan Africa into Egypt. The land also had its own wealth of gold, granite, and other natural treasures much coveted by the pharaohs in the north.

As the southernmost border of ancient Egypt, Aswan was the gateway to Nuba—the great civilization that lay between the First and Sixth Cataracts. The First Cataract (near the Aswan Low Dam) served as the natural barrier between the two lands. This shallow, granite-covered section of the Nile thwarted river traffic and, for much of history, separated the two great nations—though they took turns colonizing each other as their respective powers waxed and waned.

Unlike Luxor, Aswan never developed as a conventional city in antiquity, and instead served for most of its history as a trade outpost or military base. **Elephantine Island** was separate from Aswan (the latter confined to the East Bank) and ruled by a distinct set of governors. During the Old Kingdom (c. 2600-2150 BC) these Elephantine rulers commanded great power in southern Egypt—so much so that they eventually broke away from the central government (along with other powerful local rulers across the country), leading to the end of the Old Kingdom and years of conflict. Later pharaohs demoted the Elephantine noblemen, but they remained important figures in local politics.

During the Greco-Roman period, Aswan continued to serve as an important trade outpost and a number of temples were built or expanded (like that of **Isis** on **Philae Island**) to win favor with the local population.

By the 19th century, these treasures, older pharaonic remains, and Aswan's stunning landscape had made this frontier city a favorite destination for adventurous Western travelers. To cater to the growing demand for luxury by wealthy European visitors, English businessman Thomas Cook built the Old Cataract Hotel in 1899.

The same year, work started on construction of the **Low Dam,** which changed the topography of the city, inundating the First Cataract and nearby land beneath its reservoir. For the first time in history, the Nile's annual flood cycle would be (partially) controlled. But it wasn't until 1960-1970, with the building of the much larger **High Dam,** that the Nile floods were completely tamed, and the governorate of Aswan dramatically transformed—much of its southern settlements submerged under its massive reservoir, Lake Nasser.

Previous: camels in Aswan; fields near Aswan; Elephantine Island.

ORIENTATION

Aswan can be divided into four major sections: East Bank, West Bank, Central Islands, and South Aswan (south of the Low Dam).

East Bank

Aswan's busiest section, the East Bank is where you'll find the downtown area and most of the commerce. The central **Aswan Souq** begins just south of the Railway Station and continues for around a mile. The **Nubia Museum** and **Unfinished Obelisk** (around 3 km/2 mi south of the Railway Station) mark the southern limits of downtown that's of any interest to visitors. **Corniche el-Nil Street,** which runs along the Nile, is spotted with the various ferry landings to the West Bank and Elephantine Island.

Central Islands

ELEPHANTINE ISLAND

Of the Central Islands the largest is Elephantine (known by locals as Gezirat Aswan, or Aswan Island)—just about 2 kilometers (1 mi) long and 450 meters (1,500 ft) across at its widest. This labyrinthine island is divided into three main sections. The northern third belongs to the **Mövenpick Resort** (not accessible from elsewhere on Elephantine—must be reached by the resort's private ferry landing on the East Bank, 190 m/620 ft south of McDonald's). The middle section is a hamlet called Siou ("Sand" in Nubian)—where you'll find the **Animalia Museum** in the island center. To get here, take a ferry from the **North Ferry Landing** on the East Bank, next to the KFC. South of Siou through a maze of houses is the hamlet of Koti ("High Place," named after its elevated land), which is where the island's ancient remains lie at the **Ruins of Abu.** The **South Ferry Landing** on the East Bank (just north of Feryal Garden) will bring you here.

NABATAT ISLAND

West of Elephantine, Nabatat Island is home to the **Aswan Botanical Garden.** The other mini-islands to the south are not destinations to wander on foot, but they are nice to cruise around in a felucca or motorboat.

West Bank

The West Bank, dominated by sand dunes and mountains, is much less built up. The ferry from the East Bank—located parallel to the Railway Station along the Nile—will drop you off at the northernmost point of interest, the **Tombs of the Nobles.** Nearby is a mostly residential area called **El-Qubba** with a few nice guesthouses along the Nile. Around 2 kilometers (1 mi) south of that as the crow flies is the **Monastery of St. Simeon** (best reached by boat or, for the adventurous, hiking). Just south of the monastery, closer to the river, is the dome-topped Agha Khan Mausoleum (not open to the public, but a helpful landmark). The hamlet of **Gharb Soheil** is another 3 kilometers (2 mi) of hilly desert farther south, home to the touristic **Nubian Village** and some colorful hotels.

South Aswan

In South Aswan (beginning 7 km/4 mi south of central Aswan), the main attractions lie in the reservoir (el-Khazzaan) hugged by the **Low** and **High Dams.** Just south of the Low Dam on the East Bank, the **Philae Temple Marina** is where you can pick up tickets and a motorboat for a short ride to the temple of the same name on **Agilkia Island.** Just south of that, the rocky **Bigeh Island** has a charming Nubian hotel and restaurant, but little else. And next to that, **Heissa Island** has its own thriving, if tiny, village with a handful of Nubian guesthouses. Around 4 kilometers (2.5 mi) south of Heissa Island is the **High Dam,** and beyond that, **Lake Nasser** (locally known as Buherat el-Nuba, Lake Nubia). **New Kalabsha** with its temple and other ancient treats sits on an island (unless the water is low) just 1 kilometer (0.6 mi) south of the High Dam.

PLANNING YOUR TIME

You need at least three days to get acquainted with beautiful Nubia and its treasures.

Consider dividing your itinerary into geographic sections, visiting the East Bank and Elephantine Island one day, the West Bank and Nabatat Island (perhaps on a felucca trip) the next, and South Aswan on another. If you have a fourth day, hire a driver or hop on a short flight to Abu Simbel. With even more time, take the trip down to Abu Simbel on a 3-4-night Lake Nasser cruise.

Many travelers make a point of visiting the **Abu Simbel Temples** (270km south of Aswan along a desert highway) on October 22 and February 22, when the sun illuminates statues in the inner sanctuary. If you decide to visit at this time, note that crowd control is scant, making for a very cramped visit.

The **Daraw Camel Market** (page 213), located between Luxor and Aswan, is a unique day trip from Aswan. Hiring a car is the quickest way to get here, but waking up to the market after an overnight trip on a felucca is a special experience. You can arrange with a felucca captain along the Corniche in central Aswan as little as a day before departure, but for more trusted services try **Aswan Individual** ($65 one-way for the whole boat, holds up to 5 passengers). This trip usually takes one day and one night to reach Daraw depending on the wind (if it's slow going, Aswan Individual will send a car to get you the rest of the way in time). From there, you can return to Aswan by car ($55) or continue to Luxor via Kom Ombo and Edfu ($100). For a faster option, do the whole trip by private car from Aswan (1 hour each way; $55 round-trip). Remember: The market is only open on Saturday and Sunday 8am-1pm.

TOURS AND LOCAL GUIDES

MENA ZAKI

tel. 0127 400 8892; www.aswanluxortravel.com

The animated Mena Zaki is a fantastic guide to Aswan and Luxor and great company to have along on your travels. He's a licensed Egyptologist who enriches visits around the sites, and a reliable trip organizer who can tailor outings to your liking at reasonable prices. Aside from tours within Aswan and Luxor proper, he can arrange for a comfortable car between the two cities with stops at the Daraw Camel Market and the temples between Luxor and Aswan (8-10 hours; $200 for 1-2 people including tours and transportation, or less if you stop at fewer sites). He also does a great day trip from Aswan to Abu

view of Aswan from the Tombs of the Nobles

Simbel (about 8 hours; $180 for 1-2 people including tour and private car). Entrance tickets not included.

ASWAN INDIVIDUAL

tel. 0100 250 95 88; www.aswan-individual.com; 8am-10pm daily

Waleed and his team offer a wide range of personalized tours and/or private transportation. They are extremely punctual and professional. Recommended packages include a full day trip to New Kalabsha, the Philae Temple, Aswan High Dam, and Unfinished Obelisk ($80 for 1-2 people) or a felucca ride from Elephantine Island to the Tombs of the Nobles and Monastery of St. Simeon ($9/hour). They also do trips to Abu Simbel or Luxor (via Kom Ombo, Edfu, and Esna), each for just around $105. Entrance tickets not included.

Itinerary Ideas

DAY 1: SOUTH ASWAN, EAST BANK, AND ELEPHANTINE ISLAND

1 After breakfast, begin your day at the Philae Temple Marina on the East Bank, where you can pick up tickets and a private boat to the **Philae Temple** (5-10 minutes). Ask your boatman to wait at the temple's exit, and take your time exploring it. When you're done, the boat will return you to the marina.

2 From the marina, grab a cab to the East Bank Ferry Landing (near the KFC) where the public ferry will bring you to Elephantine Island (Siou village). Take a short walk west to the **Animalia Museum** for an introduction to Nubian culture and the flora and fauna of Aswan.

3 When you've finished at the museum, wander through the winding village streets to the **Ruins of Abu** on the south end of the island.

4 Hop on the public ferry to the East Bank (at the southern Ferry Landing just a few steps from the Ruins of Abu) and enjoy a leisurely lunch with a view at the historic Old Cataract Hotel's **The Terrace.**

5 Walk down the street (5-10 minutes) to the **Nubia Museum** to check out some of ancient Nubia's lasting treasures.

6 Take a 15-minute cab to the northern entrance of the **Aswan Souq** (near the train station) to check out the handicrafts.

7 End the day with a tasty meal of Egyptian fare at **El Masry** (near the southern end of Souq Street).

DAY 2: WEST BANK AND NABATAT ISLAND

On your second day in Aswan, get an early start to avoid the heat, and then pick up a private felucca at your agreed upon spot. (Arrange a day or two in advance with the excellent local tour operator, **Aswan Individual,** for an all-day felucca tour).

1 Set sail on your felucca for the **Tombs of the Nobles** on the West Bank. Hike up the hill to inspect the ancient burial sites and enjoy the superb views.

Itinerary Ideas

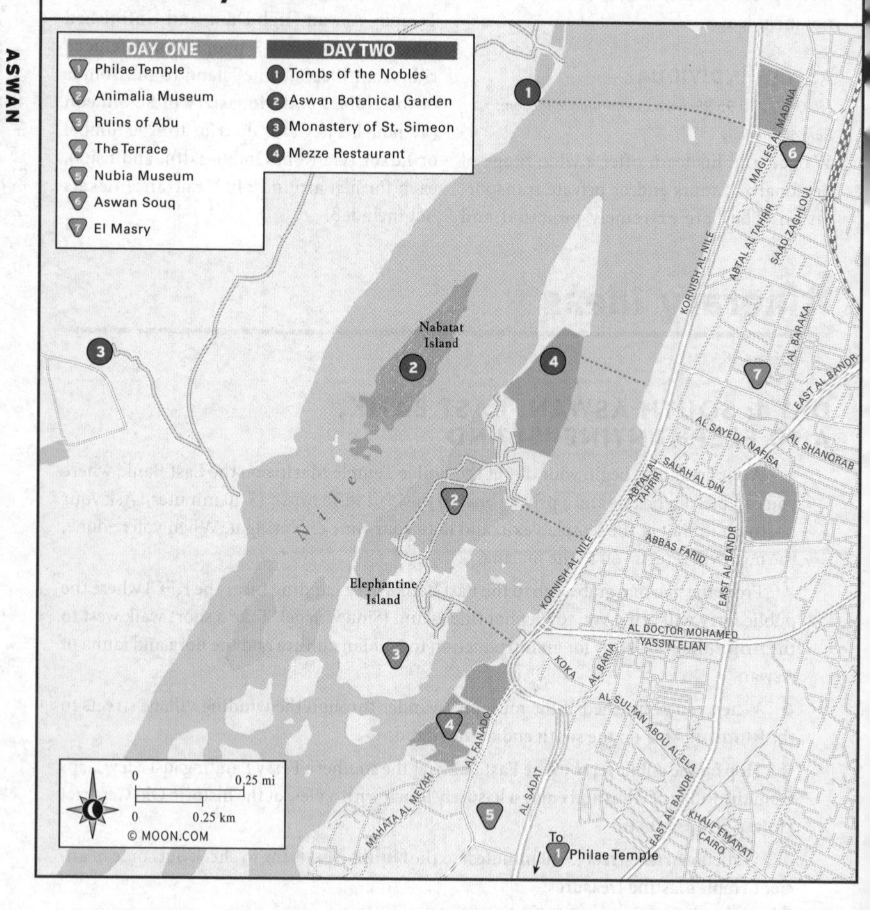

2 Sail next to Nabatat Island and the **Aswan Botanical Garden** for a peaceful walk through the greenery and some quality souvenir shopping. Then, return to the felucca to enjoy a fresh lunch on board, prepared by the Aswan Individual team.

3 Head back to the West Bank and catch a camel ride up the hill to the **Monastery of St. Simeon.**

4 Continue to sail around the central rocky islands. When you've had enough time on the water, ask to be dropped off at the eastern entrance to the Mövenpick Resort on Elephantine Island for dinner and drinks at the hotel's **Mezze Restaurant.**

Sights

EAST BANK

★ Nubia Museum

Al-Fanadek St., 400 m (1,300 ft) south of the Old Cataract Hotel; tel. 097 2319111; 9am-1pm and 4pm-9pm daily winter, 6pm-10pm daily summer; 100LE adults, 50LE students

The Nubia Museum is one of Egypt's best with an attractive layout, dramatic lighting, and excellent signage. The objects on display were saved during UNESCO's project to rescue Nubian artifacts from a watery grave during the construction of the Aswan High Dam in the 1960s. The team excavated over 3,000 items—from gold jewelry to striking statues of kings and queens made of Nubia's copious granite—many of which you can view here. An interesting section with photos from the excavations provides context for where the objects were found. Dioramas also show scenes from traditional Nubian life (dress, homes, musical instruments, etc.) as they exist today. History lovers could spend hours here reading about the waxing and waning of this lesser-known civilization. For the casual visitor, 1.5-2 hours should do.

Unfinished Obelisk

Off Dr. Abd Al-Rady Hanafe St.; no tel.; 8am-5pm daily; 60LE adults, 30LE students

Carved directly into granite bedrock, this 42-meter (138-ft) obelisk never reached verticality. There's a general consensus that Queen Hatshepsut (r. 1479-1457 BC) ordered the work, which would have been the tallest of its kind by nearly a third. Unfortunately, the pillar cracked as workers tried to lift it, bringing the project to an abrupt end. The site is particularly interesting because it sheds light on how obelisks were crafted and resurrected from their rocky beds (you can still see the textures carved out by hands and early tools some 3,500 years ago). The surrounding area, an ancient granite quarry, generated the raw materials that supplied the spectacular temples of Upper Egypt.

CENTRAL ISLANDS

Animalia Museum

Siou Village, central Elephantine Island; tel. 0100 545 6420 or 097 2314152; www.animaliaaswan.wordpress.com; 8am-7pm daily; 20LE admission, 40LE tour

The animated ornithologist Mohammed Sobhi has converted the ground floor of his traditional Nubian home into an ethnobiological museum. He and his team provide an excellent introduction to Nubian history and contemporary culture, making it a good stop early in your trip to provide context for what's to come. The museum also houses an interesting collection of taxidermied local animals, geological samples, and rare photos of pre-High Dam Nubia. Don't miss their small gift shop with a selection of colorful scarves, baskets, jewelry, and garments.

Ruins of Abu

Koti Village, southern tip of Elephantine Island; no tel.; 8am-5pm daily; 35LE adults, 15LE students

Abu, meaning "elephant's tooth" in ancient Egyptian, was the original name of Elephantine Island, likely due to the importance of ivory as a wealth-making trade item for its residents. The ruins here hold the traces of an ancient settlement dating to some 5,000 years ago, and layers of later villages and their temples. You can wander freely along the paths of the ongoing excavation site, with beautiful views from the area's highest points.

The ruins' centerpiece, the **Temple of Khnum** (signs 6, 12, and 13), was first built around the 16th century BC and became one of the most impressive in all of Egypt after successive generations expanded and embellished it. A large cult formed around Khnum—the ram-headed creator god and controller of the Nile who caused both floods

East Bank, West Bank, and Central Islands

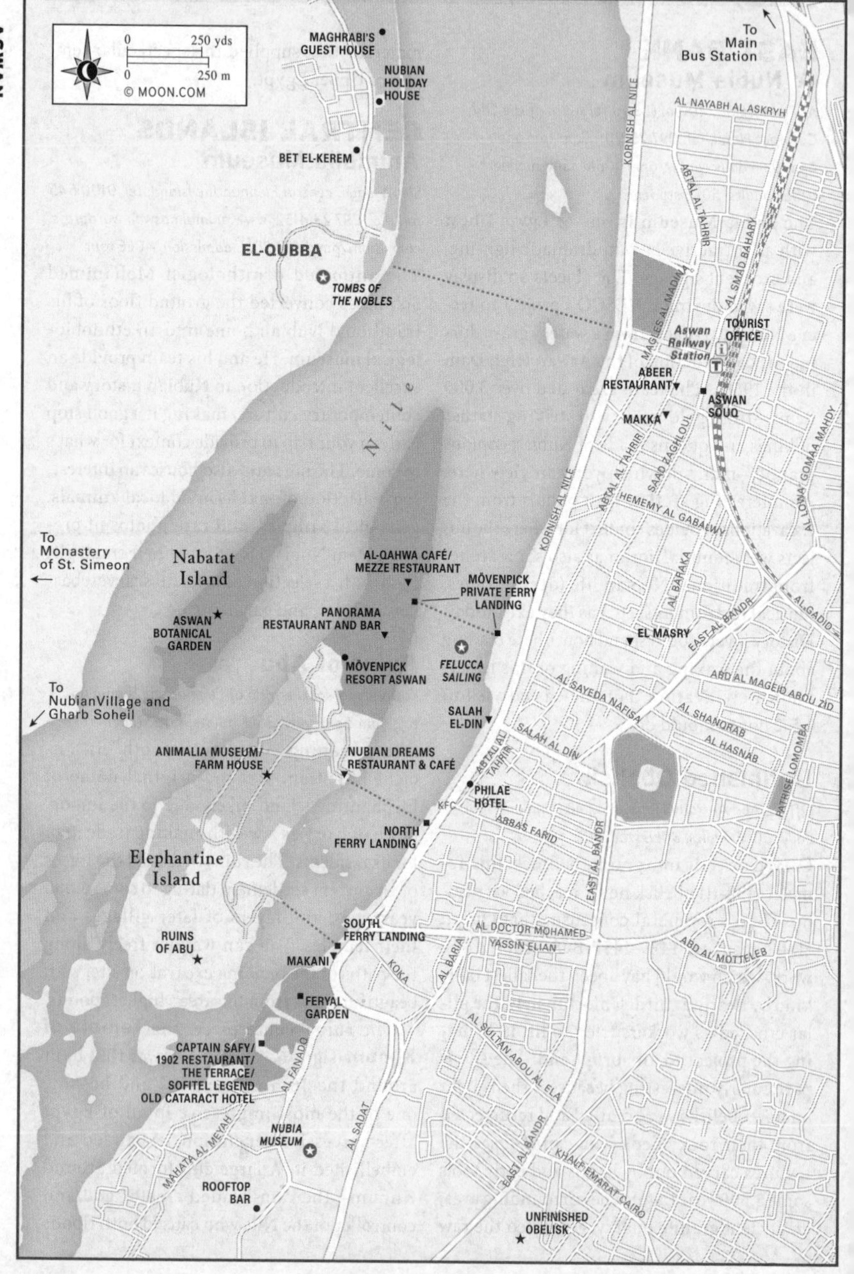

and famines. The temple also honored the goddesses Satet (Khnum's consort) and Anket (their daughter), the guardians of the cataracts. In the 4th century AD part of the temple became a church, and then military housing for the Byzantine army. When the Byzantines left, locals moved in and large sections of the temple walls were torn down. Today it's easy to miss if you don't know what you're looking for, but some pillars have been re-erected and the smaller **Temple of Satet** (sign 3) stands largely reconstructed beside it.

Be sure to check out the spectacular views from the raised platform just north of Khnum's Temple. Keep an eye out also for the mini **step pyramid** on the northern edge of the site, likely commissioned by Snefru (builder of the first true pyramid in Dahshur; c. 2600 BC), the **sacred ram cemetery** (sign 11), and the **Nilometer** (number 7, just southeast of the Temple of Khnum) dating from around the 6th century BC. You can still see inundation markings from the Roman period on the Nilometer—used to measure water levels to determine whether there would be floods, famine, or bounty. The entire area is an easy walk, with each stop no more than a few hundred meters from any other. A guard will likely offer a tour around the numbered signs (a small tip of 30-40 LE is expected) and can actually be quite helpful.

Aswan Botanical Garden

Nabatat Island; no tel.; 8am-6pm daily; 30LE

If you've been missing green space on your travels through deserts and urban jungles, a short walk across this emerald Gezirat el-Nabatat (Island of Plants) will be well-spent. Founded as a botanical garden in 1898, the island was known as "Kitchener's Island" when the eponymous British commander of the Egyptian army received the land as a gift after a successful campaign in Sudan. Kitchener imported dozens of exotic trees and plants, many of which are still standing today.

The garden is around 1 kilometer (0.6 mi) long with ample shade provided by palms and a wealth of fruit trees hung with mangos, guavas, and avocados. Patches of aromatic jasmine line the paths, perfuming the air. If you need a break, rest your feet on one of many benches looking out to the West Bank's golden slopes.

The entrance is located on the northeast side of Nabatat Island. To get here, grab a private felucca or motorboat from the East Bank. The ride takes 15-50 minutes (depending on departure point) and costs around 140LE/hour including wait time. You can also leave from the west side of Elephantine Island (arriving in just 5-10 minutes), but you might have trouble finding a boat. Ask your boatman to wait for you at the exit (southeast side of the island). WCs, souvenir vendors, and a small cafeteria can be found on the south side of the island.

WEST BANK

Monastery of St. Simeon

1 km/0.6 mi northwest of riverbank along sandy path; no tel.; 8am-4pm daily; 40LE adults, 20LE students

This maze-like Coptic monastery perched on the edge of the desert was originally dedicated to Anba Hadra, a late-4th-century hermit saint who became the bishop of Aswan. The monastery itself dates to around the 7th century (but was largely rebuilt in the 10th century) and holds layers of additions made by later monks who lived there until the complex was abandoned in the late 1200s.

A cliff separates the sprawling structure into two levels. On the lower level you can find the saints' original rock caves and the remains of the church with wall paintings and baptistry. The upper level holds the monks' living quarters, a dining hall, and a number of workshops. Don't miss the milling yard with grinding stone adorned with Coptic crosses.

A guide will likely greet you on site to share a wealth of information about the monastery (donation appreciated). To get here, hire a private boat from Elephantine Island or the East Bank. Camels are often stationed by the river where boats drop you off and can save you a walk up the sandy hill (20 minutes; 50-100 LE). You can also opt to take a camel on the way back, but the ride down is a bit uncomfortable.

★ Tombs of the Nobles

200 m/650 ft west of the of West Bank Ferry Dock; no tel.; 8am-4pm daily; 60LE adults, 30LE students

Over 100 tombs lie scattered in this patch of hillside, but only a few are open to the public. Most date to the Old and Middle Kingdoms (c. 2200-1750 BC) and house the remains of local elites. Wealthy governors of Elephantine were largely buried in the middle section of the four-level necropolis. On the top level, some of the chambers were converted into a Coptic church by a monastic settlement.

To visit the best tombs, you'll have to find the keeper of the keys (he'll probably find you first just beyond the ticket window or at the top of the stairs that lead to the tombs), who will open them for a small tip (10-15LE). Don't miss the most vibrant tomb (site 31) of Prince Sarenput II from 12th dynasty (1985-1795 BC), with the walls covered in hieroglyphs, lotuses (a symbol of rebirth), and scenes of daily life. His wife and mother are depicted on the right and left walls, respectively. Most of the other tombs have little to offer by way of decoration.

Rivaling the tombs as the main attraction are the views from the top of the hillside near **Qubbat al-Hawa** (the domed structure dedicated to a local sheikh). They're possibly the best in all of Aswan, with sloping golden sands to the west, green islands to the south, and the snaking Nile with its elegant felucca traffic disappearing into the horizon. You need to be relatively fit to get to the top (you ascend a long staircase to get to the tombs before climbing up a sandy hill to Qubbat al-Hawa) and be sure to wear your walking shoes.

To get to the tombs, catch the public ferry from the landing parallel to the Railway Station on the East Bank (runs every 10-15 minutes 6am-10pm; 3-5LE), or hire a private felucca or motorboat (about 140LE/hour). You can find them along the corniche of the East Bank and (sometimes) on the west side of Elephantine Island.

Nubian Village

Gharb Soheil; no tel.; 8am-8pm daily; free

The touristic "Nubian Village" feels a bit like Disney World, but it's a favorite excursion for many. You can visit colorful Nubian houses (many playing host to photogenic baby crocodiles), get a henna tattoo, ride a camel, and take a quick lesson in Nubian languages at a local school. Vendors line the streets—many selling more aggressively than elsewhere in Aswan—but you can find nice handicrafts if you're in the mood to haggle. Beware of running camels.

SOUTH ASWAN

★ Philae Temple

Agilkia Island; no tel.; 7am-4pm daily Oct.-May, 7am-5pm daily June-Sept.; 140LE adults, 70LE students

The original island of Philae (pronounced by locals as FAY-ya-la) now lies under water, but the sprawling complex that once stood there remains, rebuilt in all its grandeur on the neighboring island of Agilkia. Kushite King Taharqa (r. 690-664 BC) commissioned the earliest structures on Philae, while Nectenebo II (r. 360-343 BC)—the last native king of Egypt—built the first known temple here. But most of what we see now we owe to the Ptolemies and Romans (3rd-1st centuries BC). Ptolemy II (r. 285-246 BC) began construction of the main temple, the **Temple of Isis,** expanding the popular cult that worshiped the eponymous goddess on Philae.

When you arrive to the dock on the south side of the island, you'll find a small cafeteria to your right and the temple's outer court to your left, lined by dozens of columns with a hodgepodge of floral motifs courtesy of Roman emperors. The two granite lions standing at the entrance to the temple look miniature compared to the 18-meter (60-ft) pylon (monumental gateway) decorated with

---

1: Aswan Botanical Garden 2: Monastery of St. Simeon 3: Qubbat al-Hawa at the Tombs of the Nobles 4: Hathor column capital at the Philae Temple

1
2
3
4

The Cult of Isis

a bas-relief of Egyptian goddess Isis, on the Temple of Isis

Goddess of protection, healing, magic, and motherhood, Isis was the sister-wife of **Osiris** (god of the underworld) and mother of **Horus** (lord of the sky). In other parts of Egypt, followers worshiped her as part of this power triangle, but on the island of Philae, Isis reigned supreme. Her cult center here competed with the followers of Khnum on Elephantine Island to the north, and inscriptions in the Philae Temple attribute control of the life-giving Nile (long connected to Khnum) instead, to her: "You induce the Nile and lead him in due season up over the land of Egypt."

THE STORY OF ISIS

The story of Isis—daughter of **Geb** (god of the earth) and **Nut** (goddess of the sky)—is one of undying devotion. The goddess once ruled over the world alongside her brother-husband Osiris until their jealous younger brother (**Seth**) killed and dismembered Osiris, scattering his body across Egypt and usurping his role as lord of the living. Isis scoured the land, gathered the pieces of her husband, put him back together, and used her magic to revive him. But not even Isis could return her beloved to his previous post in the realm of the living and Osiris became, instead, the lord of the dead. The two had a son, Horus, and Isis raised him in secrecy, protecting him from all evils until he was old enough to avenge his father and dethrone Seth. This he did, and order was restored—no small thanks to the magical protectress.

The appeal of the good-hearted goddess spread far and wide across the ancient world during the Greco-Roman period, and Cleopatra even fancied herself Isis in earthly form. It was only with the rise of Christianity that the cult of Isis was suppressed and her temple on Philae closed.

SIGHTS THAT CELEBRATE ISIS

Philae Temple is the main sight in Aswan that celebrates Isis, but she also makes appearances at other temples.

- **New Kalabsha** (page 231)
- **Abu Simbel's Small Temple** (page 247)
- Outside of Aswan, she can also be found in the **Dendera Temple Complex** (page 158).

images of Isis, her son (Horus), and Ptolemy XII (a 1st century BC pharaoh) smiting his foes.

Enter to the left to reach the **Birth House,** commemorating the birth of Horus, from whom all pharaohs (themselves "divine") were said to have descended. Beyond the Birth House up a small set of stairs you'll encounter a vestibule that was converted into a church under Christian rule. Note the Egyptian key of life (ankh) hieroglyphs changed into crosses. During the 3rd and 4th centuries AD, Christianity was practiced on Philae beside Egypt's native cults before the temples were finally closed in the 6th century—the last cult temples to fall in Egypt.

To explore the layers of history and symbols on this island it's best to bring a guide. Either way, be sure to pass by the **Temple of Hathor** (east of the Temple of Isis; first

Aswan High Dam

Located 16 kilometers (10 mi) south of central Aswan, the Aswan High Dam—built in the 1960s under President Gamal Abdel Nasser and financed by the Soviet Union—took some 30,000 workers over a decade, operating in shifts both day and night, to complete. Lake Nasser, the reservoir created by the dam, stretches over 500 kilometers (310 mi) in length and 14 kilometers (9 mi) in width at its widest. The project regulated the Nile's floods and provided Nasser the electricity needed for his industrialization plan, but it had a range of negative environmental impacts. It also completely submerged all of Egypt's Nubia south of Aswan, displacing some 100,000 people.

VISITING THE DAM

The Aswan High Dam is not a must-see unless you have a special passion for engineering. You can check out this historic site from the roadside, or for better views head to the neighboring **Russia-Egypt Friendship Memorial** (off al-Sad al-Aali-Aswan Rd., west side of dam)—a concrete lotus with an elevator in one of its petals that brings you to an observation platform at the top.

The dam is just 6 kilometers (4 mi) directly east of Aswan International Airport and can easily be visited en route to central Aswan if you fly in. Ask the taxi to take the road that passes al-Sad al-Aali (the High Dam).

constructed around 100 BC and rebuilt under Augustus, c. 20 BC) dedicated to the goddess of the sky, from whom Isis (emerging later) took many characteristics. Just south of that, the 2nd-century **Kiosk of Trajan** stands tall with 14 columns and reliefs of Trajan (Roman emperor, c. AD 100) burning incense for Isis and Osiris.

To reach the island, hop on a boat at the **Philae Temple Marina** (off Nagaa el-Karour-Aswan Rd., 300 m/1,000 ft south of the Aswan Low Dam, East Bank). The 5-10-minute ride on a private boat should cost around 125-150LE round-trip, including wait time at the temple (payment can be made at the end of the visit when you return to the marina). Alternatively, arrange a trip through your hotel or guide. Purchase tickets from the office at the marina (no tickets available on the island).

New Kalabsha

Lake Nasser; 8am-5pm daily; 60LE adults, 30LE students

Just south of the High Dam, New Kalabsha is a lonely island home to the impressive Kalabsha Temple, as well as the temple of Beit al-Wali. A single entrance fee to the island covers both sights.

KALABSHA TEMPLE

This sandstone structure dedicated to the Nubian sun god Merul (Mandulis in Greek) once stood at Bab el-Kalabsha ("The Gateway to Kalabsha"), an ancient settlement on the West Bank that was flooded with the building of the High Dam. A German mission dismantled the temple into 13,000 blocks, together weighing around 20,000 tons, and reassembled it here.

While the temple itself dates to the reign of Roman Emperor Augustus (c. 30 BC), interior reliefs of king Amenhotep II (r. 1426-1400 BC) offering gifts to Merul indicate the 15th-century BC pharaoh likely built a temple to the Nubian sun god here some 1,400 years earlier. The Ptolemies (also predating the Romans) built the columns in the forecourt and engraved reliefs on stones used throughout the temple.

At the main entrance, look up to spot a winged solar disc flanked by two cobras—one of Merul's symbols, and a common motif in ancient Egypt. Kalabsha served as the solar god's cult center, but the temple also honored the powerful trio of Isis, Osiris (her husband), and Horus (her son)—and in some traditions, Merul was believed to be the son of Horus. Along the entrance wall are scenes of a pharaoh, likely Augustus, providing offerings to the foursome. Inside you can find graffiti of Roman soldiers—their prayers and names—who were garrisoned in Kalabsha (known as Talmis by the Romans) and also worshiped Merul. The temple was ultimately converted into a church, likely in the 6th century.

Beyond the forecourt and hypostyle hall lies the three-chambered inner sanctuary, where stairs lead to the top of the temple granting superb views of the High Dam, lake, and **Kiosk of Kertassi** (which you can visit with a short walk to the south). This Greco-Roman pavilion has six pretty columns, two of which are topped with the head of the mother goddess, Hathor.

BEIT AL-WALI

Saunter to the opposite side of New Kalabsha to find Beit al-Wali—an interesting rock-cut temple carved into a sandstone slope by Ramses II (r. 1279-1213 BC) not far from the original site of Kalabsha Temple. This was also saved from flooding by an international team of enthusiastic archeologists who oversaw the relocation. Flanking the entrance, two engraved Ramses IIs command all who enter to be pure. Inside you'll find three rooms, with the pharaoh alternating between smiting various enemies (Libyans, Nubians, Bedouins) and making offerings to the gods. After the entrance hall, there's a small columned chamber and beyond that, an inner sanctuary with reliefs of Ramses II suckled by Anuket and Isis (both goddesses of the Nile and protection)—a striking change of character for the one-man army shown in other images throughout the temple.

GETTING THERE

To get to New Kalabsha, grab a motorboat from the West Bank just south of the High Dam and ask the boatman to stay with you while you visit the sites (80-100LE). The ride will only take a few minutes and a leisurely visit should take around 1.5 hours or 2-3 if you bring a guide to explain (recommended). When the river is low, you can approach the site by land.

Recreation and Activities

PARKS

FERYAL GARDEN

Corniche el-Nil, next to the Old Cataract Hotel, East Bank; no tel.; 7am-4pm daily; 10LE

This Nile-side park with bulbous granite rocks and flowering trees is a pretty perch for watching the boats float by. Benches scattered along the park's multiple tiers are good spots to watch the sun set over the West Bank and Elephantine Island's Ruins of Abu.

KAYAKING

Paddling around in the tranquil waters of the reservoir between the Low and High Dams is a treat. Here, it's just you and nature.

HEISSA CAMP

Heissa Island; tel. 0100 500 4122; 8am-10pm daily; 250LE/day

Heissa Camp has a fleet of high-quality single kayaks that you can use to explore the nearby Tinjar Beach and surrounding rocky islands.

ANAKATO

Gharb Soheil; tel. 0100 081 8833; www.anakato.com; 8am-10pm daily; 200LE/2-hour guided tour

To paddle around Gharb Soheil on the West Bank, pick up a kayak from Anakato guesthouse.

BEACHES

After a number of drownings due to fickle currents, it's no longer permitted to swim in the Nile in Aswan. And while the Nile is much cleaner here than in Cairo, it still carries the risk of infecting swimmers with bilharzia, a disease caused by parasitic worm. But if you want to picnic on a beach or hang out near the water, you do have a few nice options.

NUBIAN BEACH

500 m/1,600 ft from Agha Khan Mausoleum, West Bank; tel. 0111 153 2280; noon-8pm daily; free

Nubian Beach is a nice sandy space run by Nubian Beach Lodge and open to the public. There's a tasty restaurant on site and WCs are available.

ANAKATO BEACH

Gharb Soheil; 8am-9pm daily; 50LE for non-hotel residents

This beach owned by Anakato Lodge is a pretty patch of sand on the north side of the touristic Nubian Village with a restaurant and WCs.

TINJAR BEACH

1 km/0.6 mi from Heissa Island; 24 hours daily; free

Tinjar Bech is located in the reservoir below the Low Dam near Heissa Island. It's only accessible by boat and makes for a nice stop on a kayak trip.

TOP EXPERIENCE

★ FELUCCA SAILING

Few activities rival the serenity of sailing around Aswan at sunset on your own private felucca (traditional wooden sailboat). Enjoy the cool evening breeze as you glide through glittering waters and weave between vegetation-rich islands. Feluccas are also a fabulous way to see parts of the West Bank and Central Islands on a day trip. Pick one up from along **Corniche el Nil Street** on the East Bank (around 150LE/hour), or choose one of the options below. It's customary to tip the boatman 10-20%. Note: Feluccas don't have motors and rely on good wind levels (not too much and not too little). Most days are suitable for sailing, but it's best to have a backup plan just in case.

ASWAN INDIVIDUAL

tel. 0100 250 95 88; www.aswan-individual.com

For assured quality, call Waleed at Aswan Individual. He has an excellent team that can take you out for 140LE/hour with an option of fresh lunch for 235LE per person.

sailing on a felucca

CAPTAIN SAFY

Old Cataract Hotel Marina; tel. 0100 647 3189; www.nubiansailing.com; 9am-9pm daily

Captain Safy offers well-run outings on his boat, the *Lion Heart* (200LE/hour). Design your own program or choose from one of his set packages, like a 3-hour cruise with a superb Nubian lunch or dinner (500LE, plus 100LE/person) or a 6-hour sightseeing trip around Aswan (1,000LE, not including admission).

CAMEL RIDES

Camels and their handlers hang out in a few spots along the West Bank. Pick one up next to the river near the **Monastery of St. Simeon** for a 20-minute ride up the sandy hill to the site (50-100LE). For a longer ride, grab a camel at the **Tombs of the Nobles** and head across the desert hills to the monastery (35-45 minutes each way; 300-350LE round-trip).

You'll also find plenty of camels in and around the touristic "Nubian Village" in **Gharb Soheil** if you just want to hop on one for a photo op or take a short stroll through the village.

BIRD-WATCHING

Aswan is one of the best spots in Egypt for a bird-watching excursion. You can spot a wealth of resident birds year-round and even more species during the cooler months (Oct.-Mar.) when the migratory birds fly through. **Saluga and Ghazal Nature Reserve,** a set of islands just a mile south of Elephantine Island, can only be navigated by motorboat and is a great place to cruise around and bird-watch. Pick up a boat on the East Bank's Corniche el Nil Street or organize a sunrise bird-watching trip.

FATMA SOBHI

Siou Village, Central Elephantine Island; tel. 0100 545 6420 or 097 2314152; www.animaliaaswan.wordpress.com; 470LE per person

Fatma takes visitors on a fun 2.5 to 3-hour tour by boat around favorite bird spots along the Nile (including alongside the islands of the Saluga and Ghazal Nature Reserve). She learned how to track them down from her ornithologist father and has since taken over the family trade. The trip ends with a visit to their homemade Animalia Museum in their village on Elephantine Island. For groups larger than two, the price per person is reduced.

ANAKATO

Gharb Soheil; tel. 0100 081 8833 or 0101 763 1212; www.anakato.com; 8am-10pm daily; 600LE per person

Anakato guesthouse offers a 6am guided sunrise tour (4 person min.) with motorboat around the First Cataract, Saluga and Ghazal Nature Reserve, and other favorite bird spots. If your group has more than four people, price is reduced to 400LE per person.

SANDBOARDING

While Aswan's sandboarding locations don't compare to the massive dunes in the Western Desert, the activity is still a fun outing for sporty travelers and can be incorporated into a multi-event tour package.

ANAKATO

Gharb Soheil; tel. 0101 763 1212; www.anakato.com; 8am-10pm daily; 200LE per person

Anakato lodge organizes trips to the West Bank's hills for sandboarding, complemented by a short camel ride, a walk through the "Nubian Village," and tea at Anakato lodge. The trip takes around 3 hours total and includes boat transportation to/from the East Bank corniche, and, of course, the board.

HEISSA CAMP

Heissa Island; tel. 0100 500 4122; 8am-10pm daily; 200LE per person

Heissa Camp offers a nice sandboarding trip to the West Bank's hills near Gharb Soheil. Call them to integrate it into a day trip that includes lunch and/or kayaking around Heissa Island.

Entertainment and Events

SOUND AND LIGHT SHOW AT PHILAE TEMPLE

Agilkia Island; tel. 0155 311 3161; www.soundandlight.show; 300LE adults, 150LE children

If you only go to one sound and light show in Egypt, check out the one at Philae. The first 30 minutes or so are spent walking through the illuminated complex with the history of the temples and their deities acted out around you as an audio drama. Like the other sound and light shows in Egypt, the narration here is somewhat dated and feels a bit like Disney World. But the British old-time radio sound does have its charms. You might want to bring a flashlight to help you navigate the dark paths, and be sure to wear comfortable footwear and something warm for the boat ride. The show lasts approximately 40 minutes.

Shows in English take place 6:30pm (Mon., Fri., and Sun.) and 7:45pm (Sat. and Wed.). You can purchase tickets online, but it's better to buy them at the ticket counter at the **Philae Temple Marina** (off Nagaa el-Karour-Aswan Rd., 300 m/1,000 ft south of the Low Dam, East Bank) as shows with fewer than 13 people will be canceled.

The easiest way to get to the show is to arrange with your hotel or a guide. **Aswan Individual** (Corniche el Nil St.; tel. 0100 250 9588; www.aswan-individual.com) offers private transportation to and from your hotel for $40 (1-2 people), including the boat trip to/from the island. Otherwise, grab a taxi to the marina and ask your driver to wait for you until the show is over (this is common practice), and make a similar deal with a boatman. For round-trip including wait time, the boat should cost around 125LE and the taxi 150-250LE depending on where you're picked up.

Shopping

Aswan isn't exactly a shopping destination, but it is the place to find unique Nubian-inspired beaded jewelry, hand-painted wooden dolls, and souvenirs crafted from palm leaves—like vibrant trivets that double as wall décor and beautifully woven baskets. Check out the Aswan Souq for the widest array of options.

Some of the best treats can be found from peddlers who spread their wares around the city. At both the entrance and exit of the **Aswan Botanical Garden** on Nabatat Island (just west of Elephantine Island), vendors sell a range of items, some high-quality goods, and others cheap trinkets. You can find everything from Panama hats and fake snakes to seashell necklaces, attractive scarves, and handcrafted alabaster statues of ancient gods. You'll find a wider variety toward the exit.

At the **Philae Temple Marina** in South Aswan, vendors sell unique jewelry, alabaster statues, handmade instruments, and wooden figurines along the dock where motorboats gather to bring visitors to the Philae Temple on Agilkia Island. A smaller group also sets up shop near the entrance to Agilkia Island.

EAST BANK

ASWAN SOUQ

Souq St., starts near Aswan Train Station; no tel.; 8am-9pm daily

Locals and visitors alike shop at this central market, its stalls piled high with dates, dried hibiscus, spice pyramids, and famous Aswani peanuts, which are roasted in sand from the surrounding hills. Keep an eye out for handwoven palm baskets, some the neutral color of dried palm leaves and others dyed in brilliant fuchsias, yellows, purples, and cyans. Down the one-mile or so street (Sharia el-Souq), you can also find pretty handmade scarves, leather goods, and appliqué alongside T-shirts with camels and cartouches.

WEST BANK

NUBIAN VILLAGE SOUQ

Nubian Village, Gharb Soheil; no tel.; 8am-8pm daily

Shopping in the market in Gharb Soheil's touristic Nubian Village is not the most peaceful experience, but you can find some nice handicrafts. Check out Aswan's other shopping spots first to get a sense of the local prices, and arrive prepared to haggle.

Food

Other than Aswan's delicious shamsi bread cooked in a clay oven and the crepe-like senasil bread made on a flat iron disc, juicy tagines (stews served in clay pots) are the quintessential local fare. Tomatoes, oil, and onions are the base ingredients for these saucy dishes that typically include meat, fish, or—for a vegetarian meal—okra, spinach, potatoes, and/or peas. These can be sampled at any of the listings under the "Nubian" headings below.

Aswan has also absorbed many traditional Egyptian dishes into its repertoire, with stuffed pigeon, grilled meats (kebab and kofta), fava beans (fuul), falafel (ta'maya), and molasses ('asl iswid) with tahini (tahina) all popular. Other favorite plates are similar to those in the north of Egypt but with an Aswan touch, like molokhia (the Egypt-wide soupy green dish akin to spinach) cooked with eggs.

For a nice snack, pick up some of Aswan's famous peanuts sold from roaming carts along the Corniche (East Bank) or in the Aswan Souq (10-20LE for a small bag). The local technique of roasting the legumes in sand from the surrounding hills not only enhances the flavor, but also makes the nutrients more easily absorbed.

Note: Restaurants in Aswan's nicest hotels have a dress code of smart casual, so if you plan on fine dining be sure to bring some close-toed shoes (anything but sneakers) and something other than a T-shirt and shorts.

EAST BANK

Most of the East Bank dining options can be found near the Aswan Souq or along the Nile.

Egyptian

ABEER RESTAURANT

Abtal el-Tahrir St., near Train Station, East Bank; tel. 0114 700 0801; noon-4am daily; 80-150LE

For a proper local hole-in-the-wall with excellent grilled meats (kebab and kofta), Abeer Restaurant is a solid choice. Mains come with salad, bread, soup, and tahini. Staff are fun and inviting. Located just one street west of the train station (2-minute walk).

MAKKA

Abtal el-Tahrir St., near Train Station, East Bank; tel. 097 2440232; noon-midnight daily; 110-150LE

A fine choice if hunger strikes while shopping in the Aswan Souq or waiting for your train. Service is a bit lacking, but the classic Egyptian dishes (grilled meats, vegetable stews, mezze) are tasty and portions are big.

EL MASRY

Al-Matar St, East Bank; tel. 097 2454576; noon-1am daily; 110-150LE

El Masry ("The Egyptian") does a good stuffed pigeon and other traditional Egyptian dishes. Mains come with a feast of soup, rice, bread, and mezze (dips and salads). Interior is nice with some wooden latticework panels and striped horseshoe arches. Located just 100 meters (300 ft) east of the southern part of Souq Street.

SALAH EL-DIN

Corniche el-Nil, 350 m/1,100 ft north of KFC, East Bank; tel. 0114 086 0000; noon-1am daily; 120-170LE

This floating restaurant nestled between moored feluccas is a great place to break for a cold beer on the Nile with some simple Egyptian fare, pizzas, or pastas. It's a nice spot to watch the sun set over Elephantine Island. Wine also served.

International

MAKANI

El-Sadat Rd., near Midan Magdi Yacoubi, East Bank; tel. 0100 918 3661; noon-1am daily; 50-160LE

Located Nile-side, this casual diner specializes in burgers and grilled chicken and meats. You can sit outside on a spacious riverside terrace, or hide indoors under the AC where beautiful murals line the walls. The food can take a while to arrive, so it's not the best option if you're in a rush. But if you have some time, sit back, enjoy the view, and tide yourself over with a fresh juice or one of their many Aswani peanut-based shakes. Good coffee and sweet snacks (like waffles with ice cream) also served.

★ THE TERRACE

At Sofitel Legend Old Cataract Hotel, Abtal El Tahrir St., East Bank; tel. 0102 222 9071; www.sofitel.accor.com; 6am-2am daily; 150-550LE

The Terrace is ones of Aswan's classiest venues with a view. Indulge in lobster ravioli with spinach chutney or lamb fillet with truffle puree while watching white-sailed feluccas dance along the Nile. Towering palm trees line the foreground with Elephantine Island's ancient ruins in the distance. Sit in the shade of umbrellas or below colonial-style ceiling fans for some extra breeze. Afternoon tea is a favorite tradition here (3pm-6pm) with tiered trays of sweet and savory goodies. Non-hotel guests will have to buy a 300LE voucher per person at the door, which will be deducted from your bill. Alcohol served. Dress code: smart casual (no shorts, no flip-flops).

1902 RESTAURANT

At Sofitel Legend Old Cataract Hotel, Abtal El Tahrir St., East Bank; tel. 0102 222 9071; www.sofitel.accor.com; 7pm-midnight daily; 380-750LE

Reminiscent of Córdoba's Mezquita—with soaring ceilings and tall keyhole arches outlined by cream and rust-colored stripes—this fancy French restaurant serves a range of seafood and well-marinated meats all with (of course) special sauces. A sommelier can assist in pairing your dishes with their wine selection (other spirits and beer also available). The colonial atmosphere is (surprise, surprise) not without its pretentions, and non-hotel guests sometimes experience less than lavish service. Visitors who aren't staying in the hotel must also buy a 300LE voucher at the door, later deducted from the bill. There's a dress code of tie and/or jacket for men (if you don't have one, they can lend you one free of charge), and a bit more flexibility for women.

CENTRAL ISLANDS

Nubian

NUBIAN DREAMS RESTAURANT & CAFÉ

Elephantine Island, next to the northern ferry landing; tel. 0127 622 0488; 7am-1am daily; 90-150LE

This shaded riverside restaurant offers delicious Nubian dishes and a fun ambiance. Most evening meals are accompanied by live Nubian music, and owner Ali "Jamaica" is a character. Mains come with homemade bread, salad, tahini, and rice or pasta, and the generous portions are enough to split. Don't miss the camel tagine. Breakfast is served 7am-11am, lunch noon-4pm, and dinner 6pm-11pm. Beer, wine, and shisha available.

Egyptian

★ MEZZE RESTAURANT

At Mövenpick Resort, Elephantine Island; tel. 097 245 44 55; www.movenpick.com; 3pm-10pm daily; 250-450LE

Enjoy brilliantly executed Egyptian fare from

a pleasant terrace looking out to the Nile and the West Bank's golden hills. Indoor seating with nice views also available, though the interior is otherwise a bit lacking in character. Portions are liberal (you might want to consider sharing), and the staff exceedingly friendly. Imported spirits and local beer and wine served. Dress code: smart casual.

International

★ PANORAMA RESTAURANT AND BAR

At Mövenpick Resort, Elephantine Island; tel. 097 245 4455; www.movenpick.com; 3:30pm-11pm daily; 200-650LE

Whether you're looking for a cheese board and a glass of wine or herb-crusted saddle of lamb, the Mövenpick's elevated Panorama Restaurant and Bar will not disappoint. The food is scrumptious and setting equally divine. Come for sunset to best enjoy the 360-degree views of Aswan through floor-to-ceiling windows. Dress code is smart casual—nothing too fancy needed, but no shorts or sweatpants.

WEST BANK

Nubian

NUBIAN BEACH

500 m/1,600 ft south of Agha Khan Mausoleum, West Bank; tel. 0111 153 2280; noon-8pm daily; 100-160LE

Enjoy tasty Nubian dishes at this sandy beach restaurant. Be sure to call ahead so Moustafa (nickname "Darsh") can provide complimentary boat pickup from the East Bank (KFC's a popular meeting point) and arrange for live Nubian music.

KATO DOOL NUBIAN RESTAURANT

Just south of Nubian Village, Gharb Soheil; tel. 0106 755 7225; www.katodool.com; 8am-11:45pm daily; 100-200LE

Hang out on bean bag chairs under palm leaf umbrellas at this colorful Nubian restaurant along the Nile. The outdoor dining area has palm wood furniture painted in vibrant yellows, greens, and blues. A wide array of Nubian tagines (meat, chicken, fish, vegetarian) are served in liberal portions. The coffee is fresh and strong. Shisha available.

SOUTH ASWAN

Nubian

OLD NUBIAN GUESTHOUSE RESTAURANT

Just south of the Philae Temple Marina, south of the Low Dam; tel. 0122 483 1838; noon-10pm daily; 80-250LE

Balanced on a hillside of bulbous rocks on the East Bank of South Aswan, this Nubian guesthouse has a delightful restaurant that serves Nubian tagines (meat or vegetarian) with fresh salads and bread. The views from the riverside dining terraces are superb, and you can choose between pillow floor seating or regular tables and chairs. The only way to get here is by boat—best to call 24 hours ahead to arrange a pick-up from the Philae Temple Marina (2 min. away). Only open in high-season (Nov-Mar).

★ SOLAIH NUBIAN RESTAURANT

Bigeh Island, at Eco Nubia Lodge; tel. 0100 123 0755 or 0103 000 0055; www.solaih-nubian-restaurant.business.site; 11am-10pm daily; 160-380LE

This shaded outdoor restaurant perched on the side of a rocky island offers marvelous views of the Philae Temple and surrounding Nile. Their menu is full of tasty Nubian dishes with plenty of vegetarian options. Try the mixed grill and Nubian mousakka (eggplant and minced meat) or the vegetable tagine. You need a boat to get to the island, so best to include it with your trip to Philae Temple (just a few meters across the water), or for a small fee the restaurant will send a boat to pick you up from the marina near the temple ticket office on the East Bank (10-minute ride). Call a day (or at least a few hours) ahead to reserve so fresh food will be waiting for you.

Bars and Nightlife

There's no real nightlife in quiet Aswan, but you'll have no trouble finding a drink. A handful of restaurants serve local beer and wine (noted in the "Food" section below), and most of the bigger hotels have a bar.

EAST BANK

ROOFTOP BAR

At Basma Hotel, El-Fanadek St.; tel. 097 248 4001; www.basmahotel.com; 10am-11pm daily; 65-80LE local beer and wine, 130LE cocktails

For unpretentious evening drinks, the Rooftop Bar at Basma Hotel offers fantastic views of the Nile and the West Bank's sloping desert hills. Local beer, wine, cocktails, and light snacks available.

CENTRAL ISLANDS

AL-QAHWA CAFÉ

At Mövenpick Resort, Elephantine Island; tel. 097 245 4455; www.movenpick.com; 8am-11pm daily; 150-250LE mains; 85-300LE drinks

This terrace café and bar looking out across the Nile to the Tombs of the Nobles is a great spot to take a break with a cold beer, fresh juice, or proper espresso. Nice sandwiches, pizzas, and mezze are served, along with a wide array of Egyptian wines. Also called the "Lobby Bar." Dress code: smart casual.

Accommodations

There are five main areas to stay in Aswan: the East Bank, Elephantine Island, El-Qubba (a hamlet on the West Bank to the north, near the Tombs of the Nobles), Gharb Soheil (home to the "Nubian Village," also on the West Bank), and South Aswan in the reservoir (el-Khazzaan) between the Low and High Dams.

You might consider staying in two different areas during your trip to get a taste of both downtown and the more isolated Nubian ecolodges to the south. Each has its own charms and advantages. East Bank accommodation is the most central—closest to the train station and easiest to navigate independently. Elephantine Island and El-Qubba are nice compromises—both a short ferry ride from the East Bank, but quieter than the center and with genuine Nubian village vibes.

Gharb Soheil is home to the made-for-tourists "Nubian Village" and might ring inauthentic (and overpriced) to some. South Aswan is the best option for those seeking an idyllic retreat. These areas are closest to the airport, but a bit of a trek from the train station/central Aswan (boat transfer required).

If you end up staying anywhere near the Nile, don't forget the mosquito repellent. And winter travelers: Be sure to bring warm clothes as the nights are chilly and not all hotels are outfitted for the cold.

EAST BANK

800-1,650LE

PHILAE HOTEL

79 Cornish El Nil St., East Bank; tel. 0111 901 1995; philaehotel@gmail.com; 1,200LE d

This basic hotel is a good option for people who like staying central. It's just around a mile from the train station and a 2-minute walk to the ferry for Elephantine Island. Rooms with a Nile view are lovely, but they overlook the main thoroughfare (Corniche el-Nil St.), which can be noisy at night. No elevator, but staff can help carry your luggage up. A nice breakfast spread included.

Over 3,300LE

★ SOFITEL LEGEND OLD CATARACT HOTEL

Abtal El Tahrir St., East Bank; tel. 0102 222 9071; www.sofitel.accor.com; 6,000LE d

The Old Cataract is the crème de la crème of hotels in Aswan for those who like their luxury with a hint of history. Built by the British at the turn of the century, the 138-room hotel boasts an aesthetic of Victorian meets Islamic. Balconies in the Nile Wing overlook green islands encircled by flocks of feluccas and the hotel's large pool perched on the pink granite bank of the Nile. Princess Diana, Winston Churchill, and President Carter all rested their heads here. And the hotel-palace fueled the imagination of Agatha Christie as she wrote her murder mystery, *Death on the Nile.* A scrumptious breakfast spread included.

CENTRAL ISLANDS

Under 800LE

FARM HOUSE

Above Animalia Museum, Elephantine Island; tel. 0100 300 5672; 530LE d

Those in search of simplicity will enjoy a stay at the Farm House. The Sobhi family converted two floors of their home on Elephantine Island into a quaint guesthouse with comfortable beds and colorful accents. There are only four rooms (three doubles and one single), all with private bathrooms. Rooms on the lower floor share a small kitchen and those on the top floor open up to a spacious terrace with views of the surrounding farmland. The ACs are not the best, so beware in the summer—it's hot. The family's Animalia Museum is located on the ground floor where you can learn about local nature and Nubian culture. Tasty traditional Egyptian breakfast available for a small extra charge. Booking through Airbnb preferred.

Over 3,300LE

MÖVENPICK RESORT ASWAN

North side of Elephantine Island; tel. 097 245 4455; www.movenpick.com; 3,500LE d

The sprawling Mövenpick Resort covers more than a third of Elephantine Island with two large swimming pools and over 400 rooms and suites. Most of the rooms are spacious with balconies and spectacular Nile views (or fine views of the gardens for a bit less). You'll be spoiled for choice with their excellent on-site restaurants serving a variety of Egyptian and international food. Staff are on top of it and always ready to assist. Request a room in the "new building" for more modern accommodation, and be sure to specify nonsmoking if that's your preference. The breakfast buffet (included) offers a nice assortment of goodies, and a complimentary hotel boat is available to bring you to and from the East Bank in just a few minutes.

WEST BANK

Under 800LE

NUBIAN HOLIDAY HOUSE

Off Awan-Giza Rd., 450 m/1,500 ft north of Ferry Dock, El-Qubba; tel. 0112 429 4349; www.nubian-holiday-house-aswan.business.site; 550LE d

Habib and his family transformed their home into a charming guesthouse with soaring barrel vault ceilings and seven spacious rooms. Most have a private bathroom attached (or just next door) and all are equipped with ACs. The shaded rooftop terrace offers bucolic views of river, farmland, and grazing animals. It's just a quick 5-minute walk to the ferry for the East Bank. Delicious breakfast included and other meals available for extra.

★ MAGHRABI'S GUEST HOUSE

Off Awan-Giza Rd., 650 m/2,100 ft north of Ferry Dock, El-Qubba; tel. 0114 771 7656; 680LE d

The rooms at this Nile-side Nubian lodge are cozy, clean, and comfortable with redbrick dome ceilings and clay wall lamps. Private bathrooms in all. Hang out on the grassy front yard or in the large sand pit that's perfect for lounging. The staff will spoil you with their hospitality and can help arrange trips around the city at good prices. Superb Nubian food served in generous portions (breakfast included). Just a 10-minute walk to the ferry for the East Bank. If you schedule in advance, the

Dancing to the Nubian Beat

Nubian music is unique and eclectic, blending sounds of sub-Saharan Africa and the Middle East. Drums and clapping are its heart, with accents of stringed instruments like the rababa (a one-stringed fiddle) and—since Nubian music legend Hamza el Din (1929-2006) introduced it to his compositions—the classical Arabic instrument, the oud (lute). But the original Nubian beat-maker is the tar, a flat drum similar to a tambourine without the metal discs.

LIVE MUSIC

No trip to Aswan would be complete without a night of Nubian music. Dancing often breaks out, and musicians encourage audience participation, teaching some simple Nubian steps. For live music, head to **Nubian Dreams Restaurant and Café** (Elephantine Island, next to the northern ferry landing; tel. 0127 622 0488; 90-150LE mains). Jam sessions typically start around 8pm daily and last until late, but call ahead to be sure.

These Nubian lodges also organize regular performances open to all (typically with the expectation that you'll stay for dinner):

- **Heissa Camp:** Heissa Island; tel. 0100 500 4122; www.heissacamp.com
- **Anakato:** Gharb Soheil; tel. 0100 081 8833; www.anakato.com
- **Bet el-Kerem:** Off Awan-Giza Rd., 350 m/1,100 ft north of Ferry Dock, West Bank; tel. 0122 391 1052; www.betelkerem.com

MAKE A PLAYLIST

To make your own playlist of Nubian sounds check out the following artists:

- **Ali Hassan Kuban** (1929-2001): Kuban's album ***From Nubia to Cairo*** is a fun fusion of Nubian-Egyptian-Western music with trumpets and saxophones dancing around the beat of the Nubian tar drum.
- **Mohammed Mounir** (aka "the King," b. 1954): A contemporary pop star from Aswan with a prolific repertoire and entrancing sound that integrates Nubian, Egyptian, jazz, and reggae.
- **Ahmed Mounib** (1926-1990): Known as "the Godfather," Mounib was Mounir's brilliant mentor. He grew up in a Nubian village near Esna before moving to Cairo, blending the sounds of the south and the big city.
- **Alsarah (b. 1982):** This talented Sudanese-born musician sings lead vocals in her Brooklyn-based band Alsarah & the Nubatones. Their unique style is traditional Nubian meets East African retro pop.

team can provide complimentary boat transfers to just about anywhere you want to go.

BET EL-KEREM

Off Awan-Giza Rd., 350 m/1,100 ft north of Ferry Dock, El-Qubba; tel. 0122 391 1052; www.betelkerem.com; 700LE d

A sweet and simple Nubian bed and breakfast that feels more like a homestay than a hotel. There's a pretty garden and shaded rooftop terrace with marvelous views of the Tombs of the Nobles. All the rooms have private bathrooms and ACs. Ping-pong table available in the common area. Just a 5-minute walk to the ferry for the East Bank.

800-1,650LE

ANAKATO

Gharb Soheil; tel. 0100 081 8833 or 0101 763 1212; www.anakato.com; 1,400LE d

Located along the Nile on the edge of the touristic "Nubian Village," Anakato ("Our House") is Aswan's most sprawling Nubian lodge with five separate houses, each with 4-15 rooms. Accommodations range from basic to boutique, but all are clean and colorful with Wi-Fi and AC (ask for a photo of your room before booking). A variety of activities are on offer around the guesthouse—from kayaking to bird-watching, hiking, and sandboarding. There's a small private beach, a private island, and three restaurants on site. Tasty Nubian breakfast included. Staff can arrange for boat shuttle (25 minutes) to central Aswan.

1,650-3,300LE

KATO DOOL NUBIAN HOUSE

Gharb Soheil; tel. 0106 755 7225; www.katodool.com; 1,900LE d

This colorful Nubian guesthouse has 18 vibrant rooms with redbrick domed ceilings and funky geometric décor. Most are quite cozy (read: small), but pristine and with comfortable beds. The multi-tiered outdoor seating area along the Nile is a highlight, as is their tasty Nubian restaurant (a basic breakfast included). In high season it's overpriced—you can find better deals for nicer places—but check their website for occasional offers. Note: The lodge is a good distance from central Aswan and a boat from the hotel to the East Bank will cost 250-300LE round-trip.

SOUTH ASWAN

800-1,650LE

★ HEISSA CAMP

Heissa Island; tel. 0100 500 4122; www.heissacamp.com; 900LE d

Perched above clear Nile waters on the edge of Heissa Island, this charming ecolodge has 15 earthen dome huts and five traditional Nubian dwellings built of stone and sundried earth bricks. Wake up to views of the East Bank's golden mountains and the Aswan High Dam towering to the south. Accommodation is simple—beds sit on raised platforms with a small table in the center—but comfortable, keeping cool on hot days and warm on cool nights. All the stone houses and six of the huts have private bathrooms attached, and the other nine share clean bathrooms and showers nearby. Island locals prepare authentic Nubian dishes (like delicious cheeses, salads, sautéed vegetables, catch-of-the-day fish, and bread fresh from the clay oven) for your breakfast and lunch (both included). Wander around the tiny island, or rent a kayak (100LE/hour or 250LE/day) to explore nearby islets and hidden beaches. Management can also arrange an excellent evening of Nubian music and dancing, enjoyed at the camp or on a private boat trip around the reservoir.

To get to the lodge, take a taxi to Heissa dock, where a boat will collect you and transport you to the lodge free of charge. Pickup from the Aswan Train Station is also available for an extra fee (about 130LE). Check their Facebook page @heissacampnubian if the website isn't working.

OLD NUBIAN GUESTHOUSE

Near Philae Temple Marina, south of the Low Dam, East Bank; tel. 0122 483 1838; 1,200LE d

Only accessible by boat, this delightful guesthouse camouflaged into the rocks on the bank of the Nile is a good option for those seeking a quiet escape. Brothers Mustafa and Ramadan are wonderful hosts and happy to share their Nubian culture with curious guests. Rooms are small but attractive with redbrick barrel vault ceilings and the option of a balcony overlooking the Nile. Choose to eat in the shade of the outdoor dining hall, or on a terrace that practically hangs over the river. Only open in the cooler months (Nov.-Mar.). Complimentary boat transfers to the Philae Temple Marina available (just a few minutes away).

ECO NUBIA LODGE

Bigeh Island; tel. 0103 000 0055; 1,300LE d

This ecolodge on the edge of a granite island affords brilliant views of the Philae Temple—just a stone's throw across the river. Rooms are rustic chic with clay walls, stone floors, log beds, and handmade palm wood furniture. Private bathrooms attached. While its simplicity is charming, the price is less so (but keep an eye out for occasional deals). There's a small "beach" (though not for swimming) and an excellent Nubian restaurant on site.

Delicious complimentary breakfast served. A boat ride for initial pickup/drop-off is included, but other boat transfers come at a small additional cost.

Information and Services

Tourist Office

Midan el-Mahatta; no tel.; 8am-3pm Sat.-Thurs.

Don't expect a wealth of information from this tourist office, but if you have specific questions about Aswan and are in the neighborhood (north side of train station) it's worth a quick stop.

ATMs

You'll find a number of ATMs along Corniche el-Nil Street and Abtal al-Tahrir Street near the train station in central Aswan on the East Bank. ATMs on the West Bank, Central Islands, and South Aswan are hard to come by, so stock up on cash before you head to those parts. (Most places accept cash only.)

Pharmacy

EL EZABY

Corniche el-Nil St.; tel. 097 246 5282; 8am-2:30am daily

This is the best pharmacy in town and can help with any stomach problems or other minor health issues. Delivery available 24/7.

Emergency Numbers

- **Tourist Police:** 126
- **Police:** 122
- **Ambulance:** 123

Transportation

GETTING THERE

Most travelers prefer to make their way down to Aswan from Cairo via air. The more adventurous enjoy taking the train to watch the small villages rush by along the way. To get to Aswan from Luxor, the most comfortable options are train or private car hire.

Air

ASWAN INTERNATIONAL AIRPORT

Aswan International Airport (ASW) is 18 kilometers (11 mi) southwest of central Aswan on the West Bank of the Nile near the High Dam. Multiple daily flights to and from Cairo (1.5 hours) are operated by **EgyptAir** (www.egyptair.com) and **Nile Air** (www.nileair.com) and typically range 1,700-4,000LE round-trip. To get from the airport to central Aswan, grab a taxi (30-45 minutes; 100-200LE) or arrange for a pickup by your hotel.

Train

Multiple trains travel daily between **Aswan Railway Station** and Cairo (13-15 hours; 200-250LE for first class), Luxor (3.5-4.5 hours; 55-95LE), and Qena (4.5-5 hours; 65-115LE). Tickets can be purchased at the station or online (when the website decides to work) from Egyptian National Railways (www.enr.gov.eg). To ride in comfort, you can book a sleeper car to/from Cairo (www.wataniasleepingtrains.com) for $80 per person for a double cabin, including dinner and breakfast. Sleeper trains typically leave from Cairo (Ramses Station) around 7-8pm and arrive to Aswan around 9-10am and return to Cairo from Aswan around 4-5pm, arriving at 6-7am. Safer to book a week or so in advance during the winter season.

Aswan Railway Station is located on the East Bank, on the north side of central Aswan in Midan al-Mahatta (Station Square), just 300 meters (1,000 ft) east of the Nile. It's an easy walk from the station to downtown, but taxis are also available (15-30LE depending on where you're going).

Bus

The government-run **Upper Egypt Bus Company** (no tel.) is your only bus option and isn't the most comfortable (4-5 hours from Luxor; 14-15 hours from Cairo). Train or plane recommended.

The Main Bus Station is 5 kilometers (3 mi) north of central Aswan on the East Bank next to the Nile (Al Khataar-Aswan Rd.). A taxi should cost 20-30LE from central Aswan.

Private Car Hire

For the fastest trip between Aswan and Luxor, hire a private car with driver. Contact Waleed at **Aswan Individual** (tel. 0100 250 9588; www.aswan-individual.com) to book comfortable transportation between the two cities (starting at either). The 4-hour trip will cost $85-90 (seats up to 3 passengers) or $115-120 (for microbus that seats up to 8) if you go direct. If you opt to visit the temples along the way in Kom Ombo, Edfu, and Esna, the 8-hour trip will cost around $120.

GETTING AROUND

The best way to get around Aswan's East Bank is on foot or by taxi. On the Central Islands (Elephantine and Nabatat), walking is your only option; and to visit the sights on the West Bank or in the reservoir in South Aswan, a private boat is the way to go.

Travel between the East Bank, West Bank, and the Central Islands is easiest via public ferry or private boat. Roads run along the Low and High Dams in South Aswan, connecting the East and West Banks, but these routes are pretty far south and usually not the quickest way to cross. To get to South Aswan, grab a taxi.

Taxi

Taxis are easily accessible and inexpensive on Aswan's East Bank. No meters here (unlike Cairo), so be sure to agree on a price before you get in. Short distances (e.g., Aswan Railway Station to the Nubia Museum, a 10-15-minute drive) should only cost around 20-35LE. Taxis are much scarcer on the West Bank (but you can likely ask your hotel to send for one if necessary) and nonexistent on the islands.

Public Ferry

Public ferries are available for a few pounds (3-5LE) to get to/from the East Bank, Elephantine Island, and the West Bank hamlet of El-Qubba (near the Tombs of the Nobles). The East Bank ferry landings for Elephantine Island are located near the KFC (this brings you to the middle of the island) and across from the EgyptAir office, just north of Feryal Garden (brings you to the south side of the island, near the Ruins of Abu). Each takes under 5 minutes. The East Bank ferry landing for the north side of the West Bank (to El-Qubba) is located parallel to the Aswan Railway Station and takes 5-10 minutes. Ferries run every 10-15 minutes 6am-10pm.

There are no public ferries between the West Bank and Elephantine Island (you must go via the East Bank).

Private Boat

You can rent a motorboat, rowboat, or felucca to get almost anywhere north of the Low Dam. Pick one up along the Nile Corniche on the East Bank or on the West Bank in El-Qubba or Gharb Soheil. South of the Low Dam (in the reservoir), you can grab a motorboat at the Philae Temple Marina. To get to the marina, take a taxi from anywhere on the East Bank.

Microbus

Microbuses are prevalent on the East Bank (but nowhere else) and cost around 3-5LE a trip. It's much easier to just grab a cab, but if you want to try out the locals' most popular mode of transportation, wave one down and check if they're heading in your direction.

Abu Simbel

This isolated village perched on the edge of Lake Nasser, 280 kilometers (175 mi) south of Aswan and just 50 kilometers (30 mi) north of the border with Sudan, is home to one of Egypt's most fabulous sites. Most visitors come on day trips from Aswan by car or by plane and stay for a few hours at the temples. But if you have the time, a night or two at a local hotel will let you see the sights at their best—when the air is still cool, the crowds are few, and the rising sun illuminates the temples in majestic golden hues.

★ ABU SIMBEL TEMPLES

280 km/175 mi southwest of Aswan; no tel.; 6am-5pm daily; 200LE adults, 100LE students

Ramses II (r. 1279-1213 BC) built this pair of lofty temples on Egypt's southern frontier to demonstrate his power in Nubia—the neighboring civilization colonized by Egypt some 200 years prior. The monuments are remarkable for their sheer size, their modern dismantling/reconstruction, and their idyllic location on the edge of Lake Nasser.

The rock-cut structures were completed around 1255 BC, 24 years into Ramses II's rule. They represent a new level of narcissism for the long-reigning pharaoh, with over a dozen soaring statues of himself and images of him bringing offerings to his own divine form. The king's early military victories, his rule of nearly seven decades (one of Egypt's longest ruling kings), and the fact that he lived into his 90s at a time when the average lifespan was 35 no doubt did little to encourage modesty.

The site is located at the southern tip of Abu Simbel village, surrounded on three sides by Lake Nasser. Just a few dozen meters separate the two temples, so feel free to start at whichever is less crowded. Near the **ticket office,** there's a small **cafeteria** (though best to bring your own snacks, as you'll find a paltry and overpriced selection) and a **visitor center** where you can watch a short video about the site. Save this for the end if you have extra time. A camera ticket (300LE) is needed if you wish to take photos *inside* the temples (photos can be taken with phones for free), but

the Great Temple at Abu Simbel

Unearthing the Abu Simbel Temples

For centuries the largest of Ramses II's rock-cut monuments (**The Great Temple**) lay forgotten, reclaimed by nature's sand dunes. Meanwhile, within its unburied sister temple (**The Small Temple**), early 19th-century locals took refuge from raiding Bedouins—paying no mind to Hathor, goddess of the sky, nor to the divine Queen Nefertari, so devoutly worshipped there some 3,000 years prior.

It wasn't until 1813 that a Swiss traveler stumbled across the smiling baboons of the pharaoh's Great Temple, creeping out of the sand, determined to fulfil their original purpose of welcoming the sun each day. Subsequent explorers dug out the colossal statues of Ramses II, and they resumed their place in the light for over a century, only to be threatened once again by the building of the Aswan High Dam in the 1960s. In a feat of engineering rivaling the original construction of the temples themselves, the monuments were cut into more than 1,000 blocks and moved some 200 meters (700 ft) west of their original site, now 60 meters (200 ft) below water.

the temple exteriors are the main attractions, so probably not worth the extra cash. WCs are located beside the visitor center.

The Great Temple

Towering nearly 30 meters (100 ft) high, Ramses II's rock-cut temple carved into a sandstone mountain with no fewer than four colossal statues of himself is one of Egypt's most commanding monuments.

EXTERIOR

At the entrance to the temple, each colossus of the larger-than-life pharaoh reaches a height of nearly 20 meters (70 ft) (sitting) with his most beloved relatives at his feet. His first and favorite bride, Nefertari, occupies the most prominent position, reaching all the way up to his knee and flanking the entrance to the temple. The rest of the small figures are mostly the other daughters and sons from this favored partnership (of the over 160 children he fathered), and his mother.

The four **statues of Ramses II,** with his characteristic Mona Lisa smile, were once nearly identical. Can you spot the differences? Aside from the second statue that lost its head, likely in an earthquake during the reign of Ramses II, the only major variations are in the crowns. Those on the right side (when facing the entrance) don the crown of Lower Egypt (North Egypt), and those on the left wear the double crown of Upper and Lower Egypt. Look up to see Re-Horakhty (a form of Horus, lord of the sky, affiliated with the sun god, Re) over the doorway, and above that, a row of baboons who welcome the rising sun each morning.

INTERIOR

Inside the **Great Hall,** eight more statues of the pharaoh hold up the ceiling. Here he imitates the god of the underworld, Osiris (who also represented the resurrected king), with his hands crossed over his chest, holding a crook and flail. Reliefs with some of their original colors decorate the walls, depicting the king's military exploits: To the north are imagined scenes from the battle of Qadesh in Syria (depicting Ramses II as a victorious leader in a battle that, in fact, ended in a stalemate), and to the south are more wars in Syria, Libya, and Nubia.

A second columned hall with four pillars gives way to a **vestibule,** and then a smaller **antechamber** with four pillars and a small **transverse hall** that leads to the **inner sanctuary,** tucked away some 50 meters (170 ft) deep into the mountain. Here, four statues sit in a niche at the rear, representing the dominant gods of each major region during this period, alongside the divine king Ramses II himself. From left to right these are Ptah from Memphis, Amon-Re from Thebes, Ramses

II, and Re-Horakhty from Heliopolis. On October 22 and February 22, the sun shines directly into the inner sanctuary and illuminates the niche statues (visiting on these dates is very popular—unfortunately, too popular for comfort as the poorly organized crowds in the thousands do dampen the magic).

The Small Temple

Ramses II built this smaller temple for his favorite wife, Queen Nefertari, and Hathor, the goddess of love and protection.

Outside, six statues standing 10 meters (33 ft) tall stride out from the mountainside—four of Ramses II and two of his beloved queen with their sons and daughters standing beside their calves. Nefertari wears the sun disc crown between cow horns in imitation of Hathor. An inscription tells us the king has cut the temple from the mountain "for his chief wife Nefertari ... for whom the sun shines."

Inside, six columns with Hathor capitals line the **Central Hall.** On the side walls, the royal couple smite a Libyan and a Nubian before Re-Horakhty and Amun-Re. Beyond that, a **vestibule** with side chamber leads to the **inner sanctuary** with a niche at the back holding a statue of Hathor in her cow form, protecting the king. On the rear wall the divine cow emerges from a rock, and along the sanctuary walls, Ramses II worships both his deified self and his divine partner.

Throughout the temple keep an eye out for reliefs of the royal pair's coronations, Nefertari crowned by goddesses Hathor and Isis—all donning the solar disc between cow horns—and Ramses II crowned by both Horus and his murderous uncle, Seth.

ENTERTAINMENT AND EVENTS

Sound and Light Show

Abu Simbel Temple; tel. 0155 311 3161; www.soundandlight.show; shows at 6:30pm and 7:30pm daily; 300LE adults, 150LE children

Not a must-see event, but if you decide to stay the night in Abu Simbel, it's a nice way to spend more time admiring the temples in dramatic lighting. The show (about 40 minutes) tells the history of the temple and only goes on if at least 10 visitors are there to watch, so try for the earlier one to have two chances. It's you and your luck for which language will be coming out of the speakers, but headphones are always available to listen in English.

FOOD AND ACCOMMODATIONS

There are only a couple of good options for sleeping and dining in Abu Simbel, but plenty enough for a brief stay. The two best hotels are also the best places to eat, and their restaurants are open to all.

★ ESKALEH NUBIAN ECOLODGE

Abu Simbel, off Ramsis Rd., 2 km/1 mi from Abu Simbel Temples; tel. 0114 744 7566 or 097 3401288; eskalehnubianecolodge@gmail.com; 1,300 d

This colorful Nubian lodge is *the* place stay in Abu Simbel. Built using mudbrick, the lodge is an attractive imitation of the surrounding hills, with domes and arches predominating. The owner and staff are friendly and happy to share their Nubian culture with guests. (Spontaneous Nubian jam sessions break out on occasion.) Domed rooms are simple but stay cool (AC also available) and comfortable, with mosquito nets for both style and practicality. If you have time, ask the staff to take you out in their motorboat for a ride on Lake Nasser. To get to the temples it's an easy 20-25-minute walk, or they can arrange for transportation. A basic breakfast included.

Come to the on-site restaurant (8am-9pm daily; 90-180LE mains) for tasty Nubian dishes like vegetable tagines and fresh fish (try the grilled tilapia) on a spacious terrace that looks out to Lake Nasser, or from a cool indoor space. Alcohol served.

TUYA HOTEL

Abu Simbel, off Ramsis Rd., 1 km/0.6 mi from Abu Simbel Temples; tel. 097 3400002; 1,400 d

The 12 basic rooms here are clean and colorful, with brick domed ceilings, splashes of wall

Cruising to Abu Simbel

This cruise route across one of the largest manmade lakes on earth, Lake Nasser, is Egypt's most peaceful, with few interruptions to miles of open water. Trips typically leave on Mondays from Aswan to Abu Simbel (4 nights) or Fridays from Abu Simbel to Aswan (3 nights).

SAMPLE ITINERARY

Typical stops include:

- **New Kalabsha:** Located just south of the Aswan High Dam, this little island is home to the **Kalabsha Temple** (dedicated to the Nubian sun god, Merul), the **Kiosk of Kertassi** (a Greco-Roman pavilion), and **Beit al-Wali** (a rock-cut temple built by Ramses II).
- **Wadi el Seboua:** The three temples on this sandy lakeside spot were moved from their original locations scattered across 50 kilometers (30 mi), which now lie under Lake Nasser. Here you'll find another **Temple of Ramses II**—approached by a pathway of sphinxes (giving the site its name, "Valley of the Lions")—with yet more statues of the self-loving pharaoh; the Greco-Roman **Temple of Dakka** dedicated to the god of wisdom, Thoth; and the **Temple of Maharraqa** dedicated to the goddess Isis.
- **Amada:** The **Amada Temple** is the oldest one you'll find along Lake Nasser—built in the 15th century BC by Thutmose III and Amenhotep II for the favorite gods of the time: Amun-Re and Re-Horakhty. It was moved here from its original home 2.5 kilometers (1.5 mi) away. The **Temple of Derr**—another rock-cut temple of Ramses II—was also rescued to this location and offers brightly colored reliefs. Nearby is the well-preserved resting place of a Nubian viceroy during the time of Ramses IV, the **Tomb of Pennut,** relocated from 40 kilometers (25 mi) away.
- **Kasr Ibrim:** Ships don't stop here, but they make a point of passing by close enough to view this Roman fortress (built atop Nubian and Egyptian monuments) from the sundeck. It stands on its original location—once an elevated part of the Nile's East Bank and now an island.
- **Abu Simbel:** The magnificent rock-cut temples built by Ramses II, moved to survive flooding by Lake Nasser.

Aside from New Kalabsha and Abu Simbel, the only way to see these sights is by boat. Entrance fees are usually included with your cruise package.

CRUISE OPERATORS

- **Steigenberger MS Omar El Khayam** (Aswan Dam Port, Aswan; tel. 0012 216 5036; www.steigenbergernilecruises.com; 6,150LE d per night): This plush hotel on water is equipped with a spa, gym, a number of chic lounge bars, hot tubs, and a good-sized swimming pool on the sundeck. All 80 cabins and suites have balconies overlooking the Nile. The restaurant has a nice variety of Egyptian and international food (full board included). Elevator on board.
- **Mövenpick MS Prince Abbas** (Aswan Dam Port, Aswan; tel. 0100 005 9590; www.movenpick.com; 5,000LE d per night): The MS Prince Abbas has a bit of a 1960s feel with AstroTurf on the sundeck and some interesting choices for carpets and upholstery. But the 65 cabins and suites are attractive and clean. There's a swimming pool, gym, and nice restaurant (all meals included) with Egyptian and international dishes.

paintings, and powerful ACs. Some of the hotel's décor is a bit tacky, but the vibrant murals in the dining room make up for the kitsch. An easy 10-15-minute walk will get you to the temples. Best to bring ear plugs or be prepared to wake up with the call to prayer from the nearby mosque. Basic breakfast included.

Hungry visitors can dine at their restaurant (8am-9pm daily; 115-200LE mains) on a terrace looking out to the lake. Decent Nubian dishes are available for lunch and dinner (alcohol served).

INFORMATION AND SERVICES

You can find a couple of **ATMs** (National Bank of Egypt) inside the temple complex and a few more (Banque du Caire, Banque Misr, and National Bank of Egypt) clustered in Abu Simbel's "downtown" off the main road (Ramses St.), 1.5 kilometers (0.9 mi) northwest of the complex.

GETTING THERE

The easiest way to get to Abu Simbel is by hiring a private car with a driver from Aswan. Flying is not substantially faster when you factor in the time of getting to the airport and waiting (the whole trip will probably take around 7 hours door to door versus 8.5-10 hours driving) and is considerably more expensive unless you're traveling alone and only have one ticket to buy. Another advantage of driving is flexibility. You can spend more time visiting the temples and depart anytime between 4am-11am, while plane departures are more limited and only allow you around 1.5 hours at the temples. Do note that the road between Aswan and Abu Simbel can be a bit harrowing in the dark, so best to make it back before then.

For those with more time (and money), a Lake Nasser cruise is a magical way to approach Abu Simbel in all its splendor.

Air

Flights from **Aswan International Airport** (ASW) typically depart at 9:25am and 9:55am (2,500-3,000LE round-trip) a few times a week and take 45 minutes to reach Abu Simbel Airport (ABS). A complimentary shuttle bus is provided by the airline to get to the temples from the airport, a short 10-minute drive (ignore the taxi drivers). The plane waits and takes passengers back at 1:10pm or 1:30pm. This option gives you around 1.5 hours to visit the site itself, which can feel a bit rushed for some. Tickets available at www.egyptair.com. Tip: Select Egypt as your country from the drop-down menu to see the prices in Egyptian pounds (LE), which tends to be substantially cheaper than the prices in USD or euros. And grab a window seat for spectacular views of the Nile and Lake Nasser.

Private Car or Microbus

Aswan Individual (Corniche el Nil St.; tel. 0100 250 9588; www.aswan-individual.com) offers a private car ($105 for up to 3 people) or a microbus ($130 for up to 6 people) with professional driver and excellent service. **Anakato Lodge** can also organize a trip with a private car (3,000LE for up to 3 people) or microbus (4,800LE for up to 10 people) including a guide. Egyptologist **Mena Zaki** (tel. 0127 400 8892; www.aswanluxor-travel.com) arranges transportation and accompanies you as a guide ($180 for up to 3 people). Note: Guides are not allowed to enter the temple, but can speak about it from outside. Most hotels in Aswan can also arrange private transportation or get you a spot in a shared microbus with other guests (550LE per person), leaving at 4am.

Alexandria and the North Coast

Between Egypt's majestic Nile and enchanting deserts, it's easy to forget about the country's brilliant Mediterranean shores. Here, the sea reigns supreme. The vast open waters connecting North Africa to Europe and the Levant has brought with it millennia of cultural and material exchange. Much of this wealth has made its way to Alexandria—Egypt's largest port and second city. Alexandria has ebbed and flowed over the ages, but in contemporary times has exploded to a population of around 5.5 million.

East of Alexandria, the Delta's emerald green farmland runs along the coast until Port Said—mainland Egypt's easternmost city on the Med. Here, the Suez Canal meets the sea, bringing a steady flow of supertanker guests that make for a colorful backdrop to the cityscape.

Highlights

Look for ★ to find recommended sights, activities, dining, and lodging.

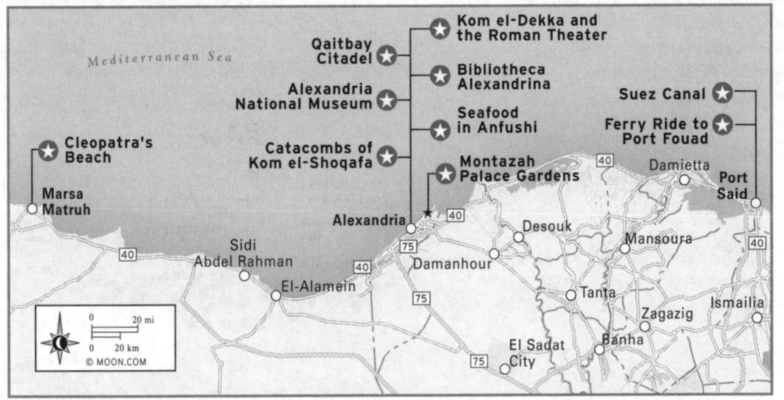

★ **Kom el-Dekka and the Roman Theater:** Explore the best remaining site of Roman-ruled Alexandria, with Egypt's only uncovered Roman theater alongside traces of ancient mansions, lecture halls, and public baths (page 259).

★ **Alexandria National Museum:** The treasures in this museum illuminate Alexandria's transformation throughout the ages, from its birth as a city through the 19th century (page 263).

★ **Bibliotheca Alexandrina:** This shiny cultural complex imitates the lost Library of Alexandria, which made the city an intellectual center of the ancient world (page 264).

★ **Qaitbay Citadel:** Wander the cavernous passageways of Mamluk Sultan Qaitbay's sturdy citadel, built in 1477 to protect Alexandria's Eastern Harbor (page 264).

★ **Catacombs of Kom el-Shoqafa:** Descend into this ancient Greco-Roman funerary complex to explore the blend of Egyptian, Greek, and Roman symbols used to help the dead navigate the underworld (page 265).

★ **Montazah Palace Gardens:** Stroll along these palm-lined royal gardens and enjoy Alexandria's most peaceful stretch of sea (page 268).

★ **Seafood in Anfushi:** Indulge in the Mediterranean's freshest dishes with a sea view from your perch of choice along the coast (page 274).

★ **Suez Canal:** In Port Said, walk along the historic waterway that cuts between continents and links great seas (page 286).

★ **Ferry Ride to Port Fouad:** Cross the Suez Canal on this short (and free) ferry ride between Africa and Asia (page 288).

★ **Cleopatra's Beach:** In Marsa Matruh, cool off in a craggy cove of turquoise waters said to have been a favorite bathing spot of Cleopatra (page 297).

Alexandria and the North Coast

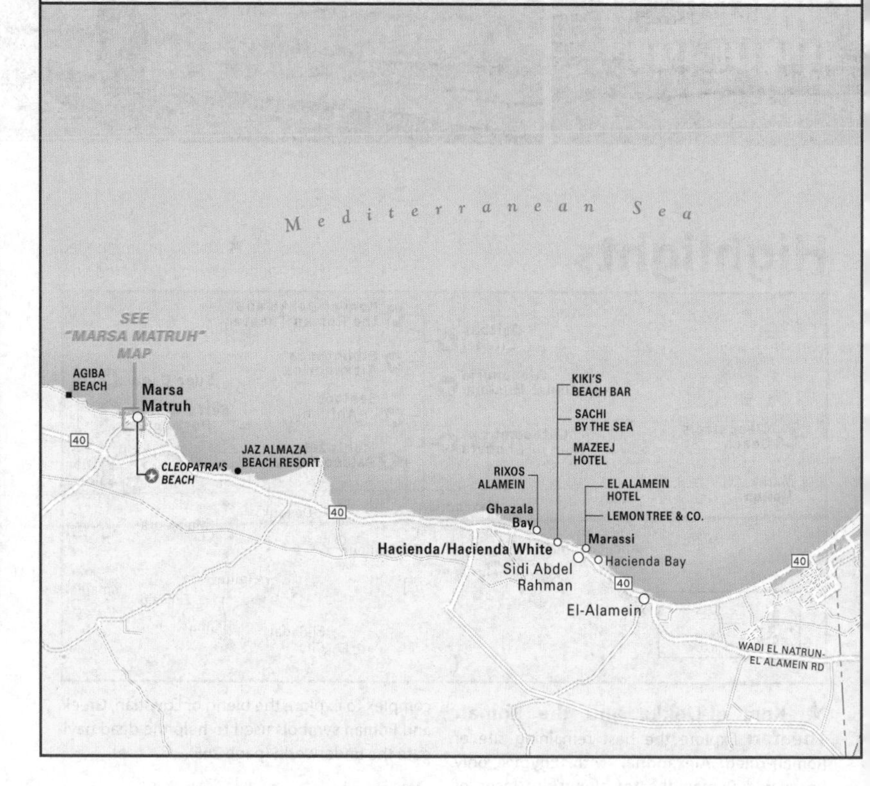

To the west of Alex, stunning coastline stretches for some 480 kilometers (300 mi) to Libya. Bordered to the south by unforgiving desert, this strip of the North Coast has been sparsely populated throughout history—most recently by resourceful Bedouin tribes until a building boom in the 1990s saw the proliferation of resort compounds and an influx of vacationing city folk. Sidi Abdel Rahman holds the prettiest (and most expensive) vacation villages. Marsa Matruh, the regional capital, feels a bit like a mini-Alexandria—boasting all the infrastructure of a modern city and a wealth of public beaches—with the added charm of luminous turquoise waters.

Each of these strips along the Mediterranean has its own distinct character, but all are connected by their debt to the sea, their salty breeze, and their endless northern border in various shades of blue.

ORIENTATION

Alexandria and **Port Said** bookend the Nile Delta, separated by a 260-kilometer (160-mi) road (3.5 hours) along the coast. Both are just about equidistant from Cairo—Alexandria 218 kilometers (135 mi; 2.5 hours) northwest of the capital and Port Said 200 kilometers (124 mi) northeast (2.5 hours).

From Alexandria heading west, **Sidi Abdel Rahman** is around 145 kilometers (90

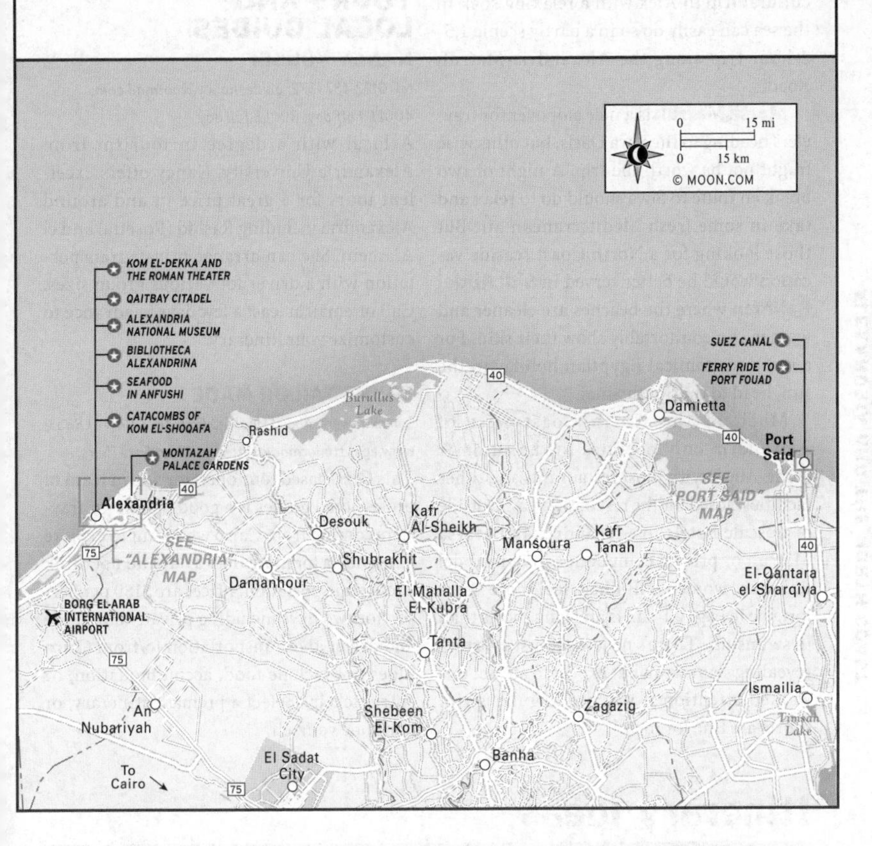

mi; 2 hours) away and **Marsa Matruh** 296 kilometers (184 mi; 3.5 hours).

PLANNING YOUR TIME

Located just 2.5 hours or so by car from Cairo, many visitors head up to **Alexandria** on a day trip from the capital. This is a fine compromise for those short on time, but the city deserves at least two days to soak in its illustrious past and pulsating present. Most activities and sights are concentrated in the Downtown area and along the coast. Come outside of summer (June-Aug.) to avoid the heat and crowds.

Port Said is best visited as a separate day trip or overnight excursion from Cairo (2.5 hours), but can also be reached by Alexandria (3.5 hours). Other than the Suez Canal and some late-19th-century architecture, there's not a ton to see, so most visitors will find one day here sufficient.

A road from Cairo (**Wadi el Natrun-El Alamein Rd.**) cuts through the desert to the best North Coast holiday destinations (Sidi Abdel Rahman) in around 3 hours, making it unnecessary to pass by Alexandria on the way. But travelers who'd like to combine the

Previous: Alexandria's Corniche; the ferry station in Port Said; beach in Port Said.

cultural trip in Alex with a relaxing soak in the sea can easily do so in a partly scenic 1.5-2-hour trip along the Alexandria-Matruh Road.

Marsa Matruh is a nice stopover for travelers heading to the Siwa Oasis, but otherwise might not be worth the trip. A night or two break en route to Siwa should do to relax and take in some fresh Mediterranean air. But those looking for a North Coast seaside vacation would be better served in **Sidi Abdel Rahman** where the beaches are cleaner and women can comfortably show their skin. For a more economical Egyptian holiday in the sun, head to the South Sinai.

Much of the North Coast west of Alexandria only operates in the summer (June-Aug.), with most restaurants and other facilities closed for the rest of the year. Outside of upscale hotels in Alexandria and Marsa Matruh or private compounds in Sidi Abdel Rahman, women will likely feel more comfortable in baggy T-shirts and long shorts than in swimsuits. There's no law against sporting revealing swimwear, but expect to attract unwanted attention if you do. Regular swim shorts are fine for men.

TOURS AND LOCAL GUIDES

NANCY YOUSEF

tel. 0122 457 1872; guide_nancy@hotmail.com; 400LE half day, 800LE full day

A local with a degree in tourism from Alexandria University, Nancy offers excellent tours for a great price in and around Alexandria including Rashid (Rosetta) and el Alamein. She can arrange private transportation with a driver for various group sizes. Call or email at least a few days in advance to customize your itinerary.

EGYPT TAILOR MADE

Sphinx Towers, Abo el Hool St., Giza; tel. 0114 441 8853; www.egypttailormade.net; 9am-10pm Sat.-Thurs.

This Giza-based tour operator with a team of professional guides is a good option for travelers coming from Cairo who want to explore Alexandria for more than a day and not think about transportation. Prices are $180 per person for two days including private tour guide and driver and transportation to/from Cairo (does not include food, accommodation, or entry tickets). Select a premade itinerary, or craft one yourself.

Itinerary Ideas

ALEXANDRIA IN TWO DAYS

Day 1

Travelers who enjoy walking can do this itinerary entirely on foot.

1 Start your day with a classic Egyptian breakfast of fuul and ta'maya at **Mohammed Ahmed Restaurant.**

2 Walk over to **Kom el-Dekka and the Roman Theater** for a peek into life in Alexandria under the Romans.

3 Grab a cab to the **Alexandria National Museum** for some of the city's best artifacts from ancient Egypt to the 19th century.

4 Make your way to **SeaSide** in Anfushi to enjoy a fresh fish lunch en plein air with a fabulous sea view (5.5 km/3.4 mi; 20-30LE cab).

5 Take a short walk (220 m/720 ft) over to the 15th-century **Qaitbay Citadel** for a bit of Mamluk history and more beautiful views of the harbor (closes at 4pm).

Itinerary Ideas

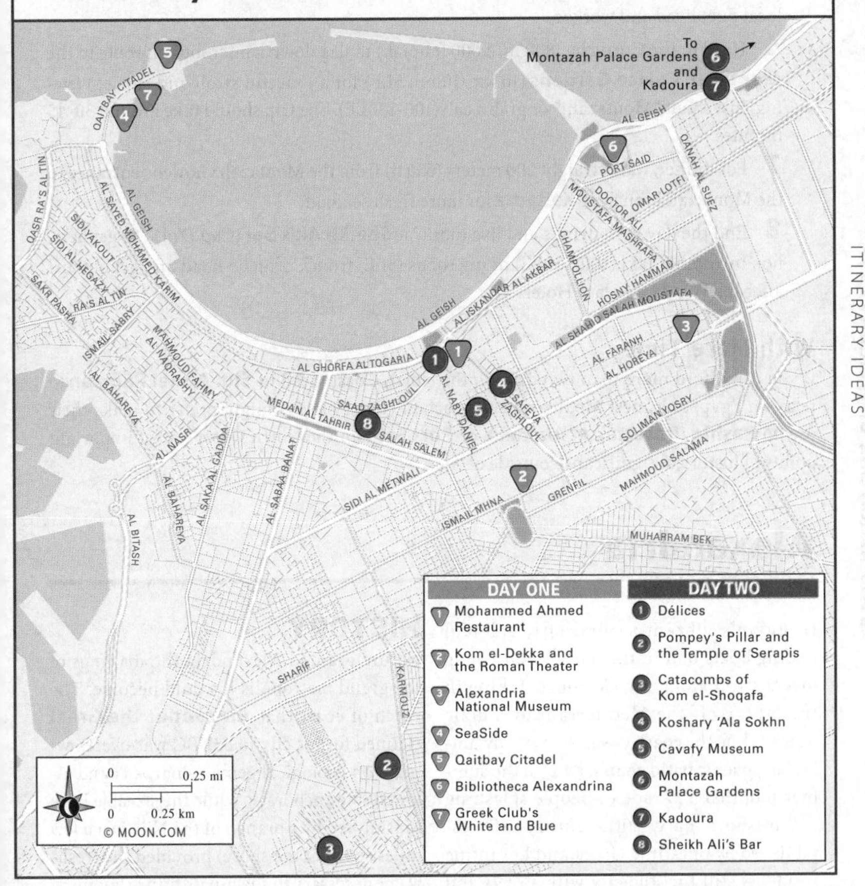

6 Head to the **Bibliotheca Alexandrina** on the opposite side of the harbor to explore the exhibits and mini museums inside. A leisurely stroll along the Corniche should take just under an hour (4 km/2.5 mi).

7 If you haven't had your fill of seafood, head back to the opposite end of the harbor for dinner and drinks at the **Greek Club's White and Blue** restaurant.

Day 2

1 Soak in the energy of the city and the sea while you enjoy a coffee and croissant from the garden seating of **Délices.**

2 Hop in a taxi (3 km/2mi; 15LE) to **Pompey's Pillar and the Temple of Serapis** to check out the remains of Greek Alexandria's former religious center (built c. 300 BC).

3 Walk 500 meters (1,600 ft) southwest to the **Catacombs of Kom el-Shoqafa** for a quick descent into Alexandria's best remaining Greco-Roman necropolis.

4 Wave down a cab for a hearty pasta lunch at **Koshary 'Ala Sokhn.**

5 Walk 350 meters (1,100 ft) southwest to the **Cavafy Museum** for a peek into how the local poet lived and worked.

6 Head to the Corniche (800 m/2,600 ft north) to flag down a microbus en route to the **Montazah Palace Gardens** (16 km/10 mi; 5LE) for a peaceful stroll and sunset viewing. Just shout "Montazah!" or grab a cab (100-130LE). The trip should take around 30-45 minutes.

7 For dinner, walk straight 200 meters (650 ft) from the Montazah Gardens entrance to the Montazah branch of **Kadoura** for more fresh seafood.

8 End the day with drinks and live music at **Sheikh Ali's Bar** (Cap D'or). To get here, hop in another taxi (100-130LE) or microbus (5LE) from Corniche Road and get out just after the Windsor Palace Hotel.

With More Time

If you can afford more than two days on the North Coast, head to **Sidi Abdel Rahman** to relax on Egypt's cleanest Mediterranean beaches. History lovers might prefer to make their way to **Rashid (Rosetta), el Alamein,** or **Port Said** for the North Coast's most important points of historical significance outside of Alex.

Alexandria

In Egypt's vibrant second city, colorful fishing boats bob in the harbor and young lovers stroll along the Corniche, taking in the breeze off the Mediterranean. Public beaches line the coast, covered in sturdy umbrellas, plastic patio chairs, and (in the summer months) a parade of people splashing just offshore. Early 20th-century cafés established by one-time Greek and Levantine residents still fuel the city with sweets and coffee (alongside newer international chains and trendy local creations), and traces of Alexandria's rich Greco-Roman past sit tucked like hidden treasures between traffic-choked streets and concrete housing complexes.

While it's perhaps no longer the "Pearl of the Mediterranean," Alexandria's gritty beauty remains, with the hubbub of 5.5 million residents energizing the coastal metropolis—buzzing around the layers of more than 2,300 years of history.

HISTORY

Nature granted Alexandria the makings of the grand metropolis it would become. The patch of coast that **Alexander the Great** claimed for his city in 331 BC was overflowing with geological gems—Pharos Island allowed safe anchorage, while the sizeable Lake Mariut (fed by a branch of the Nile just a few miles south of the shore) provided the freshwater necessary to sustain its future booming population.

Alexander's successors, the Ptolemies, built his fabulous city, made it their capital, and ruled over a golden age in Egypt. The famed **Cleopatra** (d. 30 BC) reigned as the last Ptolemy—securing help from Romans **Julius Caesar,** and then **Mark Antony** before the latter's rival (**Augustus**) eventually stole Egypt for his Roman Empire. Bitter Augustus exploited Egypt for its wheat and corn, viewing Alexandria as little more than the gateway to the grains that would feed Rome.

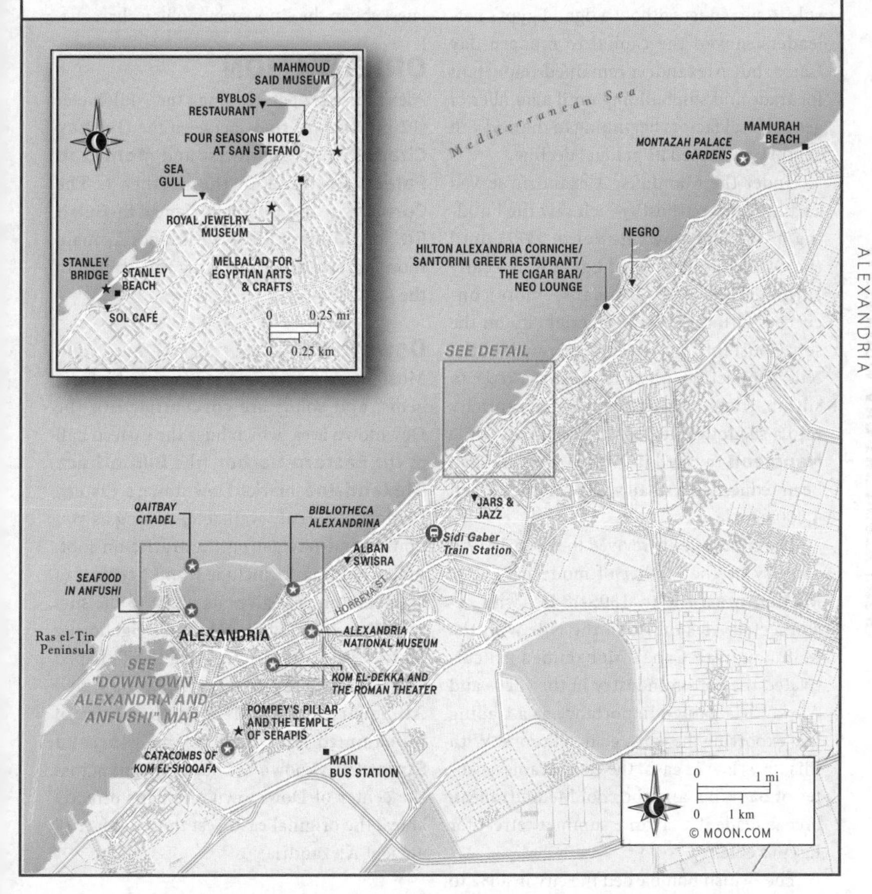

After Augustus's death, Alexandria became a respected province of the Roman Empire, serving as an important commercial hub on the Mediterranean, and regained its status as a thriving intellectual center. But the cosmopolitan character and religious tolerance of the city cultivated under the Ptolemies began to show cracks. Alexandria's Jewish population faced near complete obliteration in AD 117 when they clashed with a series of Roman emperors. Christians, who began to appear in larger numbers toward the end of the 2nd century AD (escaping persecution in Rome), suffered massacre at the hands of **Diocletian** (285-305). And when the tides turned and the Roman Empire adopted Christianity as its official religion, **Theodosius** (r. 379-395) hammered some of the final nails in the coffin of Alexandria's polytheism. The murder of the great pagan thinker **Hypatia** (415)—female mathematician, astronomer, and philosopher—at the hands of Christian zealots marked the end of the city's paganism in the public sphere. Alexandria's secular philosophical schools were usurped by the church, and the city became a global center of Christian thought.

By the time Muslim Arab invaders entered

the city in 641, Alexandria's population had become sufficiently dissatisfied by Roman rule to surrender without a fight. Egypt's new leaders moved the capital to modern-day Cairo, but Alexandria remained important for trade and shipbuilding until a number of geopolitical factors beginning in the mid-8th century prompted its gradual decline.

Under the Mamluks, Alexandria served as a military outpost (which saw the building of the **Qaitbay Citadel** in 1477) until the Ottomans conquered Egypt in the early 16th century. The Ottomans—more concerned with their own imperial city on the sea, Constantinople—left the branch of the Nile connecting Alexandria to the river to silt up, transforming the once vibrant city into a shadow of its former self. By the time **Napoleon** invaded in 1798, Alexandria had been reduced to a small village of just around 4,000 people.

The city was only revived in the early 19th century by the "father of modern Egypt," **Mohammed Ali** (r. 1805-1848), who reconnected Alexandria to the Nile with the Mahmoudiyah Canal. Mohammed Ali cultivated the cotton industry in the 1820s and Alexandria gained importance as a trading hub exporting the white gold to Europe. With this new flow of cash, the city became a center of banking, and the cool Mediterranean breeze made it a favorite summer retreat for Egypt's elite.

The British bombarded the city in 1882 to suppress a nationalist revolt, and then occupied the country for decades to come. Under British control, Alexandria's foreign population expanded and the city served as an important base for the Allied forces in both World War I and II.

After nationalist President **Gamal Abdel Nasser** came to power in 1952, he nationalized much of the economy including the Suez Canal. The 1956 Tripartite Aggression (when Britain, France, and Israel attacked Egypt in retaliation) accelerated the xenophobic spirit of the time. The state seized many foreign assets, prompting the exodus of tens of thousands of Greeks, Italians, French, Jews, and Brits from Alexandria—and marking the latest ebb in the city's cosmopolitan character.

ORIENTATION

Alexandria proper lies along the 7-kilometer (12-mi) strip of coast between the **Qaitbay Citadel** in the southwest and **Montazah Palace Gardens** in the northeast. The **Corniche Road** (officially named **El-Geish Rd.**, or "Military Rd.") is Alexandria's main thoroughfare and runs along this stretch of the sea.

Downtown

Most of Alexandria's museums, historic gems, and souqs are concentrated in the Downtown area, which hugs the eastern half of the **Eastern Harbor** (the **Bibliotheca Alexandrina** marks Downtown's eastern border). It's easily walkable, as long as you don't mind navigating the traffic on foot. Major landmarks include **Raml Station** (a tram station that gives its name to the surrounding area and includes the neighboring **Saad Zaghloul Square**) and the T-shaped **Tahrir Square**—originally Mohammed Ali Square, built in 1830 as the center of Mohammed Ali's city. Inland, **Horreya Street** (also known as Fouad St.) cuts across the center of Downtown and runs directly above the original east-west thoroughfare of ancient Alexandria.

Anfushi

West of Downtown, the Anfushi neighborhood sits on the Ras el-Tin ("Cape of Figs") peninsula—named for the fig trees that once covered the area. The peninsula separates the Eastern and Western Harbors, with **Qaitbay Citadel** at its tip. Anfushi was home to the bustling Ottoman quarters in the 17th-18th centuries, and today has some of the liveliest pockets of the coast with a carnival-like atmosphere (near the Qaitbay Citadel) in the evenings and fantastic views of the Eastern Harbor. Its seaside also has the city's densest selection of quality seafood restaurants.

Alexandria's Legendary Founding

Legend has it that **Homer** led **Alexander the Great** to these parts when he came to the warrior king in a dream. The gray-bearded poet spoke his lines from the *Odyssey* of the island of Pharos just off Egypt's shores, and Alexander—in search of a plot on which to build the most world's most magnificent Hellenic city—took the visit as a sign from the gods.

In 331 BC Alexander commissioned the city before heading east to expand his empire. As his architect laid the plans with barley flour (for lack of chalk), hungry seabirds made a spectacle of undoing them. But an exquisite city of white marble eventually rose nonetheless, becoming the "Pearl of the Mediterranean."

The celebrated island of Pharos (now the location of the **Qaitbay Citadel**) was connected to the mainland via causeway, creating two harbors. And into these ports poured great material and intellectual wealth, transforming Alexandria into a magnet for some of the ancient world's most illustrious thinkers.

Alexander died in battle before he could see his glimmering city. But his general and successor, **Ptolemy I,** founded a dynasty that would rule from Alexandria for some 300 years.

Karmus

Karmus, just south of Downtown, is the oldest inhabited part of the city—home to the original settlement of Egyptian goatherders, pre-Alexander the Great's arrival. Their village (Rhakotis) sat on the elevated hill where **Pompey's Pillar** was later erected. This area also has the city's oldest remains, dating to the earliest days of the Ptolemies (Alexander the Great's successors).

East Alexandria

Sprawling East Alexandria brings more seaside promenade and over a dozen mostly residential neighborhoods. There are a couple of sights of interest in the **San Stefeno** area (near the massive San Stefeno Mall), and another at the far east edge of Alexandria proper (**Montazah**).

SIGHTS

Downtown

★ KOM EL-DEKKA AND THE ROMAN THEATER

Ismail Mahana Rd., just north of Alexandria Railway Station; tel. 03 902904; 8am-4:30pm daily; 80LE adults, 40LE students

For nearly 200 years (4th-6th centuries AD) this ancient rec center served as the social hub of Alexandrians under Roman rule. Its centerpiece was a large complex of **baths** surrounded by grand columns, around which sprung up a sports hall, public restrooms, and a **theater** for musical performances—Egypt's only remaining Roman theater and the most impressive structure still standing at the site. In the 6th century AD, the theater was expanded and covered with a dome, and 22 **lecture halls** were added just to the north.

Before the site became a community center, it was a wealthy residential area (1st-3rd centuries AD), destroyed during a period of rebellion. Over the debris of the fabulous villas, more modest accommodations and artisans' workshops were built—the excavated remains of which are visible on the far east side of the complex.

Just south of these communal houses, fragments of one of the earlier mansions—known as the Villa of the Birds for its stunning floor mosaic of exotic birds—have been lovingly uncovered and offer the best remaining clues to how a wealthy family would have lived in Alexandria during Roman times. It dates to the rule of Emperor Hadrian (r. AD 117-138), when the city experienced a particularly prosperous period.

After the 7th-century Arab conquest, Egypt's capital shifted down to modern-day Cairo and the site fell into disrepair,

Downtown Alexandria and Anfushi

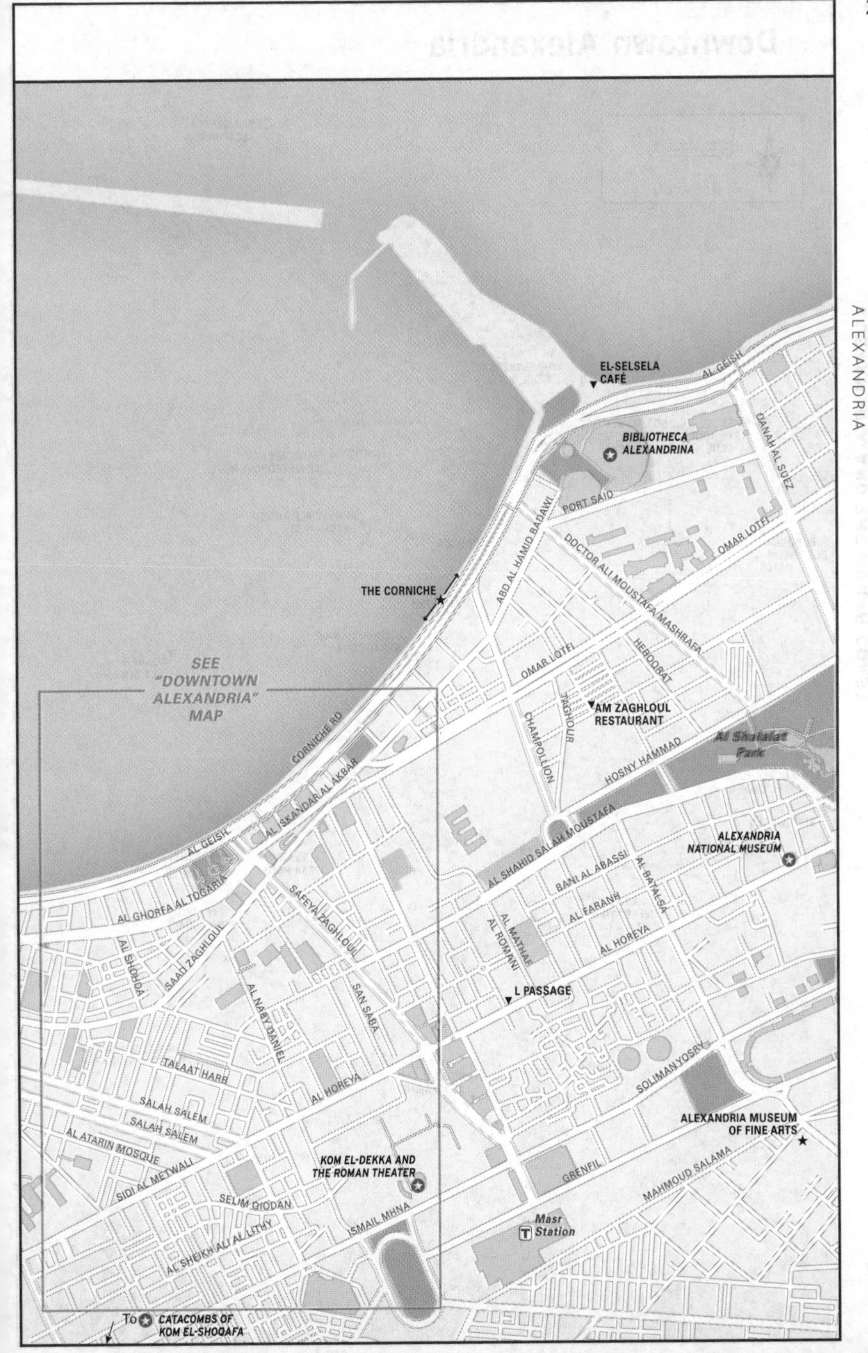
EL-SELSELA CAFÉ
AL GEISH
BIBLIOTHECA ALEXANDRINA
QANAH AL SUEZ
PORT SAID
ABD AL HAMID BADAWI
DOCTOR ALI MOUSTAFA MASHRAFA
OMAR LOTFI
THE CORNICHE
HEBOQRAT
SEE "DOWNTOWN ALEXANDRIA" MAP
AM ZAGHLOUL RESTAURANT
TAGHDUR
CHAMPOLLION
Al Shalalat Park
HOSNY HAMMAD
CORNICHE RD
AL ISKANDAR AL AKBAR
AL SHAHID SALAH MOUSTAFA
ALEXANDRIA NATIONAL MUSEUM
AL GEISH
BANI AL ABASSI
AL BATALSA
AL GHORFA AL TOGARIA
SAFEYA ZAGHLOUL
AL FARANH
AL MATHAF
AL ROMANI
AL HOREYA
AL SHOHDA
SAAD ZAGHLOUL
L PASSAGE
AL NABY DANIEL
SAN SABA
TALAAT HARB
SOLIMAN YOSRY
AL HOREYA
SALAH SALEM
SALAH SALEM
ALEXANDRIA MUSEUM OF FINE ARTS
AL ATARIN MOSQUE
SIDI AL METWALI
KOM EL-DEKKA AND THE ROMAN THEATER
GRENFIL
MAHMOUD SALAMA
SELIM QIODAN
ISMAIL MHNA
Masr Station
AL SHEIKH ALI AL LITHY
To CATACOMBS OF KOM EL-SHOQAFA

Downtown Alexandria

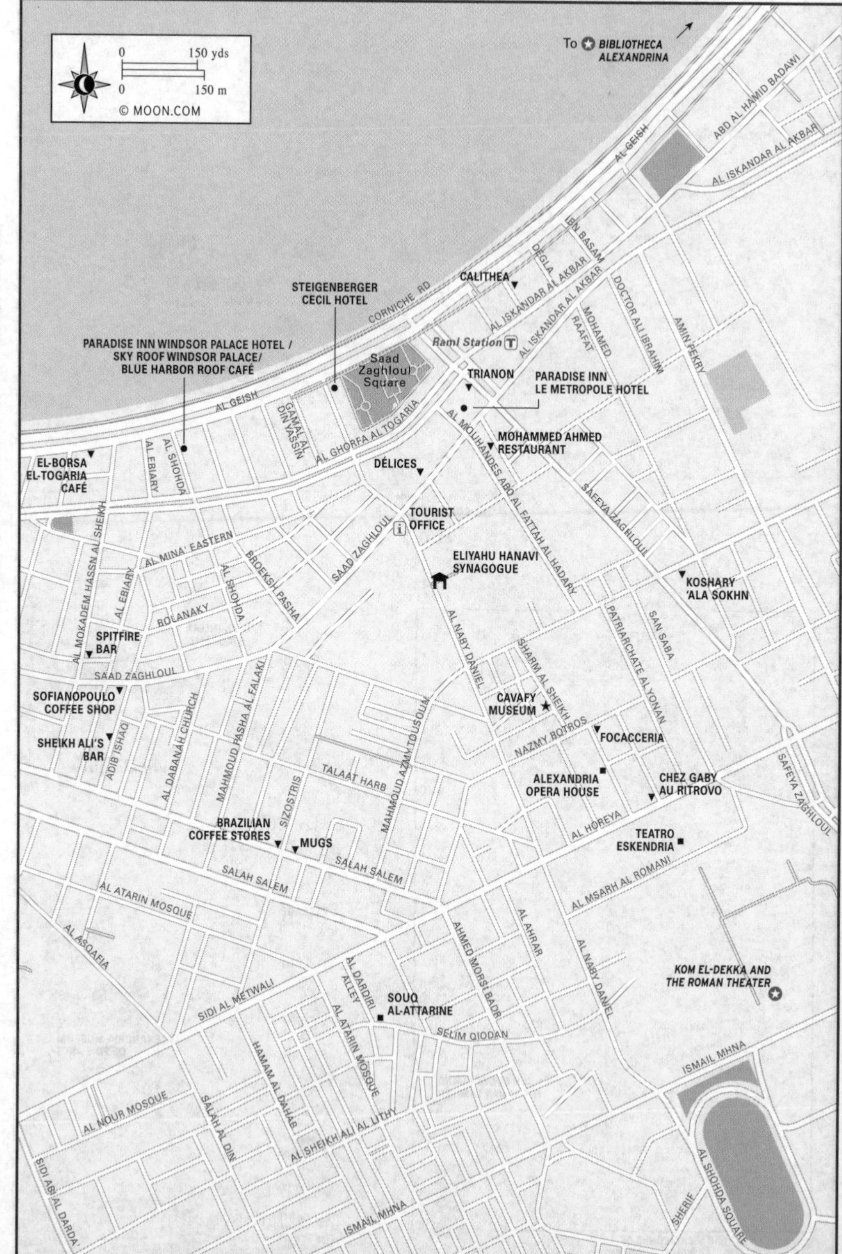

earning the name Kom el-Dekka ("Mound of Rubble"). Thanks to a Polish-Egyptian archeology mission (beginning in 1960), visitors can again enjoy a glimpse into the world of Roman Alexandrians. A leisurely visit will take around an hour.

ALEXANDRIA MUSEUM OF FINE ARTS

6 Mensha St., Moharram Bek; tel. 03 3936616; 10am-6pm Sat.-Sun. and Tues.-Thurs.; free

Alexandrian-German Edward F. Heim donated over 200 works of art to his home city in 1906 on the condition they establish a museum, and the Alexandria Museum of Fine Arts was born. Added to his international collection of mostly Romantic, baroque, and rococo pieces are a number of Orientalist paintings gifted by the politician and patron of the arts Mohamed Mahmoud Khalil, some sculptures by Egypt's beloved sculptor Mahmoud Mokhtar (1891-1934), and paintings by modern Egyptian artists. An hour or so should be enough time for a visit.

If you have extra time, check out the **Museum of Arabic Calligraphy** (same hours and tel.; also free) next to the main building with a beautiful array of just what its name suggests.

★ ALEXANDRIA NATIONAL MUSEUM

110 al-Horreya Rd.; tel. 03 4835519; 9am-4:30pm daily; 100LE adults, 50LE students

Located in the former villa of a Lebanese timber merchant, this gem of a museum holds over 1,800 objects (not all displayed) from the pharaonic era to the 19th century. The pharaonic collection—with mummies encased in gilded coffins (my personal favorite objects) and other artifacts from around Egypt—is appropriately housed in the basement. On the ground floor you'll find the Greco-Roman area, including some statues found underwater just off the city's modern-day shores and a fantastic mosaic of Medusa. Upstairs are artifacts from the early Islamic and Ottoman eras.

The space is beautifully curated with dramatic lighting and English descriptions. It's rarely crowded and big enough to have substance, but not overwhelming. Around 2 hours should do for a nice overview. WCs and a small bookshop available.

CAVAFY MUSEUM

4 C.P. Cavafy St. (aka Sharm el-Sheikh St.); tel. 03 4861598; 10am-5pm Tues.-Sun.; 25LE

Born in Alexandria to a wealthy merchant family of Greek origin, C. P. Cavafy (1863-1933) lived most of his life in obscurity before becoming one of modern Greece's most celebrated poets. He wrote in Greek but is said to have spoken the language with an English accent after spending much of his childhood in Liverpool.

Cavafy's verse combined the city's glorious ancient history and his erotic encounters with male prostitutes in the seedy corners of early 20th-century Alexandria. The house in which he lived with his mother until her death in 1899 has been converted into a museum, where visitors can get a glimpse into the poet's life and works. Two rooms were preserved as Cavafy left them and the others have display cases exhibiting his publications, letters, and photographs of him throughout his life.

ELIYAHU HANAVI SYNAGOGUE

69 Al-Naby Daniel St., al-Attarine; no tel.; 8am-5pm daily; free

One of Egypt's largest synagogues, the Eliyahu Hanavi dates to 1850—built on the ruins of a 14th-century synagogue that was leveled during Napoleon's 1798 invasion. It once catered to Alexandria's Jewish population of 30-40 thousand, nearly all of whom left following the creation of Israel in 1948 and its ensuing wars with Egypt. The synagogue was closed for almost a decade due to security concerns and then renovations before finally reopening in 2020. Inside, visitors can see soaring arch ceilings, Italian marble columns, and copper nameplates at the seats of early members of the congregation. Bring your passport to enter.

THE CORNICHE

Corniche Rd. (aka El-Geish Rd.), bookended by Manar al Islam Mosque in Anfushi and the Monatazah Palace Gardens

Sitting or strolling along Alexandria's 7-kilometer-long (12-mi-long) seaside promenade is a beloved pastime of the city's young and old. The nicest strip lies along the Eastern Harbor (between Qaitbay Citadel and the Bibliotheca Alexandrina), where you can dangle your legs over the wall for some spritzes of seawater and watch the fishing boats bounce in the waves.

★ BIBLIOTHECA ALEXANDRINA

Corniche Rd., Shatby; tel. 03 4839999; www.bibalex.org; 10am-7pm Sun.-Thurs., 2pm-7pm Fri., noon-4pm Sat.; 70LE adults, 10LE students

Alexandria of antiquity became one of the greatest intellectual centers of the ancient world, largely thanks to the city's legendary library, the famed **Library of Alexandria.** Established by Ptolemy I in the early 3rd century BC (shortly after the birth of the city itself), the library's shelves held all the known works written in Greek, many in Egyptian, and several scrolls in other languages—totaling an estimated 500,000. Euclid, the most renowned mathematician of Greco-Roman antiquity, taught and wrote here, as did Eratosthenes—Greek astronomer and poet who first calculated the diameter of the earth to near perfect precision.

The fate of the library remains an ongoing debate, but most historians guess Caesar unintentionally burned it down in 48 BC when he torched a fleet of enemy forces in the harbor. Today, travelers can visit a beautiful re-imagination of the original library at Bibliotheca Alexandrina. The soaring space is part library, part museum, part cultural center. Its international architects fused ancient themes with futuristic panache, using the Egyptian sun disc as inspiration for the structure's circular shape (which ended up looking a bit like a spaceship), and imitating the glow of the Ptolemies' legendary lighthouse with a roof of windows that reflect the sun.

The quiet, cool, naturally lit interior is an oasis from the busy (and often hot) city, and full of places to explore. Aside from the main library that can hold up to eight million books, you can also peek into the permanent exhibitions (free with entry ticket), which include a collection of Arab folk art, replicas of Arab-Muslim medieval scientific instruments, and printing machines from Egypt's first press (est. 1820). Additional temporary exhibits also bring artistic treasures (check the website to see what's on) and if you have the time you can explore the **Manuscripts Museum** (30LE adults, 10LE students), **Antiquities Museum** (50LE adults, 25LE students), **Planetarium** (50LE adults, 25LE students), and the excellent **BA Bookshop** (11am-7pm Mon.-Thurs., noon-4pm Sat.). The museums open with the library and close at 5pm Sun.-Fri. and 4pm Sat.

Don't miss out on a free tour in English offered by the library staff. It's best to call ahead a day or two to ensure your spot (especially Fri.-Sat.).

Anfushi

★ QAITBAY CITADEL

Qaitbay St.; no tel.; 8am-4pm daily; 60LE adults, 30LE students

Mamluk Sultan Qaitbay borrowed the location and remains of Alexandria's famed Pharos Lighthouse—one of the Seven Wonders of the Ancient World—to build his impressive citadel in AD 1477. The 3rd-century BC beacon for Alexandria-bound ships fell after more than 1,500 years on this site, following earthquakes in the 12th and 14th centuries. Qaitbay recycled what remained, seen for example in the five massive pillars of red granite from Aswan near the entrance and other stones layered throughout the walls.

Much of the Citadel was destroyed during the Bombardment of Alexandria in 1882—when British troops shelled the city to quell an Egyptian nationalist revolt against the Brits' puppet ruler—and restored to its polished state throughout the 20th century. The cavernous interiors are full of hidden treasures like **Qaitbay's Mosque**—the city's second oldest, with soaring ceilings and exquisite marble floors; air shafts that look out to a world of brilliant blues; and stairs leading to a roof with stunning views of the Eastern Harbor.

Try to avoid the weekends (Fri.-Sat.) when the sight is most crowded. Evenings around the Citadel are lively, with cotton candy vendors and bicycles for rent that kids take out for quick spins in exchange for a few LE.

ABU AL-ABBAS AL-MURSI MOSQUE

El-Sayed Mohammed Karim St.; no tel.; 24 hours daily; free

Designed by Italian architect Mario Rossi as part of King Fouad's plan to renovate the old Ottoman quarters of Anfushi, this ornate, neo-Mamluk mosque is dripping with the wealth of the royal coffers. Completed in the 1940s, it was built on the spot of earlier mosques dedicated to a 13th-century Sufi saint from Andalusia (al-Mursi). Al-Mursi's tomb lies beneath the mosque's soaring domes (open to visitors).

Men and women will be directed to separate entrances. Don't miss the exquisite mihrab (prayer niche) inside, with kaleidoscopic marble inlay surrounded by Kufic script.

Karmus

★ CATACOMBS OF KOM EL-SHOQAFA

Kom el-Shoqafa St.; tel. 03 4865800 or 03 3936825; 8am-4:30pm daily; 80LE adults, 40LE students

Discovered in 1900 by a hapless donkey who stumbled into the access shaft (so the story goes), these catacombs represent Alexandria's largest remaining necropolis of the Greco-Roman period. The three-tiered subterranean complex, dating to the 2nd century AD, displays a mélange of Egyptian, Greek, and Roman themes.

After 99 steps down a spiral staircase, visitors reach the first level with a **rotunda** and large **banquet hall** (to the left) where relatives would feast to celebrate their departed. The shaft in the center of the staircase served as a shortcut for the bodies as they were lowered into the tombs.

At its peak, the funerary complex accommodated over 300 corpses (there was stacking involved), but the **main tomb** held only three. You'll find this ornate resting place of unknown patrons down a small set of stairs off the rotunda.

Outside of this original tomb, Greek Medusas flank the chamber to ward off evil above serpents wearing the double crown of Upper and Lower Egypt and the pharaoh's false beard. Anubis, the Egyptian jackal-headed god who guarded the gates of the underworld, comically stands in Roman military garb just inside.

The lowest level is closed (it seems permanently) due to flooding, but a separate complex called the **Hall of Caracalla** is now connected, courtesy of tomb raiders. The walls here were once covered in vibrant paintings of the Greco-Roman and Egyptian gods of the underworld (Hades and Osiris), almost all of which have faded.

Watch your step as you explore—some of the interior ground is uneven and the stairs are abnormally shallow. Around 30-40 minutes should be enough time for a visit. WCs available.

POMPEY'S PILLAR AND THE TEMPLE OF SERAPIS

Amoud al-Sawari St.; no tel.; 9am-4:30pm daily; 80LE adults, 40LE students

Pompey has nothing to do with the red granite **pillar** that bears his name, erected around AD 300 for the Roman Emperor Diocletian. But a misreading of the column's inscription gave it the 1st-century BC Roman general's name, and it stuck. Poor Diocletian—who saved the city once from massacre and again from famine—also lost his imposing statue that stood atop the 27-meter-tall (88-ft-tall) monument. A graveyard of broken columns, some stone tablets with pharaonic reliefs, and a pair of sphinxes brought over from ancient Heliopolis (modern-day Cairo) surround the main attraction.

1
2
3
4

Centuries earlier, the Ptolemies (c. 300 BC) had built the **Temple of Serapis** on this site—an impressive complex dedicated to Alexandria's patron god, filled with statues and columned halls. As foreign rulers, the Ptolemies reinvented the god Serapis—as a mix between Egyptian deities (the sacred bull and fertility god, Apis, and god of the underworld, Osiris) and the Greek Dionysus (god of wine, ecstasy, and fertility)—to bring together the Egyptian and Greek residents of Alexandria under one chief cult deity. The temple not only served as Alexandria's most important pagan sanctuary, but also as a center of knowledge. An annex known as the "Daughter Library" to the legendary Library of Alexandria held the remaining books following the latter's destruction (c. 48 BC) and is believed to have contained over 42,000 scrolls.

The Serapeum remained a central part of Alexandrian life for nearly seven centuries until it was destroyed by a Christian mob in AD 391 and replaced by a church. Little remains of the once magnificent temple save some excavated rocks and a few underground passageways open to visitors.

Be sure to wear comfortable shoes and beware the rocky footing. The site can be covered in around an hour. WCs and a small gift shop near the entrance.

East Alexandria

STANLEY BRIDGE

Corniche Rd.

Spanning a mini bay, this 290-meter (950-ft) bridge is a nice place for a stroll or a sit (concrete benches line the sidewalk here). During peak traffic hours it's less pleasant, so try to come early (before 8am) or late (after 6pm) when the four towers flanking either end of the bridge—imitating the style of the Montazah Palace a bit farther north—are pleasantly illuminated.

1: Roman Theater **2:** Pompey's Pillar **3:** Qaitbay Citadel **4:** Bibliotheca Alexandrina

ROYAL JEWELRY MUSEUM

27 Ahmed Yehia St.; tel. 03 5828348 or 0120 363 5595; 9am-4pm daily; 100LE adults, 50LE students

Most of the royal jewels were seized after Egypt's last king was ousted in 1952 and many have since disappeared. But the less extravagant pieces on display here are still a treat for lovers of bling and gilded kitsch. The oldest items date to the days of the dynasty's founder, Mohammed Ali (r. 1805-1848)—like his diamond-encrusted snuffbox. Other highlights include the fabulous tiara of Queen Shwikar (wife of King Fouad) and the fancy chess set of King Farouk. The early 20th-century palace (former home of a princess) that houses the royal heirlooms is a sight in itself, with opulent ceilings and interesting blends of European styles. The (non-functioning) bathroom upstairs is a particular delight.

MAHMOUD SAID MUSEUM

6 Mahmoud Basha Said St.; tel. 03 5821688; 10am-6pm Sat.-Sun. and Tues.-Thurs.; free

Like so many of Egypt's best artists, Mahmoud Said (1897-1964) practiced his creative passion on the side while performing the father-pleasing duties of a civil servant. The pioneer of modern Egyptian art only dedicated himself to painting full time at the age of 50, when he retired from his work as a judge. At least three of his paintings have sold for over $1 million, making him the only Arab artist to have raked in (posthumously) such a fortune.

Said's former home, an Italianate stone mansion, is now a three-story museum, with Said's works on the ground floor, paintings by the Wanly brothers (contemporaries of Said) one floor up, and a basement full of pieces by other modern Egyptian artists. Additional traces of Said's life (like his easel, paintbrushes, and pipe) are scattered about on the ground floor as well.

When he wasn't painting landscapes, Said's favored subject was women—many of them nude and most of them commoners because, he said, they embodied unadulterated Egyptian beauty. (Said was of the aristocracy—son of a prime minister and uncle of Queen Farida.) For these more risqué painting sessions, he left his studio in the family villa for the house of a Greek friend. Both landscapes and these more provocative pieces are on display. Your passport may be required for entry, so best to bring it along.

★ MONTAZAH PALACE GARDENS

Corniche Rd., Montazah; no tel.; 8am-midnight daily; 25LE

The prettiest corner of Alexandria, the Montazah Palace Gardens cover several acres of land with the most peaceful seaside (far from the busy Corniche Rd.) you'll find in the city. Several species of palm trees dominate the gardens, alongside Mediterranean pines, manicured lawns, and other rich greenery.

Khedive Abbas II (r. 1892-1914) wasted no time in claiming this lush land for his summer residence, building the **Salamlik** as his hunting lodge shortly after he ascended the throne. The **Montazah Palace** followed, commissioned by King Fouad in 1925 and designed by an Italian architect in an Ottoman-meets-Florentine style. This served as the summer home of the royal family while the king held court 21 kilometers (13 mi) to the west at **Ras el-Tin Palace** (closed to the public). It's also where King Farouk (Fouad's son) got news that he was on the way out after junior officers staged a military coup in Cairo in the summer of 1952. He hopped in his royal yacht, *El-Mahroosa* ("The Protected One"), parked in the Montazah Harbor, and never returned. The palace grounds were converted into a public park by the socialist regime that followed.

Both the Salamlik and Montazah Palace are closed to the public, but you can admire their architecture from outside and enjoy the beautiful seaside green space. The highlight is the island on the northeast edge of the grounds, where fishermen line the rocky coast and waves spritz passersby (reached by **Montazah Bridge**).

If hunger strikes, **Zanilli's** (just to the right after Montazah Bridge; tel. 03 5479935; 9am-midnight daily; 70-120LE mains) has decent pizzas and fantastic outdoor seaside seating. But you're better off doing like the locals and picnicking under the palms.

RECREATION

Parks

EL-SHALALAT PARK

Istanbul-Salah Mustafa St., Downtown; 10am-11pm daily; free

Designed by a Frenchman in the late 19th century (with inspiration from great landscaper Frederick Law Olmsted), El-Shalalat Park surrounds what's left of the walls built by Ibn Tulun in AD 881 (known as the "Arab walls"). Ibn Tulun used materials collected around the city, layering chunks of marble and broken columns to build his fortified city. The remaining walls are about 9-10 meters (30-35 ft) tall and twice as wide. The ancient canal that once connected Lake Mariut (just south of Alexandria proper) to the sea has been reduced to a small pond beside the walls.

The park has seen better days and suffers from a daily dose of litter, but is worth a visit for a shaded stroll among the palms and banyan trees. You can find it 1 kilometer (0.6 mi) south of the Bibliotheca Alexandrina.

Beaches

Despite Alexandria's ample shoreline, it's sadly not the best swimming destination. Beaches tend to be littered, ridiculously crowded (especially June-Aug.), and not bikini-friendly (women who choose to swim will feel more comfortable in a baggy T-shirt and long shorts). For pristine beaches where you can avoid a T-shirt tan, either choose your hotel wisely (the Four Seasons and Hilton both have beautiful private beaches and pools), or extend your North Coast trip to the upper-class compounds in Sidi Abdel Rahman (135 km/84 mi west of Alexandria). Of all Alexandria's beaches, these are the best.

MAMURAH BEACH

Corniche el-Mamurah Rd., just east of Montazah Palace Gardens, East Alexandria; 8am-8pm daily; 20-150LE

Mamurah Beach is really a string of separate beaches, lined with a pedestrian walkway instead of the traffic-choked thoroughfare that hugs most of the city's shoreline. It's located in a gated compound of upper-middle-class summer homes just north of Montazah Palace Gardens and around 17 kilometers (11 mi; 35-60 minutes depending on traffic) from Downtown Alex.

For 20LE you can access the "public beach," 85LE the neighboring private beach (includes chair and umbrella), and 150LE the **Paradise Inn Beach Resort's** Flamingo Beach (on the far west side of the Mamurah complex; tel. 03 5650152). The rooms and pool aren't the cleanest, so avoid staying overnight. Unfortunately none are fantastic, but the more you pay the cleaner and less crowded the beaches, and the less uncomfortable it is to show some skin.

STANLEY BEACH

Beside Stanley Bridge, East Alexandria; 8am-8pm daily; 25LE

This patch of water in the tiny bay spanned by Stanley Bridge is a nice place to splash around. It's surrounded by roads but below street level, so you get some protection from the noise and bustle. The higher entrance price also means it's not as crowded or littered as some of the other beaches. For an extra 15LE you can grab a chair and umbrella.

PERFORMING ARTS

ALEXANDRIA OPERA HOUSE

22 Horreya Rd. (aka Fouad St.), Downtown; tel. 03 4800138; www.cairoopera.org

Enjoy some of Egypt's best musical and drama talents in the plush interior of the Alexandria Opera House (also called Sayed Darwish Theater). Performances range from Egyptian pop stars to the national orchestra, international ensembles, and local theater troops. Dress code for performances is formal/business casual with jacket and tie for men (though you should be able to rent a tie and jacket on-site if you've left yours at home). Check their Facebook page for schedule (@AlexandriaOpera).

TEATRO ESKENDRIA

25 Horreya Rd. (aka Fouad St.), Downtown; tel. 033901339; 9am-1am daily

Cultural center par excellence, Teatro Eskendria combines musical performances, art exhibitions, creative workshops, and a restaurant all under one very attractive roof. Located in an Italianate building from the 1920s, the space is decorated with bold colors, beautiful wooden panels, and kaleidoscopic tiles. There's a constantly changing set of works by local artists on display, and performances most weekends (Thurs.-Sat.). Check their Facebook page for upcoming events (@Teatro.Eskendria.Official).

Outdoor seating is available in a shaded alleyway tucked away from the bustle of historic Fouad Street. The food (Egyptian; mains 50-100LE) isn't bad, but the fresh juice and shisha are the highlights on the menu. Don't miss their excellent shop (closed Mon. 2pm-10pm).

SHOPPING

Alexandria's souqs are experiential outings—usually more interesting for their energy and mazelike layout than the products available for purchase. For high-quality souvenirs from around Egypt, head to one of the handicraft shops listed below.

Downtown

SOUQ AL-ATTARINE

Off Masgid al-Attarine St., 500 m/1,600 ft west of the Roman Theater, al-Attarine; no tel.; 10am-10pm daily

You might not end up buying anything here, but this labyrinthine souq is worth a visit for its colorful character. The shop-lined alleys are pedestrian only—a designation not typically upheld in practice in Egypt unless, as is the case here, the streets are too narrow for anything but legs. What started as a spice market (al-Attarine means "the spice sellers")

Alexandria in Books and Films

Many of the artistic works out of Alexandria come in the form of series—testament to just how inspiring the city can be for the creative eye.

THE ALEXANDRIA TRILOGY

Alexandrian native and one of Egypt's greatest filmmakers **Youssef Chahine** (1926-2008) wrote and directed the *Alexandria Trilogy:* three semi-autobiographical movies (1978-1989) that are as much about his hometown as they are about himself. If you only watch one, check out his first (*Alexandria, Why?*)—his coming-of-age story as an artist in World War II Alexandria.

ALEXANDRIA QUARTET

Twenty years earlier **Lawrence Durrell** (1912-1990), a British writer who spent time in Alexandria during World War II as press attaché to his embassy, wrote of an entirely different Alexandria. His tetralogy, *Alexandria Quartet* (1957-1960), was his most commercially successful work and is a good example of the "cosmopolitan" Alexandria so romanticized by Western audiences. He provides a window into the world of Alexandria's cosmopolitan elite just before and during the Second Word War. But accompanying his sheltered expat existence comes shameless racism and a disdain for the "native quarters" of Arabs.

CITY OF SAFFRON AND GIRLS OF ALEXANDRIA

For a more inclusive look at 1940s and '50s life in the city, read Alexandrian **Edwar al-Kharrat's** (1926-2015) *City of Saffron* and its sequel *Girls of Alexandria*, about a Coptic Christian protagonist (who resembles the author) and his experiences with the full range of religions and classes the city had to offer.

in medieval times turned into a hub of antique shops in the 1950s when most of the city's cosmopolitan residents left. These shops now offer both the beautiful and the Napoleonic gaudy, from tasteful copper lamps to gilded furniture and elaborate chandeliers. Smells of spices and fresh fish still dominate some corners of the market, while others have transformed to meet the modern demands with shisha pipes, handblown glass, and belly dancing costumes. As with any Egyptian souq, bargaining is expected.

SOUQ AL-MANSHIYA

Off Faransa St., just west of Tahrir Square, al-Manshiya; no tel.; 10am-10pm daily (but many shops close on Sun.)

Souq al-Manshiya is really more of a small village of souqs. In one street, fish chill on beds of ice, fruits and vegetables make colorful mounds, and sausages hang like curtains outside butcher shops. Another glitters with silver and gold. (Locals don't usually use street names, so if you're looking for a particular product, best to ask for it.) Zan'et el-Sitat ("Women's Narrow Street") is a mecca for young brides—bursting with cheap accessories, makeup, lingerie, bedding, and jewelry. The Thread Market (Souq el-Kheit) intersects with Zan'et el-Sitat, with rainbows of spools, textiles, and belly dancing getups. Even before you reach the bowels of the souq, the goods of street-side vendors, like flip-flops, dishware, and handbags, pour over the sidewalk.

TEATRO ESKENDRIA

25 Horreya Rd. (aka Fouad St.), Raml Station, Downtown; tel. 03 3901339; 9am-1am daily

This cultural center has an attractive shop tucked inside with unique handicrafts like framed Arabic calligraphy, vintage magazine covers, and the more typical bags, pottery, and appliqué. Closed Mon. 2pm-10pm.

THE BA BOOKSHOP

In the Bibliotheca Alexandrina; tel. 03 4839999; www.bibalex.org; 11am-7pm Mon.-Thurs., noon-4pm Sat.

Located in the Bibliotheca Alexandrina's main entrance, this shop is full of crisp English-language books covering the full range of subjects (fiction and non), but with a special focus on Egypt-related reads. It's an official bookstore of the American University in Cairo (AUC) and carries many of AUC Press's best publications and those of international publishers. You can also find some nice Egyptian handicrafts.

East Alexandria

MELBALAD FOR EGYPTIAN ARTS & CRAFTS

3 Raas el-Hekma St., off Abdel Salam Aref St., San Stefeno, East Alexandria; tel. 0122 316 6765; melbalad@gmail.com; 9am-9pm Sat.-Thurs.

This colorful shop offers Alexandria's best selection of handcrafted treasures from around Egypt. Choose from beautifully embroidered scarfs, pottery, wooden figurines, jewelry, unique clothing, and leather handbags embellished with pretty needlework of rural scenes (among other treats).

FOOD

Thanks to its proximity to the Mediterranean, in Alexandrian dining, seafood is king. Alexandrians also add their own touch to Egyptian classics like fuul (fava bean paste) and kebda (liver) with green pepper, tomatoes, onions, and a blend of spices like cumin, paprika, and chili powder.

Downtown

KOSHARY 'ALA SOKHN

On corner of Salah Moustafa St. and Safiya Zaghloul St.; 9am-midnight daily; 15-25LE

This homegrown restaurant prides itself in having no other branches and serving only koshary with the perfect ratio of pasta, rice, chickpeas, lentils, fried onions, and special sauces. Service is speedy, seating clean, and the food always fresh. Many locals swear this is the best koshary in town, and the constant crowds lend credence.

★ MOHAMMED AHMED RESTAURANT

17 Shakour St., Raml Station; tel. 03 4873576; noon-midnight daily; 15-30LE mains

This modest Egyptian diner has been serving up some of Alexandria's favorite fuul and falafel since 1957. What the venue lacks in décor it makes up for with colorful dishes (presented on stainless steel plateware). The constant flow of customers means you'll get some of the crispiest falafel around. Other classic Egyptian breakfast items also on offer (eggs, fries, eggplants) along with excellent fried cheese.

AM ZAGHLOUL RESTAURANT

9 Hasan el-Adawy; tel. 0127 669 3003; 6am-4pm Sat.-Thurs.; 15-30LE mains

With no frills but plenty of character, this hole-in-the-wall fuul and falafel joint serves a medley of classic Egyptian breakfast foods (like fried eggplants, baba ghanoush, and fries) on stainless steel cafeteria trays. Its outdoor seating in a colorful alley completes the street food experience. Be prepared to compete for a spot, especially on Fridays.

★ DÉLICES

46 Saad Zaghloul St., Raml Station; tel. 03 4861432; www.delicesgroup.com; 8am-10pm daily; 25-35LE juice and hot drinks

Sample a dazzling array of sweets at this Alexandrian institution (est. 1922) from cream-filled donuts to blueberry cheesecake, gelato, and tiramisu. Light meals (sandwiches, omelets, pastry-pizzas) also available. You can enjoy your treats with good coffee under the soaring ceilings of the posh interior, or in shaded outdoor seating on a palm-lined square. Attached to the historic patisserie, the French and Greek restaurant **La Veranda** (11am-midnight daily; 60-100LE) serves decent dishes as well as beer and wine.

Alexandria's Coffee Shops

As with most Egyptian cities, ahaawi (singular ahwa)—casual social hubs serving cheap tea, Arabic/Turkish coffee, and shisha—can be found pouring into nearly every street in Alexandria. Some of the most unique date to the early 20th century and are the less pretentious counterparts of the city's European-style cafés (though women might not feel comfortable alone in the often male-dominated spaces).

In true port city fashion, Alexandria also attracted people and beans from across the Mediterranean and beyond, bringing Greek expats and their coffee culture, along with an interesting injection of Brazilian coffee, courtesy of globetrotting immigrants from the Levant who left for Latin America in the late 19th century and brought the tasty beans to Egypt.

Below are some of the best caffeine-fueled gems from an earlier Alexandria.

Egyptian coffee served at a café

BRAZILIAN COFFEE STORES

20 Salah Salem St., Downtown; tel. 03 4865059; 8am-10pm daily; 20-40LE hot drinks

This shop dating from 1929 is one of the country's last original Brazilian coffee houses. The barrel vault ceiling striped with coffee bean plant motifs, matching red bar stools, and walls of mirrors all complement their excellent coffee beans. Both espresso drinks and their Turkish-style coffee are delicious. Newer, less atmospheric branches can be found around the city.

EL-BORSA EL-TOGARIA CAFÉ

148 Corniche Rd., Downtown; tel. 03 4802535; 9am-1am daily; 15-25LE hot drinks

El-Togaria is a popular ahwa with a host of aging male regulars. Established in 1890, the place gets its name from the many merchants (togaar) who once did business over coffee here in the commercial district of el-Manshiya. Like most ahaawi, the smell of unflavored shisha predominates and the soundscape buzzes with the clacking of dominoes, backgammon, and metal spoons clinking in glasses of syrupy tea.

SOFIANOPOULO COFFEE SHOP

21 Saad Zaghloul St., Raml Station, Downtown; tel. 0122 324 4108; 8am-10pm daily; 15-35LE coffee

Bags and barrels of coffee beans line the floor at this relic of a bygone Alexandria. Established in 1908 by a Greek Alexandrian, the café continues to serve some of the best coffee in the city. Grab some beans to try at home, or sit in the cozy atmosphere and soak in the smell of freshly ground java.

CAFÉ FAROUK

Ismail Sabry St., Anfushi; tel. 0100 230 1000; www.cafe-11032.business.site; 24 hours daily; 15-25LE hot drinks

Opened in 1928, this ahwa takes its name from King Farouk, who frequented the coffee shop (or perhaps just rode by in his carriage depending on whose story you believe). The largely male clientele has been coming to chat and play dominoes for decades. It's one of the more attractive ahaawi with large windows that let in fresh air and plenty of natural light. Shisha, of course, available.

MUGS

21 Salah Salem St.; tel. 03 4865703; 7am-midnight daily; 20-40LE hot drinks

This trendy café makes some of the best espresso drinks in Alexandria. The stylish interior suffers from lack of a nonsmoking area, but is otherwise attractive with nice lighting and good music. Tasty sandwiches, sweets, and smoothies also served.

TRIANON

54 Saad Zaghloul St., Raml Station; tel. 0128 583 9731; 8am-midnight daily; 25-45LE juice and hot drinks

Rows of glistening sweets decorate the display cases at this classic Belle Époque Alexandrian café established by a pair of Greeks in 1905. The tall wood-paneled ceilings and art nouveau wall paintings make for a colorful space to enjoy a coffee and cake, and the outdoor seating just off busy Saad Zaghloul Square is a perfect place to people-watch. It's a much-loved spot for evening outings and crowds start coming around 8pm. Light meals (soups, sandwiches, etc.) also served, but not their specialty. Shisha available.

EL-SELSELA CAFÉ

Corniche Rd., in front of Bibliotheca Alexandrina; tel. 0128 243 7477; 24 hours daily; 25-45LE juice and hot drinks

Seaside seating under grass huts is the highlight of this venue. The food can be skipped, but tea, fresh juice, and good shisha are served to the sound of crashing waves and nostalgic Arabic pop from the '60s. It's a popular hangout spot for college students from the nearby University of Alexandria.

FOCACCERIA

22 Al-Mesallah Sharq, near Alexandria Opera House; tel. 0127 303 3916; noon-midnight daily; 15-80LE mains

Tucked in a narrow alley with street-side seating, this unassuming restaurant manages to cook up some of Alexandria's best pizzas. The owner learned the craft in Italy and adds an Egyptian touch (like shawarma toppings). The cheesy fries, lasagna, and ravioli are also top picks.

CHEZ GABY AU RITROVO

22 El-Horraya Rd.; tel. 03 4874404; 1pm-11:30pm Tues.-Sun.; 75-100LE mains

For more than four decades Chez Gaby has been an Alexandrian establishment, serving pizza and classic Italian dishes in a cozy interior with red and white checkered tablecloths and matching curtains. Nonsmokers might be bothered by the lack of a smoke-free section. Beer and wine served.

L PASSAGE

52 el-Horraya Rd. (aka Fouad St.); tel. 03 4860066; 7:30am-1am daily; 50-250LE mains

This Western-style food court in a renovated Downtown mansion claims to be "the place to be," and Alexandrian youth believe it. If you don't mind the crowds, you can enjoy some of Alexandria's best sushi at **Mori Sushi,** pick up a great sandwich for a seaside picnic at **The Bakery Shop (TBS),** or snack on a sweet array of desserts at **Brew & Chew,** among a dozen or so other options.

KADOURA

Corniche Rd.; tel. 03 4800967; 11am-midnight daily; 80-250LE mains

A bed of ice with the day's haul greets you at the entrance to this modest seafood eatery. Choose your fish and crustaceans to be weighed, before heading upstairs to wait for your meal. Try to grab a seat by the window that looks out across the busy Corniche Road to the sea (outdoor seating also offered on occasion). On busy nights it can stay open until 2am. They have another branch in Montazah (Gamal Abdel Nasser St., el-Mandara Square; tel. 03 5536752; same hours and prices).

Anfushi

Anfushi is the place to go for seafood in Alexandria, with **Seaside** and **Greek Club's White and Blue** the neighborhood standouts.

☆ A Guide to Seafood on the Med

Visitors to Alexandria are spoiled for choice when it comes to seafood. Here you can find some of Egypt's freshest Mediterranean-caught critters in the most varied range of settings—from five-star fancy to street-side simple. It's not uncommon for Cairenes to make the trek up just to lunch on the catch of the day.

grilled seafood

ALEXANDRIA'S BEST SEAFOOD RESTAURANTS

The neighborhood of **Anfushi** has the densest selection of quality seafood restaurants in Alexandria, but you can also try **Kadoura** Downtown or **Sea Gull** in East Alexandria.

HOW TO ORDER

At nearly all the restaurants worth visiting, diners first select their meals from a bed of ice by the kilo (half a kilo per person will usually do the trick), and choose how to have it prepared. Sides often come with the order and include a variety of small dishes like tahini, baba ghanoush, pickled beets, and tomato-cucumber salad.

The fact that many menus are only in Arabic doesn't make the decision-making process any easier. Here's a quick guide to the most popular Mediterranean treats and preparation styles to make sure you get what you want (or at least know what you're trying).

Step 1: Choose Your Fish

- **Bouri:** mullet
- **Qarus:** sea bass
- **Danees:** gilt-head bream
- **Wi'aar:** grouper
- **Subeet:** squid
- **Gambari:** shrimp
- **Bolti:** Nile tilapia (Note: If you're looking for something from the sea, this farmed freshwater fish on almost every menu isn't your best option)

Step 2: Choose the Preparation Style

- **Maqli:** deep-fried
- **Mashwi:** grilled
- **Fil furn, sada:** baked, plain
- **Fil furn bi soos ahmar:** baked in tomato sauce
- **Singari:** split down the middle, piled with tomatoes, carrots, onions, and bell peppers, and baked

EL-SHEIKH WAFIK

34 Qasr Ras el-Tin St., Anfushi; tel. 0106 332 8930; 9am-2am daily; 10-25LE sweets

You might have trouble snagging a seat at this much-loved sweet shop, famous for its rice pudding with ice cream and nuts. Om Ali (Egyptian bread pudding with raisins, almonds, and coconut) is another top choice here—also covered with ice cream on demand.

KEBDET SAMI

26 Mohammed Karim Bahary; tel. 0122 652 7411; 4pm-3am daily; 20-100LE mains

Come hungry to this meat lovers' restaurant specializing in kebda iskandarani (Alexandrian liver prepared with bell peppers, garlic, and cumin). You can also sample some mukh (brain), alb (heart), and various types of Egyptian sausages. For the less adventurous, the mixed grill with lamb and meatballs is a good option. Indoor and street-side seating available.

ABU NOURA

Qasr Ras el-Tin St., next to Shohada Mosque; tel. 0100 800 5453; 24 hours daily; 60-120LE mains

This local favorite is less polished than many of the other seafood spots in Anfushi, but it has great views of the shipyards and large windows that let in the sea breeze. The prices are also a steal for the same freshly caught fish, shrimp, squid, and other marine treats.

SAMAKMAK

42 Qasr Ras el-Tin St.; tel. 03 4811560; 10am-2am daily; 70-120LE mains

What Samakmak lacks in views, it makes up for in fresh, expertly prepared dishes and cozy interior with blue and white checkered tablecloths. Added cachet comes from its owner, the retired Alexandrian belly dancer Zizi Salem. The seafood soup and saucy butterfly shrimp are divine. An array of mezze (potato salad, green salads, etc.) also available.

★ GREEK CLUB'S WHITE AND BLUE

Qaitbay St., at the Greek Club; tel. 0127 588 8836; noon-midnight daily; 150-250LE mains

Alexandrian elite have been enjoying this corner of the Mediterranean for decades. It's a good option for those looking to enjoy their seafood with a side of sea breeze (and perhaps a beer or glass of wine). The spacious outdoor seating offers fabulous views of the Eastern Harbor, and the stylish interior boasts tall ceilings and a color scheme of, you guessed it, white and blue. Their sister restaurant on the roof, **Olive Island,** offers more fresh air with a typically younger crowd and access to the same kitchen.

★ SEASIDE

Qaitbay St., off Qaitbay Square; tel. 0100 010 7145; www.lbay.business.site; 2pm-1am daily; 150-300LE mains

With shaded rooftop seating looking out to the rowboat-speckled harbor, this chic establishment seems to get everything right. Competing with the view (one of the best in the city) are the dishes—skillfully prepared and presented—and service, speedy and friendly. Along with the classic seafood dishes, they also make a great squid tagine and bisque. Excellent bread with sesame seeds and fennel flower served. Located inside the L Bay food court.

East Alexandria

ALBAN SWISRA

82 Port Said St.; tel. 03 5913369; 24 hours daily; 25-40LE mains

Alban Swisra (or "Swiss Dairy Products") serves up cheese, cheese, and more cheese over just about anything you can imagine, including shrimp, crab, chicken, fries, pastrami, and liver. You can also opt for a range of egg or mixed grill dishes sans dairy. Regulars soak up the gooey cheese plates with 'aish fino (long bread rolls) and share them family style. The super sweet desserts are also local favorites. On weekends (Thurs.-Fri.), finding a seat can be a challenge.

SOL CAFÉ

256 Corniche Rd.; tel. 03 5414067; 10am-3am daily; 25-45LE hot drinks and juices

Sol Café's sprawling terrace right on the sea offers a fabulous breeze and nice views of the attractive Stanley Bridge. The food is fine (pizza, burgers, pasta), but the main draws are the location, good shisha, and fresh juice. Located in the Divided Lounge complex.

NEGRO

33 Amin Khairat el-Ghandour St.; tel. 0100 692 3042; 5pm-3am daily; 120-250LE mains

This clean and colorful restaurant serves up unique seafood and sides in ample portions. There's no menu, but the owner will bring out a feast of what's fresh (typically including soup, salads, grilled fish, shrimps, crabs, and dessert). It's a great option for more adventurous diners who like to sample a bit of everything, though not ideal for picky eaters. If you're on a budget, let them know ahead of time how much you'd like to spend so you're not surprised by the bill (it's generally a good value if you come hungry). There are only a handful of tables, so best to call in advance to reserve. No WCs.

JARS & JAZZ

22 Abdel Aziz St.; tel. 0120 172 1752; info@jarsandjazz.com; 8am-1pm daily; 80-300LE mains

Industrial-chic with redbrick walls and thick ventilation pipes snaking across the ceiling, this trendy spot serves "casual American cuisine"—pancakes, burgers and fries, loaded baked potatoes, Philly cheesesteak, etc. The name comes from the long list of creative desserts and drinks served in jars, and the endless jazz music that plays as your meal's soundtrack. They host live music on occasion (check their Facebook page @jarsandjazz for schedule).

SEA GULL

Corniche Rd.; tel. 0120 008 1066; seagull.gleem@hotmail.com; noon-2am daily; 100-300LE mains

Sea Gull really embraces the nautical theme with anchors, ship wheels, shells, and seahorses covering the spacious dining hall that sits directly on the sea. Large windows open to let in the breeze as you enjoy a wide variety of mezze with warm bread and freshly prepared dishes. Try the grilled jumbo shrimp or sea bass singari-style (sliced open, de-boned, and piled high with bell peppers, cilantro, onions, and tomatoes). You can find their original branch in Alexandria's western suburb, al-Max.

SANTORINI GREEK RESTAURANT

In Hilton Alexandria Corniche, 544 Corniche Rd.; tel. 03 5490935; www.hilton.com; 1pm-midnight daily; 250-400LE mains

In this Santorini-themed restaurant at the Hilton you'll be hard pressed to find a color that's not white or cobalt blue. The Greek key pattern decorates gleaming marble floors, and floor-to-ceiling windows offer views of the sea and sky that match the interior color scheme. Its delicious Greek dishes are the best in town. Don't miss the baked feta cheese covered in phyllo pastry, sesame seeds, and honey, or the chicken, beef, and seafood souvlakia served with yogurt sauce and pita bread—artfully presented and equally tasty. Alcohol available.

BYBLOS RESTAURANT

In Four Seasons Hotel, 399 Corniche Rd., San Stefano; tel. 0 3581 8000; www.fourseasons.com; 1:30pm-1am daily; 250-500LE mains

The décor here is a bit eccentric—a kind of Colonial-meets-Oriental with thick drapes, floral wallpaper, and pistachio green accents. But the sea view and tasty Lebanese dishes make up for it. The mezze are the highlight, best enjoyed family style, and the grilled meats are also nice. Service can be slow, so come prepared to hang out for a while. Wine and beer served. Kitchen closes at 5pm and reopens for dinner at 6:30pm.

BARS AND NIGHTLIFE

Alexandrians in search of more varied nightlife often make the trip down to Cairo, but visitors looking for a drink will have plenty of options in Egypt's second city. If you'd prefer to avoid the crowds, skip the weekend evenings (Thurs.-Sat. after 10pm) when all will likely be busy. You can also pick up something from the nationwide liquor store, **Drinkies** (1 Gamal el-Din Yassin St., Downtown; tel. 19330; www.drinkies.net). Various other branches are located throughout the city.

Downtown

SKY ROOF WINDSOR PALACE

In Paradise Inn Windsor Palace Hotel, 17 El Shohada St. and Corniche Rd., Raml Station; tel. 03 4801930; 6pm-2am daily; 55-200LE drinks

Suckers for a view will enjoy this seventh-floor lounge looking out to the harbor. An outdoor section provides escape from the pervasive nightlife smoking, and inside neon lights dominate the floor with DJs or live performances on a center stage (call ahead to check). Twenty- to 30-somethings sip on technicolor cocktails or shisha pipes and sometimes move in a way that approximates dancing. Minimum charge of 160LE on Fridays and 140LE after 2pm all other days.

CALITHEA

83 Corniche Rd., Raml Station; tel. 03 4847508; www.calithea-alex.com; 10:30am-2am daily; 50-150 drinks

Opened in the 1930s, this Greek taverna hasn't managed to preserve the fine flavors of Greek cuisine, but it's a nice place to enjoy a local beer or wine. They do manage to get some simple sides right, like fries, baba ghanoush, and chicken wings. And the place is atmospheric with a mezzanine, maritime décor, and a few large windows on the upper floor that open up to nice views of the harbor.

SPITFIRE BAR

7 El-Borsa El-Qadeema St., Raml Station; tel. 03 4806503; 2pm-1:30am Mon.-Sat.; 50-100LE drinks

Operating for some 140 years, Spitfire wins the title of Alexandria's oldest still-functioning bar, but its name is newer—inspired by Britain's World War II fighter aircraft. Barely an inch of wall has been left uncovered at this dark and smoky watering hole, layered with flags, stickers, and posters left by decades of customers (possibly to hide the peeling paint). Once a hard-drinking sailors' bar, today expats and locals enjoy its eccentric ambiance.

★ SHEIKH ALI'S BAR (CAP D'OR)

4 Adib St.; tel. 0122 264 9184; 10am-3am daily; 60-150LE drinks

Opened some 120 years ago by Alexandrian Greeks, this local bar oozes character. An Egyptian (Ali) bought the place in the 1950s, and when he decided to close on Fridays (the Muslim holy day) it became flippantly known as Khamaret Sheikh Ali (Sheikh Ali's Bar). Cold Stella (Egyptian beer) is the most popular item on the menu, often ordered alongside an array of seafood mezze—try the calamari. Most evenings an aging oud (lute) player serenades with classic Arabic tunes, adding to the nostalgic air of this Alexandrian gem. Egyptian wine and liquor also served.

BLUE HARBOR ROOF CAFÉ

In Paradise Inn Windsor Palace Hotel, 17 El Shohada St., Raml Station; tel. 03 4801930; reservation@paradiseinnegypt.com; 7:30am-1am daily; 60-150LE mains

With sweeping views of the crescent-shaped harbor, the Windsor Palace's rooftop café is a great place to watch the bustle of the Corniche from above. While the food leaves room for improvement, a range of alcoholic and non-alcoholic beverages are served along with shisha. The pizza and other light snacks are fine in a pinch. For best views, come during the day or for sunset.

Anfushi

★ GREEK CLUB'S OLIVE ISLAND

Qaitbay St., at the Greek Club; tel. 0127 588 8837; 5pm-midnight daily; 150-250LE mains

This hip rooftop lounge next to the sea offers brilliant views of the Citadel and Eastern Harbor. They serve up nice cocktails and great seafood from their sister restaurant downstairs (White and Blue). It's a choice spot for upper-class engagement parties, so call ahead to check for availability. DJs play most weekends (Thurs.-Fri.), and with enough guests it can stay open until 1am.

East Alexandria

THE CIGAR BAR

In Hilton Alexandria Corniche, 544 Corniche Rd.; tel. 03 5490935; 4pm-midnight daily; 90-200LE drinks

Sip on some of Alexandria's best cocktails from stately armchairs strategically positioned around floor-to-ceiling windows looking out to the sea. The beige and brown color scheme is a bit drab, but live music and belly dancing energizes the venue (call ahead to check their schedule). Light meals and snacks are tasty complements to the long menu of drinks and shelves full of imported liquor. Service is superb. Come during happy hour (4pm-6pm) for buy one get one free beers and your best chance at snagging a prime table.

NEO LOUNGE

In Hilton Alexandria Corniche, 544 Corniche Rd.; tel. 03 5490935; 5pm-4am daily; 90-200LE drinks

This cocktail lounge turns into a sports bar when a game is on and a nightclub after 8pm on weekends (Thurs.-Sat.) with neon lights and flashing screens. Each night has a different theme with DJ or live music (you can catch belly dancing on Sat. at 1am and sing karaoke on Mon. at 8pm). Check their Facebook page (@NeoLounge.Alexandria) for full event schedule. Come early any day of the week for happy hour 6pm-7pm (buy one beer get one free). 300LE cover charge or 500LE minimum on weekends.

ACCOMMODATIONS

For such a large city, Alexandria is sorely lacking in the hotel department. If none of these options strike your fancy, check out Airbnb for the occasional catch. As always in Egypt, even at the big international hotels be sure to request a nonsmoking room if that's your preference. Stay Downtown to be close to the sights and buzz of the city, or in East Alex for a quieter stay.

Downtown

PARADISE INN LE METROPOLE HOTEL

52 Saad Zagloul Square, Raml Station; tel. 03 4861465; www.paradiseinnegypt.com; 2,000LE d

Built at the turn of the 20th century, the colonial style Le Metropole—with its tall, gilded ceilings, ornate chandeliers, and friezes of dancing Greek figures—is a good choice for travelers looking for a hotel with a bit of quirk (though not for the minimalists). Unfortunately, management and service could be better, but the location is central and some rooms have nice sea views.

PARADISE INN WINDSOR PALACE HOTEL

17 El Shohada St., Raml Station; tel. 03 4801930; www.paradiseinnegypt.com; 2,500LE d

Another relic from early 20th-century Alexandria, the Windsor Palace Hotel (built in 1906) competes with Le Metropole next door for the title of most ornamented lodging. Ceiling frescoes and Corinthian columns decorate the reception area, and the tall-ceilinged rooms have fabric wall panels, oil paintings, and bronze wall lamps. It's run by the same subpar hospitality group as Le Metropole and could use some renovating. But the location is central and close to the sea, and the rooftop café with prime views of the harbor is a fantastic place to enjoy your complimentary breakfast buffet or wind down in the evening with a drink.

★ STEIGENBERGER CECIL HOTEL

16 Saad Zagloul Square, Raml Station; tel. 03 4877173; www.steigenberger.com; 2,600LE d

This historic hotel from 1929 features in the novels of Naguib Mahfouz and Lawrence Durrell as a favorite haunt of some of their main characters. The art deco flairs, attractive position beside the harbor, and soaring ceilings in all 85 rooms and suites are the highlights. Try to reserve a room on the third floor or above for a bit of a cushion from the Downtown noise and the best sea views. Enjoy your complimentary breakfast buffet in the hotel's French-style café **Le Jardin** (7am-10:30am daily) and a nightcap in its **Monty Bar** (6pm-2am daily). Both open to hotel guests (and their guests) only.

East Alexandria

HILTON ALEXANDRIA CORNICHE

544 Corniche Rd.; tel. 03 5490935; www.hilton.com; 3,200LE d

This Hilton doesn't have much character, but its small pool, private beach, excellent staff, and comfortable (if simple) rooms make it a fine base. Try to stay on a top floor to avoid the traffic noise from the busy Corniche Road. The rooms with sea view have breathtaking balconies. Good Greek and Lebanese restaurants on site along with a couple of nice lounges for evening drinks.

★ FOUR SEASONS HOTEL AT SAN STEFANO

399 Corniche Rd., San Stefano; tel. 03 5818000; www.fourseasons.com; 6,300LE d

If you're not on a budget, the Four Seasons is far and away the nicest hotel in Alexandria. The private beach—in a small bay protected from high waves and connected to the hotel via tunnel—and three pools (one indoors, one on the fourth-floor terrace, and the third filled with saltwater beside the sea) make for a proper Mediterranean getaway. Choose from a handful of quality restaurants serving Italian, Lebanese, or seafood (try the Beach Restaurant & Lounge). Other amenities include a spa and 24-hour fitness center. Upper floors (eight and above) have the best views and quietest rooms. Staff is fantastic, and a wide spread of treats are available at the complimentary breakfast buffet. One major downside is the hotel-wide smoking.

INFORMATION AND SERVICES

TOURIST OFFICE

Saad Zaghloul Sq., Raml Station, Downtown; tel. 03 807985; www.alexandria.gov.eg; 8:30am-3pm daily

This is one of the more helpful tourist offices in Egypt. You can find a nice map of the city and get advice from knowledgeable staff. If you have trouble finding it, go to Saad Zaghloul Square and ask for el-maktab el-siyahi. Another tourist office can be found in the main train station (Mahattat Masr) but is less helpful.

TOURIST POLICE

Saad Zaghloul Sq., Raml Station, Downtown, above Tourist Office; no tel.; 24 hours daily

The Tourist Police station is located directly above the Tourist Office and can help in the case of thefts or safety complaints.

ATMs

ATMs are plentiful in the Downtown area and scattered elsewhere around the city. You shouldn't have trouble finding one, but in the event that you do, head just east of Tahrir Square along Salah Salem Street to find loads.

Pharmacies

EL EZABY

Southwest corner of Alexandria Railway Station, Downtown; tel. 19600; www.elezabypharmacy.com; 24 hours daily

The nationwide El Ezaby chain is a solid pharmacy that offers 24/7 delivery. Additional locations include: 2 Talaat St., San Stefeno; 41 Alexander the Great St., Azarita; and in the Sidi Gaber train station.

SEIF PHARMACIES

22 El Nabi Daniel St., Raml Station, Downtown; tel. 19199; 8am-11pm daily

Seif is another reputable pharmacy with multiple locations around the city that offer delivery 24/7.

GETTING THERE

Alexandria is an easy day trip from Cairo, especially with a private car. The train is also a comfortable, scenic, and relatively quick way (on the fast service) to get between Egypt's first and second cities. It doesn't really make sense to fly as wait time and travel to/from airports will likely make the trip at least as long as driving, and likely longer.

Air

BORG EL-ARAB INTERNATIONAL AIRPORT (HBE)

50 km/30 mi southwest of Downtown Alexandria; tel. 03 4591484; www.borg-el-arab.airport-authority.com; 24 hours daily

Travelers from Cairo by air will arrive at the Borg el-Arab International Airport (HBE) in around 45 minutes from lift-off. Prices are around 3,100LE round-trip. Taxi to/from Downtown Alexandria should be in the neighborhood of 250LE (50 km/30 mi; 50 minutes).

Train

The main Alexandria Railway Station, locally known as **Mahattat Masr** (Egypt Station) (Kom el-Dekka; tel. 02 25748279; www.enr.gov.eg; 24 hours daily), is located in the city center. Alexandria's **Sidi Gaber Train Station** (Sidi Gaber; 5 km/3 mi east of Masr Station) is a good option for visitors staying in East Alexandria (e.g., the Four Seasons or Hilton).

Trains take 3-3.5 hours to/from Cairo with prices for first class 53-104LE depending on the number of stops between Cairo and Alexandria. Trains depart from Ramses Station in Cairo usually starting at 6am and around once per hour 8am-10pm. The nicest and fastest train is the "Special Service," which typically leaves at 8am. Return trains leave from Masr Station around every hour 6am-10pm daily.

Bus

Alexandria's main bus station, called el-Mowqif el-Gadid (Moharram Bek; no tel.; 24 hours daily) is located 5 kilometers (3 mi) south of the Alexandria Railway Station (Mahattat Masr). **Go Bus** (tel. 19567; www.go-bus.com), **Blue Bus** (tel. 16128; www.bluebus.com.eg), **Super Jet** (tel. 02 22909013; www.superjet.com.eg), and **West & Mid Delta Bus Company** (tel. 02 25752157) all leave from this area. All buses from Cairo also arrive here. Blue Bus or Go Bus are best.

From Cairo, Go Bus leaves from Abdel Minam Riyad Square (near Tahrir Square), Blue Bus leaves from Ramses Square (in front of the Coptic Hospital), and West & Mid Delta from Torgoman Station (el-Sahafa St., near Downtown). Prices are in the range of 100LE one-way (3-3.5 hours).

Private Car Hire

With a private car you should be able to reach Alexandria from Cairo in around 2.5-3 hours depending on traffic. **Ibrahim el-Sheemy** (tel. 0122 487 8427; $120 to/from Cairo and a full day in Alexandria) has been driving people around Egypt in comfort for decades. **Moamen Khedr** (tel. 0122 362 3032; moamen_lancer@yahoo.com; $100 to/from Cairo and a full day in Alexandria) is another expert driver. Both are best reached by phone or WhatsApp.

GETTING AROUND

With the exception of the Montazah Palace Gardens, most points of interest are concentrated in the Downtown area. Transportation from sight to sight should be relatively quick (5-20 minutes) by taxi/Uber.

Taxi

Taxis are plentiful around the city. Meters haven't made their way to Alexandria, but a 10-20-minute trip generally costs around 15-30LE. Be sure to agree on a price before you get in. **Ubers** are an excellent way to get around if you don't want to think about prices (as long as you have access to phone data). They end up costing about the same price as taxis.

Microbus

Microbuses are a great option for traveling long distances along the Corniche (e.g., from Saad Zaghloul Square to Montazah). Just flag one down and expect to pay 2-6LE. For microbuses to other parts of the city, head to the main microbus station is called el-Mow'if el-Gadid (Moharram Bek; 5 km/3 mi south of city center).

Vicinity of Alexandria

Outside of Alexandria proper there are a couple of noteworthy destinations, visited on easy day trips from the city center. Ottoman-era lovers will enjoy a few hours in Rashid (Rosetta) and World War II buffs won't want to miss el Alamein. Both are less than two hours from Alexandria: Rashid to the east and el Alamein to the west.

RASHID (ROSETTA)

Inhabited since at least 3000 BC, Rashid (known as Khito by ancient Egyptians and Rosetta by Europeans) didn't become a city of significance until the Ottomans took Egypt in 1517 and turned the dual Nile and seaside village into a central trading port with Constantinople. By the mid-18th century, Rashid had far surpassed Alexandria as the main city in the north, with its population nearly three times that of its neighbor. (Alexandria had been suffering from tainted water supply accompanied by reoccurring epidemics and its residents had dwindled to only around 5,000.)

But with the opening of Mohammed Ali's Mahmudiya Canal in 1820—reconnecting Alexandria to the Nile—Alexander the Great's brainchild was back on track to become the favored coastal city, marking the start of Rashid's decline. The opening of the Suez Canal in Port Said (1869) accelerated Rashid's fall from grace as Egypt's favorite port city.

Today Rashid is a sleepy agricultural and fishing village with some great examples of 16th- to early 19th-century Ottoman townhouses and an impressive Mamluk-era fort where the famed Rosetta Stone was discovered. Many of the some two dozen old houses are closed for renovation, but they can often be accessed before 4pm for a bit of baksheesh (tips). Visitors can enjoy these parts as a quick day trip from Alexandria—just 65 kilometers (40 mi; 1 hour) away.

Sights

Make the Rashid Museum your first stop in Rashid, as staff here should be able to direct you to the other sights.

RASHID MUSEUM

El-Hurraya Square, El-Geish St.; tel. 045 2921733; 9am-4pm Sat.-Thurs.; 40LE adults, 20LE students

Housed in a beautifully renovated Ottoman villa from the early 18th century, the Rashid Museum offers a glimpse into how the city's wealthy once lived. The exterior is made of traditional red and black bricks, while inside you'll find fine samples of furniture, carpets, tiles, and mashrabiya (wooden latticework). On the ground floor you can visit a replica of the Rosetta Stone beside a bust of the French scholar who deciphered it, Jean-François Champollion.

AL-AMASYALI HOUSE

On corner of al-Tubgi St. and al-Amasyali St.; no tel.; 9am-5pm daily; 15LE adults, 10LE students

Built in 1808 by an officer in the Turkish army, Uthman Agha al-Tubgi, this spacious Ottoman-style townhouse provides a good example of accommodation for Rashid's well-to-do. What the house lacks in furnishing it makes up for in its stunning ceilings, delicate mashrabiya, and clever cooling system with thick walls to keep out the heat punctuated by strategically placed windows to let in the breeze. As with most wealthy homes during this period, the ground floor was used for business and storage, the first floor for entertaining male guests, and the second a space where women could see without being seen.

ABU SHAHEEN MILL

Beside al-Amasyali House; no tel.; 9am-5pm daily; entrance included with al-Amasyali House ticket

The officer who built al-Amasyali House had this mill constructed in the late 18th century. Donkeys once walked in endless circumambulation here to grind the city's grain into flour. A wooden mill supported by wooden beams still stands in the center (sans donkey) and gives a sense of how the process worked. Like the other old houses, locally made bricks dominate the visual space in classic Delta style with alternating red and black. If you have trouble finding, ask for Tahonat Abu Shaheen.

DUMAQSIS MOSQUE

400 m/1,300 ft south of Rashid Museum; 24 hours daily; free

Completed in 1704, the Mosque of Salih Agha Dumaqsis is also known as the Hanging Mosque (el-Masgid el-Moa'llaq) for its rare elevation (built on top of a row of old shops and storage rooms that line the ground floor). The entrance can be found at the top of a set of stairs and the interior still holds some original Ottoman tiles—a classic mix of organic and geometric shapes—and a beautiful wood-paneled ceiling.

CORNICHE

El-Bahr El-A'zam St.

Rashid's delightful palm-lined promenade along the Nile is a favorite spot for walks and picnics. It starts near Abbasi Mosque (Masgid el-Abbasi) and continues north for about a mile. The litter is an unfortunate feature, but if you keep your eyes focused on the charming fishing boats bobbing along the shore, you can almost forget it's there.

FORT OF QAITBAY

El-Bahr El-A'zam St., 8 km/5 mi north of central Rashid along the Nile; no tel.; 9am-4pm daily; 40LE adults, 20LE students

Built in 1479 by Sultan Qaitbay (of Alexandria's citadel) and renovated by the French during Napoleon's campaign in Egypt, this strategic fort guarded the entrance to the Nile from seafaring ships. It was known as Fort Julien by the French when they set up camp here in 1799 and discovered the legendary Rosetta Stone. Other reused stones from pharaonic Egypt are still visible throughout the structure, with occasional splashes of hieroglyphics as accidental décor. Don't miss the stunning views from the roof of where the river meets the sea. The 15-minute drive here from central Rashid—through the shipyards and brick factories—is also a delight. (about 35LE one-way for taxi to fort from central Rashid).

Getting There and Around

Rashid is just 65 kilometers (40 mi) east (1 hour) of Alexandria's city center, and 240 kilometers (150 mi) northwest (3.5 hours) of Cairo. The shortest route to Rashid from Cairo passes through Alex, so it's better to combine the two trips. Private car hire, taxi, or Uber are the best ways to get to (and from) these parts without fear of being stranded.

PRIVATE CAR HIRE

Ibrahim el-Sheemy (tel. 0122 487 8427; $120 to/from Cairo and a full day in Alexandria) and **Moamen Khedr** (tel. 0122 362 3032; moamen_lancer@yahoo.com; $100 to/from Cairo and a full day in Alexandria) are both highly experienced drivers with comfortable cars based in Cairo. If you choose to visit Alexandria and its surroundings as a day trip from Cairo, you can add a side trip to Rosetta (Rashid) from Alexandria for an additional $20 or so. Be sure to agree on a full plan and price ahead of time with the driver. Both are best contacted via WhatsApp.

Local tour guide **Nancy Yousef** (tel. 0122 457 1872; guide_nancy@hotmail.com; 400LE half day, 800LE full day) can also organize transportation to/from Alexandria if you take her private tour. For a private car hire to Rashid from Alexandria sans guide, ask your hotel to arrange (although taxi or Uber will likely be cheaper).

TAXI AND UBER

If you opt to take a taxi, be sure to negotiate a price for a return trip ahead of time. A round trip from Alexandria should cost around 600-700LE (including waiting and transportation around Rashid). Most Uber drivers will also

The Rosetta Stone

In 1799, soldiers of Napoleon's army stumbled across a broken slab covered in text while they were digging an extension to Qaitbay's Fort in Rosetta. For the Mamluk sultan's 15th-century builders, what would come to be known as the iconic Rosetta Stone was just another chunk of rock suitable for construction of a sturdy wall. Little did they know it held the key to deciphering nearly 4,000 years of Egyptian history.

The Rosetta Stone's decree, written in 196 BC by a council of priests, declares 13-year-old Ptolemy V divine king—bestowing the honor in exchange for an increase in stipends and a tax break. A number of these stelae were distributed to temples around Egypt. What made this one such a find was the repetition of a single text in three scripts: Greek, hieroglyphics, and Demotic (an Egyptian script that emerged long after hieroglyphics and was used for administrative, but not religious, writings). While the knowledge of hieroglyphics had disappeared around the end of the 4th century AD, plenty of scholars could still read ancient Greek. And so the unassuming stone became an essential tool for translating the wealth of ancient Egyptians' records.

The British scooped up the treasure after helping expel the French from Egypt in 1801, but it would be a French scholar (Jean-François Champollion) who finally cracked the complex set of symbolic and phonetic hieroglyphic marks some 20 years later. The original stone has been housed in the British Museum since 1802, though visitors to Rashid (Rosetta) can check out a replica at the Rashid Museum.

bring you to Rashid from Alex. Expect to pay 600-800LE return (again, including wait time and transportation around Rashid).

MICROBUS

Microbuses are by far the cheapest and most authentic option, if not the quickest or most comfortable. They leave Alexandria (1 hour; 15LE) on a rolling basis from the main microbus station (El-Mow'if El-Gadid, Moharram Bek) and will drop you off around 3 kilometers (2 mi) south of central Rashid. From there you can grab a taxi to the center for around 10LE.

EL ALAMEIN

Around 115 kilometers (70 mi; 1.5 hours) west of central Alexandria, el Alamein was the site of two significant World War II battles between British-led Allied troops and Axis armies commanded by one of Hitler's favorite generals, Erwin Rommel. "The Desert Fox," as he was known, had plans to seize the strategic Suez Canal, but only made it as far as Alamein before the Allied forces managed to push his troops out of Egypt, all the way across Libya to Tunisia. The battles led to the German surrender in North Africa and Allied control of the Mediterranean. The few sights of interest in Alamein pay homage to the soldiers who fought here.

Nearby along the coast, the government has poured billions of dollars into constructing "New Alamein City" to become a year-round hub for tourism and other industries. It was scheduled to open in June 2020, but it doesn't look like construction will be finished for at least a few more years.

Sights

EL ALAMEIN MILITARY MUSEUM

El Mathaf el Harby St., off Alexandria-Matruh Rd.; tel. 046 4100021; 9am-4pm daily; 100LE adults, 50LE students

The display cases at this museum dedicated to the battles of Alamein look a bit like an elementary school history fair (plus a few weapons and full-size dioramas of life on the frontlines). But you will find some interesting information about the battles and the international troops who fought in them.

Tanks, planes, and anti-aircraft guns decorate the garden around the museum—possibly the highlight (or second only to the crazed-looking statues inside). One of the planes (a Kittyhawk P-40) was discovered in 2012 during an oil expedition in the Western Desert after 70 years of disappearance. British authorities hoped it would be sent back to the UK to be preserved as is, but instead the relic remained in Alamein and was given what aviation historians describe as a grotesque makeover (look for the shiny plane with the shark teeth and red nose). The museum closes noon-1pm Fridays.

EL ALAMEIN WAR CEMETERY

850 m/2,800 ft south of the El Alamein Military Museum; no tel.; enquiries@cwgc.org; 7am-2:30pm daily; free

Over 7,300 fallen Allied soldiers from the WWII Western Desert campaigns lie buried in this stark patch of desert spotted with well-manicured flora and rows of matching tombstones. In the southeast corner a **cremation memorial** remembers another 600-plus soldiers, and thousands more whose bodies weren't recovered are honored at the cemetery entrance. Access is not guaranteed after 2:30pm, but you might be able to convince security to let you in before 5pm.

Getting There and Around

El Alamein is around 115 kilometers (70 mi) west of central Alexandria (about 1.5 hours by car).

PRIVATE CAR HIRE

Ibrahim el-Sheemy (tel. 0122 487 8427) and **Moamen Khedr** (tel. 0122 362 3032; moamen_lancer@yahoo.com) are well-acquainted with this route and can offer a day trip from Cairo to Alexandria with a side trip to Alamein for $120-150 round-trip. WhatsApp is the best way to contact them.

Alexandrian tour guide **Nancy Yousef** (tel. 0122 457 1872; guide_nancy@hotmail.com; 400LE half day tour, 800LE full day) can also organize transportation (around 1,200LE for driver for the day around Alexandria and Alamein) if you take her private tour.

TAXI

Be sure to negotiate a price for a return trip ahead of time. It should cost around 700-800LE round trip from central Alexandria (Saad Zaghloul Square) depending on wait time.

BUS

Bus is the most economical way to get to Alamein, but not the most convenient. You can take a **Go Bus** (tel. 19567; www.go-bus.com; 2 hours; 80LE one-way) from Alexandria's main bus station (El-Mow'if El-Gadid, Moharram Bek) to their station called "Marina 7," located just a 10-minute walk to El Alamein War Museum and 15-20 minutes to the War Cemetery. During summer (June-Aug.), a bus usually leaves around 7am every day and returns to Alexandria at 3pm from the same place where they drop you off. Be sure to reserve a round-trip ticket online or at the station.

Outside high season, you should be able to find a bus heading to Marsa Matruh and get out along the way, but return to Alexandria might be trickier. Taxis are not easily found in these parts, so best not to rely on them. Double check at the bus station to see what your options are as schedules during low season are always changing.

Port Said and the Suez Canal

Founded in 1859 to cater to the coming Suez Canal, the city of Port Said was built on an unlikely strip of sand running between the Mediterranean Sea and the shallow, brackish Lake Manzala. Workers hauled in mud, sand, and stones to create a suitable foundation for the city that would blossom into a booming entrepôt around the mouth of the canal.

French diplomat Ferdinand de Lesseps broke ground (symbolically) on the new city of Port Said, and then put the pickaxe down while laborers built a single row of huts on the beach and got digging. Thus, Port Said was born—a construction camp for the waterway that would link East to West.

These days, the destruction wrought by three wars and the wear of time have left Port Said's early architecture looking a bit tired, and the black waves that lap the shore bear little resemblance to the turquoise blues farther west. But with its wide boulevards, towering supertankers, and historic passageway between the seas, this north coast city is worth a visit.

HISTORY

Said Pasha (1822-1863)—son of Mohammed Ali and by 1854 viceroy of Egypt—granted his childhood friend, Ferdinand de Lesseps, permission to build the **Suez Canal** after the latter became obsessed with the idea. The historic shortcut connecting the Mediterranean to the Red Sea was finally finished in 1869, saving ships nearly three weeks for travel between Europe and Asia.

Though the British vehemently opposed construction of the canal, preferring instead to use railway networks for trade and travel, they ultimately benefited more than any other nation. Their ships made up some 80 percent of traffic during the first 10 years of the waterway's operation. The British government also became the largest single shareholder in the canal in 1875 when Ismail Pasha, Said's successor as viceroy of Egypt, sold them Egypt's 44 percent of shares in the Canal Company (after running into financial troubles). To protect its investment, the Empire did what it had done for centuries: British troops occupied the strategic outpost in 1882, where they remained for the next 74 years.

Port Said was cosmopolitan from the beginning, but by 1899 Europeans outnumbered Egyptians—the latter making up just under half the population of 49,000. Until the late 1940s, the rugged port city was known for its bars and international brothels with women coming from around Europe to cater to the flow of visitors, lonely sailors, and British soldiers. In 1911, with the population of Port Said booming, the Canal Company built Port Fouad across the waterway (today, a neighborhood of its older sister) with workshops and elegant villas for its mostly European staff.

By 1956—with a strong nationalist movement coursing through the country and Mohammed Ali's royal descendants ousted from power—Port Said was in for the largest transformation it'd seen since the city sprang from the sand nearly a century earlier. On July 26, military officer-turned-president Gamal Abdel Nasser nationalized the canal. He promised that erstwhile British and French owners would be compensated for their shares, but before the details could be sorted the European pair launched an attack.

Israel, which had been a key part of the secret scheme—later known as the Suez Crisis or Tripartite Aggression—charged across the Sinai to provide pretext for a British and French invasion to "protect" the strategic waterway. Before landing on the shores, the Brits rocked Port Said with aerial bombardments, leveling parts of the city. Opposition to the war by the US and United Nations (UN) forced a withdrawal, and Port Said became the first city to welcome the UN's newly established peacekeeping troops.

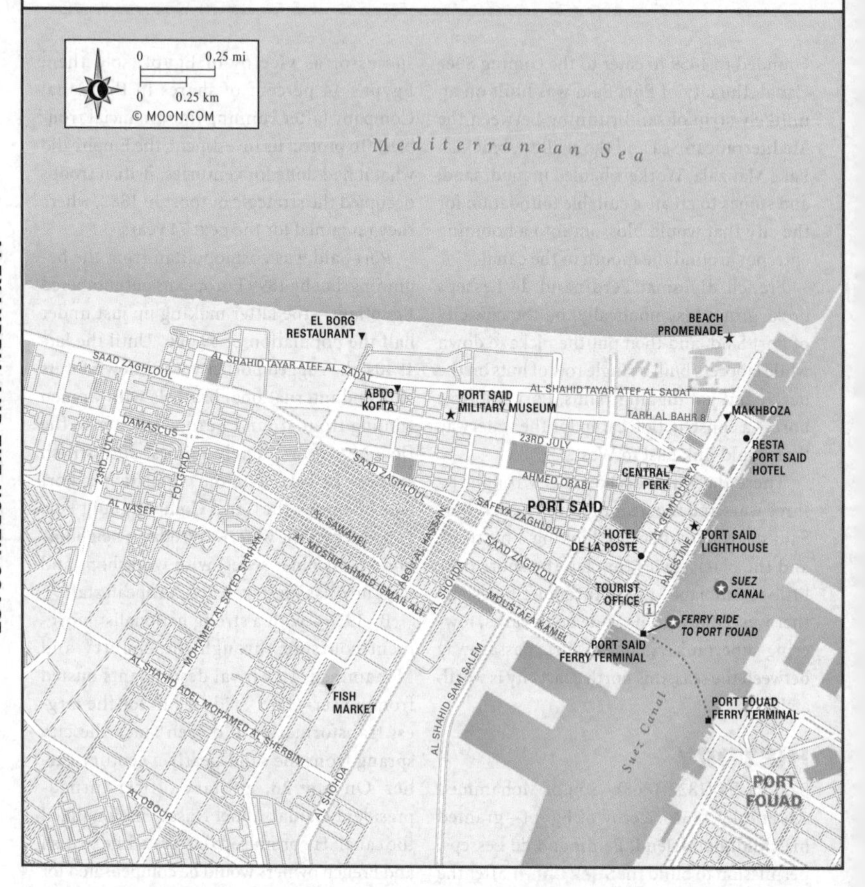

Israel would be back just over a decade later to occupy Port Fouad after its victory in the 1967 War. In 1973, the Egyptian military crossed the canal in a surprise attack, ultimately resulting in the return of the waterway and its cities. After the mines and other booby traps were removed from the canal, the 15 unfortunate ships that had been languishing in the isthmus for eight years could finally leave (so much for a shortcut!).

To entice people back to war-torn Port Said, the government granted the city a duty-free status in 1975. People came in large numbers—both Port Said natives and other Egyptians looking to take advantage of the resettlement incentives—opening profitable shops filled will products flowing into the port sans customs. Over the next few decades, Port Said's markets became a shopping mecca for Egyptians from around the country who could buy everything from car parts to jeans and packaged food at a steal, until the government revoked the city's special status in 2002.

SIGHTS

★ Suez Canal

Central Port Said; 24 hours daily; free

Running for 164 kilometers (102 mi) between

Early Canal Attempts

The idea of building a canal connecting the Mediterranean to the Red Sea has been around for millennia:

- **Ancient Egyptians** attempted to construct a canal from the Nile to the Bitter Lakes and down to the Red Sea (and possibly succeeded) as early as early as 1850 BC. Subsequent efforts throughout the centuries by other Egyptian pharaohs, the Ptolemies, and the Romans all ultimately resulted in a victory for nature, with sand clogging the waterways and rendering them useless.
- **Napoleon,** after invading Egypt in 1798, was the first on record to investigate a different kind of canal. In all of the earlier projects, the northern leg of the of the journey proceeded up the Nile and into the Mediterranean. Instead, Napoleon wanted to link the two seas directly through the Isthmus of Suez. Poor calculations by Napoleon's engineers convinced the future French emperor that the task would be too difficult even for him—the man out to conquer all of Europe and beyond. Their reports suggested, erroneously, that the Red Sea sat at a higher level than the Mediterranean, making the project too messy an undertaking.
- It would be another 32 years before **Ferdinand de Lesseps,** while preoccupying himself in quarantine in Alexandria, picked up the abandoned plans. De Lesseps's obsession marinated for another 23 years until his friend, Said Pasha, assumed the reins of power in Egypt. And the rest is history.

the Egyptian mainland and Sinai Peninsula, the Suez Canal was an epic undertaking. An estimated 1.5 million people worked on the waterway over the decade it took to complete. Tens of thousands of Egyptian peasants—made to dig with basic tools under harsh conditions—died from disease, injuries, and even hunger before Ismail Pasha, then viceroy of Egypt, banned the use of forced labor. To finish the work, de Lesseps and the Suez Canal Company had their engineers design new technology powered by steam and coal.

In 2015, President Sisi built a second lane along part of the canal to much fanfare—proclaiming it "Egypt's gift to the world." But with traffic through the waterway waning in recent years, the $8.5 billion project has so far been more successful at creating an excuse for a party than boosting Egypt's revenues. Unfortunately, the second lane didn't run alongside the section of the canal that was blocked for nearly a week when one of the world's largest container ships got stuck in March 2021, disrupting the flow of global trade for many months to follow.

Though the canal also runs through Ismailia and Suez, Port Said is the most dramatic venue to view the engineering marvel. Here you can watch the ships sweep in from the Mediterranean, while you stand in the city built to welcome them.

The **Canal Promenade** (Shokri al Kowalti St.) is a raised pedestrian pathway that follows the canal for 1 kilometer (0.6 mi). It's an excellent place to stroll and see the canal. The promenade's northern end is marked by a statue-less plinth that once held a smug de Lesseps, welcoming ships through the waterway. Egyptians toppled the monument after the attack by the UK, France, and Israel in 1956 and it has stood empty ever since. The path ends in the south at the ferry landing that will bring you across the canal to Port Fouad.

Beach Promenade

Starts at Al Gomhoriya St. on the corner of the canal and the sea

Running for around 5 kilometers (3 mi) along the beach (and perpendicular to the Canal), this paved pedestrian path is a pleasant place for a stroll. Begin a tour of town on the promenade to watch the fishermen drag in their nets, or if you prefer the feel of sand between your toes, hop onto the beach that follows the entire north coast of Port Said. Locals enjoy picnicking and swimming here—though the latter isn't recommended due to the pollution from the ships coming through the canal.

Port Said Lighthouse

Al Taef St. and Shokri Al Kowalti St.; 24 hours daily; free

As the inauguration of the Suez Canal approached in 1869, French sculptor Frédéric-Auguste Bartholdi rolled out an idea for a statue called "Egypt Bringing Light to Asia" to stand at its entrance. He envisioned a woman dressed in Egyptian peasant garb holding a torch to guide ships to the waterway. The idea never caught on in Port Said, but nearly 20 years later Bartholdi found a new home for his creation, unveiling "Liberty Enlightening the World" (the Statue of Liberty) in New York Harbor.

Instead of Lady Liberty, Port Said got this 56-meter-tall (185-ft-tall) lighthouse, the first structure ever built of reinforced concrete. Completed just before the canal's inauguration, it's the city's the only still-surviving original landmark. The octagonal column once stood on the edge of the shore, but after years of landfill expansion toward the sea it's now found nearly a kilometer inland. When still in use, the beaming light on top could be seen 30 kilometers (20 mi) away at night—perhaps not as iconic as New York's torch-holder, but it got the job done.

You can't enter the lighthouse, but you can get a nice view from the raised Canal Promenade.

Port Said Military Museum

23 of July St.; 10am-3pm Sat.-Thurs.; 50LE adults, 25LE students

For a city devastated by three wars (1956, 1967, and 1973), Port Said is a natural host for a military museum. Paintings and dioramas show key battle scenes that took place along the canal. Outside, the lawn is spotted with military hardware like US-made Israeli tanks captured during the 1973 War. Around 30 minutes should be enough time for a visit.

★ FERRY RIDE TO PORT FOUAD

Corner of Filistine St. and Abdel Minam Riyad St., 600 m/2,000 ft south of the Port Said Lighthouse; free

Cross the historic Suez Canal on a free ferry between Africa and Asia—more specifically, to the neighborhood of Port Fouad. Flitting seagulls and passing ships make for a picturesque ride. On your way over, keep an eye out for the **Suez Canal House** (located around 200 m/650 ft south of where you board the ferry) designed by a French architect in the 1890s. The regal building with white arcades and three pastel green domes served as the headquarters of the Suez Canal Company. Once you reach Port Fouad, the main attractions are the early 20th-century red-roofed villas that line many of the streets and a public beach with a row of modest coffee shops (2 km/1 mi southeast of the ferry landing).

Ferries leave every 5-10 minutes and get you across in around the same amount of time. They run 24/7.

FOOD

Like most of its Mediterranean neighbors, Port Said is famous for its seafood (prawns in particular). To sample a favorite local specialty, try sayadiyah—a kind of white fish casserole cooked in yellow rice, tomatoes, and onions.

For a cold beer or a glass of wine, head to the **Resta Port Said Hotel** where you can enjoy your beverage on a sprawling patio with a view of the canal.

Egyptian

ABDO KOFTA

7 el Shahid Atef el Sadat St.; tel. 0106 648 4848; 11am-1am daily; 70-120LE mains

When it comes to classic Egyptian dishes,

1: ship entering the Suez Canal **2:** Port Said Lighthouse **3:** Suez Canal House **4:** Port Said Canal Promenade

ARKAS
1
2
3

4

Abdo Kofta is unrivaled in Port Said. Succulent meats are their specialty—particularly, you guessed it, the kofta (spiced sticks of ground beef or lamb). The large windows make for nice natural lighting during the day, and the rare no-smoking policy keeps the air clean.

Seafood

FISH MARKET

El Sabah St.; no tel.; 7am-2pm daily; 40-90LE mains

The long rows of stalls at this covered market all sell only one thing: the catch of the day. After making your fresh seafood selection, find a station with a grill where they'll cook it up (15-20LE) with your choice of seasoning. Grab some seating there or head to the beach for a picnic. Come early for the best options. Floors can be slippery so step with care.

EL BORG RESTAURANT

Tarh el Bahr St., Beach Plaza Restaurant Complex; tel. 066 3323442; 24 hours daily; 80-120LE mains

This local favorite has the ambiance of a warehouse but serves up some fine dishes. Plastic tablecloths mean you don't have to worry about making a mess as you indulge in Port Said's famous prawns, shrimp, and other seafood delights. The outdoor seating is a perfect venue to watch people stroll along the beachside promenade while enjoying your meal with a touch of sea breeze.

Cafés and Snacks

CENTRAL PERK

El Gomhoreya St., Al-Masryeen Tower, Port Fouad; tel. 066 3411131; 8am-2am daily; 20-40LE hot drinks

The owners of Egypt's Central Perk did their best to imitate the iconic hangout of *Friends*... twice. With a branch in downtown Port Said (23rd of July St.) and another in Port Fouad, the café draws in nostalgic Port Saidians looking to watch reruns of the sitcom with a good cup of coffee and a sweet dessert named after their favorite character. Pleasant street-side seating also available.

MAKHBOZA

El Gomhoreya St., in front of El Salam Mosque; tel. 0109 200 2212; 10am-2am daily; 35-130LE

This trendy fateer shop serves all types of "Egyptian pizzas"—flaky pastries filled with sweet or savory fillings, from seafood to sliced hot dogs or honey and ishta (clotted cream). Enjoy your snacks in the colorful interior or snag a seat outside.

ACCOMMODATIONS

Port Said hasn't been an international destination for decades (save for passing ships), and the hotel options reflect that. The few decent outposts are overpriced and unimpressive. But the city is only around three hours from Cairo, making it an easy day trip. If you do wish to stay the night, these are your best bets.

HOTEL DE LA POSTE

42 El-Gomhoreya St.; tel. 066 3224048; 750LE d

Bare bones but clean, this historic hotel has lived through a lot. The wooden floors and lofty ceilings still provide a whiff of its early appeal, when visitors came here from around the world to rest their heads and dine under soaring arcades in the once-posh café downstairs. On the upside, staff are helpful and the location convenient—just around the corner from the canal and Port Fouad ferry. Basic breakfast included.

RESTA PORT SAID HOTEL

Filistine St.; tel. 066 3200511; reservations.portsaid@restahotels.com; 2,000LE d

Visitors who come to Port Said for the water will love this spot—right where the Mediterranean pours into the canal. From the sea-facing rooms, it feels like you're on a ship anchored in the harbor. The hotel itself could use an upgrade, but things are generally clean and beds are comfortable. If you're not happy with your room, don't be shy to ask for another (some are newly renovated, others not). There's a pool (though not always sparkling clean) surrounded by a sprawling patio with tables and chairs—a nice perch to watch the ships come in. Breakfast included.

INFORMATION AND SERVICES

Tourist Office

8 Filistine St.; tel. 066 3235289; 10am-7pm Sat.-Thurs.

The friendly staff here will do their best to answer questions and can offer a nice map of town.

Pharmacies

El Ezaby Pharmacy (tel. 19600; www.elezabypharmacy.com; 24 hours daily) and **Roshdy Pharmacies** (tel. 19011; 24 hours daily) are both reputable pharmacies with multiple branches around Port Said. They deliver anywhere in the city 24/7.

GETTING THERE

Bus or private car hire are your best options for making the trip to Port Said. Trains also trundle along from Cairo but stop frequently and are in need of an update.

BUS

Go Bus (tel. 19567; www.go-bus.com) takes nearly a dozen trips daily each way between Downtown **Cairo** (Abdel Minam Square, next to Ramsis Hilton) and Port Said Station (Masaken Mubarak, 3 km/2 mi south of central Port Said). The ride is 3.5-4 hours with a fare of 65-120LE depending on bus class. From **Alexandria** (Moharram Bek Station), a morning and afternoon bus head to Port Said Station each day (4-4.5 hours; 85LE).

The government-run **East Delta Bus Co.** (no tel.) also shuttles between Cairo (Torgoman Station in Downtown) or Alexandria (Moharram Bek Station) and Port Said Station just about every hour, but their buses could be cleaner. Use as a last resort.

PRIVATE CAR HIRE

A car ride to Port Said from Cairo only takes around 2.5-3 hours depending on traffic. **Ibrahim el-Sheemy** (tel. 0122 487 8427; $120 round-trip) is a kind and experienced driver who can escort visitors around Port Said on a nice day trip. Best contacted via WhatsApp or phone.

GETTING AROUND

With its wide lanes and watery borders, Port Said is a pleasant city to navigate on foot. For quicker transportation, white and baby-blue **taxis** cruise around the city. Most trips around town should cost 10-15LE.

Sidi Abdel Rahman

When Egyptians talk about the North Coast (or el-Sahel as its popularly known), they're usually referring to this 35-kilometer (22-mi) strip of seaside—lined with resort compounds that house pristine, bikini-friendly beaches. With fine white sand and turquoise waters, it's little wonder the Egyptian elite claimed this spot for their summer playground. But these luxuries come at a high cost, and unless you have a friend with a chalet expect to pay European resort prices (and up). Most facilities only operate from the start of June to end of August.

Locals in search of nightlife will often grab an Uber or private car to party-hop between clubs or parties. But visitors might find it easier to choose their compound wisely and stay put.

FOOD AND ACCOMMODATIONS

The nicest resort towns are **Hacienda Bay, Marassi, Hacienda/Hacienda White, Telal,** and **Ghazala Bay.** Check on **Airbnb** and Booking.com for private rentals in these compounds for more economical options compared to the high-end hotels available. Most of the restaurants are located within the compounds and only accessible to residents and their guests. The exceptions are two food courts/malls on the edge of the compounds near the main highway that are open to all. Both **Lake Yard** (next to Hacienda Bay, Alexandria-Matrouh Rd.; tel. 00101 096 9870; 5pm-2am daily) and **M-Porium** (next to Marassi, 129 Alexandria-Matrouh Rd.; tel. 0122 439 8511; 9am-4am daily) are favorite hangout spots with several Western-style cafés, restaurants, and shops.

Marassi

EL ALAMEIN HOTEL

Kilo 129, Alexandria-Matruh Rd., Marassi; tel. 046 4680140; www.alalameinhotel.com; 8,300LE d

This super stylish resort stretches along a prime patch of sea in the upscale Marassi compound. The immaculate beach is the uncontested highlight, but the swimming pool with sea view and superb staff add to the experience. Jet skiing, parasailing, kayaking, and more are available. Visitors who can pull themselves away from the turquoise waters can also opt for a bike ride, round of tennis, or day at the spa. The hotel is kid friendly and open year-round (low season offers excellent discounts but isn't the best for swimming). For the best food, check out the hotel's open-air **Beach Grill** (tel. 0101 111 1714; 10am-2am daily) that serves fresh seafood and Lebanese treats, or **The Smokery** (just after the Marassi compound entrance; tel. 0102 601 9175; www.thesmokery.net; 6pm-3am daily; 90-350LE drinks)—a floating restaurant and bar on a lagoon with good cocktails, wine, smoked salmon, and sushi.

Hacienda/Hacienda White

★ MAZEEJ HOTEL

Hacienda White; tel. 0101 911 8199; www.mazeejhotels.com; 6,000LE d

The 38 rooms and suites at this boutique hotel surround a glowing blue lagoon, with a beautiful beach just a stone's throw away. Each deluxe cabana has unique décor (in the same ultra-chic style), with supremely comfortable beds. As an adults-only resort, Mazeej caters mostly to 20-40-somethings looking to relax by the sea or enjoy the nightlife of their hip venue, **Kiki's Beach Bar** (1pm-7pm and 10pm-3am daily; 80-350LE drinks), host to live music events and much-loved DJs. The hotel's main restaurant, **Sho.ku.ku** (10am-midnight daily; 150-400LE mains), prides itself as being a "gastronomical experience" and offers Egyptian food with a Mediterranean fusion flair.

The hotel is located within the swank Hacienda White compound (connected to the Hacienda compound), which also offers a variety of food options with some favorites including **The BRGR Truck** (Hacienda; 10am-9pm Sat.-Wed. and 10am-4am Thurs.-Fri.; 60-80LE mains) and healthy food from **Be Good to You** (Hacienda; tel. 0128 085 0607; www.begoodtoyoueg.com; 10am-midnight daily; 200-250LE mains).

Ghazala Bay

RIXOS ALAMEIN

Ghazala Bay Village; tel. 0110 000 0244; www.alamein.rixos.com; 3,500LE d

This sprawling resort with nearly 250 rooms and suites has two enormous outdoor swimming pools (along with a few smaller ones), an indoor pool in a faux stalactite cave, and a beautiful beach lined with lounge chairs and umbrellas. Other amenities include a spa, tennis courts, play areas for kids, and seaside bars. For dining, chose from one of their three main restaurants serving seafood, Lebanese, or international fusion. The rooms aren't as sleek as some of the other North Coast hotels, but they're clean and comfortable—all with either a pool or sea view.

BARS AND NIGHTLIFE

El-Sahel is synonymous with summer nightlife in Egypt. Many of these venues serve as restaurants by day and continue late into the night with DJs and dancing. Unlike most regular restaurants, bars and clubs can be accessed by non-compound guests with advanced reservation (required).

1: The BRGR Truck **2:** Mazeej Hotel

BRGR
BRGR
1
2

Hacienda Bay

IVORY

Next to Hacienda Bay, along Alexandria-Matrouh Rd.; tel. 0122 456 6666; 7pm-4am daily; 100-350LE drinks

This sizeable nightclub looks like a small open-air stadium with multiple tiers of standing tables surrounding a center stage where live music, belly dancers, or DJs perform nightly. The venue prides itself on its elaborate lighting and pyrotechnics. Call ahead for events schedule and reservations.

Marassi

LEMON TREE & CO.

In Marassi; tel. 0112 163 3666; info@thelemontree.co; 2pm-3am daily; 80-350LE drinks

Cairo's high-end restaurant and bar made its way to the North Coast with the same Instagram-able dishes and drinks, plus an added soundtrack of crashing waves. Fairy lights and sheer white curtains decorate the breezy beachside lounge, where you can relax on comfortable cushioned seating or dance to the nightly DJs and live music. Weekends bring Las Vegas lite entertainment with bedazzled dancers and occasional circus tricks. Additional branches can be found in Hacienda White and Telal.

Hacienda/Hacienda White

SACHI BY THE SEA

In Hacienda; tel. 0103 003 0055; www.sachirestaurant.com/by-the-sea; 3pm-3am daily; 100-500LE drinks and 200-1,000LE mains

Enjoy gourmet cuisine and good music at this swanky beachside bar and restaurant that turns into a dance club on the weekends. The extensive drinks menu includes mules of various nationalities and creative cocktails like wasabi martinis and cucumber matcha punch. Food options range from fresh sushi to octopus carpaccio and chateaubriand. Kitchen closes from 6pm-10pm. Call ahead to reserve.

KIKI'S BEACH BAR

In Hacienda White; tel. 0103 000 5205; www.kikis-beach.com; 1pm-7pm and 10pm-3am daily; 80-350LE drinks

During the day, Kiki's serves colorful cocktails and gourmet snacks like braised octopus and chimichurri beef in shaded open-air seating just a stone's throw from the sea. From 10pm it turns into a nightclub with DJs, dancing, and colorful lighting. The ultra-trendy bar is popular with the 20-30-something crowd. If you have trouble reaching them for a reservation, message their Facebook page @kikisbeach.

GETTING THERE

The easiest way to get to this stretch of the North Coast from Cairo is by private car hire (290-310 km/180-192 mi; 3-3.5 hours). If you're starting from Alexandria, a taxi or Uber is your best option (140-160 km/87-99 mi; 2 hours).

Private Car Hire

Ibrahim el-Sheemy (tel. 0122 487 8427) and **Moamen Khedr** (tel. 0122 362 3032) can get you safely and comfortably here and back from Cairo. Prices will be around $120-150 for a day trip to/from Cairo. If you want to stay overnight (which is more realistic) it will cost around that amount each way. Both are best reached via WhatsApp.

Taxi

A taxi should cost around 600-700LE one-way from Downtown Alexandria (Saad Zaghloul Square). Be sure to negotiate a price ahead of time. If you like your driver, save his number so he can pick you up on your way back to Alexandria.

Bus

During high season (June-Aug.) you can catch a **Go Bus** (tel. 19567; www.go-bus.com) from Cairo (Abdel Minam Riyad

Square, beside Ramses Hilton Hotel, Downtown) to Marassi (3.5-4 hours; 180LE). There are usually two a day that leave around 7am and 10am. Buses don't go inside the compounds, so arrange with your accommodation for pickup at the bus station (just off Alexandria-Matruh Rd.). The bus station is just an easy 5-minute walk from the Marassi compound entrance (and another 20-minute walk to the shore from there), but the other compounds are a 1-4-hour walk away.

GETTING AROUND

Uber is the transportation of choice in these parts during summer season. Otherwise you'll need a **private car.** Locals use this service to party-hop between compounds. As a visitor, you might prefer to plant yourself at your resort and avoid the extra commute.

Marsa Matruh

While Egypt's cosmopolitan elite have claimed much of the North Coast for their private compounds, Marsa Matruh is a rare strip of crystal-clear waters accessible to the public. During the warmest months (June-Sept.), busloads of Cairenes and other city dwellers flood the streets and beaches. But for the other two-thirds of the year, the luminous sea and sandy beaches remain relatively empty, making it a nice stopover on the way to the Siwa Oasis 310 kilometers (190 mi) to the south.

SIGHTS

Corniche

Corniche St., Downtown

Take in the salty breeze with a stroll along the Corniche. Mini carnivals with dizzying rides line the promenade and make for entertaining people-watching. If you want to sit, the McDonald's (10am-4am daily) has staked out a prime spot with pleasant outdoor seating right on the sea—probably the nicest place to rest along the corniche.

Matruh Archeological Museum

Gaber Al Magaway Al Shamai St., inside Misr Public Library, Downtown; no tel.; 9am-5pm daily; 60LE adults, 30LE students

This hidden gem opened in 2018 after the city reclaimed artifacts uncovered in Matruh that had been taken to museums around the country. Housed in a corner of the Misr Public Library, the collection spans two floors with unique pieces from early ancient Egypt to Greco-Roman times. The items—statues, pottery, weapons, jewelry, figurines, stone tablets, and the like—offer hints of the history lived along this border region between Egypt, Libya, and Europe across the sea. The museum is small with a decent amount of English signage. A visit should only take around 45 minutes to an hour.

Rommel Cave Museum

Rommel Bay, near Rommel's Beach; no tel.; 9am-5pm daily; 40LE adults, 20LE students

Nazi general Erwin Rommel (aka "Desert Fox"), who led Germany's North Africa campaign, used this cave as a base to launch his incursions east toward the Suez Canal, but never made it past the British-led Allied forces in el Alamein. Inside the cave, small displays show the general's jacket, weapons, military maps, photographs, and medals from Hitler.

The museum is officially opened year-round but usually closed Oct.-May (low season). A suggestion of baksheesh (tips) may grant entry.

BEACHES

Like Alexandria, Marsa Matruh's public beaches suffer from litter and overcrowding, and female bathers who aren't fully covered will receive unwelcome attention. But the sea in Matruh is far more striking than it is in Alexandria, with vibrant blues and

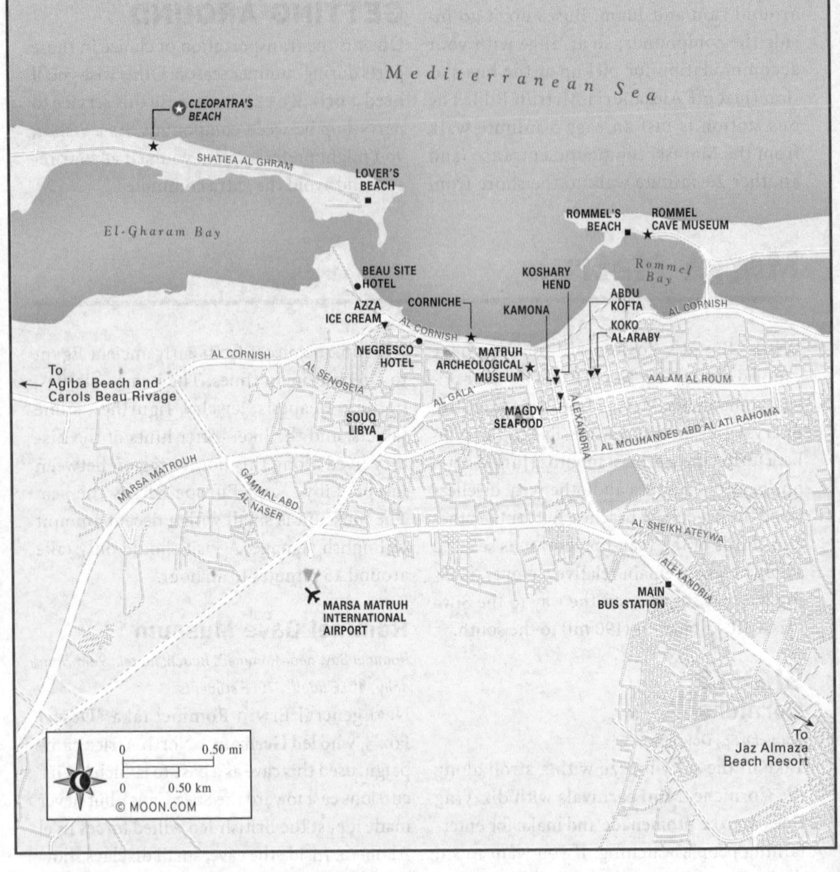

transparent waters. These beaches are also a nice way to see how local families enjoy their summer holidays. And paddleboats (with slides!) available for rent at Rommel's Beach and Lovers' Beach provide an opportunity for some privacy and your own floating playground (50-60LE/hour). Outside of season (Oct.-May) and early in the morning, these spots are cleaner and far less crowded.

Visitors looking for a more manicured experience (e.g., less litter, fewer people) in or around Matruh should choose accommodation with a private beach (like the Jaz Almaza Beach Resort, Beau Site, or Carols Beau Rivage). Beau Site also offers a day-use pass for 200LE per person, but their beach is small and only gets sunlight for the first half of the day.

ROMMEL'S BEACH (SHAT' ROMMEL)

Rommel Bay; 7am-sunset daily; free

Taking its name from the German general who led his World War II North African military campaign from a nearby cave, this beach bears little trace of those troubled times. The turquoise waters are bordered on the north by a rocky hill that protects swimmers from the whims of the open sea, making it a great place

The Real Cleopatra

Modern imaginations turn Cleopatra (r. 51-30 BC) into a striking beauty and the quintessential femme fatale. But she was in fact notable less for her appearance than for her highly skilled statesmanship, which advanced the Ptolemaic interests through smart alliances with Rome.

A woman of great intelligence and legendary charm, Cleopatra was the last of the Ptolemaic rulers. She survived civil war in Egypt against her younger brother (who was bitter their dad made them co-rulers) by joining forces with Julius Caesar. When the Roman general came to Alexandria to hunt down a rival, the clever queen—by this time exiled from the city—gained his audience by hiding in a rolled carpet (so the story goes). Unfurled before Caesar to dramatic effect, Cleopatra convinced him to help return her to the throne, and they became both political allies and lovers.

They had a son (according to Cleopatra, though never acknowledged by Caesar), Caesarion or "Little Caesar," whom she made co-regent, herself becoming the divine mother—like the Egyptian goddess Isis whose affiliation she embraced to win favor with the Egyptian people.

By 41 BC, Caesar was assassinated and his protégé, Mark Antony, had made his way to Alexandria to form an alliance with the 27-year-old queen against Caesar's adopted son, Octavian, for control of the Roman empire. Over the next decade Cleopatra bore Mark Antony three children and ruled over a relatively prosperous Egypt. Octavian's feud with Mark Antony eventually came to a head in 30 BC, when the Roman emperor captured Alexandria, leading to the power couple's suicides and a Roman-controlled Egypt.

for kids. Plenty of shade with patio chairs available for rent (5-10LE). Bubble-gum pink paddleboats with slide available for rent. To get here, grab a taxi. A ride from the city center should take around 15 minutes.

★ CLEOPATRA'S BEACH (SHAT' CLEOPATRA)

Gharam Bay, Gharam-Cleopatra Rd.; 7am-sunset daily; 10LE

Legend has it Cleopatra herself chose this spot for romantic swims with Mark Antony. While the story is likely apocryphal, the striking waters, protected cove, and unique rock formation do indeed make this patch of sea fit for a queen. It's also the cleanest public beach you'll find in the city.

Most visitors come to see **Cleopatra's Rock,** the large climbable rock with a hollow interior that's now connected to the shore by a glass walkway. On calm days, the cove directly past the formation is a prime swimming spot (bring your water shoes for the rough entrance). Views from the top of the neighboring cliffside are spectacular, and the accessible coastline continues west for over a mile, offering a nice secluded walk past the occasional group of friendly fishermen. In the summer small cafés sell snacks near the entrance, but be sure to bring plenty of water just in case. Finding a return taxi might be challenging so consider asking your driver to wait for a negotiated price.

LOVERS' BEACH (SHAT' EL GHARAM)

Gharam Bay, Gharam-Cleopatra Rd.; 7am-sunset daily; free

Egyptian movie star Leila Murad sang of her love for Matruh's sea and wind on this spot for the popular 1950 film *Shat' el-Gharam* (Lovers' Beach), giving this strip of sand its name. Located at the end of a peninsula, the rocky north side looks out to the wide-open sea, while the sandy east side opens up to the protected bay. Paddleboats with slides available for rent. A quick ferry to/from central Marsa Matruh runs continuously during the summer 8am-sunset (5 minutes; 10LE), offering a nice shortcut to the 20-minute drive.

AGIBA BEACH (SHAT' AGIBA)

Agiba-Alabiyad Rd.; 7am-sunset daily; free

This sandy public beach on a protected cove of

1

2

crystal-clear waters 25 kilometers (16 mi) west of central Marsa Matruh is a favorite local spot. During summer (June-early Sept.), visitors flock here to explore the watery caves and enjoy the views from the surrounding cliffsides. Try to get here for opening to beat the crowds, or come during low season to enjoy this patch of paradise in peace. Basic cafés and WCs available near the parking lot.

SHOPPING

SOUQ LIBYA

Galaa St., Downtown; no tel.; 9am-midnight daily

This sprawling covered market blossomed in the 1980s when it was easy to drive cheap goods from Europe and North Africa across the border from Libya. The selection isn't quite what it used to be since the regional uprisings in 2011, but you can still find a wealth of local olives, olive oil, and spices (along with cheap made-in-China knickknacks).

FOOD

Egyptian

KOSHARY HEND

Off Alexandria St., across from Kamona, Downtown; tel. 0100 116 0088; 24 hours daily; 20-40LE mains

Aluminum tables and chairs full of hungry locals pour onto the sidewalks at Marsa Matruh's best koshary joint. Watch the bustle of Downtown as you enjoy your filling plate of pasta, legumes, friend onions, and sauces.

★ KAMONA

Off Alexandria St., Downtown; tel. 046 4932107; noon-midnight daily; 50-80LE mains

It's hard to go wrong with anything on the menu at this grill, but their specialties are lamb kebab and kofta (meatballs). Dishes are best enjoyed family style with a spread of mezze for starters. Upstairs is separated into small private dining rooms with a few tables in a communal space. The outside tables are technically only for waiting, but if you ask nicely they might let you eat there on quiet days.

1: Cleopatra's Rock at Cleopatra's Beach **2:** Lovers' Beach

★ KOKO AL-ARABY

Tahrir St., on corner with Ahmed el-Rateb St., Downtown; tel. 0109 111 9058; 24 hours daily; 50-80LE mains

Snag your own private dining area with floor pillow seating, saloon-style doors, and large windows that open to a (relatively) quiet street below. The private seating in this Bedouin restaurant is designed so niqab-wearing women can enjoy their food without having to take furtive bites beneath their face veils. Their specialties are grilled chicken and meats, but the vegetable tagines are also tasty. Try one of their fabulously fresh fruit juices for dessert.

ABDU KOFTA

Tahrir St., on corner with Zaher Galal St., Downtown; tel. 0111 772 4888; 24 hours daily; 50-80LE mains

Just down the street from Koko al-Araby, Abdu Kofta is another popular grill with a large open dining hall on the upper floor and a few outdoor tables (where you can escape the smell of cigarettes). The decoration is a bit drab, but the kitchen competes for the title of best kebab and kofta in town. Dips and salads also fresh and tasty.

Seafood

MAGDY SEAFOOD

Gool Gamal Qibli St., off Alexandria St., Downtown; tel. 0109 098 5558; 6am-1am daily; 80-100LE mains

Magdy's has the best seafood in town. The two-floor dining space embraces the nautical theme complete with porthole windows and sea life swimming across the walls. Across the street, locals line up to get fish fresh off the ice to cook up at home at the restaurant's fishmonger branch. Smoke-free.

Sweets and Snacks

AZZA ICE CREAM

Corniche St., near Negresco Hotel, Downtown; no tel.; 10am-midnight daily; 10-30LE ice cream and sweets

The ice cream at this ice cream shop is fine (skip the chocolate), but the rice pudding with nuts and raisins is the real treat. Grab your sweet of choice and bring it across the street to enjoy seaside. A smaller branch can be found 300 meters (1,000 ft) to the west on Corniche Street, off Beau Site Square.

BARS AND NIGHTLIFE

There's no nightlife to speak of in Marsa Matruh, but if you're desperate for a drink in this near-dry town head to the **Beau Site Hotel Bar** (Corniche St., Downtown; tel. 046 4932066; 10am-midnight daily; 60-90LE drinks) where you can sip your beverage of choice in their gardens near the sea, or to the lush red **Yanni Lobby Bar** at Carols Beau Rivage Hotel (El-Obayed Bay, Agiba-Alabiyad Rd.; tel. 046 4851000; 10am-2am daily; 80-150LE drinks).

ACCOMMODATIONS

Central Marsa Matruh is unfortunately dominated by a number of overpriced, subpar hotels run by retired military generals and their relatives. Check Airbnb for the occasional find. Around 40 kilometers (25 mi) east of Marsa Matruh you have a few fancy resort options with stunning private beaches. Out of season (late Sept.-late May) prices are significantly lower.

800-1,650LE

NEGRESCO HOTEL

Corniche St., Downtown; tel. 046 4934492; 1,600LE d

Negresco's style is a bit pedestrian, but its clean rooms, friendly staff, and central location with sea view make the stay here comfortable enough. Try to book through the hotel directly for best prices. Breakfast included.

1,650-3,300LE

BEAU SITE HOTEL

Corniche St., Downtown; tel. 046 4932066; www.beausiteegypt.com; 2,050LE d

Beau Site is the nicest hotel in central Marsa Matruh, though still pretty standard. The balconies looking out to the sea and clean private beach are the best features. But in the summer their relatively small patch of shore fills with guests from the hotel's 200 rooms and loses its sun in the late afternoon. Most packages include a mediocre breakfast and dinner.

Over 3,300LE

CAROLS BEAU RIVAGE

El-Obayed Bay, Agiba-Alabiyad Rd.; tel. 046 4851000; www.carolsbeaurivage.com; 3,700LE d

With tacky flourishes of cheetah print furniture and the like, Carols is considerably overpriced. But visitors pay for the dreamy private beach with thatch umbrellas, cushioned lounge chairs, and sand like talcum powder. Other highlights include palm tree groves and two large pools (indoor and outdoor).

★ JAZ ALMAZA BEACH RESORT

Almaza Bay, off Alexandria-Matruh Rd.; tel. 02 3854 1111; www.jazhotels.com; 4,400LE d

The Jaz Hotel Group's shiny beach resorts some 40 kilometers (25 mi; 40 minutes) east of central Marsa Matruh share a long strip of flawless seashore with white sand and turquoise waters protected by a bay. The Jaz Almaza Beach Resort is the nicest of the three with two outdoor pools that look like enormous blue ink splotches and an indoor heated pool for the rare winter visitors. In the summer there's live music and entertainment at their **Nafora Bar.** Other highlights include tennis courts and a health club with sauna, Jacuzzi, and gym. The super swanky **Pier 88** restaurant (tel. 0127 480 0022; www.pier-88group.com; noon-1am daily; 300-600LE mains) has a branch here right on the beach. Neighboring resorts located within the same compound—Jaz Oriental Resort and Jaz Crystal Resort—are similar in quality so you might want to price compare before booking. You'll need private transportation to get here, or take the bus headed to Marsa Matruh and arrange with the hotel in advance to pick you up off the Alexandria-Matruh Road (1.5 km/0.9 mi from resort).

INFORMATION AND SERVICES

ATMs

A handful of ATMs line al-Galaa Street near

Wist el-Balad Square (there are also plenty elsewhere throughout the city). One street over is the Bank of Alexandria (al-Hekma St.; tel. 19033; 8:30am-2pm Sun.-Thurs.).

Pharmacies

HUDA PHARMACY

Alexandria St., across from Marsa Matruh Public Hospital, Downtown; tel. 046 4934902; 24 hours daily

There are a number of pharmacies throughout the city, but this one has a good variety of imported sunscreens and basic medications.

GETTING THERE

If you're traveling from Cairo or Alexandria, bus is the easiest way to get to Marsa Matruh. Between Matruh and Siwa, bus or microbus are the best options.

Air

Very few flights are offered to the **Marsa Matruh International Airport (MUH)** (3 km/2 mi south of central Marsa Matruh), but you might find something if you go in season (June-Sept.). Check at www.egyptair.com. Flights typically cost around 3,000LE round-trip to/from Cairo. Flight time: 1.5 hours. From the airport, taxis to the center of the city should only cost around 15LE.

Bus

Buses travel daily between Marsa Matruh and Cairo (7-7.5 hours; 165LE), Alexandria (4.5-5 hours; 85LE), or Siwa (4-4.5 hours; 70LE) year-round, but are far more frequent June-September. **Go Bus** (tel. 19567; www.go-bus.com) is generally your best option, followed by **Super Jet** (tel. 02 22909013; www.superjet.com.eg). The **West Delta Bus Co.** (no tel.) is fine as a last resort and the only bus company that travels between Marsa Matruh and Siwa.

Matruh's **Main Bus Station** (Alexandria St.) is located 3 kilometers (2 mi) south of the Corniche. From here, a taxi to center of town should cost 15LE.

Microbus

The **Main Microbus Lot** is located directly north of the bus station. Microbuses to Siwa (4 hours; 75LE) and Alexandria (3.5 hours; 65LE) leave on a rolling basis as soon as the 15 seats fill. You can buy extra seats to expedite the departure and have a roomier ride, or even rent the whole microbus for the price of 15 seats. Microbuses also leave Siwa and Alexandria to Matruh daily (same system). The microbus lot in Alex is just beside the main bus station, el-Mow'if el-Gadid (Moharram Bek; no tel.; 24 hours daily).

GETTING AROUND

There are no meters in Marsa Matruh, but to get almost anywhere around Downtown a **taxi** should cost 15LE or so. Destinations a bit farther afield (such as Cleopatra's Beach) should be in the range of 35-50LE from Downtown. Expect to pay around 100LE to Agiba Beach (25 km/16 mi; 35 minutes). Taxi drivers here tend to be much more relaxed than their counterparts in the big cities and are not likely to overcharge.

Red Sea Coast

Just over 160 kilometers (100 mi) east of the Nile Valley at the desert's narrowest strip, Egypt's Red Sea Riviera seems a world away from the country's densely populated cities. The entire Red Sea Governorate, covering over 20% of Egypt's land mass, holds a mere 0.4% of the country's population. Most of the area is comprised of the mountainous Eastern Desert, streaked with dried riverbeds once traversed by trade caravans headed for the Arabian Peninsula. Today, the Red Sea Coast's sprawling backyard serves as a beautiful backdrop to life on the water and beckons the adventurous to explore by desert safari.

Along the coast, more stretches of barren sand separate a handful of towns. Those in the north are dominated by the petroleum industry,

Highlights

Look for ★ to find recommended sights, activities, dining, and lodging.

★ **Big Giftun Island:** Hurghada's best beaches, surrounded by turquoise waters, patches of coral, and animated fish, are located on this sandy island an hour offshore (page 316).

★ **Gota Abu Ramada:** Teeming with sea life, this site off the Hurghada coast is suited for all levels of divers (page 317).

★ **Abu Dabbab Beach:** The sheltered bay off this beach of fine white sand is home to dozens of sea turtles, grazing dugongs, and two stunning house reefs (page 326).

★ **Samadai Reef ("Dolphin House"):** Swim with pods of spinner dolphins in this protected lagoon hugged by a crescent-shaped reef (page 328).

★ **Fury Shoals:** Dive among some of the Red Sea's most immaculate corals in this chain of reefs with underwater caves and canyons (page 328).

★ **Beaches in Wadi el Gemal National Park:** Marvel at the region's most unspoiled coastline, and enjoy an authentic meal prepared by members of the local Ababda tribe (page 333).

★ **Hamata Islands:** Hop on a boat to walk the fine white sand of these desert islands and explore their vibrant fringing reefs (page 334).

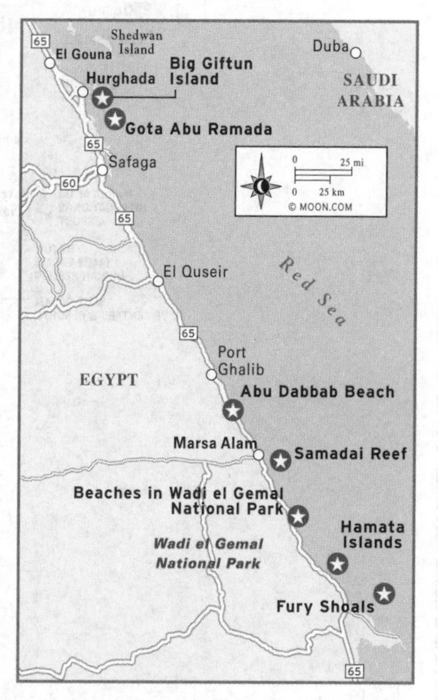

Red Sea Coast

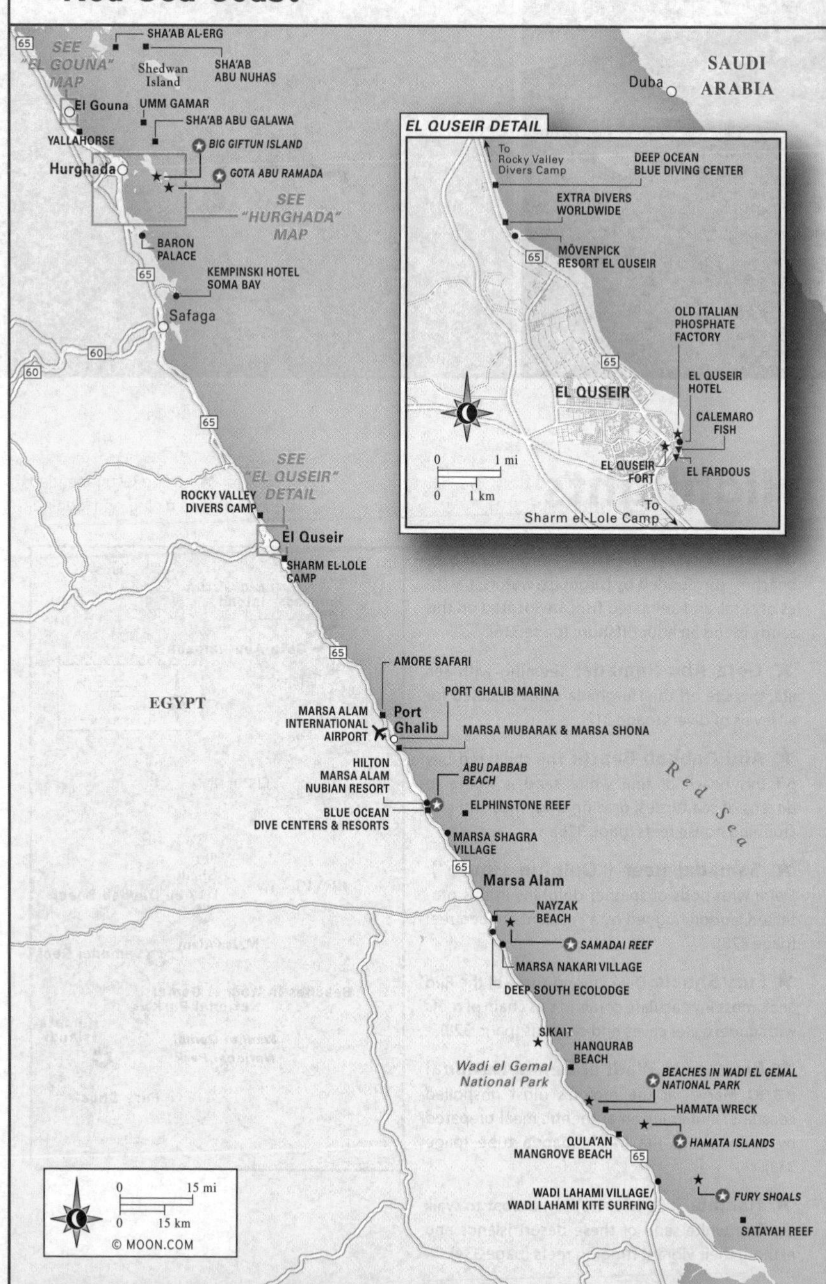

Recreation on the Red Sea Coast

Travelers to the Red Sea Coast have no shortage of activities to choose from. Lounge on the beach with a book, step into your hotel's private corner of the sea, head out by speedboat on an excursion deeper into the blue, or explore the peaks and valleys of the Eastern Desert. Here are some of the best spots to enjoy the region's most popular recreation options.

DESERT SAFARIS

For real desert dreamers, **Marsa Alam** is the place to go. Its sprawling **Wadi el Gemal National Park** holds a wealth of wadis, mountains, and wide-open space spotted with antiquities and rare animals. For a brief jaunt into the desert on quad bike or horseback, the more easily accessible **El Gouna** or **Hurghada** are fine entry points.

DIVING AND SNORKELING

Divers can't go wrong anywhere along the Red Sea Coast, but **Marsa Alam** has the most unique stretches of reefs (like the Fury Shoals), and **Hurghada** offers the most economical diving packages. Snorkelers should head to Marsa Alam and choose accommodation with an excellent house reef (any of the listings below). In the Hurghada area, the **Oberoi Beach Resort** (Sahl Hasheesh) and **Kempinski** (Soma Bay) are both excellent choices.

KITESURFING

The best kitesurfing spots along the Red Sea Coast can be found in **El Gouna** (on Buzzah Beach), **Hurghada** (Soma Bay), and **Marsa Alam** (Wadi Lahami). Each is great for beginners to advanced, with options of surfing in shallow lagoons or more difficult waters. Kitesurfing is a year-round sport in these parts, but the best time to go is April-October when the water is warm and the wind most consistent.

before the resort town of El Gouna marks the start of touristic terrain.

Hurghada, capital of the Red Sea Governorate, welcomes dozens of international flights each week and bursts with activities—from diving to boating, kitesurfing, desert safaris, and horseback riding. Farther south, the string of resorts trickle off and visitors find a quieter scene—with small-town El Quseir's historic charm, and the untouched beaches in Marsa Alam, Egypt's "Deep South." This is also your best chance to explore pristine coral reefs that stretch for miles, and swim with the dugongs, sea turtles, and spinner dolphins that call this corner of the Red Sea home.

ORIENTATION

Visitors traveling to the Red Sea Coast from Cairo by plane will fly into either the **Hurghada International Airport** (just a 1-hour flight) to access El Gouna or Hurghada, or into **Marsa Alam International Airport** (1.5 hours) to reach El Quseir or Marsa Alam.

A more economical option is to grab a bus. Buses head to these coastal towns from Cairo daily and take 7-12 hours depending on destination. **El Gouna** is closest to Cairo (455 km/282 mi), followed by **Hurghada** (475 km/295 mi), **El Quseir** (605 km/375 mi), and **Marsa Alam** (670 km/415 mi).

From Luxor, buses only travel to Hurghada (300 km/186 mi) but travelers can hire a

---

Previous: Abu Dabbab Beach; Bullet Speedboats; spinner dolphins.

private car to reach El Quseir (225 km/140 mi), Marsa Alam (300 km/186 mi), or El Gouna (327 km/203 mi).

PLANNING YOUR TIME

Each region along the Red Sea Coast offers a distinct flavor, and few visitors venture far from their base of choice. **El Gouna** is the well-manicured culinary capital; **Hurghada** the busy hub for economical all-inclusive resort packages; **El Quseir** the quaint and quiet village with a handful of striking dive and snorkel spots; and **Marsa Alam,** the rugged "Deep South," with ecolodges, a few resorts, and miles of pristine shoreline fringed with coral reefs. The rare travelers hoping to visit all these coastal towns can do so by bus, starting in El Gouna and making their way south. A flight into Hurghada with day trips to El Gouna (a 40-minute drive to the north) and El Quseir (a 2-hour drive to the south) is an easy way to see one chunk of the coast, while Marsa Alam's sprawling shoreline—including Wadi el Gemal National Park—should be enough to explore on its own.

El Gouna

Brainchild of real estate tycoon and scion of Egypt's richest family (Samih Sawiris), El Gouna is the year-round playground of Egyptian elites. When the North Coast gets too cold, they flock to this resort town, interlaced with artificial lagoons and marinas with the country's finest yachts. If you're looking for long stretches of beach and untouched land, you won't find it here—Gouna is all about high-end property development. But travelers in search of luxury, glam, and fine dining won't be disappointed.

SIGHTS

El Gouna Library

Kafr el Gouna, Downtown; tel. 065 3580023; info@elgounalibrary.com; 9am-9pm daily; 20LE

Also known as the "Embassy of Knowledge," Gouna's library is an official branch of the Bibliotheca Alexandrina—Alexandria's expansive house of books and culture. Like its mother library, this one doubles as a cultural center, hosting language classes and art exhibitions along with its hundreds of books available to borrow. Other highlights include a small museum with replicas of ancient Egyptian artifacts and the Culturama—a 45-minute presentation about Egyptian history projected on panoramic screens. If you can find some shade, the courtyard is a nice place to hide with a good book. Café and internet also available.

FESTIVALS AND EVENTS

Gouna hosts Egypt's most popular festivals outside Cairo.

SANDBOX MUSIC FESTIVAL

North edge of El Gouna; tel. 0101 215 2054; www.sandboxfestival.com; typically held in June; 2,800LE for 3-day pass

Egypt's young and wealthy partygoers make an annual pilgrimage to this three-day electronic music festival on the beach. Dozens of local and international DJs gather to entertain crowds decked out in glam beachwear, glitter, and costumes. The festival is typically held during a weekend in June, with Friday hosting the hottest gigs. Check their website for exact dates, lineup, and hotel packages (Airbnbs also widely available). One day passes go for 1,200LE. Age minimum: 21 years old.

EL GOUNA FILM FESTIVAL

El Gouna; tel. 0 227378034; www.elgounafilmfestival.com; typically held in Sept. or Oct.

Another creation of the Sawiris family, the annual El Gouna Film Festival (GFF) is the most glamorous event for Egypt's film industry.

El Gouna

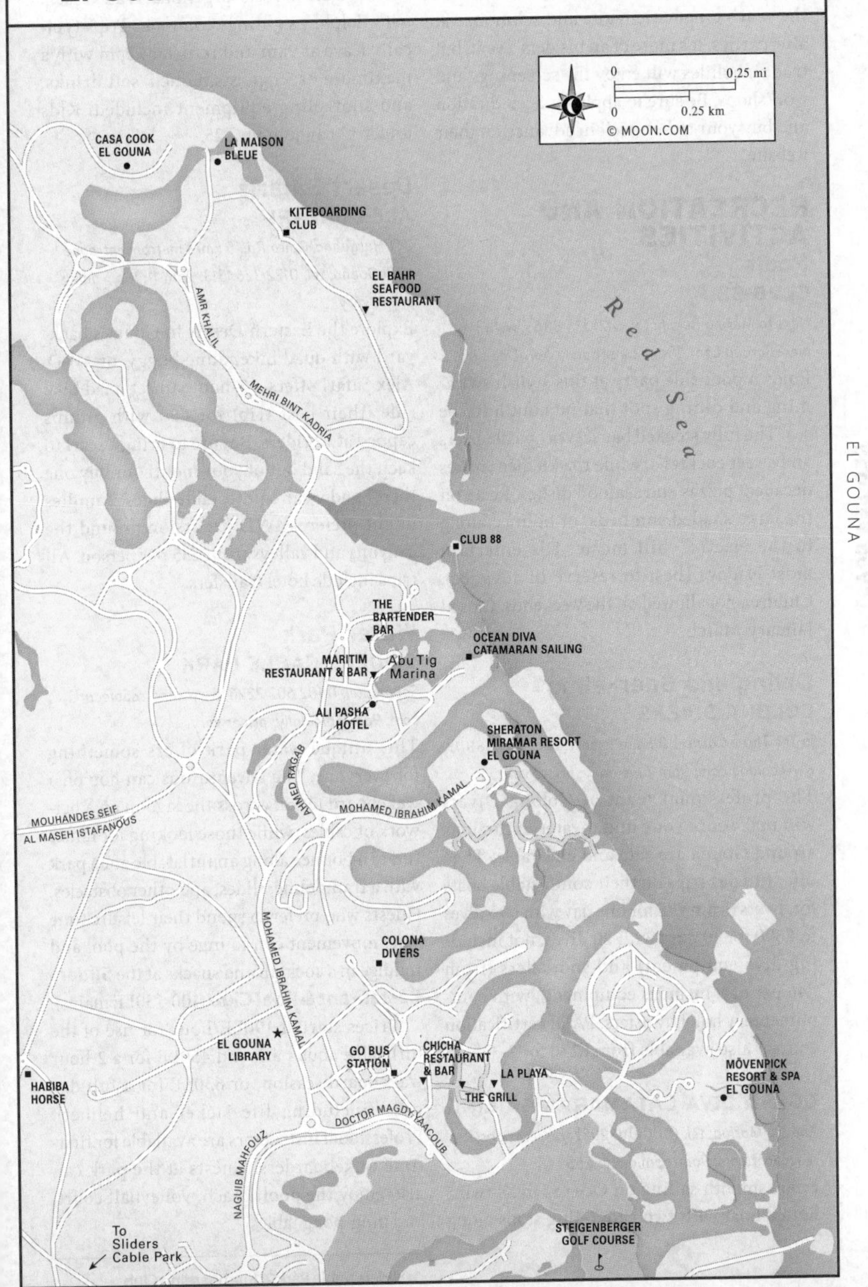
0
0.25 mi
0
0.25 km
© MOON.COM
Red Sea
CASA COOK EL GOUNA
LA MAISON BLEUE
KITEBOARDING CLUB
EL BAHR SEAFOOD RESTAURANT
AMR KHALIL
MEHRI BINT KADRIA
CLUB 88
THE BARTENDER BAR
OCEAN DIVA CATAMARAN SAILING
MARITIM RESTAURANT & BAR
Abu Tig Marina
ALI PASHA HOTEL
SHERATON MIRAMAR RESORT EL GOUNA
AHMED RAGAB
MOHAMED IBRAHIM KAMAL
MOUHANDES SEIF
AL MASEH ISTAFANOUS
COLONA DIVERS
EL GOUNA LIBRARY
GO BUS STATION
CHICHA RESTAURANT & BAR
LA PLAYA
THE GRILL
MÖVENPICK RESORT & SPA EL GOUNA
HABIBA HORSE
DOCTOR MAGDY YAACOUB
NAGUIB MAHFOUZ
STEIGENBERGER GOLF COURSE
To Sliders Cable Park

The red-carpet affair sees the country's top movie stars and film crews gather to watch the year's cinematic fruits and schmooze at afterparties. It's more of an insiders' event, but true cinephiles will enjoy the screenings and workshops. Be sure to apply for accreditation and buy your tickets well in advance on their website.

RECREATION AND ACTIVITIES

Pools

CLUB 88

Next to Marina Beach; tel. 0121 128 8866; www.pier88group.com; 10am-sunset daily Apr.-Dec.; 175LE

Enjoy a pool-side party at this stylish swimming and dining spot that juts out into the sea. The fully stocked bar serves up cold beers and sweet cocktails, while the kitchen makes decadent pizzas and seafood dishes. Relax on the large shaded sun beds, or bounce along to the electro chill music. DJs entertain most Fridays (best to reserve in advance). Children not allowed on the weekends. Closed January-March.

Diving and Snorkeling

COLONA DIVERS

In The Three Corners Rihana Resort; tel. 065 3580113; www.colona.com; 9am-6pm daily; prices vary

The professional team at Colona Divers will make sure your underwater excursions around Gouna are safe and enjoyable. They offer full day trips on their comfortable boats for divers (from €75 for one day with two dives to €600 for 10 days with 20 dives, not including dive equipment) and snorkelers (from €46 per day, includes equipment), with complimentary hotel transfers. PADI certification courses also available from €230 for 2-3 days.

OCEAN DIVA CATAMARAN SAILING

Abu Tig Marina; tel. 0100 010 2952; reservations@redseacat.com; 9am-6pm daily; €55

Enjoy smooth sailing on Ocean Diva's twin-hulled boat with two snorkeling stops along the way. The catamaran's low draft means it can navigate to reefs larger boats can't reach, with dolphin sightings common. Trips typically leave at 9am and return at 2pm with a maximum of 55 guests. Lunch, soft drinks, and snorkeling equipment included. Kids under 12 can join for €25.

Desert Safaris

ALEX SAFARI

Off Hurgahda-Cairo Rd., 5 km/3 mi from entrance to El Gouna; tel. 0122 326 1313; 9am-11:30pm daily; prices vary

Explore the Eastern Desert in Gouna's backyard with quad bike, dune buggy, or 4WD. Alex Safari offers a 3-hour sunset quad bike ride (their best trip) for €50 with groups capped at 12 riders. Be sure to bring a scarf to keep the sand out of your mouth (or buy one there) and wear comfortable shoes. Families might prefer a 4WD excursion around the canyons and valleys from €35 per person. All trips include hotel transfers.

Water Park

SLIDERS CABLE PARK

Sabina; tel. 0 102 602 2226; www.sliderscablepark.com; 9am-6pm daily; prices vary

This unique water park offers something for everyone. The adventurous can hop on a wakeboard to sail across the lagoon on a network of cables, while those looking for tamer fun can bounce along an inflatable aqua park with a trampoline, slides, and other obstacles. Guests who prefer to spend their leisure time sans movement can lounge by the pool and indulge in a cocktail and snacks at the **Sliders Restaurant & Pool Club** (100-130LE mains).

Prices start at 190LE/hour for use of the inflatable aqua park and 450LE for a 2-hour wakeboard session, or 630LE for a full day pass (including life jacket and helmet). Professional instructors are available for first-time wakeboarders. Guests at the park can also enjoy the pool, beach, volleyball court, and ping-pong tables.

1: Sliders Cable Park **2:** Kiteboarding Club

1

2

Kitesurfing

KITEBOARDING CLUB

Buzzah Beach/Northern Mangroovy Beach, Kite Center Rd.; tel. 0122 661 0878; www.kiteboarding-club.com/el-gouna; 8:30am-7pm daily; prices vary

The Kiteboarding Club (KBC) offers excellent equipment and instructors for beginners to advanced. They snagged a prime location for their outpost on Buzzah Beach, where reefs protect kiteboarders from the open sea in a large lagoon of crystal-clear shallow waters. When you're not flying through the air, cool off in the pool or relax on the beach. The skilled kitchen and bar are added treats, making it a perfect spot to camp out for the day. Beginners' course starts from 6,700LE per person for 8 hours over 2-3 days in a group of 2-4 people.

Horse and Camel Rides

HABIBA HORSE

Habiba Horse Circle; tel. 0106 439 3709; www.habibahorse.de; 8am-7pm daily; prices vary

Explore El Gouna's deserts and beaches on a 1-4-hour horseback ride. Choose from a range of trips at sunrise or sunset, climbing mountains, or swimming in the sea. The German owner, Kerstin, has a true passion for horses and ensures their well-being in the stables and on the trail. Prices start at €30/hour or €50/2 hours, and all trips include a guide, water, photos, riding gear (helmets, gloves, chaps, and pants) and transportation from/to any Gouna hotel. Trips are suitable for beginners to advanced riders with group numbers capped at 7. Best to call or message on WhatsApp to reserve (they don't always see their emails).

YALLAHORSE

Off Hurgahda-Ismailia Rd., 15 km/9 mi south of central Gouna; tel. 0101 585 5099; www.yallahorse-elgouna.com; prices vary

Another high-quality stable catering to Gouna visitors, YallaHorse offers an excellent 2-hour sunset ride through the desert and along the beach for €40. An extra €10 will get you a short swim with the horses for some Insta-worthy pics. If you want more time in the saddle, try their 5-hour trip to the mountains with a stop in a Bedouin camp for tea, followed by a barbecue back at the stables (€90). Camels also available for €10/hour. Hotel transfers included.

Golf

STEIGENBERGER GOLF COURSE

Steigenberger Resort; tel. 0122 7464712; golf.club@elgouna.com; 7am-5pm daily; €85

Be sure to bring some extra balls on this 18-hole golf course woven with water hazards. The desert mountains in the distance are an added visual treat to the milky blue lagoons and sprawling greens (made of a special type of grass that can live off sea water). The course is suitable for beginners to advanced players. Carts and clubs available to rent. Best to make a tee time in advance.

FOOD

El Gouna is the gastronomic capital of the Red Sea Coast. Choose from a wide variety of international fare and fantastically fresh seafood. Most of the best restaurants are concentrated in the Downtown area (Kafr el Gouna) and at the Abu Tig Marina.

Egyptian

THE GRILL

Kafr el Gouna, near pedestrian bridge; tel. 0122 178 5555; 1pm-midnight daily; 100-300LE mains

The Grill's succulent meats and fresh bread straight from the brick oven make it the best spot in Gouna to indulge in your favorite Egyptian dishes. Try the lamb chops with a hummus starter (more a Levantine addition than an Egyptian classic), or sample other international fare like burgers and chicken wings.

International

★ LA PLAYA

Kafr el Gouna; tel. 0102 422 0440; www.laplaya-elgouna.com; 9am-midnight daily; 100-300LE mains

La Playa serves up excellent pizzas, pastas, burgers, and brunch on its own little patch of sandy beach. Sip on a fresh fruit smoothie between dips in the lagoon, or enjoy artfully presented plates on the shaded terrace. The ice cream and desserts are also delicious. Alcohol and shisha available.

CHICHA RESTAURANT & BAR

Kafr el Gouna, across from Ebeid Supermarket; tel. 0122 775 5888; noon-midnight daily; 120-300LE mains

Named after a corn-based beer from the Andes, this Latin American fusion restaurant makes some of the best guacamole in Gouna. The tacos, churros, and funky cocktails are also a treat, best enjoyed in the stylish outdoor seating under rattan lamps. Music from the continent adds to the good vibes.

Seafood

★ MARITIM RESTAURANT & BAR

Abu Tig Marina; tel. 0102 888 8926; www.maritim.elgounarestaurants.com; 10am-10pm daily; 150-500LE mains

Cook your own seafood or steaks on volcanic lava stone at this classy restaurant on the edge of the marina. Nestled beside a string of yachts, the outdoor seating canopied with sails makes for an attractive dining experience. A range of other fresh seafood, pasta, and meat dishes also on offer from the kitchen. Try their eggs and smoked salmon for breakfast. Tasty cocktails and other alcohol served (4pm-6pm happy hour, buy one get one free).

EL BAHR SEAFOOD RESTAURANT

Kite Center Rd., Mangroovy Beach; tel. 0127 852 7530; 2pm-10pm daily; 200-400LE mains

This sleek restaurant on the beach serves up fresh seafood while nearby kitesurfers provide colorful entertainment. Select your fish from a bed of ice and choose how you want it prepared—grilled, baked, or fried. Dishes are artfully presented to match the coastal chic décor. No alcohol served, but feel free to bring your own.

BARS AND NIGHTLIFE

Most of Gouna's restaurants serve alcohol and double as chill nightlife venues.

THE BARTENDER BAR

Abu Tig Marina, at Captain's Inn Hotel; tel. 0122 783 6337; 4pm-1am daily; 70-300LE drinks

The Bartender's ample outdoor seating hugs a corner of the hip Abu Tig Marina. Neon cocktails decorate tables made of truck tires or brightly colored barrels imprinted with portraits of John Lennon and the like. The servers pride themselves on their pouring performance, and live musicians entertain most weekends. Call ahead to see what's on the schedule. Tasty bar food also available. Be sure to check the price of imported liquor before ordering to avoid any unpleasant surprises.

ACCOMMODATIONS

Before you book, check out Gouna's official website (www.hotels.elgouna.com) where they guarantee the lowest prices. For more economical options, take a look at Airbnb for some excellent flats starting from 750LE/night.

1,650-3,300LE

ALI PASHA HOTEL

Abu Tig Marina; tel. 065 3580088; www.hotels.elgouna.com; 2,000LE d

Moorish elegance meets Scandinavian chic in this boutique hotel nestled in the heart of Gouna's hottest marina. Cool off in the private pool (heated in the winter), or take a short walk to the Marina Beach Club where hotel guests get free entrance, a sunbed, and umbrella. A delicious breakfast spread is included.

SHERATON MIRAMAR RESORT EL GOUNA

Mohammed Ibrahim Kamel St.; tel. 065 3545606; www.marriott.com; 2,650LE d

Scattered across a cluster of islands, the Sheraton Miramar is another sprawling seaside resort with a large pool, clean beach, and excellent food. Each of the 300-plus rooms—most with attractive barrel vault ceilings—boasts a private balcony or terrace. The enthusiastic animation team makes the hotel uniquely entertaining.

MÖVENPICK RESORT & SPA EL GOUNA

Off Hill Villas Rd.; tel. 065 3544501; www.movenpick.com; 2,750LE d

This vast Mövenpick with over 400 rooms covers nearly an entire island, giving guests plenty of shoreline to enjoy. Add to that three pools, a private lagoon, beautiful landscaping, and excellent on-site restaurants and you have an idyllic self-contained vacation spot. Adventurous guests will appreciate the high-quality kitesurfing and diving centers located within the complex. The rooms are a bit awkwardly designed, but clean and comfortable with either a balcony or terrace.

★ CASA COOK EL GOUNA

North El Gouna; tel. 065 3545163; www.casacook.com; 2,900LE d

Tucked away at the north end of town, this adult-only boutique hotel offers an escape from the hubbub of central Gouna. Rooms are decorated with earthy colors, raw wood furniture, and accents of rattan. All 100 have a private terrace and small pool at their doorstep. For communal bathing, guests can head to the hotel's larger pool or private beach—both with comfortable lounge chairs, thatch umbrellas, and the occasional rope hammock. Quality kitesurfing and dive centers are within walking distance.

Over 3,300LE

LA MAISON BLEUE

Kite Center Rd.; tel. 065 3545604; www.lamaison-bleue.com; 7,300LE d

Anything but understated, this mansion-cum-hotel offers an eclectic mélange of baroque, neoclassical, art deco, and North African designs. Its decadent attention to detail extends even to your pillow, which you can choose from a menu. The mosaic columns and kaleidoscopic marble floors aren't for the minimalist, but ensure your eyes are never bored. Lounge at the private lagoon beach, take a dip in the pool, or spend a few hours in their spa and Turkish hammam. Extensive cigar menu on offer, and fantastic breakfast included (think smoked salmon and avocado toast). No children under 16 allowed.

INFORMATION AND SERVICES

Check out the official El Gouna website (www.elgouna.com) for maps and a full directory of restaurants, accommodation, and activities around the town.

ATMs

Gouna has no shortage of ATMs. You'll find them in nearly every hotel and most densely concentrated around Downtown (near the Go Bus station) and Abu Tig Marina.

Medical

For medical emergencies, head to the **El Gouna Hospital** (Off Mohammed Ibrahim Kamel St.; tel. 065 3580011; www.elgouna-hospital.com.eg; 24 hours daily). Their facilities include a hyperbaric chamber for diving accidents.

GETTING THERE

The best way to get to Gouna from Cairo is by bus or plane, depending on your budget. The bus from Cairo takes around 7 hours. If you fly, you'll arrive to Hurghada International Airport in around an hour. Take a taxi or private car from the airport (40 minutes).

Air

El Gouna is located just 40 kilometers (25 mi) north of **Hurghada International Airport** (El-Nasr St., Hurghada; tel. 065 3414213; www.hurghada-airports.com). A taxi to most hotels in Gouna should cost around 185-200LE. To avoid the hassle of haggling, book an **Uber** or call **ABC Taxi** (tel. 0100 222 8294) to arrange a ride in advance for a fair price.

Bus

Go Bus (tel. 19567; www.go-bus.com; 225LE) is your most comfortable option and offers multiple trips a day from Cairo, leaving from Abdel Minam Square (next to Ramses Hilton). The Gouna Go Bus station is conveniently located in Downtown.

GETTING AROUND

The best way to get around Gouna is on foot or by tuk tuk. To travel outside of the resort town elsewhere along the Red Sea Coast, taxi or Uber is best.

Tuk Tuk

Call **Tuk Tuk Mini Cab** (tel. 0111 900 4500) to get just about anywhere around Gouna for 10-30LE. Each motorized rickshaw can hold up to two people. Your hotel can also arrange.

Taxi and Private Car Hire

ABC Taxi (20 Mohamed Hawaydek St., Hurghada; tel. 0100 222 8294; www.abctaxi.com; 24 hours daily) has a fleet of comfortable cars with expert, nonsmoking drivers and fair prices. To reserve, call or message them on WhatsApp. Their responsive team will give you an exact price in advance depending on your location. **Uber** is also active for travel between El Gouna and elsewhere along the Red Sea with a trip to or from the airport around 160LE.

Hurghada (el-Gharda'a)

Hurghada began its transformation from a sleepy fishing village into a resort mecca in the 1980s. For more than a decade prior, nearly the entire Red Sea Coast was an off-limits military zone following the 1967 war with Israel. The unplanned building bonanza that followed has resulted in a jarring contrast between the inland (lined with concrete skeletons and resort gates), and the beauty offshore—where sandy islands interrupt the meeting of the sky and the sea, and pleasure boats briefly dot the expanse of blue on blue, before disappearing over the horizon.

Visitors seldom spend much time in town (save for downtown dining), preferring to relax at their resort's private beach, journey into the desert, or explore the Red Sea's striking underwater worlds on diving or snorkeling day trips.

ORIENTATION

Hurghada—the largest city in the Red Sea Governorate—extends for around 30 kilometers (20 mi) along the coast with the main neighborhoods **Al-Dahar** in the far north (home to most of the locals) and the downtown **Sakala,** which includes the restaurant-filled **Hurghada Marina.** South of Sakala a long row of wall-to-wall resorts compete for the shoreline, followed by more clusters of hotels outside of the city proper in the resort towns of **Sahl Hasheesh, Makadi Bay,** and **Soma Bay.**

SIGHTS

Hurghada Marina

New Marina Blvd.; www.hurghada-marina.com; no tel.; 10am-midnight daily; free

Hurghada's sleek marina hosts a boardwalk of the city's best restaurants and bars with a view of resting yachts. It's mostly a dining destination, but also a nice spot for an after-dinner stroll.

Hurghada Museum

Airport Rd., Mubarak 6; tel. 0111 111 8891; www.hurghadamuseum.com; 10am-2pm and 5pm-11pm daily; 250LE adults, 125LE students

The brand new Hurghada Museum opened its doors in 2020, hosting gems from the pharaonic era all the way up to Mohammed Ali's dynasty. The well-curated space is divided by themes like ancient beauty routines and the pharaonic obsession with the afterlife.

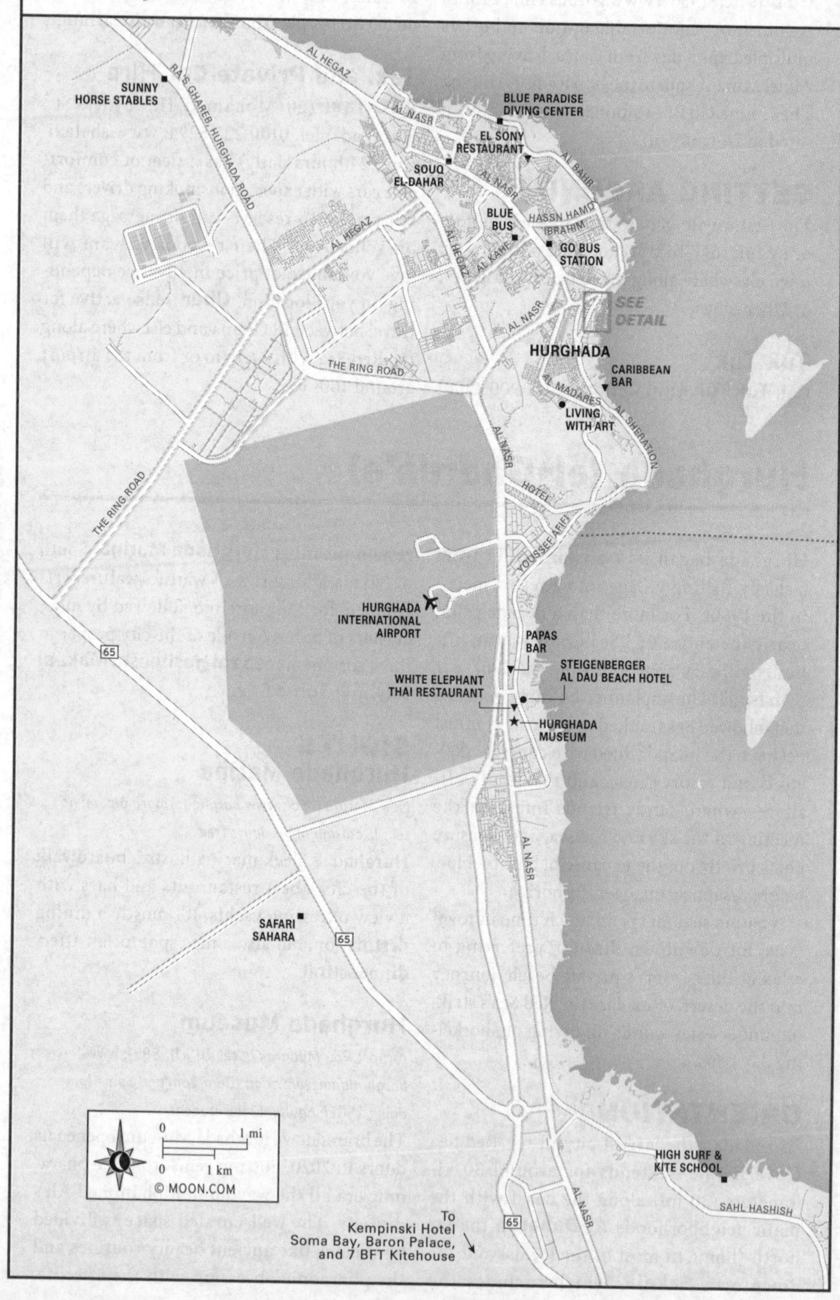
Hurghada
SUNNY HORSE STABLES
AL HEGAZ
RA'S GHAREB, HURGHADA ROAD
AL NASR
BLUE PARADISE DIVING CENTER
EL SONY RESTAURANT
SOUQ EL-DAHAR
AL BAHR
BLUE BUS
HASSN HAMDY
IBRAHIM
GO BUS STATION
AL KAHF
SEE DETAIL
HURGHADA
CARIBBEAN BAR
THE RING ROAD
AL MADARES
LIVING WITH ART
AL SHERATION
HOTEL
YOUSSEF AFIFI
HURGHADA INTERNATIONAL AIRPORT
65
PAPAS BAR
STEIGENBERGER AL DAU BEACH HOTEL
WHITE ELEPHANT THAI RESTAURANT
HURGHADA MUSEUM
SAFARI SAHARA
0
1 mi
1 km
© MOON.COM
HIGH SURF & KITE SCHOOL
SAHL HASHISH
To Kempinski Hotel Soma Bay, Baron Palace, and 7 BFT Kitehouse

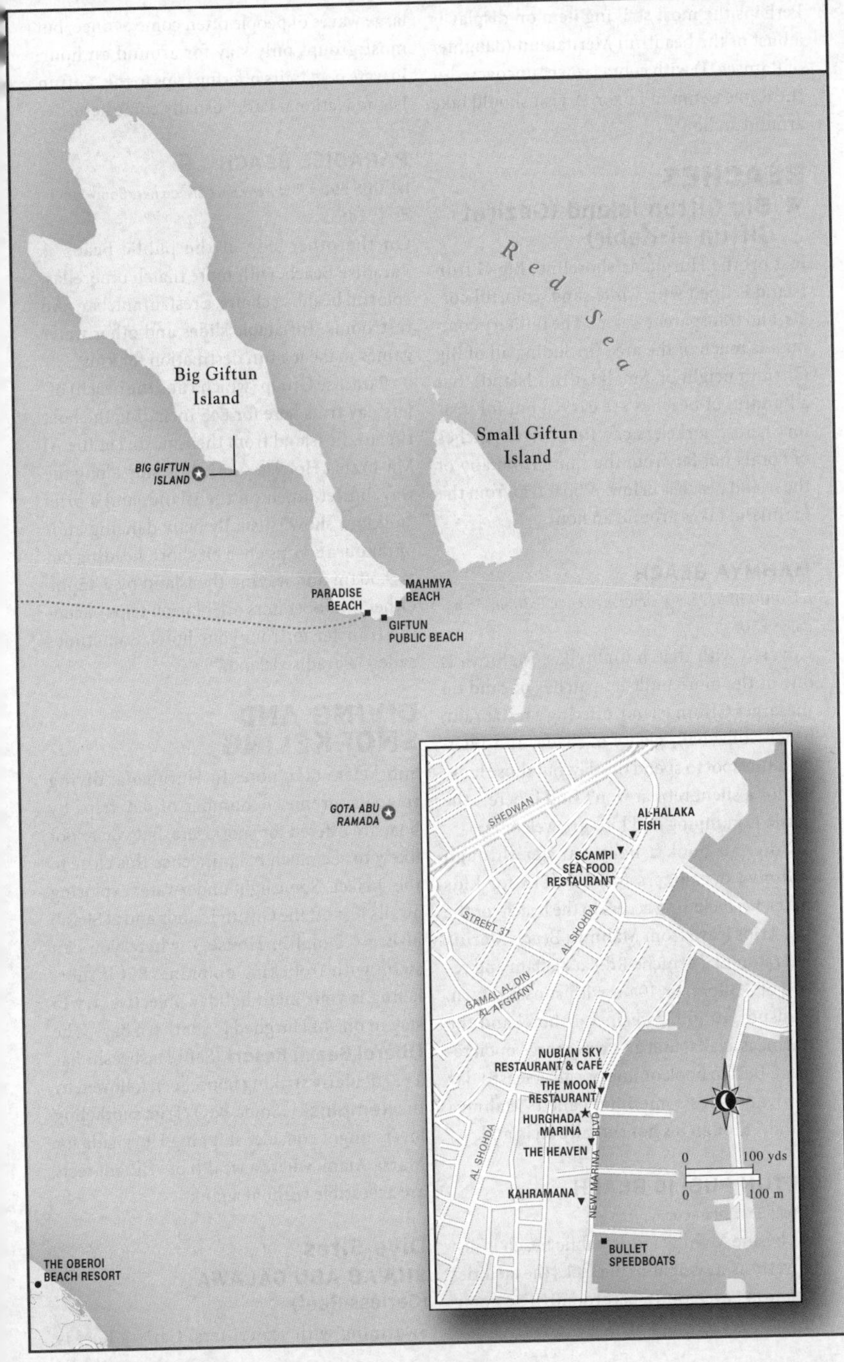
Red Sea
Big Giftun Island
Small Giftun Island
BIG GIFTUN ISLAND
PARADISE BEACH
MAHMYA BEACH
GIFTUN PUBLIC BEACH
GOTA ABU RAMADA
THE OBEROI BEACH RESORT
SHEDWAN
AL-HALAKA FISH
SCAMPI SEA FOOD RESTAURANT
STREET 37
AL SHOHDA
GAMAL AL DIN AL AFGHANY
NUBIAN SKY RESTAURANT & CAFÉ
THE MOON RESTAURANT
HURGHADA MARINA
THE HEAVEN
NEW MARINA BLVD
AL SHOHDA
KAHRAMANA
BULLET SPEEDBOATS
0
100 yds
0
100 m

Perhaps the most striking item on display is a bust of the beautiful Meritamun (daughter of Ramses II) with cobra crown, uncovered at the Ramesseum in Luxor. A visit should take around an hour.

BEACHES

★ Big Giftun Island (Gezirat Giftun el-Kebir)

Just off the Hurghada shoreline, Big Giftun Island is lined with white sand, colorful corals, and transparent waters. The military commands much of the area (including all of Big Giftun's neighbor, Small Giftun Island), but a handful of beaches are carved out for visitors here. Snorkelers can find pretty patches of corals not far from the shore from any of the island beaches below. A boat trip from the mainland takes around an hour.

MAHMYA BEACH

tel. 0100 111 9792; www.mahmya.com; 8:30am-6pm daily; €30

Covered with thatch umbrellas, Mahmya is one of the more built-up patches of sand on the larger Giftun Island, offering a restaurant, beach volleyball, plenty of shade, and WCs. It's a fun spot to spend the day, but those looking for a silent retreat won't find it here—the music is pumping and kids are welcome.

You can book a boat transfer through Mahmya organizers for €30 (€15 for kids under 12) including access to the beach for the day. Trips leave from Mahmya Beach Marina (Sheraton El Corniche Rd.) at 8:30am and return at 4:30pm, or 10am with sunset return. Transportation between your hotel and the Marina is available at an extra charge upon request. Best to book online or call at least a day in advance. It's sometimes called "Mahmya Island," though it's not actually an island.

GIFTUN PUBLIC BEACH

No tel.; 8am-sunset daily; free

Just beside Mahmya, this public beach is just as pretty as its neighbor but lacks the facilities (you won't even find a bathroom). It's a popular stopover for big tour boats, which means large waves of people often come at once, but most groups only stay for around an hour. Private boat tours offering trips to the "Giftun Island National Park" usually come here.

PARADISE BEACH

tel. 0115 600 7755; www.paradiseco.net; 8am-4pm daily; €45

On the other side of the public beach is Paradise Beach, with more thatch umbrellas, colorful beanbag chairs, a restaurant, bar, and restrooms. Inflatable slides and other water games make it a fun destination for kids.

Paradise Group (which runs the beach) offers day trips here for €45 including the boat ride to the island from their marina at the Al Mashrabia Hotel, a snorkeling stop along the way, buffet lunch on the island, and a brief "folklore show" (usually belly dancing and/or tanoura). Trips are a bit short, heading out at 9:30am and leaving the island by 3:45pm. Other tour operators offer longer trips including transfer to/from your hotel. Sometimes called "Paradise Island."

DIVING AND SNORKELING

Snorkelers take note: In Hurghada, diving reigns supreme. A number of day trips by boat are offered for snorkelers, but you're not likely to see much magnificence this close to the surface. Some light underwater exploring awaits just off the Giftun Islands and at Sha'ab al-Erg ("Dolphin House"), where you can swim with frolicking dolphins. But if snorkeling is your main holiday objective, try to stay in one of Hurghada's southern bays. The **Oberoi Beach Resort** (Sahl Hasheesh) has a particularly striking house reef, followed by the **Kempinski** (Soma Bay). True snorkeling lovers might consider skipping Hurghada for Marsa Alam, where a wealth of brilliant reefs are accessible without a tank.

Dive Sites

SHA'AB ABU GALAWA (Carless Reef)

Swarming with sea critters, Carless Reef is

notable for its two large pinnacles that jut out from a coral garden plateau. Large fish (tuna and reef sharks) swim among moray eels, neon-colored sea slugs, and other miniature marine life. The site is located between Umm Gamar and Big Giftun Island, about 1 hour from Hurghada by boat. Suitable for all levels if waters are calm, but during windy days even advanced divers will want to avoid the unsheltered site. Caves start at around 30 meters (100 ft) depth (ripe for the exploration by the experienced), but the main attractions are no deeper than 16 meters (52 ft).

★ GOTA ABU RAMADA

Nicknamed "The Aquarium" for its wealth of sea life, this spot is a joy for all levels of divers. Butterflyfish, eagle rays, and coral compete in an aquatic beauty pageant, their vibrant colors popping against the white sand. Boats from Hurghada reach the site (south of Abu Ramada Island) in around an hour.

UMM GAMAR

North of the Giftun Islands, Umm Gamar (or "Mother of the Moon") gets its name from the crescent-shaped island that borders the reef. The plateau on the south side has pretty corals that play occasional host to turtles and (almost always harmless) whitetip reef sharks. Suitable for beginners to advanced. Site reached in around 90 minutes by boat from Hurghada.

SHA'AB AL-ERG ("Dolphin House")

On the north side of Hurghada, directly east of El Gouna, this horseshoe-shaped reef has a sandy bottom at 12 meters (39 ft), which gradually slopes down into a coral garden that keeps the company of unicorn fish, blue-spotted ribbontail rays, Napoleon fish, and turtles. As a dive site it's mediocre, but the resident dolphins are the highlight, making it a popular spot for snorkeling outings as well. It's not uncommon to see dozens at a time, playing and communicating with their trademark chatter. Suitable for all levels. Depth: up to around 20 meters (65 ft).

SHA'AB ABU NUHAS

Just a few kilometers north of Shadwan Island, this three-sided reef is Egypt's own Bermuda Triangle. No fewer than five shipwrecks lie nearby, victims of the shallow corals invisible from the surface. The oldest—the British *SS Carnatic,* which sank in 1869 en route from Suez to Bombay—is also the most majestic, with shattered glass from its large wine cargo still visible on the ship's floor. Sea life has now reclaimed the wrecks, and the corals that brought the boats down are still pretty and unassuming. On calm days all levels can enjoy four of the ships, but more skill is needed when the currents are strong to reach the fifth. The site is a good journey from central Hurghada, about 2.5-3.5 hours by boat.

Outfitters

BLUE PARADISE DIVING CENTER

14 el-Bahr Rd.; tel. 0111 350 84 00; www.blueparadise.be; 10am-6:30pm daily; prices vary

The European-run Blue Paradise Diving Center offers fun and safe outings on their comfortable boat, "Basyl." Their team is extremely professional and group sizes are kept to just 15-20 people. Prices start at €30/day for snorkeling, €60/day for diving, and €303 for 2 days of a PADI course for beginners. Best to book a week or two in advance (especially during high season, Apr.-Nov.), but last-minute reservations by noon the day before are sometimes possible. Hotel transfers included.

BULLET SPEEDBOATS

Hurghada Marina; tel. 0102 404 8277; www.bulletspeedboats.com; 7am-9pm daily; prices vary

To avoid the crowds, rent your own speedboat for a 4-hour snorkel tour. Prices start from €128 for up to 4 people. Choose from the "Dolphin Spotting" trip (recommended), "Three Islands" tour—including the reefs off Giftun Island and two lesser visited desert islands, Magawish and Abu Munqar—or customize your own schedule. Larger boats for up to 8 people also available, and each additional hour is €35. Best to contact them via phone, WhatsApp, or Facebook.

1
2
WWW.BLUEPARADISE.BE
BASYL

OTHER RECREATION AND ACTIVITIES

Safaris

SAFARI SAHARA

Safari Land, Ring Rd.; tel. 0122 747 2358; www.safari-sahara.com; 8am-9pm daily; prices vary

Safari Sahara arranges excellent sunset quad bike trips to a Bedouin village (€23), and other desert excursions in 4WDs (€19) or dune buggies (€49). All outings include transportation to/from your hotel and a buffet lunch or dinner. Helmets and glasses are provided for the quad bike and dune buggy trips, but be sure to bring a scarf and comfortable shoes.

Kitesurfing and Windsurfing

HIGH SURF & KITE SCHOOL

In Long Beach Resort, off Sahl Hasheesh Rd., 23 km/14 mi south of central Hurghada; tel. 0101 120 2227; www.highsurf-kite.com; 9am-6pm daily; prices vary

Protected by a cove, this shallow kite and windsurfing spot provides ideal conditions for beginners. The high-quality equipment and professional, patient instructors are added bonuses. Beginner lessons start at €110/3 hours for kitesurfing and €75/3 hours for windsurfing. More advanced guests can go out on their own with rentals from €55/2 hours for kitesurfing or €20/hour for windsurfing. They have a second location closer to central Hurghada called **Magic Kite** (14 El-Nasr Rd., in Grand Seas Hostmark Resort; tel. 0100 404 9406; www.magickitehurghada.com; same hours and prices) of equal quality.

7 BFT KITEHOUSE

Soma Bay, 56 km/35 mi south of central Hurghada; tel. 0127 755 5025; https://kitehouse-somabay.com; 8am-6:30pm daily; prices vary

The protected Soma Bay is an excellent place to kitesurf. This kite school and rental house offers professional instructors and the latest equipment. Two-day courses (6-8 hours) go for €320, whether for beginner, intermediate, or advanced levels. Group sizes are limited to four people maximum. Private lessons also available for €89/hour. Kitesurfers just looking to rent equipment can get a kite and board for a half day (4 hours) for €62. Free transportation provided from any hotel in the Soma Bay area.

1: reefs off the Giftun Islands **2:** boat trip with Blue Paradise Diving Center

Horseback Riding

SUNNY HORSE STABLES

Off Hurghada-Ismailia Rd.; tel. 0111 008 2804; hamadatito@gmail.com; 5am-8pm daily; prices vary

Journey to Hurghada's desert, mountains, and/or sea on healthy horses with the pleasant company of brothers Tito and Mido or their cousin Mahmoud. Choose from a quick 1-hour ride (€25), a 6-hour mountain trek with lunch (€120), or something in between. Helmets, chaps, and riding pants included.

SHOPPING

SOUQ EL-DAHAR

El-Dahar Square, off El-Nasr St.; no tel.; 11am-11pm daily

This bustling covered market is a fun place to explore in the evenings when locals come out to shop. Browse fresh fruits and veg, fish, spices, live animals, and handicrafts.

FOOD

The well-manicured **Hurghada Marina** (New Marina Blvd.) is the city's top dining destination for holidaymakers who venture outside the resorts. Take a stroll along the boardwalk to check out the full menus. Just to the north, restaurants on and around **El-Shohada Street** serve up some of the best seafood in town, catering to locals and visitors in the know (but don't expect to find alcohol).

Egyptian

EL SONY RESTAURANT

Off el-Bahr St., across from Safwa Mosque, el-Dahar; tel. 065 3553778; noon-midnight daily; 40-120LE mains

For a no-nonsense Egyptian grill, this local favorite is the best in town. Try the grilled chicken or succulent lamb with complimentary sides of bread, tahini, and salad. The interior (though not likely to inspire) is kept clean.

NUBIAN SKY RESTAURANT & CAFÉ

New Marina Blvd.; tel. 0111 838 3188; 10am-1am Sat.-Thurs. and 2pm-1am Fri.; 70-200LE mains

If you're looking for Egyptian food in the Marina, head here. Along with the countrywide favorites of falafel and fuul, Nubian delicacies are served fresh. Try the juicy tagines (stews cooked and served in a clay pot) like okra with veal, or minced meat with mousakka'a (an eggplant-based blend). Seating is open-air and shaded. Alcohol and shisha available.

International

★ KAHRAMANA

New Marina Blvd.; tel. 0122 242 8204; 2pm-2am daily; 70-200LE mains

Kahramana is one of the more atmospheric restaurants on the Marina strip, with a large outdoor seating section of colorful couches and an attractive interior. The menu is eclectic with a smattering of Indian and Chinese food alongside their specialty—locally farmed steaks (beef or camel). The lounge feel makes it a nice place for an evening with drinks or a shisha (some of the best around).

THE HEAVEN

New Marina Blvd.; tel. 0122 242 8204; noon-1am daily; 70-250LE mains

Dine al fresco on a wide variety of delicious. Try the catch of the day, camel, or locally farmed T-bone steak for the freshest dishes (skip the shrimp). The music is a bit cheesy, but service is on point. Excellent cocktails, other alcohol, and shisha served.

THE MOON RESTAURANT

New Marina Blvd.; tel. 0122 457 4533; 10am-2am daily; 70-250LE mains

Mostly a Lebanese restaurant, the Moon also serves up a bit of local fare like (a huge) camel steak that comes out sizzling on a hot stone. It's hard to go wrong with anything on the menu, so sample an array of options with the mixed mezze platter and mixed grill. Inside there's a bit of a sports-bar atmosphere (especially when a game is on), but some days are quieter than others. Alcohol and shisha available.

★ WHITE ELEPHANT THAI RESTAURANT

Youssef Afifi Rd., in front of Steigenberger Al Dau Beach Hotel; tel. 065 3442156; noon-10:30pm daily; 130-250LE mains

Let your tastebuds explore the hints of ginger, lemongrass, and coconut milk in the White Elephant's fresh and flavorful Thai dishes. Food is artfully plated, matching the pleasant ambiance with cushioned booths and sumptuous accents. Ample outdoor seating also available. The fried ice cream makes for a special desert. Alcohol served.

Seafood

SCAMPI SEA FOOD RESTAURANT

El-Shohada St., Sakala; tel. 0100 440 2209; noon-2am daily; 60-170LE mains

Just a few paces south of al-Halaka Fish, Scampi is a close competitor for the title of Hurghada's seafood restaurant. Ingredients are fresh, and a good selection of seafood stews (tawagin) are on offer alongside more traditional options. Don't miss the grilled grouper (waqaar) served with shrimp and calamari.

★ AL-HALAKA FISH

El-Shohada St., near Al-Mina Mosque, Sakala; tel. 0100 456 2800; noon-midnight daily; 50-220LE mains

Head to al-Halaka for the freshest fish in town. Select your meal from a bed of ice and choose how you want it cooked. The grilled prawns and fried calamari are the highlights, with traditional mezze (try the hummus) and hot bread an added treat. Sit upstairs for a sea view.

BARS AND NIGHTLIFE

Travelers staying in one of Hurghada's many resorts will likely have bars to choose from on site. The Hurghada Marina is another pleasant option for a calm night out, with nearly all the restaurants serving alcohol and shisha. For proper bars around the city, check out one of these options.

★ CARIBBEAN BAR

El-Fondoq St., inside Bella Vista Resort; tel. 0111 049 7436; 7am-midnight daily; 55-110LE drinks

This gorgeous open-air venue jutting out into the sea serves up a mean cocktail with a spritz of sea breeze. Live music usually plays on Saturdays, and karaoke on Tuesdays from 8pm. Fresh juice and decent food (pizza, burgers, sandwiches, etc.) also on offer. Around sunset is the nicest time to visit, when the sea and sky change colors and the crowds haven't arrived yet. Reservations necessary by phone or WhatsApp.

PAPAS BAR

Mamsha Rd., al-Hambra Building, beside Carrfour Market; tel. 0106 883 3552; 3pm-3am daily; 55-110LE drinks

Dimly lit with liquor bottle lamps, Papas is part sports bar, part nightclub, part live music venue, depending on the evening. Call ahead to see what's on the schedule. Sisha, draught beer, and a long list of cocktails available. As with nearly all bars in Egypt, be prepared for smoke.

ACCOMMODATIONS

Choose your accommodation wisely in Hurghada: The lack of clean, female-friendly public beaches means you might be confined to your resort or compound for swimming. If you plan to spend most of your time on boat trips or other excursions, check Airbnb for cheaper, more diverse options. But if you want to lounge at the beach and enjoy fine dining without a commute, the large resorts are your best bet.

Under 800LE

LIVING WITH ART

Hadaba Hill, next to former German Consolate; tel. 065 3448 003; www.livingwithart.biz; 750LE d

Run by two art collecting Germans who've lived in Hurghada for over 35 years, this eclectic B&B has 16 suites—each with kitchenette and locally made wrought iron furniture. The tree-lined courtyard and rooftop terrace with Jacuzzi looking out to the sea are the highlights. Hosts Karin and Peter also keep a fully stocked bar and a kitchen that cooks up fantastic food. The one downside is the lack of private beach, but it's a great option as a base for divers or those planning to spend their days at sea.

1,650-3,300LE

BARON PALACE

S. Marina Drive, Sahl Hasheesh; tel. 0112 666 6280; www.baronhotels.com; 2,550LE d

This truly palatial hotel boasts a long sandy beach and rich landscaping with lush green grass and rows of palms. The lobby drips with opulence, and the rooms (though less luxurious) are spacious and comfortable. Several pools spot the premises, including a massive one that seems to pour into the sea.

★ KEMPINSKI HOTEL SOMA BAY

Soma Bay, 53 km/33 mi south of Hurghada International Airport; tel. 010 6880 1990; www.kempinski.com; 3,000LE d

Tucked away in a charming bay on the far southern border of Hurghada, the Kempinski claims a beautiful stretch of the shore. The resort looks across the water to craggy mountains in the distance, best enjoyed from the sandy beach lined with lounge chairs and umbrellas (an adults-only section allows for a quiet escape). Second only to the sea and house reef are the two large pools and lazy river with waterfalls. Rooms and common spaces are built in an elegant blend of Islamic and European architecture.

Over 3,300LE

STEIGENBERGER AL DAU BEACH HOTEL

Youssef Afifi Rd., El Mamsha El Seyahi; tel. 065 3465400; www.steigenbergeraldauresort.com; 3,200LE d, all inclusive

With its massive swimming pool, meandering lazy river, and long stretch of private beach, the Steigenberger has no shortage of special features. Guests can borrow canoes and paddleboats for free, and hop over to the Steigenberger Aqua Park just across the street. Unlike at many all-inclusive resorts, the food here is excellent and varied, with a delicious sushi bar and Lebanese restaurant, among other options. All 390 rooms and suites are spacious and attractive, each with a balcony looking out to green lawns, palm trees, and the turquoise sea.

★ THE OBEROI BEACH RESORT

117 Sahl Hasheesh; tel. 065 3461040; www.oberoihotels.com; 4,650LE d

Luxury is your only option at the Oberoi. All accommodations are suites, with soaring domed ceilings, soft colors, and "traditional" touches like handwoven Bedouin wall art. The house reef here is probably the best in all of Hurghada, making diving and snorkeling excursions as easy as a walk to the beach. A pier off the long sandy shore leads to the reef edge for easy access. Restaurants are exceptional with fantastic breakfast included.

INFORMATION AND SERVICES

ATMs can be found in most hotels and elsewhere around the city.

Medical

For emergencies, **El Salam Hospital** (Corniche Rd., Sakala; tel. 065 3615012; www.elsalamhospital.com; 24 hours daily) is one of the better options around.

Pharmacies

Hurghada has no shortage of pharmacies. **El Ezaby** (tel. 19600; www.elezabypharmacy.com; 24 hours daily) delivers 24 hours a day and has multiple branches around the city. **Abdeen Pharmacy** (Nasr St.; tel. 19036; 24 hours daily) is another reputable nationwide store always available for delivery.

GETTING THERE

The easiest way to get to Hurghada from Cairo is by plane. Bus is a great option for travelers on a budget. To reach Hurghada from Luxor, bus or private car hire is the way to go.

Air

HURGHADA INTERNATIONAL AIRPORT

Airport St.; tel. 065 3414213; www.hurghada-airports.com

Hurghada International Airport is located just a few kilometers west of Hurghada city center. A flight from Cairo takes 1 hour, starting at around 4,500LE round-trip with multiple flights a day on **Egypt Air** (www.egyptair.com).

Getting to your hotel from Hurghada International Airport should cost 75-290LE depending on distance. Arrange with **ABC Taxi** (20 Mohamed Hawaydek St., Hurghada; tel. 0100 222 8294; www.abctaxi.com; 24 hours daily) for safe and reliable drivers. Their team will give you an exact price in advance depending on your location.

Bus

The bus takes around 7.5 hours from Cairo. **Go Bus** (El-Nasr St., Hurghada; tel. 19568; www.go-bus.com; 225LE) is the best, departing Cairo from Abdel Minam Riyad Square (next to Ramses Hilton), Downtown. **Blue Bus** (El Nasr St., 500 m/1,600 ft north of Go Bus Station, Hurghada; tel. 16128; www.bluebus.com.eg; 499LE), a close second, departs Cairo from Ramses Station, Downtown. **Upper Egypt Bus Co.** (El-Nasr St., 1.4 km/0.9 mi north of the Go Bus Station, Hurghada; no tel.; 200LE) departs Cairo from Torgoman Station, Downtown. All three companies also offer daily trips to Cairo and Luxor (4-5 hours; 120-135LE).

All three bus stations are located within one mile of each other on El-Nasr Street in Hurghada's El-Dahar neighborhood on the north side of the city.

GETTING AROUND

Taxis and Ubers are plentiful around Hurghada, and they're best way to get around the city and beyond.

You'll find plenty of taxis around central Hurghada for local transportation. Safe and reliable, **ABC Taxi** (20 Mohamed Hawaydek St., Hurghada, tel. 0100 222 8294; www.abc-taxi.com; 24 hours daily) offers private transportation within and between Red Coast cities (usually for much less than hotels provide). To reserve, call or message them on WhatsApp. **Uber** is also active in and around Hurghada.

El Quseir

The sleepy port city of El Quseir is a rare preserved piece of history along the Red Sea Coast. Its name ("The Short" in Arabic) comes from its strategic location at the end of a dried riverbed, Wadi Hammamat, that cuts across the Eastern Desert and offers the shortest route between the Nile and the Red Sea.

Some historians believe Queen Hatshepsut's famous expedition to the Land of Punt in the 15th century BC left from here, returning with a wealth of gold, exotic plants, and incense. The Ptolemies built their own port city on this spot in the 3rd century BC called Myos Hormus ("Harbor of the Mussel"), serving as the main entrepôt for trade with India and the Arabian Peninsula.

With the advent of Islam in the 7th century AD, El Quseir became a popular departure point for pilgrims performing the hajj to Mecca. And in the 19th century, Mohammed Ali sent ships full of soldiers (to wage his war in Arabia) and subsidized wheat—a gift to the Holy Cities across the sea—from Quseir's port. The town became something of a little Italy in the 20th century, when an Italian phosphate mining factory set up shop in 1916. A colony of Italian workers populated the area until the late 1950s, when President Nasser nationalized the company and sent them packing.

Today Quseir is a quiet and dusty town—a far cry from Hurghada's hyper-developed strip of coast—spotted with inconspicuous relics of the past and relatively untouched reefs.

SIGHTS

El Quseir Fort

El-Gamhoria St., central El Quseir; no tel.; 8am-5pm daily; 40LE

Smack dab in the middle of Quseir, this 16th-century Ottoman fort was built to protect against threats from the Portuguese, who traded heavily across nearby waters. When Napoleon invaded Egypt in 1798, the French occupied and refitted the structure—making it strong enough to survive bombardment by the British Navy (before the French got the boot from Egypt just a couple of years later). In the 1810s, Mohammed Ali took it over to use as a base for his incursions into the Arabian Peninsula against the fundamentalist Wahhabis.

After decades of disuse, the fort was restored by the American Research Center in Egypt (ARCE), with mini exhibitions and good signage added in the towers. The courtyard holds a locally made pearl diving boat, trucks from the phosphate factory, and cannons dating to the Napoleonic era that held off the Brits. Don't miss the view from the top of the round tower in the middle that looks down on a large floor map of the region. Bring a flashlight to get the best out of the exhibits.

Old Italian Phosphate Factory

North end of Abdel Khalik Tharwat St., central El Quseir; no tel.; 7am-sunset daily; free

Residents of Quseir keen on protecting the town's history have managed to save (for now) this shell of the Italian phosphate factory first built in 1916. You can still wander around the abandoned plant, shut down for decades, which has become something of an open-air museum with vintage refrigerators, scales, and other vestiges of a bygone era. Ask the guards at the entrance if you can take a look around.

DIVING AND SNORKELING

Dive and Snorkel Sites

ROCKY VALLEY DIVERS CAMP

Safaga-El Quseir Rd., 13 km/8 mi north of central Quseir; tel. 0100 653 2964; www.rockyvalleydiverscamp.com; 8am-6pm daily; 40LE day use

Located on the edge of a small bay north of central Quseir, Rocky Valley is home to the stunning **Abu Sawatir** reef. With an easy entrance and gradually sloping ground that descends to more than 40 meters (130 ft), this site is a great option for both snorkelers and divers. Colorful corals swarming with sea life line the bay on both sides. The camp itself consists of cone-shaped thatch huts on the beach and simple bungalows on a hill across the street. Minimalists might enjoy spending the night, but most will content themselves with use of the facilities for the day (WCs, café, umbrellas, and chairs) while exploring the reef.

SHARM EL-LOLE CAMP

El Quseir-Marsa Alam Rd., 10 km/6 mi south of central Quseir; tel. 0109 264 3474; 8am-6pm daily; 100LE day use

On the south side of Quseir, this simple camp sits alongside the **Zerib Kebir** reef (also known as **"Kahf,"** or Cave, for its many caves and canyons). This site also lies in a vibrant coral-lined bay with a gradual entrance, descending to 30 meters (100 ft)—suitable for snorkelers and all levels of divers. Along with WCs, you can take advantage of the café with fresh juices and snacks. For lunch (70-100LE), reserve a day in advance and choose between fish, chicken, or vegetarian dishes. A chair and umbrella come with the day-use pass.

Old Italian Phosphate Factory

Outfitters

DEEP OCEAN BLUE DIVING CENTER

Safaga-El Quseir Rd., in Silver Beach Resort; tel. 0101 050 4700; www.deep-ocean-blue.com; 8:30am-5pm daily; prices vary

Deep Ocean Blue is a local dive center with international standards. Nader, Sabina, and the rest of their team ensure safe and fun outings. Shore dives start at just €28 or €10 for snorkeling. Enjoy a full-day boat trip with two dives for €65 or €40 for snorkeling (includes guide, equipment, lunch, and hotel transfers). PADI courses available for beginners starting at €149 for two days (includes equipment). Numbers are capped at a 6 people per dive guide, and 38 people max.

EXTRA DIVERS WORLDWIDE

Safaga-El Quseir Rd., in Mövenpick Resort; tel. 0127 551 6267; www.extradivers-worldwide.com; 8am-6pm daily; prices vary

Located in the Mövenpick, this international dive center offers highly professional guides and equipment. The price for diving starts at €37 for one dive to €225 for six dives at the beautiful house reef. Snorkelers can rent equipment (mask, snorkel, and fins) for €11/day. Boat day trips (8-9 hours) available, leaving from Port Ghalib (1hour to the south). Guests not staying at the Mövenpick will be charged an extra 20%. Be sure to reserve in advance, especially during high season (Oct. and Apr.).

FOOD

Most meals will likely be enjoyed in your hotel, but there are a couple of nice seafood restaurants in central Quseir near the water. Outside the resorts, don't expect to find alcohol.

★ CALEMARO FISH

Port Saed St., next to El Quseir Hotel; tel. 0106 420 0914; 10am-11pm daily; 60-120LE mains

This unassuming restaurant doesn't have the seaside seating of its competitor down the street (El Fardous), but the food here is just as good and half the price. Plus, you can admire the work of local artists in the aquarium-like dining room with Red Sea life adorning the walls. Try the calamari and catch of the day.

EL FARDOUS

Port Saed St.; tel. 0128 332 4884; 10:30am-10pm daily; 120-250LE mains

Dine to the soundtrack of the waves on El Fardous's little patch of seashore. A range of seafood dishes on offer. Ask what's fresh to avoid disappointment.

ACCOMMODATIONS

Under 800LE

★ EL QUSEIR HOTEL

138 Port Said St., central El Quseir; tel. 0103 314 0049; elquseirhotel@gmail.com; 500LE d

Built in 1908 by a local sheikh from the Ababda tribe, this renovated stone house with wooden accents is the most unique accommodation option in Quseir. The hotel—now operated by the sheikh's grandson, Mustafa—sits directly beside the sea, offering stunning views and a constant breeze. Historical photos of old El Quseir decorate the walls, adding to the museum feel of the place. Mustafa and his team are also excellent guides, happy to give guests a walking tour around their hometown. Breakfast included. The one downside is the lack of a private beach.

1,650-3,300LE

MÖVENPICK RESORT EL QUSEIR

Safaga-El Quseir Rd., 7 km/4 mi north of central El Quseir; tel. 065 3350410; www.movenpick.com; 2,000LE d

The house reef at this Mövenpick is the best in Quseir, with brilliant marine life including a wealth of colorful corals. The resort's long beach hugs a private bay (once the site of an ancient port), perfect for loungers, divers, and snorkelers alike. Rooms here are a bit small, but have attractive features like barrel vault ceilings and bright accents. For the best food and ambiance, head to the Seagull's Restaurant perched on a seaside terrace. Other highlights include an excellent on-site dive center, hammocks strategically hung between palm trees, and two large swimming pools (one heated in the winter). Breakfast included.

GETTING THERE

Air

The easiest way to get to Quseir from Cairo is by flying into **Marsa Alam International Airport** (flight time 1.5 hours) and taking a private car arranged by your hotel (1-hour drive). For more frequent flights, fly to **Hurghada International Airport** (1 hour) and hire a private driver to Quseir (1.5-2 hours).

Bus

A bus ride from Cairo takes around 10 hours. Your most comfortable option, **Go Bus** (tel. 19567; www.go-bus.com; 255LE), boards at Abdel Minam Riyad Square (next to the Ramses Hilton) and typically leaves around midnight. The **Upper Egypt Bus Company** (no tel.; 200LE) also offers multiple trips a day to/from Cairo, leaving Cairo from the Torgoman Bus Station in Downtown.

Both bus companies also make daily trips to Quseir from Hurghada (2.5-3 hours; 70 LE). In Quseir, the **bus station** is located 1 kilometer (0.6 mi) west of the town center on Falaki Road.

A handful of buses head back to Cairo out of Quseir each afternoon, but buses to Hurghada are infrequent. To get to Hurghada, hop in a shared taxi—a seven-seater Peugeot—to make the pretty 2-hour trip along the sea. The cars leave as soon as all seats are filled from a parking lot off the Ring Road to the northwest of Downtown Quseir. Expect to pay 40-50LE per person, and feel free to buy up more space to hurry the car on the road.

GETTING AROUND

Downtown Quseir is very walkable. To get to the dive/snorkel sites farther afield, ask your hotel to arrange for a **private car** (you won't find any official taxis in the city).

Marsa Alam

Stretching for some 190 kilometers (120 mi) along the coast, Marsa Alam is a divers' paradise. The mass tourism of Hurghada hasn't yet made its way this far south, and untouched reefs teeming with vibrant sea life line the shore. Visitors don't spend much time in the town center (a small and dusty desert outpost), preferring instead to base themselves in one of the ecolodges or resorts that spot the coast. Between them, miles of unspoiled land kiss the azure waters of the Red Sea to the east and rugged mountains to the west.

As such relatively uncharted territory, "Marsa Alam" has become something of a catch-all name for Egypt's coast south of Quseir—including Port Ghalib (near the Marsa Alam International Airport), Marsa Alam Town, Wadi el Gemal National Park, and Hamata. Anything south of this strip is usually off limits to visitors (with a high military presence), especially the southernmost territory of the Halayib and Shalateen, also known as the Halayib Triangle, claimed by both Egypt and Sudan.

BEACHES

Marsa Alam is all about beaches, diving, and snorkeling. Aside from whatever private patch of the coast your resort or ecolodge will offer, these are the best spots open to the public.

★ ABU DABBAB BEACH

Abu Dabbab Bay, El Quseir-Marsa Alam Rd., 35 km/22 mi north of Marsa Alam Town; www.abudabbab.com; 8am-midnight; 190LE

With its soft white sand, cyan waters, and shaded lounge chairs, Abu Dabbab is the crown jewel of Marsa Alam's beaches. Just off the blissful shore, visitors can swim in a sheltered bay with a wide sandy bottom and

TOP EXPERIENCE

Dugongs

dugong

Cousins of the manatee, dugongs get their name from the Malay word for mermaid (duyung). Though not as sleek as the mythical sea creatures, these friendly giants share their fluked tails and elegant swimming style. Reaching an average size of 3 meters (10 ft) and 400 kilograms (900 lbs), the herbivores sustain their figures on a diet of seagrass, sucking it up with their purpose-made snouts and earning them the nickname "sea cows." Because of their exclusive diet of these mostly coastal plants, dugongs have become a vulnerable species—threatened by degradation of their eating grounds and exposure to boat collisions as they graze. But efforts to protect the gentle giants have led to rising numbers, especially off Australia's Great Barrier Reef.

WHERE TO SPOT DUGONGS

Keep an eye out for these serene sirenians off the Red Sea Coast, often accompanied by golden trevally who snack on critters in sediment stirred up by the dugong's probing snout. Your best chance at spotting one is at their grazing grounds just off **Abu Dabbab Beach.**

explore two vibrant house reefs (one on each side) that burst with pinks, purples, and yellows. It's home to more than two dozen sea turtles and two friendly dugongs who feed on the bay's beds of sea grass. A chair and umbrella are included with the cost of entrance. WCs and a small snack bar available.

NAYZAK BEACH

Off Halayib wa Shalateen Rd., 10 km/6 mi south of Marsa Alam Town; 24 hours daily; free

This rugged beach gets its name ("Meteorite" in Arabic) from the large crater-like pool jutting into the coast that locals say was made by a prehistoric space rock hitting the earth. Whatever its origin, the spot is an excellent place for a dip in turquoise waters protected from the open sea. No facilities or shade nearby, so be sure to bring enough snacks, water, and sunscreen for your trip.

DIVING AND SNORKELING

Dive and Snorkel Sites by Boat

Marsa Alam has a wealth of exquisite coastal

reef walls accessible from the shore (like those of Abu Dabbab Beach and nearly every hotel or ecolodge's house reef), but travelers looking to adventure out to the deep blue might enjoy a trip to these special spots, which bring opportunities to spot spinner dolphins, shipwrecks, and (for divers) more dramatic underwater landscapes filled with larger sea life.

ELPHINSTONE REEF

Off Abu Dabbab Beach; 24 hours daily; free

Divers come from around the world to explore this reef, known for oceanic whitetip and hammerhead shark sightings. Other features include vibrant soft coral, sheer walls, and fun sea life like tuna, manta rays, and Napoleon fish. It's located just 30 minutes by speedboat from Abu Dabbab Beach. For advanced divers only (the current is strong), and not suitable for snorkeling.

MARSA MUBARAK AND MARSA SHONA

Boats leave from Port Ghalib Marina; 24 hours daily; free

These two bays located just south of Port Ghalib are often visited together. Lined with colorful reefs and frequented by sea turtles, the sheltered inlets are popular outings (sometimes too popular) for both snorkelers and divers. Summers can be crowded.

★ SAMADAI REEF ("Dolphin House")

Boats leave from Marsa Alam Marina; 24 hours daily; 105LE

This horseshoe-shaped reef hugs a shallow lagoon, creating an ideal resting place for spinner dolphins—and a perfect spot for both snorkelers and divers to observe the majestic creatures up close. Turtles, clownfish, and other colorful sea life are added treats (and fine consolation if the main attraction is a no show). Advanced divers can also enjoy a swim through underwater caves and explore rich pinnacles.

The area was named a protected reef in 2001 due to overcrowding, and the daily numbers of visitors has since been limited. Snorkelers are also required to wear a life jacket to prevent aspiring underwater cowboys. Reached by a 45-minute boat ride from the Marsa Alam Marina.

★ FURY SHOALS

Boats leave from Hamata Marina; 24 hours daily; free

This sprawling network of reefs in Egypt's deep south is home to some of the Red Sea's most pristine coral. Stretched over nearly 30 kilometers (20 mi), the reefs hold hidden gems like underwater caves, dense coral gardens, and multiple shipwrecks. Though mostly a divers' playground, some sections are also suitable for snorkelers.

SATAYAH REEF ("Dolphin House")

Boats leave from Hamata Marina; 24 hours daily; free

This lesser-visited "Dolphin House" is located at the southeastern edge of the Fury Shoals reef network. Stretching for around 5 kilometers (3 mi), the reef curves around a shallow lagoon and provides sanctuary to numerous pods of spinner dolphins. To get there is a bit of a trek (especially for travelers staying on the north side of Marsa Alam)—2 hours by boat from Hamata Port south of Wadi el Gemal National Park. Of course, dolphin sightings can't be guaranteed, but there's a high chance you'll get to swim with dozens. The reef itself is also a beautiful place to explore from the surface or deep down below with a tank.

Outfitters

BLUE OCEAN DIVE CENTERS & RESORTS

Abu Dabbab Bay, 35 km/22 mi north of Marsa Alam Town; tel. 012 0753 5555; www.blueocean-eg.com; 8am-5pm daily

Blue Ocean's knowledgeable snorkel and dive guides are based at Abu Dabbab Beach

1: a diver explores the reefs of Fury Shoals **2:** boat trip with Blue Ocean Dive Centers & Resorts

1

2

Swimming with Spinner Dolphins

Marsa Alam's two "Dolphin Houses"—Samadai and Satayah Reefs—offer unique opportunities to observe dozens of spinner dolphins in their natural habitat. It's important to keep in mind these reefs provide rare refuge for the nocturnal animals to rest and recover after long nights hunting in the wide-open sea. Samadai Reef is monitored by the Hurghada Environmental Protection and Conservation Association (HEPCA), which has divided the reef into zones (some off limits to people) and limited the number of daily visitors to protect the dolphins and their sanctuary. Satayah Reef, farther afield, isn't monitored. If you want to swim with these magical creatures:

- Be sure to choose an **ethical tour operator** (Blue Ocean and Red Sea Diving Safari are good ones).
- **Do not touch or swim after the animals,** and avoid making loud noises.
- If possible, **plan a trip outside summer** to avoid the largest groups.

and inside the nearby Hilton Nubian Resort. Their team gets you to the best spots and ensures a magical time in the water. Boats and dive equipment meet high-quality international standards, and PADI courses are available for beginners to advanced. Prices are good value for the quality of services, starting at €45 for one dive, including equipment. Contact them by email or phone to arrange for a wide array of trips for snorkelers, divers, or mixed groups. Some of their best trips include visits to **Satayah Reef** or **Samadai Reef** (each 8-10 hours; €60 per person). All excursions include hotel transfers, lunch, guides, and snorkeling equipment.

RED SEA DIVING SAFARI

tel. 065 3380021; www.redsea-divingsafari.com; 8am-6pm daily

Red Sea Diving Safari have three superb dive centers located at their ecolodges: Marsa Shagra, Marsa Nakari, and Wadi Lahami Villages. A dive at the house reef at any of the three costs €55, or €80 for one day unlimited diving (includes equipment). Larger packages come at a small discount (e.g., €370 for a 5-day package including equipment). These prices are for guests at any of their ecolodges. Non-resident guests pay around 30% extra.

OTHER RECREATION AND ACTIVITIES

Kitesurfing

WADI LAHAMI KITE SURFING

Halayeb wa Shalateen Rd., just south of Wadi El Gemal National Park; tel. 0122 174 4271; www.wadilahamikitesurfing.com; 8am-6pm daily; prices vary

Tucked away in Egypt's deep south, Wadi Lahami Kite Surfing offers a stunning backdrop for flying through the calm, shallow bay. Rolling mountains border the area to the west, with a mangrove forest to the north and the open sea to the east. The center got a facelift in 2020 and now matches the quality of the equipment and team of instructors. Beginner courses start from €280 for 6 hours to €450 for 12-hour course. Book a diving and kitesurfing package through Red Sea Diving Safari for a discount.

Safaris

AMORE SAFARI

El Quseir-Marsa Alam Rd., 4 km/2.5 mi east of the Marsa Alam Airport; tel. 0100 191 9999; www.amoresafari.com; 8am-8pm daily; prices vary

Take a ride on a camel, quad bike, or in a 4WD. Amore Safari offers a range of excursions—the best a 90-minute sunset quad bike trip along the beach and through the desert, ending with a buffet dinner, a belly dancer or tanoura show, and stargazing at their base, the Camel Yard (4.5 hours; €40). They're located in the north of Marsa Alam (just east of the airport), so it might not be the best choice for those staying in the deep south. Best to reserve a few days in advance during high season (Apr. and June-Oct.).

FOOD AND ACCOMMODATIONS

Accommodation in Marsa Alam is scattered along some 180 kilometers (110 mi) of coast to the north and south of the town center (where you're not likely to spend much time). Before choosing your accommodation, take into account your preferred activities. Do you want to visit Abu Dabbab Beach? Maybe stay in the north at the Hilton Marsa Alam Nubian Resort right next door. Do you want to spend a day or more exploring the land and sea in the Wadi el Gemal National Park? You might want to stay farther south at Wadi Lahami Village. Want to visit both? Perhaps choose somewhere in the middle, like Deep South Ecolodge or Marsa Nakari Village. If good food is important, be sure to take that into account when choosing accommodation. You'll likely eat most if not all meals in your lodge or resort.

Divers and snorkelers might also want to take into consideration the quality of the "house reef" at their lodging when choosing accommodation. (The house reefs at all of the below are excellent.) Other dive sites can be reached by boat or car through diving centers, but come at an extra cost in terms of both time and money.

Ecolodges and Beach Glamping

Travelers in search of simplicity will enjoy these seaside ecolodges (listed in order from north to south), which offer more of a return to nature than the shiny resort compounds. The three dive/snorkel villages below (Wadi Lahami, Marsa Nakari, and Marsa Shagra) all offer the option of staying in luxury tents right on the sandy seashore, while at Deep South Ecolodge you can rough it in a proper sleep-on-the-floor tent, also right on the beach.

★ MARSA SHAGRA VILLAGE

Al Quseir-Marsa Alam Rd., 24 km/15 mi north of Marsa Alam Town; tel. 065 3380026; www.redsea-divingsafari.com; 2,270LE d full board

The seaside tents at Marsa Shagra are a glamper's dream. Made of strong canvas and furnished with a fan, palm wood furniture, and proper beds, the tents sit just a few meters from the water. Open the flap to let in the cool sea breeze and watch the sun peek up over the horizon. Those looking for a bit more traditional comfort can opt for the deluxe chalet with private bathroom, AC, and flat screen TV (3,300LE d).

The village is run by Red Sea Diving Safari—a professional diving center and tour operator that's been working in Marsa Alam for decades—and has one of the best house reefs around, ideal for both diving and snorkeling. Dive equipment, kayaks, and stand-up paddles available for rent. Meals are prepared fresh by highly skilled chefs (prices are full board), and a BaroMedical Hyperbaric Center can be found on site in case of diving accidents. Located just 20 minutes from the bus station in Marsa Alam Town, and 40 minutes from the Marsa Alam airport. Book directly through their website for the best rates.

★ DEEP SOUTH ECOLODGE

Um Tondoba Bay, 16 km/10 mi south of Marsa Alam Town; tel. 0111 181 2277; www.deepsouthredsea.com; 900LE d

The long untouched beach and dazzling house reef set in the sheltered Um Tondoba Bay are the highlights of this well-run ecolodge. Simple chalets (sans AC) some 800 meters (2,600 ft) from the sea serve as comfortable outposts for daily walks to the water. Tents with shared bathrooms are also available (a more economical option at 400LE d). The outstanding staff can help organize trips over land to other beaches, and excellent speedboat excursions to surrounding reefs through their professional dive center (PADI recognized).

Beach barbecues are common dining options, or enjoy fresh fish, vegetarian dishes, and more at their house restaurant. Delicious breakfast included.

MARSA NAKARI VILLAGE

Halayib wa Shalateen Rd., 20 km/12 mi south of Marsa Alam Town; tel. 0128 216 6511; www.redsea-divingsafari.com; 1,780LE d full board

Also operated by Red Sea Diving Safari, Marsa Nakari Village is a bit smaller than Marsa Shagra, but offers the same excellent food, service, and range of lodgings—from sturdy tent to deluxe chalet and everything in between. The house reef is also spectacular, full of coral and sea life that can be enjoyed by snorkelers and divers alike. It's a great outpost for visitors keen to explore the beaches and mountains of Wadi el Gemal National Park, located just a 20-minute drive to the south, without straying too far from the Marsa Alam bus station (20 minutes) and airport (70 minutes). Samadai Reef ("Dolphin House") is also a quick Zodiac boat ride away (20 minutes).

WADI LAHAMI VILLAGE

Halayib wa Shalateen Rd., 120 km/75 mi south of Marsa Alam Town; tel. 0106 577 9300; www.redsea-divingsafari.com; 1,700LE d full board

The southernmost of Red Sea Diving Safari's villages, Wadi Lahami is the perfect option for travelers looking for an escape into nature. Choose from the same classic tents with handmade furniture and electricity outlets; royal tents (1,900LE d) for a bit more space, a fan, and mini fridge; or deluxe chalets (2,600LE d) with AC and private bathroom. A mangrove forest (brilliant for bird-watching) borders the village to the north, and just off the coast lies the Fury Shoals—a network of pristine reefs that includes Satayah Reef, known for its resident dolphins. Along with the classic diving options and excellent house reef, Wadi Lahami also offers a professional kitesurfing center. It's located near the southern border of the Wadi el Gemal National Park, granting easy access to the area's untouched beauty. The one downside is its distance from Marsa Alam's bus station (1.5 hours) and airport (2.5 hours).

Resorts

HILTON MARSA ALAM NUBIAN RESORT

Abu Dabbab Bay, 37 km/23 mi north of Marsa Alam Town; tel. 065 3740060; www3.hilton.com; 1,900LE d

Tucked away on the north side of the brilliant Abu Dabbab Bay, the Hilton Nubian Resort offers stylish rooms with tasteful accents like vase-filled niches, chiffon curtains, and ceilings striped with wooden panels. Four pools—the largest elegantly ringed with palm trees—spot the compound, and a private beach lined with umbrellas and lounge chairs is located just down the street (still within the resort). Swimmers can safely cross the protected bay in search of the resident turtles and dugongs, or stay closer to shore to explore the fantastic Abu Dabbab reef just off the beach. Food not remarkable but fine, and there's no shortage of bars.

GETTING THERE

Fly into **Marsa Alam International Airport** from Cairo for the quickest, most comfortable trip. For a more economical option, grab a bus.

Air

MARSA ALAM INTERNATIONAL AIRPORT

tel. 065 3700029

Marsa Alam International Airport (RMF) is located 71 kilometers (44 mi) north of Marsa Alam Town. Check **Egypt Air** (www.egyptair.com) for schedule and prices. Flights from Cairo take 1.5 hours.

Steven's Taxi (Port Ghalib; tel. 0128 433 2337; www.MarsaAlam.com; 24 hours daily) has a team of friendly and reliable drivers based near the airport, making them a good option for transfers to your accommodation—often much cheaper than hotel services. Book online for best prices (no need to pay in advance).

Bus

Go Bus (www.go-bus.com; tel. 19567; 275LE) offers overnight trips from Cairo, leaving from Abdel Minam Riyad Square (next to Ramses Hilton) around 11:45pm and 1am and arriving in Marsa Alam Town around 11 hours later. Their buses make the return trip to Cairo from Marsa Alam at 2:30pm and 4:30pm (check the schedule in advance in case of changes). The government-run **Upper Egypt Bus Co** (no tel.) also offers multiple trips between Marsa Alam and Cairo (though this option is less clean and comfortable than the alternatives). Check at the bus station for a full schedule as it often changes.

Marsa Alam's bus stop is located in the center of tiny Marsa Alam Town.nYour lodge or resort can arrange for transportation to/from the bus stop.

GETTING AROUND

Steven's Taxi (Port Ghalib; tel. 0128 433 2337; www.MarsaAlam.com; 24 hours daily) can bring you anywhere around sprawling Marsa Alam but is most economical for travel to/from the airport. For transportation around the south, your lodge will likely be able to offer cheaper alternatives. Expect to pay around €50-60/person for most day trip outings by speedboat or car (including lunch and guide).

Wadi el Gemal National Park

On the southern edge of Marsa Alam, Wadi el Gemal ("Valley of the Camels") National Park holds a trove of treasures both on land and at sea. Spanning some 6,700 square kilometers (2,600 sq mi) of desert and water, the park plays host to thousands of plant and animal species. The undulating coast dances along a luminous sea, creating sheltered bays with fringing reefs and exquisite sea life. Along the shore, mangrove forests house scuttling crabs. And in the desert, elegant gazelles roam the valleys, Nubian ibex scale the craggy mountains, and wild camels snack on the fruit beneath acacia trees.

Traces of antiquity still spot the interior from when the Ptolemies and Romans mined the rich mountains for gems and precious metals over 2,000 years ago. To reach these parts, an off-road vehicle with expert guide is necessary. Aside from these ancient outposts, a single coastal road (Halayib wa Shalateen Rd.), and a few small villages (Abu Ghusun and Qula'an), all is nature.

The park is open from sunrise to sunset. Your trip organizers will likely include the **entrance ticket** (200LE by land, 100LE by sea) in your package.

SIGHTS

Sikait

Eastern Desert; no tel.; sunrise-sunset daily; free with park entrance

Tucked away in a craggy mountain valley 45 kilometers (28 mi) from the coast, this ancient Roman settlement grew up around the world's earliest known emerald mine, active from at least the 1st-6th centuries AD. Called Mons Smaragdus ("Emerald Mountain") by the Romans, the area produced the Roman Empire's only source of the cherished gem. The town is made up of several hundred stone houses and a few rock-cut temples—built on the hillsides to stay clear of the occasional winter floods that poured through the valley. Though the site remains under active excavation, some 200 structures can be seen, including a **rock-cut temple** dedicated to Isis.

★ BEACHES

HANQURAB BEACH

Off Halayib wa Shalateen Rd., 18 km/11 mi south of Gorgonia Beach Resort; sunrise-sunset daily; free

Also known as Sharm el-Loli after the small marina located a few miles to the north, this

The Ababda People

Long before the area of **Wadi el Gemal** became a national park, the Ababda have called this land home. For centuries, their nomadic ancestors roamed the rugged terrain between the Nile Valley and the Red Sea with herds of goats and camels. But major changes to Egypt's landscape have endangered their way of life. After construction of the Aswan High Dam in the 1960s, the permanent pastures for the Ababda livestock were submerged, while the nearby desert was hit with decades of drought.

Today most of the Ababda have resettled along the Nile, but some continue to live in this southeastern corner of Egypt—in the coastal town of **Abu Ghusun** and the small fishing village of **Qula'an.** Visitors to Wadi el Gemal will likely meet these friendly locals at the main beaches or as guides on desert excursions, and enjoy a peek into their unique culture over a cup of their super-sweet jebena coffee.

pristine sandy beach spotted with rugged desert plants is an excellent first stop in Wadi el Gemal National Park. On calm days, the snorkeling is superb—the protected patch of sea a brilliant, transparent blue, and the corals eye-poppingly vibrant. Members of the local Ababda tribe have set up a small café, offering shade, WCs, snacks, and water (though best to bring your own just in case). A few chairs and umbrellas are available for 25LE, and you can usually snag some handicrafts from local women. Summers are often crowded, but during the rest of the year you might even have the beach to yourself.

QULA'AN MANGROVE BEACH

Off Halayib wa Shalateen Rd., 30 km/20 mi south of Hanqurab Beach; sunrise-sunset daily; free

Surrounded by a mangrove forest, this sandy white beach lines a shallow lagoon, perfect for a protected dip. The nearby corals are often off limits, so be sure to get your snorkeling fill at Hanqurab before heading this way. Locals from the Qula'an fishing village just inland have set up a small restaurant and café, where you can try their traditional coffee (jebena) and relax in the shade. For food, try to order at least 2 hours in advance (typical menu includes delicious fried fish, rice, and salads for 150LE). WCs and showers also available. A great place to watch the sunset.

DIVING AND SNORKELING

To dive or snorkel at the Hamata Wreck or Hamata Islands, book with a dive center in Marsa Alam (page 328).

HAMATA WRECK

Off Abu Ghusun Beach; sunrise-sunset daily; free

This cargo ship met its watery fate in 1993 on a journey from Jeddah (Saudi Arabia) to Suez. The sea has since reclaimed it—covering its corpse in colorful coral, at once eerie and beautiful. The Hamata is one of the very few wrecks visitors can reach from the shore, making it suitable for both divers and intrepid snorkelers. Also known as Abu Ghusun Wreck.

★ HAMATA ISLANDS

boats leave from Hamata Port; sunrise-sunset daily; 80LE

Also called the Qula'an Archipelago, this chain of desert islands springs out of the water not far from the coast, surrounded by brilliant sea life just below the surface. Gradients of blue ripple out from the patches of fine white sand—from the cyan of the shallow beside the shore to the azure of the open sea. The farthest and largest of the islands, **Jezirat Siyul** (also known as "Island of the Birds"), is a favorite sanctuary for birds and nesting place for turtles (May-Nov.). Located 1 hour by boat from Hamata Port (111 km/69 mi south of Marsa Alam Town).

GETTING THERE

To get to these parts visitors must enlist the services of a local tour operator. They'll provide transportation and guidance to the expansive park desert and shore. If you want to explore the desert and ancient sights, a 4WD is necessary. But if you just want check out the park's beaches, a regular car will do.

Tour Operators

Amore Safari generally sticks to the desert section of the park, but if you wish to add the beaches along the coast, they might be able to accommodate. **Blue Ocean Dive Centers & Resorts** organizes trips to the sea part of the park.

AMORE SAFARI

Port Ghalib; tel. 0100 191 9999; www.amoresafari.com; 24 hours daily; 900LE per person

Amore Safari offers a trip around the national park for 900LE per person in an off-road vehicle, including transportation to/from your hotel. They have a 6-person minimum per car, so if your group is smaller than that you'll join other travelers (or pay a premium). Best to reserve around a week in advance, but last-minute bookings are sometimes possible.

BLUE OCEAN DIVE CENTERS & RESORTS

Abu Dabbab Beach, 35 km/22 mi north of Marsa Alam Town; tel. 012 0753 5555; www.blueocean-eg.com; 8am-5pm daily; prices vary

Blue Ocean organizes nice trips by minibus to Hamata Port, and then by boat to the sea part of the park. An 8-10-hour outing to Hamata Islands costs 900LE per person (including hotel transfers, lunch, and snorkeling equipment). Expect between 20-35 other guests on board.

Private Car Hire

Your lodge or resort should be able to arrange for a private car to visit the park's beaches. Depending on your starting point, expect prices in the range of 1,000LE for the day in a car that seats up to 3 passengers.

South Sinai (Janoob Sina)

Embraced by two arms of the Red Sea, the South Sinai is the triangular jewel in Egypt's crown. From its dramatic interior of granite and sandstone mountains to its coastal strips of sandy beaches and brilliant underwater worlds, the peninsula's beauty shines in all directions.

Inland, wadis (dried riverbeds) run between bare mountains like veins in the earth—often the only suggestion of life for miles around. Along the Gulf of Aqaba, fringing reefs line turquoise shores for nearly 240 kilometers (150 mi), bordering hyper-developed resorts, small vacation towns, and untouched beaches. Aside from St. Katherine in the mountainous interior, most of the South Sinai's 106,000 residents live in these coastal towns or along the Gulf of Suez on the west coast,

Highlights

Look for ★ to find recommended sights, activities, dining, and lodging.

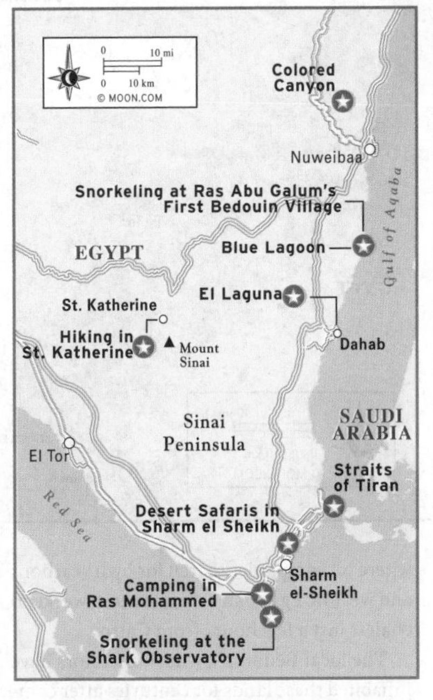

★ **Straits of Tiran:** Dive through dazzling underwater landscapes along a string of reefs, snorkel around Tiran Island, or just enjoy the scenery from the boat as you zip along the narrow Red Sea passage (page 344).

★ **Desert Safaris in Sharm el Sheikh:** Hop on a quad bike for a rush of adrenaline as you careen through the desert at sunset (page 346).

★ **Snorkeling at the Shark Observatory:** Explore some of Egypt's most stunning sea life between a dense wall of corals that lines the shore and the mysterious dark blue of the open sea (page 352).

★ **Camping in Ras Mohammed:** Sleep on the beach under the stars and wake up to the sun rising over the sea in this haven of tranquility (page 352).

★ **El Laguna:** Lounge on this long, sandy beach surrounded by mountains that's loved by locals and visitors alike (page 356).

★ **Snorkeling at Ras Abu Galum's First Bedouin Village:** Take a quick boat ride to this camp-lined village for secluded snorkeling (page 364).

★ **Blue Lagoon:** Enjoy a sheltered swim or watch the kitesurfers perform their tricks at this brilliant turquoise lagoon in Ras Abu Galum Protectorate (page 364).

★ **Hiking in St. Katherine:** Summit Mt. Sinai—or another of several less-crowded mountains—in this rugged patch of untouched nature (page 366).

★ **Colored Canyon:** Hike along colorful swirls in uniquely carved cliffsides—wind and water's artwork, millions of years in the making (page 371).

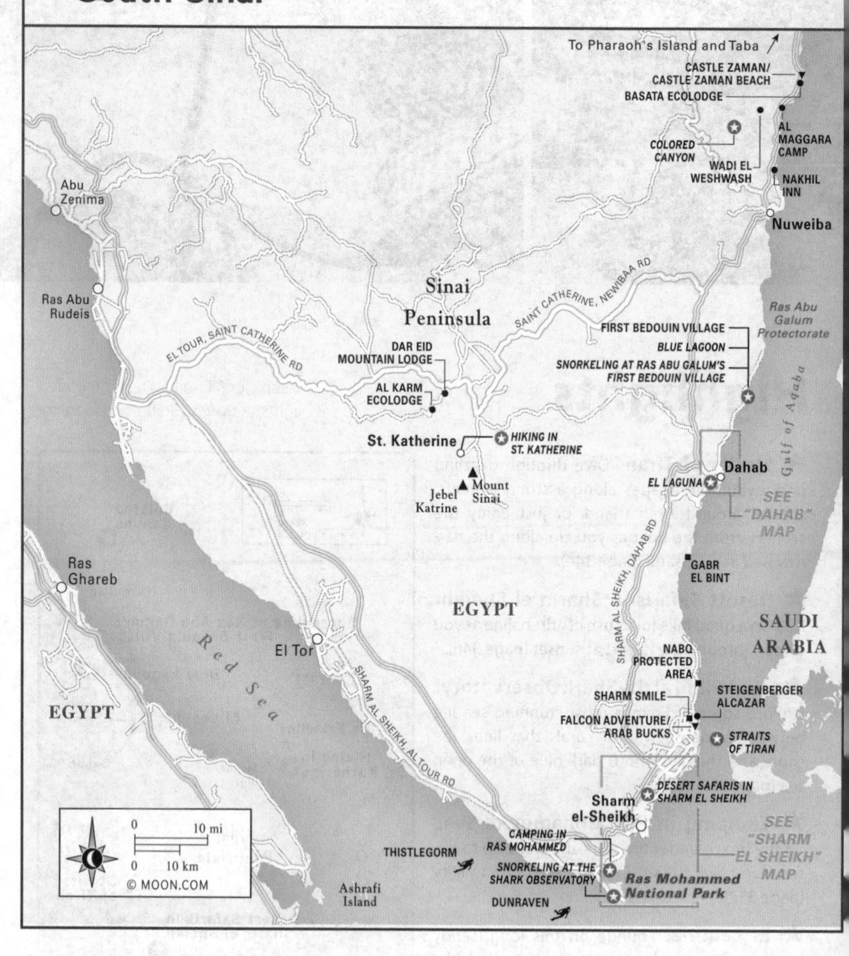

where oil companies search for hydrocarbons and wealthy Egyptian urbanites keep weekend chalets just a few hours from Cairo.

The local Bedouins, whose ancestors have inhabited these lands for centuries after coming over from the Arabian Peninsula (for the most part), are some of Egypt's most generous hosts. They will be your guides on mountain hikes, expert drivers on unmarked desert terrain, and suppliers of super sweet sage tea around campfires under the stars.

HISTORY

The Sinai (in Arabic, "Sina") gets its name from the moon god Sin from ancient Babylonia (modern-day Iraq). As the sole land bridge between Africa and Asia, the Sinai has been a place of passage, and contestation,

Previous: snorkeling at Shark Observatory; hiking in the South Sinai interior; driving an ATV in Sharm el Sheikh desert.

Violence in the North Sinai

The Sinai Peninsula may not look that large on a map, but the border that separates North and South Sinai marks the boundary between two very different worlds. Since 2011 an insurgency in the north—and the Egyptian military's heavy-handed response—has left thousands dead and many more displaced. A jihadist group called Sinai Province pledged its allegiance to ISIS in 2014 and has staged a number of attacks on Egypt's security forces.

But don't let this deter you from visiting the South Sinai, where the security situation is far more stable. As with elsewhere around the world, terrorist attacks are not unheard of in these parts. The 2015 downing of a Russian passenger plane out of Sharm el Sheikh International Airport killed everyone on board and resulted in a major overhaul of the airport's security. Bombings have occurred in Taba (2004), Sharm el Sheikh (2005), and Dahab (2006). But, to put it in perspective, there have been far more terrorist attacks in Paris over the past decade than in the South Sinai. And the local Bedouins, together with the rugged mountain border, do their best to protect their territory from any spillover of violence.

for thousands of years. By around 2600 BC, Egyptians began mining the valleys of the South Sinai for turquoise and copper. With the invasion of the Hyksos (Greek for "rulers of foreign lands," in this case Western Asia) around 1700 BC, Egyptians retreated from the peninsula for many centuries.

Undoubtedly the most famous events in the Sinai's ancient history—those surrounding the biblical stories of Moses in the 14th-13th centuries BC—may never have actually happened. Despite decades of digging, archeologists have been unable to find any evidence that Moses ever led anyone, let alone millions of followers for 40 years, through the Sinai desert. Nor that he parted the Red Sea (a mistranslation from the Hebrew Bible that should be "Reed Sea"), only to have it swallow up his pursuers.

The peninsula's turbulent 20th-century AD history, understandably, is far better documented. Most of the Arab-Israeli Wars played out in part on the Sinai. While the 1948 War didn't reach far beyond the Palestinian/Israeli border, during the 1956 Tripartite Aggression—an attack on Egypt by Israel, France, and the UK after President Nasser nationalized the Suez Canal—Israeli troops moved as far south as Sharm el Sheikh before the US called for a ceasefire.

Israel captured the entire Sinai in the 1967 War, and Egypt launched the 1973 War to get it back. The territory wasn't returned until 1982, three years after the Egypt-Israel Peace Treaty.

Over the 15 years of occupation, Israelis built the first beach camps and tourist villages along the Gulf of Aqaba. Egyptian developers poured in to participate in the building bonanza following Israel's withdrawal in 1982 (the Israeli exit from Taba on the border took another few years). One of these early vacation villages has since boomed into the resort city of Sharm el Sheikh near the southern tip of the peninsula.

All along, the local Bedouins have been living under their own rules and honor codes, adapting as needed to the foreign military presence of either Israelis or Cairenes, and trying to preserve their homes and homeland in the beautiful Sinai.

ORIENTATION

The shiny resort city of **Sharm el Sheikh** is located near the southern tip of the Sinai Peninsula. In the southern tip proper (19 km/12 mi south of Sharm), you'll find the pristine **Ras Mohammed National Park.** A 1-hour drive north of Sharm will get you to **Dahab,** a former Bedouin fishing village that has maintained its small-town feel. It's filled with more modest lodging and a long promenade that hugs the coast. The **Ras Abu Galum Protectorate,** directly north of Dahab, is most often reached by boat from the **Blue Hole** on Dahab's northern border.

Continuing along the coast, the port city of **Nuweiba** comes next. Between Nuweiba and the border town of **Taba,** dozens of beach camps lie scattered for many miles along the coast (starting around 150 km/93 mi, or just under 2 hours, north of Sharm).

The St. Katherine-Nuweiba Road branches off the Dahab-Nuweiba Road heading inland at around 25 kilometers (16 mi; 20 minutes) south of Nuweiba. Another 83 kilometers (52 mi; 1 hour) through the mountains will get you to the small town center of **St. Katherine** (called El Milga), which is just down the street from the trailhead to **Mt. Sinai.**

To get to the region from Cairo, Sharm el Sheikh is the easiest entry point. Visitors short on time or not keen on a 9-12-hour bus ride will prefer to fly direct to Sharm and take a bus or private car to the surrounding points of interest.

PLANNING YOUR TIME

Whether you're looking for a short stay in seaside luxury or a summer's worth of beach bumming, the South Sinai can accommodate. Visitors spend anywhere from a few days to a few decades enjoying the sun, sand, and waves in this beautiful corner of Egypt. Most travelers will be content with **a week** or so of soaking in the Sinai's natural wonders. Ambitious travelers can visit all of the peninsula's highlights in 5-6 days.

Itinerary Ideas

The South Sinai is an outdoors destination. You'll be in the water for every day of this itinerary, so be sure to wear a swimsuit and plenty of sunscreen. Dahab is the best base for the first two nights. For the trip to Ras Mohammed National Park, Dahab is also a fine starting point, but to minimize travel time, spend the night in Sharm or camp in the park itself.

DAHAB IN TWO DAYS

Day 1: Blue Hole and the Ras Abu Galum Protectorate

1 Pick up a breakfast, coffee, and a sandwich for lunch at **Ralph's German Bakery.**

2 Flag down a pickup truck taxi to the **Blue Hole** for a snorkel in the sheltered ring of corals. Ask your driver to stay for the day to make sure you have a ride home (300LE round-trip).

3 Hop in a speed boat to the Ras Abu Galum Protectorate (120LE round-trip) and hitch a short ride with a pickup truck taxi to the calm waters of the **Blue Lagoon** (250LE round-trip). Park yourself in the shade of any of the camp cafés for your packed lunch and a tea before taking a dip.

4 Grab a taxi back to the spot where the boat dropped you off at Ras Abu Galum's **First Bedouin Village** to snorkel among some of Dahab's most pristine corals. Bring snorkel gear with you, or rent from central Dahab in advance.

5 Take the boat back to the **Blue Hole** at sunset to meet your pickup truck taxi and head back to central Dahab.

6 End your evening beside the sea at **Nemo's Restaurant** for delectable seafood dishes with a view.

Itinerary Ideas

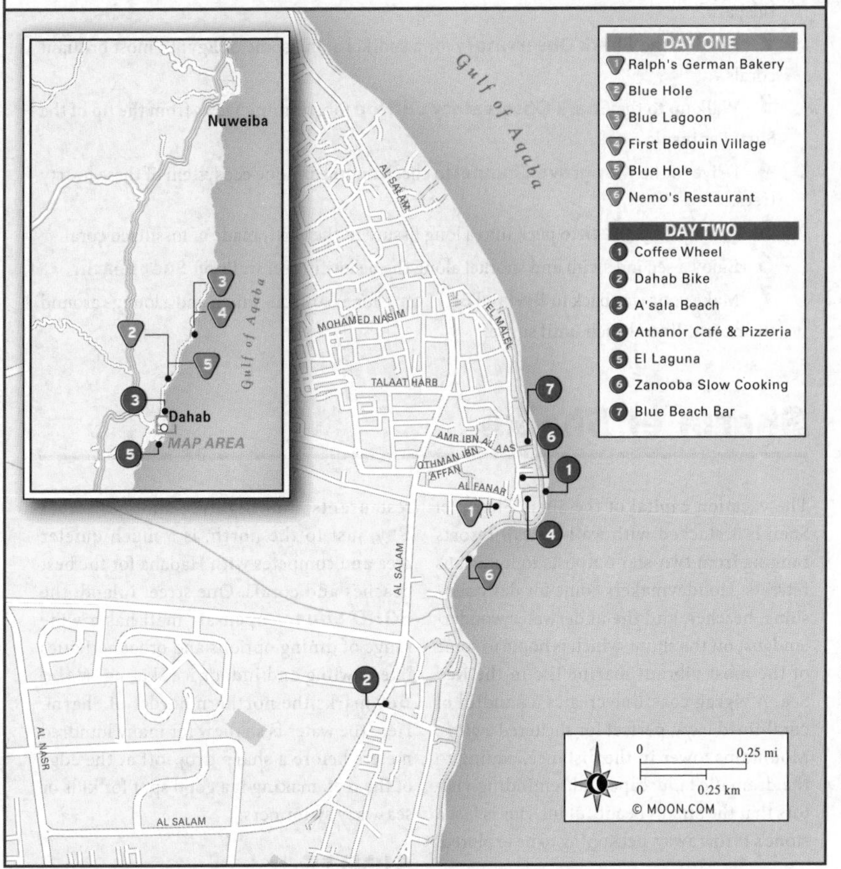

Day 2: A'sala Beach and El Laguna

1 Enjoy your breakfast and morning caffeine by the sea at **Coffee Wheel.**

2 Walk over to **Dahab Bike** to rent some wheels for the day.

3 Cycle north to **A'sala Beach** to relax on the sand, swim in the shallows, or explore the hidden fringing reef around 100 meters (330 ft) out.

4 When hunger strikes, cycle down to **Athanor Café & Pizzeria** for a cheesy pizza and afternoon coffee.

5 Make your way to the promenade for a 4-kilometer (2.5-mi) ride along the sea to **El Laguna.** Cool off in the water as you wait for the sunset lightshow.

6 Head back to your accommodation for a quick shower before indulging in a hearty meal at **Zanooba Slow Cooking** (be sure to reserve at least 6 hours in advance).

7 Sip on a seaside nightcap at the **Blue Beach Bar.**

RAS MOHAMMED NATIONAL PARK IN ONE DAY

1 Connect with your guide at **Bedawi Eco Camp** around 8am to start your trip around the park.

2 Head to the **Shark Observatory** for a snorkel along some of Egypt's most brilliant corals.

3 Walk up to the **Shark Observatory Clifftop** for stunning views from the tip of the Sinai Peninsula.

4 Drive to the **Mangrove Channel** to check out the unique ecosystem of these hearty trees.

5 Pass by **The Crack** to peek into a long fissure in the earth made of fossilized coral.

6 Enjoy a second swim and snorkel along the beautiful reef walls off **Suez Beach.**

7 Make your way back to **Bedawi Eco Camp** for a barbecue lunch and a lounge around their coral-lined beach until sunset.

Sharm el Sheikh

The vacation capital of the Sinai, Sharm el Sheikh is stacked with wall-to-wall resorts ranging from two-star outposts to luxurious retreats. Holidaymakers come for daily sunshine, beaches, and the underwater wonderland just off the shore, which is home to some of the most vibrant marine life in the Red Sea. A zigzag coastline creates a handful of coral-lined bays, perfect for sheltered swims. Mountains tower in the distance, adding to the dramatic landscape and reminding visitors that the Sinai's beautiful interior is just a stone's throw away, beckoning to be explored.

ORIENTATION

Like most of Egypt's seaside vacation spots, the neighborhoods here hug the water. All lie along the main thoroughfare **El Salam Road** that starts near the **Old Market** (for souvenir shopping) in the south and runs the length of Sharm, terminating at the northern edge in **Nabq Bay.** From the south after the Old Market, **Hadaba** is the first neighborhood of note—home to the **Ras Um el Sid** area with marvelous corals and crystal-clear waters. Next is **Na'ama Bay,** Sharm's bustling downtown area with a 2-kilometer (1-mi) pedestrian boardwalk lined with cafés, restaurants, and nightlife spots. **Shark's Bay,** just to the north, is a much quieter area and competes with Hadaba for the best beaches and corals. One street inland, the **SOHO Square** open-air mall has a wide range of dining options and other activities like bowling and indoor ice skating. **Nabq Bay** marks the northern border of Sharm. Here the water is shallow for many hundred meters before a sharp drop-off at the edge of the reef, making it a good spot for kids or sea-wary swimmers.

SIGHTS

Sharm el Sheikh Museum

Off El Salam Rd., 2 km/1 mi north of Na'ama Bay; 10am-1pm and 5pm-11pm daily; 200LE adults, 100LE students

Brand new and beautifully curated, this museum of ancient Egyptian artifacts is a welcome cultural addition to Sharm el Sheikh's natural treasures. The objects—ranging from mummified animals to ancient games and flip-flops, pharaonic busts, and a recreated Roman bathhouse—are well-lit with brief descriptions. The museum stays open late to cater to daytime beachgoers and deserves a solid hour or two.

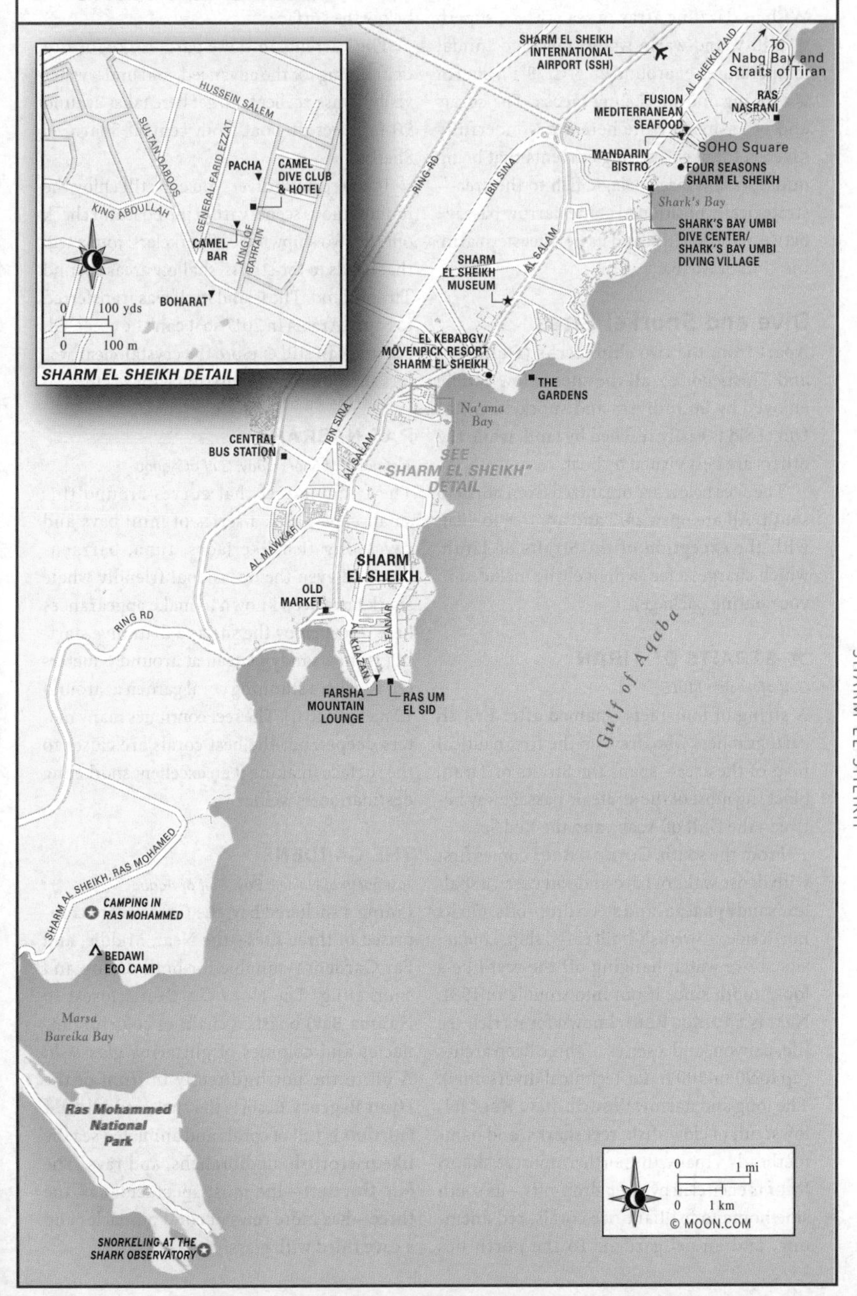
Sharm el Sheikh
HUSSEIN SALEM
SULTAN QABOOS
GENERAL FARID EZZAT
PACHA
CAMEL DIVE CLUB & HOTEL
KING ABDULLAH
CAMEL BAR
KING OF BAHRAIN
BOHARAT
0 100 yds
0 100 m
SHARM EL SHEIKH DETAIL
SHARM EL SHEIKH INTERNATIONAL AIRPORT (SSH)
AL SHEIKH ZAID
To Nabq Bay and Straits of Tiran
RAS NASRANI
FUSION MEDITERRANEAN SEAFOOD
SOHO Square
MANDARIN BISTRO
FOUR SEASONS SHARM EL SHEIKH
Shark's Bay
SHARK'S BAY UMBI DIVE CENTER/ SHARK'S BAY UMBI DIVING VILLAGE
RING RD
IBN SINA
AL SALAM
SHARM EL SHEIKH MUSEUM
EL KEBABGY/ MOVENPICK RESORT SHARM EL SHEIKH
THE GARDENS
Na'ama Bay
CENTRAL BUS STATION
SEE "SHARM EL SHEIKH" DETAIL
AL MAWKAF
SHARM EL-SHEIKH
OLD MARKET
AL KHAZAN
AL FANAR
FARSHA MOUNTAIN LOUNGE
RAS UM EL SID
Gulf of Aqaba
SHARM AL SHEIKH, RAS MOHAMED
CAMPING IN RAS MOHAMMED
BEDAWI ECO CAMP
Marsa Bareika Bay
Ras Mohammed National Park
SNORKELING AT THE SHARK OBSERVATORY
0 1 mi
0 1 km
© MOON.COM

DIVING AND SNORKELING

With its dazzling array of sea critters, superb visibility, and warm waters (average annual temperatures of around 25.5°C/78°F), Sharm is a diving and snorkeling mecca. The corals and other marine life here are wonderfully diverse, thanks to strong currents that bring nutrients and large pelagic fish to the area—strategically positioned at the narrow passage between the Red Sea and its northeastern arm, the Gulf of Aqaba.

Dive and Snorkel Sites

Apart from the two shipwrecks (Dunraven and Thistlegorm), all the sites below can be enjoyed by both divers and snorkelers. Ras Um el Sid is easily reached by land, while the others are best visited by boat.

The sites below are organized from north to south. All are open 24/7 and are free to visit, with the exception of the Straits of Tiran, which charges a fee (will likely be included in your outing package).

★ STRAITS OF TIRAN

Gulf of Aqaba; 140LE

A string of four reefs—named after British cartographers who drew up the first nautical map of the area—spans the Straits of Tiran, blocking most of the strategic passageway between the Gulf of Aqaba and the Red Sea.

From the south, **Gordon Reef** comes first with dense walls of hard and soft coral, a shallow sandy plateau, and steep drop-offs. On its north side, a Swedish-built cargo ship, *Loullia,* sits above water, hanging off the reef like a loose tooth since it ran into trouble in 1981. Next is **Thomas Reef,** known for its rich sea life, canyon, and a series of three deep arches (up to 90 m/300 ft, for technical divers only). The long and narrow **Woodhouse Reef** follows, full of clownfish, reef sharks, and hammerheads. Finally, the northernmost **Jackson Reef** is encircled by steep drop-offs—its south side home to brilliant fire corals, red anemone, and an eel garden. To the north lies another shipwreck from the early 1980s, the German-built *Lara,* visible both above and below the surface.

The currents in these parts make for fun drift diving for the advanced, and underwater visibility is excellent. To get here takes around 90 minutes by boat from central Sharm el Sheikh.

If you're not a diver, you can still enjoy the mountainous scenery from the boat and check out the two shipwrecks. Snorkelers: Join a trip that heads to the straits' shallow areas around Tiran Island. The island itself was transferred to Saudi Arabia in 2017 so it can't be accessed, but you can still explore the crystal-clear waters surrounding it, bursting with sea life.

RAS NASRANI

Just north of Shark's Bay, Gulf of Aqaba

The fringing reef that curves around this small cape forms a series of mini bays and caves. Big fish like jacks, tuna, barracudas, and even the occasional friendly whale shark have been known to make appearances here. Most enjoy the site as a drift dive starting from a sandy plateau at around 6 meters (20 ft) with a stunning coral garden at around 12 meters (40 ft). The reef continues many meters deeper, but the best corals are closer to the surface (making it an excellent snorkeling destination as well).

THE GARDENS

Just north of Na'ama Bay, Gulf of Aqaba

Lining a sheltered bay, the Gardens are comprised of three sites—the Near, Middle, and Far Gardens—suitable for both diving and snorkeling. The **Near Garden** (closest to Na'ama Bay) boasts a chain of colorful pinnacles and colonies of glittering glassfish. A bit to the north (directly in front of the Hyatt Regency Resort) the sheltered **Middle Garden** is full of corals and animated sea life like parrotfish, nudibranchs, and rays. The **Far Garden**—the most spectacular of the three—has more rows of coral pinnacles and a cave filled with glassfish.

RAS UM EL SID

Hadaba

Excellent for both diving and snorkeling, this fish-filled reef with a striking gorgonian forest runs along the shore for nearly a kilometer. Private resorts line most of the coast, but dive centers take regular trips here by boat. **El Fanar Beach and Restaurant** (El Fanar St., Ras Umm el Sid, Hadaba; tel. 0120 222 6760; 9am-midnight daily; 100LE) on the eastern side of the reef is also open to the public and a great place to make your entrance. Sunbeds and umbrellas (included in the price of admission) line the craggy coast, and a long wooden pier leads to the edge of the reef for easy access to a wall of vibrant corals. If hunger strikes, walk a few steps up to the restaurant (50-200LE mains) for a wide variety of snacks and drinks, including beer and cocktails.

DUNRAVEN

Off Ras Mohammed National Park

The SS *Dunraven* has been gathering barnacles since it sunk here en route from Bombay to Liverpool in 1876. Divers can explore the British cargo ship's remains starting at 18 meters (60 ft) to around 30 meters (100 ft) deep. Much of the wreck is now covered in corals and filled with marine life, making it extra fun to explore. Beacon Rock, the colorful reef that downed the Dunraven, is an added treat. To get here from central Sharm el Sheikh takes around 2 hours by boat.

THISTLEGORM

Gulf of Suez

Sunk by the Germans during WWII, the SS *Thistlegorm* is an underwater museum accessible only to advanced divers. The British navy ship was headed for Alexandria to resupply Allied soldiers when a German aircraft bombed it, resulting in an even larger explosion when the ammunition on board caught fire. Nine men were killed but 41 others managed to abandon ship in the few minutes before it sunk to the seafloor.

Today the wreck sits at around 32 meters (105 ft) deep and still has much of its cargo inside, including motorcycles and armored vehicles. Two steam locomotives also lay nearby, blown off deck by the blast. Not far from Dunraven, the two can often be combined for wreck-lovers. To enjoy more time at the site (with fewer people), check out liveaboard options. For more information and to experience a virtual dive around the wreck, check out the British Council-funded Thistlegorm Project (www.thethistlegormproject.com).

Dive Centers

Snorkelers: Try to skip the large tour operators offering snorkel trips and stick with the dive centers, which usually go out in smaller groups.

SHARK'S BAY UMBI DIVE CENTER

Shark's Bay, in Shark's Bay Umbi Diving Village; tel. 0120 000 1558; www.sharksbay.com; 8am-6pm daily

This PADI 5 Star Dive Center has a fleet of boats and a private jetty, making trips to all of Sharm's dive and snorkel sites quick and easy. Their knowledgeable guides keep group sizes small (5 people max). A 4-day PADI Open Water Course for beginners costs €270, a guided dive starts at €30, and snorkelers can enjoy a boat day trip for €30. They also offer great prices for dive and accommodation packages for guests at their Diving Village.

CAMEL DIVE CLUB & HOTEL

Na'ama Bay; tel. 069 360 0700; www.cameldive.com; 8am-6pm daily

Another PADI 5 Star Center, the Camel Dive Club has been taking visitors around Sharm's underwater sites for decades. The 4-day PADI Open Water Course for beginners goes for €310 if booked online in advance, a guided shore dive €45, and a full-day trip by boat for snorkelers for €36 (including equipment). Groups are limited to 6 people for all courses and guided dives. Their dive center is attached to a hotel not far from the beach in Na'ama Bay that offers comfortable accommodation and makes a nice outpost for divers (good dive and accommodation combo packages are available).

Nabq Protected Area

Just 30 kilometers (20 mi) north of central Sharm el Sheikh, the Nabq Protected Area spans 600 square kilometers (232 sq mi) of desert and sea. Highlights include a small mangrove forest and some superb, seldom swum snorkel spots. Unfortunately, the tourist police often prevent visitors from venturing too far into the protected area out of an abundance of caution for visitors' safety, and there are far fewer options of getting here than to Ras Mohammed National Park in the south. Check with your Sharm accommodation to see if they offer trips. Otherwise, **Sinai Gate** (Fanar St., Dahab; www.sinaigate.com; tel. 0106 633 0415) is one of the few tour operators that bring guests here, including a day trip for 1,050LE per person with a guide, lunch, snorkel gear, and hotel transfers. One-night camping trips are also available for 1,600LE per person, including transfers, guide, snorkel gear, three meals, and camping equipment. Park entry: 80LE.

★ DESERT SAFARIS

Venture into Sharm's desert interior for sunrise or sunset, when the air is cool and the mountains are illuminated by a golden glow. Feel the wind on your face as you zip along by quad bike (recommended) or dune buggy, enjoy a slow saunter on horse or camel, or let a guide do the driving in an off-road vehicle. Be sure to wear comfortable shoes and bring a scarf to protect your face from sand.

FALCON ADVENTURE

El Salam Rd., next to McDonald's, Nabq Bay; tel. 0100 158 8922; www.falconadventure.com; 9am-11pm daily

Falcon Adventure has its own quad bike center on the north side of Sharm that offers safe and fun trips into the desert. A 2-3-hour excursion with a short stop for tea at a Bedouin village starts at just 425LE per person, including helmet and hotel transfers. Sunset rides are recommended. Horse, camel, and dune buggy trips also available.

SHARM SMILE

El Salam Rd, Nabq Bay, in Sea Beach Hotel; tel. 0106 077 5377; www.sharmsmile.com; 24 hours daily

This professional tour operator offers a range of desert outings, by quad bike (2-3 hours; 200LE/person), dune buggy (2-3 hours; 200LE/person), camel (1 hour; 320LE/person), or horse (1 hour; 400LE/person). They can also organize private speed boat excursions (2 hours; 950LE/person) and snorkeling in Ras Mohammed (6-8 hours; 580LE/person, including lunch). All trips include hotel transfers and friendly guides.

SHOPPING

OLD MARKET (El-Souq El-Adim)

Old Town Sharm; no tel.; 9am-1am daily

Mostly filled with unnecessary trinkets, the Old Market can still be a fun place to stroll in the evening. This is the place to come if you're in the market for spices, produce, arabesque lamps, or your very own shisha (don't forget to haggle). The ornate Al Sahaba Mosque, inaugurated in 2017 and built in a Disney-World-meets-Ottoman style, towers over the souq in the northeast corner next to a park and wide promenade.

BARS AND NIGHTLIFE

Sharm is the South Sinai's nightlife hub. Most of the bars and clubs are located in Na'ama Bay or SOHO Square near Shark's Bay.

★ CAMEL BAR

Malek El Bahrein St., in Camel Dive Club & Hotel, Na'ama Bay; tel. 069 3600700; www.cameldive.com; 6pm-2am daily; 75-200LE drinks

Located in the busy center of Na'ama Bay, this rooftop bar is a popular spot to sip a cold

1: snorkellers on Jackson Reef in the Straits of Tiran **2:** spices for sale at the Old Market **3:** desert tour by quad bike **4:** Camel Bar

1
2
3
4

beer or smoke a shisha under the stars. Their mezze, pizzas, burgers, and fish-and-chips are all tasty treats for when hunger strikes. The indoor area has a sports-bar vibe with a handful of screens lining the walls. Head over for happy hour (5pm-8pm Mon.-Fri.) when you can grab a bottle of beer for just 40LE and strawberry daquiris or mojitos for 85LE.

PACHA

Malek El Bahrein St., Na'ama Bay; tel. 0128 215 1010; 9pm-4:30am daily; 100-250LE drinks

If you're in search of a proper nightclub, check out Pacha's massive dance floor with tall ceilings, an indoor pool, and occasional foam parties. Be sure to buy your tickets at the door (350LE/person) rather than from vendors in the street to avoid a surcharge. Table service available. They play a range of music from hip-hop to house depending on the day. Check their Facebook page (@pacha.egypt) for the week's schedule.

★ FARSHA MOUNTAIN LOUNGE

Umm el Sid, Hadaba; tel. 0120 030 0162; 11am-midnight daily; 30-60LE drinks

Perched on a cliffside overlooking the sea, the multi-tiered Farsha Lounge offers a superb view, comfortable seating, and eccentric décor like antique doors and blown-glass baubles. Sunset from the elevated café is a treat, and in the evenings arabesque lamps illuminate the space with soft glow. Beer, wine, cocktails, shisha, and snacks served. Best to reserve in advance (especially Thurs.-Sat.). Daytime visitors can hang out on the Lounge's own patch of sandy beach. Come early (11am) to snag a chair and umbrella.

FOOD

Most of the resorts offer all-inclusive options, but this is rarely the tastiest way to go. For some of the best restaurants, head to Na'ama Bay or the open-air mall, **SOHO Square** (tel. 0100 010 9109; www.soho-sharm.com; 6pm-1am daily).

Egyptian

BOHARAT

Al Sultan Qaboos St., next to Tropitel Hotel, Na'ama Bay; tel. 0106 417 2755; 1pm-3am daily; 90-250LE mains

Boharat ("Spices") serves up all your favorite Egyptian dishes like stuffed pigeon, okra and lamb stew, and grilled meats that come out steaming on mini beds of charcoal. Enjoy your meal al fresco on the large patio, or in the attractive interior with wood paneled walls and ceilings, geometric floor tiles, and shelves of spices on decorative display. Try the konafa (a syrup-soaked shredded filo pastry) with cream for a divine dessert. Alcohol served.

★ EL KEBABGY

In Mövenpick Resort, Na'ama Bay; tel. 069 3600081; 6:30pm-10:30pm daily; 120-350LE mains

For dinner with a view, head to El Kababgy where you can find more Egyptian favorites by the sea. Grilled chicken and lamb artfully served on portable copper grills with pita bread fresh out of the brick oven are their specialties. Come just before sunset to grab a nice seat on the patio and enjoy the view. Alcohol served. Dress code: smart casual.

International

ARAB BUCKS

El Salam St., Nabq Bay; tel. 0101 500 2324; 10am-2am daily; 75-300LE mains

A favorite eatery for locals and expats, Arab Bucks has a bit of everything. Whether you're in the mood for seafood or pasta, Italian or Egyptian, coffee or beer, the friendly staff will deliver it with a smile. Don't miss the steak and creamy seafood soup. There's a spacious patio for outdoor dining. Good shisha and alcohol served.

MANDARIN BISTRO

SOHO Square; tel. 069 3602500; 6:30pm-1am daily; 200-350LE mains

The dishes at this Asian fusion restaurant are bursting with flavors. Choose from a wide variety of cuisines off four different menus, including Indian, Chinese, Thai, Japanese, and Egyptian. The Thai noodles, curries, and coconut soup are particularly tasty. Plentiful outdoor seating available. Alcohol and shisha served. Dress code: smart causal (no shorts or flip-flops).

Seafood

FUSION MEDITERRANEAN SEAFOOD

SOHO Square; tel. 0100 010 9109; 7pm-midnight daily; 100-300LE mains

With keyhole archways, pink bougainvillea, and beaded chandeliers, Fusion makes for an attractive dining space. Select your fresh seafood from a bed of ice and choose how you want it prepared. The grilled seabass and shrimp are particularly tasty. Outdoor seating available. Beer and wine served.

ACCOMMODATIONS

Sharm el Sheikh is dominated by large resorts and compounds, with a few smaller hotel options. If the resort life isn't your style, you might want to check out the small-town vibes of Dahab 1 hour to the north. Alternatively, you can find dozens of highly rated, economical flats on Airbnb. To stay close to the action, look for a place in Na'ama Bay. Shark's Bay, close to the restaurant-filled SOHO Square, is another good option.

800-1,650LE

SHARK'S BAY UMBI DIVING VILLAGE

Shark's Bay; tel. 0120 000 1558; www.sharksbay.com; 900LE d

Built into a hill overlooking the sea, Umbi Village's few dozen simple rooms offer excellent views and a comfortable sleep. Just off their small private beach, a long pier brings guests out to the reef edge for easy access to exquisite corals. Super basic beach cabins on the ground floor go for just 730LE d, and excellent diving and accommodation packages offer some of the best prices for quality around. Breakfast included.

★ MÖVENPICK RESORT SHARM EL SHEIKH

Na'ama Bay; tel. 069 3600081; www.movenpick.com; 1,600LE d

The Mövenpick has carved out a pretty patch of the shore, with a long sandy beach nestled between rocky hills and a fantastic house reef. Palm trees spring up in all directions, and rooms sit staggered on a hill, wrapping around a large pool and looking out to the sea. Each of the 298 rooms has a balcony or terrace, with attractive interior—all arches, wood, and marble in "Arabic style." Superb restaurants and bars on site. Complimentary breakfast, airport transfers, and excellent Wi-Fi included.

1,650-3,300LE

STEIGENBERGER ALCAZAR

Nabq Bay; tel. 069 3710950; www.steigenberger.com; 2,400LE d

On the northern edge of Sharm el Sheikh, the Steigenberger Alcazar keeps its grounds green and immaculate. Its 610 rooms are spacious with supremely comfortable beds that look out to the sea, gardens, or one of three enormous pools. Off the fine sandy beach, a long pier brings snorkelers to the edge of the house reef, but its unprotected waters (and very shallow area closer to the shore) means swimming is sometimes off limits on choppy days. Tennis courts, beach volleyball, and a superb spa all offer fine alternative activities. Breakfast included.

Over 3,300LE

FOUR SEASONS SHARM EL SHEIKH

1 Four Seasons Blvd., Shark's Bay; tel. 069 3603555; www.fourseasons.com; 5,500LE d

The Four Seasons is a step above even the most luxurious of Sharm's resorts. Its sprawling grounds with hundreds of palm trees and bright bougainvillea resemble a small village, which guests can navigate via golf carts and funicular. Perched on a hill, the resort offers superb views of the sea and the rocky Tiran

Island—best enjoyed from the private beach and main pool area. The nine on-site bars and restaurants serve excellent food and drinks in attractive settings (five-star breakfast included). And each of the 200 rooms is super spacious with down pillows, an elegant marble bathroom, and a balcony or terrace. Staff are on point.

INFORMATION AND SERVICES

Sharm is spread out and does not have a major tourist information center. If you need advice, ask at your resort.

ATMs

ATMs are prevalent around Sharm el Sheikh, especially in Na'ama Bay, Shark's Bay, and in most resorts.

Medical

Most of the big resorts have quality doctors on site for an extra charge, but in a medical emergency head to **Sharm el Sheikh International Hospital** (Al Mustashfa Al Dowli St. and Al Salam Rd.; tel. 069 3660893; www.sharmih.webs.com; 24 hours daily). Their facilities are the best in the Sinai and include a hyperbaric chamber for diving accidents.

For the best pharmacy in town, visit **El Ezaby Pharmacy** (Il Mercato Mall, Hadaba; tel. 19600; www.elezabypharmacy.com; 24 hours daily). They have two other branches around the city (one in Na'ama Bay and the other in Nabq Bay) and deliver anywhere 24/7 for nominal fee.

TRANSPORTATION

Getting There

Flying is by far the easiest way to get to Sharm from Cairo. EgyptAir runs several direct flights to/from Cairo each day. Those who don't mind spending 8-9 hours on the road can save by taking a bus.

AIR

Sharm el Sheikh International Airport (SSH) (El Salam Rd., Sharm el Sheikh; tel. 069 3601140; www.sharm-el-sheikh-airport.com) is centrally located, just 10-15 minutes from most hotels and resorts. A taxi from the airport to just about anywhere in Sharm el Sheikh should be around 70-200LE. Flight time from Cairo: 1 hour.

BUS

The **central bus station** is located on Rowyasat Road, 8 kilometers (5 mi) southwest of Na'ama Bay. **Go Bus** (tel. 19567; www.go-bus.com) and **East Delta Bus Co.** (no tel.) both leave from here. Go Bus is a much more comfortable option, but East Delta offers more trips. Tickets to/from Cairo should cost around 235LE each way (8-9 hours). And to/from Dahab 90LE each way (1 hour).

Getting Around

Taxis are generally the best way to get around Sharm. If you stay in the central Na'ama Bay, many of the restaurants, cafés, and shops will be walkable.

TAXIS

Taxis are prevalent all over Sharm el Sheikh. Most have meters—be sure to ask that they're used—or agree on a price before getting in.

PRIVATE CAR HIRE

Most hotels can arrange private transportation in and around Sharm. The tour operator **Falcon Adventure** (tel. 0100 158 8922; www.falconadventure.com) also offers reliable and hassle-free transfers to/from the airport (520LE round-trip) and private cars/guides for other trips around the city and its outskirts.

Ras Mohammed National Park

As Egypt's oldest national park (est. 1983), Ras Mohammed has enjoyed decades of protection—evident in the pristine condition of its reefs and beaches. Covering some 480 square kilometers (185 sq mi) of land and sea, the park sits at the southern tip of the Sinai with coral walls following the coastline and a handful of coral islets spotting the waters just offshore.

Most of the sights can be found on the skinny peninsula (around 10 km/6 mi long) that juts off the mainland into the Red Sea where the Gulf of Suez meets the Gulf of Aqaba. The unique underwater conditions where the bodies merge—the Gulf of Suez is relatively shallow and the Gulf of Aqaba extremely deep—bring a wide variety of sea life. Inland, encroaching pools of water and mangrove trees spot the rugged terrain.

Visiting the Park

The park is an easy day trip from central Sharm el Sheikh—located just 19 kilometers (12 mi) south of the resort town. Visitors must leave the grounds by sunset (unless they're camping) and enter no later than 3pm. Tickets cost 80LE per person for the day (8am-sunset) or 160LE per person to camp.

The best time to visit is May, when the fish come in swarms and the temperatures aren't yet soaring. March-April and October-November are also delightful, with daytime temperatures around 27-32°C (80-90°F). Temperatures in summer (June-Sept.) reach over 38°C (100°F), but also bring rich sea life, making it a fine time to visit for divers and snorkelers who plan to spend most of their time in the water.

SIGHTS

Shark Observatory Clifftop

(Masidat el 'Aroosh)

A few dozen rocky steps bring visitors to this platform with striking views of the surrounding mountains and sea where the Gulf of Suez and Gulf of Aqaba meet. The water is so clear you can see the outline of the coral wall below. Contrary to what the name suggests, you're not likely to spot many sharks.

Mangrove Channel

(Shagar el Mangrove)

Lines of hearty mangrove trees break up the stark landscape in this channel, playing host to a unique ecosystem. Fiddler crabs—the males with one oversized claw to attract the ladies—scurry among the mangroves' aerial roots, and in September thousands of white storks and other migratory birds stop by for a snack.

The Crack

(Sha' el Zalzal)

An earthquake in the 1960s tore a 40-meter-long (130-ft-long) hole in the fossilized reef here. "The Crack," as it's been dubbed, is filled with water (though not for swimming) that descends more than 13 meters (45 ft). You can find it just west of the Enchanted Lake.

TOP EXPERIENCE

DIVING AND SNORKELING

To visit the dive spots around Ras Mohammed, book with a dive center in Sharm el Sheikh (page 345). They make regular day trips by boat to the park's marine sites.

For a snorkel tour, contact **Bedawi Eco Camp** (tel. 0100 698 3031; www.bedawi.com). If you don't feel like camping, Bedawi can pick you up at your Sharm hotel at 8am in a private car, take you to the best sights and snorkel spots around the park, prepare an excellent lunch at their campgrounds, and have you back at your hotel in Sharm by 5pm (740LE/person, plus entrance ticket).

Beaches and Snorkeling Sites

MARSA BAREIKA BAY

Small camps line the northwest coast of Marsa Bareika Bay, where stunning corals and their fishy friends live just a few feet off the shore. It's possible to jump in at **Marsa Bareika Beach** (follow the arrows), but a more comfortable option is to use the shade and services of one of the camps. **Bedawi Camp's** sandy beach is an excellent place to spend the day (200LE day use including lunch and access to bathroom and showers).

SUEZ BEACH
(Shat' Swiss)

Along the main road 2 kilometers (1 mi) south of the archway of large concrete slabs ("Stone Gate"), this long sandy beach leads to shallow waters for around 100 meters (330 ft) before arriving to a healthy wall of corals. Early morning is the best time to visit, before big groups arrive.

★ SHARK OBSERVATORY
(Musidat el 'Aroosh)

Dragonflies zip around this idyllic cove hidden behind rocky hills and boulders. A short walk into the water leads to a dramatic drop in the seafloor and a sprawling wall on either side with some of Egypt's most brilliant fish and corals. The reef starts just below the surface and makes a steep descent for more than 40 meters (130 ft), making it perfect for both snorkelers and divers. Sharks do make infrequent appearances, but those that do are typically harmless, like the friendly whale shark. There have been no recorded attacks here.

THE ENCHANTED LAKE
(El Buhera el Mashoura)

Swimmers wary of the open sea will find their happy place in this shallow saline lake filled with water that pours in at high tide. The lake looks out to rolling mountains in the distance and changes various hues of blue throughout the day depending on the sunlight.

Dive Sites

RAS GHOZLANI

Located on the northeast side of the park, Ras Ghozlani is bursting with table corals, anemones, and pinnacles encased in swarms of glassfish. It's a lesser visited dive site and suitable for all levels. Depth: 7-30 meters (23-100 ft).

SHARK AND JOLANDA REEFS

Divers come from around the world to visit these two patch reefs that sit side by side just off the tip of the Ras Mohammed Peninsula. The drift dive typically starts at Shark Reef's sheer walls before the current pushes visitors along to Jolanda Reef's coral gardens. Both spots get their names for good reason. Sharks are common sightings at the former while the latter is named after the Spanish-built cargo ship, *Jolanda,* that sank here in 1980. Most of the boat's frame disappeared into the deep blue during a storm, but its shipment of toilets, bathtubs, and sinks—along with a vintage BMW—now make up an accidental contemporary art exhibit ripe for exploring. The reefs are not suitable for snorkelers (in a rare occurrence, an oceanic whitetip shark attacked a group of snorkelers here in October 2020).

★ CAMPING

Stargaze under clear skies, slumber to the sound of soft waves, and wake up with to the sun turning the sky purple. If you want to spend the night inside the park, camping on the northwest side of Marsa Bareika Bay is your only option. There are small campgrounds here where you can set up your own tent, or stay at Bedawi Eco Camp's pre-pitched accommodation (recommended). Sunrise until around 10am—before most visitors arrive and the sun gets too strong—is the ideal time to explore the park.

1: Ras Mohammed National Park **2:** fish off Suez Beach **3:** snorkeling at Shark Observatory **4:** Bedawi Eco Camp

1
2
3
4

BEDAWI ECO CAMP

Marsa Bareika Rd., Site 3, Ras Mohammed Park; tel. 0100 698 3031; www.bedawi.com; 9am-9pm daily; 1,200LE d full board

Mohammed Harby and Rayya keep a clean campground on a sandy patch of the shore. A handful of high-quality tents sit nestled between two rocky mounds on the side of a protected bay, and brilliant corals line the coast. There's a spacious common area with Bedouin-style seating (floor pillows) where visitors can enjoy a breakfast and superb lunch in the shade (dinners are served beside a campfire under the stars). Makeshift showers in plastic tanks are available to wash off salty sea water, and a composting toilet is kept surprisingly clean. Best to reserve at least a week or two in advance.

INFORMATION AND SERVICES

Be sure to bring your passport and a photocopy of your passport photo and visa pages to leave with security. The closest ATMs, pharmacies, and stores are in central Sharm el Sheikh around 40 minutes away, so stock up on essentials before your visit.

VISITORS CENTER

Sharm el Sheikh-Ras Mohammed Rd.; no tel.; 8am-4pm daily

Located just off the main road into Ras Mohammed (at Marsa Ghozlani), the Visitors Center has some nice informational displays about the area's marine life and unique geological features. It's worth a brief stop if you have the time, though despite the official opening hours, it's often closed. Ask at the park's ticket office (you'll pass through it like a toll booth on your way into Ras Mohammed) to see if it's open.

GETTING THERE

Getting There

A taxi or private car from central Sharm el Sheikh (40 minutes) should cost around 100-200LE depending on where you're starting. From Dahab to Ras Mohammed expect to pay 500-600LE (2 hours). Best to organize this a day in advance with your host in Dahab. **Bedawi Eco Camp** (tel. 0100 698 3031; www.bedawi.com) offers transfers from central Sharm el Sheikh to their campgrounds for 150LE each way.

Getting Around

You need a car to get around the park. Either book a private tour with Bedawi Eco Camp (740LE per person including lunch and transportation to/from your Sharm hotel, plus entrance ticket) or ask your hotel in Sharm to arrange a day trip.

Dahab

It's not hard to imagine where Dahab (Arabic for "Gold") gets its name: The town outshines even the precious metal itself with golden mountains that pour into an azure sea. Saudi Arabia, just 24 kilometers (15 mi) across the Gulf of Aqaba, also lends its beauty to Dahab's skyscape with more phantasmal mountains rising out of the horizon. The natural splendor along the shore is rivaled only by Dahab's rich underwater worlds, attracting divers and snorkelers from around the world with its unique submarine topography. While there's no shortage of activities for the adventurous—from kitesurfing to diving and desert safaris—Dahab is also a perfect place to lay in the sand, watch the waves come in, and soak up the sea breeze.

ORIENTATION

The town of Dahab lies along a small strip of the coast, running only around 5 kilometers (3 mi) from north to south. **A'sala** is the northernmost neighborhood of Dahab proper—its interior home to locals, while the

Dahab

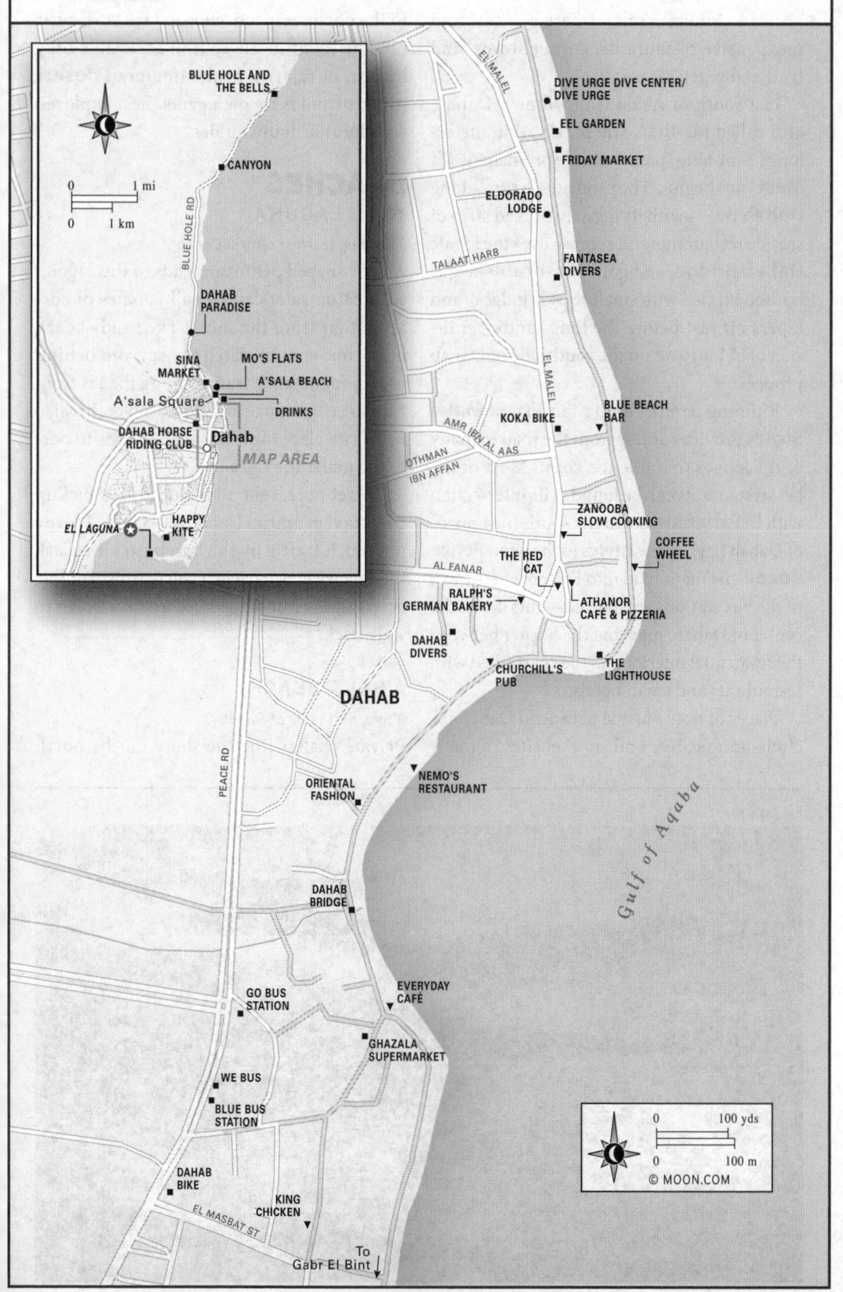

BLUE HOLE AND THE BELLS
CANYON
0 1 mi
0 1 km
BLUE HOLE RD
DAHAB PARADISE
SINA MARKET
MO'S FLATS
A'SALA BEACH
A'sala Square
DRINKS
DAHAB HORSE RIDING CLUB
Dahab
MAP AREA
EL LAGUNA
HAPPY KITE
EL MALEL
DIVE URGE DIVE CENTER/ DIVE URGE
EEL GARDEN
FRIDAY MARKET
ELDORADO LODGE
TALAAT HARB
FANTASEA DIVERS
EL MALEL
BLUE BEACH BAR
KOKA BIKE
AMR IBN AL AAS
OTHMAN IBN AFFAN
ZANOOBA SLOW COOKING
COFFEE WHEEL
THE RED CAT
AL FANAR
RALPH'S GERMAN BAKERY
ATHANOR CAFÉ & PIZZERIA
DAHAB DIVERS
CHURCHILL'S PUB
THE LIGHTHOUSE
DAHAB
PEACE RD
NEMO'S RESTAURANT
ORIENTAL FASHION
Gulf of Aqaba
DAHAB BRIDGE
EVERYDAY CAFÉ
GO BUS STATION
GHAZALA SUPERMARKET
WE BUS
BLUE BUS STATION
0 100 yds
0 100 m
© MOON.COM
DAHAB BIKE
KING CHICKEN
EL MASBAT ST
To Gabr El Bint

shore is lined with private chalets for rent. "Downtown" A'sala centers around **A'sala Square** (Midan A'sala), where you can find inexpensive restaurants, corner stores, and fruit and vegetable stands.

Just south of A'sala is downtown Dahab, also called **Masbat,** where the 3-kilometer-long (2-mi-long) paved seaside promenade (**El Mamsha**) begins. The promenade runs along **Dahab Bay**—with its densely packed strip of seaside restaurants and shops—over the iconic **Dahab Bridge,** along the **Mashraba** neighborhood (lined with small seaside lodges), and tapers off just before the long sandy peninsula of **El Laguna** on the south side of Dahab proper.

Running parallel to El Mamsha, **El Malel Street** provides access from the road to many of the lodges that line the coast. Most of the best restaurants can be found at its intersection with **El Fanar Street** to the south (just north of Dahab Bay). A few streets to the west, **Peace Road**—the main road into Dahab where most of the bus stations are located—cuts down the center of Dahab, marking the border between the residential interior and the coast filled with restaurants and small hotels.

Places of note outside of central Dahab include unique dive and snorkel sites, namely the **Canyon** and **Blue Hole,** both reached via **Blue Hole Road** (7 km/4 mi and 10 km/6 mi to the north, respectively); and **Gabr el Bint** (28 km/17 mi to the south), accessible only by boat or safari. The mountainous **desert interior** holds its own gems, best explored with local Bedouin guides.

BEACHES

★ EL LAGUNA

3 km/2 mi south of central Dahab

A boot-shaped peninsula leads to this lagoon with calm waters and small patches of corals not far from the shore. The sandy beach is a prime spot to watch the sun dip behind nearby mountains, transforming the sea from turquoise to orange and liquid silver. It's also a favorite place for locals and visitors to barbecue under the stars.

To get here, rent a bike or grab a pickup truck taxi in central Dahab (20-35LE). There's not much traffic by the beach, so either ask the driver to return when you're finished, flag down another beachgoer for a ride, or plan to walk back.

A'SALA BEACH

A'sala, north side of Dahab

Private chalets line the shore on the north

El Laguna

side of Dahab, but the long, skinny beach between them and the sea is open to the public. The water here is shallow (2 m/6 ft or less) for around 100 meters (330 ft) before the seafloor drops into an infinite blue. A good number of colorful fish make their way near the shore, but the real treat is the wall of brilliant corals that follows along the drop-off. Both the shallower sections and the drop-off area are excellent places to swim.

DIVING AND SNORKELING

Dive and Snorkel Sites

The sites below are organized from north to south. All are open 24/7 and are free to visit, with the exception of Blue Hole and the Bells, which is open 8am-sunset and charges an entry fee.

BLUE HOLE AND THE BELLS

Blue Hole Rd., 10 km/6 mi north of central Dahab; 8am-sunset daily; 160LE

This sinkhole—descending for over 110 meters (360 ft) and surrounded by a ring of jagged rocks and corals—is an underwater playground for casual snorkelers and advanced divers alike. The entrance lies a short (but rocky) walk to the north at a narrow channel called the Bells.

Recent years of overcrowding has left many of the corals near the surface worse for wear. But plenty of vibrant sea life can still be seen near the Bells entry and for many meters along the ridge to the right. Divers who prefer to stay close to the surface can enjoy the colorful "Saddle" that leads into the Blue Hole at 7 meters (23 ft) deep. And diving experts with multiple tanks can reach the "Arch" at around 56 meters (184 ft) that connects the Blue Hole to the open sea. Plaques on a nearby cliffside commemorate some of the hundreds who died trying to achieve the feat—a dark reminder not to dive beyond your limits.

Along the shore, Bedouin-run cafeterias offer refreshments, WCs, and showers for a small fee. The **Bedouin Star** (8am-5pm daily; 100-150LE mains) is a good choice. You can leave your belongings here while you take a dip and come back for lunch or tea (best to leave valuables at home). Snorkeling equipment available to rent.

The Blue Hole is also the gateway to the Ras Abu Galum Protectorate and shares the same entrance ticket. To get to the protectorate, pick up a boat just a few meters north of the Bells entry. Be sure to bring your passport to enter both the Blue Hole area and Ras Abu Galum.

CANYON

Blue Hole Rd., 7 km/4 mi north of central Dahab

One of Dahab's most dramatic dive sites, this canyon that starts at around 20 meters (65 ft) below the surface descends to more than 40 meters (130 ft) in semi-darkness. A resident octopus makes frequent appearances, and glassfish glitter around a coral dome near the surface. From the bottom, the entrance becomes a distant sliver—creating a sensation that the earth might just swallow you whole. **Abdul Café** (no tel.; 8am-6pm daily; 65-120LE mains) offers refreshments and WCs just on the beach.

EEL GARDEN

El Malel St., Masbat

Dozens of eels sway hypnotically on the sandy seafloor at this dive and snorkel site. Those not fond of this feature can still enjoy the long entry channel filled with glassfish and healthy coral gardens. Avoid it on windy days as currents can be dangerous.

THE LIGHTHOUSE

Lighthouse Promenade, Masbat, Dahab Bay

Smack dab in the center of town, the Lighthouse—with its gradual sandy slope entrance—is always busy with swimmers and novices in search of an easy dive (though the site doesn't offer much to snorkelers). More advanced divers can also enjoy the deeper corals (at around 30 m/100 ft) and night excursions, when a new cast of critters come out to play. Other unexpected characters include a life-size elephant made of scrap metal and a few pharaonic (imitation) statues—placed here in 2017 as part of an underwater museum.

GABR EL BINT

18 km/11 mi south of Three Pools

Despite its ominous name, Gabr el Bint ("Grave of the Girl") is an excellent dive site—full of table corals and majestic gorgonians. Deep in the south and accessible only by foot, bike, boat, or camel, it's one of Dahab's least visited gems. While much of the underwater beauty lies far below (descending over 50 m/160 ft), a shallow lagoon spotted with colorful coral islands is a great place to snorkel. Most dive centers offer trips here by boat or camel for around €100 per person (including dive guide, equipment, food, and transportation).

Outfitters

FANTASEA DIVERS

El Malel St., just north of Eel Garden; tel. 0100 260 1312; www.fantasearedsea.com; 8am-7pm daily

This PADI certified dive center has a professional group of guides and high-quality gear for rent. Guided dives start at €65 per person for two dives, and a 4-5-day beginner course with certification goes for €335 (both including full equipment). Group sizes are limited to a maximum of 4 people to ensure every diver gets close attention from the instructors.

DAHAB DIVERS

El Fanar St.; tel. 069 3640233; www.dahabdivers.com; 8am-7pm daily

The fun team at the PADI certified Dahab Divers offers guided outings with full equipment starting at €65 per person for two dives. The 3-4-day PADI Open Water Course for beginners is available for €350, and serious divers can check out the 3-4-week PADI Dive Master Course (€750). Equipment is kept clean and up to date. Group sizes limited to 4 people max.

DIVE URGE DIVE CENTER

El Malel St., just south of Eel Garden; tel. 0155 051 8038; www.dive-urge.com; 8am-6pm daily

Another of Dahab's well-established PADI certified centers, Dive Urge offers excellent services and diving gear. They come at a premium but keep their customers happy. Two guided dives cost €108 per person and a 4-day beginner course will set you back €518 (equipment included for both). Group sizes up to 4 people.

RECREATION AND ACTIVITIES

Kitesurfing and Windsurfing

The wind that funnels through the narrow Gulf of Aqaba makes Dahab a fabulous place to kite or windsurf. Dahab's sheltered lagoon (El Laguna) is a great corner for beginners to cut their teeth, and more advanced surfers can also find plenty of spots for a challenge.

HAPPY KITE

El Laguna, at Happy Inn Hotel; tel. 0106 056 1912; www.happy-kite.com; 9am-5pm daily; prices vary

This kitesurfing center located on the northeast side of El Laguna has a stock of first-rate equipment and professional instructors. Prices start at €35 for a one-hour kitesurfing rental and €310 for a private 6-day beginner course. Windsurfers can rent equipment from their on-site partner organization for just €15 for one hour and can try a private two-hour beginner lesson for €70.

Desert Safaris

Venture into Dahab's desert and mountains on foot, on a quad bike, or in an off-road vehicle. Plenty of trip options are available—from a quick morning jaunt to multiday excursions.

MO'NAS DAHAB

tel. 0100 194 3027

If you want to avoid groups and enjoy the guidance of a fantastic local, contact Mo'nas via phone, WhatsApp, or Facebook Messenger

1: Dahab **2:** local guide Mo'nas **3:** A'sala Beach

1
2
3

(@MonsDhab). He can organize a variety of day trips to the mountains by 4WD with lunch (2,000LE for 2 people; 8 hours) or a desert trip with one night of camping (4,000LE for 2 people; 32 hours). He knows the region by heart and makes for very entertaining company. For a more economical option, contact Mo'nas to see if you can join another small group (the 4WD can hold 7 passengers).

SINAI GATE

tel. 0106 633 0415; www.sinaigate.com

Sinai Gate offers professional guided day trips to the mountains (€25 hiking; €35 quad bikes; €45 4WD; €35/hour horseback) and off-road bike rides along the shore from south Dahab to **Gabr el Bint** for some snorkeling (23 km/14 mi round-trip; €70).

Horseback Riding

DAHAB HORSE RIDING CLUB

Abu Mina St.; tel. 0100 141 7906; dahab.horseridingclub@gmail.com; 7am-11pm daily

Sirgun and Ali keep their horses happy and healthy. Prices start at 300LE per person for a 1-hour ride on the beach (with a swim), or 2,700LE per person for an overnight trip in the mountains including around 7 hours of riding, food, drinks, and camping. All rides include the company of an expert guide.

SHOPPING

Little shops with handicrafts, beachwear, and other clothes can be found along the seaside promenade (El Mamsha) on Dahab Bay.

ORIENTAL FASHION

El Mamsha, next to Ali Baba Hotel; tel. 0100 589 5470; 10am-midnight daily

If you only make one stop, head to Oriental Fashion to browse their unique handmade clothes from the Sinai. The shops continue inland at the southern end of Dahab Bay (just south of Ghazala Market) on Tawfik el Hakim Street.

FRIDAY MARKET

Near Eel Garden, El Mamsha; no tel.; 11am-5pm Fri.

On Friday afternoons, visitors can also swing by the Friday Market, where local and expat Dahab residents sell home-cooked food and handicrafts. The market starts earlier and ends later some weeks.

FOOD

Seaside restaurants line the promenade (El Mamsha) along Dahab Bay, offering fresh seafood and international fare. Diners who don't mind sacrificing the view can head one street inland for a wider variety, and usually much cheaper prices. Few restaurants in Dahab serve alcohol due to the hefty cost of a license, but you can usually bring your own (just ask before cracking open the bottle). For shisha, head to nearly any of the dining spots along the Mamsha.

Egyptian

KING CHICKEN

Tawfik el Hakim St., Mashraba; tel. 0100 909 0628; 10am-2am daily; 40-100LE mains

Succulent rotisserie chickens are the star attraction at this modest Egyptian restaurant favored by Cairenes. Plentiful outdoor seating pours into the (mostly pedestrian) street, and busy waiters speed by to cater to the crowds. Mains come with an array of salads and dips.

International

★ ATHANOR CAFÉ & PIZZERIA

Off Al Fanar St., Masbat; tel. 0106 950 3541; noon-3am daily; 45-70LE mains

With its layers of fresh toppings and crust crisped to perfection, the brick oven pizza at Athanor is the best in town. They also serve solid pasta dishes and roast their own coffee beans (the iced latte with ice cream is a sweet pick-me-up). Head to the courtyard in the back to enjoy your meal al fresco in the company of trees, or take it away for a picnic on the beach.

Dahab Groceries and Liquor Shops

Whether you're staying in an accommodation with a kitchen or just need supplies for daily outings, Dahab has a handful of good corner stores and liquor shops to provide the essentials. Check out:

- **Sina Market** (450 m/1,500 ft north of A'sala Square; no tel.; 9am-11pm daily) to stock up on water and snacks.
- **Gennat el-Fowakah** (A'sala Square; no tel.; 9am-11pm daily) for fresh fruits and veg.
- **Drinks** (A'sala Square; tel. 0100 583 5274; 9am-midnight daily) for Egyptian beer, wine, and spirits.
- **Ghazala Supermarket** (just south of Dahab Bridge, Masbat Square) for a wide variety of groceries.

THE RED CAT

Off Al Fanar St., Masbat; tel. 0109 114 0113; 1pm-10pm Wed.-Mon.; 105-155LE mains

Famous for its fresh Russian and Ukrainian dishes, the Red Cat injects new flavors into Dahab's dining scene. Try the dumplings stuffed with potatoes and fried onions, the fried chebureki filled with lamb, or a cold beetroot soup with eggs and cucumbers. There are plenty of options for vegans and vegetarians, and a nice range of wood oven pizzas and calzones.

★ ZANOOBA SLOW COOKING

El Malel St., next to Dahab Divers Lodge, Masbat; tel. 0109 699 2699; www.zanoobaslowcooking.business.site; 6pm-10:30pm daily; 130-250LE mains

Tender turkey legs in gravy, succulent roasted duck, coconut curry vegetables—each dish at Zanooba is a daylong project of stewing juices. Order a day (or at least 6 hours) in advance by phone or WhatsApp to allow enough time for the staff to gather fresh ingredients and to ensure you get a spot in the cozy interior.

Seafood

★ NEMO'S RESTAURANT

El Mamsha, Masbat; tel. 0122 949 5318; 9am-1am daily; 100-280LE mains

Indulge in your pick of fresh seafood from a bed of ice and choose how you want it cooked. Sautéed veggies, fries, and a handful of dips (baba ghanoush, feta cheese and tomatoes, tahini) come along with the meal. Try to snag a seat on the upstairs deck under the stars or on the ground floor platform jutting into the sea.

Cafés and Snacks

COFFEE WHEEL

Lighthouse area, Masbat; tel. 0111 801 9462; 9am-9pm daily; 15-25LE hot drinks

In search of your caffeine fix? Look no further. This little beachside café has some of the best coffee in Dahab. The skilled baristas can make all your favorite espresso-based drinks. Delicious waffles and other snacks also on the menu.

EVERYDAY CAFÉ

Masbat Square, Masbat; tel. 0111 999 2571; 8am-2am daily; 15-25LE hot drinks

This eclectic café decorated with brightly painted antique doors and old bicycles serves up excellent milkshakes, smoothies, and fresh juices. Their back porch basically hangs over the water—a great place to soak up the sun and snap some Insta-worthy pics on a strategically placed swing. Evenings bring live music. There are a few "Everyday Café" imitations around town, so be sure to visit the one near Ghazala Market.

★ RALPH'S GERMAN BAKERY

Al Fanar St., Masbat; tel. 0100 233 9994; www.ralphsgermanbakery.com; 7am-8pm daily; 40-100LE sandwiches

The Germany Bakery is a landmark in Dahab—known for its wholesome breads, chewy pretzels, and delectable pastries. They also serve excellent coffee, breakfasts, and sandwiches on your choice of baguette. For ample outdoor seating and the buzz of brunchers, head to their original location on Fanar Street. Their newer branch (just south of A'sala Square) tends to be much quieter with a few tables outside and a cozy interior.

BARS AND NIGHTLIFE

Much like the rest of Dahab's vibes, nightlife here is pretty chill—consisting mostly of a seaside beer or shisha.

CHURCHILL'S PUB

El Mamsha, at Red Sea Relax Resort; tel. 069 3641309; 10am-2am daily; 50-100LE drinks

This rooftop bar is set back a few meters from the water but still offers a nice breeze and sea views. Ice cold beers (classic Stella or Heineken on draft) and flavorful shisha are the main attractions, but they also make solid burgers and other pub snacks.

★ BLUE BEACH BAR

El Mamsha, at Blue Beach Club; tel. 0128 501 0429; noon-midnight daily; 50-100LE drinks

A row of picnic tables lines the sand at this beachside bar that buzzes with life in the evenings. Additional seating can be found on the roof—a perfect place to enjoy sunset with a drink. Pub food also served.

ACCOMMODATIONS

Small hotels, lodges, and private chalets line Dahab's shore for some 4 kilometers (2.5 mi). The **Mashraba** neighborhood in south Dahab is quiet and speckled with unfinished hotels—many halted after the 2011 Revolution. **Masbat** in central Dahab is the busiest area with most of the shopping, restaurants, and cafés. And **A'sala,** just north of Masbat, is a peaceful part of town full of beachside chalets. Check out Airbnb for some superb (and economical) accommodation options next to or near the sea.

Under 800LE

★ MO'S FLATS

A'sala Beach, A'sala; no tel.; mwereida@gmail.com; 750LE d

After managing a boutique hotel in Dahab for six years, Mo Wereida struck out on his own to design a handful of gorgeous chalets right on A'sala Beach. Jazz, Blues, Soul, and Bossa Nova are all uniquely decorated one-bedroom flats starting at 750LE a night. The Beachfront Penthouse and Norwegian Wood (top pick) are the nicest, each with two rooms (1,100-1,300LE). The latter sleeps up to six people and includes a private roof with hammock, lounge chairs, al fresco shower, and unbeatable views of the mountains and sea. Each flat is filled with special touches like a wide range of kitchen appliances and snorkeling gear. Book through Airbnb.

DIVE URGE

El Malel St., next to Eel Garden, Masbat; tel. 0155 051 8038; www.dive-urge.com; 760LE d

The 10 attractive rooms at this boutique hotel enjoy views of either vibrant green gardens or the sea. Its location is ideal—on a private patch of the shore between A'sala Beach and downtown Dahab, each just a few minutes' walk away. Excellent restaurant and dive center on site.

800-1,650LE

ELDORADO LODGE

El Malel St., next to Eel Garden, Masbat; tel. 0106 160 3418; eldoradodahab@gmail.com; 900LE d

The centrally located Eldorado Lodge offers cozy, colorful rooms with wood paneled ceilings and a first-rate outdoor restaurant. Their small private beach—just across a pedestrian path—is kept pristine.

★ DAHAB PARADISE

Blue Hole Coast, 3 km/2 mi north of central Dahab; tel. 0100 700 4133; www.dahabparadise.com; 1,200LE d

Travelers looking for a quiet escape will enjoy this boutique hotel flanked by mountains and sea. The stylish rooms—each with a balcony—wrap around a well-manicured lawn and palm-lined pool. A 24-hour restaurant is available on site for whenever hunger strikes (superb breakfast included), and staff could not be more helpful. The minor cons are the road that runs between the hotel and the beach (though with little traffic) and the distance to central Dahab—around 35 minutes on foot.

INFORMATION AND SERVICES

ATMs

A handful of ATMs spot the Mamsha in central Dahab and Tawfik el Hakim Street (which turns into El Mashtaba St.) a bit farther south. You won't find any in the areas to the far north (Blue Hole and Ras Abu Galum Protectorate) or south (El Laguna).

Medical

For emergencies, head to **Dahab Medical Care Hospital** (El Mashraba St.; tel. 0122 348 6209; www.dahabpolyclinic.com; 24 hours daily)—a new hospital set up by a veteran doctor, Ahmed Sadek. Facilities are basic, but it's your best option in Dahab. For drug store essentials, check out any of the **pharmacies** in central Dahab along the promenade (El Mamsha).

GETTING THERE

The quickest and most comfortable way to get to Dahab from Cairo is by flying to Sharm el Sheikh and taking a private car (with driver) from there.

Bus

Go Bus (tel. 19567; www.go-bus.com) and **Blue Bus** (tel. 16128; www.bluebus.com.eg) are both comfortable options for traveling between Dahab and Cairo (10-11 hours; 215LE); Sharm el Sheikh (1.5 hours; 85LE); or Nuweiba (1 hour; 95LE). Both companies' stations are centrally located 100 meters (300 ft) apart along Peace Road, just southwest of the Dahab Bridge.

If you're in a bind, when you're ready to leave Dahab head to the government-run East Delta Bus Co. ticket office (Peace Rd., 180 m/590 ft south of the Blue Bus station; no tel.) to see their schedule. They typically offer more frequent trips for cheaper, but their buses could use a deep clean. The station (with another ticket office) is located 3 kilometers (2 mi) to the west of their downtown ticket office.

Microbus

WE Bus (Peace Rd., next to Blue Bus station; tel. 0111 118 8021; www.webusegypt.com) has a fleet of comfortable microbuses that travel to Dahab from Downtown Cairo (Abdel Minam Riyad Square) for 280LE first class and 380LE VIP—carrying 13 and 8 passengers, respectively. This is a much quicker option than the bus and only takes around 8 hours from Cairo. They also offer trips between Dahab and Sharm el Sheikh, St. Katherine, and Nuweiba. For questions and reservations, call or contact them on Facebook Messenger (@webusEG).

Air

Sharm el Sheikh International Airport (El Salam Rd., Sharm el Sheikh, 90 km/56 mi south of Dahab; tel. 069 3601140; www.sharm-el-sheikh-airport.com) is located just over an hour south of central Dahab. Your accommodation in Dahab should be able to arrange airport pickup, or if you don't mind haggling you can grab a taxi. The price to central Dahab should be around 600-1,000LE.

GETTING AROUND

Taxi

Dahab's taxis are pickup trucks. Don't expect to find any meters, so be sure to agree on a price before you get in. Anywhere around town should cost 15-30LE.

Bicycle

Cycling is an excellent way to get around the small town of Dahab, especially in the cooler months. For the best rides, check out **Dahab Bike** (on corner of Peace Rd. and El Masbat St., next to East Delta Bus Co. station; tel. 0109 314 9508; 8am-midnight daily; 75LE/day). A decent alternative is **Koka Bike** (El Melal St., Mashraba; tel. 0128 012 2815; 9am-10pm daily; 75LE/day). You're not likely to find many superb options at either, but their stock is sufficient for a pedal around town. Rentals available for an hour to multiple weeks.

Ras Abu Galum Protectorate

Covering 400 square kilometers (155 sq mi) of mountains and shore, the Abu Galum Protectorate (est. 1992) is best known for its pristine corals and untouched shores. The vast mountain interior is rarely explored but holds more than 100 unique species of desert plants, along with agile Nubian ibex, who scale the steep cliffsides with ease.

Not long ago, the only way for visitors to reach these parts was by hopping on a camel or hiking along the narrow path between the mountains and sea (which is still an option). Motorboats have since been employed to get people from the Blue Hole to the isolated Bedouin villages and beach camps to the north. It's an easy day trip from Dahab, but those who prefer to spend the night can pick a camp at either the First Bedouin Village or the Blue Lagoon. They offer very basic beach huts, makeshift WCs, and cafeterias with floor pillow seating. If you do stay the night, be sure to bring bug spray and extra water to rinse off the salty seawater. Both day trippers and campers should pack their passports, sunscreen, water, and snacks. The protectorate shares an **entrance ticket** with the Blue Hole (160LE).

FIRST BEDOUIN VILLAGE

Whether you reach Ras Abu Galum by boat, camel, or on foot, this row of beach camps will be your introduction to the protectorate. Here, mountains kiss the azure sea and thatched huts are the only manmade structures around. Pick a shaded place to relax with a tea before exploring the beautiful underwater worlds just offshore with a snorkel and fins.

★ Snorkeling

A wealth of unique coral formations and vibrant fish can be found along the coast right at the start of Ras Abu Galum Protectorate (just north of where boats drop you off). Most camps provide lifejackets and snorkel equipment for a small fee (25-60LE), but best to rent at any of the dive centers in central Dahab (page 358) for a wider selection and better quality.

For **diving,** book with a dive center in Dahab and come to the protectorate as part of a package.

★ BLUE LAGOON

Nestled between mountains and sea, this dazzling turquoise pool is an excellent spot for swimmers who prefer some shelter from the open water. On windy days, kitesurfers entertain as they fly across the lagoon with their colorful sails. A number of camps line the beach, offering shade, snacks, and basic restrooms. Located around 4 kilometers (2.5 mi) north of the First Bedouin Village, it's reached by pickup truck taxi (250LE return) or on foot.

Kitesurfing and Windsurfing

The Blue Lagoon is a favorite kitesurfing and windsurfing spot in Dahab. Check out **El Omda Camp** (Blue Lagoon; tel. 0100 744

3421; elomdacamp@hotmail.com) to try some lessons and/or rent equipment. Prices start at €15/hour for windsurf rental or €45/half-day kitesurf rental.

INFORMATION AND SERVICES

The closest ATMs, pharmacies, and other essential services are located in central Dahab, so be sure to bring along enough cash, snacks, water, and anything else you might need.

GETTING THERE

The Blue Hole is the gateway to the protectorate. From this point your options for arriving are via boat (fastest), hiking, or camel. Once you arrive at the First Bedouin Village at the entrance of the Ras Abu Galum Protectorate, pickup trucks will be waiting to take visitors to the Blue Lagoon 15-20 minutes to the north. The price per car should be around 250-300LE round-trip and can be split between as many people as can pile into the bed of the pickup truck.

Boat

Motorboats take the 20-minute trip from the Blue Hole to Ras Abu Galum throughout the morning (10am-2pm) as soon as they gather a minimum of 6 passengers. There's a small shaded area on the far north side of the Blue Hole area where people wait for the boat. Head here first to let the organizers know you want a spot before enjoying a swim in the Blue Hole. The price of a return trip per person should be in the range of 120LE, and the last boat comes back to the Blue Hole just before sunset. Try not to miss it!

Hike or Camel

From the Blue Hole, active travelers can take a magnificent (moderate) 8-kilometer (5-mi) hike to Ras Abu Galum along a path that's flanked by mountains and sea. Alternatively, you can solicit the assistance of a camel around the Blue Hole area to transport you (about 150-200LE one-way). Either option should take around 90 minutes. The mountains will protect you from the sun on your way back in the late afternoon, but expect to be in the sun for most of the time on the way there. Best to set out early (at 8am when the Blue Hole opens) and avoid the trek in the summer months.

Blue Lagoon

Mt. Sinai and St. Katherine Protectorate

Mountains—jebel (singular) or jebaal (plural) in Arabic—spring out from the earth as far as the eye can see in the St. Katherine Protectorate. Covering some 4,350 square kilometers (1,680 sq mi) of the South Sinai interior, the protected area (designated such in 1986) holds both natural and historical treasures. Red granite mountains formed 700 million years ago dominate the skyscape and hardy medicinal plants creep out from between the rocks. Hiking routes weave through the valleys and up more than two dozen summits, each with a unique vantage point to admire the region's magnificent landscape. The most popular route up **Mt. Sinai** attracts thousands of visitors each year, many in religious pilgrimage.

At the center of the protectorate is **St. Katherine Town,** also called El Milga—a small village with one main (unnamed) road and simple houses built into the hills. The 6th-century St. Katherine Monastery and trailhead to summit Mt. Sinai are located just 3 kilometers (2 mi) down the street, in the village of Wadi el Deir. Other smaller villages can be found deep in the mountains, scattered around the protectorate.

SIGHTS

St. Katherine Monastery (Deir Sant Katrine)

Wadi el Deir; tel. 069 3470353; www.sinaimonastery.com; 9am-11:30am Mon.-Thurs. and Sat.; free

St. Katherine Monastery (officially, The Greek Orthodox Monastery of the God-Trodden Mount Sinai) is the oldest continuously inhabited Christian monastery in the world. The fortress-like structure dates to AD 530, when Byzantine Emperor Justinian commissioned the building to protect cave-dwelling monks from theft and harassment. Hermits (predominately Greek) had settled in the area centuries earlier to live near the site where they believed God first appeared to Moses at the Burning Bush. Christian pilgrims journeyed to the monastery throughout the Middle Ages, buying relics like the enchanted oil that seeped from "Saint Katherine's tomb," and supporting the monastery's coffers in the process.

Inside, the basilica (some 1,500 years old) still stands, rich with Byzantine artwork like a glittering mosaic of the Transfiguration with Jesus surrounded by five apostles. Nearby, a small museum holds a collection of centuries-old icons, and a library houses thousands of early manuscripts. The complex is closed to the public on Fridays, Sundays, and official holidays of the Greek Orthodox Church, but visitors can admire the paradisical gardens of olive and pomegranate trees any day of the year. If you plan on entering the monastery, note that shorts and sleeveless tops are not permitted (for both men and women).

★ HIKING

St. Katherine holds Egypt's best hiking routes. The views from the summits are spectacular and the routes themselves—through rocky valleys and Bedouin orchards—are a rejuvenating retreat into nature.

Local Guides

Local guides are required for all hikes in the protectorate. Contact Sheikh Mousa and his sons at the **Bedouin Camp** (tel. 0100 688 0820) or Youssef (tel. 0109 640 8883) and his brothers at **Dar Eid Mountain Lodge.** Both organize professional trips at fair prices. Choose from short walks or multiple-day mountain treks. They offer premade packages, or you can tailor the trip to your liking. No need to worry about trailheads—your guide will pick you up at your accommodation and bring you back at the end of the hike. Be sure

Katherine of Alexandria

The St. Katherine Protectorate and surrounding region gets its name from the legendary martyr Katherine of Alexandria who fought against the persecution of Christians in the 4th century before being tortured and beheaded at behest of Roman Emperor Maxentius, and flown by angels to the top of Mt. Katherine. Known for her purity and intellect, the virginal princess was said to have debated 50 pagan philosophers at once, emerging victorious against all. Modern scholars cast doubt on her existence (no known records of her story appear until five centuries after her alleged execution), but that didn't stop her from becoming one of the most venerated saints across medieval Europe. Her wide appeal has brought millions of pilgrims to the Sinai mountains to supplicate.

to bring something warm on overnight trips (even on the hottest days, the nighttime temperatures at the summits are chilly).

TOP EXPERIENCE

Mt. Sinai
(Jebel Sina)

Distance (round-trip): *13.5 kilometers (8.5 mi)*
Duration (round-trip): *4 hours*
Effort level: *easy*

Legend has it Moses received the Ten Commandments at the peak of this mountain, known by locals as Jebel Musa (Mt. Moses). At 2,285 meters (7,497 ft) above sea level, it's a pleasant 2-2.5-hour hike up and a bit quicker on the way down. The most popular way to make the journey is with a 2am start time to hike under the stars and enjoy sunrise at the top. Sunset climbs are equally beautiful, but can be hot in the summer months. A small church and mosque sit side by side at the summit, and the views (together with the last few dozen steps to the top) are truly breathtaking.

A local guide is required and should charge around 400LE for your whole group. Cafeterias spot the route, offering overpriced snacks, water, and blankets for rent (nights at the top range from chilly to freezing all year round). Fridays and Sundays—when the monastery is closed—are good times to go to avoid the crowds (there can be hundreds). For less traveled paths, try one of the other summits.

Other Routes

Visitors have no shortage of summits and valleys to explore in the St. Katherine Protectorate. While the quick trip up and down Mt. Sinai is the most popular route, to get a better taste of interior Sinai's untouched beauty, choose from the below. Each trip costs 700-800LE per person per day including a guide, food, water, camels to carry supplies, and camping equipment (when applicable). The price per person decreases for groups larger than five.

JEBEL ABBAS (ABBAS'S MOUNTAIN)

Distance (round-trip): *14.5 kilometers (9 mi)*
Duration (round-trip): *6 hours*
Effort level: *easy-moderate*

Egypt's 19th-century ruler and grandson of Mohammed Ali, Abbas Pasha, chose this spot to build his mountain retreat. The viceroy's untimely death in 1854—officially by stroke, but possibly murdered by his maltreated servants—meant his palace project was abandoned, but some of the unfinished stone walls still stand. From the top, views of rolling mountains can be seen in all directions.

JEBEL KATRINE (ST. KATHERINE MOUNTAIN)

Distance (round-trip): *20 kilometers (12.5 mi)*
Duration (round-trip): *8-10 hours*
Effort level: *moderate*

The peak of Jebel Katrine—the highest point

1
2

3

The Sinai Trail

Eight Bedouin tribes run a network of trails through South Sinai's mountains, wadis, and palm-lined oases. The original 12-day trek weaves through 209 kilometers (130 mi) of stunning desert terrain, leaving from **Ras Shaitan** on the Gulf of Aqaba, through the **Colored Canyon** and to the peak of **St. Katherine Mountain.**

The Bedouin-run initiative, called **Sinai Trail** (www.sinaitrail.net; tel. 0100 505 4119), began in 2015 and now covers 550 kilometers (340 mi) of paths—from Gulf to Gulf with many more zigzagging routes in between. You'll be in good hands with their knowledgeable team that can traverse the land sans maps and get you across the mountains in a safe and enriching experience. Check out their website to browse a range of treks and choose which works best for you.

in all of Egypt at 2,642 meters (8,668 ft) above sea level—can be reached in around 6 hours from central St. Katherine (including a leisurely lunch break), with a 4-hour descent. At the top sits a chapel dedicated to the mountain's namesake on the spot where it's said her body appeared. The moderate hike up this unique formation, made of black volcanic rock, is often done as a full-day trip with an early start, or a two-day trip with camping.

4-5 DAY CIRCUIT

To sample a wider variety of the landscape, try a 4-5-day circuit that includes highlights like summiting **Jebel Abbas** and **Jebel Bab el Donia** at sunset, swimming in **Galt el Azraq** (a large natural pool), and sleeping in the garden campsites that spot the mountains.

FOOD

Most meals will likely be enjoyed at your lodge or on the trail. You might want to bring snacks to tide you over between meals or on hikes. You can also pick up some fruits and basics at the corner stores in central St. Katherine along the (unnamed) main road, but the selection is limited. You're not likely to find any alcohol around town, but feel free to bring your own and consume discreetly.

1: St. Katherine Monastery **2:** a cat at Sheikh Mousa Bedouin Camp **3:** Mt. Sinai

ACCOMMODATIONS

Under 800LE

DAR EID MOUNTAIN LODGE

El Tarfa, 25 km/16 mi north of central St. Katherine; tel. 0106 518 4930; eidlodge@gmail.com; 320LE d

Built in vernacular style with materials gathered from the surrounding hills, this mountain lodge blends into the landscape. Its six rooms are attractive, with stone walls and redbrick barrel vaulted ceilings, but basic—beds are foam pads on raised stone platforms and bathrooms are shared. The dozen or so Eid brothers, with Youssef, Younis, and Mohammed leading the charge, are fantastic hosts and skilled guides who can take guests on hikes to all of St. Katherine's best spots. They can also provide transportation to the lodge from central St. Katherine or elsewhere in the South Sinai. Breakfast included and other meals available at a small extra cost.

★ SHEIKH MOUSA BEDOUIN CAMP

El Milga; tel. 0100 688 0820; www.sheikmousa.com; 500LE d

Located in the tiny central town of St. Katherine, Bedouin Camp (known by locals as Mukhayem Sheikh Mousa) offers cozy rooms with comfortable beds, wood paneled ceilings, private bathrooms, and small balconies looking out to stunning mountain views. No ACs, but each room has a fan and manages to stay cool even on hot summer days. The lodge encircles a courtyard of small rocks, raked with Zen garden-like

Moses in the Sinai?

For the followers of the Abrahamic faiths (Judaism, Christianity, Islam), the Sinai Peninsula oozes religious significance. According to the scriptures, it's the land that Moses crossed, leading the Israelites out of slavery under an oppressive Egyptian pharaoh in the famous Exodus. Once in the desert, Moses climbed **Mt. Sinai,** where God delivered the Ten Commandments and later instructed Moses and his two million followers to take Canaan (modern Israel and Palestine). But before they headed into war, the Israelites wanted reassurance that they could capture the Promised Land and sent 12 spies to scout the territory for 40 days. When the spies returned, they brought news that indeed the "land flows with milk and honey," but a strong people lived there who couldn't be conquered. As punishment for their doubt, God condemned the Israelites to spend the next 40 years wandering the rugged Sinai.

The tale of the Hebrews' departure from Egypt is told in the Hebrew Bible and Old Testament in the Book of Exodus. But historians have long debated just about everything in this biblical narrative—from the location of Mt. Sinai to the route of the fleeing Hebrews, to whether or not their en mass departure actually occurred, and down to the very existence of Moses himself. Nevertheless, the land remains of sacred significance to millions of believers around the world.

perfection, and pale green olive trees. Tasty complimentary breakfast and other meals (at a small extra cost) are served in their rustic dining hall or shaded outdoor seating area with floor pillows and low tables. Sheikh Mousa and his son, Mohammed, are perfect hosts and can organize guided hikes anywhere around St. Katherine. Cheaper room options are available with shared bathrooms or in dormitories.

AL KARM ECOLODGE

Wadi Gharba, 30 km/20 mi northwest of central St. Katherine; tel. 0100 132 4693; www.sheikhsina.com; 500LE d

Nestled deep into the mountains, this ecolodge with compost toilets and no electricity is a charming retreat. Their eight rooms—each accommodating up to six people in a squeeze—are very basic with thin foam pads for beds, candles for lights, and showers heated with solar power. A surprising amount of greenery surrounds the lodge in the otherwise beige-colored terrain, with date palms and acacia trees lining the sides of the wadi (dried riverbed). Transportation to the lodge from central St. Katherine is available upon request.

800-1,650LE

MONASTERY GUESTHOUSE

Wadi el Deir, at the St. Katherine Monastery; tel. 069 3470353; www.sinaimonastery.com; 1,050LE d half board

Decoration is apparently superfluous, but cleanliness next to godliness in the small, simple rooms (each fitted with AC and private bathroom) at the Monastery Guesthouse. Outside, a pleasant stone courtyard lined with olive trees sits in the shade of towering granite mountains. Located adjacent to the 6th-century monastery at the start of the path to Mt. Sinai, the guesthouse is a good option for pilgrims who want to be close to the area's most important religious sites. A simple dinner and breakfast with fresh bread are included.

INFORMATION AND SERVICES

Visitors Center

The Visitors Center (no tel.) is located on the south side of the main road into St. Katherine Town, just before the roundabout and road to the St. Katherine Monastery. Inside are nice informational displays about the culture and history of the area. Unfortunately, the hours are fairly random (9am-3pm Sat.-Thurs. are your best bet), but if it's closed, ask at the monastery to see if anyone has a key.

ATMs

Best to come to St. Katherine with enough cash for your stay. There's a Banque Misr ATM in central St. Katherine near the CO-OP gas station, but it doesn't always work. Most lodges don't accept credit cards.

Police

In the very rare event of security issue, plenty of police officers are stationed beside the St. Katherine Monastery at the entrance of the path leading to Mt. Sinai (Jebel Mousa).

GETTING THERE

From Cairo

BUS

Your bus options between Cairo and St. Katherine are unfortunately limited to the government-owned **East Delta Bus Co.** (no tel.; 150LE), which is routinely late and not the cleanest around. Daily trips typically leave from Torgoman Station at 9:30am and 11:30am and arrive in central St. Katherine across from the Sacred Valley Mosque (Masgid el Wadi el Qadees) in around 8 hours. Best to reserve your ticket a day in advance at the station's office as some trips are canceled due to low demand.

MICROBUS

Much quicker than the bus, **WE Bus** (tel. 0111 118 8021; www.webusegypt.com) operates a fleet of comfortable microbuses that travel to St. Katherine from Downtown Cairo (Abdel Minam Riyad Square, near the Ramses Hilton) in 6-7 hours for 280LE first class and 380LE VIP—carrying 13 and 8 passengers, respectively. For questions and reservations, call or message them on Facebook (@webusEG).

From Dahab or Sharm el Sheikh

Your accommodation in St. Katherine should be able to arrange a private car from Dahab (1.5 hours; 700LE) or from Sharm el Sheikh (2.5 hours; 1,200-1,300LE).

GETTING AROUND

To get around St. Katherine, visitors rely on local hosts. Most lodges offer complimentary pickups from the bus station and include transportation to/from trailheads as part of your hiking package.

Nuweiba to Taba

Along the northernmost stretch of the Gulf of Aqaba, the road from Nuweiba to Taba runs between sheer granite slopes of the Sinai mountains and the turquoise waters of the Red Sea. This stunning 70-kilometer (44-mi) strip of coast is bookended by the scruffy port town of Nuweiba to the south, and tiny border town of Taba to the north. Travelers don't tend to spend much time in either—preferring instead to retreat into nature at the beach camps and lodges between the two. With easy access to some of the most beautiful rock formations in the Sinai and life-filled fringing reefs all along the shore, the area is an outdoor lover's dream.

The main activities in these parts (aside from lounging on the beach) are snorkeling and desert safaris. All the seaside camps and lodges of note have private beaches, house reefs, and guides who can organize day trips into the neighboring desert and mountains with 4WD.

SIGHTS

★ Colored Canyon

Off Nuweiba-Taba Rd., 20 km/12 mi north of Nuweiba Town

Striking reds, yellows, and purples swirl in the rocks of the Colored Canyon, where dried riverbeds run between dramatic sandstone

Slow-Cooked Food with a View

Midway between Nuweiba and Taba, **Castle Zaman** (Nuweiba-Taba Rd.; tel. 0128 214 0591; www.castlezaman.com; noon-9pm daily; 800LE) offers a unique dining experience. The modern fortress built of local materials looks across the sea to Saudi Arabian mountains from its perch on a rocky hill. Slow-cooked Egyptian and Bedouin meals bursting with flavors are served on the terrace or in the rustic dining hall after stewing for up to five hours. While visitors wait for their dishes—like veal shoulder roasted with dates and figs or a vegetarian banquet of sautéed vegetables and molokhia (soupy greens)—they can enjoy the pool, sauna, and beautiful grounds. Be sure to reserve a day in advance on their website and prepare yourself for large servings. Adults only. Alcohol available. Across the street, the **Castle Zaman Beach** with its fine sand and striking coral reef is free and open to the public—a perfect stop before a shower and dinner in the fortress, or a more economical outing alternative.

cliffsides. Molded over millions of years, this unique geological formation with colorful mineral deposits makes for a spectacular sight. Be sure to wear comfortable shoes—you'll hike for around an hour (round-trip) to see the best spots. Off-road vehicle day trips come here regularly from Nuweiba, Taba, and Dahab.

Wadi el Weshwash

Ras Shaitan; off Nuweiba-Taba Rd., 23 km/14 mi north of Nuweiba Town

The wind that slips through the large granite boulders in this corner of the mountains—with echoing sounds of *wesh-wash*—gives the onomatopoetic Wadi el Weshwash (Valley of the Weshwash) its name. Rainwater gathers periodically throughout the year to form a natural bright green pool, reached by 4WD, a short hike, and a bit of a scramble over rocks. Be sure to ask your local Bedouin guide if the pool is full (and the water clean) before making the trek. And don't forget your swimsuit! Trips leave from Nuweiba, Taba, and Dahab.

Pharaoh's Island (Gezirat Far'aon)

Off Nuweiba-Taba Rd., 6 km/4 mi south of Taba Town; no tel.; 9am-5pm daily; 160LE adults, 80LE students

Rising out of waters, a beige-colored fortress snakes along this small island just 250 meters (820 ft) off the coast. Built by Crusaders in the early 12th century, **Salah el Din Citadel** (as it's now called) was seized and refurbished by the eponymous sultan in 1170. Egyptian officials controlled the traffic of goods and people through this strategic corridor—then bordered by Syria and Palestine to the north, the Arabian Peninsula to the east, and Egypt to the west—providing safe passage to Muslim pilgrims performing the hajj.

The citadel likely fell out of use toward the end of the 13th century, but thanks to modern restoration projects the structure can be visited once again. Some highlights include the governor's quarters, mosque, and pigeon house (their 12th-century post office). Rivaling the fortress itself are the elevated views and surrounding corals—earning the spot the moniker Coral Island.

Most hotels and lodges in and between Nuweiba and Taba organize trips here, many including a snorkel stop. The boat ride to the island takes just a few minutes.

FOOD

Chances are you'll be enjoying most of your meals at your accommodation, so if good food is important to you be sure to check out their menus ahead of time. Similarly, travelers on a budget might want to factor in food prices before booking. Meals are offered throughout the day. For the best food, head to Al Maggara Camp.

ACCOMMODATIONS

Under 800LE

★ AL MAGGARA CAMP

Ras Shaitan, Nuweiba-Taba Rd., 24 km/15 mi north of Nuweiba Port; tel. 0101 487 1909; 750LE d half board

Nestled in the foothills of the Sinai mountains beside crystal-clear waters, the basic huts and bungalows at Al Maggara Camp offer an idyllic return to nature. Lounge on the private beach of fine sand, explore the house reef just a few feet off the shore, and indulge in the healthy, fresh, and flavorful meals (superb breakfast and dinner included). The kitchen caters to vegetarian and vegan guests in particular, but also offers delicious meat and seafood dishes. At night, visitors can see where the camp gets its name—Al Maggara, or "Galaxy"—as they gaze into star-speckled skies. Friendly hosts Rana and Misho keep the place spotless and can help organize trips around the Sinai. Shared bathrooms.

800-1,650LE

BASATA ECOLODGE

Nuweiba-Taba Rd., 75 km/47 mi north of Nuweiba Port; tel. 0127 537 9570; www.basata.com; 950LE d

Egyptian engineer-turned-camp-creator Sherif el Ghamrawy chose this strategic spot on a stretch of fine white sand between the mountains and sea to build his little patch of paradise in 1986. Guests can choose between a basic bamboo hut with shared bathroom (950LE d), or splurge on a beautiful chalet with vaulted ceilings, stone accents, and a private bathroom—but still no AC (1,750LE d). Nature-made paths make for easy hikes up the neighboring hills, and nice corals lie just off the shore. The Egyptian-German couple who run the camp keep it well-ordered and clean and can help organize trips around the area. A 24-hour kitchen is available, where guests can prepare their own meals with provided staples (or bring their own) and pay at the end of their stay. No meals included and alcohol not permitted.

NAKHIL INN

Tarabeen Bay, Nuweiba-Taba Rd., 11 km/7 mi north of Nuweiba Port; tel. 069 3500879; www.nakhil-inn.com; 1,100LE d

Situated on the northern bend of Tarabeen Bay, Nakhil Inn boasts a sandy private beach and beautiful house reef sheltered from the open sea. Dried palm leaf umbrellas line the shore—their live parent trees are nearby in the gardens alongside fuchsia bougainvillea. Rooms are spacious and clean with private bathrooms, ACs, and mini fridges (try for one with a balcony and sea view). The welcoming staff can help organize trips to the mountains or other snorkeling and diving sites around the area. Complimentary kayaks, snorkel gear, and swim shoes are a nice touch, and a great breakfast is included.

INFORMATION AND SERVICES

If you're staying in a camp along the Nuweiba-Taba Road, be sure to bring enough cash (most camps don't accept credit card) and basic medical necessities with you—the closest ATMs and pharmacies will likely be many kilometers away in Nuweiba Town or Taba Town.

ATMs

You can find a handful of ATMs in the Nuweiba Port area along Nuweiba Street near the East Delta Bus Co. station. Nuweiba Town (9 km/5.5 mi to the north) also has a functioning ATM or two.

Medical

The **Nuweiba Central Hospital** (tel. 069 3500302; 24 hours daily) and **Taba Central Hospital** (tel. 069 3530231; 24 hours daily) are both government-run facilities located just off Nuweiba-Taba Road in each respective town.

GETTING THERE

From Cairo

BUS

Go Bus (tel. 19567; www.go-bus.com) runs a daily trip to the Nuweiba Port area from Cairo leaving around midnight (315LE; 11-12 hours). A bus departs Nuweiba for Cairo around 4pm daily. **East Delta Bus Co.** (no tel.) offers more options but less comfort. Check the schedule at their station in Cairo (Torgoman Station), Dahab, or Nuweiba. The Go Bus and East Delta Bus Co. Nuweiba stations are located a few hundred meters from each other near the port.

MICROBUS

WE Bus (tel. 0111 118 8021; www.webusegypt.com) microbuses travel daily to Ras Shaitan (passing through central Nuweiba) from Downtown Cairo (Abdel Minam Riyad Square) for 280LE first class and 380LE VIP—carrying 13 and 8 passengers, respectively. The ride is as comfortable as it is quick, taking only around 8 hours (compared to about 12 hours on the bus). They can usually drop you off right at your camp for no extra charge. For questions and reservations, call or contact them on Facebook Messenger (@webusEG).

From Dahab or St. Katherine

BUS

Go Bus (tel. 19567; www.go-bus.com) buses depart Dahab for to the Nuweiba Port area around 11am daily (1 hour; 95LE). A bus departs Nuweiba for Dahab around 4pm daily.

The less comfortable **East Delta Bus Co.** (no tel.) offers more options. Check the schedule at their station in Dahab or Nuweiba.

PRIVATE CAR HIRE

Your accommodation will be able to organize a private car with driver to Nuweiba Town from St. Katherine (1.5 hours; 600-700LE) or Dahab (1 hour; 350-450LE). Expect to pay around 50-350LE extra to get to any camp along Nuweiba-Taba Road depending on the distance.

Western Desert

Egypt's Western Desert is vast and sparsely populated—its long stretches of sand spotted by a handful of inhabited oases that offer unique cultures and gushing natural springs. Here you'll encounter a different pace of life from Egypt's urban centers. Locals harvest dates, work fields of alfalfa, and socialize in the watering holes scattered throughout their sleepy villages.

Beyond the oases, each patch of desert feels like a planet unto itself. In the land between Bahariya and Farafra, blackened rocks of volcanic deposits give way to golden hills before becoming a chalky white wonderland of wind-carved sculptures. And the undulating dunes outside of Siwa arrange themselves into distinct patterns, indecipherable to the

Highlights

Look for ★ to find recommended sights, activities, dining, and lodging.

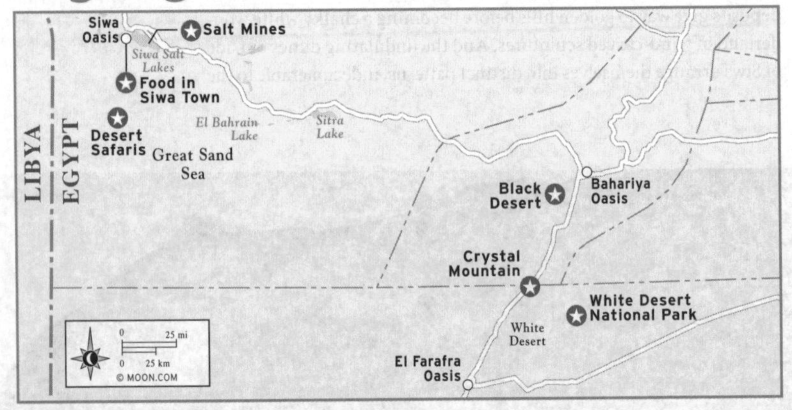

★ **Black Desert:** Hike up and around the black hills covered in volcanic rock from lava that poured over the land some 20 million years ago (page 384).

★ **Crystal Mountain:** Climb rocky ridges scattered with shimmering crystals in this trove of geological treasures (page 385).

★ **White Desert National Park:** Wander among nature's abstract sculptures in this unique patch of windswept land (page 387).

★ **Food in Siwa Town:** Try some of Egypt's tastiest food, like the local specialty Abu Mardam—meat or poultry slow-cooked underground (page 393).

★ **Siwa Oasis Salt Mines:** Float in dramatic pools of turquoise waters surrounded by beaches of snow-white salt (page 402).

★ **Desert Safaris in the Great Sand Sea:** Ride the waves of endless dunes and watch them change from gold to pink as the sun dips beyond the horizon (page 403).

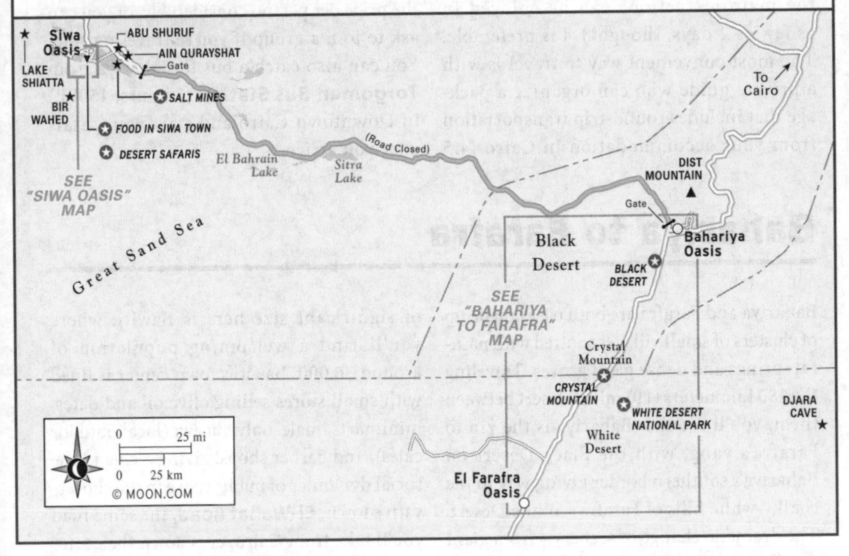

untrained eye, with sand separated according to grain size by nature's meticulous sorting.

In these parts, modern distractions disappear, leaving you alone with the elements—with the wind that continues to shape the landscape as it has for hundreds of millions of years; the mineral-rich waters, heated by subterranean rocks, that spout forth from the earth; and the stars that seem to explode out of infinitely black skies. This is a place to reconnect with the living universe, contemplate its wonders, and meditate on your place within it.

ORIENTATION

The Western Desert spans the entire area west of the Nile Valley and south of the Mediterranean coast, with its sands pouring into Libya and Sudan. **Bahariya and Farafra** are located just 375 kilometers (230 mi) and 545 kilometers (340 mi) from Cairo, respectively. Farther afield is the **Siwa Oasis** 760 kilometers (470 mi) from Cairo via the nearest North Coast town, Marsa Matruh (325 km/200 mi from Siwa).

PLANNING YOUR TIME

The road between Bahariya and Siwa has been closed due to security concerns since the 2011 uprisings in Egypt and Libya, but if and when it reopens, combining a trip to Siwa and Bahariya to Farafra will be a fabulous desert excursion. Until then, it makes most sense to enjoy each region separately, with Cairo as your starting point.

If you have a good chunk of time, make your way to **Siwa**—a 10-11-hour bus ride from Cairo. To break up the commute you might consider spending 2-3 nights in Marsa Matruh, the last Mediterranean town en route before continuing south into the desert. Make sure you have at least 3 nights in Siwa to hit the must-see spots, but 5-6 nights are preferred to properly bask in its enchanting nature.

Previous: Agabat Valley; old town of the Siwa Oasis; the Great Sand Sea.

A trip to Bahariya and Farafra is much less of a time commitment than Siwa, and the main attractions can be enjoyed in as few as 2 days, though 3-4 is preferable. The most convenient way to travel is with a private guide who can organize a package that includes round-trip transportation from your accommodation in Cairo (4.5 hours; 1,800-4,000LE for 6-passenger car). Gathering a group of 5-6 people will reduce the price per person considerably, or you can ask to join a group if you're traveling solo. You can also catch a bus to Bahariya from **Torgoman Bus Station** (5 hours; 150LE) in Downtown Cairo and start your safari once you arrive.

Bahariya to Farafra

Bahariya and Farafra are both oases made up of clusters of small villages spotted with natural springs and dense palm groves. Traveling the 180 kilometers (110 mi) of desert between them, you'll see that Bahariya is the yin to Farafra's yang, with the Black Desert on Bahariya's southern border giving way to the chalky-white hills of Farafra's White Desert. The dramatic change of scenery—from giant vanilla cakes dripping in chocolate sauce to the cotton-colored fairyland of Farafra—is due to the shift in the land's foundation from sandstone to limestone, the former made of compressed sand, and the latter of remains from prehistoric marine life. These aquatic creatures once thrived in a deep sea that covered the land here tens of millions of years ago. Bahariya also holds traces of pharaonic and Greco-Roman civilizations that once flourished in this green sanctuary, adding interesting layers of human history to its fascinating geological past.

Aside from spring-hopping in Bahariya, the deserts between the two oases are the main attraction. Bahariya's main village, **Bawiti,** is full of small hotels and makes for a nice base to explore the oasis before setting out on your desert adventure. If you're short on time, Qasr el-Farafra and Farafra's smaller villages can be skipped, but don't miss the **White Desert** that sits on Farafra's northern border.

BAWITI

Bahariya is the first patch of green you'll reach outside Greater Cairo. The only town of significant size here is Bawiti, where you'll find a welcoming population of around 36,000. Bawiti's town center is lined with small stores selling olive oil and dates, minimarts, male-only ahaawi (local outdoor cafés), and barber shops, giving a clue to the social dynamics of public space in the conservative town. **El-Wahat Road,** the same road you'll take from Cairo, cuts down the center of town.

Sights

The ticket office for the multi-site pass that will get you into all Bawiti's antiquities is located at the entrance to the **Golden Mummies Hall Museum.** Visit here first before visiting the other three main historical attractions (Qarat Qasr Salim, Ain el-Muftilla, and the Temple of Alexander the Great).

GOLDEN MUMMIES HALL MUSEUM

Al-Mathaf St., off al-Wahat Rd.; 8am-4pm daily; Bawiti multi-site ticket 100LE adults, 50LE students

Nine glass cases line this tiny hall, cooled by tired air-conditioners doing their best to preserve the remains of its 2,000-some-year-old Greco-Roman residents. The mummies were discovered in 1996, 6 kilometers (4 mi) south of Bawiti by a donkey—according to Zahi Hawass, Egypt's resident archeologist diva who led the expedition to dig up hundreds of Bahariya's former inhabitants. The team unearthed a cemetery covering around 6 square kilometers (2.3 sq mi), holding an estimated 10,000 bodies.

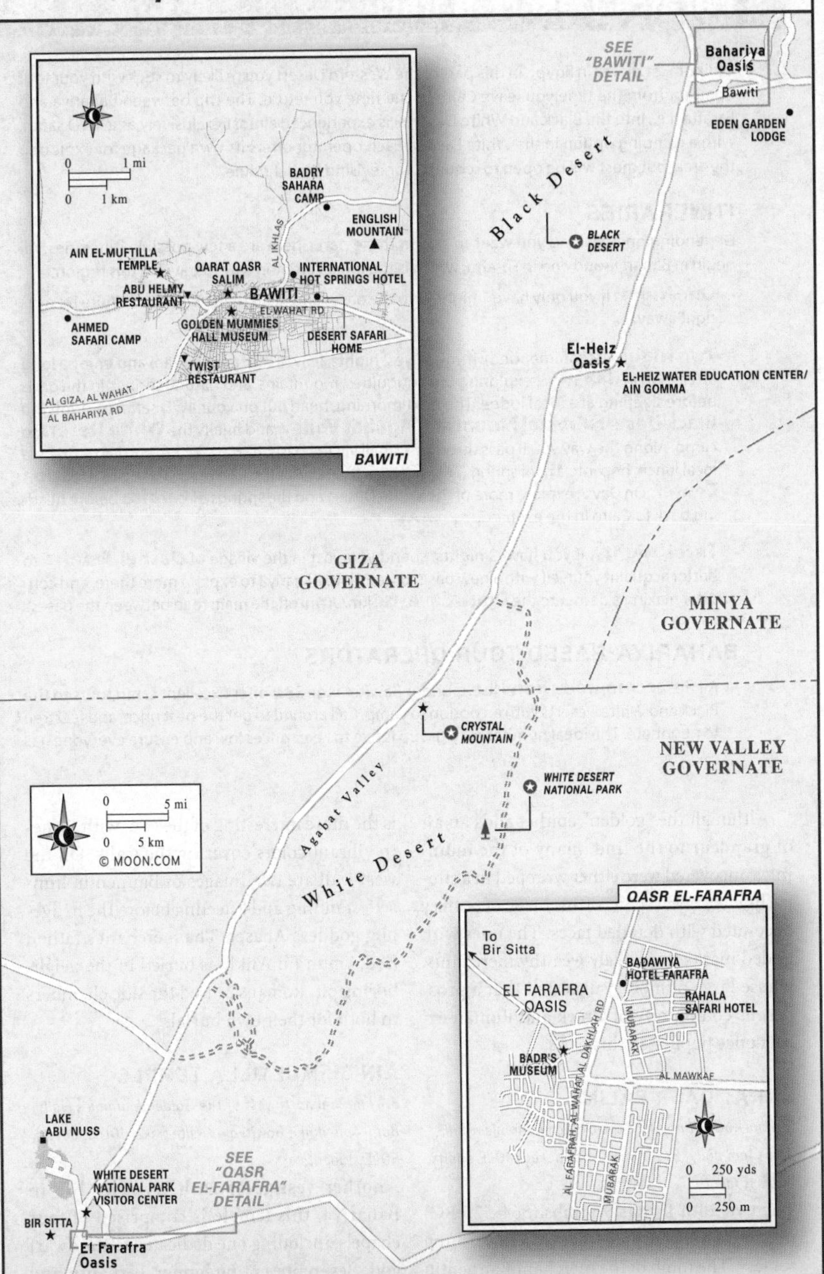
Bahariya to Farafra
SEE "BAWITI" DETAIL
Bahariya Oasis
Bawiti
EDEN GARDEN LODGE
Black Desert
BLACK DESERT
El-Heiz Oasis
EL-HEIZ WATER EDUCATION CENTER/ AIN GOMMA
BADRY SAHARA CAMP
ENGLISH MOUNTAIN
AIN EL-MUFTILLA TEMPLE
QARAT QASR SALIM
AL IKHLAS
INTERNATIONAL HOT SPRINGS HOTEL
ABU HELMY RESTAURANT
BAWITI
EL-WAHAT RD
AHMED SAFARI CAMP
GOLDEN MUMMIES HALL MUSEUM
DESERT SAFARI HOME
TWIST RESTAURANT
AL GIZA, AL WAHAT
AL BAHARIYA RD
BAWITI
0 1 mi
0 1 km
GIZA GOVERNATE
MINYA GOVERNATE
CRYSTAL MOUNTAIN
NEW VALLEY GOVERNATE
WHITE DESERT NATIONAL PARK
Agabat Valley
White Desert
0 5 mi
0 5 km
© MOON.COM
QASR EL-FARAFRA
To Bir Sitta
BADAWIYA HOTEL FARAFRA
EL FARAFRA OASIS
RAHALA SAFARI HOTEL
BADR'S MUSEUM
AL FARAFRAH, AL WAHAT AL DAKHLAH RD
MUBARAK
AL MAWKAF
0 250 yds
0 250 m
LAKE ABU NUSS
WHITE DESERT NATIONAL PARK VISITOR CENTER
SEE "QASR EL-FARAFRA" DETAIL
BIR SITTA
El Farafra Oasis

Designing Your Bahariya-to-Farafra Desert Safari

Unlike most places in Egypt, in this part of the Western Desert you're likely to stick with your tour operator from the time you leave Cairo to the time you return. The trip between Bahariya and Farafra (i.e., into the Black and White Deserts) is experienced almost exclusively as a 4WD safari, with a camping option in the White Desert. Each operator offers its own package for exploring the area, but most will be open to requests for revising the schedule.

ITINERARIES

Depending on how long you want to stay in these parts, here are a few possible itineraries. All begin in Bahariya and end in Farafra, which is the most common way to travel in this region.

- **One Night:** If you only have 1 night, skip the oases and head to the Black and White Deserts right away.
- **Two Nights** (recommended): If you have 2 nights, leave Cairo around 7am and enjoy a long afternoon in **Bahariya** exploring the antiquities, mountains, and natural springs in the oasis before sleeping at a local lodge. The next morning, head out on your 4WD safari through the **Black Desert, Crystal Mountain, Agabat Valley,** and finally the **White Desert** to camp. Along the way you'll pass through a small village oasis, el-Heiz, where you can stop for a local lunch, hop into a cool spring (**Ain Gomma**), and visit the **el-Heiz Water Education Center.** On Day 2, explore more of the White Desert and the springs of **Farafra** before heading back to Cairo in the evening.
- **Three Nights:** If you have 3 nights, spend your last in the village of **Qasr el-Farafra** to better acquaint yourself with a new oasis, or return to Bahariya to explore more there, and consider making a detour to the **Djara Cave** (150 km/90 mi off the main road between the oases).

BAHARIYA-BASED TOUR OPERATORS

- All the **accommodations** listed under Bawiti (page 383) offer excellent safari tours to the Black and White Deserts with an option to camp. Call around to get the best price, and feel free to negotiate. The ideal number for a group is five to keep prices low and ensure everyone has

Although the "golden" epithet adds an air of grandeur to the find, many of the mummies uncovered were either wrapped in a simple linen or encased in coffins made of pottery decorated with detailed faces. The ones with gilded masks were likely wealthy merchants, whose large numbers suggested that a prosperous community of Greek and Roman expats once populated this oasis.

QARAT QASR SALIM

500 m/1,600 ft north of the Golden Mummies Hall; 8am-4pm daily; Bawiti multi-site ticket 100LE adults, 50LE students

The two 26th Dynasty tombs (664-525 BC) dug into a hill here hold traces of a flourishing society. The tomb of the merchant Bannentiu is the more interesting of the two, with scenes in vibrant colors covering the walls. On the west wall are two images of Bannentiu himself, standing and kneeling before the hedgehog goddess Abaset. The merchant's father, Zed Amun Iuf Ankh, is buried in the neighboring pit. Romans reused the side chambers in both for their own burials.

AIN EL-MUFTILLA TEMPLE

3.2 km/2 mi northwest of the Golden Mummies Hall; 8am-4pm daily; Bawiti multi-site ticket 100LE adults, 50LE students

Another vestige of 26th Dynasty life in Bahariya, this temple is comprised of four chapels, including one dedicated to the dwarf god, Bes, representing humor, sexuality, and

enough space in the car, but you can also opt to join a group of strangers or pay a premium for a private trip for two. For a group of five, expect to pay around 2,000-3,000LE per person for two nights including one night in a lodge in Bawiti, one night camping in the White Desert, tours around Bahariya and the Black and White Deserts, all meals, and round-trip transportation in a private car from Cairo. Typical safari itineraries include: Black Desert, Crystal Mountain, Agabat Valley, sandboarding, White Desert, and a few hot and/or cold springs.

- It's common practice for tour operators to severely underpay the driver/guide who does all the work. If you prefer to cut out the middleman and book directly, contact **Mahmoud Abdel Zaher** (tel. 0122 809 5223)—a Renaissance man who can navigate to hidden spots in the desert, set up camp in record speed, and prepare you a feast on the fire as you relax after a long day of exploring. He has a comfortable 4WD vehicle, all the necessary food, water, and camping equipment (sleeping bag, tents, etc.), and a great sense of humor. All you have to do is show up ready for an adventure. Message him on WhatsApp for best communication. As with many drivers/guides, English is not his specialty but he can communicate.
- Other good options are family-run businesses that do the trips themselves, like **Badri Khozam's Desert Safari Home** (tel. 0127 570 9430; www.desertsafarihome.com) and Badry of **Badry Sahara Camp** (tel. 0122 792 2728).

FARAFRA-BASED TOUR OPERATORS

You'll have many more options for tour operators out of Bahariya, but if you prefer to leave for a White Desert excursion from Farafra, consider the following. Both can also arrange for **multi-day trekking trips** through the desert by foot or on camel.

- **Rahala Safari Hotel** (tel. 0100 306 4733; www.rahala-safari.com) is very accommodating and can make you a tailored package for anything from an afternoon in the desert to a multi-day excursion.
- **Badawiya Hotel** (tel. 0128 287 9695; www.badawiya.com) also has experienced guides to take you out. You can call ahead or arrange for your safari when you get there.

music among other things. Only his legs and tails remain, but it's likely that his chubby naked body once covered the walls here. A wooden roof now covers the complex, making it a cool place to escape the desert sun.

TEMPLE OF ALEXANDER THE GREAT

Southwest of Bawiti; 8am-4pm daily; Bawiti multi-site ticket 100LE adults, 50LE students

A grid of rock walls now barely rising above the ground once formed a much grander entrance leading to the temple here. Not much remains of the temple either, believed to have been founded by Alexander the Great (c. 332 BC) on his way back to the Nile Valley after declaring his divinity in Siwa. Interesting side attractions are a stone pillar chair beside a large mortar, shards of broken pottery, and ancient copper coins.

Natural Springs

BIR EL-SIGAM

8.5 km/5 mi east of central Bawiti, just off el-Wahat Rd.; 24 hours daily; free

Bir el-Sigam is probably the best hot spring in town. Tucked into a palm grove about 16 meters (52 ft) off the main road, the small pool fed by groundwater is a perfect temperature for those who enjoy an intense soak, but it's not unbearable like many of the other scorching springs that locals still manage to kick around in. You can take a dip whenever, but fresh water is propelled from the ground by a

Soaking in Natural Springs

You'll find springs for soaking in both Bahariya and Farafra, as well as on the road between the two oases. A few tips for visiting them:

- It's best not to wear your favorite suits, as the minerals might turn them orange.
- Ladies might feel more comfortable swimming in T-shirts and waiting for any locals (men) to leave before jumping in.
- Some springs are extremely hot—ask your local guide to bring you to the springs with more moderate temperatures if that's your preference.

motor that's controlled by the keeper of the keys, and usually turned off soon after sunset. If you want the full effect of flowing water, ask your guide or hotel to call the guard to turn it on it in exchange for a small tip (20-30LE).

BIR EL-AMRIKAN

North side of English Mountain, across the street from Badry Sahara Camp; 24 hours daily; free

To cool off, head to Bir el-Amrikan with a great view of the mountain and surrounding palms.

BIR EL-JAFFARA

7 km/4 mi east of central Bawiti, 5 km/3 mi south of Wahat Rd., next to Eden Garden Camp; 24 hours daily; free

At Bir el-Jaffara you can choose between hot or cold springs in an idyllic patch of palms.

Camel Rides

Hamada Omer (tel. 0128 682 4751; https://desert-safari-egypte.com) can organize a day trip around Bahariya for 500LE per person including guide, or arrange a longer trek in the desert. **Badri Khozam** (tel. 0127 570 9430; www.desertsafarihome.com) can also set up desert excursions on camel for an extra 400LE per person per day on top of the trekking costs.

Food

The easiest and most common dining experience in Bahariya is to get a package with your lodge that includes full board. If you want to venture out by yourself, you do have a couple of good options. And if you're desperate for a drink, the restaurants at the **International Hot Springs Hotel** (tel. 023 8473014; 6pm-10pm daily), **Desert Safari Home** (tel. 0122 731 3908; 4pm-10pm daily), and the **Eden Garden Lodge** (tel. 0100 071 0707; www.edengardentours.com) can accommodate with some beer and wine (50-75LE). Call ahead.

ABU HELMY RESTAURANT

Siwa-Bahariya Rd., Al-Qasr; tel. 0122 250 1423; 9am-3am daily; 60-80LE

This hole-in-the-wall is a local favorite. Enjoy a feast of various grilled meats, chicken, and pigeon alongside tasty traditional dips like tahina and baba ghanoush. The dining space is very basic but clean. Located just off the main road (Siwa-Bahariya Rd.) in the village of Al-Qasr, 1 kilometer (0.6 mi) west of central Bawiti in an unnamed square with a large pigeon statue in the middle.

★ TWIST RESTAURANT

El-Wahat-Farafra Rd., 2.5 km/1.5 mi southwest of central Bawiti; tel. 0128 020 2321; 9am-1am daily; 80-90LE

At this Bedouin restaurant you can find a tasty array of local dishes like fuul, fried eggplant, grilled chicken, rice, and plenty of fresh bread. You have a choice of outdoor seating or floor pillows in a large open room that lets in the cool breeze while protecting you from the sun.

Accommodations

DESERT SAFARI HOME

200 m/650 ft north of al-Wahat Rd., Bawiti; tel. 0122 731 3908; www.desertsafarihome.com; 350LE d

This family-run operation has been in business for decades. Badri started as a guide over 40 years ago and has since built his own humble hotel to serve as a base for his excellent excursions. His son Mohammed has taken the reins and inherited his father's knowledge and passion for their desert surroundings. Rooms are simple but clean with traditional domed roofs, and the gardens are lush with pink bougainvillea, palms, and other shades of green. Cheaper options available without AC (250LE d). Includes breakfast. Beer and wine available at their restaurant.

★ BADRY SAHARA CAMP

Northern base of English Mountain, Bawiti; tel. 0122 792 2728; WhatsApp: +201007459591; 430LE d

Those in search of simplicity will find their happy place here. Twenty little grass huts with sparse rooms line the campground that sits at the foot of English Mountain and looks out onto fields of palm trees. Common spaces are constructed of materials that match the surroundings, with palm tree trunks as pillars and thatched roofs. Badry and his family offer a warm welcome and can organize great trips around Bahariya and into the desert. Cheaper options available without AC (230-300LE d). Bathrooms and showers are shared. Breakfast included.

AHMED SAFARI CAMP

Off Siwa-Bahariya Rd.; tel. 0122 117 9521; https://ahmedsafaricamp.business.site; 480LE d

One of Bahariya's oldest inns, Ahmed Safari Camp has clean and comfortable rooms with domed brick ceilings that, aside from looking attractive, also keep the room cool. The reception lodge with tall stone walls and domes also provides deliciously cool refuge from the midday sun, and the palm-lined garden offers a pleasant place to sit when the weather is right. Most rooms have ACs for hot summer weather, and space heaters for cold desert nights. Tasty traditional Egyptian breakfast of eggs, fuul, and ta'maya included.

EDEN GARDEN LODGE

El-Jaffara, 7 km/4 mi east of central Bawiti, 5 km/3 mi south of Wahat Rd.; tel. 0128 245 0975; www.edengardentours.com; 500LE d

Tucked between a patch of green and the desert, Talaat Moulaa's lodge is a wonderful place to relax. Two natural springs—one hot and one cold—sit just beyond the lodge grounds and make for a convenient evening excursion. Accommodation options include simple huts (500LE d), beautiful peach-colored rooms with domed ceilings (1,000LE d), or spacious chalets with kitchens (1,500 d). Prices include breakfast and dinner.

★ INTERNATIONAL HOT SPRINGS HOTEL

Southwest side of English Mountain, Bawiti; tel. 023 847 3014; https://whitedeserttours.com; 1,300LE d

Run by a German and Japanese couple, this little retreat enveloped by green trees has plentiful outdoor and rooftop seating where you can enjoy mountain views. Rooms are basic but pristine, with wooden floors and a Santorini color scheme that matches the rest of the hotel. Their private hot springs bubbling into a large jacuzzi at around 35°C (95°F) is the highlight. While their rooms are probably the most expensive in town, if you book your desert safari and Cairo-Bahariya transportation as a package, prices are very reasonable. Includes breakfast and dinner. Beer and wine available.

Information and Services

ATMS

There are a few ATMs in central Bawiti near the police station. Nearly everyone in these parts accepts cash only, so be sure to have plenty on you.

POLICE

For emergencies head to the police station off Wahat Road in central Bawiti or call the tourist police at **126.**

Getting There

BUS

Upper East Bus Co. buses to Bahariya (central Bawiti) depart Cairo's **Torgoman Station** every morning at 7am and 8am (5 hours; 150LE). To get back to Cairo, hop on at the **Bawiti Bus Station** (180 m/590 ft west of the police station) at 10am or 3pm. Best to buy tickets a day or two in advance to make sure you get a seat and to double check the times. Most hotels in Bahariya offer free pickup from the station.

PRIVATE CAR HIRE

All the accommodations listed above offer the option of private transportation from Cairo to Bahariya and back for 1,800-4,000LE roundtrip (4.5 hours each way). Call around to find the best price—**Desert Safari Home** (tel. 0122 731 3908) is likely the most economical—and feel free to ask them to send you a photo of the car that will be picking you up to ensure it's up to your standards. The road between Cairo and Bahariya is full of giant trucks and can be a bit unnerving at night. Travelers might feel more comfortable making the trip during the daylight hours.

Getting Around

You need a 4WD to get the fullest experience out of Bahariya and its surrounding desert. The easiest way to get around is to arrange for a package with your accommodation that includes all the major sights, or message the wonderful driver/guide **Mahmoud Abdel Zaher** (tel. 0122 809 5223). Your driver will accompany you for your whole trip in and around Bawiti and into the desert.

VICINITY OF BAWITI

Dist Mountain (Gebel el-Dist)

13 km/8 mi northeast of central Bawiti; 24 hours daily; free

This pyramid-shaped mountain holds evidence suggesting Bahariya was a thriving coastal area some 66-100 million years ago. In the early 20th century, German explorers found Egypt's first recorded dinosaur fossils here and sent the massive claws and vertebrae of carnivores (likely larger than the T. rex) to Munich. Unfortunately, their collection was destroyed in a British air raid during World War II. But in 2000 a team from the US uncovered 7 more tonnes of fossils, including additional giant dinosaurs alongside the remains of turtles, fish, and crocodiles. Today the flat sandy area that surrounds it makes for a great hike, and experts may even wish to climb the mountain itself (though beware the sliding stones).

English Mountain (Gebel el-Ingliz)

Covered in bulbous mounds made of 20-some-million-year-old lava flows, this hilltop in northeast Bawiti offers stunning views over neighboring volcanic fields, Bahariya's palm groves, and the surrounding desert. Enjoy an easy walk up to watch the sunset from the remains of a World War I outpost that gives the mountain its name. British officers used this vantage point to scan the desert for Senussi troops from Libya who were waging a campaign against Egypt's British occupiers, encouraged by the Germans and Ottomans. Your guide will drive you to the base of the mountain, and from there it's just a few minutes' walk to the top.

Camel Farm

Between Gebel el-Dist and Gebel el-Maghrafa there's a small camel farm (without a formal name, as it's not a tourist attraction) where you can pet the beautiful creatures and maybe even watch a birth. The owners, Ali and Abdullah, are very welcoming but don't speak English. Ask your tour operator to bring you.

BAHARIYA-FARAFRA ROAD

★ Black Desert (El-Sahara el-Sooda)

10 km/6 mi south of Bawiti

Just around 10 kilometers (6 mi) after leaving Bawiti, the plots of green farmland start to fade, and black mounds like enormous

Guided Hikes in the White Desert

You can do some short hikes around Bahariya by yourself near **Gebel el-Dist** and **Gebel el-Maghrafa** on the north side of the oasis, but if you're interested in some proper desert trekking, you'll want to bring along a local guide.

- Badri Khozam's team at **Desert Safari Home** (tel. 0127 570 9430; www.desertsafarihome.com) offers 2-7-day treks starting from **Agabat Valley** into the **White Desert** for €50 per day per person if you get a group of four together.
- Hamada Omer and his team at **Desert Safari Egypte** (tel. 0128 682 4751; https://desert-safari-egypte.com) also lead professional trekking tours for 2-10 days for $110 per person per day for a group of four. The prices include all meals, water, and camping equipment, set up ahead of time by a driver who meets the group at designated spots.

anthills rise out of the desert. The coal-black basalt that covers the conical mounds here are remnants of volcanic activity that occurred between 16 and 22 million years ago.

You can see the desert from the car window, but to really soak it in, a better option is to ask you driver to pass by one of the region's main volcanic fields, **Gebel el-Marsoos,** for a scenic 5-10-minute hike up and along the mini mountain to check out the prehistoric debris up close and look out across the open desert.

El-Heiz Oasis

43 km/27 mi south of Bawiti

After the Black Desert, your next stop en route to the White Desert is the little el-Heiz Oasis on the outer limits of Bahariya. Here, you can combine a stop at el-Heiz Water Education Center with a dip in the Ain Gomma cool spring, and lunch at the neighboring cafeteria.

EL-HEIZ WATER EDUCATION CENTER

tel. 0122 992 2226; 10am-4pm daily; 15LE adults, 10LE students

This mini museum dedicated to water and the geological history of the surrounding landscape is a nice detour on your way to the White Desert. Jump in a time machine to see what the area looked like 10,000 years ago and read up on how oases come to exist. The small-town tourist attraction also doubles as a learning center, where locals teach students from surrounding villages about water management.

AIN GOMMA

24 hours daily; free

Enjoy a soak in the mineral-rich Ain Gomma, surrounded by farmland, desert, and distant mountains. The loud motor used to pump the water into the pool makes it not the most relaxing of spots, but it's still a nice place to cool off while you wait for lunch (neighboring cafeteria open daily).

★ Crystal Mountain

94 km/58 mi south of Bawiti

A short detour off the main road between Bahariya and Farafra brings you to unassuming rocky hills that upon closer examination hold a mesmerizing array of crystals and funky formations. Contrary to popular belief, these glittering rocks are not quartz, but likely barite and calcite (softer minerals), formed under a volcano between 23 and 33 million years ago. You only need around 20 minutes to explore the area, but each patch of land has its own unique treasures to admire.

Djara Cave

Djara Cave Desert Path, 150 km/90 mi east off the Bahariya-Farafra Rd.

Located deep into the desert about midway between Farafra and the Nile Valley, this

1
2
3
4

isolated dripstone cave is an explorer's dream. Beneath the enormous stalactites, sharp eyes will spot over 100 (very) faint engravings of gazelles, antelopes, ostriches, and other animals that likely roamed the area. Experts haven't been able to date the cave art for certain, but estimates place the earliest at around 8,500 years old.

Agabat Valley (Wadi Agabat)

123 km/76 mi south of Bawiti

According to locals, this stunning spot was once the main passageway for travelers moving between Bahariya and Farafra on camel, giving the valley its name, Agabat, meaning both "mountain passes" and "difficulties." The golden oblong mounds rising from the ground look straight from the set of a *Star Wars* movie and cast imposing shadows in the late afternoon hours. Scramble up the rocky hill for the best views of the now-exposed prehistoric seabed. A hidden canyon beside the main route through Agabat Valley holds a limestone theater with sand dune stage and a great echo chamber. A knowledgeable guide can lead you to the hidden canyon. (It might help to show them a photo.)

TOP EXPERIENCE

★ White Desert National Park

125 km/78 mi south of Bawiti; 24 hours daily; 100LE entrance

Rocks that look like craggy dollops of meringue decorate this lunar patch of earth. Wander among the wind-carved formations and frozen waves of limestone that make the scorching land resemble an icy tundra. The protected area covers over 3,000 square kilometers (1,160 sq mi) of dramatic desert that you can explore with an expert guide and 4WD. Arrange your trip ahead of time or when you get to Bahariya (the tour operator will secure your entrance ticket).

Camping is the best way to experience the park—to enjoy both sunset and sunrise when the changing light illuminates the chalky white figures in golden hues, and the darkness of night reveals a star-speckled sky.

WHITE DESERT NATIONAL PARK VISITOR CENTER

Just before entrance to Qasr el-Farafra town; 9am-2pm Sun.-Thurs.; free

This little center set up by a joint Egyptian-Italian mission is well worth a short trip if you're already heading to Qasr el-Farafra. Inside you'll find some posters with information on local customs, landscapes, and native flora and fauna. When entering the White Desert from Bahariya, the visitor center is found *after* the national park.

QASR EL-FARAFRA

Qasr el-Farafra is the only village of note in the Farafra Oasis and was, for centuries, the only settlement in the whole depression. Its name comes from the medieval fortress (el-Qasr) that once protected inhabitants from attack by desert invaders. The fort now lies in ruins in the town's center—most of its 125 rooms gone after succumbing to the elements in the 1950s.

Few tourists make their way to this tiny town deep in the Western Desert, making it an ideal escape for those in search of solitude or a glimpse of isolated oasis life. At the doorstep of the White Desert, this is also an excellent base for travelers keen on enjoying sunrise or sunset in the stunning landscape without spending the night under the stars.

Sights

BADR'S MUSEUM

Qasr el-Farafra center, 230 m/770 ft west off Farafra-Wahat Rd.; 8:30am-6pm daily; 20LE

The paintings, wood carvings, and clay sculptures made by local artist Badr Abdel Moghny are the main attraction in this sleepy village. Other corners of the museum hold dioramas depicting traditional village life alongside local tools, instruments, and woven crafts made of palm tree wicker. If you find it closed,

---

1: Agabat Valley **2:** Dist Mountain **3:** natural rock formation in the White Desert **4:** Crystal Mountain

ask a nearby shop to call Badr and he'll head over if available.

Natural Springs

You have fewer options in Farafra than Bahariya to enjoy the gift of desert water, but **Bir Sitta** (6 km/4 mi east of Qasr el-Farafra; 24 hours daily; free) is a pleasant hot spring just off a dusty road beside fields of green, and **Lake Abu Nuss** (17 km/10.5 mi northwest of al-Qasr el-Farafra), a swimmable lake sandwiched between farmland and desert, is perfect for hot days.

Food and Accommodations

Qasr el-Farafra's two best hotels have excellent hosts who can show you around the gardens and palm groves of their idyllic hometown. You'll likely enjoy all meals at your lodge or around the campfire. Best to negotiate a full-board package at your hotel.

BADAWIYA HOTEL FARAFRA

Gamal Abdel Nasser St.; tel. 0128 287 9695; www.badawiya.com; 400LE d

There's a lot of potential at this attractive hotel that's all domes and archways, but it's suffered neglect since the dip in tourism post-2013. The 20 rooms are beautifully decorated with traditional rugs and mosquito nets, common areas are comfortable, and there's a nice pool to cool off in from the harsh desert sun. Unfortunately, cleanliness levels vary—but don't hesitate to ask them to throw on a clean set of sheets if those present don't meet your standards.

★ RAHALA SAFARI HOTEL

Qasr el-Farafra; tel. 0100 306 4733 or 0122 950 0473; www.rahala-safari.com; 500LE d

This oasis within an oasis is without a doubt the best place to stay in Farafra. Comfortable domed rooms (just 12 in all) stay cool under the beating sun, and the gardens full of olive trees and bougainvillea offer plenty of shade. The spacious stone patio with attractive lighting is a nice spot to enjoy the cool evenings. Ahmed and his family who run the hotel are delightful and can organize great trips to the desert. Breakfast included.

Information and Services

Banque Misr (north side of Qasr el-Farafra, off Bahariya-Farafa Rd.; 9am-2pm Sun.-Thurs.) is your only chance for an ATM here. For tourist police, call **126.**

Getting There

If you aren't arriving from Bahariya with a guide, it's possible to reach Farafra by bus. Also, both **Rahala Safari Hotel** (tel. 0100 306 4733; www.rahala-safari.com) and **Badawiya Hotel** (tel. 0128 287 9695; www.badawiya.com) can arrange for round-trip transportation to Farafra from the Cairo airport or your hotel in Bahariya or Cairo.

BUS

Buses from Cairo to Farafra (8 hours; 200LE) leave from the **Torgoman Bus Station** (Upper Egypt Bus Co.) and pass through Bahariya. Trips usually leave at 10am and 10pm (the road between Cairo and Bahariya is well-traveled by large trucks and more comfortable during the daytime), but it's best to book your tickets at the station a day or two in advance to secure a seat and double check times.

To get to Farafra from Bahariya by bus, hop on one coming from Cairo. Check at the Bawiti Bus Station to see when it's expected to come through as times vary.

Getting Around

There's no public transportation in these parts, so you'll have to depend on your hotel (or your legs) to get around. They can arrange for 4WD desert safaris, or cars to take you to Farafra's Lake Abu Nuss and Bir Sitta hot spring.

Siwa Oasis

One of Egypt's most far-flung destinations (50 km/30 mi from the Libyan border), the Siwa Oasis holds a world unto itself. The dozens of natural springs hidden among date-laden palm trees give the town a paradisiacal air of plenty. Endless desert surrounds this patch of green, making the verdant groves and pools of water spouting from the earth and all the more magical.

Siwa Town is also the gateway to the Great Sand Sea, one of the country's most fascinating natural wonders. A 4WD safari into this dune-filled desert is an essential excursion and can be enjoyed as an afternoon outing with evening barbeque by campfire, or as a multiday adventure with nights under the stars.

SIWA TOWN

Once reachable only by 6-7-day camel ride, Siwa was first linked to the country's roads in the 1980s. Since then, its population has jumped from just around 8,000 to more than 28,000. To the village elders, the oasis must now feel like a bustling city. But outside of the busy central square, Siwa Town still has a sleepy village feel. Children play in sandy streets and donkeys bray from their resting spots beside mud brick pigeon houses.

Be sure to set aside a few hours to swim in the turquoise Salt Mines (el-Mallahaat) and a few more to explore Shali Fortress and climb the Mountain of the Dead (Gebel el-Mawta). To acquaint yourself with Siwi culture, head to the House of Siwa Museum or reserve an afternoon to dine in a local home—ask if your lodge or guide can arrange.

Orientation

Siwa is a small town and easy to navigate with tuk tuk or, in the cooler months, by bike. Residents of Siwa have a mental map of their hometown so have skipped the street names, but major landmarks can help the casual visitor. The town centers around **Market Square** (Souq el-Medina) and the towering **Shali Fortress** (Qala'at Shali). Olive orchards and palm groves dotted with dozens of mini-hotels and ecolodges envelope the rest of the village. The **Mountain of the Dead** (Gebel el-Mawta) marks the northern edge of downtown; **Dakrur Mountain** (Gebel el-Dakrur) stands in the southeast corner; and **Lake Siwa** (Birket Siwa) and the **Middle Lakes** (Buheraat el-Awsat) bookend the town on the west and east, respectively.

Sights

SHALI FORTRESS (QALA'AT SHALI)

Just west of Market Square; free

The Shali Fortress is quintessentially Siwan—built in the town's signature style out of a rock-salt mixture (karshif) sourced from surrounding lake beds. What remains of this early 13th-century walled city resembles a jagged mouse maze of beige shards. Head to the highest point of the fortress for the best views of the structure and modern-day Siwa Town, which was built around it. After serving as locals' homes for some 700 years, the once impenetrable stronghold dissolved under heavy rains in the 20th century—the first in 1928.

The **Old Mosque** (located at the main entrance to Shali just off Market Square) is the world's oldest karshif mosque, dating to AD 1203, and is still used for religious celebrations. There's not much to see inside, save a ceiling made of palm trees.

HOUSE OF SIWA MUSEUM (EL-BEIT EL-SIWI)

400 m/1,300 ft northwest of Market Square; 9am-2pm Sat.-Thurs.; 10LE

This traditional karshif house holds a small museum with some beautiful Siwi wedding dresses, silver jewelry, and a section set up to imitate a local living room with carpet and floor pillows. Signs (in English) offer

Siwa Oasis

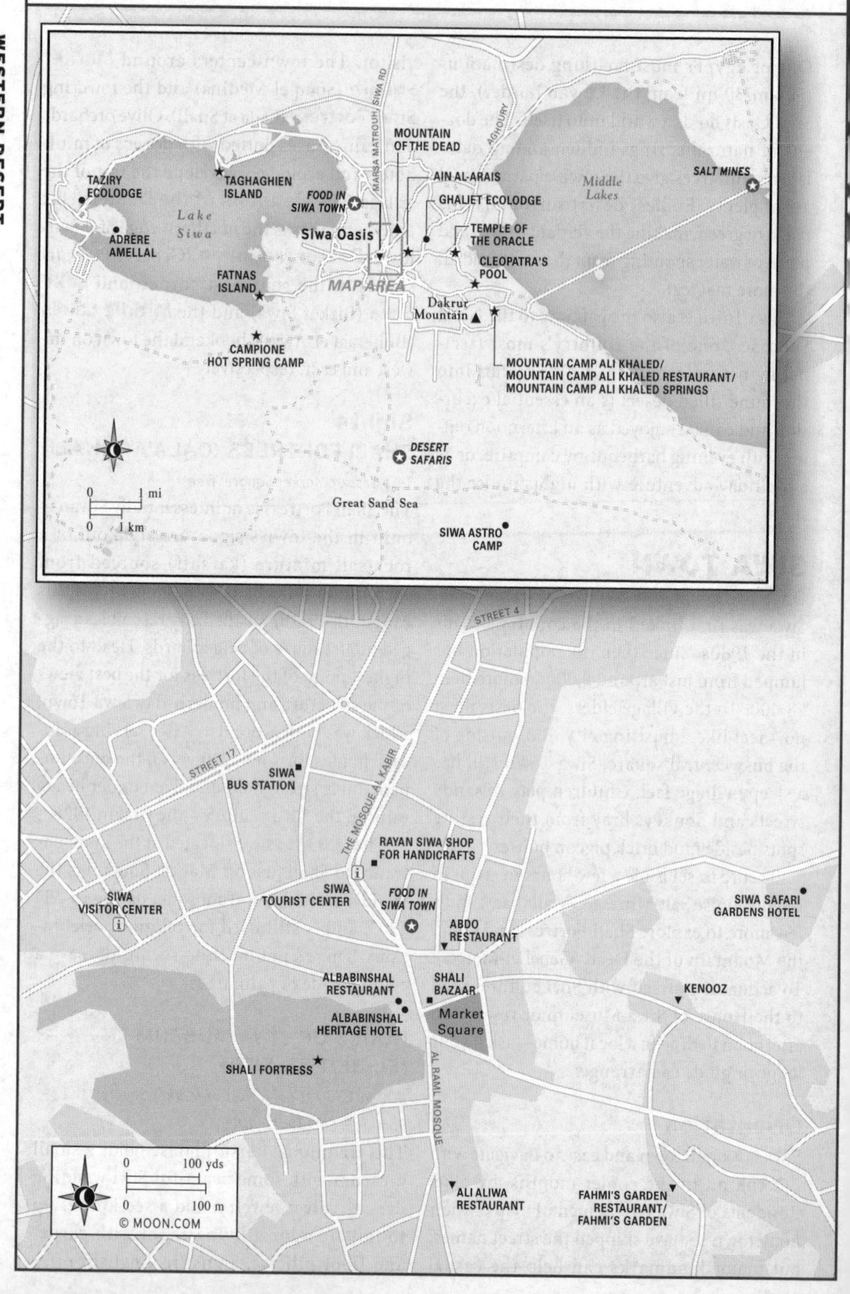
MARSA MATROUH / SIWA RD
AGHOURY
MOUNTAIN OF THE DEAD
AIN AL-ARAIS
GHALIET ECOLODGE
TEMPLE OF THE ORACLE
CLEOPATRA'S POOL
SALT MINES
Middle Lakes
TAZIRY ECOLODGE
TAGHAGHIEN ISLAND
FOOD IN SIWA TOWN
Lake Siwa
ADRÈRE AMELLAL
Siwa Oasis
FATNAS ISLAND
MAP AREA
Dakrur Mountain
CAMPIONE HOT SPRING CAMP
MOUNTAIN CAMP ALI KHALED/
MOUNTAIN CAMP ALI KHALED RESTAURANT/
MOUNTAIN CAMP ALI KHALED SPRINGS
DESERT SAFARIS
0 1 mi
0 1 km
Great Sand Sea
SIWA ASTRO CAMP
STREET 4
STREET 17
SIWA BUS STATION
THE MOSQUE AL KABIR
RAYAN SIWA SHOP FOR HANDICRAFTS
SIWA VISITOR CENTER
SIWA TOURIST CENTER
FOOD IN SIWA TOWN
ABDO RESTAURANT
SIWA SAFARI GARDENS HOTEL
ALBABINSHAL RESTAURANT
SHALI BAZAAR
KENOOZ
Market Square
ALBABINSHAL HERITAGE HOTEL
SHALI FORTRESS
AL RAMIL MOSQUE
0 100 yds
0 100 m
© MOON.COM
ALI ALIWA RESTAURANT
FAHMI'S GARDEN RESTAURANT/
FAHMI'S GARDEN

Women in Siwa

Siwi culture is notably more conservative than most of the country, with women all but absent from public spaces. In fact, it's not unusual for visitors to spend their entire trip without seeing a single Siwi woman. The few who pass through town will likely be wearing a niqab or even more complete coverage, with even the eyes invisible.

ADVICE FOR FEMALE TRAVELERS

After decades of tourism, locals have become accustomed to encountering more liberal cultures, which they welcome as oddities so long as they don't disrupt their own way of life. Still, women will likely feel more comfortable swimming in clothing rather than bikinis. Some exceptions include the secluded **Salt Mines (el-Mallahaat), Lake Shiatta,** and **Bir Wahed** in the **Great Sand Sea.** Many hotels also have natural spring pools on their premises where you can swim at your leisure.

interesting information about Siwi architecture and history. A visit should only take around 20 minutes.

TEMPLE OF THE ORACLE

2.5 km/1.5 mi east of Market Square; 9am-5pm daily; 50LE adults, 25LE students

Dating to around the 6th century BC, this elevated temple once housed the oracle of Amun (ancient Egypt's king of the gods). Kings sent delegations across unforgiving deserts to consult the priests here who relayed the prophecies of Amun. The most famous visitor, Alexander the Great, traveled to Siwa himself to consult the oracle just after his conquest of Egypt in 332 BC. Priests conveniently confirmed Alexander's godliness and legitimacy as Egypt's pharaoh, and the young king continued his military campaign, successfully expanding his empire deep into the East.

The crumbled **Temple of Umm Ubayd,** which lies around 400 meters (1,300 ft) to the south, was once connected to the main Temple of the Oracle. Not much remains of either today, but a healthy imagination can conjure how impressive it may have looked over 2,000 years ago. The panoramic views from the top are also a treat.

Natural Springs

The natural springs—'ain (singular) or 'ayoon (plural)—scattered around Siwa are the town's most unique feature. Without these life-giving waters that trickle up from the earth, there would be no oasis. Locals have dug dozens of pools fed by the underground springs—many of them open to the public. Grab your suit (and perhaps an oversized T-shirt and shorts to avoid wandering eyes) and head to these watering holes—some of Siwa's best.

CLEOPATRA'S POOL (AIN CLEOPATRA)

3.5 km/2.2 mi east of Market Square; 24 hours daily; free

Cleopatra's Pool, the town's main natural spring, can be found nestled between palm groves just east of Market Square. With its clear blue-green waters surrounded on all sides by trees, this large pool is loved by locals and visitors alike. Park yourself in the shade of the palms or stake out a spot on the floor cushions at the **juice bar** (8am-8pm daily) next door. A bathroom is available to change into your suit.

AIN AL-ARAIS

750 m/0.5 mi northeast of Market Square, Ain al-Arais St.; 24 hours daily; free

Tucked away in a sprawling palm grove, this natural spring with crisp, cold waters is a great place to take a quick dip if you're pressed for time. Its proximity to the center of town means the pool can be a bit crowded, but

A Cycle Tour of Siwa Town

While cycling through hot and dusty summer streets in Siwa is less than appealing, bikes are a great way to get around in the cooler months. The town is flat (save the occasional mountain, which can be easily avoided) and small enough to navigate on two wheels. You can pick one up (with a lock) in **Market Square** next to Albabinshal Hotel (50-60LE per day) and try out this itinerary:

- From Market Square, weave your way northeast down a palm-lined lane to the **Temple of the Oracle** (2.4 km/1.5 mi).
- Cycle south (1.5 km/0.9 mi) to cool off in **Cleopatra's Pool** and have a fresh juice at its neighboring café.
- Continue to the east side of Dakrur Mountain and park your bikes in **Mountain Camp Ali Khaled** (1.5 km/0.9 mi).
- Climb **Dakrur Mountain** (20 minutes) for panoramic views.
- Head back to Mountain Camp Ali Khaled for a dip in their cold or hot **natural springs** as you wait for them to prepare a delicious Siwan lunch (call 5-6 hours ahead).
- Make your way back to **Market Square** (4.2 km/2.6 mi northwest) by following the street at the base of Dakrur Mountain for 1 kilometer (0.6 mi), and then taking a right for 500 meters (1,600 ft), and a left for 2.6 kilometers (1.6 mi).

you might get lucky and have it to yourself. A small café and restroom are available.

MOUNTAIN CAMP ALI KHALED SPRINGS

Across from Gebel el-Dakrur on east side of Siwa; tel. 0109 042 3255 or 0100 632 6253; 8am-11pm daily; 25LE

Mountain Camp Ali Khaled is one of the few places in Siwa where you can easily hop between hot and cold springs. The beautifully manicured hot tub and pool are fed by natural springs, clean as can be, and surrounded by chairs, chaise longues, and nature. As you soak, admire Dakrur Mountain towering next door and take in the greenery of the camp's gardens. Don't miss the kitchen's delicious food and fresh juice options. WCs available.

CAMPIONE HOT SPRING CAMP

6.2 km/3.9 mi southwest of central Siwa; tel. 0106 466 0200; 8am-11pm daily; 30LE

This hidden gem on the edge of the desert has a large hot spring surrounded by tall grasses. There's not much shade around, but you can seek refuge from the elements (and enjoy refreshments) in the colorful lodge with Arabic-style seating. For food, best to call 5-6 hours ahead so they can prepare something fresh. WCs available.

AIN QURAYSHAT AND ABU SHURUF

20 km/12 mi and 27 km/17 mi east of Siwa, off Al-Bahariya-Siwa Rd.; 24 hours daily; free

These two cool natural springs lie past the Salt Mines (el-Mallahat) 20 kilometers (12 mi) and 27 kilometers (17 mi) east of central Siwa, respectively. They're worth seeking out, as they're both more unique and generally less crowded than the ones in town. The expansive **Ain Qurayshat** is the closer and more idyllic of the two with a view of the lake, palm trees, and an ancient cemetery. **Abu Shuruf** is also tucked into a palm grove, but it's a bit too close to a water bottle factory for the ideal return to nature (though it is home to some interesting big-eyed fish).

Unless you're a serious biker, you'll need a car to get here. Your hotel can arrange for a driver, or call **Youssef Dahman** (tel. 0100 615 4383), **Fathi Benhagar** (tel. 0122 490 7806 or 0109 683 0728; https://siwawi.com), or **Youssef Sarhan** (tel. 0122 305 3314) to arrange a day trip that includes a visit to these parts.

Shopping

It will come as no surprise to anyone who's stepped foot in Siwa that its main products involve dates and olives. There's date paste, date syrup, date cookies, date jam, olive jam, olive oil, olive soap... You get the idea. All are superb and can be found at a number of small shops scattered around **Market Square.** More lasting treasures include the colorful Siwi embroidery, intricate rugs, salt lamps, and beautiful baskets.

SHALI BAZAAR

Next to Shali Fortress, near Market Square; tel. 0106 860 3428; 9am-midnight daily

Enjoy a wide selection of Siwa's impressive handicrafts in this small shop overflowing with goodies. Shelves are stacked with traditional rugs, palm frond baskets, vibrant scarves with detailed embroidery, and salt lamps molded into various shapes.

RAYAN SIWA SHOP FOR HANDICRAFTS

Next to the Great Mosque, near Market Square; tel. 019 388 2828; 10am-10pm daily

Head here if you're in search of a Siwi wedding dress, festooned with unique patterns, colorful beads, and probably more buttons than all of your clothes combined. You can also choose from simpler garments, tasteful leather wallets, bedazzled bags, salt lamps, and baskets.

Hiking

Both of the hikes below are relatively easy and offer stunning panoramic views of the oasis and its outskirts. Hardcore hikers can head out to the desert for a day or more to explore the landscape at a more leisurely pace. **Fathi Benhagar** (tel. 0122 490 7806; https://siwawi.com) is an excellent guide who knows where to find shade for a nap during the midday heat and can arrange tailored trips including all food, water, and equipment for a minimum of 5 people (1,400LE per person per day).

DAKRUR MOUNTAIN (GEBEL EL-DAKRUR)

Take a quick hike up **Dakrur Mountain** for fabulous sunrise views over the Salt Mines. The ascent is fairly easy and should only take 15-20 minutes, but good shoes are recommended. Start on the east side of the mountain, near Mountain Camp Ali Khaled for the easiest angle.

MOUNTAIN OF THE DEAD (GEBEL EL-MAWTA)

1.2 km/0.7 mi north of Market Square; 9am-5pm daily; 50LE adults, 25LE students

Climb to the top of this honeycombed hill for phenomenal views of the Salt Mines to the east, Lake Siwa to the west, and the thousands of palm trees that stand between the two. On your way up you'll pass dozens of tombs, some dating back to the 7th century BC. Most of the interiors are empty, but ask the guard to direct you to the decorated tombs (for a small tip), particularly that of Si Amun, which depicts immortal Egyptian gods and man's less than divine aging process. The hike to the top of the hill takes 10-15 minutes.

★ Food

The food in Siwa is some of the tastiest you'll find in all of Egypt. Dates and olives are creatively incorporated into almost every meal, along with cloves and desert herbs. Traditional breakfast here, like most everywhere else in the country, includes a savory smattering of fuul (fava bean paste), ta'maya (falafel), eggs, and bread, with the homemade jams a special Siwi addition. Lunch is the most elaborate meal—often including salad, bread, and rice alongside tagines, couscous, or grilled chicken—and dinner is typically light, with fruits, vegetables, bread, and cheese (though you'll still have a full range of options at restaurants).

Tanta Waa
1
2

Siwa's Festival of Peace

The Festival of Peace, or **Asihaite** in the local Siwi language, takes place over three days during October's first full moon (check www.timeanddate.com to see when this will be in any given year). Local men and children (women are not invited) gather on Dakrur Mountain (Gebel el-Dakrur) to feast and forgive, resolving old spats over shared plates of meat and rice. Rows of aluminum pots line the mountainside as meals are cooked on open fires before the platters are passed around. In the evenings, there's music and dancing as they perform Sufi rituals. The event is also known as the Siyaha ("Tourist") Festival, even though few tourists attend (but all tourists, including women, are welcome).

Siwa is a dry town (save the locally brewed date liquor surreptitiously passed around at jam sessions), but it's perfectly acceptable to bring your own alcohol to enjoy at your lodge or in the desert if consumed discreetly.

★ FAHMI'S GARDEN RESTAURANT

Torar St., 350 m/1,100 ft southeast of Market Square; tel. 012 482 9421; 8am-11am breakfast and 5pm-8pm dinner; 45-75LE mains

This hidden gem offers some of the freshest food in town. Fahmi sources much of his ingredients from his own garden (which also serves as the attractive dining area), including delicious olives, goat cheese, and date syrup-drizzled fruit salads. The main dishes are typically grilled chicken and meats. Call at least three hours in advance to reserve and check what's in season. Breakfast also available if you call the day before. The date pancakes are delectable.

★ ABDO RESTAURANT

Market Square; tel. 0100 812 6833; 8:30am-midnight daily; 40-80LE mains

Smack dab in the center of town, Abdo Restaurant is a great place to watch downtown Siwa's (relative) bustle. The décor is all stones and palms with an open front that looks out to the street. Choose from a wide selection of traditional dishes, like tagines (highly recommended), fuul, and couscous piled high with roasted veg. Pizza, pasta, and crepes also available. Don't miss out on their sahleb (a thick white drink made of orchid tubers, sugar, and cinnamon).

1: Cleopatra's Pool 2: Mountain of the Dead (Gebel el-Mawta)

★ ALI ALIWA RESTAURANT

Batookhi Street, 350 m/1,100 ft south of Market Square; tel. 0106 177 3085; 9am-11pm daily; 60-80LE mains

The traditional Abu Mardam dishes served here are some of Siwa's best. The mains typically come with a generous spread of rice, salad, and vegetables or molokhia (Egypt's traditional soupy green vegetable)—all almost as good as the fall-off-the-bone meats. You can choose to dine in their spacious courtyard with dancing palm trees, or inside on Arabic-style seating with pillows and a low table.

ALBABINSHAL RESTAURANT

At Albabinshal Hotel next to Shali Fortress; tel. 0100 625 7140 or 0100 812 6833; 8am-10:30pm daily; 50-85LE mains

Enjoy fresh local food like camel stew, chicken and olive tagine, or the famous slow-cooked Abu Mardam. Their breakfasts are also delicious with a variety of local jams on offer alongside the traditional fuul, ta'maya, bread, and eggs combination. You can choose between indoor seating with large windows that let in a cool breeze, or a rooftop area that looks out to the side of Shali Fortress, the busy central square, and (in the evenings) up to a star-filled sky. Both spaces are pleasantly lit (with the rooftop sometimes illuminated only by candles and the moon). Best to call a few

Abu Mardam: Siwa's Slow-Cooked Specialty

Complementing the pace of life in Siwa, slow-cooked Abu Mardam is a classic dish in the oasis. The chefs who've perfected this specialty dig a hole in the sand about half a meter (2 ft) deep before lighting a fire in the pit that's left to burn for around 1.5 hours. The meat of choice (duck, chicken, lamb, beef, or camel) is then flavored with a blend of local seasonings in a covered pot, placed on the fire, and buried under the sand for another 90 minutes. The technique keeps the meat juicy and gives it a light smokey flavor that mingles with the desert herbs and spices.

Abu Mardam is available at multiple restaurants in town. For some of Siwa's best, head to **Ali Aliwa Restaurant.**

hours in advance to give them time to prepare dinner, but they can usually accommodate walk-ins as well.

KENOOZ (SIWA SHALI LODGE)

At Siwa Shali Lodge, 250 m/820 ft east of Market Square; tel. 046 4601299; 9am-11pm daily; 50-85LE mains

This pleasant rooftop restaurant under the shade of palms and above Shali Lodge offers a range of tasty Siwi dishes with fresh farmed ingredients. Try their crepes with date syrup for breakfast or their chicken and olive dish for dinner. Their molokhia is some of the best in town. Comfortable inside dining area also available.

MOUNTAIN CAMP ALI KHALED RESTAURANT

Across from Gebel el-Dakrur on east side of Siwa; tel. 0109 042 3255 or 0100 632 6253; 9am-9pm daily; 100-150LE mains

This mini farm with bunnies, birds, and utopic orchards also serves up some mouthwatering food. If you come for breakfast, sample their colorful array of homemade jams (orange, olive, date, and hibiscus) with fresh bread, eggs, and traditional fuul and ta'maya options. For dinner you can choose from a selection of Siwi specialties like couscous with vegetables, Abu Mardam, or macarona ba'ba'a (pasta with meat juice). Dinner typically served around 6-7pm. Best to call a few hours in advance to let them know you're coming (especially if you want to try the Abu Mardam). You can take a dip in their crystal clear hot and/or cold springs before or after dinner.

Accommodations

Most of the lodges in Siwa serve as mini oases, with their own lush gardens and natural spring-fed pools. Stay somewhere relatively central if you prefer independence; otherwise, the hotels on the outskirts of Siwa Town (including Mountain Camp Ali Khaled and Campione Hot Spring camp) can arrange your transportation for a small extra charge.

FAHMI'S GARDEN

Torar St., Harat Muqbal, next to Market Square; tel. 012 482 9421; fahmiprince@gmail.com; 300LE d

Enjoy the simple life at Fahmi's Garden—one of the most economical and central locations in town. From the palm trees that shade his verdant garden, Fahmi also builds his furniture and harvests dates to make his syrup. Choose from one of four cozy accommodation options, all built by Fahmi himself: a bungalow made of palm fronds; a house with two rooms and a kitchen; a basic room; or a tent in the garden surrounded by orange, fig, pomegranate, and olive trees. All but the house have shared bathrooms. His goats and chickens complete the idyllic scene. Don't miss Fahmi's farm-to-fork meals.

ALBABINSHAL HERITAGE HOTEL

Next to Shali Fortress, near Market Square; tel. 0100 625 7140; salama.albabenshal@hotmail.com; 650LE d

Built into the side of the medieval Shali Fortress, this rustic chic lodge is constructed Siwi-style with karshif (rock, salt, and mud) walls, palm wood furniture, log-lined ceilings, and traditional niches in lieu of shelves. The 14 rooms are minimalistic (no ACs, but the mud walls keep it fairly cool even in the hot summers) and comfortable, with options for singles, doubles, or triples. A tasty breakfast is included with homemade jams, fresh bread, fuul, eggs, and ta'maya. The downside: no garden or pool.

CAMPIONE HOT SPRING CAMP

6.2 km/3.9 mi southwest of Market Square; tel. 0106 466 0200; 500LE d

There are only three double rooms at this campground where most guests opt to sleep in tents or under the stars (150LE per person). The few rooms are beautifully crafted with brick dome ceilings, neutral colors, and accents of locally made rugs and pillows. Meals are enjoyed in a shared space with dramatic arches, handmade tassel décor, and more brick-lined vaults. The camp's hot spring is sublime in the cool desert evening. Attractive garden lined with olive trees and herbs out front. Breakfast included.

★ MOUNTAIN CAMP ALI KHALED

Across from Gebel el-Dakrur on east side of Siwa; tel. 0109 042 3255 or 0100 632 6253; 550LE d

At the eastern base of Dakrur Mountain, this camp offers a row of rooms tucked into a garden brimming with palms, olive trees, and other thriving greenery. Cool off in their pool, or warm up in their hot tub—both sourced from flowing spring water. The rooms are simple but clean, with domed ceilings and comfortable beds, or you can opt for a tent (150LE per person). There's plenty of shade in the camp's sprawling garden, where you can enjoy your scrumptious complimentary breakfast with homemade jams of dates, olives, orange, or hibiscus grown on site, and fresh bread, falafel, and fuul. Impromptu Siwi music-making is known to break out in the evenings in the common area.

★ GHALIET ECOLODGE

1 km/0.6 mi east of Gebel el-Mawta; tel. 0100 920 2346; ghaliet@ecobilities.com; 700LE d

This lodge in the middle of a palm grove has 12 stylish rooms with various wood and stone accents, all full of natural light. On the top floor, glass ceilings let you stargaze from the comfort of your bed. Most rooms look out onto the courtyard's pool (replenished by constantly flowing spring waters) that surrounds a small island, home to happy palm trees and benches perfect for reading. Fire pit available for cool nights. Breakfast included.

★ SIWA SAFARI GARDENS HOTEL

Ain al-Arais St., 500 m/1,600 ft northeast of Market Square; tel. 0115 842 1897; www.siwagardens.com; 800LE d

From the brick-domed rooms tastefully decorated with traditional rugs to the palm-lined courtyard with crystal clear spring-fed pool, this family-run operation is on point. The reception welcomes you with a marble fountain and sweeping arches, and Manager Susi is a delight. It's just a 10-minute walk to the center of town, but still a world away from the bustle. Breakfast included.

Information and Services

Siwa Town's sole **bank, police station,** and **bus stop** are located 400 meters (1,300 ft) north of Market Square. **Banque du Caire** (400 m/1,300 ft north of Market Square, beside the Police Station) is the only **bank/ATM** in town. Best to bring a bit of cash with you just in case. Head to the **police station** (across from the Siwa Tourist Center; 24 hours daily) in case of emergency or call the tourist police at **126.**

Siwa's Luxury Ecolodges

Adrère Amellal ecolodge

Nestled in the foothills of the Red and White Mountains, the Taziry and Adrère Amellal ecolodges are really more like self-contained villages—each with its own organic gardens, palm groves, and springs. Visitors in search of an escape into nature with all the comforts of a luxury hotel will find their happy place here on the western edge of Lake Siwa. Both lodges are sans electricity, but candles illuminate the grounds in the evenings—imitating the stars in the sky with a faint flicker—and traditional building techniques keep temperatures pleasant all year round.

TAZIRY ECOLODGE

16 km/10 mi west of downtown Siwa; tel. 0101 633 3201; https://taziry.com; 3,600LE d

This ecolodge blends into its surroundings with karshif walls, palm trunk ceilings, and some rooms actually carved into the side of the mountain. Each of the 30 rooms is unique with handcrafted furniture, vibrant rugs, and candles instead of lightbulbs. A large natural spring looks across the lake to the stunning White Mountain. The Moroccan owners and their staff offer the warmest of welcomes, and their compatriot chef makes scrumptious Moroccan food alongside Siwi dishes (breakfast included). Don't miss the chance to head to the desert on one of their camels or pure-bred Arabian horses.

ADRÈRE AMELLAL

17 km/11 mi west of downtown Siwa; tel. 0122 315 8110; www.adrereamellal.com; 9,500LE d

With mud brick walls and no electricity, this ecolodge still manages to be one of the country's most luxurious getaways. The location is picture perfect—tucked between Lake Siwa and the White Mountain (or Adrère Amellal in Siwi). Like the rest of the lodge, the rooms are minimalistic and elegant, built using local materials. The spring-fed pool surrounded by palms is divine, and the food is exquisite with gourmet interpretations of traditional Siwi dishes made with ingredients fresh from their gardens. Price includes all meals and beverages (beer, wine, and prosecco included), a desert safari, and other excursions. They can also arrange for flights from Cairo on limited dates ($630 per person round-trip).

SIWA TOURIST CENTER

Across from the bus station; tel. 0100 546 1992; 9am-2pm Sat.-Thurs., also open 5pm-8pm Oct.-Apr.

Pop into the Siwa Tourist Center for a short video about the area and to collect some maps and brochures before exploring Siwa. The helpful staff can arrange desert safaris or day trips around Siwa (though check with your hotel or the guides recommended above to compare prices).

SIWA VISITOR CENTER

Behind Banque du Caire; tel. 0106 560 9042; 9am-2pm daily

At the Siwa Visitor Center, find information about the Siwa Protected Area that covers over 7,000 square kilometers (3,000 sq mi) and includes everything west of Siwa to the Libyan border, the Great Sand Sea, and neighboring Qattara Depression.

Getting There

For solo travelers on a budget, the bus is the best way to get to Siwa. Groups of two or more might prefer to indulge in a private car hire. Do note: Buses to Siwa typically don't have a toilet on board, and they stop around four times during the 10-11-hour trip. Be sure to bring your own toilet paper, hand sanitizer, coins (use of rest stop bathrooms is around 3LE), and a flashlight (there aren't always lights).

AIR

By far the most comfortable (and expensive) option for getting to Siwa is with a group chartered flight (about $630 per person round-trip if plane is filled). Contact **Adrère Amellal** ecolodge (tel. 0122 315 8110; info@eqi.com.eg) to grab a seat on their next scheduled flight, even if you don't choose to stay with them. Trips leave from Cairo International Airport and arrive at a military airstrip close to central Siwa.

BUS

From Cairo your only option for a direct bus trip to Siwa is with the **West & Mid Delta Bus Co.**, boarding downtown at **Abdel Minam Riyad Station** next to the Ramses Hilton (10-11 hours; 230LE). Buses typically leave at 10pm on Saturdays, Mondays, and Thursdays, but check ahead as trips can be canceled and times changed. To avoid disappointment, buy your tickets 2-3 days in advance from the station (though you can sometimes get away with same-day booking).

If you're coming from Alexandria with the **West & Mid Delta Bus Co.** (9 hours; 100-150LE), board at the **Main Bus Station** (Moharam Bek; al-Kabary al-Saree'a Rd.). Buses usually head to Siwa 3-4 times per day, but again their schedules are always changing so go a day before to book and double check times.

Siwa's **Bus Station** is located on Marsa Matruh-Siwa Road (500 m/1,600 ft northwest of Market Square, across from the police station). Trips back to Cairo leave at 8pm on Sundays, Tuesdays, and Fridays. Buses to and from Alexandria are more frequent (7am, 10am, 8:30pm, or 10:30pm on Sun., Tues., and Fri., depending on demand). In Siwa you usually *must* book your ticket on the same day from the station, and the ticket office is closed between noon and afternoon prayers (about 11:30am-4pm depending on the time of year), so try to go early.

BUS AND SHARED MICROBUS

Another option for reaching Siwa from Cairo is to take a **Go Bus** (also boarding at **Abdel Minam Riyad Station** next to the Ramses Hilton) to Marsa Matruh (6-7 hours; 200LE), and then grab a shared 15-person microbus to Siwa (4 hours; 70LE). This route is usually only available in the warmer months (May-Sept.), when transportation to the north coast town is in high demand.

The Matruh microbus stop is directly next to the West & Mid Delta Bus Co. ticket window on its northwest side. You'll have to wait for the microbus to load, which can take over an hour depending on your luck. Or you can be the hero (and have a more comfortable ride) by paying for any last remaining seats to hit the road quicker. The microbus will drop you off in the center of Siwa Town near the police station.

To return to Cairo, do the same in reverse. Hop in a microbus to Marsa Matruh, where you'll be dropped off right next to the ticket office/bus station for West & Mid Delta Bus Co. and Go Bus.

PRIVATE CAR OR MICROBUS

Fathi Benhagar (tel. 0122 490 7806; https://siwawi.com), Siwa guide extraordinaire, can organize private transportation from Cairo. A car that holds up to 4 passengers costs 3,250LE one-way, or you can splurge on extra room and get a microbus with 14 seats for 3,500LE (the minimal price difference is because the microbus runs on diesel).

Getting Around

TUK TUK

Tuk tuks are the main form of transportation around Siwa Town and can take you almost anywhere you'd want to go, including to west to Siwa Lake and east to the Salt Mines. Pick one up in **Market Square** or ask your hotel to call one. The driver will usually be happy to stay with you for the day, but it's best to negotiate a price in advance. For longer trips, be sure to choose one with cushions (it can be a bumpy ride) and a canopy roof to protect you from the desert sun. Prices should be in the range of 400LE for 5 hours.

BIKE

In the cooler months, bikes are a great way to get around. Rent one with a lock in **Market Square** next to Albabinshal Hotel (30-50LE/day).

4WD AND PRIVATE CAR HIRE

A 4WD with driver/guide is necessary to reach the sandier parts of Siwa, including the Great Sand Sea and Lake Shiatta. You can also hire a normal car (with driver) for longer trips around the outskirts of the town (e.g., to Taghaghien Island or the natural springs beyond the Salt Mines, Ain Qurayshat, and Abu Shuruf). Contact one of the guides listed above or ask your hotel to arrange.

LAKE SIWA (BIRKET SIWA)

Flanking Siwa's center to the west is Lake Siwa, a shallow body of saline water from irrigation runoff. Fatnas Island (actually a peninsula) is located in the lake's southeast corner, and Taghaghien Island in the north is connected to the mainland via causeway. These are some of the best places in the Siwa Oasis to watch the sunset.

Fatnas Island (Gezirat Fatnas)

This little peninsula-cum-palm grove juts into Lake Siwa. At the western tip you'll find **Hagg Omran's Cafeteria** (noon-just after sunset daily; 15LE juice), where you can enjoy a tea or fresh juice as you wait for dusk. Lake Siwa isn't the best for swimming, nor is Fatnas Spring (which looks a bit grimy), but there's plenty to entertain you on this pseudo-island. Request a performance from the café's eponymous owner, a professional storyteller (hakawati), or ask permission to collect some of the hundreds of freshly fallen dates. A paddle boat is also available for rent (100LE/hour) and a treat to take out as the sun dips beyond the horizon.

The best way to get here is by tuk tuk, which should cost around 150LE round-trip from Market Square (including 1-1.5-hour wait time). Biking is also an option, but try not to get stuck in the dark.

Taghaghien Island (Gezirat Taghaghien)

If you want to watch the sunset with a cold beer or a bottle of wine, Taghaghien Island is the place to be (it's one of the only places in town that serves alcohol). Head to **Taghaghien Island Resort Restaurant** (tel. 0120 004 3379; Info@taghaghienisland.com; 9am-10pm daily; 60-85LE mains) and sit outside for beautiful vistas over Lake Siwa to the distant mountains. Their food is good

1: Fatnas Island **2:** the Salt Mines (El-Mallahaat)

1
2

enough, with a traditional menu of grilled chicken and meat, salads, rice, and vegetables. You can take a boat ride to their surrounding islands (ask the resort to organize—should cost around 100-150LE/hour) and even camp if you wish.

A causeway connects the island to the mainland and can be reached in 25 minutes from central Siwa by car (your hotel can arrange; expect to pay around 200-250LE round-trip including wait time). Don't forget the bug spray!

TOP EXPERIENCE

★ SALT MINES (EL-MALLAHAAT)

The Middle Lakes (Buheraat el-Awsat) border Siwa Town to the east, sliced down the center with a rocky road that leads to the super-saline pools of the Salt Mines (locally known as el-Mallahaat). This patchwork of blinding turquoise waters is formed by ongoing mining of the crystalline mineral—dug out by massive excavators and bulldozers. Fortunately, the area is large enough for visitors to steer clear of the machinery and enjoy the silence of the pools they leave behind.

You can't help but float in these crystal-clear waters surrounded by snow-white salt in lieu of sand. To find the best spots for swimming, head along the gravel road that cuts through the Middle Lakes (6 km/4 mi east of central Siwa). After 6.2 kilometers (3.9 mi) you'll come across three luminous pools on your left. Jump in to cool off before continuing about 350 meters (1,100 ft) to take the first right. After 1 kilometer (0.6 mi) you'll find hills of pure white salt and larger baths to kick about in.

Don't forget plenty of water for drinking and rinsing off the salty residue. There are no toilets or establishments around, so be sure to bring snacks and come wearing your suit.

The Great Sand Sea (Bahr el-Rimaal el-A'zam)

4 km/2.5 mi south of Siwa's Market Square; 24 hours daily; 300LE entrance permit

Covering an area of around 72,000 square kilometers (27,800 sq mi), the rolling dunes of the Great Sand Sea are a stunning sight to behold. The landscape here has been meticulously shaped over millions of years by nature's forceful winds, which have arranged the piles of sand in nearly perfect rows. To the untrained eye, the majestic dunes have a disorienting sameness, but local Siwis learn the terrain as children and navigate their home's sandy surroundings as if traversing a grid plan, using the dunes themselves, the sun, the stars, and the moon.

Many of the dunes are over 100 meters (330 ft) high and 100 kilometers (62 mi) long, making for a fun drive through the dramatic scenery. The shorter hills are perfect for sandboarding (or sand sledding if you prefer to start your descent closer to the ground)—best enjoyed during the desert's golden hour just before sunset.

You can hike to the Great Sand Sea, or visit on a 4WD desert safari. Either way, you'll need a guide.

SIGHTS

Just a few patches of water spot the vast expanse of desert that makes up the Great Sand Sea, with the **Bir Wahed Cold Lake** and **Hot Spring** just around 12 kilometers (7 mi) southwest of central Siwa. According to locals, a foreign oil company found the underground water source in the 1980s. Lucky for us all, instead of oil pumps we get to enjoy these healing pools open to the public (free of charge with your entrance ticket to the Great Sand Sea).

BIR WAHED COLD LAKE

Reeds and tall grasses line the Bir Wahed ("Well No. 1") Cold Lake, where schools of small fish swim near the shore, eager to be fed. It's really more of a large pond than a lake, with the deepest sections around 2 meters (6 ft)—still impressive considering its location in the middle of the desert. The crisp, clear water is a nice place to cool off mid-safari.

BIR WAHED HOT SPRING

A natural hot spring pours into this large tub, surrounded by palm trees and golden sand. Its sulphureous waters are a perfect 37°C (98°F), with all the minerals' healing properties sans eggy odor that sometimes comes along with them. The spot is a special place to enjoy dusk after watching the sunset from the nearby hill.

TOP EXPERIENCE

★ DESERT SAFARIS

A 4WD desert safari into the Great Sand Sea is a must. The fabulous undulating landscape is a destination in itself, but typical itineraries also include a visit to the Cold Lake, Bir Wahed Hot Spring, sandboarding (accessible for beginners and children; your guide should bring everything you need), and a desert barbecue under the stars. **Youssef Dahman** (tel. 0100 615 4383) and **Fathi Benhagar** (tel. 0122 490 7806 or 01096830728; https://siwawi.com) are two of Siwa's best driver/guides. **Youssef Sarhan** (tel. 0122 305 3314; ysfsiwa@gmail.com) also organizes nice outings and can offer a complimentary tour of his date syrup factory. Alternatively, you can arrange a trip through your hotel or at Abdo Restaurant. Prices should be in the range of 1,400LE for a day trip with 4WD (seats up to 5; price of the vehicle doesn't change regardless of the number in your party), plus 300LE per person for ticket entrance to the protected area. Camping in the open desert or at Fathi's Astro Siwa campgrounds are also options.

CAMPING

All guides can organize camping under the stars in a private patch of the desert as part of your safari. If you prefer to stay at a permanent campground (with other campers), head to Siwa Astro Camp.

SIWA ASTRO CAMP

10.5 km/6.5 mi southeast of central Siwa; tel. 0122 490 7806; https://siwawi.com; 300LE d

If you want to camp in the Great Sand Sea but prefer to have access to a bathroom and a kitchen, Fathi Benhgar's Astro Camp is the place to stay. The tents are clean and comfortable and protected by a rocky hill that provides shade during (some of) the day. Still, one night under the stars here is probably enough as the days can get unbearably hot. Price includes breakfast and transportation by 4WD from central Siwa to the desert camp.

LAKE SHIATTA (BUHERAT SHIATTA)

50 km/30 mi northwest of central Siwa; 24 hours daily; free

Travelers looking to spend more time in the desert can start their 4WD safari a day early with a trip to Lake Shiatta, a lonely salt lake north of the Great Sand Sea. Lucky visitors might spot flamingos and other migratory birds who break here, or just enjoy a secluded swim in this ancient lake surrounded by shrubs and mini mountains in the distance. In pharaonic times, this patch of water likely connected to Lake Siwa and reached all the way to today's downtown.

History

Humans have inhabited the land that is modern Egypt since at least 55,000 BC. It wasn't until around 5500 BC that some of these prehistoric hunter-gathers started to settle down to farm. **Fayoum's** fertile land with its fish-filled Lake Moeris (now known as Lake Qarun), fed by a natural waterway off the Nile, became the spot of choice for Egypt's first agricultural communities. And by 5000 BC, people began to set up camp along the Nile itself.

Heliopolis (modern northeast Cairo) emerged around 4200 BC as home to the cult of the sun god Re, and would continue to serve as an important religious center well into the Roman period. In the southern city of **Abydos,** another important cult center from predynastic days, scribes recorded Egypt's first known text around 3250 BC—among the earliest writing in the world.

Ancient Civilization

EGYPTIAN AND NUBIAN RULE (3000 BC-525 BC)

Early Dynastic Period

The origin of ancient Egypt begins with the origin of recorded history, around 3000 BC. It was then that King Menes united the regional capitals scattered throughout Upper and Lower Egypt to create what some call the first ever nation-state. He chose a spot at the base of the Delta to establish his new capital **Memphis**—earlier called Ankh-tawy, or "That which Binds the Two Lands."

The legacy of this once glorious city, mostly erased by floods and time, is best seen today in its sprawling Memphite necropolises. The pyramids at **Saqqara, Dahshur,** and **Giza** are all sacred burial spots for the pharaohs and high-ranking officials who ruled from Memphis during the Early Dynastic Period and Old Kingdom.

Old Kingdom (c. 2575-2150 BC)

Saqqara, directly west of Memphis on the desert's edge, became the new capital's royal burial site. It's here King Zoser built his **Step Pyramid** (c. 2665 BC)—the precursor to the more famous pyramids to come.

The pharaohs of the 4th Dynasty, also known as the Golden Age of the Old Kingdom, chose new patches of desert to lay their bones. Snefru headed south to what's now known as **Dahshur** to build Egypt's first true pyramid, the **Red Pyramid** (c. 2600 BC), as well as an earlier attempt, the **Bent Pyramid** with its rounded sides. Snefru's son and successor, Khufu, sent workers many miles north to the virgin Giza Plateau to construct his monumental resting place, the **Great Pyramid of Giza** (c. 2560 BC). Khufu's son and grandson, Khafre and Menkaure, each built another sky-scraping burial spot here.

That such grand tombs were built so early in Egyptian history and never again surpassed in size or precision is testament to how advanced the 4th Dynasty kings and their architects were. The massive monuments also demonstrate the extent to which power was concentrated in the hands of the pharaohs—a phenomenon that would be undone by the end of the Old Kingdom.

First Intermediate Period (c. 2125-1975 BC)

The First Intermediate Period was marked by power struggles and famine. Kings lost control over the country and local governors took the opportunity to expand their rule. Tensions ran particularly high between power centers in Upper and Lower Egypt—namely, at Thebes (modern Luxor) in the south and Herakleopolis (near Fayoum) in the north. Although many historians describe this period as anarchic, other material finds suggest there was still a good amount of prosperity in some of the provinces (nomes).

Middle Kingdom (c. 2000-1640 BC)

Around 1970 BC the ruler of Upper Egypt, **Mentuhotep II** (r. 2010-1960 BC), triumphed over his northern counterparts and reunited the country—inaugurating the Middle Kingdom. He moved the royal residence to **Thebes** (modern Luxor), which also became the country's religious capital, home to the cult of Amun ("the hidden one" or "king of the gods").

Amenemhet I (r. 1938-1908), a local administrator from Thebes, founded the 12th Dynasty and moved the royal residence back

Previous: The Red Pyramid in Dahshur was Egypt's first true pyramid.

north to the Memphite area to help hold the country together. His son, **Senusret I** (r. 1918-1874 BC), ruled alongside him for the last decade and helped usher in the Middle Kingdom's Golden Age—expanding Egypt's borders deep into Nubia (modern Sudan) through military conquests. The king exploited the region's gold and other mineral wealth to finance major building projects across Egypt, including the **"White Chapel"** in Thebes—the oldest structure uncovered at the **Karnak Temple Complex.** Senusret I also began the trend of replacing older mud-brick cult temples with durable stone, and built a string of fortresses along newly captured Nubian territory (lost under Lake Nasser since the building of the High Dam in the 1960s).

His grandson, **Senusret II** (r. 1844-1837 BC), turned his attention to **Fayoum** in the north, commissioning the first canal in the area to expand the land available for farming. He was buried after a relatively short reign at his **Lahun Pyramid** just outside Fayoum, now reduced to a sand-covered mound. The pharaoh's son and successor, **Senusret III,** enjoyed a much longer rule—making enemies along the way as he reconsolidated power and reduced the privileges of the governors (nomarchs) around the country. In the foreign policy realm, he expanded the territorial gains of his great-grandfather through violent campaigns into Nubia.

Senusret III's son, **Amenemhet III** (r. 1818-1770 BC), by contrast presided over a relatively peaceful period. He expanded his predecessors' agricultural and monumental building projects—especially keen on following in his grandfather's footsteps to enrich lush Fayoum. Through additional irrigation schemes, he transformed even more of the area into fertile farmland, and founded the city **Medinet Maadi** in the nearby desert to host a beautiful sandstone temple dedicated to the cobra goddess Renenutet and the crocodile god Sobek. Amenemhet III's sacred burial place, the **Hawara Pyramid,** was once a marvel of the ancient world with a sprawling mortuary temple and thousands of chambers. He had to abandon an earlier attempt in Dahshur (the **Black Pyramid**), when it began to crumble due to structural flaws.

Sobeknefru, daughter of Amenemhet III, became the first fully fledged female pharaoh on record and continued to rule over a thriving Egypt. Her father named her after one of his most revered gods and the symbol of royal strength, the crocodile god Sobek.

The final dynasty (13th) of the Middle Kingdom was characterized by a quick turnover in leadership, with more than 60 pharaohs wearing the crown over the next 150 years or so. The country continued to enjoy peace and prosperity for much of this period, but by the end of it, the land had again fallen into divisions between Upper and Lower Egypt.

Second Intermediate Period (c. 1630-1520 BC)

While local governors stole power from the pharaohs during the First Intermediate Period, the second major interruption to Egypt's unified rule was characterized by foreign encroachments. The **Nubians** (the Kingdom of Kush) gained strength in the south and allied with the Hyksos from Western Asia, who dominated the Delta. Native Egyptian rule shrank to its last stronghold in Thebes. This state of affairs lasted for around a century before the kings of Thebes managed to reverse their fortunes, retake Nubia, and expel the Hyksos.

New Kingdom (c.1520-1075 BC)

AHMOSE

Military-general-turned-pharaoh Ahmose (r. 1539-1514 BC) led the charge into the Hyksos heartland, forcing them out of the Delta and back into the Levant. His troops used the momentum to take new territory in modern Syria, all the way to the Euphrates River. But first, they headed south to reconquer Nubia and its overflowing gold mines. Egypt was unified once again, its major sources of wealth restored, and the New Kingdom—said to be the Golden Age of all Egyptian history—commenced.

Thebes, birthplace of the 18th Dynasty and heroes of Egypt's War of Independence, took a commensurate status and enjoyed the zenith of its affluence and power during this period. We owe most of the stunning tombs and temples in modern Luxor to the next four centuries of prosperity.

AHMOSE-NEFERTARI AND AMENHOTEP I

When Ahmose died, his sister-wife Ahmose-Nefertari ruled as regent for their young son, Amenhotep I. They worked to reunify the country politically and culturally once the dust settled from the wars and were worshiped as deities for centuries after their deaths. Nowhere was devotion for them greater than at the workers village of **Deir el-Medina** (on modern Luxor's West Bank). These artisans would fashion the first resting places in the **Valley of the Kings,** which either the mother-son pair or their successor, Thutmose I, consecrated as new the royal burial grounds, protected by the undulating hills outside Thebes.

THUTMOSE I

When Amenhotep I died young and without an heir, Thutmose I (born to an unknown father and commoner mother) took the crown. Known as a great warrior king, Thutmose I pushed Egypt's borders even deeper into Nubia and the Levant—the first Egyptian ruler to extend his reach past the Euphrates. With his riches from war, he built temples around the country, lavishing particular attention on his hometown, Thebes, and its cult center to Amun at the modern **Karnak Temple Complex.** Here he erected imposing pylons, columns, and granite obelisks to the increasingly grand structure.

HATSHEPSUT AND THUTMOSE III

Prolific in his offspring, Thutmose I's most important progeny was his eldest daughter, Hatshepsut, who took the position of high priestess and God's Wife in the Temple of Amun in Karnak. She married her brother, King Thutmose II, whose reign proved short and unimpressive. When he died, his toddler son of another wife, Thutmose III, became king (Hatshepsut producing no male heir). But rather than have the child's mother serve as regent per tradition, the Theban elites rallied around Hatshepsut to assume the post. After a few years as substitute ruler for the child king (her stepson/nephew), she took on the full title of pharaoh—fitting for her leadership, which she performed over a stable and prosperous Egypt.

For the first time since Sobeknefru reigned as pharaoh queen at the end of the 12th Dynasty, Egypt came under the control of a woman. Hatshepsut, like her successful predecessors, inaugurated a temple building spree, adding layers to Amun's cult center (**Karnak**) with pylons, grand obelisks, and new chambers for sacred rituals. It was here that the first image of Hatshepsut as King of Upper and Lower Egypt would appear, the young leader donning a sleek dress and a headdress of ram horns and two ostrich plumes.

During her 20-some years as pharaoh, she also built temples north along the Nile, often in honor of her favorite goddesses like the lion-headed Pakhet and sky goddess Hathor to whom the rock-cut tomb of **Speos Artemidos** at Beni Hasan is dedicated. Hatshepsut and Thutmose III likely laid some of the first stones at the **Luxor Temple** when they built a small temple to the "Theban Triad"; and they built a temple for Amun on the West Bank of Thebes at **Medinet Habu.** But Hatshepsut's nearby mortuary temple (**Temple of Hatshepsut**) would be her grandest building achievement.

Hatshepsut continued to reign as pharaoh even when her stepson/nephew came of age (once a divine king, always a divine king) at which point they ruled together. While Thutmose III led military campaigns in the Levant, Hatshepsut consolidated her rule in Nubia. More importantly, she traded with her

Timeline of Ancient Egyptian History

Ancient Egyptians marked years based on the reigns of pharaohs (e.g., year 10 of Ramses II) and by astronomical observations, making exact dating difficult for modern historians. In the 3rd century BC, an Egyptian high priest/historian named Manetho created the dynastic system, dividing ancient Egypt into around 30 dynasties largely based on changes in ruling families. These dynasties were then divided into three kingdoms, each succeeded by an "intermediate period" that marked years of disunity. (Note: Because of the difficulties in determining exact dates, estimated years for events and the birth/death of pharaohs often vary between publications by as much as a century.)

The following timeline shows the approximate breakdown of dates and dynasties (still used today), highlighting some of Egypt's most important pharaohs who will likely reappear during your travels.

EARLY DYNASTIC PERIOD: DYNASTIES 1-2 (C. 3000-2710 BC)

- **Menes (c. 3000 BC):** First king to unify Egypt

OLD KINGDOM: DYNASTIES 3-6 (C. 2710-2181 BC)

- **Zoser** (r. 2691-2625 BC): Built the Step Pyramid in Saqqara

Dynasty 4: Golden Age of the Old Kingdom:

- **Snefru** (r. 2600-2575 BC): Built the Red and Bent Pyramids in Dahshur and Meidum Pyramid
- **Khufu** (r. 2575-2552 BC): Snefru's son; built the Great Pyramid of Giza
- **Khafre** (r. 2542-2516 BC): Khufu's son; built the second largest pyramid in Giza
- **Menkaure** (r. 2512-2494 BC): Khafre's son; built the third largest pyramid in Giza

FIRST INTERMEDIATE PERIOD: DYNASTIES 7-10 (C. 2175-2010 BC)

MIDDLE KINGDOM: DYNASTIES 11-13 (C. 2010-1640 BC)

- **Mentuhotep II** (r. 2010-1960 BC): Rreunited Egypt and moved the capital to Thebes (Luxor)

Dynasty 12: Golden Age of the Middle Kingdom:

- **Amenemhet I** (r. 1938-1908 BC)
- **Senusret I** (r. 1918-1874 BC): Expanded territory into Nubia and Western Desert
- **Senusret II** (r. 1844-1837 BC)
- **Senusret III** (r. 1837-1800 BC)
- **Amenemhet III** (r. 1818-1770 BC)

SECOND INTERMEDIATE PERIOD: DYNASTIES 14-17 (C. 1630-1539 BC)

NEW KINGDOM: GOLDEN AGE OF ANCIENT EGYPT, DYNASTIES 18-20 (C. 1539-1070 BC)

Dynasty 18:

- **Ahmose** (r. 1539-1514 BC): Reunified Egypt after expelling the Hyksos
- **Amenhotep I** (r. 1514-1494 BC): Son of Ahmose
- **Thutmose I** (r. 1493-1482 BC)
- **Queen Hatshepsut** (r. 1473-1458 BC): Daughter of Thutmose I
- **Thutmose III** (r. 1479-1425 BC): Hatshepsut's stepson/nephew
- **Amenhotep II** (r. 1425-1400 BC)
- **Amenhotep III** (r. 1390-1353 BC)
- **Akhenaten,** originally **Amenhotep IV** (r. 1353-1335 BC): Married to Queen Nefertiti (c. 1370-1330)
- **Tutankhamun** (r. 1335-1327 BC): Son of Akhenaten
- **Horemheb** (r. 1319-1292 BC): General and advisor of Tutankhamun

Dynasty 19:

- **Ramses I** (r. 1292-1290 BC)
- **Seti I** (r. 1290-1279 BC)
- **Ramses II** (r. 1279-1213 BC): Married to Queen Nefertari (c. 1300-1255 BC)
- **Tawosret** (r. 1189-1187 BC): Last female pharaoh of Egyptian origin

Dynasty 20:

- **Ramses III** (r. 1187-1156 BC)

THIRD INTERMEDIATE PERIOD: DYNASTIES 21-24 (C. 1070-715 BC)

LATE PERIOD: DYNASTIES 25-30 (C. 715-332 BC)

Dynasty 25:

- **Nubian rulers** (r. 715-665 BC)

Dynasty 27:

- **Persian rulers** (r. 525-404 BC)

Dynasty 30:

- **Nectanebo II** (r. 360-343 BC): Last native king before Persian, Greek, and Roman rule

neighbors, bringing a wealth of exotic goods from Punt (likely modern Somalia), especially myrrh—much-cherished for its fragrance, healing properties, and essential role in the embalming process.

When Hatshepsut passed into the afterlife, Thutmose III finally took center stage. The warrior king extended Egypt's borders farther than ever before, capturing land well over the Euphrates River into modern Syria and south into the Land of Gold (Nubia). He poured his spoils of war into the Temple of Amun at **Karnak,** adding more obelisks, pylons, buildings, and engravings—particularly of his conquests. Thutmose III's built another mortuary temple (now reduced to ruins) next to Hatshepsut's and reappropriated hers, carving images of his father over those of his late stepmother.

This period toward the end of Thutmose III's rule also marked the start of a concerted campaign to wipe out his late co-regent's images as pharaoh—possibly in attempts to secure his son's claim to the throne instead of someone from the long-standing royal bloodline that ran through the pharaoh queen.

AMENHOTEP II

Amenhotep II (r. 1425-1400 BC), Thutmose III's son, did indeed succeed his father and emulated his military victories, quelling uprisings in Syria and maintaining Egypt's newfound empire. To balance the power of the Theban priests of Amun (so favored under Hatshepsut's reign), Amenhotep II foregrounded the sun god, Re, along with Re's clergy based in his northern cult center at Heliopolis. Amun had already long been worshiped as Amun-Re—the blended form of the two gods—in Thebes, but under Amenhotep II, this latter manifestation would take even greater prominence. The king took the title "ruler of Heliopolis," harkening back to Old Kingdom greats who built the famed pyramids at Giza and were called "Sons of Re." He was also the first king to bring the sun disc god, Aten, to the fore, which his great grandson, Akhenaten, would transform into the nation's central god in his religious revolution.

THUTMOSE IV

The great **Sphinx** at the Giza plateau spoke to the young Thutmose IV (grandson of Thutmose III) in a dream, bestowing on him divine kingship—a marked departure from the time of Hatshepsut when Amun (communicating through the Theban priests) determined who would next rule. The young king embellished both the cult center of the sun god Re at Heliopolis and the Temple of Amun at Karnak to keep the two gods (and their clergies) content.

AMENHOTEP III

Amenhotep III (r. 1390-1353 BC), son of Thutmose IV, ruled over nearly four decades of peace and prosperity. With few battles to fight, he used his free time to commission epic building projects, especially in Thebes, earning the title Menwy, or "Monument Man." The **Colossi of Memnon** on the West Bank stand as a reminder of how grand his mortuary temple once was—the largest ever built in Egypt, though almost entirely destroyed by an earthquake in antiquity. The nearby **Deir el-Medina** workers village more than doubled in size during his reign to accommodate the artisans needed to decorate his temples, tombs, and royal palace—the latter relocated from Memphis and unconventionally placed on the West Bank ("Land of the Dead"). And we owe much of **Luxor Temple** to his efforts, where the king paid tribute to Amun-Re.

Under Amenhotep III, who took the throne name "Re, Lord of Truth," the privileging of Heliopolis's gods continued. The sun god Re and warrior goddess Sakhmet ("destroyer of the enemies of Re") enjoyed increased favor. The king became Re's manifestation on earth and commissioned hundreds of statues of Sakhmet—the sleek part woman, part lioness—for his mortuary temple on the West Bank and in **Mut's Temple** across the river in **Karnak.** He also built the first temple to the sun disc god, Aten, in Heliopolis. But the pharaoh, ruling from Thebes, was still wise to show his piety toward the Theban patron god, Amun, albeit in the form of Amun-Re, most notably at the grand **Luxor Temple.**

AKHENATEN AND NEFERTITI

Amenhotep III's son and successor, Amenhotep IV (r. 1353-1337 BC), worked to undo the long-standing national worship of Amun-Re—ushering in the most radical period in ancient Egyptian culture and earning the moniker the "heretic king." First named after his royal predecessors and indeed Amun himself, Amenhotep IV ("Amun is Satisfied") changed his name after five years as pharaoh to Akhenaten ("Beneficial to Aten") in honor of the sun disc god. He grew up in Heliopolis, the cult center of the sun god, and perhaps owing to this early exposure to the preeminence of sun worship, inaugurated a religious revolution characterized by the near monotheistic devotion to *the* Aten as the god was later called. Not only did Akhenaten favor Aten over Amun (or Amun-Re), but he even led a campaign of destruction against images of the latter—heretic indeed.

The King's revolutionary ideas reverberated beyond religion into art and architecture. The **Amarna style**—named after the capital that Akhenaten built 200 miles north of Thebes, **Tell el-Amarna**—decorated the temples of his new city with the sun disc god shining rays of light (terminating in small hands) on Akhenaten and his famous queen of legendary beauty, Nefertiti. Human depictions took a unique style as well, with characteristic features including conical heads, curvy hips and thighs (even for the king himself), and chubby bellies in place of the rock-hard abs of his royal ancestors.

Images of Nefertiti suggest she was much more than Akhenaten's beloved queen, commanding great authority within the court and even shown smiting enemies—a depiction previously enjoyed only by pharaohs. Indeed, it's widely believed that Nefertiti ruled briefly as pharaoh (r. 1337-1335 BC) after Akhenaten's death, and during his tenure she enjoyed the elevated status of co-ruler.

Akhenaten's mother (Amenhotep III's main wife), Queen Tiye, also played an important role in her son's court as she had in her husband's. A woman of noted intelligence and diplomatic skill, she beseeched early allies in the Levant and Mesopotamia to continue their friendship with her son and maintain the lucrative peace. These correspondences and many others were found in a cache of clay tablets in Tell el-Amarna, later dubbed the **Amarna Letters,** that offer invaluable insight into ancient international relations in the region.

TUTANKHAMUN

Perhaps Egypt's most famous pharaoh—far more widely known than his radical father—Tutankhamun (r. 1335-1327 BC), aka King Tut, ascended the throne soon after Akhenaten's death when he was still a child. His fame comes less from deeds during life than from fate after death—the entrance to his tomb in the **Valley of the Kings** was buried under fallen rocks and hidden from the sticky fingers of tomb raiders for millennia. The boy king's opulent treasures for the afterlife captured the imagination of the Western world when they went on tour in the 1960s and '70s after being unearthed a few decades earlier (in 1922).

Following the advice of his counsels, the young Tutankhaten (or "Living Image of Aten," as he was named by his father) undid much of Akhenaten's legacy. He changed his name to Tutankhamun ("Living Image of Amun"), abandoned his father's experimental new capital and cult center for Aten, and relocated to the administrative capital, **Memphis.** With the country's clergies split, its people suffering economically, and the Hittites (a strong empire in modern Turkey) threatening Egypt's northern borders, there was a need for national unity. Tutankhamun worked to rehabilitate the old gods (and their priests), particularly Amun, while reintegrating Aten as a god among many.

HOREMHEB

Horemheb (r. 1319-1292 BC), military commander and advisor to King Tut, ascended the throne as last king of the 18th Dynasty. He had been away at war to recover the northern reaches of Egypt's empire when the young King Tut died, and the Egyptian military (along with the priests of Amun) supported his rise to divine kingship. **Karnak** regained its former prestige, and Horemheb added even more pylons to Amun's main cult center while dismantling the temples to the sun disc god built by Akhenaten. Not of royal blood himself, he was sure to depict himself as both regal and godly, sitting, for example, beside Amun-Re, Sobek, and other favored deities at his rock-cut temple, **Great Speos,** along the Nile at **Gebel el-Silsila.** Horemheb also carved his name over those of his immediate predecessors, the young King Tut and Queen Tiye's brother Ay, erasing them from the official king list and claiming their modest achievements as his own. His death marked the end of the long and prosperous 18th Dynasty, but there were still more great kings to come.

RAMSES I AND SETI I

Ramses I (r. 1292-1290 BC), Horemheb's successor and founder of the 19th Dynasty, also rose to prominence as a military leader and later, the king's trusted vizier. Already advanced in age by the time he became pharaoh, Ramses I soon made his son Seti I (r. 1290-1279 BC) co-regent. The father directed his attention to Thebes, decorating Horemheb's pylons at **Karnak** and building part of the colonnaded hall there, while his son advanced Egypt's interests through military campaigns in the Levant.

Ramses I died after just two years as pharaoh and Seti I built them both a "mansion of millions of years" (**Mortuary Temple of Seti I**) on the West Bank of Thebes dedicated to themselves and Amun. Honoring Osiris, god of the afterlife, Seti I built yet another grand mortuary temple in **Abydos (Temple of Seti I).** But more striking yet was his **Great Hypostyle Hall** in Amun's Temple at **Karnak** with over 130 towering papyrus columns. All were decorated with the delicate raised reliefs for which his artisans were famed. His artists also demonstrated their skills in the warrior king's tomb—one of the most vibrant resting places in the **Valley of the Kings (KV 17).**

RAMSES II

Ramses II (r. 1279-1213), Seti I's son, reigned next for nearly 70 years. After occasional fighting with the Hittites over the first 20 years of his rule, the two great powers signed a peace treaty, leaving Ramses II free to fend off invading Libyans who preferred the Delta to their sandier homes.

When not at war, Ramses II's long rule gave him plenty of time for his prolific building projects. His favorite object to be artistically rendered seems to have been his own image—particularly in massive form. His colossi were unearthed across the country, the most notable ones now found in the **Grand Egyptian Museum, Memphis Complex, Karnak Temple Complex, Luxor Temple,** and **Abu Simbel.** Ramses II completed his father's unfinished work like decorating the **Great Hypostyle Hall** at **Karnak** and his mortuary temples in **Thebes** and **Abydos.** Nearby each of his father's "mansions for millions of years," Ramses II built one for himself—his main mortuary temple, the **Ramesseum,** on the West Bank in Thebes dedicated to Amun and the **Temple of Ramses II** in **Abydos** honoring Osiris.

Ramses II did embellish Amun's temple at **Karnak,** but perhaps because he felt this northern hub was becoming too cluttered, he headed to the "Southern Sanctuary" (**Luxor Temple**) to add his not-so-understated touch there. Along with colossi of himself, he erected obelisks and the sprawling column-lined courtyard. Up in the administrative capital of **Memphis,** he decorated the grand temple of the patron god of Memphis, Ptah (little remains save Ramses II's limestone statue), and his son, a priest of Ptah, expanded the original burial sites for the sacred Apis bulls in Saqqara to create the labyrinthine **Serapeum** in **Saqqara.**

But Ramses II's most magnificent architectural project was the **Abu Simbel Temples** built for himself and his favored wife, Nefertari, to project their power over their Nubian subjects in the south. He buried his beloved in the **Valley of the Queens (Tomb of Nefertari),** the shining jewel in this corner of the Theban hills.

MERENPTAH AND TAWOSRET

With his handful of preferred wives, including a couple of Hittite princesses, and a harem full of consorts, Ramses II produced some 100 children. His son, Merenptah, was already advanced in age when he ascended the throne and reigned for 10 successful years. But succession feuds among Ramses II's grandsons and regional power struggles among their courts led to a period of unrest and civil war. Adding to the tumult, "Sea Peoples"—or migrants coming from the north likely due to droughts and famine—had begun invading the Delta, making an alliance with the Libyans who had long wanted to claim the fertile patch of land as their own.

A granddaughter of Ramses II, Tawosret (r. 1189-1187 BC), stepped up in this turbulent period to rule in place of a young and sickly king (possibly her stepson), and eventually became full pharaoh herself—the final ruler of the 19th Dynasty and the last female ruler of Egypt for nearly a millennium.

RAMSES III

Ramses III (r. 1187-1156 BC) was the last notable king of the New Kingdom. He defended the Delta from a wave of invading Libyans and the continuing onslaught of Sea Peoples who came with ever greater force after the fall of the Hittite Empire. Although the state's coffers held far less gold than they did during the previous two dynasties, Ramses III still added more layers to **Karnak** like **Ramses III's Temple** branching off the Temple of Amun. He built his mortuary temple at **Medinet Habu** on the West Bank of Thebes and converted it into a fortified city. Like his immediate predecessors, the king economized by recycling the fallen mortuary temple of Amenhotep III (behind the **Colossi of Memnon**) to build much of his works.

Ramses III's eight successors of the 20th Dynasty all took the name Ramses, harkening back to "Ramses the Great" (Ramses II) and his long and prosperous rule. But the name

carved columns of the Great Hypostyle Hall in Karnak Temple Complex

alone could not return the kings to Egypt's Golden Age, and the next century was marked by declining power of the pharaohs and increasing authority of the Karnak priests. Egypt's great empire crumbled. At home, food prices increased, the state failed to pay employees on time, Libyans made sporadic incursions, and tomb raiders scoured the Theban hills for treasure. Seeing the tombs of their predecessors violently dismantled in the **Valley of the Kings,** the last pharaohs of the New Kingdom abandoned the sacred burial grounds. Meanwhile, skilled workers whose predecessors lived in **Deir el-Medina** for some 500 years fled to the fortified city of **Medinet Habu.**

Third Intermediate Period (c. 1075-715 BC)

Again, Egypt fell into disunity with the high priests of Amun in Thebes controlling the south, and kings ruling over the north from a new capital in the east Delta called Tanis. By this time, Egyptian royals had begun to employ Libyan mercenaries to help fight their battles, and some of the favored generals eventually rose to the rank of pharaoh. Libyans ruled Egypt for the next 200-some years (the 22nd and 23rd Dynasties; 945-712 BC), taking control of the country from the inside as intimates of the fractured kings. But these Libyan pharaohs proved equally fragmented. A new power center in the western Delta called Sais sprang up, with more Libyan princes vying for control of the country and multiple petty kings ruling at the same time for much of this period.

Late Period (c. 715-332 BC)

NUBIAN DYNASTY

Long subjugated by their northern neighbors, the Kingdom of Kush took advantage of local power struggles to conquer southern Egypt, inaugurating the 25th Dynasty and the start of the Late Period. **King Piye** (r. 743-712 BC) claimed Thebes as his capital and was named pharaoh of Egypt and Nubia. He appointed his sister, **Amenirdis I,** God's Wife of Amun at **Karnak,** and she ruled Upper Egypt in his stead while he was away.

When the Libyan royals in the Delta headed south to confront the Nubian invaders, Piye and his troops crushed their offensive, pushing all the way to Memphis. All of Egypt now came under Nubian rule—the Libyan princes in the Delta serving as mere vassals of King Piye, who moved back to his beloved homeland in the south.

Taharqa (r. 690-664 BC), son of King Piye, ruled over more than a decade of prosperity from his royal palace in Memphis. But trouble was brewing again to the north, this time from the rising power of Assyria (modern Iraq).

When the Assyrians invaded Egypt in 674 BC, Taharqa's well-trained troops turned them away. But a few years later they returned to sack Memphis, and subsequent invasions sent Taharqa all the way back to Nubia. His nephew and successor, **Tantamen** (r. 664-656 BC), regained territory briefly, before the Assyrians returned with a vengeance, plundered Thebes's gold-soaked temples, and expelled the kings of Kush from Egypt once and for all.

SAITE AND PERSIAN DYNASTIES

With rebellion back in Babylon (modern Iraq), the Assyrian troops moved east, appointing **Psamtik I** (r. 664-610 BC), a Libyan prince from Sais, as their vassal king. Psamtik I reunited the country and sent his daughter, Nitocris, to keep an eye on Thebes as God's Wife of Amun in **Karnak.** For his military campaigns, he became the first king to employ Greek mercenaries—a trend that continued for the next 300 years and forebode future Greek rule over Egypt.

But first, it was the Persians' turn. After around a century of successfully defending their borders against kingdoms in the Levant and Nubia, the kings from Sais (the Saite Dynasty) fell to the Persian **King Cambyses** in 525 BC. The new pharaoh ruled from Memphis for just a few years, but his countrymen would control Egypt as a province of their empire for most of a century (Dynasty 27; 525-404 BC).

Darius (r. 522-486 BC) came next, developing trade routes to facilitate the flow of Egyptian treasures to his capital, Persepolis (in modern Iran). He completed a canal linking the Nile to the Red Sea and began the widespread use of camels laden with goods to traverse new desert paths.

Revolts popped up across the sprawling Persian Empire, first in Greece, then Egypt. **Xerxes** (r. 486-465 BC), Darius's son, crushed the rebellions before the Greeks managed to free themselves, again followed by the Egyptians. But Egypt's independence lasted for less than a decade, and the Persians regained control for the next 50 years.

It was a prince from Sais who again stole back Egypt in 404 BC while the Persians were busy with uprisings across their empire. The country then came under the control of a string of rulers from the Delta who continued to defend their territory from the Persians with the help of Greek mercenaries.

A military general, **Nectanebo I** (r. 380-362 BC), declared himself pharaoh, ruling over a period of relative stability. During his reign, the arts began to flourish once more and he returned to the embellishment of Theban temples that were long neglected—building the outermost pylon at **Karnak** and the **Avenue of Sphinxes** leading between Karnak and the **Luxor Temple,** among other projects across the country.

His son, **Teos** (r. 362-360 BC), enjoyed a much shorter reign—forced off the throne when he raised taxes and slashed the priests' financial benefits bestowed on them by his father. **Nectanebo II** (r. 360-343 BC), Nectanebo I's grandson, took over—ruling as the last native Egyptian king. He reinstated the clergies' economic privileges and initiated a building campaign not seen in Egypt for nearly a millennium. Construction boomed across the country from **Philae Island** in the south (Aswan)—where he built the first known temple (**Hall of Nectanebo**)—to Tanis in the north and just about every major settlement in between.

But after nearly two decades on the throne, Nectanebo II ultimately fell to the Persians who occupied Egypt once again. A Persian governor ruled from Memphis, while religious centers—like the much-revered Heliopolis (in modern Cairo)—were burned and plundered.

GREEK, ROMAN, AND BYZANTINE RULE (332 BC-641 AD)

Another decade of Persian pillage paved the way for the warm welcome of Macedonian King **Alexander the Great** (r. 332-323 BC) who entered Egypt in 332 BC and defeated the sacrilegious invaders. Unlike the Persians, Alexander embraced Egyptian culture and even trekked across the Western Desert to the **Temple of the Oracle** in the Siwa Oasis—the first pharaoh to make the visit—to confirm his divine rule after the priests crowned him in Memphis. He commissioned the building of new sanctuaries in Thebes at **Karnak** and the **Luxor Temple,** where the divine Pharaoh Alexander gets wall space beside Amun.

The young king's time in Egypt was brief (he had empires to conquer!), but before he set off again for war, he picked a spot on the Mediterranean for a new city that would take his name and emulate his greatness, **Alexandria.**

Upon Alexander's death in 323 BC, his military officers divvied up the late emperor's sprawling territory and **Ptolemy I** (r. 304-284 BC) headed to Egypt. Power struggles between Alexander's successors devolved into war. But Ptolemy I held onto his share of empire tightly and governed in alliance with local priests, eventually becoming full pharaoh in 304 BC and inaugurating a dynasty that would last for nearly 300 years.

Ptolemaic Period (304-30 BC)

Ptolemy II (r. 285-246 BC) ascended the throne alongside his father, and then ruled alone for just a few years before marrying his older sister, **Arsinoe II** (r. 278-270 BC)—sharing with her the throne and the title of pharaoh. They continued the work started by their father, most famously the Great

Library of Alexandria and the Lighthouse of Alexandria (one of the Seven Wonders of the Ancient World)—each the most glorious of its kind ever known. Alexandria was now the royal capital of the Ptolemaic Kingdom, and the wealth from the pair's prosperous rule poured in to adorn it.

In **Fayoum,** the royal couple promoted Greco-Macedonian settlements alongside Egyptian villages, best seen today in the ruins at **Karanis** and **Qasr Qarun** on either side of Lake Qarun. They followed the irrigation schemes of Middle Kingdom pharaohs, expanding the land available for grape growing (among other staples) to sate the increased demand spurred on by the Greek settlers' wine habits. At the southern border of their kingdom on the **Island of Philae** in Aswan, they built the grand **Temple of Isis**—dedicated to the Egyptian goddess of protection and motherhood and to the Pharaoh Queen Arsinoe II, worshiped around the country as Isis herself.

When Ptolemy II's son, **Ptolemy III** (r. 246-222 BC), became king, he followed his father's example of taking a powerful queen as his partner, marrying his cousin, **Berenice II,** ruler of Cyrene (Libya). They reigned together for the next quarter of a century as equals, both pharaohs like their predecessors. Under the power couple's rule, the Ptolemaic Empire gained its most expansive territory, reaching well across the Levant, Cyprus, and Libya and into parts of modern Turkey and Greece.

Back home in **Alexandria,** they rebuilt the **Temple of Serapis,** dedicated to the capital's patron god (a blend of the Egyptian gods Apis and Osiris and the Greek Dionysus), and continued to sponsor leading scholarship at the Great Library. Down in **Edfu,** they commissioned the magnificent **Temple of Horus** to surround a shrine built by Egypt's last native king, Nectanebo II.

This golden age of the Ptolemies would start to tarnish with the reign of their successor, **Ptolemy IV** (r. 222-205 BC). His tenure was bookended by femicide—beginning with the murder of his mother (to avoid sharing power) and ending with the execution of his sister-wife, Arsinoe III. In between, his reign was similarly unimpressive, fashioning himself as "Dionysus Reborn" (Greek god of wine and pleasure) and consuming commensurate amounts of the divine liquid. Native rebellions threatened his power from the inside, while battles on his northern borders led to loss of territory.

Much of the next 175 years of Ptolemaic rule would be characterized by more fratricide, matricide, and filicide as infighting between the royal family members gradually destroyed their empire. (Nearly all of the subsequent kings and queens would be named Ptolemy and Cleopatra or Berenice, passing on not only the favored family names but also their incestuous DNA.) But they still had Egypt's riches and lucrative trade routes at their fingertips, facilitating impressive building projects like the **Hathor Temple** in Dendera (Qena), the **Temple of Kom Ombo** north of Aswan, and the **Temple of Khnum** in Esna.

By the time the legendary **Cleopatra** (actually number VII) became pharaoh in 51 BC, her family's kingdom was well into its decline. In true Ptolemaic fashion, she and her siblings fought over control of the throne, with Cleopatra prevailing—murdering a brother and sister in the process. The clever queen made strategic romantic allies with Roman rulers, first Julius Caesar, then Mark Antony, to squeeze out another 20 years of Ptolemaic control over Egypt.

But Rome had infighting of its own, and Antony's rival Octavian (later called Augustus) declared war on Cleopatra and her second Roman lover, eventually sacking Alexandria in 30 BC and annexing Egypt into the newly minted Roman Empire.

Roman and Byzantine Period (30 BC-AD 641)

Now a province of the Roman Empire, Egypt was ruled by a prefect who reported directly to **Emperor Augustus** (r. 30 BC-14 AD). Roman legions set up camp around the country to maintain order, and Egypt became

"Rome's breadbasket," pouring its wheat into silos on the other side of the Mediterranean.

Temples still sprang up around Egypt for another century or so, particularly under Augustus, but Egyptian priests no longer enjoyed great political power—relying on Roman masters for security and finances to sustain their sacred homes.

Roman emperors embellished and expanded Egyptian and Ptolemaic cult centers, most notably the **Dendera Temple Complex** in Qena, **Temple of Khnum** in Esna, and the **Temple of Kom Ombo, Philae Temple,** and **Kalabsha Temple** in and around Aswan—depicting themselves as gods on the temple walls, like those who came before them. (Other Roman handling of Egypt's heritage was less gentle, like the quarrying of Amenemhet III's fabulous cult complex outside of Fayoum at the **Hawara Pyramid,** and the conversion of **Luxor Temple** into military barracks for their wars in Nubia.)

Meanwhile, the social status of native elites reached a new low. Descendants of Greek settlers from the Ptolemaic period enjoyed privileges not offered to Egyptians (like pensions and lower taxes). And while there was earlier a good deal of intermarrying between Greeks and Egyptians, the trend would decrease under Roman rule.

In Alexandria especially, the Greek-speaking elites continued to live well. The best remaining example of upper-class life in Roman Egypt can be found at **Kom el-Dekka** (Alexandria) with its ruins of villas from the rule of **Emperor Hadrian** (r. AD 117-138) and later remnants of their ancient recreation center built in the 300s-500s AD including public baths, a Roman theater, and lecture halls. Tombs from the 2nd century AD, like the **Catacombs of Kom el-Shoqafa** in Alexandria and **Tuna el-Gebel** near Minya, also demonstrate the wealth enjoyed by some during this period.

By around this time (c. AD 180), Christianity had made its way to the banks of the Nile, adding yet another religion to the pot. But the novel faith would be illegal for more than a century—until **Constantine** (r. AD 324-337), the first Christian Roman emperor, decreed tolerance for his adopted religion alongside the dominant polytheism.

For a time, the pagans and Christians of Egypt coexisted peacefully. The temples to Egyptian gods continued to be tended by priests, while the number of bishops increased dramatically—Alexandria becoming an important theological center of Christianity. Egypt's first monasteries also emerged in the Eastern Desert, with **St. Antony's Monastery** built as early as AD 361 and the nearby **Monastery of St. Paul** established soon thereafter (both near modern Ain Sokhna).

But Emperor Theodosius's (r. AD 379-395) war on paganism crushed much of what remained of Egypt's native religion, destroying temples and their clergies along the way. When the Roman Empire split definitively in AD 395, Egypt came under the Eastern Empire (Byzantine Empire) and its Christian rulers. More monasteries popped up in the desert under official patronage, and Egypt's ancient temples were increasingly taken over by these new religionists.

Some excellent examples of art and architecture from the Byzantine era can still be seen at the **White Monastery** (c. AD 450) and the **Red Monastery** (c. AD 500) in modern Sohag on the outskirts of the Northern Nile Valley; and the **St. Katherine Monastery** in the South Sinai (c. AD 530). Other relics from Christian centers that didn't survive can be seen in the **Coptic Museum** in Cairo, like column capitals and niches from 7th-century monasteries in Saqqara and the Northern Nile Valley.

Christianity's relatively short-lived preeminence in Egypt (of around 300 years) would soon come to an end as a new religion made its way across the Red Sea.

Early Islamic and Medieval Eras

EARLY ISLAMIC PERIOD (AD 641-969)

The Muslim conquest of Byzantine territory began soon after the death of the Prophet Mohammed in 632. Just a few years later, Arab general **Amr Ibn al-As** marched down from Syria to besiege the Byzantines' **Babylon Fortress** in modern Cairo.

Once secured, he headed for **Alexandria,** swiftly achieving a full Byzantine surrender by 642. But the opulent capital's position on the Mediterranean left it exposed to potential raids by sea, so Ibn al-As returned to the Babylon Fortress, founding Muslim Egypt's new capital in **Fustat** (modern Old Cairo).

In these early years, the Muslim conquest had little impact on the everyday lives of Egyptians. The Arab settlers lived apart from the native population, few Christians converted to Islam (the Muslim occupiers didn't push the matter), and treaties offered protection in exchange for taxes, which Egyptians had been paying to the Byzantines anyway.

Egypt was still a province in a foreign empire—only now ruled by a series of Muslim governors appointed by caliphs. This would remain the case for over 200 years until a soldier of Turkish descent, **Ahmed Ibn Tulun,** was sent to govern Egypt in 868 and claimed it (more or less) as his own.

Ibn Tulun's fleeting dynasty lasted for just under 40 years (868-905). But during this period, Egypt would begin its transformation from province to power center. The **Ibn Tulun Mosque** in modern Cairo is all that remains from the ambitious ruler's once grand capital city, which he built just north of Fustat.

All this would soon be back under the rule of Baghdad (capital of the Abbasid caliphate), with the country's wealth—which had piled up in the recent years of semi-autonomy—pouring out, once again, beyond its borders. A period of unrest followed as soldiers went without pay and rebellions became widespread.

FATIMIDS TO MAMLUKS (AD 969-1517)

Fatimids (969-1171)

Taking advantage of the power vacuum in the country, the **Fatimids** (Shia Muslims who had their capital in modern Tunisia) made occasional incursions into Egypt throughout the early 10th century. Egypt's string of ephemeral rulers managed to fight them off until General Jawhar, serving under **Caliph al-Mu'izz,** successfully took Fustat and its surrounding area in 969—founding Cairo (in Arabic al-Qahira, "The Victorious") just to the north.

The Fatimid caliphate moved its capital to al-Qahira (the area of **Mu'izz Street**) to challenge the Abbasid caliphate in Baghdad. General Jawhar ordered the construction of **Al-Azhar Mosque** as a place of worship for followers of their Ismaili sect of Shia Islam and a center of theology to teach and spread their religion.

While zealous in their missionary work to convert Sunni Muslims to their preferred sect of Islam, the Fatimids showed tolerance toward Jews and Christians, who continued to work in government under their rule. An extreme exception was the reign of **al-Hakim** (r. 996-1021)—builder of **al-Hakim Mosque** on Mu'izz Street and known as the "Mad Caliph"—who ordered forced conversions and the demolition of churches throughout the caliphate.

At the zenith of its power in the early 11th century, the Fatimid caliphate spanned the entire North African coast, reaching across the seas to Sicily, the Levant, and the Arabian Peninsula. They expanded trade and commerce in Egypt and spread their religion widely, even beyond Fatimid territory.

Eventually, military rebellions and internal

power struggles between high officials led to a string of invasions, most notably of an army from Syria led by a Kurdish military commander, **Shirkuh,** in 1169.

The Fatimid caliph, fighting off invading Franks, invited Shirkuh to enter Egypt to lend a hand. Shirkuh's forces expelled the foreign aggressors, and in return, the Kurd received the position of wazir (senior minister). His victory was short lived—he died just two months later, leaving the position to his nephew, Salah el-Din (aka Saladin).

Ayyubids (1171-1250)

Salah el-Din, envied by others who vied for his seat, acted quick to consolidate power. He swiftly ousted the Fatimid caliph, abolishing the 200 some year-old Fatimid dynasty and inaugurating his own—the Ayyubid dynasty, named after his father. His empire would stretch across Egypt, Yemen, and much of Syria and Mesopotamia, bringing a return of Sunni Islam as the official religion of his territories.

Salah el-Din commissioned the heavily fortified **Citadel** in 1176—not far from the Fatimid's former capital city—to protect against Crusader invasions and internal revolts. This would serve as the Egyptian seat of power for nearly 700 years to come.

Power struggles weakened the dynasty after Salah el-Din's death, but the threat of the Crusaders kept the Ayyubids together for nearly 60 more years.

By the time the last Ayyubid sultan, **al-Salih Ayyub,** took the throne in 1240, castle intrigues and messy successions (his own included) led him to rely even more heavily on foreign slave soldiers called mamluks to protect his power. (For centuries, rulers in the region had used mamluks—mostly Turkic people from Central Asia who were taken into slavery as children and trained as warriors—to build their armies.) To house his newly purchased soldiers, al-Salih built a fortress and barracks on Roda Island (modern Cairo's **el-Manial** district) in the middle of the Nile—a base that earned this group the title Bahari ("of the sea," referring to the river) Mamluks.

Al-Salih died just as Egypt was suffering yet another set of Crusader invasions, leaving his clever concubine, **Shagarat al-Durr,** to fill his shoes as sultana. She was murdered after just 80 days on the throne, marking the end of the Ayyubid dynasty. With her short-lived reign, she became the only woman to ever rule over Islamic Egypt and the last woman to rule Egypt until today.

Mamluks (1250-1517)

The Mamluks took advantage of this instability to overthrow their masters in 1250. They took control of the expansive empire they had earlier helped secure, and maintained Cairo as their capital. Egypt became a cultural center of the Muslim world during the Mamluk period, renowned for its scholars and monumental architecture. The first true Mamluk sultan, a military commander of Turkic origins, **al-Zahir Baybars,** inaugurated what would later be called the **Bahari Period (1250-1382).** He successfully protected Egypt's borders from Crusaders and Mongols, organized the first Mamluk system of governance, and launched a building campaign around Cairo. We owe most of the ornate architecture that still exists along Cairo's **Mu'izz Street** to Baybars's Mamluk successors.

The first of them, **al-Mansour Qalawun,** left a particularly grand footprint with his **Qalawun Complex.** Along with this material legacy, he's also credited with introducing the use of Circassian mamluks from the Caucasus. He housed these slave soldiers in the Citadel, which later gave them the name Borgi ("of the tower") Mamluks.

Qalawun's son and successor, **al-Nasir Mohammed,** ruled over the Mamluk golden age, using the wealth and stability secured by his predecessors to continue support for art, medicine, and religious institutions—like mosques and madrasas (religious schools). But these gilded years would soon come crashing to a halt with a succession of plagues and famines hitting Egypt hard beginning in the

1340s. Despite his brief reign and the ongoing public health crisis, al-Nasir's son (**al-Nasir Hasan**) continued the grand building projects, commissioning the towering **Mosque & Madrasa of Sultan Hasan** at the foot of the Citadel. Hasan, who was killed by one of his soldier slaves, would be the last Bahari ruler of note.

Out of the bloody succession struggle emerged **Barquq**—a mamluk of Circassian origin who inaugurated the **Borgi Period (1382-1517).** Imitating Qalawun's majestic complex, Barquq built his own grand mosque-madrasa-Sufi lodge (**Sultan Barquq Complex**) just down the street.

He also started the trend of being buried in Cairo's desert outskirts in the **Northern Cemetery** (or Qarafa), where his son built the stunning **Sultan Faraj Ibn Barquq Complex** to house their family's corpses and serve as a mosque and madrasa among other functions. Subsequent Mamluk rulers would imitate the grandeur with mausoleum-mosque-madrasa combos nearby, like the **Sultan Barsbay Complex** (built 1432) and **Sultan Qaitbay Complex** (built 1472).

The early years of **Qaitbay**'s rule (1468-1496) represented the zenith of Borgi power. Along with his opulent complex in Cairo, he built Alexandria's most notable medieval monument, the **Qaitbay Citadel,** and the smaller fortress at the estuary in Rashid (Rosetta), the **Fort of Qaitbay,** to protect Egypt from a growing power to the north.

Indeed, the neighboring Ottomans were on the rise. The last major Mamluk sultan, **al-Ghouri,** died on the battlefield trying to fend them off (not before building his grand mausoleum, the **Ghouri Complex** in Islamic Cairo). And the Ottomans managed to defeat the Mamluks definitively in 1517, hanging their last sultan from a southern gate of fortified Cairo, **Bab Zuweila.**

Early and Late Modern Eras

OTTOMAN ERA (1517-1867)

With the start of Ottoman rule, Egypt was reduced once again to a province under a foreign empire. Cairo's role as a cosmopolitan cultural center continued its decline as the Turks exported Egyptian wealth to their own imperial capital, Constantinople (modern Istanbul). Still, the beautiful Ottoman mansions in Islamic Cairo, such as those that house the **Gayer-Anderson Museum,** are testament to how well the country's elite continued to live during this period.

While Ottoman governors ruled over Egypt, they allowed Mamluk elite to continue to serve high-ranking roles in the army and government. By the early 1700s, Mamluks once again began to dominate politics, and before the end of the century, they had retaken control of the country. But this Mamluk resurgence did not last long.

EUROPEAN OCCUPATION AND MOHAMMED ALI DYNASTY (1798-1953)

Napoleon invaded Egypt in 1798 in what would prove to be a short-lived occupation. He had wanted to hamper British trade with India and turn Egypt into a lucrative colony, but with opposition on all sides—revolts in Cairo, British naval attacks, and Ottoman resistance—Napoleon was forced to abandon his project after just a few years.

With the French out, the Mamluks and Ottomans resumed their contest for power. The latter's occupying army employed skilled Albanian troops, who soon mutinied to vie for power for themselves. One of their commanders, Mohammed Ali, rose to become the Ottomans' viceroy in Egypt, which he governed with substantial autonomy.

Mohammed Ali Dynasty (1805-1953)

Sometimes called the father of modern Egypt, **Mohammed Ali** (r. 1805-1849) inaugurated sweeping administrative, agricultural, and educational reforms. But first, he decisively purged the Mamluk elite who had ruled the country to varying degrees for five and a half centuries—inviting them to a party at the **Citadel** and slaughtering them on the way out.

With his political rivals neutralized, Mohammed Ali turned to other projects. He appropriated most of Egypt's land for the state, revamped the country's irrigation system, introduced cotton, and built schools and public infrastructure. Abroad, he led successful military campaigns in the Arabian Peninsula, Sudan, and Syria—expanding his rule over neighboring lands.

Mohammed Ali's son, **Said Pasha** (r. 1854-1863), took over as viceroy a few years after his father's death (Said's older brother, and then nephew ruled first), leaving his most lasting mark with the **Suez Canal.**

Next came another of Mohammed Ali's grandsons, **Ismail** (r. 1863-1879), who finished the canal in 1869 and launched more massive projects, racking up commensurate debts along the way. Ismail's profligacy led to growing pressure from his European financiers—ultimately leading to his ouster by the Ottoman sultan, and replacement by his young son, **Tawfiq.**

Meanwhile, a nationalist movement was stirring. Egyptian colonel **Ahmed Urabi** led a group of compatriot officers to revolt—against the Turkish and Circassian higher-ups in the military, Franco-Anglo political involvement, and Tawfiq himself—under the slogan "Egypt for the Egyptians." The Urabi Revolt (1881-1882) ultimately failed, resulting in British occupation.

BRITISH OCCUPATION (1882-1952)

The British invasion in 1882 proved to be the inverse of the French one in 1798—intended to be brief but lasting for three-quarters of a century. The Brits entered Egypt to protect their strategic interests (especially debt repayment and the Suez Canal), but stayed to "reform" the country, extracting resources along the way.

While descendants of Mohammed Ali continued to rule in name, it was British Consul General **Lord Cromer** who controlled Egypt's policies for the next 24 years (1883-1907).

At the start of World War I, the British turned Egypt into an official protectorate. Egyptians suffered four years of wartime deprivations and martial law—fueling another nationalist movement, this time led by Egyptian statesman **Saad Zaghloul** and his Wafd Party. Their efforts eventually secured nominal independence from the British in 1922, heralding the start of Egypt's constitutional monarchy.

MONARCHY (1922-1952)

Fouad (r. 1922-1936), the youngest son of Ismail, became the first king of modern Egypt. But the Brits had agreed to Egyptian independence on their own terms—most important of which included keeping military forces in the country.

When King Fouad died, his son **Farouk** (r. 1936-1952) took the throne as the last king to rule over Egypt. During World War II, King Farouk cooperated with the British to fight the Axis powers on Egyptian soil. But after the war, nationalist groups demanded a full withdrawal of British troops. Anti-British demonstrations broke out frequently in Cairo and around the Suez Canal.

Out of the turbulence, a group of military officers led by **Gamal Abdel Nasser** staged a coup on July 23, 1952—overthrowing the monarchy and ending Mohammed Ali's nearly 150-year dynasty. King Farouk fled the country on the royal yacht from his seaside **Montazah Palace** in Alexandria, only returning after his death to be buried alongside his father and grandfather (Fouad and Ismail) in Cairo's **Al-Rifa'i Mosque.**

Independence and Contemporary Times

Egypt officially became a republic in 1953, and for the first time in over 2,000 years native Egyptians held the reins of power. After infighting among the coup-makers (and the brief tenure of Egypt's first ever president, General Mohammed Naguib), Nasser became undisputed leader.

GAMAL ABDEL NASSER (R. 1954-1970)

The pride of nationalist revival consumed the country, fueled by Nasser's bold actions like nationalizing the **Suez Canal** (1956), building the **Aswan High Dam** (starting 1960), socializing healthcare and education, and implementing a major industrialization campaign.

But a series of wars weighed heavily on Nasser's projects. The 1956 invasion of the Suez Canal area by Britain, France, and Israel (the Tripartite Aggression) ultimately worked in Nasser's favor after the US and UN condemned the action—rallying Egyptians behind him with ever greater enthusiasm. However, his foray into Yemen (1962-1967) proved a great failure and played a role in Egypt's even more devastating defeat by Israel in the 1967 Six-Day War. Israel occupied the entire **Sinai Peninsula,** and the Suez Canal closed for nearly a decade. A brokenhearted Nasser resigned, only to be reinstated as president after an outpouring of popular support. But he died a few years later, never recovering from the humiliation of the war.

ANWAR SADAT (R. 1970-1981)

Nasser's vice president and former military comrade Anwar Sadat took over in 1970 in what his peers thought would be a short-lived presidency. But Sadat turned out to be more of a politician than they expected, and he consolidated power, ruling for over a decade. A turning point early in his tenure was the launching of the 1973 October War against Israel, which proved a political victory for the new president. The conflict ended in a US-brokered ceasefire (although the less-than-neutral US was supplying Israeli troops) and paved the way for the 1979 Egypt-Israel Peace Treaty, a new relationship with the US, and the eventual return of the Sinai.

In 1974, Sadat inaugurated sweeping economic reforms with his infitah, or "economic opening," undoing many of the socialist projects of the Nasser era. Sadat's reforms benefited a small group of elites, while most Egyptians suffered. His peace with Israel and military mishandling of the 1973 war also made him unpopular among many. At the anniversary parade of the October War in 1981, a group of soldiers-turned-Islamic extremists assassinated the president, leaving the country to be ruled by yet another military man, Sadat's vice president, Hosni Mubarak.

HOSNI MUBARAK (R. 1981-2011)

As an air force general who fought in the 1973 war, Mubarak commanded early respect from his countrymen. But the continuation of Sadat era trends—like his abusive security state, imprisonment of opponents, cronyistic partnerships with business elites, and peace with Israel—along with 30 years of authoritarian rule, ultimately led Egyptians to call for his ouster.

Thousands gathered in Cairo's **Tahrir Square** on January 25, 2011 to protest these decades of grievances. During the 18 days of demonstrations, hundreds were killed in clashes with the police. Mubarak ultimately stepped down on February 11 and celebrations erupted across the country. But the victory would not last long.

REVOLUTION AND COUNTER-REVOLUTION (2011-TODAY)

The Supreme Council of the Armed Forces (SCAF), comprised of senior military officers, ruled for over a year before yielding to Egypt's first ever democratically elected government in 2012. After decades of oppression, Egypt's political opposition was fragmented, and the well-organized Muslim Brotherhood—an Islamist group established in 1928—won elections with Mohammed Morsi as their president.

Many Egyptians, particularly liberal youth who had been a driving force behind the uprising, resented the Brotherhood's lack of inclusivity in the post-Revolution order. The military and sidelined members of the Mubarak regime (including his business cronies and security apparatus) were also unhappy with their demotion.

After just one year of Morsi's presidency, the newly appointed Minister of Defense Abdel Fattah el Sisi led a military coup on July 3, 2013, backed by many of these excluded groups. In response, thousands of protesters camped out in squares around Cairo calling for a return of their democratically elected government. Security forces moved in to crush the camps on August 14 in what many call the "Raba'a Massacre," referring to the main square where demonstrators had gathered. An estimated 1,000 people were killed in the dispersal of the sit-ins. Sisi won the presidency soon after in widely criticized elections (2014), becoming the latest ruler to join Egypt's long line of pharaohs.

Background

The Landscape

GEOGRAPHY

Desert and Coast

Desert covers some 95 percent of Egypt's territory. The sprawling **Western Desert**—bordered by the Mediterranean Sea to the north, Sudan to the south, Libya to the west, and the Nile to the east—accounts for around two-thirds of the country's land (but only houses around 0.5 percent of the population). Another quarter of Egypt's land is comprised by the much slimmer **Eastern Desert,** running between the Nile and the Red Sea. These are both sections of the **Sahara,** the

largest desert in the world. Most of this land is uninhabitable, but a handful of oases spot the sandy expanses, and the coastal areas (along the Mediterranean and the Red Sea) each have notable towns and cities separated by long stretches of untouched desert land.

The Nile

The Nile cuts between the Western and Eastern Deserts, flowing north for around 1,200 kilometers (750 mi) from Lake Nasser to the Mediterranean. Rich agricultural lands line either side of the river, blossoming after Cairo into the beautiful green lotus that is **the Delta.** This last leg of the Nile branches into distributaries, irrigating the V-shaped Delta that spans 240 kilometers (150 mi) at its widest point along the coast. In Cairo—and throughout Egypt—you'll note that **"Corniche el-Nil"** is the name given to most riverside roads along the Nile.

Sinai Peninsula

The Sinai Peninsula, hugged by two arms of the Red Sea (Gulf of Suez and Gulf of Aqaba) and bordered by the Mediterranean to the north, was once linked to the Egyptian mainland by a 160-kilometer-long (100-mi-long) strip of land—now cut down the middle by the **Suez Canal.** Rugged mountains roll through South Sinai's interior with the summit of Mount Katherine the highest point in Egypt at just over 2,600 meters (8,500 ft). And along the eastern coast (in the Gulf of Aqaba), stunning corals sit just off the land's edge.

CLIMATE

Sunshine dominates Egypt's forecast year-round. It does **rain** on occasion during the winter in Cairo, the Sinai, and the Delta (especially on the coast), but almost never in the summer or the south. **Sandstorms,** known as khamasin, typically blow in 1-3 times a year between March and April, often bringing with them temperatures of over 38°C (100°F).

Summers (May-Sept.) are hot across the country, hovering in the 32-38°C range (high 90s-low 100s F) in Cairo—with humidity between 15 and 75%—and reaching daytime temperatures of 46°C (115°F) in southern cities, with much less humidity (under 20%). The Western Desert is also particularly hot and dry during summer days, often breaking 38°C (100°F), but dropping down to around 24°C (the mid 70s F) at night. Cities on the North Coast are typically many degrees cooler than inland, averaging around 30°C (in the high 80s F). The South Sinai and Red Sea Coasts see daytime temperatures around 32°C and up (in the 90s F).

The brief **spring** (Mar.-Apr.) and **fall** (Oct.-Nov.) are moderate—around 25°C (in the high 70s F) in Cairo and 27°C (the low 80s F) in the Luxor and Aswan. **Winters** (Dec.-Feb.) are cool, with average daytime temperatures around 20°C (in the high 60s F) in Cairo and 22°C (70s F) in Luxor and Aswan.

Nighttime temperatures can drop significantly throughout the year with average lows around 4°C (in the 40s F) during the winter and 22°C (70s F) in the summer. In winter, temperatures at night can even dip below freezing.

ENVIRONMENTAL ISSUES

Air Pollution

Air pollution is a serious problem in Egypt and is the environmental issue most likely to affect travelers. Most of this will be experienced in big cities (especially Cairo/Giza and Alexandria), where car exhaust and pollutants from nearby factories are most intense. The Western Desert, Red Sea Coast, and South Sinai have refreshingly clean air most of the time.

Waste Management

Egypt's poor waste management is deeply connected with the country's air quality problems. A common way to get rid of waste is by

Previous: felucca sailing in Aswan.

burning it, which of course releases harmful chemicals. This unfortunately happens just about everywhere around the country. Visitors to Egypt can expect to see mounds of trash outside city centers, burnt garbage lining the banks of canals, and litter almost everywhere—a constant eyesore.

Food and Water Security

Climate change and decades of government neglect have battered Egypt's agricultural sector and freshwater sources. Weather has been hotter and drier in recent years, requiring more water for growing; and rising sea levels are increasing salinity in the Nile Delta, compromising the country's most fertile land. Urban sprawl has added to the onslaught, encroaching on farmland for years unchecked and covering some of the country's richest soil with concrete.

Ethiopia's recent completion of its megadam on the Nile upstream of Egypt threatens to deliver an additional blow to the country's food and water security. Egypt, which relies almost entirely on the Nile for its freshwater, has so far been unsuccessful in securing a deal with its upstream neighbor to guarantee sufficient water flow in the event of a drought. In the absence of Ethiopia's cooperation, a multi-year drought could devastate Egypt's agricultural sector, which employs and more than a quarter of Egyptians and feeds much of the country.

Tips for Minimizing Environmental Impact

To minimize negative environmental impact, travelers who plan to dive/snorkel may want to bring some **reef-safe sunscreen** (you're not likely to find any in Egypt) and, of course, exercise extreme caution not to touch any of the corals or other sea life. Choosing an **ethical tour operator** for boat trips is also important, as some have been known to traumatize dolphins by chasing them or harm coral reefs by getting too close.

Plants and Animals

TREES AND FLOWERS

Greater Cairo has a striking array of greenery for such a densely populated city. Banyan trees over 100 years old dangle their aerial roots over encroaching asphalt in the upscale neighborhoods of Zamalek and Garden City. Jacaranda, royal poinciana, weeping bottlebrush, pink silk (albizia julibrissin), and bougainvillea trees add splashes of brilliant colors—violet, scarlet, pink, yellow, fuchsia—around the concrete jungle. Fragrant jasmine flowers hang over walls in some corners of the city, while they're harvested by the basketful in the Delta. But palms are Egypt's most conspicuous trees, with over a dozen species found in thick groves across the country from the Delta to the desert oases and all along the Nile Valley, Cairo included. Eucalyptus trees also tower in parts of Giza and the Delta. And acacia trees spot the Sinai and Eastern Desert near the Red Sea, with mangroves found in these parts along the coast.

LAND MAMMALS AND REPTILES

Greater Cairo's most numerous four-legged friends are its thousands of street cats and dogs. Egyptian weasels also scurry across the city streets, while in the air, fruit bats flit between trees beginning around dusk. Horses, donkeys, goats, and camels can be seen in corners of the city—most often near the pyramids in Giza or on the city's rural outskirts, but not uncommonly in central Cairo. And friendly fan-footed geckos scamper across windows, issuing the occasional chirp.

Rural areas in the Delta and along the Nile Valley are home to even more horses, donkeys, goats, and water buffalos. Camels are the favorite animal of Aswan, followed by crocodiles—the babies are sometimes kept at home as pets, with full sized crocs in Lake Nasser south of the High Dam. Lucky visitors to the Western and Eastern Deserts might come across an adorable hyrax, dorcas gazelle, Nubian ibex, or fennec. Unlucky ones might encounter the rare horned viper (though you're much more likely to spot one painted on the walls of ancient tombs).

SEA LIFE

The Red Sea holds a dazzling array of critters, best enjoyed off the South Sinai coast in the Gulf of Aqaba or on the mainland Red Sea Coast in Marsa Alam or Hurghada. In these parts you can find hundreds of species of vibrant corals visited by several types of sea creatures, with some of my personal favorites: sohal surgeonfish, parrotfish, lionfish, Napoleon wrasse, glassfish, coral grouper, clownfish, and blue-spotted rays.

Certain areas (particularly Marsa Alam) are known for their sea turtles, dugongs, dolphins, and the occasional friendly whale shark. Thrill-seeking divers hoping to spot the Red Sea's shark inhabitants—like oceanic white tip sharks, tiger sharks, and hammerheads—should head to select reefs typically far from the shore (though sharks do make occasional incursions closer to land).

BIRDS

During the migration seasons in spring and fall, more than 200 species of birds can be spotted passing through Egypt. The pseudo-oasis of Fayoum (especially Lake Qarun), Aswan (around the river islands and in Lake Nasser), the South Sinai (Ras Mohammed National Park), and Red Sea Coast (Marsa Alam) are excellent bird-watching spots.

Egypt also plays host to a wide variety of resident birds. In Greater Cairo, pigeons, doves, and hooded crows are the most visible, but this urban jungle also holds a surprising range of feathered friends like iridescent green rose-ringed parakeets, hoopoes (with woodpecker-like beak and orange crown), stocky white cattle egrets, slender sunbirds, and brilliantly blue collared kingfishers.

You can find many of these birds all along the Nile Valley and in Fayoum along with black kites and great white egrets. In Aswan you can enjoy glimpses of white-eyed ferruginous ducks and long-necked purple herons. And in the South Sinai and Red Sea coast keep an eye out for the rounded, spotted bodies of sand grouses, elegant white storks, and long-winged western reef herons.

Government and Economy

GOVERNMENT

While Egypt is nominally a republic (its official name is the "Arab Republic of Egypt"), elections are neither fair nor free and the president and his security apparatus command supreme power. After the 2011 Revolution, the country held its first and only genuinely democratic elections, which resulted in a win for the Muslim Brotherhood-backed presidential candidate, Mohammed Morsi.

Morsi appointed Egypt's current president, Abdel Fattah el-Sisi, as minister of defense in 2012, only to be ousted by his inferior less than a year later in a military coup. When thousands of anti-coup protestors occupied squares around Cairo, security forces violently cleared their camps, killing an estimated 1,000 civilians within hours.

In 2013, the military-backed interim government declared the Muslim Brotherhood terrorists, and members of the group and their families have since been killed, imprisoned, or forced to flee the country. The state has used accusations of affiliation to the group as an excuse to imprison thousands more civilians who have expressed opposition to the current military-backed regime. An estimated 60,000 political prisoners have been sent to languish in Egyptian jails since 2013, many of them young people who have done little more than post anti-regime comments on social media.

The judiciary, which once had relative independence under former president Hosni Mubarak, is now firmly under the thumb of the Sisi regime. Amendments to the constitution in 2019 gave the president power to appoint the heads of the country's most important judicial bodies. The military can also step in whenever there's a perceived threat to "national security," and routinely sends opponents to military tribunals instead of civilian courts.

The Parliament—consisting of an upper and lower house, the Senate (Maglis el-Shiyoukh) and House of Representatives (Maglis el-Nowaab)—serves a rubber stamp function. Egypt's intelligence agencies have played a significant role in funding and organizing pro-regime parties, which now dominate both houses of Parliament. Meanwhile, the few opposition parties that are allowed to exist face constant harassment and hold little power.

ECONOMY

For the past half century, Egypt's economy has been deeply entangled with "economic liberalizing" reform packages backed by the International Monetary Fund (IMF).

Following nearly two decades of socialist policies under former president Gamal Abdel Nasser (r. 1954-1970), his successor, Anwar Sadat, pivoted toward the US and signed Egypt's first major agreement with the IMF to begin dismantling the state-run economy. This was done in a highly untransparent manner, resulting in major windfalls for the president's cronies as state resources were shifted into private pockets.

The trend continued under Sadat's successors. Mubarak signed additional agreements with the IMF in the 1990s, resulting in continued benefits for connected elites and cuts to social spending for the majority. Sisi also implemented sweeping austerity measures to secure a $12 billion IMF loan agreement in 2016. (His government clinched an additional $5.2 billion loan from the fund in 2020 to support continued economic liberalizing reforms during the pandemic.)

Macroeconomic indicators like gross domestic product (GDP) growth have improved under the reforms, but they fail to translate to broadly shared benefits. Instead, while Egyptian elites are among the world's wealthiest, around 30% of the population lives below the national poverty line.

In terms of sectors, agriculture is extremely important to the Egyptian economy, accounting for over 20% of all employment and around 11% of GDP. Tourism is also a major contributor, employing around 10% of working Egyptians. While it's difficult to measure the full extent of tourism's impact—which includes all types of in-country spending by tourists on hotels, tours, transportation, meals, shopping, etc.—estimates place its GDP contribution at around 11%.

The energy sector—while not nearly as important to Egypt as it is across the Red Sea in the Gulf—accounts for the largest share of foreign direct investment (FDI) in the country. Fossil fuels (mostly crude and refined petroleum and natural gas) are also Egypt's largest export products, comprising over a quarter of all exports.

Finally, remittances—or money sent back to family members in Egypt by workers earning wages abroad—play a notable role in Egypt's economy, amounting to some $29.6 billion in 2020, or around 8% of GDP.

People and Culture

DEMOGRAPHY

Most of Egypt's 100 million-plus citizens live along the Nile Valley or in the fertile Nile Delta, which together account for just around 4 percent of the country's territory. Smaller populations are scattered throughout Egypt's desert lands, mainly along the coasts or in oasis towns.

Greater Cairo (Cairo and Giza) holds some 20 million people alone, and Alexandria, the next biggest city, follows far behind with around 5.5 million residents. These larger metropolises are Egypt's most diverse and liberal spots, attracting people from all corners of the country.

The populations outside of Egypt's urban centers are typically more ethnically and culturally homogeneous (though vary from region to region) and more conservative. They often have their own informal systems of governance and law enforcement alongside the country's official institutions. Many communities are organized in tribal systems with a locally appointed sheikh, or tribal leader, to settle disputes.

LANGUAGE AND DIVERSITY

While **Arabic** is the official language of Egypt, each region has its own linguistic nuances—usually a dialect of Arabic, but in a few cases a different language altogether. The names of the dialects are often the same as the names of the people who speak them, reflecting the extent to which language and culture are intertwined.

Native residents of Egypt's capital, second city, and other urban centers in the Nile Delta speak the country's dominant language—a dialect of Arabic known as **Egyptian Arabic,** or Masri (which also means Egyptian) or a'maya (meaning "colloquial")—with only slight variations in accents.

Coptic—the latest version of ancient Egyptian, which is written in the Greek alphabet and incorporates several Greek words—is spoken by a small number of popes and scholars, and is used on occasion in religious services of the Coptic Orthodox Church (much like the rare Catholic mass still conducted in Latin).

Sa'ada and Fellahin

The Delta's farmers (fellahin) and village dwellers speak Egyptian Arabic with a distinct accent, called Fellahi—for example, pronouncing the "g" of urban Egyptians as "j," and the "q" as a "g." Upper Egyptians, or Sa'ada (singular Sa'idi), inhabit the strip of the Nile Valley that runs from Minya down to Aswan. Their Arabic dialect, also called Sa'idi, is similar to Fellahi, and indeed many Sa'ada are also farmers (or fellahin). But Sa'idi (more than Fallahi) can be considerably different from traditional Masri in both accent and word choice. Still, their dialects are (for the most part) mutually intelligible.

Bedouins

Egypt's sprawling desert land is inhabited by various Bedouin tribes—formerly nomadic people, most of whom have now settled. Bedouins have a range of regional dialects, which are often generalized as Bedouin Arabic (Bedawi). Most Bedouin trace their roots to the Arabian Peninsula, and their dialect is closer to those spoken across the Red Sea in Saudi Arabia than to traditional Masri.

The Bedouins from the Sinai—known as Sinawiin (singular Sinawi)—share considerable linguistic traits with their neighbors to the north in Palestine and Jordan.

Nubians

Aswan is home to Egypt's largest Nubian population (Nubiin) who share more physical characteristics with their sub-Saharan neighbors than with other Egyptians to the north.

…ve darker skin and their own lan-… e most common in Aswan called …adija, named after the tribes that …n. Both are from the Nilo-Saharan …age family and are entirely distinct from Arabic (though loan words have crept in).

Nubians used to live along the Nile from Aswan down into Sudan, but after the building of the Aswan High Dam in the 1960s many were displaced, forced to relocate to other towns and cities on either side of the border. Most of their homes now lie under Lake Nasser.

Siwis

The far-flung Siwa Oasis near the border of Libya is home to an ethnically Berber population (a people from North Africa who predate Arabs in the region, also called Amazigh) that speaks a Berber language called Siwi. While Siwi is traditionally spoken at home, young Siwa natives learn Arabic in school, and Siwi has been influenced by Arabic (especially Egyptian and Bedouin) through intermarriage and other cultural contact.

RELIGION

Islam

Sunni Islam is the official religion of the state, followed by around 90 percent of the Egyptian population. Travelers to Egypt will quickly notice the prominence of Islam through the tens of thousands of mosques that spot the country, their illuminated minarets issuing the call to prayer five times a day—at dawn (fagr), noon (duhr), midafternoon (a'sr), sunset (maghrib), and evening (a'sha).

Many Egyptians take off work on Friday, the Muslim holy day. The streets before afternoon prayer on Fridays are typically quiet throughout the country—even in hyper-crowded Cairo/Giza and Alexandria. (Expect stores to open around 1pm-2pm.)

Islam also influences the country's menus with pork items conspicuously absent from nearly all the country's restaurants. Pork, like alcohol, is haram (forbidden), but the latter is consumed far more often and is easy to find around Egypt.

Christianity

A large Christian minority comprises most of the remaining 10 percent of Egypt's population. Nearly all Egyptian Christians are **Coptic**—an ethno-religious group of indigenous Christian Egyptians whose origins date back to the 1st- 2nd century AD. Most Copts are followers of the Coptic Orthodox Church, though there also smaller groups of Catholics and Protestants.

The word Coptic ("Qibti" in Arabic) comes from the Greek word for Egyptians, Aigyptios. While this has led some to suggests Copts to be the "original Egyptians," it's worth remembering that Christianity replaced the pagan religions of ancient Egypt (sometimes quite violently) just as Islam later replaced Christianity (also at times violently) as Egypt's main religion.

LITERATURE

Modern Egypt's literary poster child **Naguib Mahfouz** wrote *hundreds* of short stories, novels, plays, and movie scripts. His most widely acclaimed work, *The Cairo Trilogy* (1956-1957), consists of three novels that follow a Cairene family during a period of dramatic political and social changes in Egypt (1919-1944). He won the Nobel Prize for Literature in 1988, becoming the first Arab writer to be awarded the accolade.

For more recent works taking deep dives into the lives of Cairenes, check out **Alaa al-Aswany**'s *The Yacoubian Building* (2002) and **Khaled Alkhamissi**'s *Taxi* (2006). The first is a novel set in the 1990s and revolves around a downtown apartment building and its colorful inhabitants. The second is a collection of short stories based on the author's equally colorful conversations with Cairo's taxi drivers.

A flood of literature, both fiction and non, came out following the 2011 Revolution. If you only read one, try **Omar Robert**

Hamilton's novel *The City Always Wins* about a group of young activists and journalists navigating the Revolution and its fallout.

MUSIC AND CINEMA

Egypt has a rich history of music and cinema. Beginning in the 1930s—and really taking off after the country's independence in the 1950s—Egypt became the regional hub for these artistic forms. The voices of legendary pop stars like **Umm Kulthum, Mohammed Abdel Wahab,** and **Abdel Halim Hafez** reverberated across the Middle East. Many of these well-loved singers also took leading roles in films alongside other movie stars of Egypt's cinematic "golden age" like **Soad Hosny, Faten Hamama, Nadia Lotfi, Rushdy Abaza,** and **Omar el Sherif.**

State censorship has played a major role in determining what's "acceptable" in Egyptian art since the beginning. But the nationalization of the film industry in 1966 marked the start of firm state control over Egyptian cinema, which has waxed and waned over the decades. After a period of relative liberalism in the 2000s, censorship has reached new highs. The state security apparatus has taken over a large chunk of Egyptian media, using it to create pro-regime propaganda. And films attempting to address controversial contemporary issues are swiftly banned. Still, Egypt's small independent film community manages produce some gems (usually at great difficulty or by filming abroad).

The music industry hasn't fared much better in terms of censorship, but its artists can more easily work around constraints. While Egypt's most famous pop stars have been put to use by the regime for propaganda purposes, plenty of musicians still operate independently. There's a growing appetite for music that speaks to social issues and challenges of contemporary life through popular genres like rap, hip-hop, and mahraganat—a kind of electro street music that emerged out of working-class districts in Cairo in the late 2000.

DANCE

Belly dancing (raqs sharqi) was a central element of Egypt's golden age of cinema and nightlife in the 1930s-1970s. Many films included dance interludes performed to classic Arabic music at parties or nightclubs attended by the main characters, and sometimes, the film's female protagonist would do the dancing herself. Some of Egypt's most celebrated stars from this era include **Samia Gamal** (my personal favorite), **Taheyya Kariokka,** and **Naima Akef.** (Do a quick search for them on YouTube to find a treasure trove of scenes from their films.)

Fifi Abdou and **Dina,** who got their start in the 1970s and '80s, respectively, caught the tail end of the belly-dancing-as-essential-film-scene phase, and continued their art on the stage in nightclubs. It was around this time that a conservative current began to pulse through Egypt, and belly dancing became seen among many as disreputable. Aside from Fifi Abdou and Dina who still perform on occasion, Egypt's most famous belly dancers these days are foreigners—often from Eastern Europe. They typically dance at weddings of the well-to-do and at upscale nightclubs in Cairo or on the North Coast. Plenty of Egyptian women still perform, but due to the culture of the times, most are relegated to the seedy cabarets of Downtown Cairo or along Giza's Haram Street near the Pyramids.

SOUND AND LIGHT SHOWS

Sound and light shows are tourist attractions that take place at historic temples and sights in Egypt, including the Giza Pyramids, Luxor's Karnak Temple, Philae Temple in Aswan, and Abu Simbel Temple. As the name suggests, shows take place after dark and generally involve lights and music accompanied by some narration on the sight's historical significance. The narration can be somewhat dated and cheesy, but the spectacle is worthwhile for some. If you'd like to see one, the show at Philae Temple is the best.

Essentials

Transportation

GETTING THERE

Air

Most visitors arrive to Egypt by air, landing at either **Cairo International Airport (CAI)**, **Sharm el Sheikh International Airport (SSH)**, **Hurghada International Airport (HRG)**, or **Marsa Alam International Airport (RMF)**.

FROM NORTH AMERICA

The only direct flights to Egypt from the US leave from New York's JFK Airport (JFK; 10.5 hours) and Washington, DC's Dulles Airport (IAD; 10.5 hours), both arriving in Cairo with **EgyptAir** (www.egyptair.com). Travelers departing from any other US city to Cairo should expect a layover in Europe or Istanbul. Those traveling between any US city and Sharm, Hurghada, or Marsa Alam will have at least one layover in Cairo, Istanbul, and/or somewhere in Europe.

From Canada, EgyptAir flies direct between Toronto's Pearson Airport (YYZ) and Cairo (10.5 hours) at least once a week. Flights from all other Canadian cities to any airport in Egypt will have at least one layover.

FROM THE UK

EgyptAir and **British Airways** (www.britishairways.com) fly daily nonstop trips between Heathrow Airport (LHR; 5 hours) and Cairo. **EasyJet** (www.easyjet.com) travels nonstop 2-3 times a week between London Gatwick (LGW) and Sharm el Sheikh (4.5 hours). **TUI Airways** (www.tui.co.uk) flies nonstop 1-3 times a week from London Gatwick, Manchester (MAN), and Birmingham (BHX) to Sharm el Sheikh or Hurghada, plus once a week from London Gatwick and Birmingham to Marsa Alam.

FROM NEW ZEALAND AND AUSTRALIA

There are no direct flights between Egypt and New Zealand or Australia. **Emirates** (www.emirates.com) airline offers the best route with one stop in Dubai Airport (DXB) en route between Auckland (AKL) or Sydney (SYD) and Cairo.

FROM SOUTH AFRICA

EgyptAir flies direct between Johannesburg (JNB) and Cairo (8 hours). Flights from Cape Town (CPT) require at least one layover—the best options are either **Turkish Airlines** (www.turkishairlines.com) with a stop in Istanbul or Emirates with a stop in Dubai (both a minimum flight time of 14-15 hours).

Land

It's rare for tourists (other than Israelis) to come to Egypt by land, but when they do the only real option is to cross at the Taba border in the South Sinai. Note: Visas obtained here are free but only grant admission to the South Sinai for 14 days. This includes as far south as Sharm el Sheikh (but not Ras Mohammed or anywhere along the Gulf of Suez). If you plan to travel to these parts, Cairo, or elsewhere on the Egyptian mainland after entering at Taba, be sure to secure an eVisa ahead of time (www.visa2egypt.gov.eg).

GETTING AROUND

To travel around Egypt, buses and private cars are generally your best bet. Flying, when available, is the quickest option. Trains are a good option too, but only serve Cairo, Alexandria, and the Nile Valley region.

Air

Flying is often the fastest way to shuttle between Egypt's major cities. Expect prices of around $90-600 for a round-trip ticket depending on destination and season. Flights travel between **Cairo** and **Alexandria, Sharm el Sheikh, Hurghada, Marsa Alam, Luxor, Aswan,** and even **Abu Simbel** (via Aswan).

Train

Trains only run north and south for the most part, so they can be used to reach Alexandria or the Nile Valley area as far south as Aswan. First class trains (choose "Special Service") are generally comfortable, spacious, and inexpensive. Tickets can be booked at the station, preferably a day or two in advance, or (when it's working) on the **Egyptian National**

Previous: Ramses Station in Cairo.

Railways website (www.enr.gov.eg). For trips down to Luxor or Aswan you can also book a relatively comfortable sleeper car at the station or online at www.wataniasleepingtrains.com. Single cabins go for $120 and doubles for $160.

Bus

Between cities, the bus is usually the way to travel. You can get almost anywhere you'd want to go to (and many places you wouldn't) with the various bus companies. **GoBus** offers frequent, inexpensive, and safe travel options from a central location in Downtown Cairo (Abdel Minam Riyad Square) to as far as Marsa Alam in the south, Alexandria in the north, Marsa Matruh in the west, and Nuweiba (South Sinai) in the east. Their buses vary significantly in quality, so try to choose the slightly more expensive options of "Elite Plus" or "Elite D.D." (and avoid the "Classic" or "Deluxe Plus" buses) when you buy your ticket online (at www.gobus.com) or at the station.

Blue Bus is another good option offering similar routes. Its main station in Cairo is located Downtown in Ramses Square. Purchase tickets online (www.bluebus.com.eg) or at the station.

Other less efficient buses are run by the state-owned companies **Upper Egypt Bus Co., East Delta Bus Co.,** and **West & Mid Delta Bus Co.** Tickets must be purchased at the station, preferably a day or two in advance. In Cairo, their main station is **Torgoman** (in Downtown).

Taxi

Taxis are omnipresent and inexpensive in all major cities (Cairo/Giza, Alexandria, Port Said, Marsa Matruh, Sharm el Sheikh, Hurghada, Luxor, and Aswan), but only taxis in Cairo/Giza and Sharm have meters (request the drivers use them). For all others, be sure to agree on a price before getting in. If you're going a set route, you might want to ask your hotel how much to pay before heading out.

Uber and **Careem** (now a subsidiary of Uber) operate in Cairo, Alexandria, Port Said, and Hurghada. They typically cost around the same as regular taxis, but the prices are more transparent.

Hiring a Private Car

Hiring a private car with professional driver is probably the most comfortable way to move around and between cities. This option can save a lot of time and hassle for those not inclined to haggle with taxi drivers or navigate public transportation. You also get more time to get to know your driver, who can act as an unofficial guide. It's a particularly attractive idea for antiquity lovers who'd like to road-trip at their leisure down the Nile Valley to visit tombs and treasures without the crowds of the main attractions. Prices vary depending on distance traveled, but the cost of a private car with driver should be around 800LE (e.g., for a day around Cairo/Giza) to 2,400LE (e.g., Cairo to Alexandria and back).

Ibrahim el-Sheemy (tel. 0122 487 8427) and **Moamen Khedr** (tel. 0122 362 3032; moamen_lancer@yahoo.com) are both excellent drivers with comfortable cars. Both best reached by WhatsApp. Your hotel should also be able to arrange a driver for you (but expect to pay extra).

Microbus

Microbuses are probably the most common form of transportation in Egypt. The 14-seater shared taxis travel both within (3-7LE) and between (50-100LE) cities. There are no maps, but locals easily navigate the system with a series of hand signals to indicate their destinations. The prevalence of inexpensive private taxis means tourists don't typically take microbuses, but if you're keen to, ask for help at a microbus stations or flag one down and tell them where you want to go.

Metro

Cairo is the only city with a metro system. Though the cars can get jam packed at rush hour (around 8-10am and 5-7pm), the metro is a generally clean, cheap, and speedy way to get around. Trains run 5am-midnight, and ticket prices range from 5-10LE depending on how far you're going. Ladies-only train cars are available. Check their website for maps and details (https://cairometro.gov.eg/en).

Cruises

River cruises are a great way to explore the Nile Valley at a relaxed pace. The most popular routes are between Luxor and Aswan (3-6 nights), or from Aswan through Lake Nasser to Abu Simbel (3-4 nights). A longer trip (around 14 nights) is also offered by a few operators to sail between Cairo and Aswan. Choose between a larger cruise ship with 22-80 cabins, boutique dahabiya (large two-masted sailboat) with 4-12 cabins, or private felucca (traditional wooden sailboat) where you camp on deck.

Driving

Driving in Cairo is an extreme sport. The city has its own unwritten rules of the road that aren't necessarily (ever) intuitive. Outside Cairo is more manageable, but still comes with many dangers for those not familiar with Egyptian roads. Drivers often position their cars straddling lines on the highways so they can quickly move to the left or right as needed if, for example, a semitruck decides to drive into oncoming traffic, or some large debris happens to invade a lane.

Given the situation, not too many car rental companies have set up shop in Egypt, but you will find a handful in Cairo. If you do decide to drive, be sure you have insurance, and before taking any road trips, ask your hotel to make sure special permission from the military isn't necessary to drive your intended route as a foreigner.

Visas and Officialdom

VISAS

US, Canada, UK, EU, New Zealand, and Australia

Visas are available to citizens of the US, Canada, UK, EU, New Zealand, and Australia upon arrival at any Egyptian airport for $25 or the Egyptian Pound equivalent. You must have at least six months left on your passport before expiration to be granted the visa. Tourist visas are valid for up to 30 days (single entry), and you're given a grace period of 14 days after the visa expires. If you overstay, you'll have to pay a fee (around 1,500LE) upon departure that increases the longer you stay. To extend your visa, you can either leave the country and re-enter with a new tourist visa, or apply for a 3-6-month extension at the Passports, Emigration and Nationality Administration in el Abbassiya, Cairo (off Radwan Shokry St.; ask for the Old Police Academy).

EVisas are also available to citizens of these countries at Egypt's official government visa website (www.visa2egypt.gov.eg). These are only available for visitors not yet inside Egypt. Beware: There are many unofficial sites that are either scams or charge exorbitant fees. EVisas are not advised at this point, and long delays and hassles have been reported. Securing a visa upon arrival for eligible nationalities is a simple process.

South Africa

Visitors from South Africa will have to apply for a visa well in advance of travel to Egypt at the Egyptian Embassy in Sunnyside, Pretoria. Applications are only accepted 9am-11am Monday-Thursday, and visas should be collected after 6-10 days. To apply, bring your passport and a copy of your photo page, two color passport photos, proof of a round-trip flight itinerary, hotel booking, and bank statements for the past three months. Travelers can also enlist the services of a tour operator and need not be present to secure the visa. There has been talk of adding South Africans to the list of nationalities who can secure visas on arrival, but at the time of writing this unfortunately wasn't the case. Check for updates before making the trek to the embassy.

EMBASSIES AND CONSULATES

The embassies of the **US, Canada, UK, EU, New Zealand, Australia,** and **South Africa** are all located in Cairo. The US and a handful of European countries (France, Austria, Spain, Netherlands, Italy, Greece, Denmark) also have consulates in Alexandria.

CUSTOMS

Before entering Egypt from any airport, you'll be asked to place your bags on an X-ray scanner. Be sure you haven't packed any firearms, narcotics, more than 200 cigarettes, 25 cigars, 200 grams of tobacco, or 1 liter of perfume. You can purchase up to three liters of alcohol at duty free. The maximum currency amounts permitted upon entry are 5,000LE and $10,000 (or the equivalent in all other currencies).

Recreation

Between its deserts, mountains, and seas, Egypt is full of activities for adventure seekers. Travelers keen on exploring Egypt's interior (deserts and/or mountains) might prefer to avoid the summer months, when the sun is strong and the heat inescapable.

HORSE AND CAMEL RIDES

Horse and camel riding are popular activities in Giza near the pyramids, Fayoum's Tunis Village, Dahab, Sharm, Hurghada, Gouna, and on Luxor's West Bank. There are quality stables in each spot (recommended in this book), where you can be sure the animals are treated well. Unfortunately, the same can't be said for most of the horses and camels around the pyramid complex in Giza.

BOATING AND KAYAKING

Felucca rides are popular outings in Cairo, Luxor, and Aswan. A trip on one of these traditional wooden boats with large white sails is one of the best ways to enjoy the Nile. **Kayaking** is also a treat in Aswan where the Nile waters are at their cleanest.

DESERT SAFARIS AND SANDBOARDING

If you're keen to explore the mountains and deserts but not a fan of walking, try a desert safari by **4WD** (with driver) or **quad bike.** These trips are widely offered in the Western Desert, South Sinai, and Red Sea Coast. Children must be 12 or older to ride a quad bike by themselves.

While on safari in the deserts of Fayoum or Siwa, don't miss the chance to try your skills at **sandboarding** (think snowboarding but on sand dunes). Most driver/guides bring the board along, but it's best to request one if you're interested. With different sized dunes (mini to huge) and the option of sitting on the board like a sled, sandboarding can be enjoyed by all ages and skill levels. There's nowhere to rent sandboards independently, so if you'd like to try this activity, sign up for a 4WD safari.

DIVING AND SNORKELING

The best outposts for Egypt's number one recreation draw—diving and snorkeling—are Marsa Alam and Hurghada on the Red

Sea Coast, and Sharm el Sheikh and Dahab in the South Sinai. All of these spots are suitable for everyone: beginners and pros, solo travelers and families alike. Most of the best hotels and ecolodges have picked prime strips along the coast, with brilliant "house reefs" just offshore. Some travelers feel no need to venture far from the beauty of these private fringing reefs.

You can enjoy diving/snorkeling throughout the year, but many prefer to schedule their trips for September-early December when the weather's nice and the water's warm. May-July is hot but brings a wealth of sea life not seen outside the summer months. If you plan to visit in winter (late Dec.-Feb.), a wetsuit and a fleece will come in handy.

Travelers planning to snorkel might want to bring their own gear (mask and fins) for convenience, but there will be plenty of places from which to rent or buy in these major dive/snorkel towns. Divers will also have no trouble finding equipment to rent from their dive centers.

KITESURFING AND WINDSURFING

Kitesurfing is the second water sport of choice in Egypt, with prime destinations including the often-windy Red Sea Coast (El Gouna, Hurghada, Marsa Alam) and Dahab in the South Sinai. Each spot offers excellent kitesurfing centers with rentals and courses for beginners to advanced. Most also have windsurfing equipment and lessons available. May-October are the best months for these sports, but you can do them all year round.

HIKING AND TREKKING

The St. Katherine Protected Area in the South Sinai has dozens of routes up and around mountains with options for all levels. A less traveled (but flatter) option is to hike in the Western Desert—specifically, the Black and White Deserts between Bahariya and Farafra. Both places offer opportunities for short hikes or multiday treks and require that you enlist the services of a local guide.

Festivals and Events

Egypt's most popular festivals take place in Cairo and the Red Sea Coast resort town of El Gouna. Each spot hosts a glitzy annual film festival that brings international filmmakers and Egyptian movie stars. For a less flashy experience, head to Siwa during October's first full moon to celebrate the **Festival of Peace** (Asihaite), which includes a three-day gathering on a mountain with communal cooking and feasts.

CAIRO INTERNATIONAL FILM FESTIVAL

www.ciff.org.eg; Nov. or Dec.

The Cairo International Film Festival takes place in theaters around the capital in either November or December, with main events at the Cairo Opera House Complex.

GOUNA FILM FESTIVAL

www.elgounafilmfestival.com; Sept. or Oct.

Gouna's film festival is even swankier than Cairo's, typically held in purpose-made theaters in September or October. Be sure to buy your tickets in advance from their website.

SANDBOX MUSIC FESTIVAL

www.sandboxfestival.com; June

Gouna is the site of "Egypt's Burning Man": the Sandbox Music Festival. The three-day electronic music party on the beach usually happens in June, with one-day passes starting at 1,200LE. Get your tickets well in advance on their website.

Food

DINING OUT IN EGYPT

The relatively few venues in Egypt that enforce a **dress code** typically call for "smart casual" wear—basically no shorts, sweatpants, flip-flops, or sneakers. **Alcohol** is not typically served in restaurants except for the upscale spots. Unless stated otherwise in the listings throughout this book, assume alcohol is not on the menu.

TYPICAL EGYPTIAN DISHES

Egyptian food is not for dieters. Savory dishes are often fried or otherwise dense with ghee, butter, or oil, and sweets are soaked in syrup and then sprinkled with sugar. But it can be quite delicious…

Throughout most of the country you'll find these Egyptian street food staples:

- **Fuul:** a fava bean dish usually made into a paste with oil, tahini, and spices.
- **Ta'maya:** Egyptian falafel with fava beans as the main base instead of chickpeas, served with a'esh (round pita-like bread).
- **Koshary:** a carbtastic dish of spaghetti noodles, rice, lentils, and chickpeas topped with fried onions, a red sauce, and optional additions of hot sauce and a garlic juice.
- **Hawawshi:** spiced meat cooked inside a pita.
- In the winter, wandering carts with make-shift ovens sell **batata** (pure, unadulterated baked sweet potatoes), and other street vendors sell freshly grilled **dura** (corn).

Traditional dishes often cooked at home but also available in restaurants include:

- **Molokhia:** a green similar to spinach in appearance, but made into a viscous broth to be eaten with bread or rice.
- **Mahshi:** vegetables—usually zucchinis, eggplants, or peppers—stuffed with spiced rice and/or meat. Another common version also includes the rice/meat mixture rolled into cabbage or grape leaves.
- **Bamiya:** okra stew, sometimes made with lamb.

ta'maya

Ahaawi (Popular Street Cafés)

Ahaawi (singular ahwa) are Egypt's most ubiquitous social gathering hubs. These popular cafés with characteristic plastic patio chairs pouring into the streets serve shisha, soft drinks, juices, shay (tea) and, of course, ahwa (coffee). It's common for customers to stay for hours at a time, bringing their own food from nearby restaurants to enjoy between drinks or puffs on their waterpipes.

Once male-only spaces, many ahaawi now welcome all—and it won't be hard to tell which ones haven't made the jump into co-ed socialization spaces. To find some of the best, head to **Downtown Cairo** where dozens line the side streets. **Downtown Alexandria** also has its fair share of unique ahaawi, ranging from social institutions established in the late 19th century to ad hoc enterprises set up along the sea.

- **Kebda:** usually fried cow liver, but camel liver is also a favorite.
- **Hamam mahsi:** pigeon stuffed with spiced freekeh, a cracked wheat.
- **Macarona bechamel:** similar to lasagna—a baked pasta with a layer of spiced beef, topped with creamy white béchamel sauce.
- **Goulash:** meat pie in flaky phyllo dough.

DRINKS

Be sure to try:

- **Sahleb** in the winter—a warm liquid that's more like a snack than a beverage made from the flour from dried tubers of wild orchids, coconut flakes, cinnamon, sugar, nuts, and raisins.
- **Karkade** in the summer—a sweet, hibiscus iced drink.

DESSERTS

Desserts in Egypt are for the real sweet tooths out there.

- **Kunafa:** a syrup-soaked treat with a soft cream filling and layers of shredded phyllo dough made crunchy on the outside.
- **Basbousa:** a moist, buttery, melt-in-your-mouth semolina cake, also syrup-soaked and often topped with crushed nuts or clotted cream.
- **Harissa:** the Alexandrian version of basbousa—a bit thicker and often made with coconut, raisins, and nuts.
- **Um Ali:** Egyptian bread pudding, made of torn-up pastry mixed with raisins, pistachios, coconut flakes, and sugar, topped with cream and cinnamon before being popped into the oven for a golden-top finish.
- **Roz bi laban:** rice pudding (sometimes with coconut) served cold.

Accommodations

The quality of accommodations in Egypt varies greatly depending on the city. The major tourist destinations (Cairo, Luxor, Sharm el Sheikh, and Hurghada) have a wealth of options—from luxury **hotels** to boutique **guesthouses** and quality **Airbnbs.** Other spots have much less to offer when it comes to lodging (like the North Coast and Northern Nile Valley), with just a handful of decent outposts for the casual visitor. For attractive **ecolodges,** check out Fayoum, Siwa, the St. Katherine Protectorate, Aswan, and Marsa Alam; for sprawling all-inclusive **resorts,** head to Sharm el Sheikh, Hurghada, El Gouna, or Marsa Alam; for **camping,** make your way to Fayoum's Wadi el-Rayan Protectorate, Ras Mohammed National Park in the South Sinai, or the Western Desert (the Black and White Deserts between Bahariya and Farafra or Siwa's Great Sand Sea); and for glamping in **beach huts** or fancy tents, your best options will be in the South Sinai between Nuweiba and Taba or in Marsa Alam.

You can expect most accommodations (except for the beach huts/tents) to have **air conditioning.** All listings included in this book do unless otherwise noted.

BOOKING TIPS

When choosing your accommodations, there are a few important points to keep in mind.

- It's usually cheapest to **book your hotel** directly via phone or website, but www.booking.com is another popular platform for making reservations. Be sure to read the fine print as taxes and other fees are often added to the advertised room price. Some hotels and lodges also use Airbnb, but again this comes with added fees. The smaller establishments (ecolodges, beach huts, campgrounds) will often prefer booking via Facebook. In this case, you can usually pay upon arrival (often cash only).
- Most hotels permit **smoking** in at least some of the rooms and often even in the lobbies. Be sure to request a nonsmoking room if that's your preference.
- Egyptian law forbids unmarried Egyptians from **sharing accommodations with the opposite sex.** In practice, this applies to both Egyptians and other Arabs who wish to stay in the same room in hotels, resorts, lodges, or even Airbnbs. Unmarried foreigners who both hold passports in Western countries shouldn't have a problem.

Conduct and Customs

SMOKING

Smoking in Egypt is widespread (at least 40% of Egyptian males smoke tobacco products) and is ubiquitous in public spaces, including hotels, restaurants, bars, and cafés. When establishments do have "nonsmoking sections" they're usually just tiny corners of the room, and inevitably fill with smoke during busier times. Nonsmoking venues are rare, and I've tried to note those that qualify as such in this book, or to mention if a venue has outdoor dining space available (more common). The legal smoking age in Egypt is 18.

ALCOHOL

In Egypt, the legal drinking age is 21.

Local beer, wine, and spirits are easy to get in most cities around Egypt, whether at bars or liquor shops. **Drinkies** (tel. 19330; www.drinkies.net) is nationwide chain that can deliver to your accommodation with dozens of branches in Cairo/Giza and Alexandria, and a few others in Sharm el Sheikh, Hurghada, and Luxor. You typically can't bring your own alcohol to restaurants, except for upscale establishments where you'll be charged a corkage fee (call ahead to ask). Drinking in public spaces (streets, parks, etc.) is not allowed.

Imported alcohol can be found at select bars, restaurants, and hotels, but is usually absurdly expensive—it's not uncommon for a single drink to go for $50 or more. If you have a favorite spirit, you might want to pick up a bottle or two at duty free on your way in at the airport. You have 48 hours after arrival to purchase up to three liters of alcohol at any duty-free shop around Egypt (be sure to bring your passport, and they might also ask for your boarding pass). Check out www.dutyfree.egyptair.com for a list of locations around Egypt.

Some areas of the country are drier than others. Travelers heading to the Western Desert (Siwa, Bahariya, Farafra, Fayoum), Northern Nile Valley (Minya, Sohag, Abydos, Qena), Marsa Matruh, Port Said, or the beach camps between Nuweiba and Taba might want to bring their own booze.

SHISHA

Shisha, a waterpipe used to smoke tobacco (called hookah or nargile in other countries), is ubiquitous throughout Egypt. You'll find it at many cafés and restaurants, often in a variety of flavors like watermelon, peach, mint, melon, or apple.

Almost by definition, ahaawi (street-side coffee shops) offer shisha, but theirs is typically of a strong variety and not all have the fruity flavors more common at cafés. If you choose to partake, be sure to ask for a fresh, disposable pipe (most venues offer this). The legal age for partaking in shisha is 18.

TIME

The near constant traffic of Egypt's big cities has given their residents a lifelong excuse for being late. An "Egyptian minute" can take hours, and trains and buses are perpetually tardy (but always on schedule when you're running late!). Try not to get too frustrated and just take it as part of the cultural experience.

Thursday night-Saturday is considered the **weekend** in Egypt. Expect Thursday and Friday nights to be the busiest at bars and restaurants.

TOUCHING

Touching between the opposite sexes can sometimes be taboo. Not all women will want to shake the hands of men and vice versa. If in doubt, feel free to express your greetings with a hand to the heart. PDA (even between foreigners) is typically frowned upon, unless you're in the confines of your hotel or resort grounds.

TIPPING AND BAKSHEESH

There's sometimes a fine line between tipping and bribing—the Arabic word "baksheesh" can really mean either—and both are usually acceptable. A dollar or two can open a number of doors at the various temple sites, mosques, and museums. Bathroom attendants will usually ask for (or expect) a few Egyptian pounds. At restaurants a 10-15% tip is the norm. The same goes for drivers and guides. People are often seriously underpaid, so a little extra here and there is very much appreciated.

"KHALEEH"

As a sign of politeness, Egyptians will often refuse payment for goods and services, saying "khaleeh" ("keep it"). As generous as Egyptians are, this is almost never meant sincerely. Try to pay *at least* three times (maybe more) if a stranger tries to give you something for free.

Coronavirus in Egypt

At the time of writing in late 2021, Egypt was moderately impacted by the effects of the coronavirus, but the situation was constantly evolving. Face masks were required in some museums, supermarkets, and on public transportation, but there was little enforcement.

Now more than ever, Moon encourages its readers to be courteous and ethical in their travel. We ask travelers to be respectful to residents, and mindful of the evolving situation in their chosen destination when planning their trip.

BEFORE YOU GO

- Check local websites (listed below) for **local restrictions** and the **overall health status** of the destination and your point of origin. If you're traveling to or from an area that is currently a COVID-19 hotspot, you may want to reconsider your trip.
- Get **vaccinated** if your health status allows, and if possible, take a **coronavirus test** with enough time to receive your results before your departure.
- Check with your airline and the destination's health authority for updated **travel requirements.** Some airlines may be taking more steps than others to help you travel safely, such as limited occupancy; check their websites for more information before buying your ticket. Flights may be more infrequent.
- Check the website of any museums and other venues you wish to patronize to confirm that they're open and if their hours have been adjusted.

Health and Safety

EMERGENCY NUMBERS

- **Tourist Police:** 126
- **Ambulance:** 123
- **Fire Department:** 180

Aside from the tourist police, operators are not likely to speak English. Best to have a local bystander call if possible.

VACCINATIONS

The US Centers for Disease Control and Prevention (CDC) recommends travelers to Egypt get vaccinated against hepatitis A and B, typhoid, rabies, measles, and tetanus. Proof of COVID vaccination and/or a negative PCR test are required for entry at the time of writing. Check the **International Air Transport Association (IATA) Travel Center** website (www.iatatravelcentre.com) for updated information about COVID-related travel requirements.

MEDICAL SERVICES

Medical services in Egypt range from good to dire. There's an overburdened public healthcare system, which travelers will want to avoid. Major cities have decent private hospitals in case of emergencies, though visitors from countries with the world's finest facilities might be unimpressed with even the best Egypt has to offer.

For non-emergency care, Cairo is the country's medical hub with an abundance of relatively inexpensive private clinics—some with outstanding specialists. For a consultation with the best doctors, expect to pay around $50. As with all trips, **travel insurance** is a wise addition in case of emergencies.

- Pack **hand sanitizer,** a **thermometer,** and plenty of **face masks.**
- **Assess the risk** of entering crowded spaces, joining tours, and taking public transit.
- Expect **general disruptions.** Events may be postponed or canceled, and some tours and venues may require reservations, enforce limits on the number of guests, be operating during different hours than the ones listed, or be closed entirely.

RESOURCES

- **World Health Organization:** www.who.int/emergencies/diseases/novel-coronavirus-2019/travel-advice
- **International Air Transport Association:** www.iatatravelcentre.com/world.php
- ***New York Times* Coronavirus Map:** www.nytimes.com/interactive/2020/world/coronavirus-maps.html
- **CDC:** www.cdc.gov/coronavirus/2019-ncov/travelers
- **U.S. State Department:** https://travel.state.gov/content/travel/en/traveladvisories/ea/covid-19-information.html
- **U.S. Embassy in Egypt:** https://eg.usembassy.gov/u-s-citizen-services/covid-19-information

AIR QUALITY

Air quality in Cairo and Alexandria can be quite bad. Outside of these two large cities, the air is generally *much* cleaner, but many places still do burn their garbage. It's always helpful to have a scarf or bandana to breathe into when passing through particularly congested areas. People with respiratory problems will want to keep inhalers on hand.

DRINKING WATER

The water that comes out of Egypt's taps is typically highly treated with chlorine and other chemicals, which means it's usually fine for brushing teeth, but not for drinking. Though most Egyptians do drink the tap water, it's not recommended. Bottled water is easy to find in all major cities at kiosks and corner stores for around 5LE for 1.5 liters. You might want to stock up on a few bottles to keep at your hotel or for longer outings. Unlike some destinations, hotels don't tend to have filtered water for guests to refill bottles, so you really do have to rely on bottled water.

FOOD POISONING

Food poisoning (bacterial diarrhea) is an unfortunate but common experience for many visitors to Egypt. Stick to bottled water, patronize recommended restaurants, avoid street food, and perhaps pass on fresh salads or other raw foods to minimize the chances of exposure. For adventurous eaters, keep an eye out for pharmacies (singular saydalaya) in case you need to stop in for some antibiotics. Pharmacists will often recommend Flagyl (metronidazole), Antinal (nifuroxazide), or for very bad cases Cipro (ciprofloxacin). These are all widely available without a prescription in Egypt. Avoid taking loperamide (Imodium) or other medications that only treat the symptom (diarrhea) and not the cause (likely bacteria) as that can slow the recovery process.

TRAFFIC AND ROAD SAFETY

The biggest threat to your health and safety in Egypt is probably traffic. Exercise extreme caution when crossing streets in Cairo. The best strategy might be to walk beside (not behind) a local who's crossing, or to ask someone to help you get to the other side. If you go it alone, try to make eye contact with the drivers and whatever you do, don't run—if you give drivers enough time to react, they'll likely avoid hitting you. Also, try not to cross in front of microbuses (they'll probably be speeding and might not have their eyes on the road).

CRIME AND SAFETY

Egypt is generally a very safe country. The level of gun violence is extremely low and pales in comparison to the US. The country does experience occasional terrorist attacks, but then again, so do many major cities around the world.

Do be vigilant of phone and bag snatchers who occasionally speed by on motorcycles. And as always, common sense safety precautions should be taken (e.g., best to avoid dark, empty streets; watch your pockets in crowded areas; keep your valuables in a safe spot, etc.). It's also good to avoid wandering into unknown neighborhoods at night. (Any area listed in this book should be perfectly safe at most hours.)

The North Sinai is the one place in Egypt that is a strict no-go zone. Since 2011 there has been an ongoing war between the state security forces and a combination of Islamic militants and locals radicalized by the state's indiscriminate use of force. Despite the relative proximity, South Sinai remains a safe place to travel. There have been incidents of terrorist attacks in the south, but they are as random as anywhere else. The worst incident was in 2015 when a flight departing from Sharm el Sheikh Airport to Russia was downed by a bomb, killing over 220 people. Since then, Egyptian authorities have upped the airport security significantly.

As safety levels change from time to time, check your government travel warnings before your trip. Note they often err on the side of caution and tend to inflate the security threats.

Travel Tips

BUDGETING

Prices around Egypt are generally inexpensive compared to the US and Europe but can vary drastically depending on the venue. A cup of coffee at an ahwa (street-side café) will go for between 5-15 LE, while it can cost four times as much at an upscale café or hotel. Local staples like fuul (fava bean paste) or ta'maya (Egyptian felafel) sandwiches go for just 5-10LE, and a filling meal of koshary (pasta-based dish with lentils, chickpeas, and sauces) can be enjoyed for 15-30LE. Fancier restaurants around the country have more Western prices, with some charging 500-800LE for a meal with a drink. Alcohol prices also have a dramatic range, with 50-60LE for a local beer in more casual bars, and imported shots at swish venues going for 800LE or more (these swankier spots also usually have the local beer option for around 100LE).

Taxis are extremely cheap relative to the US and Europe. Expect to pay around 15LE for 4 kilometers (2.5 mi) and 100-150LE for 20 kilometers (12 mi) (depending on traffic). The meters in Cairo's white taxis start at 7.50LE. Ubers cost around the same, about 2.7LE/kilometer plus 0.40LE/minute and the 7.25LE start price during regular hours and increasing during peak times.

MONEY

Egypt's currency, the **Egyptian Pound** ("gineh masri" in Arabic) is represented by the symbols LE, EGP, E£, or ج.م. Paper currency denominations come in 1, 5, 10, 20, 50, 100, and 200LE. The 1LE coins are useful to have on hand for small tips.

Packing Checklist

CLOTHING

Light colored, loose fitting, breathable clothes are ideal. Specific items to pack include:

- **T-shirts:** Pack extra—you'll likely soak through a couple a day.
- **Layers:** The best antidote for hot days and cold winter nights (or excessive air-conditioning other times of year).
- **Light scarves:** Always good to have on hand to protect yourself from cold, sun, sand, or car exhaust.
- **Comfortable shoes**
- **Swimsuit**
- **Water shoes**
- **Ankle-length dresses or skirts:** Outside the South Sinai, Red Sea Coast, or compounds on the North Coast, women may not feel comfortable in shorts. These are a good alternative.

OTHER ITEMS

- **Light umbrella:** It does rain on occasion in the winter.
- **Hat**
- **Sunglasses**
- **Sunscreen:** Also available at Egyptian pharmacies, but if you plan to snorkel, try to bring some reef-safe sunscreen along with you.
- **SPF lip balm**
- **Camera and mobile phone***
- **Power bank**
- **Goggles**
- **Flashlight:** Useful for exploring tomb interiors and dimly lit museums.
- **Plug adaptors:** For UK, US, and Canadian electronics (US and Canadian electronics may also require a voltage converter).
- **Female sanitary products:** Pads are easy to find in pharmacies across the country, with tampons also available in most big cities—they're both called *Always* (after the Procter & Gamble brand that's cornered the market). But if you have a preferred type, you might want to bring your own.

* A note on **cameras:** Most sites require you to buy an additional camera ticket (50-300LE), which can add up. At the time of writing there were no fees for taking photos with phones, so if you have good image-snapping capabilities on your mobile you might consider leaving the camera in your bag at these stops.

The pound has been volatile over the years, particularly when it was devalued in November 2016 and jumped from 8.5LE to the (US) dollar to over 18LE/$1 in just a few days. In more recent years it's been relatively stable, hovering around the following rates:

- **US$1**=15.5-16.5LE
- **€1**=18-20LE
- **£1**=20-21.5
- **AUS$1**=10-12LE
- **NZ$1**=9.5-11.5LE
- **ZAR1**=0.83-1.3LE

Check www.ex.com before you travel for the latest exchange rate.

Credit Cards

Cash is king at the average Egyptian establishment, but **Visa** and **Mastercard** are accepted at nearly all upscale hotels, shops, and restaurants. If you do use a credit card, ask to be charged in the local currency to avoid markups and check your policy before you travel to make sure there aren't high international transaction fees.

ATMs

ATMs are abundant in most cities around the country and will likely be your best way to access cash (unless your bank charges astronomical fees). If possible, try to bring an extra debit card in case your primary one gets lost, stolen, or eaten by the occasionally hungry machine. Most banks place a 6,000LE daily withdrawal limit, but some (like HSBC) will allow you to take out 8,000LE per day. You'll usually have to do this in two transactions of 3,000-4,000LE each. Don't forget to let your bank know you're traveling.

Exchanging Money

It's typically far less expensive to change money in Egypt than at your country of origin, where reserves of Egyptian Pounds are not likely high. There are plenty of currency exchanges in major cities. Banks will also usually change your cash at a fair rate, but they have limited hours (around 8:30am-3pm) and only operate Sunday-Thursday. There should also be bank windows at the airport with extended hours. You might want to shop around, but generally don't expect to pay too much more than the official exchange rate.

Note: You're not supposed to bring more than 5,000LE in cash into the country, but can bring up to $10,000 (USD) or the equivalency in other foreign currencies.

Student Discounts

Students are offered discounts on admission to most sites. Be sure to bring your student ID card. Technically, you're supposed to have the official International Student ID Card (available for $20 at www.isic.org) to get the discount, but some sites are more lenient than others.

OPENING HOURS

Before COVID-19, Cairo never slept. It was not uncommon to see 24/7 cafés and restaurants, and bars/nightclubs open until the early hours of the morning. The resort towns of Sharm el Sheikh, Hurghada, and El Gouna kept their nightlife venues open until around 2-3am, while venues in most other destinations around Egypt closed around midnight.

Cairo might return to its 24/7 schedule someday, but the military-backed regime has long wanted to instill "discipline" into the country's population with an early to bed, early to rise system and might try to extend the new hours even after the pandemic subsides. At the time of writing, most shops had a mandatory 10-11pm weekday closing time (typically opening between 9-11am) and could stay open an hour later on weekends (Thurs.-Sat.). Grocery stores could stay open until 1am; and restaurants, bars, and cafés until 2am, with takeaway still often offered at all hours. Some establishments have managed to maintain their 24/7 habits discreetly.

PUBLIC HOLIDAYS

Egypt's major public holidays that create notable changes in daily life include:

Traveling During Ramadan

The Islamic holy month of Ramadan is a period of fasting and prayer for many Egyptians. Traveling at this time is not an issue—in fact, it's a unique time to visit, when an air of festiveness spreads across the country. At sunset, streets in usually chaotic Cairo and Alexandria become free of traffic for the hour or so during the breaking of the fast (iftar), and in many areas, colorful Ramadan tents are set up for free iftar meals for those in need.

WHAT TO KNOW

Most shops and restaurants—and all sights—do remain open during Ramadan (though hours may vary), and non-Muslims are not expected to fast. However, travelers who visit at this time should expect some inconveniences in addition to **truncated hours** for sights and restaurants, including **limited nightlife** and difficulty finding **alcohol.** All liquor stores close for the month (save a few discreet vendors), as do many bars. You can bring your own liquor into the country from duty free, and most international hotels do still serve alcohol. (A law bans the sale of alcohol to Egyptians during Ramadan, but it doesn't apply to foreigners.)

In general, expect a **slower pace:** Fasting (and un-caffeinated) guides might not be as animated as usual, and early morning starts might be challenging for them after staying up for sohour (the last meal just before sunrise when fasting resumes). It may also be difficult to find a **taxi** during the time around iftar (at sundown), but the streets will be delightfully empty—great for walking around Egypt's normally traffic-choked cities.

UPCOMING DATES FOR RAMADAN

Ramadan follows the lunar calendar, so it falls on different dates each year. Here are the approximate start dates for this month of fasting and prayer for the next few years:

- **2022:** April 1
- **2023:** March 23
- **2024:** March 10
- **2025:** February 28

- **Sham el Nassim** (Spring Festival that coincides with Orthodox Easter) takes place on a Sunday to Monday in April or early May. (Should fall on April 24-25 in 2022 and April 16-17 in 2023.)
- **Eid el-Fitr** (Festival of the Breaking of the Fast) takes place over three days at the end of Ramadan. It should begin on May 2 in 2022 and April 21 in 2023 and shifts around 11 days earlier each year.
- **Eid el-Adha** (Festival of the Sacrifice): Like Ramadan and Eid el-Fitr, this Muslim holiday is based on the lunar calendar and similarly shifts depending on the year. It lasts for four days, and will begin around July 10 in 2022 and June 29 in 2023.

The week of each holiday often sends Egyptians flocking to the coasts—so best to avoid Egypt's seaside destinations during these times (unless you prefer crowds).

Other official holidays that still get people a day off work but aren't as dramatically celebrated are:

- **Eastern Orthodox Christmas:** January 7
- **Revolution Day/National Police Day:** January 25
- **Sinai Liberation Day** (commemorated nationwide): April 25
- **Labor Day:** May 1
- **June 30 Revolution Day:** June 30
- **July 23 Revolution Day:** July 23

- **Armed Forces Day:** October 6
- **Mawlid el-Nabi** (Prophet's Birthday): This is another one based on the lunar calendar with shifting dates each year. Oct. 7, 2022, and Sept 26, 2023.

COMMUNICATIONS

The dialing code in Egypt is +20. The best way to call abroad is by using FaceTime, Facebook Messenger, or Skype via Wi-Fi or phone data.

Phones and Cell Phones

Even if you'll only be in Egypt for a week, it's probably worth buying a local SIM card. Packages with 4G are cheap and great to have for navigating the country, making reservations, or in case of emergency. Make sure your phone is unlocked.

There are a handful of telecom companies, but **Vodafone** is probably the easiest to work with and their staff should speak English. Head to a Vodafone branch when you arrive (there are also branches in some airport terminals around the country). Typical operating hours are 9am-midnight Saturday-Thursday and 1:30pm-10pm on Fridays. Be sure to bring your passport. A good package for a month (including the cost of the SIM card) should go for around 200-300LE.

Internet Access

Most hotels will offer some kind of Wi-Fi ranging from excellent to barely functioning. Wi-Fi is also available in many restaurants and cafés—again, ranging in quality and reliability. If internet access is essential, it's best to get a SIM card with data.

Shipping and Postal Service

Don't bother shipping anything in or to Egypt. It likely won't get where it's supposed to go.

WEIGHTS AND MEASURES

Egypt uses the **metric system** for its weights and distances.

Electricity in Egypt is the same as in Europe with standard voltage of 220V, 50 Hz frequency, and two-prong plug. A simple plug adapter is necessary for UK electronics, while both an adapter and voltage converter are required for use of electronics from the US or Canada (with the exception of chargers for laptops, cellphones, and all other appliances that say "INPUT: 100-240V, 50/60 Hz").

Egypt follows **Eastern European Time** (EET) and stopped observing daylight savings in 2016.

Traveler Advice

ACCESS FOR TRAVELERS WITH DISABILITIES

Unfortunately, the Egyptian government makes little attempt to accommodate people with disabilities, whether locals or visitors. The city sidewalks are usually broken and/or blocked and ramps are rare. That being said, many travelers with disabilities do visit Egypt, and with some help can have an enjoyable experience. The best strategy is to arrange with a tour operator ahead of time, explaining the nature of your disability and confirming they have a suitable guide. Transportation by private car with driver/guide will likely be the best way to move about the country. Many of the best river cruises also have experience with travelers with disabilities and can help accommodate.

TRAVELING WITH CHILDREN

Depending on the destination, traveling with children in Egypt can be a challenge. The chaotic traffic in Cairo and Alexandria can make keeping children safe from speeding vehicles stressful. Elsewhere around Egypt should be much easier to keep an eye on little

Visiting Mosques

Nearly all mosques in Egypt are open to visitors of any faith. Smaller neighborhood mosques are often the domain of men/boys and it's rare for non-Muslims to visit, but the larger ones—and especially the historical monuments that double as tourist attractions, including all listed in this book—are typically open to men, women, and children alike. A few things to keep in mind before you visit:

- Non-Muslims should avoid visiting during Friday noon prayers—the busiest prayer time of the week.
- To enter mosques, both sexes must cover legs and shoulders and remove their shoes. The mosques better known to tourists will usually have elastic waistband pants for men and women whose legs are not covered.
- Women must cover their hair.

ones, and some resorts on the Red Sea Coast and in the South Sinai are particularly child friendly.

FEMALE TRAVELERS

Even though nearly all women in Egypt—both locals and foreign visitors—experience sexual harassment of some sort, women should not let this deter them from visiting Egypt or even traveling solo. The most common type of harassment will be verbal expressions of "appreciation." Physical sexual assault of tourists is, fortunately, extremely rare. If you do encounter any issues, call the tourist police (126) or head to the nearest police station.

In terms of dress, it's best to avoid shorts and low-cut shirts. To enter mosques, in addition to covering legs and shoulders (also required of men), women must cover their hair. The most popular touristic mosques will have fabric to borrow.

Women will likely feel more comfortable sitting in the back of taxis (men often sit beside the driver in front) and riding in the ladies-only cars on the metro in Cairo. Regular beachwear is fine for most beaches on the Red Sea Coast and Sinai, but not advised on public beaches in the cities (e.g., Alexandria, Port Said). Solo women might receive unwanted attention at bars but are unlikely to feel unsafe. Some ahaawi (street side cafés) are male-dominated, but women can visit freely if they're comfortable.

SENIOR TRAVELERS

There are plenty of ways for travelers to experience Egypt—from rough and tumble backpacking on trains and buses to luxury hotel-hopping and private transportation. Senior visitors wary of Egypt's frenetic cities can easily visit the country in comfort with the second option. The best approach is to contact a professional tour operator to make a full package, from airport transfers to daily excursions with local guides. Discounts are generally not available for senior travelers.

GAY AND LESBIAN TRAVELERS

While there is an underground gay and lesbian community in Cairo and Alexandria, homosexuality is not socially accepted in most Egyptian circles and remains under constant attack by the state. There's no explicit law against same sex practices, but hundreds of Egyptians have been arrested in recent years on grounds of "debauchery" for alleged homosexual acts. Tourists in Egypt aren't likely to run into trouble with the state for their sexual orientation. In case you do need assistance from the tourist police, it's best to leave out any mention of sexuality.

PEOPLE OF COLOR

Many Egyptians will tell you there's no racism in Egypt, but that's unfortunately not the case. There's a clear hierarchy in the country, with the darker skinned Egyptians from the south often treated poorly by lighter skinned northerners. Travelers of color from North America or Europe will likely encounter disbelief when they tell Egyptians where they're from and can expect a follow up question about where they're *really* from. People of Asian background will be assumed to come from China. Though the comments can be annoying, people typically don't mean any harm and often don't realize they're being offensive. If their "joking" crosses the line, head to the nearest tourist police or call them at 126 to report any incidents.

Resources

Glossary

ablaq: stripes created by alternating stone colors; a common architectural motif used by the Mamluks
'aish: round pita-like bread
a'in (plural a'youn): natural spring
ahwa (plural ahaawi): outdoor coffee shop
arabaya sandouk: box car (used for transit in Fayoum and rural towns/villages)
asab el-sukkar: sugarcane
bab (plural bibaan): door
baksheesh: tips
batata: sweet potatoes
batatas: potatoes (often used to mean fries)
cenotaph: a monument to someone who is buried somewhere else
dura: corn
fateer: flaky savory or sweet pastry; sometimes called Egyptian pizza
fattah: boiled lamb or beef on a bed of rice and fried pita bread with tomato sauce
fuul: fava bean stew
galabeya (plural galaleeb): full-length gown typically worn by men in rural Egypt
gibna ma'laya: fried cheese
hantour (plural hanateer): horse carriage
haramlik ("forbidden place"): a typical component of Ottoman architecture comprised of a women-only space
hawawshi: spiced meat in pita
iwan: vaulted chamber
jebel (plural jebaal): mountain
ka: the concept of a divine spirit passed on from ruler to ruler (in the ancient Egyptian language)
karshif: mud, rock, and salt mixture used as a building material in Siwa
khan: inn for travelers (historic term)
khanqah: Sufi lodge and place of worship (historic term)
koshary: pasta-based dish with lentils, chickpeas, and sauces (sometimes spelled koshari)
Kufic: a style of Arabic script characterized by sharp angles
kuttab: elementary school that focused on literacy and memorization of the Quran (historic term)
madrasa (plural madaaris): Historically, a madrasa was a center of learning that focused on theology and law through study of the Quran and Hadith (sayings attributed to the Prophet Mohammed). In contemporary Arabic, madrasa means school.
mahragan (plural mahraganat): festival; also a popular type of music that emerged from Cairo's working-class districts
mahshi: vegetables stuffed with rice or meat
makhalal: pickled vegetables
mamluks: people, mostly Turkic, from Central Asia who were enslaved as children and trained as warriors. The phenomenon emerged in the 9th century, and mamluks eventually overthrew their masters in the 13th century—ruling over Egypt and Syria for nearly three centuries.
maristan: hospital (historical term)
mashrabiya: wooden window screens
mastaba: flat-topped tomb
mihrab: prayer niche
minbar: the mosque pulpit from which religious leaders deliver sermons
molokhia: green soupy dish akin to spinach
mousakka: eggplant and minced meat

muqarnas: miniature pointed niches
necropolis: a sacred burial site of an ancient city
niqab: a face covering that conceals all but the eyes
om ali: bread pudding with coconut, raisins, nuts, and cream
oud: a classic instrument in Middle Eastern music; similar to a lute
qibla: the direction of the Ka'ba (a building in the center of Islam's most important mosque) in Mecca, which Muslims face when they pray; each mosque has a qibla wall (the one the faces Mecca)
rababa: one-stringed fiddle
roz bi-laban: rice pudding
sabil: public drinking fountain (historic term)
sada: plain (often used to describe food preference or to specify sugar-free coffee)
sahleb: a thick white drink made of orchid tubers, sugar, and cinnamon
saj: Syrian bread akin to a tortilla
salamlik ("greeting place"): a typical component of Ottoman architecture comprised of a room for entertaining male company
saydalaya (plural saydalayat): pharmacy
sheikh (plural shiyoukh): tribal leader
shish tawook: grilled chicken shish kebab
shisha: waterpipe (known in other countries as hookah or nargile)
sobia: a sweet drink made from rice and coconut, sprinkled with cinnamon
souq (plural aswaq): market
ta'maya: Egyptian falafel (made with fava beans instead of chickpeas)
tagine (plural towagen): stews cooked and served in a clay pot
tar: a flat drum similar to a tambourine
taza: fresh
wadi: valley; dried riverbed

Egyptian Arabic Phrasebook

Many of Arabic's 28 letters are pronounced similar to their English counterparts. Some major exceptions include the letter **'ain** (ع)—pronounced as a sweeping sound deep in the throat, as in *a'fwan* (you're welcome); **ghain** (غ), pronounced as a kind of gargling sound in the back of the throat, as in *shighaal* (works); and **qaaf** (ق)—the Arabic "q," a guttural sound with a bit of a click, as in *fondoq* (hotel). This is often pronounced as a glottal stop by Egyptians, similar to the **hamza** (ء)—a quasi-letter not included in the 28 main letters, as in the last letter of *masa'* (evening).

There are also two "h" sounds—one pronounced like an English "h" (ه) and the other a deeper kind of hissing sound (ح), indicated below with a capital "H"; two "s" sounds—again one pronounced like an English "s" (س) and another a deeper sounding "s" (ص) produced at the front of the mouth, written with a capital "S" below; two "d" sounds—an English-sounding "d" (د) and a deeper one (ض), written as a capital "D" below; and two "t" sounds—an English-sounding "t" (ت) and a deeper one (ط), written below as a capital "T."

The letter **sheen** (ش) is pronounced as "sh"; and the letter **kha** (خ) as "kh"—a scratchy sound in the throat (the way Spaniards pronounced their J's). The Arabic "r" (ر) is also rolled similar to a Spanish "r."

The letter **tha** (ث), pronounced as "th" in classical Arabic, becomes an "s" or "t" sound in Egyptian Arabic. Egyptian Arabic also simplifies other letters like the letter **Za** (ظ), which together with the letter **zain** (ز), sounds like an English "z"; and the letter **dhal** (ذ), typically also pronounced by Egyptians as a "z" or "t."

ESSENTIAL PHRASES

Hello ahlan
Good morning SabaH el-kheir
Good evening masa' el-kheir
Goodbye ma'a salama
Please low samaHt (said to male) / low samaHti (to female)
Thank you shukran
You're welcome a'fwan
Yes aywa
No la
How are you? ezzayak? (to male) / ezzayek? (to female)
I'm well, you? kowyes (said by a male) / kowyesa (female), enta (to male) / enti (to female)?
Nice to meet you forSa sa'eeda
My name is... ismi...
What's your name? ismak (said to male) / ismik (to female) ay?
Excuse me ba'd iznak (said to male) / ba'd iznik (to female)
Sorry aasif (said by a male) / assfa (by a female)
I don't understand mish faahim (said by a male) / fahma (female)
Where is... feen...
...the bathroom? el-Hammam?
...the exit? el-khuroog?
...the entrance? ed-dakhool?
Do you speak English? bi-titkalem (said to a male) / bi-titkalemi (to a female) inglizi?
Is there Wi-Fi? fih wifi?
What's the password? el basswordeh?
Is it allowed? masmuH?
Is it forbidden? mamnu'?

EMERGENCIES

Help! il-Ha'ooni!
Call the police! ITlub el-bolees
I want the tourist police. a'eyz (male) / a'eyza (female) shorTat es-siyaHa
Please take me to the hospital. wadi-ni el-mustashfa low samaHt.

MONEY

Money faloos
Cash cash
Bank bank
Credit card kart *or* fisa
Do you take credit card? kart shighaal? *or* yinfa' kart?

TRANSPORTATION

Where is...? feen...
...the bus el-autobees?
...the train station maHatat el-'atr?
...the ticket office maktab el-tizaaker?
Ticket tazkara (plural tazaaker)
Taxi taksi (plural takaasi)
What time does the bus leave? el-autobees bi-yitla' es-saa'a kam?

DIRECTIONS

Go straight imshi 'ala Tool
Take the next left khush esh-shimal ili gae
Take the next right khush el-yimeen ili gae
...at the traffic light ...'and el-ishaara
...at the intersection ...'and et-taqaaTa'
Close to urayib min
In front of oo-daam
Behind wara
Next to gamb
Can I get out here? mumken anzil hina?
Pull over here please 'ala gamb low samaHt
On the corner 'ala en-nawSiya

PLACES

I want to go to... a'eyz (male) / a'eyza (female) arooH...
...the beach esh-shaT'
...the restaurant el-maTa'm
...the hotel el-fondoq
...the airport el-mataar
Mosque gaama' (plural gowaama') *or* masgid (plural masaagid)
Church kineesa (plural kinay-es)

FOOD

May I have... mumken...
Menu men-you
Water (bottled) my-a (m'adinaya)
Tea shay
Anise (herbal tea) yansoon

Mint (herbal tea) n'anaa'
Hibiscus (herbal tea, hot) karkaday (sukhn)
Hibiscus (herbal tea, cold) karkaday (saa'a)
Coffee ahwa
...without sugar sada
...with a bit of sugar 'ala er-reeHa
...with a lot of sugar sukkar ziyada
Juice 'aSeer
Orange juice 'aSeer burtu'aan
Mango juice 'aSeer manga
Strawberry juice 'aSeer fraowla
Beer bira
Red wine nabeet aHmar
White wine nabeet abiyaD
Alcohol khamra
Bread a'esh
Meat laHma
The bill el-Hisaab
I'm a vegetarian ana nabaati (male) / nabataya (female)

SHOPPING

How much does it cost? bi-kam?
I'm just browsing. batfarag bas.
I'm looking for... ana badowar 'ala
...a scarf shaal
...a mother-of-pearl box Sandoo' Sadaf
...a bag shanTa
...a pharaonic statue timsaal far'aooni
...a gold necklace silsila dahab
...a silver necklace silsila faDa
That's expensive da ghaali
Are there other styles / designs? fih ashkaal tania?

HEALTH

Pharmacy saydalaya
I'm sick ana ta'baan (male), ta'baana (female)
I'm hurt ana mowgowa' (male), mowgowa'a (female)
I have... a'ndi...
...a fever sokhnaya
...a headache Sodaa'
...a stomachache maghas
...diarrhea is-haal
...constipation imsaak
I have a toothache Dirsi bi-yiw-ga'ni
I feel like I'm going to throw up Haassis (male) / Hass-sa (female) ini ha-rag-ga'
I'm allergic to... a'ndi Hassasaya min...
I need a doctor miHtaag (male) / miHtaaga (female) doktoor
Medicine dawa (plural ad-waya)

ACCOMMODATIONS

Do you have a room...? a'ndak oDa fawDia...?
...for one person li-fard waHid?
...for two people li-fardain?
...for three people li-talat afraad?
Nonsmoking min gheer tadkheen
Does the room have AC? el-oDa mu-kay-yef-a?
Is there AC? fih takeef?
Is there a pool? fih pisine?
Is the hotel near downtown? el-fondoq urayib min wist el-balad?
Is the hotel next to the sea? el-fondoq gamb el-baHr?
Can I have a room with a nice view? mumken oDa bi manzer Helw?
I want a room for... a'eyz (male) / a'eyza (female) oDa li-
...one night laila waHda.
...two nights laila-tain
...three nights talat layali

NUMBERS

0 sifir *or* zero
1 waHid
2 itnain
3 talaata
4 arba'a
5 khamsa
6 seta
7 saba'a
8 tamania
9 tasa'
10 'ashira
11 Hidasher
12 itnasher
13 talatasher
14 arba'tasher

15 khamastasher
16 setasher
17 saba'atasher
18 tamantasher
19 tasa'tasher
20 'ashreen
21 waHid wa 'ashreen
22 itnain wa 'ashreen
...
30 talateen
40 arba'een
50 khamseen
60 setteen
70 saba'een
80 tamaneen
90 tasa'een
100 maya
1,000 alf

TIME

What time is it? es-saa'a kaam?
Morning es-Subh
Afternoon ba'd ed-Duhr
Evening el-maghrib
Night el-leil
Today el-naharda
Tomorrow bukra
Yesterday imbaaraH

DAYS

Sunday yom el-Had
Monday yom el-itnain
Tuesday yom et-talat
Wednesday yom el-arba'
Thursday yom el-khamees
Friday yom el-goma'a
Saturday yom es-sabt

MONTHS

Egyptians often refer to the months by *shahr* (month) followed by their number. For example, January is *shahr waHid* (month one), February is *shahr itnain* (month two), and so on.

January yinayer
February febrayer
March maaris
April abreel
May mayo
June younio
July youlio
August aghostos
September sebtember
October october
November nofember
December dee-cember

Internet Resources

TRAVEL INFORMATION

EGYPTIAN TOURISM AUTHORITY

http://egypt.travel

Official site of the Egyptian Tourism Authority, with information broken down by region.

MINISTRY OF TOURISM AND ANTIQUITIES

https://egymonuments.gov.eg/en

The Ministry's official website includes listings of just about all of Egypt's museums and sights, along with little history blurbs about Egypt throughout the ages. (Note: opening hours on the website are often wrong.)

TICKETSMARCHE

www.ticketsmarche.com

Find tickets to a variety of music and theater events in Cairo or on the North Coast.

SOUND & LIGHT EGYPT

https://soundandlight.show/en

You can use this website to book tickets online for most of Egypt's sound and light shows at various monuments throughout the country.

TRANSPORTATION

Train Travel

EGYPTIAN NATIONAL RAILWAYS

https://enr.gov.eg

ERNST SLEEPING TRAINS (CAIRO-LUXOR/ASWAN)

https://wataniasleepingtrains.com

CAIRO METRO

https://cairometro.gov.eg

Bus Travel

GO BUS

https://go-bus.com

BLUE BUS

https://bluebus.com.eg

WE BUS

https://webusegypt.com/public

APPS

- **WhatsApp:** Use this free app to call or message local guides and recreation outfitters listed in this book.
- **Facebook Messenger:** Another useful method for contacting local guides and outfitters.
- **Uber:** Use this app to get around Cairo/Giza, Alexandria, and Hurghada.

Index

A

B

C

G

H

IJ

Q

R

S

T

UV

WXZ

List of Maps

Photo Credits

All interior photos © Sarah Smierciak except: title page photo: Calin Stan | Dreamstime.com; page 4 © Guernica | Dreamstime.com; page 5 © Elena Frolova | Dreamstime.com; page 6 © (top left) Evgeniy Fesenko | Dreamstime.com; (top right) Maryna Konoplytska | Dreamstime.com; (bottom) Ginasanders | Dreamstime.com; page 7 © (top) Jakezc | Dreamstime.com; (bottom left) Evgeniy Fesenko | Dreamstime.com; (bottom right) Wing Travelling | Dreamstime.com; page 8 © (top) Anton Aleksenko | Dreamstime.com; page 9 © (top) Maksym Gorpenyuk | Dreamstime.com; (bottom left) Andrej Privizer | Dreamstime.com; (bottom right) Giko | Dreamstime.com; page 10 © Anton Aleksenko | Dreamstime.com; page 13 © Lu Yang | Dreamstime.com; page 14 © Znm | Dreamstime.com; page 15 © Navarone | Dreamstime.com; page 18 © (top) Mikhail Kokhanchikov | Dreamstime.com; (middle) Cristian Tecu | Dreamstime.com; (bottom) Vkilikov | Dreamstime.com; page 20 © (bottom) Liveandstereo | Dreamstime.com; page 23 © (bottom) Steirus | Dreamstime.com; page 25 © (bottom) Emily Wilson | Dreamstime.com; page 27 © Emanuele Mazzoni | Dreamstime.com; page 29 © Jackmalipan | Dreamstime.com; page 31 © Arapix | Dreamstime.com; page 32 © Robert Smierciak; page 33 © (top right) Flopezold | Dreamstime.com; page 49 © (right middle) Robert Smierciak; page 71 © Evgeniy Fesenko | Dreamstime.com; page 72 © Anton Kudelin | Dreamstime.com; page 77 © Jackmalipan | Dreamstime.com; page 79 © (bottom) Robert Smierciak;page 102 © Robert Smierciak; page 111 © (top) Robert Smierciak; (bottom) Dj Long Smierciak; page 114 © Chrupka | Dreamstime.com; page 132 © Mohamed Hatem; page 133 © (top left) Mohamed Hatem; (top right) Real Egypt Tours; page 137 © Sergey Strelkov | Dreamstime.com; page 144 © (top left) Sergey Strelkov | Dreamstime.com; (top right) Sergey Strelkov | Dreamstime.com; (bottom) Sergey Mayorov | Dreamstime.com; page 149 © (top) Sergey Strelkov | Dreamstime.com; (bottom) Sergey Strelkov | Dreamstime.com; page 153 © (top) Rania Hegazi | Dreamstime.com; (bottom) Prapton | Dreamstime.com; page 157 © (top left) Sergey Strelkov | Dreamstime.com; (top right) Amanda Lewis | Dreamstime.com; (bottom) Artur Maltsau | Dreamstime.com; page 160 © (top left) Mohamed Hatem; (top right) Mohamed Hatem; (bottom) Mohamed Hatem; page 164 © (top left) Robert Smierciak; (top right) Robert Smierciak; page 176 © (top left) Robert Smierciak; (top right) Robert Smierciak; (bottom) Joey Shea; page 180 © (bottom) Robert Smierciak; page 185 © Joey Shea; page 196 © (top) Gustavo Rosa | Dreamstime.com; (bottom) Sergey Strelkov | Dreamstime.com; page 210 © (top) Joey Shea; (bottom) Robert Smierciak; page 229 © (top left) Cristianzamfir | Dreamstime.com; (top right) Freeprod | Dreamstime.com; (bottom left) Albertoloyo | Dreamstime.com; (bottom right) Robert Smierciak; page 230 © Wrangel | Dreamstime.com; page 245 © Wisconsinart | Dreamstime.com; page 266 © (top) Robert Smierciak; (left middle) Robert Smierciak; (right middle) Robert Smierciak; (bottom) Evren Kalinbacak | Dreamstime.com; page 272 © Emily Wilson | Dreamstime.com; page 274 © Monika Hodáňová | Dreamstime.com; page 293 © (top) Community Restaurants; (bottom) Abdelrahman Hussein; page 302 © Blue Ocean Dive Centers & Resorts; page 303 © (top left) Bullet Speedboats; (top right) Caan2gobelow | Dreamstime.com; page 309 © (top) Sliders Cable Park; (bottom) Kiteboarding Club; page 318 © (bottom) Blue Paradise Diving Center; page 327 © Berndneeser | Dreamstime.com; page 329 © (top) Tim Gurney | Dreamstime.com; (bottom) Blue Ocean Dive Centers & Resorts; page 337 © (top left) Ekaterina Polyashova | Dreamstime.com; (top right) Patryk Kosmider | Dreamstime.com; page 347 © (top) Rob Atherton | Dreamstime.com; (left middle) Photographerlondon | Dreamstime.com; (right middle) Oleg Doroshenko | Dreamstime.com; (bottom) Dreamstime.com; page 368 © (top left) Kylie Nicholson | Dreamstime.com; (bottom) Jacek Sopotnicki | Dreamstime.com; page 376 © (top left) Presse750 | Dreamstime.com; page 394 © (top) Zaramira | Dreamstime.com; page 398 © Khaled Arafa | Dreamstime.com; page 404 © Rui G. Santos | Dreamstime.com; page 413 © Donyanedomam | Dreamstime.com; page 424 © Gunold | Dreamstime.com; page 432 © Evgeniy Fesenko | Dreamstime.com; page 438 © Ppy2010ha | Dreamstime.com.

Acknowledgments

A special thanks to the world's best travel partner, Mohammed Fouad, whose unfaltering response of *yallah bina* ("let's do it") enriches every adventure.

Many thanks to my brother and sister, Rob and Cate, for joining me on travels to Egypt's farthest corners, my mom for her adventurous genes, my dad for his beautiful photo contributions, and to both of my parents for teaching me the joy of travel and exploration.

For when your friends want your recommendations.
Keep track of your favorite...

Cairo Al Qahera

Restaurants and Meals

1 Cairo Ibn tulum mosque
2 Muzz street soug Soug el atteba
place of koshary
jebenna - traditional coffee
Nile seperates Cairo/Giza
3 Tahrir Square
4 Tentmakers Soug
Mokhatam Corniche - sunset

Neighborhoods and Regions

Shabi musu - of the people
Egyptian pound / dollar 1 USD/24.3787EGP
Egyptian Arabic

Cultural Experiences

Beaches and Recreation

Day Trips or Scenic Drives

Travel Memories

MAP SYMBOLS

Line symbols	Point symbols	Icons	Icons
Expressway	City/Town	Information Center	Park
Primary Road	State Capital	Parking Area	Golf Course
Secondary Road	National Capital	Church	Unique Feature
Unpaved Road	Highlight	Winery/Vineyard	Waterfall
Trail	Point of Interest	Trailhead	Camping
Ferry	Accommodation	Train Station	Mountain
Railroad	Restaurant/Bar	Airport	Ski Area
Pedestrian Walkway	Other Location	Airfield	Glacier
Stairs			

CONVERSION TABLES

°C = (°F - 32) / 1.8
°F = (°C x 1.8) + 32
1 inch = 2.54 centimeters (cm)
1 foot = 0.304 meters (m)
1 yard = 0.914 meters
1 mile = 1.6093 kilometers (km)
1 km = 0.6214 miles
1 fathom = 1.8288 m
1 chain = 20.1168 m
1 furlong = 201.168 m
1 acre = 0.4047 hectares
1 sq km = 100 hectares
1 sq mile = 2.59 square km
1 ounce = 28.35 grams
1 pound = 0.4536 kilograms
1 short ton = 0.90718 metric ton
1 short ton = 2,000 pounds
1 long ton = 1.016 metric tons
1 long ton = 2,240 pounds
1 metric ton = 1,000 kilograms
1 quart = 0.94635 liters
1 US gallon = 3.7854 liters
1 Imperial gallon = 4.5459 liters
1 nautical mile = 1.852 km

MOON EGYPT
Avalon Travel
Hachette Book Group
1700 Fourth Street
Berkeley, CA 94710, USA
www.moon.com

Editor: Nikki Ioakimedes
Managing Editor: Hannah Brezack
Graphics Coordinator: Rue Flaherty
Production Coordinator: Rue Flaherty
Cover Design: Faceout Studio, Charles Brock
Interior Design: Domini Dragoone
Moon Logo: Tim McGrath
Map Editor: Albert Angulo
Cartographers: Brian Shotwell, John Culp, Karin Dahl
Proofreader: Megan Anderluh

ISBN-13: 978-1-64049-395-7

Printing History
1st Edition — April 2022
5 4 3 2 1

Front cover photo: Khan el Khalili souk, Cairo © Richard Taylor / Sime / eStock Photo
Back cover photo: Karnak Temple, Luxor © Ginasanders | Dreamstime.com

Printed in Malaysia for Imago